Principles of Earthquake Resistant Design of Structures and Tsunami

B.L. Gupta
M.E. Civil Engg. (Roorkee)
Formerly Head of Civil Engg. Dept. & Principal
and
Amit Gupta
B.E. (Hons) I.R.S.E.

STANDARD PUBLISHERS DISTRIBUTORS
1705-B NAI SARAK, POST BOX No. 1066, DELHI-110 006
www.standardpublishers.com Email: stpub@vsnl.com

Published by:
A.K. Jain (Prop.)
For Standard Publishers Distributors
1705-B, Nai Sarak, Delhi-110 006
Ph.: 23262700, 23285798 Fax : 23243180

First Edition : 2010
Edition: **2013**
Reprint **:** 2017

Price ₹ 300.00

ISBN : 978-81-8014-148-5

Laser Typesetting by:
Bhargave Laser Printers, Delhi.
Printed at :
Lomus Offset Press, Delhi

PREFACE

Earthquakes are one of the most destructive natural phenomenon and their occurrence is beyond the human control, but their results are man made. Thus man is responsible to provide protection measures against earthquake, by way of providing earthquake resistant structural design and safety measures. Earthquakes shakes the foundations of the buildings and cause their destruction. About 67% land of India lies in severe seismic zone and approximately 90% population live in masonry structures. The masonry has a number of serious draw backs in earthquake resistance. It has high inertial response to earthquake due to its brittle nature and heavy mass. Thus masonry structures suffer severe damage during an earthquake causing large miseries to the people and loss of property.

This book has been written with a view to spread awareness of mass destruction of structures due to earthquakes and safe guards against this destruction. The large scale destruction due to 26.1.2001, Bhuj earthquake has increased the importance of construction of earthquake resistant structures.

This book deals with the basic principles of earthquake resistant construction of structures. In preparing this text authors have drawn matter freely from the published literature on the subject, which is gratefully acknowledged. The matter has been presented in a simple and lucid language at one place serially. We hope that this book will prove useful for under graduate students preparing for Civil Engineering degree. However it will also prove useful for practicing engineers. For figures we express our gratitude to faculty IIT Kanpur, USGS, E.Q.E., C. Arnold, Building system development Inc. and Shri S.K. Dugal, Shri Jai Krishna and Shri D.V. Mallick.

Though every care has been taken to rectify composing and printing error. even then some errors might have been left. Readers are requested if they come across any error, they should bring it to the notice of the publisher. At the end we are thankful to M/s Standard Publishers and Distributors, who brought out such a nice book in a very short period.

Ellenabad
25th Dec., 2009

B.L. GUPTA
AMIT GUPTA

CONTENTS

1
The Earthquakes

1.1. INTRODUCTION

Human being has faced the fury of natural disasters like earthquakes, floods, tornadoes, hurricanes, droughts and volcanic erruptions from time immemorial. Even in the face of such catastrophic natural Phenomenon, human beings have tried to coexist with them and control nature. Of all the natural disasters, earthquakes are least under stood and most destructive. Earthquakes are dreaded by human beings because they strike suddenly and destructively causing injuries, deaths and damage to properties. Though average annual losses due to floods, tornadoes and hurricanes etc. are much more than those caused by earthquake. But totally unexpected and nearly instantaneous occurrence of major earthquakes and their devastation has a peculiar or unique Psychological impact on the human beings. Hence earthquakes need serious consideration.

Though earthquakes are natural phenomenon, but the results are of man made. The consequences of earthquakes are often disastrous, particularly in developing countries with large population. Much damages due to injuries, deaths and loss of property can be prevented if appropriate earthquake resistant design and preparedness measures are taken. An earthquake itself does not kill any body, but the human acts of poorly designed and constructed buildings do that job for earthquakes. The devastation due to 26th January 2001 of Bhuj (Gujarat) earthquake would have been avoided, if only the guide lines available since 1960, for the construction of earthquake resistant buildings would have been adopted in the building construction.

1.2. DEFINITION OF EARTHQUAKE

The vibrations caused by the waves generated by forces in constant turmoil under the earth surface is called earthquake. These waves travel in all directions through the earth's crust. This earth crust is known as Lithosphere. In other words it can be defined as the vibrations (some times violent) of the earth's surface caused by the release of energy in the earth's crust. The release of energy may be due to sudden dislocation of segments of the earth's crust, violent erruptions or explosions created by humans. How ever the dislocations of segments lead to the most destructive earthquakes. In the process of dislocation vibrations are caused, which are called seismic waves. These waves travel out wards from the source of the earthquake with varying speeds causing the earth to quiver like a tunning fork. During an earthquake a large amount of energy is released. The relation of magnitude of earthquake and energy released would be discussed in chapter 3.

1.3. SEISMIC ZONES OF INDIA

In India about 67% land lies in severe seismic zones. Till 1984, India was divided into five earthquake zones as shown in Fig. 1.1. After 1984, India has

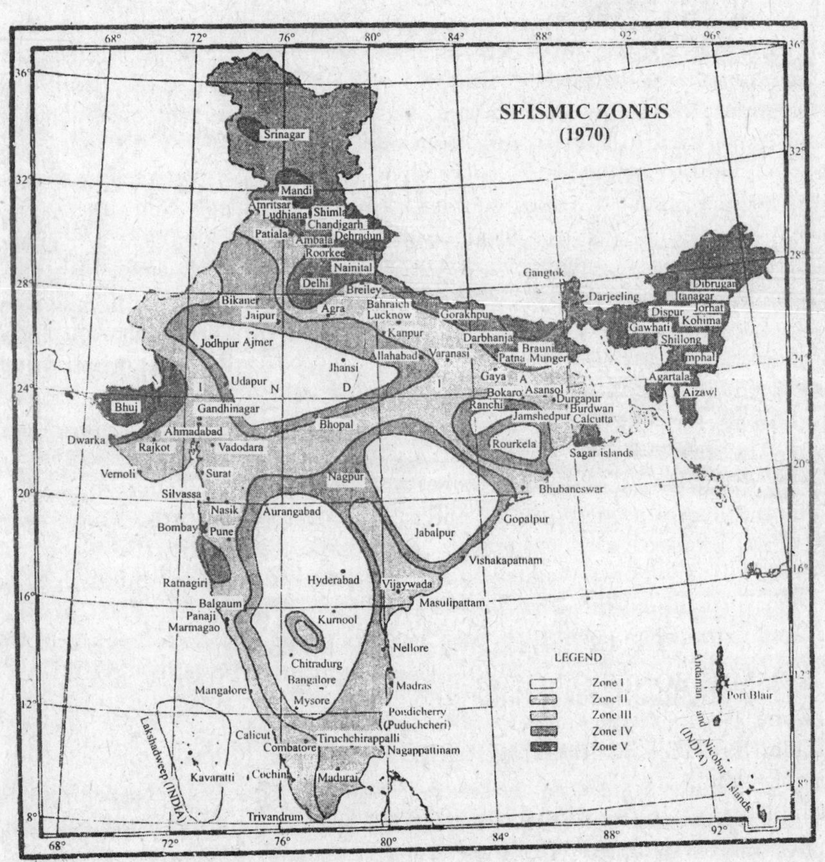

Fig. 1.1. Seismic Zoning Map of IS: 1893-1970

been divided into four seismic zones. The original zones I and II have been merged together. Now zone I does not exist. New zones are II, III, IV, and V. The new zones are shown in Fig. 1.2.

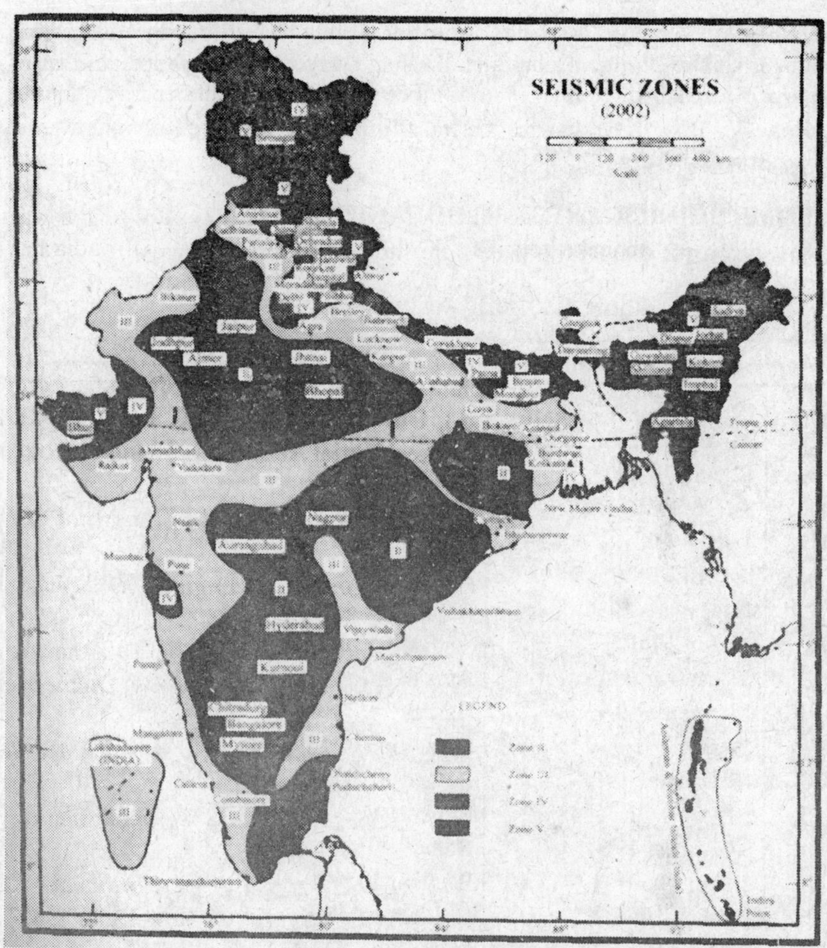

Fig. 1.2. Seismic Zoning Map of IS: 1893-2002

1.4. SEISMIC ZONES OF IMPORTANT CITIES OF INDIA

Zone II. Ajmer, Allahabad, Aurangabad, Banglore, Bhilai, Bhopal, Chitradurga, Gulburga, Hydrabad, Jaipur, Jamshedpur, Jhansi, Jodhpur, Kota, Kurnool, Madurai, Mysore, Nagpur, Nagarjunasagar, Pandichery, Raipur, Ranchi, Rourkela, Sironj, Thanjavur, Tiruchirappali, Udaipur, Vishakapatnam.

Zone-III. Agra, Ahmedabad, Asansol, Bareilly, Belgaum, Bhatinda, Bhuneshwar, Bijapur, Bikaner, Bokaro, Burdwan, Calicut, Channi, Coimbatore, Cuddalore, Cuttak, Dharampuri, Dharwad, Durgapur, Gaya, Goa, Jabalpur, Kakrapara, Kalpakkam, Kanchipuram, Kanpur, Karwar, Kolkatta, Lucknow, Mangalore, Mumbai, Nasik, Nellore, Osmanabad, Panjim, Patiala, Pune, Salem, Solapur, Surat, Tarapur, Thane, Thiruvananthapuram, Tiruvannamalai, Vadodra, Varanashi, Vellore, Vijawada.

Zone-IV. Almora, Ambala, Amritsar, Bhariach, Barauni, Bulandsher, Chandigarh, Darjeeling, Dehradun, Delhi, Gangtok, Gorakhpur, Ludhiana, Manghyr, Moradabad, Nanital, Patna, Pilibhit, Roorkee, Simla.

Zone-V. Bhuj, Darbhanga, Guwahati, Imphal, Jorhat, Kohima, Mandi, Sadiya, Srinagar, Tezpur.

1.5. SOME SIGNIFICANT EARTHQUAKES OF INDIA

The details of these earthquakes are shown in Table 1.1 below:

Table 1.1. Details of earthquakes of India

S. No.	*Date of year*	*Region*	*Magnitude*
1.	16 June 1819	Kutch Gujrat	8.0
2.	26 August 1833	Bihar	7.7
3.	12 June 1897	Assam	8.7
4.	8 Feb. 1900	Palghat Kerla	6.0
5.	4 April 1905	Kangra H.P.	8.0
6.	3rd July 1930	Dhubri Assam	7.1
7.	15 January 1934	Bihar	8.3
8.	26 Jun 1941	Andamans	8.0
9.	23 october 1943	Assam	7.2
10.	15 August 1950	Assam	8.6
11.	21 July 1956	Ajnar Gujrat	7.0
12.	10 October 1956	Bulandsher U.P.	6.7
13.	28 December 1958	Kapkota U.P.	6.3
14.	27 August 1960	Delhi	6.0
15.	2 Sept 1963	Badgam J & K	5.5
16.	27 June 1966	U.P. Nepal	6.3
17.	15 August 1966	Moradabad (U.P.)	5.3
18.	2 july 1967	Nicobar	6.2
19.	11 Dec. 1967	Koyna (Mahrastra)	6.5
20.	14 April 1969	Bhadrachallam (A.P.)	6.0
21.	23 March 1970	Broach (Gujrat)	5.7
22.	19 Jan. 1975	Himachal Pradesh	6.5
23.	29 July 1980	U.P. Nepal	6.5
24.	20 Jan. 1982	Nicobar	5.7
25.	26 April 1986	H.P.	5.7
26.	6 August 1988	Manipur (Burma)	6.8
27.	21 August 1988	Bihar (Nepal)	6.5
28.	20 Oct. 1991	Uttar Kashi (U.P.)	6.6
29.	30 Sept 1993	Latur-osmanabad (Mahrastra)	6.3

S. No.	*Date of year*	*Region*	*Magnitude*
30.	21 May 1997	Jabalpur (M.P.)	6.0
31.	29 March 1999	Chamoli Dist. (U.P.)	6.8
32.	26 Jan. 2001	Bhuj (Gujrat)	7.9

1.6. FREQUENCY OF OCCURRENCE OF EARTHQUAKES IN INDIA (From Indian data)

1. During 1819-1950, the frequency of occurrence was once in 13 years.
2. During 1950-1975, the frequency of occurrence was once in 6.5 years.
3. During 1975 to 2001 the frequency remained once in 2 years.
4. Earthquakes of magnitude of 8.0 or more are not uncommon in India.
5. The main north-east-boundary fault and the main control thrust fault are active.

1.6.1. From global seismic data

From the world seismic data, it has been observed that:

1. World experiences on an average 18 major earthquakes every year whose intensity on Richter scale measures 7.0 to 7.9. About 20% of such major earthquakes take place in India.
2. About 800 moderate earthquakes of 5.0 to 5.9 intensity take place every year, some where or the other.

The frequency of occurrence of earthquakes based on observations of United States Geological Survey (USGS) is shown in Table 1.2 below:

Table 1.2. Frequency of earthquakes

S. No.	*Description*	*Magnitude on Richter scale*	*Annual average*
1.	Great	8.0 and higher	1
2.	Major	7.0 to 7.9	18
3.	Strong	6.0 to 6.9	120
4.	Moderate	5.0 to 5.9	800
5.	Light	4.0 to 4.9	6200 (Estimated)
6.	Minor	3.0 to 3.9	49000 (Estimated)
7.	Very minor	< 3.0	11000 per day

1.7. EFFECTS OF EARTHQUAKES

Earthquakes are major hazards to human beings. They can cause catastrophic damage to life and property. The effects of earthquakes may be classified into the two following effects.

1. Direct effects. These effects cause damage directly and include ground motion and faulting. These are discussed as follows:

(*a*) *Damage by seismic waves.* The seismic waves, especially surface waves which pass through surface rock layers cause ground motions. Such motions can damage or completely destroy buildings. If a structure such as a road or building crosses or built across a fault, then the ground displacement occurred during a earthquake will break that structure in parts or rip apart.

(*b*) *Surface faulting.* It is caused or it is the out come of the differential movement of the earth's surface across a fault. These movements shear and tear the structures built on the faults. Surface faulting, generally is accompanied by horizontal and/or vertical distorsion of the earth's surface that can distort or tilt structures constructed near the fault.

(*c*) *Land slides.* In regions consisting of hills and steep slopes, vibrations developed due to earthquakes can cause land slides, mud slides and collapse of cliffs which can damage buildings and may lead to glosal loss of life and burry buildings.

(*d*) *Damage to foundations.* Ground or soil vibrations can either shake a building off its foundation or modify its support or disintegrate its foundation.

(*e*) Strong surface seismic waves make the ground to heave and move side ways (lurch) and damage the structures. Regional uplift and subsidence may accompany earthquakes caused by large displacements on shallow faults. Such changes may damage the harbour facilities, roads, canals, rail, roads and other structures.

Ground failures accompanying earthquakes include land slides, lateral spreads, differential settlements, liquefaction of soil and ground cracking. Earthquake shaking often dislodges rock and debris on steep slopes, resulting in rock falls, avalenches, and land slides. Some times these slides bury the entire town and may be the most damaging aspect of the earthquake event.

Liquefaction

Liquefaction occurs in cohesionless fine grained soils where the soil is saturated or ground water table is very high or in filled lands near the coast. When an earthquake shakes the wet soil, the soil particles move apart allowing the water to seep in between them. This phenomenon reduces greatly the friction between the soil particles, which is responsible for the strength of the soil The saturated soils become viscous fluid losing their bearing capacity. This phenomenon is called liquefaction of soils. In this condition of soil due to sudden reduction in their shear resistance occurred due to temporary increase in pore water pressure, ground behaves like quicksand and buildings start to lean and can topple over or sink partially into the liquefied soil as soil loses all its strength to support the buildings. Sinking of buildings has been observed from 5 cm to over one metre during the past earthquakes.

After the earthquake as the soil consolidates, further damage to buildings can occur due to further settlement and soil erruptions. Liquefaction can also cause increased lateral pressure on retaining structures causing their displacement. Due to liquefaction large masses of soil can be displaced laterally, known as lateral spreading with serious consequences. The displaced ground suffers cracks, rifting and buckling.

The light structures as petrol tanks and under ground gas and water pipe lines may be thrown on the ground and may break. The lateral spreading also disrupts the foundations of the buildings built across the fault. It also causes bridges to buckle.

2. Indirect effects of an earthquake. Following are the indirect effects of an earthquake.

(*a*) *Development of tsunamis.* Tsunamis are the by products of an earthquake. When an earthquake causes vilonent movement of a sea floor, a series of sea waves are developed, whose time period is extremely long ranging from 5 minutes to 90 minutes Fig. 1.3. These waves are known as Tsunamis. The word Tsunami is composed from the Japanese word "Tsu" (means harbour) plus "nami" (mean wave). Some times they are called seismic sea waves. Tsunami wave energy extends up to the ocean bottom and water flows straight. Usually tsunamis occur along the sub duction zone and are very common in pacific ocean. In an open sea, a tsunami is only an unusually broad swell on the water surface. Similar to all waves, tsunamis only develop in a large wave covered with white bubbles moving towards the shore, called breaker as they touch the shore and the undulating waters touch the bottom. Near the shores, the energy of a tsunami gets concentrated in the vertical direction due to reduction in depth of water as well as in horizontal direction due to shortening the wave length due to reduction in velocity. In case of large earthquakes, the height of tsunami waves associated with breakers may rise upto 15 m near the shore and their effects correspondingly are disastrous. Several breakers may strike the coast in succession. Between waves, the water may be pulled back swiftly to sea wards, emptying the harbour or bay and pulling unwary

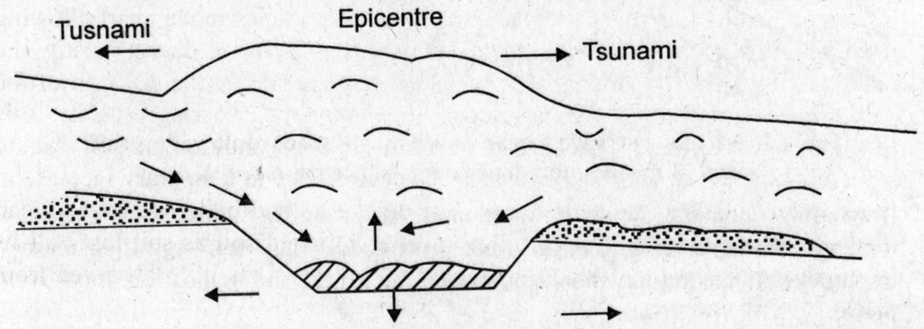

Fig. 1.3. Generation of Tsunami

on lookers along with it. The speed of travel of tsunami waves may vary from 0.14 km/sec to 0.28 km/sec *i.e.* from 500 to 1000 km per hour. The velocity of tsunami with large wave lengths *i.e.* wave length is 25 times the depth of water may be determined by the relation.

$$V = \sqrt{gh} \quad \text{where } h \text{ is the depth of water.}$$

(*b*) *Run-up and inundation.* Though tsunamis are infrequent occuring phenomenon, but they are most terrifying and complex physical phenomenon. They have been found responsible for great-loss of life and extensive destruction of property. The great-loss due to tsunami is caused due to large run up (height of waves above the sea level) and inundation (distance of submerged land from the shore), wave impact on structures and erosion.

As stated earlier also, as the tsunami waves approach the coast, their wave length is decreased and wave energy is directed upwards, increasing the wave height considerably *i.e.* kinetic energy is converted to static energy. Near the shore the tsunami wave amplitude may go upto 30 to 35 m as shown in Fig. 1.4. Depth of water and wave speed and length are shown in Table 1.3.

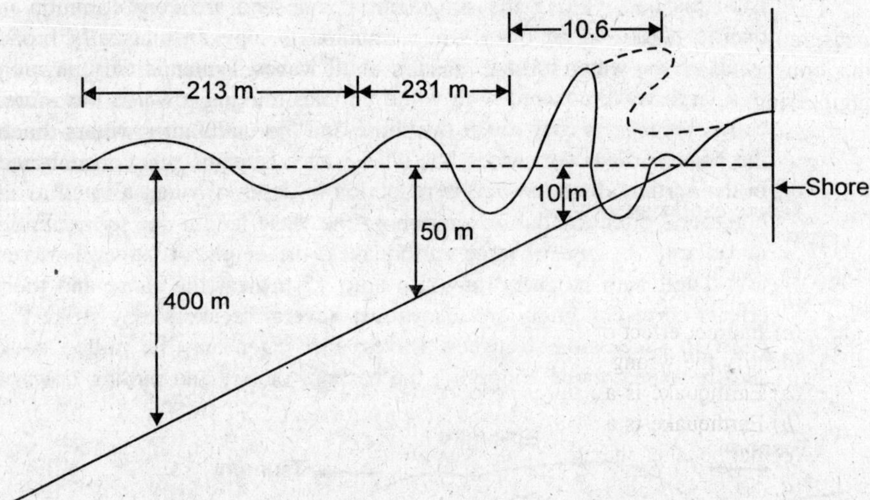

Fig. 1.4. Velocity and wave length variation with water depth with period of about 18 minutes, for amplitude amplification near the shore

Depending upon the depth of water and coastal configuration, the wave may undergo extensive refraction, an other process that may converge their energy to particular areas on the shore, increasing the height and inundation areas even more.

Sieches. These are small tsunamis generated due to shaking of water by the earthquake in enclosed water bodies such as reservoirs, lakes and harbours.

Fire damage. During an earthquake fire may broke out due to the damage of gas lines and snapping of electric wires.

Generation of floods. Earthquakes may rupture dams, and levees causing floods, resulting in damage to structures and considerable loss of life and property.

Table 1.3. Wave Parameters

Depth water meters	*Wavelength (km/h)*	*Wave speed km/h*	*Remark*
10.0	10.6	35.6	
50.0	23.0	79.0	
200.0	47.7	159.0	
2000.0	151.0	504.2	
4000.0	213.0	712.7	
7000.0	282.0	942.9	

Earthquake Engineering

The science which deals to predict the effects of earthquake motions measured with the help of different seismic instruments and suggests the design and construction of earthquake resistant structures is known as earthquake engineering.

QUESTIONS

1. Define earthquake and discuss its effects fully.
2. Write short notes on the following:
   (*a*) Tsunami
   (*b*) Liquefaction of soil
   (*c*) Indirect effect of earthquake
3. Identify the wrong statement:
   (*a*) Earthquake is a natural phenomenon
   (*b*) Earthquake is a man made or artificial phenomenon
   (*c*) Earthquakes themselves do not kill any body
   (*d*) The loss of life and property is caused due to the man non adoption of earthquake resistant building design and construction.
4. Usually Great earthquakes of magnitudes 8.0 or greater than 8.0 occur.
   (*a*) 5 a year (*b*) 10 a year
   (*c*) 1.0 a year (*d*) 15 a year
5. Earthquake of magnitude between 7.0 to 7.9 occur annually through out the world
   (*a*) 30 (*b*) 20
   (*c*) 27 (*d*) 18
6. Tsunami is developed due to
   (*a*) Atmospheric disturbance

(*b*) Disturbance in sea water due to earthquake
(*c*) Due to blasts on surface
(*d*) Due to any of the above causes

7. On an average about....% of earthquake of magnitude 7.0 to 7.9 occurs in India
(*a*) 25% (*b*) 20%
(*c*) 30% (*d*) 45%
8. Near the coast of sea the height of tsunami waves
(*a*) Decrease (*b*) Increase
(*c*) Remain constant
(*d*) All are correct
9. The area of India......is earthquake infected
(*a*) 30% (*b*) 65%
(*c*) 50% (*d*) 80%
10. Due to liquefaction, pore water pressure......
(*a*) Increases (*b*) Decreases
(*c*) No effect (*d*) All are correct
11. Due to liquefaction of soil, it shear strength ....
(*a*) Increases (*b*) Decreases
(*c*) No effect (*d*) All are correct

ANSWERS:

3. (*b*)	6. (*b*)	9. (*c*)
4. (*c*)	7. (*b*)	10. (*a*)
5. (*d*)	8. (*b*)	11. (*b*)

2

Brief History of Past Earthquakes

2.1. INTRODUCTION

Earthquakes are natural phenomenon, much about which yet to be known. It is believed that stressed earth releases its energy in the form of earthquakes and volcanoes. Though man is facing earthquakes fury from the very beggining of his existence, but he is most dreaded from earthquakes than all other natural disasters as volcanoes erruptions, tornados, floods, hurricanes etc. as least is understood about the earthquakes and as they cause nearly ins- tantaneous total devastation. In this chapter we shall discuss in brief the devastation caused by past earthquakes.

2.2. KOYANA EARTHQUAKE OF 10-12-1967

The magnitude of Koyana earthquake of 10th December 1967 was M 6.3. It is believed to be caused by the reservoir formed by construction of dam there. This earthquake caused much damage in the area. In this earthquake about 200 persons lost their lives and about 1500 persons got injured. It caused extensive damage to property. This dam is constructed on hard rock foundation. The Accelerogram of 1967 earthquake of Koyana dam is shown in Fig. 10.1.

2.3. SOUTHERN ITALY EARTHQUAKE OF 23-11-1980

After the 23rd November 1980 earthquake, the sight in the southern Italy was more shoking. Nearly 80% villages of the southern region were destroyed and hundreds of people were burried under the debris and no rescue operations could be started for the first 48 hours after the disaster.

This earthquake was the deadliest of the Europe in the last 65 years. The intensity of the tremor on Richter scale was 6.8. Every where in the the region buildings collapsed in this earthquake and many people died instantly. The tremor occurred from sicily to Alps. In southern Italy around the epicentre about one hundred towns turned into debris. There was misery every where. The official figures of dead was 3000 and the unofficial figure stood at 10,000.

2.4. EL-ASNAM (ALGERIA) EARTHQUAKE OF 10.10.1980

The city of EL-Asnam is situated in the Central-Northern Algeria. On 10th October 1980 the city of El_Asnam and its surrounding area were struck by two major earthquake tremors. The intensity of these tremors on Richter scale was found as 7.3 and 6.4. These tremors destroyed more than half the city of El-Asnam and killed or injured about 11000 persons and rendenred more than 3×10^5 people home less. In addition to this, many settlements in the rural area of about 900 square kilometer area around the city were also badly damaged or totally destroyed. These tremors, were remarkable for the following reasons.

1. The epicentre of these tremors was very near to that of 9th September 1954 major earthquake in Algeria of magnitude 6.7. This earthquake also caused great destruction and loss of life in the city of EL-ASNAM.
2. This earthquake was particularly unusual than others as the strongest movement was in the vertical direction, especially in the region of epicentre.
3. During these tremors nature's miracle came to light in the form of a surface fault extending about 40 km from a point about 10 km south south-east of EL-ASNAM to the hilly area in north-east of EL-Abbadia.
4. During this earthquake a vertical shift of 5 m has been reported. The initial shock was vertical, which was followed by horizontal oscillations after few seconds mainly in a east-west-direction lasting for more than 10 seconds.
5. Eighty five schools were destroyed in these tremors in the city El-Asnam alone.

One shudders at the thought, what would have happened had the earthquake occurred during the school time. A large number of modern buildings including multi-storeyed residential blocks, industrial structures, public buildings including schools suffered severe damage or collapsed during this earthquake. Most of these structures were constructed of R.C.C. framcs with masonry in fill walls.

The study of damaged structures in El-Asnam revealed that buildings constructed before 1954 earthquake remained standing in 1954 earthquake as well as in 1980 earthquake.

New three to four storey residential apartments made of R.C.C. frames with masonry in fill walls and some other medium high structures constructed as per provision of French Code remained standing, but other higher buildings collapsed totally. The study of damaged concrete showed that the accelerations developed during the 1980 earthquake were almost double than those suggested in the French Code. Hence the failure. Further the local subsoil and topography had the effect of amplifying the effect of ground motions.

2.4.1. Structural Failures

The study of damaged structures in earthquake showed that many of the failures occurred by the unusual high vertical accelerations and improper design provisions such as shear failure of short columns between footings and ground floor beams and slab, long span beam failures and buckling of columns and crushing of in fill masonry walls in concrete frame buildings. Fig. 2.1 shows

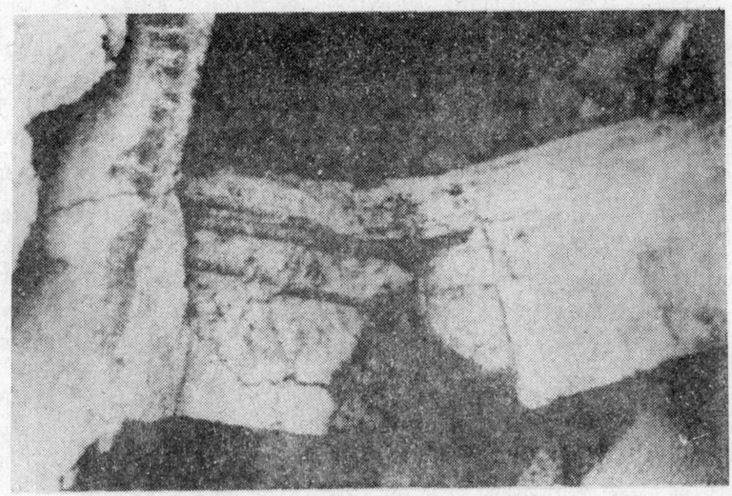

Fig. 2.1. Crushing of concrete column

crushing of concrete of the column. The other causes of structural failures have been found as:

(*a*) Building orientation with respect to fault.

(*b*) Discontinuity of rigidity along the height of the building.

(*c*) Soft storey concept.

(*d*) Column failure.

(*e*) Structural detailing, construction, quality and supervision of construction.

(*a*) Building Orientation

In certain buildings the extent of damage has been found dependent on the orientation of the building with respect to the fault. The damage survey revealed that the buildings having their long axis along the north-west to south-east direction suffered maximum damage than those having their axis in orthogonal direction (perpendicular direction). As the direction of future earth quake vibrations can not be predicted in advance, hence it becomes obligatory to provide adequate strength about both the axes. Fig. 2.2 shows the shear mode of failure along the longitudinal axis.

(*b*) Rigidity distribution

The study of damaged structures revealed that non uniform distribution of structural and non structural elements such as shear walls and masonry panels in the buildings was an other predominant cause of damage to buildings during the earthquake. This type of non uniform typical distribution of elements was found in recently constructed R.C.C. multi-storey blocks. Some of the buildings collapsed in a shear mode with plastic hinges in the columns due to insufficient

Fig. 2.2. Shear failure of columns

strength in the direction of longitudinal axis along which the ground shaking was excessive. In the central part of the city four storey buildings were constructed with a special structural system. The buildings had two bay frames in the transverse direction with semi pre cast floor system. The height of the sanitary floor was kept lower than other storeys.

The reinforced concrete transverse walls of the stair wells were constructed upto the sanitary floor. During the earthquake the short columns of the sanitary floors of all the buildings totally collapsed and the structures suffered large deformations. The sanitary floors having smaller height columns as compared to other floors produced discontinuity of rigidity along the height of the building. Thus the presence of an over strong part or element in a structure results in the ductility demand to be concentrated into the local region of the structure. This leads to collapse due to the development of very high inelastic deformations there. The prediction of mode of failure is impossible unless the structural rigidity in horizontal and vertical directions is well distributed. To eliminate the effects of discontinuity of rigidity, the rotational effects due to the earthquake should be incorporated into the design. To provide reasonable rigidity along both directions, the location of shear walls and infill panels should be planned judiciously. At the same time to minimize the torsion effects, efforts should be made to keep the centre of mass and centre of rigidly as close to each other as possible.

(*c*) Soft storey effect

When an individual storey in a building, often the ground level storey is made taller and/or more open in construction is called a soft storey. The soft storey effect can also occur at an upper level, but it is more common at the ground level between a rigid foundation system and a relatively stiffer upper level system. Any storey whose lateral stiffness is less than 60% of that of the storey immediately above it or less than 70% of the combined stiffness of the three storeys above it, is classified as soft storey. Some authors have suggested above percentages as 70% and 80% instead of 60 and 70%. A storey having few partitions and/or open exterior wall is also called a soft storey. This large open space such as in garages makes it more vulnerable to damage during earthquake. Soft storeys are universally recognised as dangerous as earthquake energy gets concentrated in the more flexible areas. This needs stronger columns and walls of the building to resist the huge earthquake energy.

Column failure

Four typical mode of failure of columns were observed during the study of damage after the earthquake:

1. Side sway mechanism of the column. Fig. 2.3.

Fig. 2.3. Failure of the column at the junction due to the wide spacing of tielinks

2. Crushing of concrete at the top due to the impact of the vertical load. Fig. 2.4.
3. Shear and flexure failure as shown in Fig. 2.2.
4. Local buckling of longitudinal has near the top 2.5.

Fig. 2.4 shows the typical failure of a column in flexure and shear. The widely spaced ties could not contain the concrete core. All post elastic deformations were due to plastic rotations at the hinges in the columns at the critical sections. Fig. 2.5 shows the local buckling of longitudinal bars and the falling out of the concrete core stresses the need of providing closer ties near the top and bottom sections of the columns.

Fig. 2.6 shows the failure of bottom short column of the factory building due to shear.

Fig. 2.4. Part of the building totally collapsed

Fig. 2.5. Damage at ground floor level

Construction related failures

The strength of joints in a building reduces considerably during a cyclic loading due to the following factors.

(*a*) Abrupt cutting of reinforcement bars.

(*b*) Insufficient length of anchorage of reinforcement bars.

(*c*) Poor detailing of joints.

Quality of material and construction

The study of damaged structures after earthquake also revealed that earthquake damage is dependent upon the quality of materials and the construction of the structure. It was observed that some parts of the structures came down like a lump of debris while the adjoining parts were slightly damaged.

Fig. 2.6. Failure of bottom short columns of the factors building due to shear

2.5. MEXICO CITY EARTHQUAKE OF 19.9.1985

An earthquake of magnitude of 8.1 on Richter's scale occurred along the pacific coast of the Maxico. The damage due to this earthquake was concentrated to an area of about 25 km^2 of Maxico city about 350 km away from the epicentre. The population of the city was about 18×10^5. During this earthquake 10,000 people were killed and 50,000 were injured. In addition to this 250×10^3 people were rendered home less. The property damage was estimated as 5 billions U.S. dollars. More than 800 buildings including hospitals, schools, hotels and other business centres were crumbled. The communication system between Maxico capital and the out side world remained cutoff for many days.

The geological reasons of the vulnerability of Maxico and Maxico city are as follows:

1. The Cocos plate along the west coast of southern Maxico and central America dips beneath the North American plate producing a very active seismic zone. In this zone 35 earthquake of magnitude more than 7.0 have occurred since the beginning of the twentieth century.
2. Maxico city it self lies in a broad basin formed approximately 30 million years ago by faulting of the uplifted plateau. The volcanic activities closed the basin and resulted in the formation of a lake. The gradual draining of the lake made available unconsolidated lake bed sediment for the expansion of the Maxico city. These soft sedimentary clay deposits in the bed amplified the seismic waves and subsided carrying buildings down with them. In some areas double resonance coupling between the earthquake waves, the subsoils and the buildings caused shaking intensity as IX lasting upto three minutes.

In the greatest damage area in the Maxico city, some type of structures failed more frequently than other types. In the highest damaged category were the buildings with six or more floor.

Resonance frequencies of these buildings were found similar to the resonance frequencies of the sub soil. Thus due to the un usual flexibility of the structures and inverted pendulum effect, the upper floors of the buildings swayed as much as one metre and frequently collapsed. Differential movements of adjacent buildings also caused damage. It was observed that a tall flexible building often failed when it was held by a more rigid adjacent lower building. Failure or damage occurred when two swaying building came in contact. Corner buildings were also vulnerable to damage.

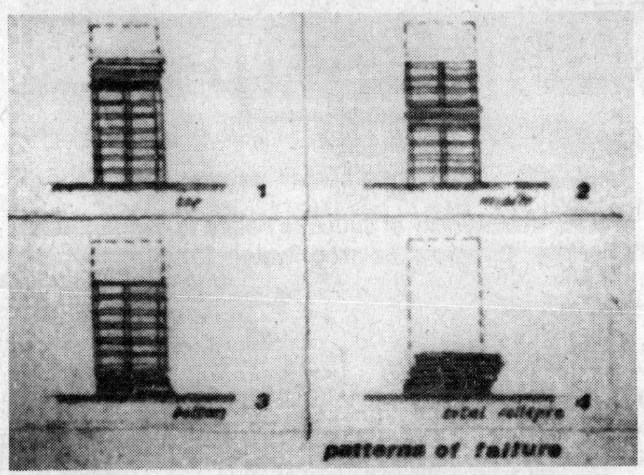

Fig. 2.7. Four common pattern of failure for buildings (Courtesy Arnold building systems development. inc.)

Four common pattern of failure of severely damaged buildings are shown in Fig. 2.7. Pattern 1 shows failure of top storeys. The second pattern describes the collapse of middle storeys. Pattern three shows collapse of bottom storeys and the fourth pattern shows complete failure of the structure. Main causes of building damage were observed as:

(*i*) Corner building failure = 42%

(*ii*) Collapse of intermediate floors = 40%

(*iii*) Collapse of upper floors = 38%

(*iv*) Pounding (striking of two buildings) = 15%

(*v*) Foundation failure = 13%

In this earthquake of 19 September 1985, the medium height buildings were most vulnerable as shown in Fig. 2.8. About 60% buildings having 6 to 15 storeys either collapsed or got severe damage. The reason of such large damage was that the resonance frequency of such buildings coincided with the frequency range amplified most frequently in the sub soil. Buildings which were not designed as earthquake resistant buildings failed where as these high

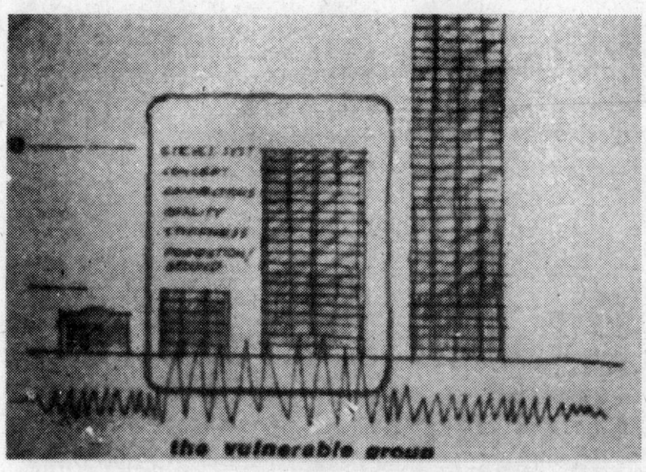

Fig. 2.8. Vulnerability of structure height to earthquake damage (Courtesy: C. Arnold, Building system development, inc.)

Fig. 2.9 (*a*). Building in the front totally collapsed. But the highrise in the background survived.

rise buildings designed as earthquake resistant survived as shown in Fig. 2.9 (*a*) and (*b*).

A 6 storey combined residential and commercial building sank more than one metre into the partially liquefied soil as shown in Fig. 2.10. Other buildings whose pile foundations rested on a hard layer of soil protruded from the surrounding terrain after the ground around the building subsided more than the buildings themselves.

Fig. 2.11. shows the mid height floor of a hotel building by pounding from a building at left side sway of the building on its right. The building was

Fig. 2.9 (*b*). Structure in the front collapsed but the communication and the highrise tower in the background survived.

Fig. 2.10. Sinking of a residential cum commercial structure (Courtesy: Reinsurance Company, Munich, Germany)

constructed of concrete frames. The two buildings were constructed too closely with equal heights. The natural periods of the two buildings were very close to the period of earthquake causing lateral displacement large enough to cause them hammer each other.

Fig. 2.12 shows the failure of the top floors of a flexible building between two rigid buildings.

Fig. 2.11. Failure of a mid height floor of Hotel de Carlo
(Courtesy: C. Arnold, Building System Development, inc.)

Fig. 2.12. Collapse of a flexible building between two rigid blocks
(Courtesy: C. Arnold, Building Systems Development, inc.)

2.6. ARMENIAN (USSR) EARTHQUAKE OF 7-12-1988

An earthquake of magnitude of 6.9 occurred in north-western Armenian at 11.41 a.m. on 7.12.1988. Four minutes later another shock of magnitude 5.8 followed it. This earthquake hit an area of about 5100 square kilometer. (80km dia)

This region is a part of broad seismic zone stretching from Turkey to the Arabian sea near India. Here the Arabian land mass is colliding slowly with the Eurasian plate and thrusting up the caucasus mountain in the north. The earthquake occurred along a small thrust fault running north west to south east right under spitak. During the earthquake the spitak section to the north east of the fault rode up over the south west side. At the point where the fault movement broke the surface, Geologists have located a 8 km long and 1.6 m high scarp (Steep slope).

The epicentre of the earthquake was located 80 km south of the main range of the caucasus maintain. Historic data shows that this area has experienced many damaging earthquakes during 1899 to 1940. Most of the earthquakes occurred with in 100 km of the 1988 earthquake epicentre. The magnitudes of these earthquakes ranged from 5.3 to 6.0.

Though the magnitude of 7th December 1988 earthquake was moderate, but the death and damage it caused, made it the largest earthquake disaster after 1976 earthquake of magnitude 7.8 in Tangshan (China), in which more than 250,000 people were killed. The town of spitak of population 25000 was nearly leveled and in the city of Laninakan of population 2,50,000 more than 50% structures were damaged or destroyed. Much damage also occurred in other nearby cities and smaller towns. Direct economic losses were estimated as 14.2 billion U.S. dollars. In this earthquake 25000 persons were killed and 15000 injured and about 517000 people were rendered home less. However 15000 people were rescued.

2.6.1. Factors Contributing to so large human disaster

Following factors contributed to this large magnitude of human disaster:

(*a*) Near freezing temperature at the time of earthquake.

(*b*) Time of the day when earthquake occurred.

(*c*) Soil conditions of the region.

(*d*) Inadequate building construction.

(*e*) Large scale destruction of medical facilities. About 80% of the medical professionals were killed.

The study of damaged structures revealed that the design deficiencies and poor construction practices in the area caused so large a collapse of buildings and resulting deaths. In this earthquake even modern multi storeyed buildings also did not survive.

In the region the load bearing walls were constructed of stone masonry with out the provision of binding wall elements together. This type of buildings were unable to resist the lateral shaking due to inadequate bond beams or R.C.C. bands necessary for tying the entire building together. The components of the buildings were not connected with the tie beams at roof level or with steel reinforcement. The grouted joints proved to be inadequate to hold the buildings together.

Apart from the poor design and construction of buildings, the soil condition of the region and the way of felling building apart also contributed to the high rate of deaths. It was observed that the ratio of survivors among people trapped in the rubble of multi storeyed buildings was about 3.5 times more for the ground floor than the higher floors *i.e.* the death rate of higher floors was more.

In this region mostly precast concrete frame composite structures were built. In these buildings the floors were constructed with individual hollow core

Fig. 2.13. Damage to a four storey building in Leninakan resulting from poor ties between floors and walls (courtesy: USGS)

pre cast planks with no (or inadequate) connections between them to tie the floors together. The lack of adequate floor ties allowed the middle portions of the buildings to collapse as shown in Fig. 2.13, while end portions remained standing.

Most of the building in the area were built on shallow foundations on thick

Fig. 2.14. A portion of the thrust fault showing uplift of 1.3 m (Courtesy: USGS)

sections of clay, sandy soils and tuffs which amplified vibrations and increased the duration of the ground motion, resulting in large scale destruction.

A surface fault as shown in Fig. 2.14 was found between 8 to 13 km long. This is an unusually short rupture for a reverse event of this magnitude and depth. The reversed thrust and right lateral movement occurred along the surface of the rupture. A maximum vertical displacement of 1.6 m and 0.5 m of right lateral displacement was observed on the fault.

2.7. LOMA PRIETA EARTHQUAKE OF 17.10.1984

An earthquake of 7.1 magnitude occurred in the Santa Cruz mountain on 17th October 1989 at 6.05 p.m. The main shock was located 16 km north-east of the city Santa Cruz and 100 km south-east of San Francisco on the secondary fault of Zayante, very closely parallel to the famous San Andrea fault. Due to this earthquake movement occurred from south-west of Los Gatos to north of San Juan bautista along a 40 km segment of the San Andrea fault. After the earthquake, measurements taken along the surface of the earth showed that pacific plate moved 1.9 m to the north west and 1.3 m upwards over the north American plate.

The upward motion resulted from deformation of the plate boundary at the bend in the San Andreas fault. At the surface the fault motion was clear as a complex series of cracks and fractures as shown in Fig. 2.15.

Fig. 2.15. Surface cracks, Santa Cruz Mountains, California (Courtesy USGS).

Recording made available by USGS show that this earthquake produced maximum acceleration at upper ground level equal to 0.6 g in the epicentre region. Acceleration at four different places were found as follows:

(*i*) 0.64 g at Corralitos

(*ii*) 0.55 g at Gilroy

(*iii*) 0.39 g at Watsonville

(*iv*) 0.38 g at Holster.

The vertical accelerations were often above normal observed at 0.66 g at Watsonville and 0.47 g at Corralitos.

A remarkable feature of Loma Prieta earthquake was the revelation of significant amplification of ground motion at a great distance from the epicentre on sites having poor geotechnical properties. About 30% buildings constructed on unconsolidated deposits were severely damaged due to amplification of ground shaking and deformation in the pacific garden shopping malls in down town santa cruz.

One hundred thirty buildings about more than one hundred years old were damaged in this historic section. Many houses that were not bolted to their foundations were partially found damaged. Thus several hundred houses were either severely damaged or destroyed. The worst ground shaking occurred in the santa cruz. Mountain closed to the epicentre, where many buildings were damaged or destroyed by ground cracking and shaking and land slides.

Apart from above thousands of land slides occurred through out the area blocking roads and highways and causing damage to structures. Land slides particularly were prevalent in the Santa Cruz Mountains, where they occur regularly even with out earthquakes.

In Watsonville two adjacent buildings sustained extensive structural damage due to a weak storey effect, insufficient shear reinforcement in columns and pounding of adjacent buildings.

At the stanford university campus about 50 km north-west of the epicentre of the earthquake 60 buildings sustained varying degree of damage with an estimated repair cost of 160 million U.S. dollars.

Concrete side walks and curbs were systematically fractured and buckled on north-east streets through out Los Gatos. In this city Los Gatos one of the very old house was damaged due to its movement off its foundation *i.e.* it slipped away from its foundation Fig. 2.16. Hollister also experienced severe damage. Sand boils appeared in the irrigated fields near the city of Hollister. Collapse or damage of buildings were reported from other cities also. These buildings suffered large scale damage due to the following reasons:

(*a*) Poor reaction of foundation soil.

(*b*) Soft storey effect *i.e.* in the ground floors or storeys walls between columns were not provided for providing space for parking of vehicles or other such purposes, or large glass panels were provided for show. These were unable to withstand the lateral forces induced by earthquake tremors.

All big towns such as Boulder Creek, Red wood estates, Los Gatos. Santa Cruz, and Watsonville experienced strong ground shaking and had high percentage of damage of buildings. All these towns were only 16 to 32 km

Fig. 2.16. One of the very old damaged houses in Los Gatos, California when it moved off its foundation (Courtesy USGS).

away from the epicentre. The old structures were vulnerable for one or the other following reasons.

(*a*) Lack of ties to the foundation.

(*b*) Deterioration of the structure.

(*c*) Non reinforced stone or brick masonry.

(*d*) Lack of shear resistance in the ground floor.

(*e*) Pounding of adjacent buildings.

(*f*) Timber diaphragms not tied to un reinforced masonry walls, which allowed separation or pushing out of walls.

In the epicentral region most of the buildings got damaged due to the strong ground shaking and land sliding. Ground shaking primarily affected the un reinforced masonry structures. This effect further enhanced in areas of fine grained sand. Land slide occurred on steep slopes where ground shaking was most severe.

2.7.1. Effect of Loma Preita Earthquake in San Francisco, Oakland

Though the Loma Prieta earthquake occurred in the remote Santa Cruz mountains, but it caused severe damage in San Francisco and Oakland 80 km towards north. This is some what unusual for an earthquake of this magnitude. In this earthquake 18306 homes, 97 business establishments and 3 public buildings, 414 single family units, 104 mobile homes were destroyed. 2575 businesses damaged, 12000 people displaced from homes, 3757 people got injured and 67 people died.

The most spectacular damage occurred in the residential neighbourhood of Marina in San Francisco. Here a four storey building constructed in 1920 on hydraulic fill reclaimed from the bay following the worst earthquake of 1906 collapsed. In San Francisco region, Marina area suffered the major damage. At the time of 1906 earthquake of San Francisco, this area was a lagoon. After the 1906 earthquake the lagoon was filled with sand and rubble of collapsed structures to make a fit ground for panama pacific international exhibition. The unconsolidated soils of the Marina district amplified the shaking and became liquefied causing permanent deformation of the ground. This was one of the main causes of the increased damage in this area.

Construction practices also contributed to the damage. In the area some four storey buildings built above garages were not adequately laterally braced. Due to this reason thirty five buildings in the marina district collapsed and 150 other buildings suffered structural damage.

Main reasons for these failures were found as follows:

(*a*) Poor soil conditions

(*b*) In adequate structural design

(*c*) Liquefaction of soil.

On the other hand carefully designed against earthquake high-rise buildings perfectly withstood the fury of the earthquake.

In Oakland several mid rise buildings suffered severe damage and many old brick masonry buildings collapsed primarily due to the liquefaction of the soil. Apart this, under ground burried utilities such as gas pipe lines, water lines, and sewer lines also suffered heavy damage. This damage also added to the miseries of the people as fire broke out after the earthquake could not be fought due to want of water.

2.7.2. Communication hazard

In this earthquake 1500 bridges were affected in five towns and cities. There was a spectacular collapse of 2.4 km stretch of Cypress overpass. It was

Fig. 2.17. Side view of the collapsed Cypress section of the interstate 880 (Courtesy EQE)

a double decker bridge. The upper deck of it fell on the lower road way in Oakland causing 41 deaths. The side view of the collapsed of over pass double decker bridge failure is shown Fig. 2.17. An other spectacular failure occurred on the Oakland bay bridge, one of the longest bridge of the world connecting San Francisco with Oakland is shown in Fig. 2.18.

Fig. 2.18. Damage to San Francisco Oakland Bay bridge (Courtesy USGS).

The Cypress overpass has two levels of R.C.C. decks resting on a series of concrete portal frames about 24 m apart, standing on piles sunk in Bay shore mud. On this viaduct two types of portal frames have been used. The portal frames supporting the lower deck, which carries one way four lane highway, are all made of reinforced concrete. The upper portal frames which carry the top deck are built either of R.C.C. or pre-stressed concrete Fig. 4.17. The two lower nodes of these portal frames contain keys, which form a neck in the cross-section area with four bars that pass through the key.

The collapse of the Cypress overpass occurred due to the development of ground level acceleration of the order of 0.26 g due to the earthquake. The fourth node in the upper portal frame, the only resistant cross section to balance the inertia forces due to heavy weight of the upper deck could not dissipate all the energy generated with out developing a plastic hinge in itself, converting the frame into an unstable condition. The shearing of this cross-section further worsened due to inadequate spacing of tie bars which was found more than 30 cms. This caused the upper deck to fall on the lower deck Fig. 2.19.

The Oakland Bay bridge consists of various different spans, ranging from a suspension bridge to truss spans. The Bay bridge has structural steel frame work and the deck is made of concrete slabs, simply supported on a net work of steel girders. Suspension bridges behaved well during the earthquake as they had their natural periods varying from 3 to 5 seconds, where as 13 spans of 88

Fig. 2.19. Failure of columns of 1880 expressway. Note lack of adequate spacing of stirrups

m each made of truss girders and with double deckes suffered serious movements. Damage occurred to the 15 m long section is shown in Fig. 2.18.

It is interesting to compare this earthquake with that of Armenian earthquake of M 6.9 of December 1988 that killed 25000 people and destroyed entire towns. Good construction and good engineering practices in the Loma prieta area contributed to the preservation of property and human lives.

2.8. NORTHERN IRAN EARTHQUAKE OF 21.6.1990

Iran is located in a region formed by the slow collision of huge geological masses and studded with volcanic ridges. In fact this region is one of the world's deadliest earthquake zone and rests on several tectonic plates. Earthquake fault lines are the edges of the tectonic plates. Since 700 A.D. 14 disastrous earthquakes of magnitudes ranging from 6.0 to 7.7 have been recorded in this area. In the past about 36 years more than 50 significant earthquakes have been recorded in Iran. These earthquakes occurred due to the compression of Iran by the movement of Africa and Arabian peninsula. The Africa-Arabian Peninsula moves to wards Eurasia with a speed of about 16 mm per year.

During the earthquake of 1968, atleast 18000 people were killed in northern Iran near the border of Russia. In 1978, 25000 people were killed in the southern Iran. In December 1988 earthquake 25,000 people were killed in soviet Armenia. This earthquake originated a few hundred kilometer north west of the epicentre of June 1990 earthquake, which was located just off the caspian shore.

A earthquake of magnitude of 7.7 occurred on June 21, 1990 in the northern Iran. The largest ever earthquake recorded in the region of caspian sea might have been amplified by two or more closely spaced tremors occurring in rapid succession. The event which was exceptionally close to the surface for this region was un usually destructive.

The epicentre of 1990 earthquake was located in the collision zone between the Arabian plate and the Eurasian plate. This area, the northern seismic zone runs east and west-along the southern shore of the caspian sea. The June 1990 earthquake caused wide spread damage in a area of 100 km radius of the epicentre near the city of Rasht and about 200 km north west of Tehran. The cities of Manjil, Rudbar and Lushan and 700 villages were distroyed and atleast 300 more villages were slightly damaged.

In Gilan and Zanjin provinces south west of caspian sea a damage of seven million U.S dollar was estimated. 10^5 Kuccha houses (Adobe house) were collapsed resulting 40,000 dead and 60,000 injured. 5×10^5 people were rendered home less. Telephone lines, electricity and water supplies were cut off. Most of the victims were buried under the concrete walls and ceilings as the earthquake occurred at night.

The rescure operations were hampered due to:

(*a*) Earthquake occurred at mid night.

(*b*) Adverse weather conditions.

(*c*) Rugged terrain of mountain villages. Roads and highways were blocked by extensive land slides further hampered the rescure operations.

Following factors contributed to the large scale damage:

1. **Construction materials:** In the construction, brittle materials such as bricks, blocks, adobe, wooden timber and modern materials of in appropriate quality were used in traditional structures.
2. **Construction techniques and workmanship.** The use of un reinforced masonry and un reinforced shear walls, poor welding connections in steel frames, failure to tie steel support beams together, use of heavy masonry with out adequate support in flooring, ceiling and roofs.
3. **Inadequate design and detailing.** Lack in symmetry in traditional type of structures. Earthquake resistant principles of design were not applied. Reinforcement detailing near the joint and in column were inadequate. Building code provisions were inconsistent or were not applied.
4. **Liquefaction and failure of soils.** This factor specially was prominent on the shores of the caspian sea. The soil lost its strength and behaved as a viscous liquid during earthquake due to liquefaction. The structures sank or spread away by the liquefaction in the absence of any firm support. The un-consolidated soils may have amplified the seismic vibrations Fig. 2.20 shows the damage to building by liquefaction.
5. Often several factors contributed to the failure of a single structure. In building failure the single most important factor was found the use of un reinforced masonry walls. The efficient use of the lessons learnt from the

Fig. 2.20. House building damaged by liquefaction (Courtesy Dames & Moore)

past earthquake will result in saving lives and property in the future earthquakes.

Wall crack as shown in Fig. 2.20 developed due to the settlement in liquefied soil during the earthquake. As already discussed soils liquefy when the ground water near the surface of the ground is forced in between the grains of fine grained sandy soil during earthquake. The sandy soil behaves as a very thick liquid called viscous liquid like syrup. In this condition structures settle down or tip in the liquefied soil or ripped apart as ground spread laterally or flows during the earthquake.

In towns of Rudbar, Manjil and Lushan many building were collapsed or damaged beyond repair. In the epicentral region many residential and commercial buildings were destroyed. Higher damage was observed in the areas of unreinforced masonary bearing wall construction.

In the area mostly buildings were constructed of un reinforced masonry bearing walls. The masonry material used was brittle, which performed very poorly during the strong seismic vibrations. The heavy weight of the masonry floors and roofs also contributed significantly to the failure of such buildings.

In the mountain villages near Manjil buildings collapsed were of un reinforced masonry. The construction was mainly of irregularly shaped lava blocks set in dried mud or sun dried mud bricks with similar cement. The roofs of these village houses consisted of thick layers of dried mud spread over reeds laid across closely spaced horizontal poles. Such a construction is highly vulnerable to earthquake damage.

In Manjil area some buildings having jack arch roofs without adequate support for its weight also collapsed. The failure of these roofs contributed unuually high deaths and failure of buildings.

Fig. 2.21. Lateral drift of a 8 storeyed apartment building
(Courtesy Dames & Moore)

Fig. 2.21 shows tilt from verticality of an 8 storey steel structure. This structure was under construction at the time of earthquake. In the direction in which the tilt occurred, there were insufficient moment frames. The damage to the structure occurred due to inadequate design and detailing and poor construction workmanship.

During this earthquake many R.C.C. buildings and R.C.C. overhead tanks also collapsed. But all these damages were the result of inadequate design and poor reinforcement detailing.

During the earthquake though a pier of a bridge displaced at the ground

Fig. 2.22. Large lateral pier displacement of undamaged concrete bridge
(Courtesy: Dames & Moore)

level by 25.4 cms, but the bridge remained intact. Fig. 2.22 Similarly a buttress dam located within one km of the fault remained un affected during this earthquake. The length of the dam was 425 metres with a base width of 100 metres. The height of the dam was 106 metres. At the time of earthquake the reservoir was full and experienced very intensive ground motion (0.6 g). Horizontal and diagonal cracks developed at the top of some buttresses, but the dam remained intact.

2.9. NORTH RIDGE EARTHQUAKE OF 17.1.1994

An earthquake of magnitude of 6.8 occurred in Southern California on 17th January 1994. The epicenter of the earthquake was beneath the San Farnando valley 32 km West-North west of Los Angeles. The rock on the south side of the fault surged upwards and over the rock on the north side. As a result of the earthquake the crust of the earth on the south of the San Farnando valley moved slightly closer to the earth crust on the north side of the valley, making mountains on the north side of the valley a little higher.

2.9.1. Damage

The damage due to this earthquake was most extensive in San Farnando valley, Simi valley and in the northern parts of the Los Angeles basin. Though the death toll was only 57, but after the earthquake 24000 dwellings were vacated. The total cost of the earthquake was estimated atleast 10 billion U.S. dollars. This earthquake was significant in the sense that it proved most expensive in terms of money and natural disaster both in the history of united states. This earthquake occurred on a previously unknown fault.

The damage to buildings outside the epicenter area was severe and spotty in geographical distribution, but spread over a large area. The type and density

Fig. 2.23. Collapse of a three storey apartment building with a first level garage.

of the construction and the strength of the earthquake shaking affected the distribution of the damaged buildings. Here also un reinforced masonry and older concrete frame constructions suffered structural damage. However newly constructed structures, particularly parking garages, commercial buildings and apartment complexes also suffered damages. A apartment building constructed on a garage sank at its garage level and another three storeyed building totally collapsed at its garage level is shown in Fig. 2.23. Heavy damage occurred in Santa Monica about 24 km from the epicenter and across the Santa Monica mountains. In this area 134 buildings were damaged to the un safe limit of occupancy and 396 were damaged enough to limit occupancy.

(*a*) Damage to infra structure

After the occurrence of this earthquake 680,000 people were rendered without power, gas and phone service in the Los Angeles area. Power cuts swept through out the Los Angeles basin and much far off areas. Phone service was disrupted due to damage to equipments and power cuts.

Water trunk lines were broken and water flooded some streets of the town and 40,000 people remained with out water. Gas from ruptured gas lines ignited and the resulting fire destroyed several homes which caused heavy damage.

(*b*) Damage to transportation

This earthquake closed several highways. Rock slides also blocked many roads and caused disruption to traffic for many hours. Due to this earthquake southern pacific train was also derailed near the epicenter of the earthquake spilling about 20×10^3 litres of sulphuric acid and 5×10^3 litres of diesel oil fuel. Nations busiest free way remained disrupted for many hours.

2.10. KOBE (JANPAN) EARTHQUAKE OF 17.1.1995

An earthquake of magnitude of 6.9 on Richter scale struck the region of Kobe and Osaka in the south central Japan on 17.1.1995. The Region of Kobe and Osake is the second most populated and industrialized area after Tokyo in Japan. The total population of the region is estimated as 10 million. The shocks of the earthquake occurred at a shallow depth on a fault running from Awaji Island through the city of Kobe, which has a population of about 1.5 million. The strong ground shaking lasted far 20 seconds and caused severe damage to a large area. The greatest intensity of shaking was in a narrow strip of two to four kms stretching 40 km along the coast of Osaka Bay. In some places ground moved as much as five metres. The worst destruction occurred along the previously undetected fault on the coast, east of Kobe. In this strip, Kobe's major business, industrial and port facilities and residences are located.

2.10.1. Damage

The earthquake caused extensive damage to the coastal cities that border Osaka Bay and to the northern portion of Awaji Island. The inland cities located near the northern end of the fault rupture sustained significant damage. This earthquake caused 5480 deaths, the highest toll in Japan after the Great Kanto earthquake of 1923. In 1923 earthquake about 140,000 people were killed, and 94900 people were injured and 317000 people were moved to evacuation centres.

From the epicentre the damage was recorded over an area of 100 km radius. Kobe being the nearest area from the epicenter suffered most severely. The damage was severe particularly in the central Kobe in an area roughly 5 × 20 km area parallel to the port of Kobe. This coastal area is composed primarily of soft alluvial soils and artificial fills. Severe damage extended well upto north east and east of Kobe into the out skirts of Osaka and its port.

Before the ground shaking stopped, fire broke out every where in the pre dawn darkness due to the leakage of gas from the ruptured gas mains and pipe lines and the broken timber pieces of old timber houses. In first 20 seconds every thing except misery disappeared from the area.

2.10.2. Damage to buildings

By this earthquake more than 192700 buildings and houses were totally destroyed. Most of the damaged buildings were rendered un safe to occupy and later were demolished. In many buildings either first storey or fifth storey collapsed. Such failure occurred in buildings that appeared from out side to have floors of equal strength and identical construction. The first and fifth floors were specially vulnerable as they were at the internodes of the sine wave. Many buildings were leaning on one side or were out of plumb. This was usually caused by partial collapse of a storey or floor on one side of the building or by permanent off set of the structural system.

The highest concentration of damage in mid rise buildings was observed in the area of Kobe's central business district. Most of the collapse were towards north. Evidently this was due to the long period velocity pulse perpendicular to the fault. This effect has also been observed in other earthquakes. The major failures of commercial and residential buildings were noted at far off places also.

The majority of partially or complete collapse was found in older reinforced cement structures built before 1975. However, significant non structural damage was also observed in relatively recent constructed composite or steel structures. The base of larger buildings appeared a couple of centimeters higher than the adjacent streets or side walk. The horizontal gaps between the base of buildings and adjacent streets and side walks were common. This shows that the response of buildings might have been influenced by the following factors:

1. Soil structure interaction.
2. Age of the construction.
3. Soil and foundation of structure condition.
4. Proximity to the fault.
5. Type of structural system. This factor was found prominent of the factors influencing the performance of structures.

The damage was worst in areas bordering the ports or rivers and streams, where soils were either alluvial deposits or fill or poorly consolidated. The liquefaction of soils or unequal or equal settlement might have been the reason of worst damage. On the contrary there was minor damage in the foot hills of mountain, where soils either were very shallow or there were rock out crops. Loose and soft soils amplified the ground motion in comparison to bed rock, especially ground motions with in a certain frequency range. Duration of shaking is also large on soft and loose soils.

Most of the heavily damaged buildings were traditional timber frame one or two storey residential or small commercial buildings of Shinkabe or Okabe construction.

Shinkabe Construction. This type of structures have mud walls reinforced with bamboo lattice. The roofs are very heavy made of mud and tiles. This type of roofs are found effective in preventing damage due to typhoon. The roofs are supported on post and beam construction. The foundations are of stone or concrete blocks. The wood framing is not well attached to the foundation.

Okabe Construction. This construction has thin spaced wood sheathing, spaning between wooden posts and attached with limited nailing. The exterior plaster is not reinforced with a wire mesh or well attached to the wood framing. Thus it falls off in sheets when cracked. After 1981 construction nominal diagonal bracing is provided to resist the lateral loads. Rest of the construction of roof and foundation is same as that of shinkabe.

Traditional wood frame construction had the most wide spread damage through out the region, resulting in the largest number of casualties. The house collapse led to the rupture of many gas lines.

Large inertia forces due to the heavy roofs typically caused failures of these buildings. This inertia force exceeded the lateral earthquake load resisting capacity of the supported walls. The relatively weak storeys created by the open fronts typically collapsed. In Japan there are no interior partitions in houses, to help resist the earthquake forces or loads. In older houses many framing members had been weakened by wood rot. The soil failures increased the damage as the foundations virtually have no strength to resist the settlement and the connections between structures and their foundations were weak.

In Kobe's area impact of falling roof of one house caused destruction of an other house. The interaction usually caused the lateral collapse of traditional houses by impinging upon the neighbouring structure. The repair cost of buildings was estimated as 100 billions of U.S. dollars. The damage of buildings is shown in Fig. 2.24 to 2.27.

Fig. 2.24 shows the badly damaged (4th storey collapsed on 3rd storey) communication building.

Fig. 2.25 shows the collapse of fifth floor of a multi storeyed building.

Fig. 2.26 shows the leaning of a office building with partially destroyed first storey.

Fig. 2.27 shows the collapse of concrete framed structure with a mid storey collapsed fifth floor due to soft 5th storey in the business centre of Kobe.

Fig. 2.24. Badly damaged communication building (the fourth floor collapsed on the third floor).

Fig. 2.25. Collapsed fifth floor of a multi-storeyed office block.

During Kobe's earthquake more than dozens of R.C.C. commercial buildings partially or fully collapsed at one or more floor levels. The buildings which collapsed typically were 6 to 12 storey tall. The failure in these buildings often occurred with in middle third of the building height. One possible reason of such failures could be that the period of the strong ground motion pulses might have been in a range that generally coincided with higher vibration modes for these buildings. This would have amplified stresses in the middle portion of the buildings.

An other possible factor could be that there might have been changes in

Fig. 2.26. Leaning office building with partially destroyed first floor.

Fig. 2.27. Concrete framed structure with a mid-storey collapsed fifth floor in the business centre of Kobe-Cause Soft 5th storey.

the building strength or stiffness at these levels. For example if shear walls or the steel columns encased in concrete that extend up from the foundation discontinued at a certain floor level, the strength and stiffness of the structure above that floor level may be significantly less than at the floor below.

Instances of concrete structures failures in the ground floor were also fairly common. These failures resulted from the typical soft storey effect. As already discussed the soft storey effect developed by the need of garages and the desire to have numerous large open windows for store fronts at the bottom floor. In Japan high cost of land and general congestion has enhanced or increased this problem. Very narrow multi storey buildings with open store fronts are very common in Japan. Irregular distribution of shear walls or concrete frames resulted in substantial torsion, causing the structure to twist as well as sway due to earthquake.

Another most common mode of damage to structures was brittle shear failure of concrete columns leading to collapse of the floor level above. The brittle failure occurred due to inadequate reinforcement detailing.

In general it was observed that the failure of columns occurred due to the spacing of ties at greater distance than the required. Secondly the hooks provided at the ends of the ties were bent at 90° instead of 135°. The hook bent at 90°, opened out at the time of earthquake and could not provide confinement to the central core and the concrete cover out side the ties spalled off, resulting in the collapse of the buildings. Further in Kobe region un deformed bars were used as reinforcement. Further the length of ties were not extended by 10 times the diameter of tie bar into the core. This requirement is a must for ductile design of buildings.

2.10.3. Damage to transportation

One of the most disturbing and far reaching aspects of this earthquake was the severe and extensive damage to the transportation system. Kobe is situated with in the main transportation corridor between central and southern Honshu. The Hanshin express way supported over large hammer shaped R.C.C. piers failed over more than 20 km length. The supporting steel girders of the Wangan express way along the harbour shore were dislodged from their seats and few of them collapsed. It was observed that this collapse occurred at the location where the road deck was changed from steel to heavier section of concrete. Fig. 2.28. Had the earthquake occured during rush hours, unimagible loss of life and wealth would have occured.

Rail facilities. Rail facilities particularly were hit very hard. All the three main lines passing through the corridor sustained embankment's failure, over

Fig. 2.28. Collapsed Kobe Hanshin Expressway

pass collapses and distorted rails and other sever damages. The elevated viaduct that carried the bullet trains was severely damaged due to the shear failure of the supporting columns. There was damage to the subway systems including a rare instance of severe earthquake damage to a modern tunnel for reasons other than fault displacement near the portal.

Kobe's subway system. During a earthquake, the damage to underground facilities such as mines, tunnels or subways is a rare phenomenon. An unusual example of severe damage to the underground facility occurred in the Kobe's subway system.

This subway system was a two track line running under central Kobe. This system was generally built by cut and cover method in the mid of 1960s. The double track is carried typically through a concrete tube 9 m wide and 6.4 m high, which widens to 17 m at the site of stations. The tube typically has about 5 m over burden, which is supported by 40 cms thick walls and roof slabs. The walls and roof slabs are supported between the tracks by a series of 5 m high, 1.0 m long and 0.4 m wide R.C.C. columns.

Port damage. Kobe port has one of the largest container facilities in the world sustained major damage. Ships had to be diverted to other ports. The functioning of port remained suspended for days together. The suspension of port's functioning impeded the shipment of raw materials and parts between businessess in Japan and their partners over seas.

There was severe and wide spread liquefaction in the area due to earthquake. In some areas liquefaction caused settlement or subsidence ranging from 0.5 m to 3.0 m and large volume of silt was ejected due to this settlement. Local lateral spreading of soils occurred along quay walls in many parts of the extensive port facilities. The lateral ground deformation caused the piers of the highway bridge and electric rail bridge between port Island and Kobe to tilt or lean about 2 to 3 degrees towards the water front. However the pile supported structures remained at their original elevations; while the surrounding ground settled substantially. Significant quantities of sand were ejected due to liquefaction and spread over large portions of the pavements.

Many gantry cranes were damaged. The damage to gantry cranes was in the form of leg and cross beam buckling and rupture at the wheels. The extent of Buckling varied depending upon the relative horizontal displacement due to the movement of caissons. Few cranes jumped off the track and one crane collapsed due to the displacement of the caisson. Numerous other cranes through out port were damaged due to the damage of their foundations.

Quay wall caisson displacements took place due to many factors. Earthquake accelerations applied to the massive sand filled caissons resulted in large horizontal forces, which might have exceeded the sliding resistance offered by the base of the caissons. The rocking motion of the caissons would have further aggravated the situation which might have created excessive bearing pressure at the toe of the base. Further many caissons tilted in the Island. The tilting of caissons may be due to the liquefaction of the soil. In the

Island, the fill placed under water was dumped from barges. It was relatively un compacted. Thus the settlement occurred due to lateral spreading and compaction. Such settlements continued during the first few days after the earthquake. After this earthquake out of 186 heavy shipping berths, 179 berths remained inoperative for days together.

Infrastructures. In this earthquake though telecommunications and Electric power services were not disrupted, but water supply, water treatment and gas utilities were disrupted. Water lines were restored in fifteen days and gas lines in 30 days. In this earthquake about 150 fires started with in minutes of the start of earthquake. Fires mainly started in densly populated low rise areas of the city. These fires destroyed one million square metre residential area of the city Kobe.

2.11. BHUJ (Gujrat-India) EARTHQUAKE OF 26.1.2001

An earthquake of magnitude of 7.7 at Richter scale occurred at 8.46 a.m., when the Nation was preparing to celebrate its 52nd Republic day. The epicentre of this earthquake was in Bhuj town about 15 m below the earth surface.

This earthquake was the strongest of all earthquakes that hit India during the last 40 years. Parts of Bhuj town disappeared from the face of the earth for ever. Buildings were damaged in Ahmedabad, Surat and Bhav nagar. The death toll in towns and villages of Gujrat was estimated as 50,000 or more. After one month of the earthquake Govt. of India put the figures as follows.

Death total as 19727, injured as 166000, home less rendered 6,00,000 people, houses destroyed 34800, and 844,000 damaged. People affected directly or indirectly 15.9 million out of the total population of the state of Gujrat being 37.8 million. Cattle perished figure is 20,000. Government estimates total loss as 1.3 billion U.S. dollar where as unofficial Fig. is as high as 5 billion U.S. dollars. The Anjar town almost completely destroyed.

In Ahmedabad a town situated about 250 km from the epicenter of the earthquake about 69 concrete buildings collapsed killing about 700 people. The buildings that collapsed during the 26th January earthquake were so poorly designed and constructed that they were incapable of resisting lateral forces caused by the earthquake. About 80 buildings caved in with in a span of three minutes. None of these buildings which collapsed were built by known builders. The most gruesome incident happened when a new four storeyed school building in the city's Maninagar area collapsed killing 33 children instantiy.

Causes of mass destruction of buildings

Following causes may be attributed to this large scale destruction of structures:

(*a*) Kutch region is comprised of soft alluvial soils and buildings were built on loose and soft alluvial soils. Such soils might have liquefied causing mass destruction of buildings.

(*b*) Use of sub standard construction material in the construction work.

(*c*) Poor execution of building work by non technical people.

(*d*) Faulty design.

(*e*) Construction of buildings on reclaimed and soft soils.

In Bhuj and nearby region some villages have been wiped off completely. The reason of such dangerous consequences are as follows:

(*i*) *Poor quality of construction.* The walls of the houses were made of quarry stones, bricks or mud, laid in a weak cement mortar or lime mortar. No earthquake resistance measures were adopted.

(*ii*) In majority of the cases the houses were constructed on soft soils and alluvial deposits with out consolidation.

(*iii*) *No reinforcement was used in the masonry.* Thus in the absence of any measure of bonding the different units together, the load bearing walls collapsed leading to the total collapse of the building. Fig. 2.28 to 2.32 show the destruction of poorly designed and constructed buildings.

Fig. 2.28 shows the total collapse of a 10 storeyed residential building in Ahmedabad.

Fig. 2.28. Total collapse of a 10 storey residential building in front in Ahmedabad.

Fig. 2.29 shows the collapse of one half of 14 storeyed R.C. frame building in Ahmedabad.

Fig. 2.30 shows the collapse of a two storeyed R.C. frame building.

Fig. 2.31 Four storeyed L shaped building (in plan) completely collapsed.

Fig. 2.32. Partially collapsed apartment in Ahmedabad.

Causes of failure of R.C.C. buildings

Following causes may have affected the destruction of R.C.C. buildings:

Fig. 2.29. Collapse of one half on the 14 storeyed R.C. frame building in Ahmedabad.

Fig. 2.30. Collapse of ground floor of a two storeyed R.C. frame building.

1. Soft foundation soil. As explained above, the region of Ahemadabad is comprised of alluvil soft soil. The soft soil on which the houses have been founded would have affected the response of the building in the following ways:

(*i*) Amplification of the ground motion at the base of the structure.

(*ii*) Relative displacement between individual column foundation vertically and horizontally in the absence of either foundation struts as per IS 4326 or plinth beams. In the absence of beam at plinth or ground level, the length of ground storey columns get increased, which increases the flexibility of the ground storey. If the column become long, the

Fig. 2.31. Four-storey 'L' shaped building (in plan) completely collapsed in Ahmedabad.

Fig. 2.32. Partially collapsed apartment building in Ahmedabad.

buckling moment will increase the bending causing, collapse of the column.

(*iii*) If the soil is sandy and water table is high, liquefaction of soil may develop and cause wide spread damage as explained earlier also due to subsidence and tilting.

(*iv*) Absence of foundation on raft and piles may cause excessive settlement of foundation or movement of spread foundation causing collapse of the structure.

QUESTIONS

1. Explain the phenomenon of liquefaction of soil and its ill effects on the structure.
2. Name different causes of damage to buildings during earthquake and suggest measures to check such damages.
3. What is soft storey effect? How it can be removed?
4. Explain in brief the effect of Kobe (Japan) earthquake.
5. Discuss the Bhuj earthquake of 2001. What can be done to check the effects of such earthquakes.
6. Discuss in brief the earthquake of El. Asnam giving its special features.
7. Give the factors which cause structural failure during a earthquake.
8. Discuss the factors which caused large scale destruction during Armenian (USSR) earthquake.
9. What structural deficiencies were found in the building construction in Loma Prieta which caused so large a damage to buildings.
10. Identify the incorrect statement/statements.
    (*a*) Buildings founded on strong soils or rocks are less affected by earthquake.
    (*b*) Buildings founded on soft soils are more affected by earthquakes.
    (*c*) Orientation of building with respect to fault affects it severely during an earthquake.
    (*d*) Distribution of structural as well as non structural members is a prominent cause of damage of buildings during an earthquake.
    (*e*) Soft-storey is a major cause of damage to buildings during an earthquake
    (*f*) All are correct
    (*g*) All are incorrect.
11. Identify the correct statement/statements.
    (*a*) Earthquake damage depends on the quality of materials and construction of the building
    (*b*) The strength of joint is reduced considerably due to abrupt cutting of reinforcement.
    (*c*) The strength of joint is reduced considerably due to insufficient length of anchorage.
    (*d*) Cycling loading affects the strength of the joint of a building.
    (*e*) All are correct.
    (*f*) All are incorrect.
12. Identify the incorrect statement/statements.
    (*a*) Distance from the Epicenter has no influence on the damage of buildings during an earthquake
    (*b*) Geotechnical properties of soil have no effect on the damage of the buildings during an earthquake.
    (*c*) Soft soils do not amplify ground shaking and ground deformations.
    (*d*) Hard rocks amplify ground shaking more than soft soils.
    (*e*) All are incorrect.

13. The damage of buildings during an earthquake occurs due to.
    (*a*) Quality of construction materials
    (*b*) Due to construction techniques and workmanship
    (*c*) Inadequate design and detailing
    (*d*) All the above
14. Identify the incorrect statement/statements
    (*a*) Liquefaction of soil causes major damages to the buildings during earthquakes
    (*b*) Liquefaction of soil has no effect on damage of buildings during earthquakes
    (*c*) Unconsolidated soils amplify seismic vibrations
    (*d*) Usually more than one factor cause damage to buildings during earthquakes

ANSWERS:

10. (*f*)
11. (*e*)
12. (*e*)
13. (*d*)
14. (*b*)

3

Earthquakes Causes, Severity and Forecasting

3.1. INTRODUCTION

Earthquakes are natural phenomenon. It is believed that over stressed earth planet releases its energy in the form of earthquake and volcanoes. Thus it can be said that the vibrations of the earth surface caused from a source of disturbance inside the earth are called earthquakes. Earthquakes strike suddenly, violently and with out warning. For this reason the earthquakes are dreaded by human beings. The most important sources of earthquakes from Engineering point of view are those of tectonic origin. Though earthquakes occur daily in the world some where or the other but big earthquakes of magnitude of 8.0 or more on Richter scale occur only 18 in a year and about 20% of them occur in India. In this chapter causes of earthquake, their severity and forecasting shall be discussed. Before discussing earthquake, it will be proper to know our planet 'earth'.

3.2. EARTH AND ITS INTERIOR

Long long ago, a large amount of material accumulated together to form still larger layers to form the earth. A large amount of heat was generated by the fusion of this material. Slowly as the earth cooled down heavier and denser materials sank down to the centre and the lighter materials rose to the top. The equatorial radius of the earth is about 6378 km. The constituents of earth surface are as follows:

1. Oxygen ... 49.5%
2. Silicon ... 25.8%
3. Aluminium ... 7.5%
4. Iron ... 4.7%
5. Calcium ... 3.4%
6. Sodium ... 2.6%
7. Potassium ... 2.4%
8. Magnesium ... 1.9%
9. Hydrogen ... 0.09%
10. Titanium ... 0.06%
11. Other ... 0.07%

About 75% of the earth surface is covered with water. At some places of the earth the depth of water bodies is about 11.2 km, but the average depth of water bodies is estimated as 3.2 km. Further about 75% nitrogen is found on the earth surface along with other gases.

3.3. STRUCTURE OF THE EARTH

The earth consists of the following four parts:

1. **Earth crust.** The outer most layer of the earth is known as earth crust. The thickness of this layer is said to vary from 5.0 to 56.0 km. Some authors have suggested its thickness varying from 5.0 to 40 km. However the average thickness of this layer is assumed as 33.0 km. The radius at equator is taken as 6378 km. The density of this part is 1500 kg/m^3 or 1.5 gms/cc, pressure at the crust is taken as 1 atmospheric or 1 kg/cm^2 and temperature as 25°C.
2. **Lithosphere.** The crust and the upper most part of the mantle down upto a depth of about 70 to 100 km under deep ocean basin and upto 100 to 150 km under continent is rigid forming a hard outer shell. This outer shell is called lithosphere. Thus the earth's crust together with the upper most part of the mantle of about 200 km thickness forms the lithosphere. Its properties are same as that of earth crust.
3. **Asthenosphere.** Beneath the lithosphere exists Asthenosphere. Its thickness is taken as 150 km. According to some authors, its lower and upper boundaries are not well defined. It is believed that in this layer the seismic velocities are decreased, suggesting its lower rigidity. This weaker layer is thought to be partially molten. This layer may be able to flow over long periods of times like a viscous fluid or plastic solid depending upon temperature and composition. This layer plays an important role in plate tectonic, as it makes possible the relative motion of over lying lithosphere plates.

   Some authors suggest the thickness of Asthenosphere as 2685 km surrounding the core. This portion is composed of hot, dense ultra basic igneous rock in a plastic state. The density of this part varies from 5 to 6 gram per cm^3 (5000 to 6000 kg/m^3). The temperature at the periphery of mantle is 2600°C and at its centre temperature is around 4000°C. The thickness of mantle is about 2900 km.

4. **Barysphere.** It is also called as core. This core is further divided into two parts as inner core and outer core:

   (*i*) *Inner core.* The thickness of this core is 1224 km and mainly composed of nickle and iron. It's density varies from 13.5 to 16.0 gm/c.c. (13000 to 16000 kg/m^3) and it behaves as a solid. Its radius has been indicated as 1221 km. Some authors have suggested this value as 1290 km.

   (*ii*) *Outer core.* This core surrounds the inner core. The thickness of outer core is 2200 km. Again some authors have suggested this thickness as 2249 km. However the combined thickness of inner and outer cores has been suggested as 3473 km. Actually all these depths are based on hypothetical judgement of different scientists as actual measurements are not possible. So some contradiction. The outer core is comprised of, nickle and iron alloys with silica. This exists as a liquid of density 12 gm/c.c. or 12000 kg/m^3 The temperature of the core is 2500°C and pressure of 4×10^6 atmosphere Fig. 3.1.

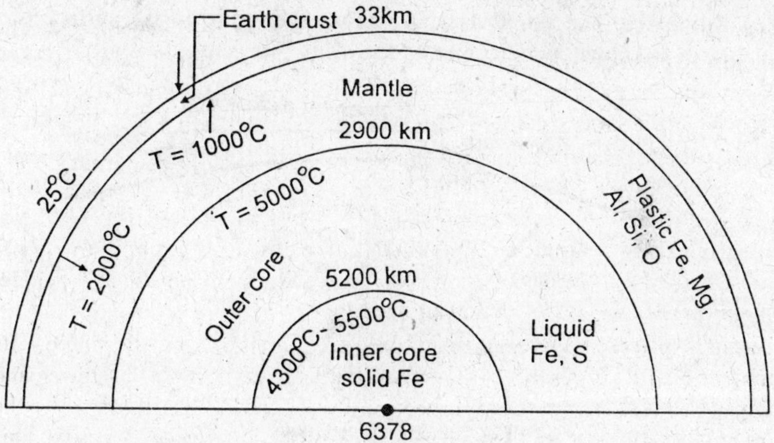

Fig. 3.1. Earth interior

These figures are guide lines not the absolute values.

3.3.1. Rocks of earth's crust

There are two types of rocks on the surface of the earth crust:

(*a*) **Sial rocks.** Thee rocks are Aluminium-silicon rocks. These are lighter rocks. Their sp. gravity is 2.7. They contain 65 to 75 silica and rest aluminium. Granite rocks which are sedimentary rocks come under this type of rocks. Researchers have proved that these rocks have not been found in sea bed.

(*b*) **Sima rocks.** These rocks are silica-magnesia rocks. Basalt rocks come under this category of rocks. These rocks are comprised of 40 to 45% of silica, and also contain magnesia and iron oxide. These rocks are dark in colour and are heavy. Their sp. gravity varies from 2.8 to 3.0. These rocks are found at sea beds. Thus it is clear that earth crust is made of a combination of sial and sima type rocks.

3.4. Definitions

(*a*) **Focus.** The point on the fault from where the slip starts is called focus or hypocentre. The location of the focus of an earthquake is very important as it indicates the depth at which rupture and movement develops. Though movement of material with in the earth occurs through out the mantle and core, but earthquakes are concentrated in the upper 700 km depth of the earth only. Most frequently earthquakes originate from a depth upto 70 kms from the crust surface. Such earthquakes are called shallow focus earthquakes. Earthquakes which originate or occur between 70 km and 300 km depth are called intermediate focus earthquakes. Earthquakes having focal depth more than 300 km are called deep focus earthquakes.

(*b*) **Epicentre.** The point vertically above the focus on the surface of the earth is known as epicenter as shown is Fig. 3.2.

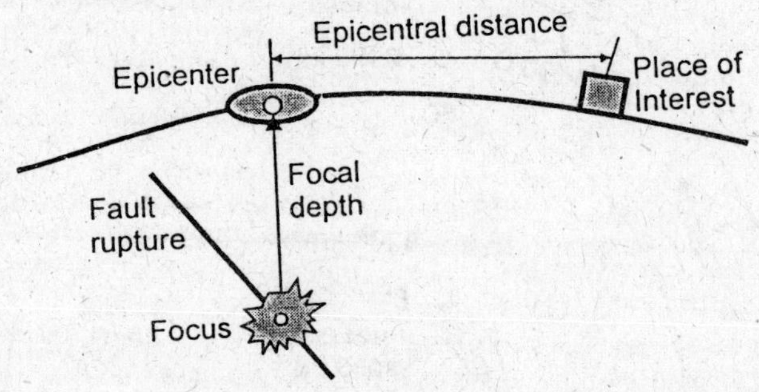

Fig. 3.2. Basic termology

(*c*) **Focal depth.** The vertical distance between the focus and the epicenter is called focal depth. It is an important parameter for determining the damaging potential of a earthquake. Most of the damaging earthquakes have been found of shallow focus with the focal depths less than about 70 km. As the focal depth increases, the energy released by the earthquake decreases progressively. Also seismic energy released from a source deeper than 70 km gets largely dissipated by the time it reaches the surface.

(*d*) **Epicentral distance.** The distance between the focus and the point of determining the effects of damage of the earthquake is known as epicentral distance.

Fore shocks. The smaller tremors which take place before the big or main earthquake are called fore shocks. These can be caused either by small ruptures or plastic deformations.

After shocks. The smaller tremors which take place after the big or main earthquake are called after shocks. These shocks are caused either by fresh ruptures or the readjustment of the fractured mass.

Major shock. A major shock may result from a rupture of rock over a length of 100 to 400 km and several km wide and thick. The energy released by a damaging earthquake is of the order of 10^{20} to 10^{25} ergs.

The bigger is the mass of rupture at one time, bigger is the earthquake.

Magnitude of earthquake. The magnitude of an earthquakes is a quantitative measure of the actual size of the earthquake.

Intensity of earthquake. The intensity of an earthquake is a measure of the actual shaking at a location during an earthquake. These shall be discussed in details in this chapter afterwards.

Focal region. From the focus, a small region of earth through which the seismic destruction propagates is called *focal region.*

ISO seismic lines. The lines joining the places or locations of experiencing earthquake of the same intensity are called *iso seismic lines.*

Homo seismal lines. The line or lines joining the locations or places which receive the seismic waves simultaneously or at the same times are called homo seismal lines.

3.5. THE CIRCULATION

In the viscous mantle convection currents develop due to prevailing high temperature and pressure gradient between crust and the core. These convection currents are similar to the convective flow of water when heated in a beaker as shown in Fig. 3.3. The energy for the development of convection currents is derived from the heat produced from the continuous or incessant decay of radioactive elements in the rocks through out the interior of the earth's crust. These convective currents result in a circulation of the earth's mass. The hot molten lava comes out of the earth and the cold rock mass goes into the earth. This cold mass absorbed, eventually melts under the high temperature and pressure and forms a part of the mantle. This material one day comes out of the earth at some or other place. Many such local circulations take place at different regions under the earth crust, leading different portions of the earth moving in different directions along the surface.

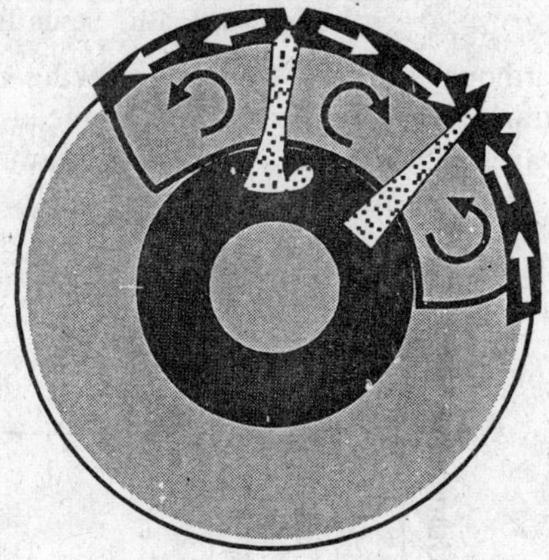

Fig. 3.3. Local Convective Current in the mantle

3.6. THE EARTHQUAKE

The rocks on earth usually are made of elastic materials. Hence during deformation due to gigantic tectonic plates action that occurs in earth, elastic strain energy is stored in these rocks. How ever the material contained in rocks is also brittle. Thus when the rocks along a weak region in the Earth's crust develop strain energy upto their bearing capacity, a sudden movement takes place to the opposite side of the fault (A fault is a crack in the rocks where movement has taken place) suddenly slip and release large elastic strain energy stored in the interface of the rocks. The elastic strain build up and brittle rupture is shown in Fig. 3.4. The sudden slip at the fault causes earthquake. When

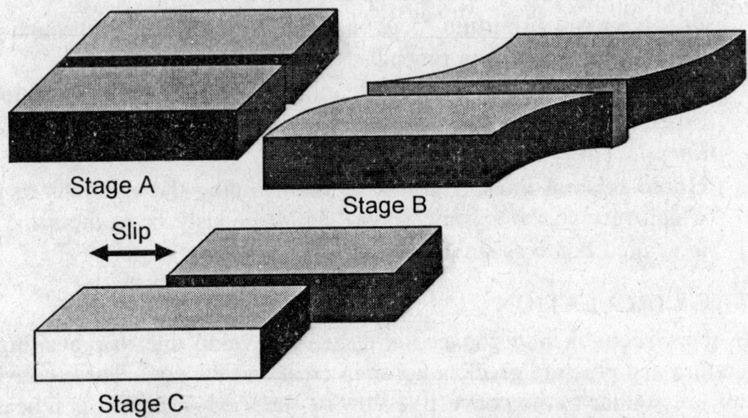

Fig. 3.4. Elastic Strain Buildup and Brittle Rupture

earthquake occurs, a violent shaking of the earth takes place and large elastic strain energy is released which spreads out in all directions through the seismic waves. The seismic waves travel through the body and along the surface of the

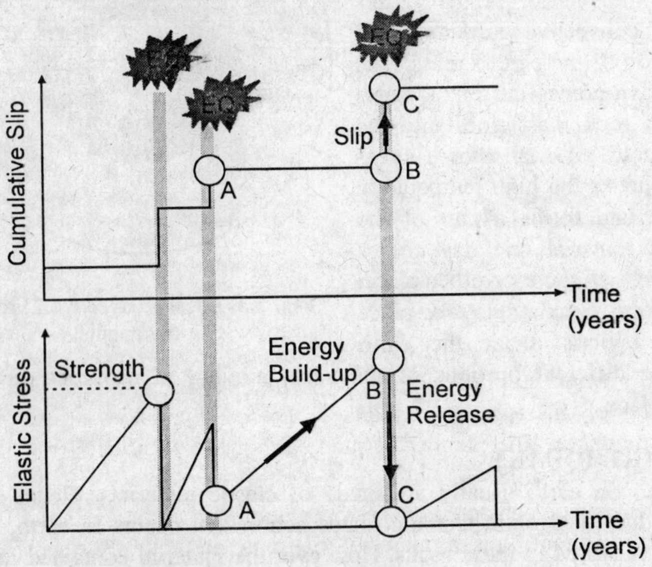

Fig. 3.5. Elastic Rrbound Theory (Courtesy—IITK)

earth. After the earthquake is over the process of strain energy build up starts again at the modified interface between the rocks as shown in Fig. 3.5. Earth scientists call it *Elastic Rebound theory.* The material at the fault over which the slip occurs points out that slip usually constitute an oblong three dimensional volume, with its long dimension. Sometimes its length may be tens of km.

During an earthquake a slip is generated at the fault in both vertical as well horizontal directions. These slip are called Dip slip. The slips developed in lateral direction are called strike slip as shown in Fig. 3.6 some times one of

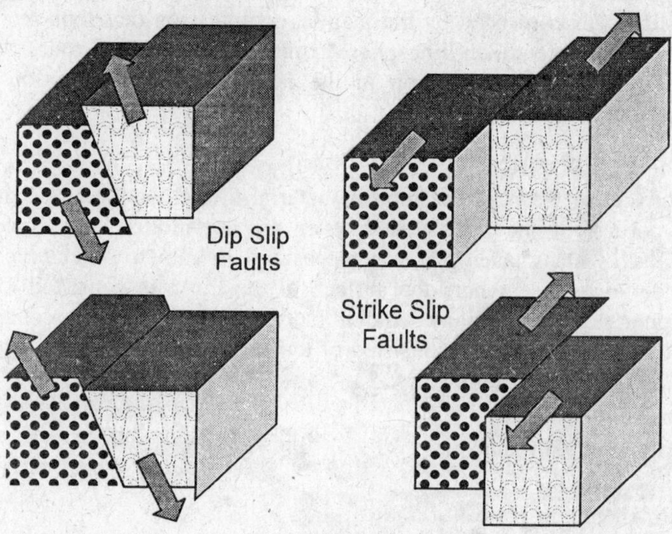

Fig. 3.6. Types of Faults

the two slips dominate the phenomenon. The thrust faults cause the ground to move vertically and break the earth surface, where as strike slip fault's cause the earth to move horizontally. Convergence of plates also cause earthquake.

3.6.1. Types of earthquakes

In the world most of the earthquakes about 90% earthquakes occur along the boundaries of the tectonic plates. These earthquakes are known as inter plate earthquake. Earthquake of 1897 in Assam (India) is an example of such an earthquake. Besides inter plate earthquakes many earthquakes occur in the plate itself away from the plate boundaries. (The 1993 Latur Maharastra, India earthquake) was of this type of earthquake. These earthquakes are known as inter plate earthquakes. The number of such earthquakes is about 10%.

The type of earthquakes may also be described as follows:

Though the surface characteristics of oceanic trench earthquake and Islands arcs are quite different, but a majority of such earthquakes seems to be confined to a narrow dipping zone. Earthquakes occurring on the oceanic side of the trench where normal faulting develops due to tensional stresses generated by the initial bending of the plates are called tensional earthquakes. Earthquakes developed due to dip slip motion in the thrust faulting as descending plates slide under the overlying plates are known as shallow earthquakes. The shallow earthquakes develop upto a depth of about 100 km.

At intermediate depth, earthquakes are caused either by compression or extension depending upon specific characteristics of the subduction zone. When a descending denser slab than the surrounding mantle sinks due to its own weight; normal and extension faulting occurs. When the downward motion of the descending slab is resisted by the mantle, compression develops there. This compression in descending lithosphere zone indicates the zone of deep earthquake zone. This compression in the mantle shows the motion of the descending plate at that depth.

3.7. PLATE TECTONIC

The convective flows of hot molten material of the Mantle cause the crust and some portion of the mantle slide over the hot molten outer core. This sliding of earth's mass takes place in pieces and is known as *tectonic plates*. According to some researchers the surface of the Earth is consisted of seven major tectonic plates and many smaller plates. Some other researchers have suggested that earth surface is consisted of ten major tectonic plates. The seven major tectonic plates are as follows:

1. Eurasian plate
2. North American plate
3. Pacific plate
4. Indo-Australian plate
5. South American plate
6. African plate
7. Antarctic plate

These plates are shown in Fig. 3.7.

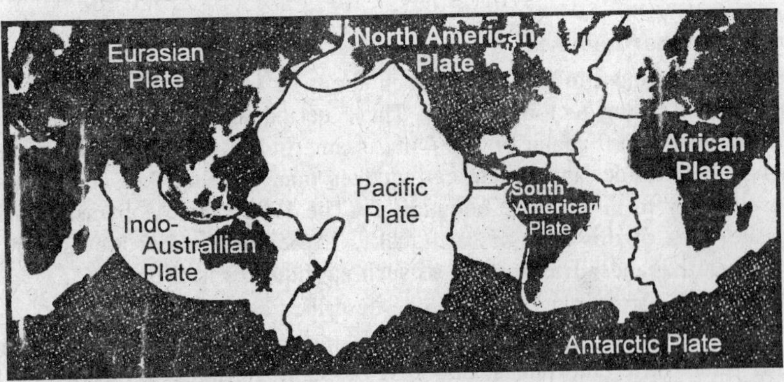

Fig. 3.7. Major Tectonic plates of the earth surface

These plates move in different directions at different speeds from those of the neighbouring one. Some times the speed of the front plate is slower than the plate behind it. In some situations the behind plate collides with the front plate forming mountains. On the other hand in some cases the two plates move away from each other forming rifts. In some situations the two plates move side by side either in the same direction or in opposite directions. These three types of interactions are convergent, divergent and transform boundaries. Fig. 3.8.

3.8. PLATE BOUNDARIES

The tectonic plate boundaries or inter plate sections are formed due to the relative motion of the crustal plates or tectonic plates. These boundaries are also known as *marginal zones.* These zones are of the following types:

1. Zone of divergence (Constructive margin)

These zones are also known as spreading or rift zones. These zones are of tension in which the lithosphere or earth crust splits, separates and moves apart. The hot magma rises up through cracks and solidifies. New material gets deposited on the edges of the oceanic plates. This material forms oceanic ridges. Due to the deposition of new material and forming oceanic ridges, it is called constructive margin or zone. This process is also known as sea floor spreading. Thus the occurrence of earthquakes is associated with volcanic activity along the axes of ridges.

This process does not cause uniform stretching all along the oceanic ridges. The movement of the pole along a plate of rotation causes differential stretching of the earth's crust. The minimum velocity of movement develops at the poles and it increases towards the equator. Hence the ocean ridges are offset by many transform faults. The shallow foci earthquakes are generated by the movement along these transformed faults.

2. Zone of convergence (Destructive margin)

The boundaries along which the edge of one plate rides over the other are known as convergent zones. When two plates from opposite direction come closer and collide are called as convergent plates. On collision, the leading edge of the higher density plate may get bent down wards, causing it to descend under the other plate. This undergoing plate enters the hot asthenosphere. At the high temperature the material of this plate gets heated and melts. This melted material mixes completely with the material of the upper mantle and forms new magma. This process is called *subduction.* The new magma rises to the surface and errupts again to form a chain of volcanoes around the edges of the plate boundaries. These boundary areas are known as subduction zones. These subduction zones cause deep ocean trenches and major earthquakes. When on collision, the two plates are pushed upwards, mountains are formed. In such a collision one of the plates is destroyed, hence such a boundary is called destructive margin.

Most intense and wide spread earthquakes occurr at the sites of subduction zones. Besides producing shallow to deep focus and volcanic earthquakes, these boundaries also produce deep trenches, basins, and folded mountain chains.

3. Fracture zone (Conservative margin)

Fracture zones are also called transformed faults. In these zones the lithosphere plates slide past each other with out any destruction or creation. The edges of the two sliding plates scrape each other very closely, creating tension along the boundaries. The scrape of the faces of the two plates cause shallow focus earthquake activities. Thus this boundary is also called a parallel or transformed fault boundary. The transform faults approximately move parallel to the direction of the plate movements. These zones are shown in Fig. 3.8.

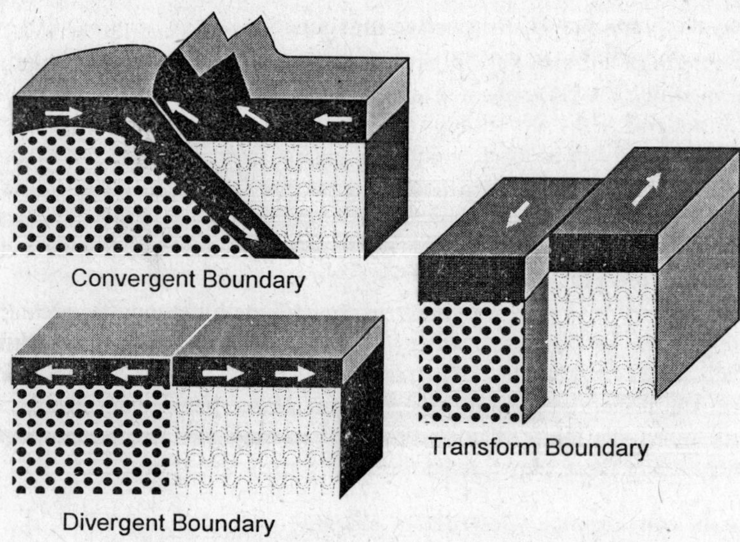

Fig. 3.8. Types of inter boundries (Courtsey—IITK)

3.9. VOLCANIC EARTHQUAKES

It is a special feature of explosive eruption. These earthquakes release very small energy in comparision of conventional earthquakes and are seldom damaging. Now it is felt that earthquakes and volcanos may have a common origin in the deep movement of mantle material. The coincidence of belts of major earthquake activity and belts of active volcanoes support this idea. The most obvious common cause of volcanic activity and seismic activity relates to the plate interactions. In the process volcanic material from the lower crust of the mantle rises up through the fracture zones. These boundaries are also the areas, in which earthquakes would occur naturally due to plate interaction in zones of convergence or divergence or areas where two plates slide past one another along the parallel boundaries.

3.10. EARTHQUAKE THEORY

Though many phenomenon may cause earthquake, but from engineering point of view the most important sources of earthquakes are those of tectonic origin, which are associated with large scale strain in the earth's crust. Earthquake phenomenon may be divided into the following three categories.

1. Elastic Rebound theory.
2. Tectonic plate theory.
3. Seepage of water into the earth's crust from large water bodies.

1. Elastic rebound theory

Rocks on earth's crust are made of elastic materials. Due to the deformation in the earth mass during the gigantic tectonic plates action large amount of strain energy is accumulated in the rocks. However there are some brittle materials also in the body of the rocks. When the rocks along the weak region of the earth's crust develop energy in excess of their bearing capacity, a sudden movement takes place on the opposite side of the fault and the stored energy is released through the rupture. The energy released is propagated in the form of seismic waves, which impart energy to the medium through which they propagate and vibrate the structures standing on the earth's surface. The phenomenon of rupture is attributed to the elastic rebound theory as shown in Fig. 3.9.

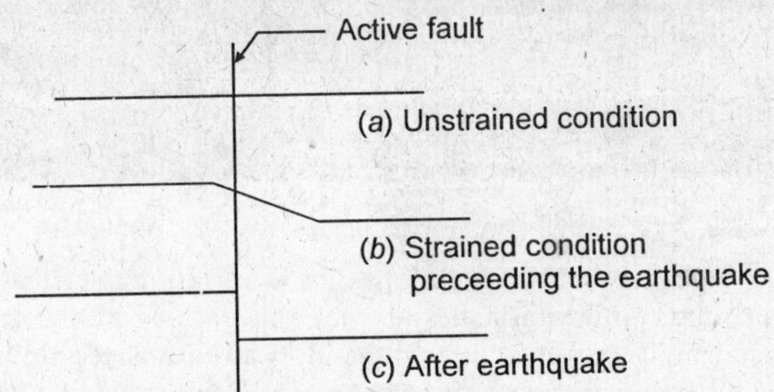

Fig. 3.9. Elastic Rebound Theory of Rupture

(*i*) Originally before deformation the section is unstrained. In this condition the section is straight as shown in Fig. 3.9 (*a*).

(*ii*) As deformation starts accumulation it starts straining as shown in Fig. 3.9 (*b*)

(*iii*) As soon as rupture takes place, it breaks as shown in Fig. 3.9 (*c*). resulting in a relative shift on the fault line.

In due course of time, after a major earthquake, the ruptured mass heals and binds up its self. Also during this period the friction along the ruptured surface permits the mass to accumulate energy again. When the accumulated energy exceeds the bearing capacity of the materials, earthquake occurs once again. Thus earthquakes may occur again and again from the same region.

2. Tectonic plate theory

As stated above also, the convective flows of mantle materials cause the earth crust and some portion of the mantle to slide over the hot molten material of the outer core. This sliding of earth's mass takes place in pieces. The molten magma cools forming the solid plates of rocks. These plates are known or called as *Tectonic plates.* These plates spread away from the ridges. Ultimately these cooled plates become heavy and are pulled back into the mantle by the gravity. This process is called *subduction* as shown in Fig. 3.10.

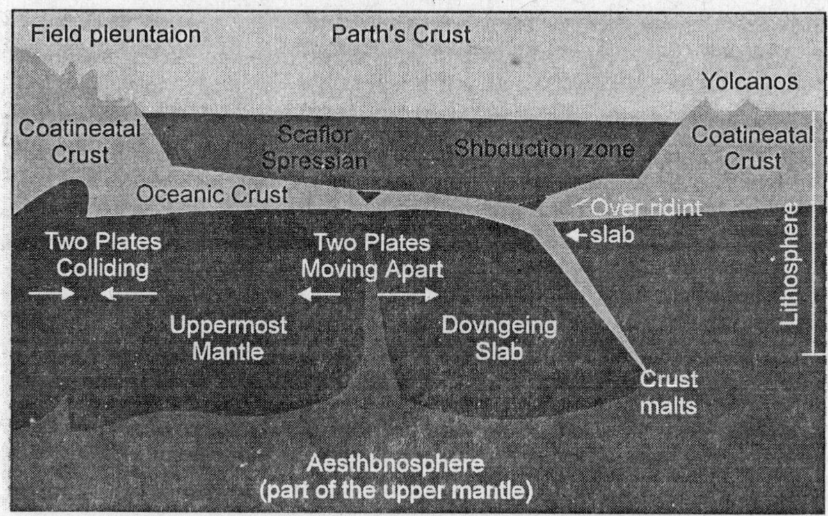

Fig. 3.10. Subduction Process (Courtesy—D.V. Mallick)

The rocks that make continental plates, however are lighter than those on sea floor. hence the continental plates are not pulled down by the gravity. But these plates are simply propelled around the globe. These plates are in constant motion on the viscous material of the mantle, over riding, plunging beneath one an other, and colliding each other or bruising past one other. Some parts of adjacent plates however remain in stationary position and locked together for years. They break in great faults producing earthquakes and seismic vibrations along the boundaries.

The movement in earth's crust is caused by the tectonic plates motion. This movement usually occur along the boundaries of the plates and over large faults in the interior of the plates.

The Indian continental plate is pushing into and under the Eurasian plate at the rate of 5 cm a year. When the plates collide head on, usually one of them slip beneath the other and the enormous force developed can cause great changes on the surface of the earth. About 90% earthquakes occur along the boundaries of the plates where the rocks are usually weaker and yield more readily to the stress than the rocks with in the plates. The remaining 10%

earthquakes occur in areas far away from the present boundaries of the plates and are called intra plate earthquakes.

There are certain regions on the earth where major earthquakes occur periodically and are called danger zones, where disasters have occurred during the past centuries due to earthquakes. These zones are as follows:

1. Pacific coast of North, central and south America.
2. Morroco, Algeria, Libya, and Mediterrancn sea bed.
3. Italy, Yugosalaviya, Greece, and Turkey belt.
4. Iran, Afghanistan, Northern, Western and Eastern parts of Indian sub continent, Nepal, Tibet region, Burma, China, Japan, South sea Islands, Indonessia and Philipines.

3. Seepage from large water bodies

Besides elastic rebound theory and plate tectonic theory, some scientists are of the view that earthquakes occur due to seepage from large water bodies such as large lakes, and reservoirs into the soil below. When this seeping water reaches in the mantle zone, water vaporises due to large amount of heat there. The vaporisation of water increases pressure there. When this vapour pressure becomes higher than the bearing power or strength of the earth there, the earth bursts at the weakest spot releasing this pressure. This process of releasing the inside pressure of the earth is known as earthquake.

Two major reservoirs at Koyna (Maharastra) and Tehri Garhwal have been constructed in India. Both these places have witnessed two major earthquakes. Thus people have started believing that these earthquakes have occurred due to the construction of these reservoirs, from where the water seeped into the earth causing large pressure inside the earth, which burst the weak spot of the earth and caused earthquake.

3.11. FORMATION OF THE HIMALAYAS

India lies at the north western end of the Indo-Australian plate. This Indo-Australian plate contain or encompasses, India, Australia, a major part of Indian ocean and other countries. This plate is colliding against the huge Eurasian plate and slipping under the Eurasian plate. The process of one tectonic plate slipping under the other is called 'Subduction'. Before collusion these plates are separeted by sea. A part of the lithosphere, the earth's crust is covered by oceans and rest by the continents. The part of the lithosphere may undergo subduction at great depths when it converges against an other plate. and the latter is raised or buoyed. Thus it remains close to the surface. When continents converge, large amounts of shortening and thickening of the earth takes place. About some 50 million years ago Himalayas and Tibet were formed due to the collision of Indo-Australian and Eurasian plate Fig. 3.11.

3.12. SEISMIC WAVES

The large strain energy released during a earthquake travels in the form of

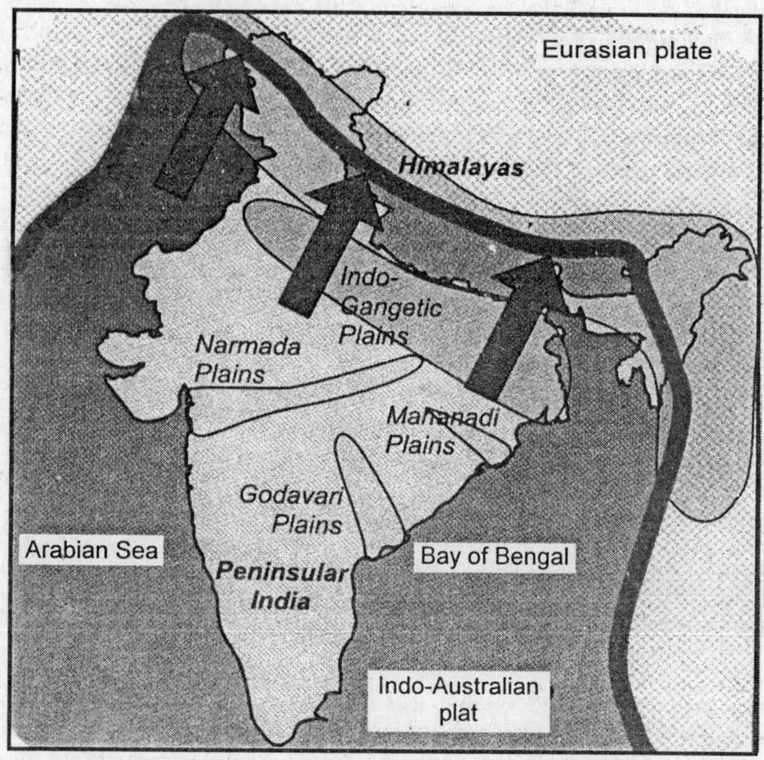

Fig. 3.11. Layout and Tractonic Geo Graphical Plate Boundries of India (Courtesy—IITK)

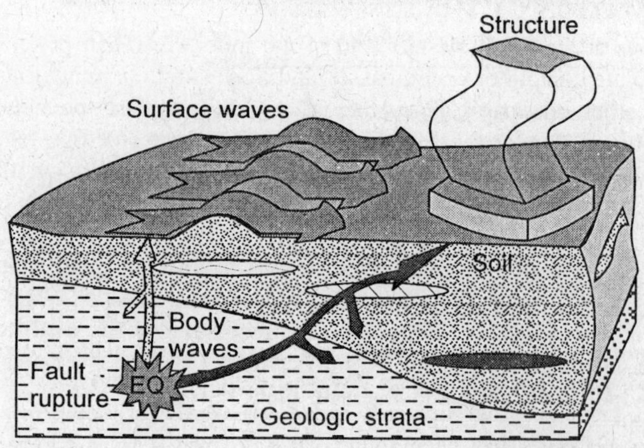

Fig. 3.12. Arrival of Seismic Waves at a site (Courtesy—IITK)

waves in all directions through the earth's layers, reflecting and refracting at each surface. Fig. 3.12. These waves are of two types, namely body waves and surface waves. Mostly waves developing between the terrain situated between the focus and the place of observation of earthquakes effects are elastic. These waves are recorded on seismographs. Greater the distance of travel, lower the energy of the wave. Different types of waves are shown in Fig. 3.13 to 3.16.

3.12.1. Classification of waves

Seismic waves can be classified as follows:

Seismic wave

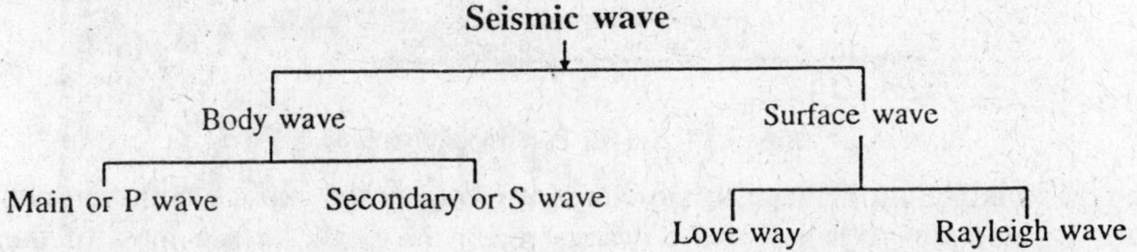

1. Main or P waves. These are the first kind of body waves and are known as primary or P waves or main waves. These are the fastest seismic waves. The primary waves can travel through the inner layers of the earth. Thus P waves can travel through solid rocks as well as through fluids like water and liquid layers of the earth. P waves push and pull the rock through which they travel just like sound waves pull and push air as shown in Fig. 3.13. The speed of P

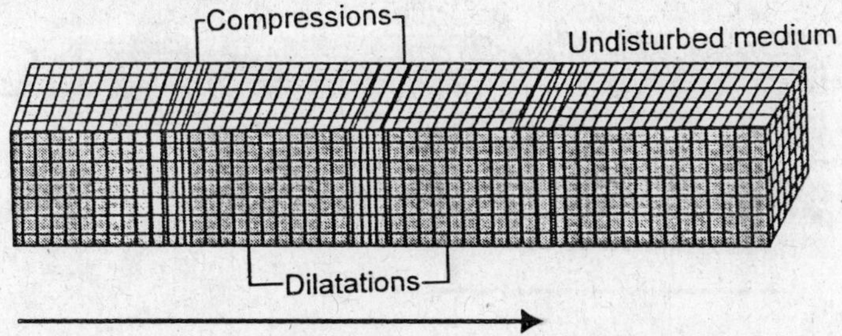

Fig. 3.13. Travel Pattern of P waves

waves has been found varying from 5 km to 15 km per second. When a thunder occurs in the atmosphere, we hear sound of thunder and rattling of windows at the same times. The rattling of windows occurs due to the pushing and pulling of the window on the window's glass panes by the sound waves like P waves pushing and pulling the rock. P waves are also called longitudinal or compressional waves.

2. Secondary or S waves. These are second waves which are felt in a earthquake. S waves are slower than P waves and can only move in solid rocks. These waves move the rock upwards and down wards as shown in Fig. 3.14. The speed of S waves has been found varying from 4 to 7 km per second. These are also called transverse or shear waves. These waves do not travel in liquids as they do not have any shear strength. In association with P waves they

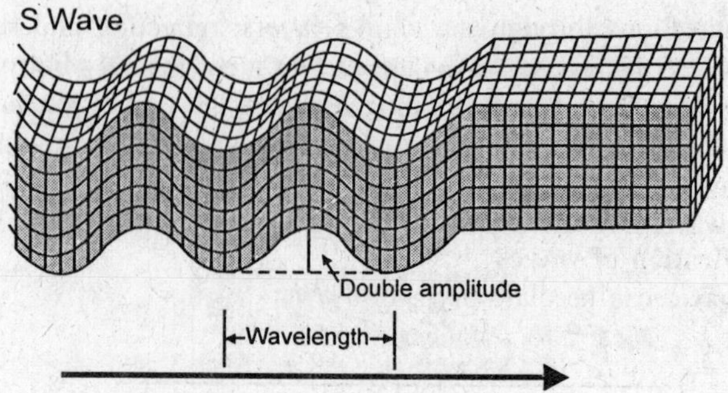

Fig. 3.14. Travel Pattern of S waves

produce maximum damage to structures by rocking the surface both vertically and horizontally. When P and S waves reach the earth surface most of their energy is reflected back. The shaking at earth surface is about twice than at a depth substantially below the earth surface.

3. Love waves. This wave is known after its inventor's name A.E.H. Love a British mathematician who worked out a mathematical model for this kind of wave in 1911. This is the first of surface waves. It is the fastest surface wave and moves from side to side as shown in Fig. 3.15.

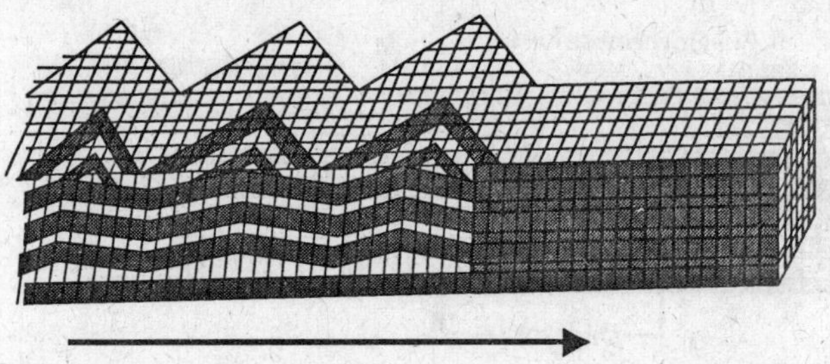

Fig. 3.15. Travel Pattern of Love waves

4. Rayleigh waves. This is the second type of surface wave. These are named after the name of their inventor John William strutt and Lord Rayleigh, who mathematically predicted the presence of this type of waves in 1885.

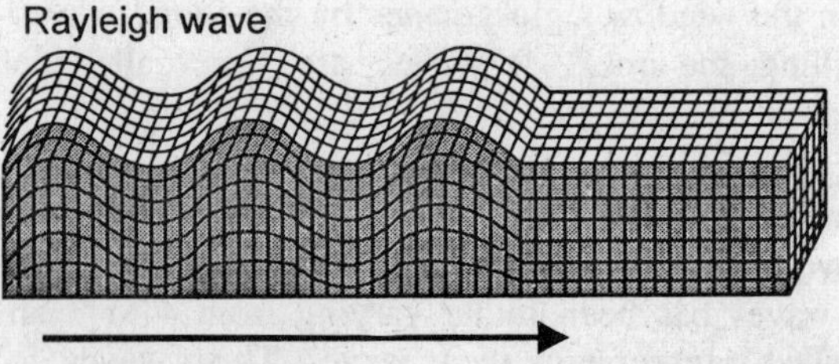

Fig. 3.16. Travel pattern of Rayleigh waves

Rayleigh waves roll along the ground like waves in lakes or an ocean as shown in Fig. 3.16. As these waves roll, they move the ground up and down and also side to side in the same direction that of wave motion. Most of the shaking felt during an earthquake is due to Rayleigh wave, which can be larger than other waves. Fig 3.21 shows seismograph record of Kobe 1995 earthquake in which, P, S and body waves as well as surface waves love wave (L) and Rayleigh wave LR have been clearly shown.

3.13. EQUATIONS FOR VELOCITY OF BODY WAVES

Velocity for P wave. The velocity of travel V_P of P wave in an elastic isotropic solid is given by the relation

$$V_p = \left[\frac{\lambda + 2\mu}{\rho}\right]^{1/2} \qquad \ldots(3.1)$$

The velocity V_s for S wave is given by relation

$$V_s = \left(\frac{\mu}{\rho}\right)^{1/2} \qquad \ldots(3.2)$$

where in both equation (3.1) and (3.2)

ρ = mass density of the material.

λ and μ = Lame's elastic constant.

μ = Modulus of rigidity of material and λ is given by the following relation

$$\lambda = K - \frac{2\,\mu}{3}$$

where K is bulk modulus.

These two constants μ and λ are expressed in terms of elastic modulus E and Poisson's ratio σ as

$$\mu = \frac{E}{2\,(1+\sigma)}$$

$$\lambda = \frac{E\cdot\sigma}{(1+\sigma)\,(1-2\,\sigma)}$$

The equation (3.1) can be pressed in Elastic modulus E and Poisson's ratio σ and mass density ρ as

$$V_P = \left[\frac{\lambda + 2\mu}{\rho}\right]^{1/2} = \left[\frac{\lambda}{\rho} + \frac{2\,\mu}{\rho}\right]^{1/2}$$

$$\left[\frac{E}{\rho} \times \frac{\sigma + 1 - 2\,\sigma}{(1+\sigma)\,(1-2\,\sigma)}\right]^{1/2} = \left[\frac{E}{\rho} \times \frac{1-\sigma}{(1+\sigma)\,(1-2\,\sigma)}\right]^{1/2}$$

$$V_s = \left(\frac{\mu}{\rho}\right)^{1/2} = \left(\frac{E}{2\,(1-\sigma)} \times \frac{1}{\rho}\right)^{1/2}$$

$$= \left(\frac{E}{\rho} \times \frac{1}{2(1+\sigma)}\right)^{1/2} \qquad \ldots(3.3)$$

Taking the value of σ (Poisson's) ratio for earth as 0.25 we get

$$V_P = \sqrt{\frac{3}{2.5}} \cdot \sqrt{\frac{E}{\rho}} \qquad \ldots(i)$$

$$V_s = \sqrt{\frac{E}{P}} \cdot \sqrt{\frac{1}{2.5}} \qquad \ldots(ii)$$

$$\therefore \quad V_P = \sqrt{3} \cdot V_s$$

$$\text{or} \quad \frac{V_P}{V_s} = \sqrt{3} = 1.734 \qquad \ldots(3.4)$$

From equation (3.4), $\frac{V_P}{V_s} = 1.734$

Ratio of Rayleigh wave velocity secondary wave velocity *i.e.*

$$\frac{V_R}{V_S} = 0.9194 \approx 0.92$$

From these values Dr. Jai kishan and associates have given a relation between ratios of V_P/V_S, poisson's ratio, and V_R/V_S and poisson's ratio in the Fig. 3.17.

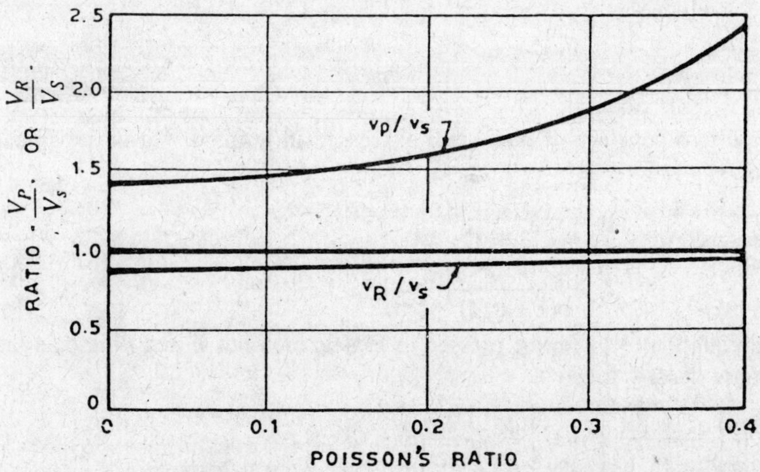

Fig. 3.17. Relative Velocitiies of Different Waves

3.14. DURATION OF PRIMARY TREMORS T_{SP}

The time interval between the arrival of primary (*P*) waves and secondary (*S*) waves at the specific observation location is called *Duration of primary tremor* T_{SP}. The value of T_{SP} can be calculated by the relation.

$$T_{SP} = \left(\frac{1}{V_S} - \frac{1}{V_P}\right)\Delta \qquad \text{...(3.5)}$$

where Δ is the distance from the focus to the observation station. Thus the epicenter can be calculated. The depth of focus can be obtained graphically by the earthquake record of atleast three locations.

The velocities through the interior of the ground are shown in Fig. 3.18.

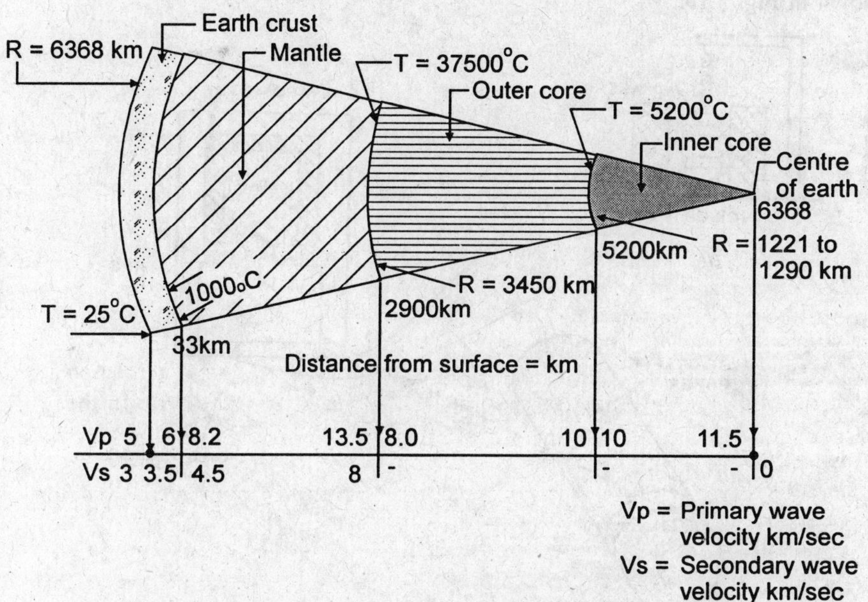

Fig. 3.18. Velocities Through the Interior of Earth

3.15. MEASUREMENT OF GROUND MOTIONS

For measuring ground motions due to seismic activities broadly two types of instruments are used as follows:

1. Seismograms
2. Accelographs

1. Seismograms. This type of instruments are used by seismologists to record even weak motions. These instruments are very sensitive and even can record weakest earth's motion. The records are called seismograms and are useful in interpreting earthquakes occurrence and help in locating epicenter, focal depth and other parameter of the event. However these instruments are not useful for measuring strong ground motions which are important to a design engineer for designing the earthquake resistant structures.

Design principle. In the design of the instrument seismogram, the simple electromagnetic principle has been used. According to this principle when a coil moves in magnetic field, a voltage is generated as an output, which is proportional to the relative velocity between the magnet and the coil. By suitable mechanical design of the coil and magnet mounting, the relative velocity may be made directly proportional to the ground velocity. Such a unit is called as *velocity pickup.*

The velocity pickup may be connected to a galvanometer, where mirror would rotate in proportion to the voltage input. The rotation of the mirror may be recorded by photographic recording process employing a light source as shown in Fig. 3.19.

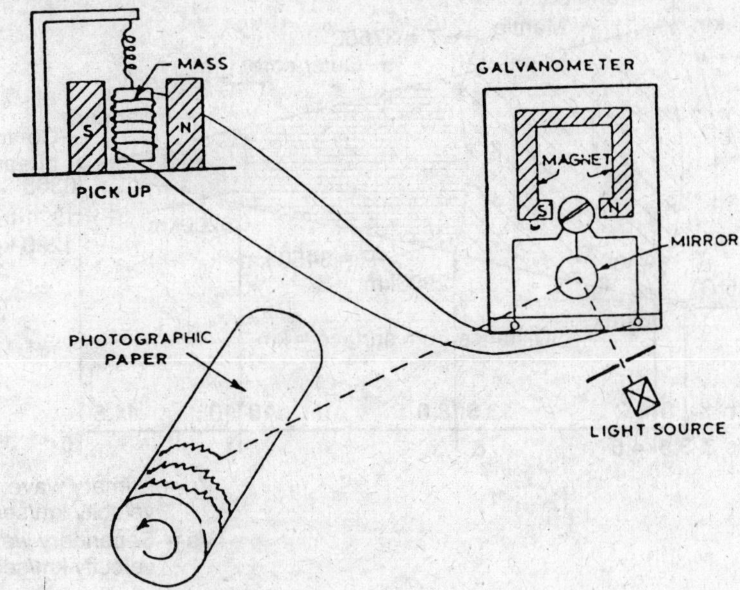

Fig. 3.19. A Typical Seismograph System

This method which does not require electronic circuritry was first used in the beginning of nineteenth century, still is used even in the twentieth century. The mechanical properties such as natural frequency and damping of the seismometer and galvanometer decides which frequency range would be magnified by a particular set of equipment. Some times such equipments are classified as short period or long period seismographs. The sensitivity is the main requirement of the seismographs to record weak motions. If strong motions occur in the vicinity of the seismograph, they would be thrown off of the scale.

In order to identify the arrival of various phases of ground motion, these instruments record continuously and need an accurate time base. These instruments are located on isolated foundations resting on hard rock, such that instruments are insulated against spurious ground noise.

Accelerographs. The strong motions which are needed to design the earthquake resistant structures are recorded by accelerographs. These instruments operate when ground motion exceeds an initial or threshold value of a ground motion of 0.01 to 0.02 g and are expected to record the stronger ground motion. Seismograms and Accelerographs are complementary to each other and provide useful data in earthquake engineering. The speed of recording of Accelerographs is much more than seismograms instruments. The speed is of the order of 20 mm/sec. Now more sophisticated variety seismic instruments are available. *Principle of working of accelerographs.* Accelerographs also work on the same principle as that of seismograms.

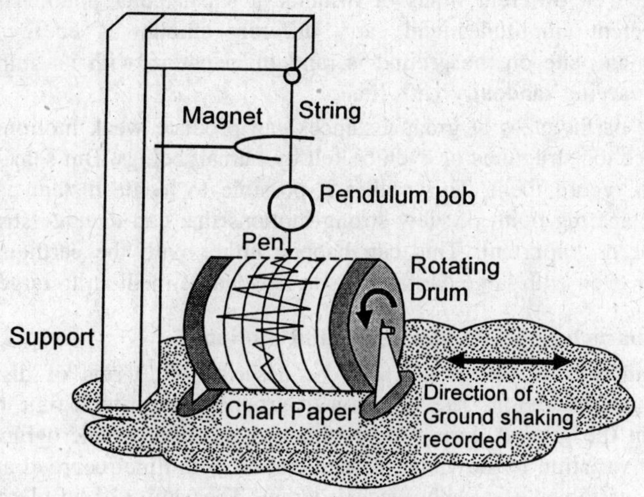

Fig. 3.20. Schematic of Early Seismograph

An other type of seismograph is shown in Fig. 3.20. This instrument has three components and its principle of working also is same as explained above.

Components. It has the following components:

1. **Sensor.** The string, pendulum mass, magnet and support together form the sensor.
2. **Recorder.** The drum, pen and chart from the recorder.
3. **Timer.** The motor that rotates the drum at constant speed forms the timer.

Working. As shown in Fig. 3.20 a pen is attached at the tip of an oscillating simple pendulum (a mass hung by a string from a support) marks on a chart-paper held on a drum rotating at a constant speed. A magnet around the string provides required damping to control the amplitude of the oscillation.

One such instrument is required in each of the two orthogonal horizontal directions. For measuring the vertical oscillations, the string pendulum is replaced with a spring pendulum oscillating about a fulcrum. Some instruments do not have a timer component and provide only the maximum extent of the motion during the earthquakes. Such instruments are called *Seismoscope*. To day digital instruments using modern computer technology are commonly used.

The digital instrument records the ground motion on the momory of the microprocessor that is in built in the instrument.

3.16. STRONG GROUND MOTIONS

The rupture at the fault point in the three dimensional volume of the earth releases energy. The release of energy creates seismic waves which cause shaking of earth's surface. This is the net consequence of a earthquake. These waves reach at different times or instants at a particular point. These waves have different amplitudes and carry different amount of energy. Thus the motion at any site on the ground is random in nature with its amplitude and direction varying randomly with time.

Large earthquakes at great distances can produce weak motions that may not damage the structures or even be felt by human beings. But sensitive instruments can record them. This makes it possible to locate distant earthquakes. From engineering point of view strong motions that can damage structures are of interest or important. This can happen either with the earthquake in the vicinity or even with large earthquakes at reasonable medium to large distances.

3.16.1. Characteristics of strong ground motions

The motion of the ground can be described in terms of displacement, velocity or acceleration. The variation of ground motion with time recorded at a point on the ground during an earthquake is called accelerogram. In other words the variation in the value of acceleration with time recorded at any point during an earthquake is called accelerogram. The nature of accelerogram may vary depending upon the following factors.

(*a*) Energy released at source by the earthquake.

(*b*) Type of slip at fault rupture.

(*c*) Geology along the path of travel from fault rupture to the earth's surface.

(*d*) Local soil characteristics.

They carry distinct information regarding ground shaking as follows:

(*i*) Peak amplitude.

(*ii*) Duration of strong shaking.

(*iii*) Frequency content *i.e.* amplitude of shaking associated with each frequency.

(*iv*) Energy content or energy carried by ground shaking or each frequency.

These factors often are used to distinguish shaking peak amplitude (peak ground acceleration PGA) in physically intuitive (sence). For instance a horizontal PGA of value 0.6 g indicates that the movement of the ground can cause a maximum horizontal force on a rigid structure equal to 60% of its weight. In a rigid structure all its points move with the ground by the same amount, hence experience the same maximum acceleration of peak ground acceleration. Horizontal peak ground acceleration values greater the 1.0 g were recorded during 1994 North ridge earthquake in U.S.A. Generally the maximum amplitude of horizontal motions in the two orthogonal directions are nearly equal. However maximum amplitude in the vertical direction usually is taken less than horizontal amplitude. Design codes suggest the value of vertical amplitude as 0.5 to 0.67 of the horizontal design acceleration. But it has been found that such relationship between horizontal and vertical ground accelerations does not hold good in the vicinity of the fault rupture.

3.17. SEVERITY OF EARTHQUAKES

Severity of an earthquake convey the sense of size of the earthquake whether bigger or small. Seismologist express the size in terms of magnitude of the earthquake. There are several different methods for determining the size of the earthquake. Some of the methods are based on body waves (which travel deep with in the structure of the earth), some are based on surface waves (which mainly travel along the upper layers of the earth) and some are based on completely different methodologies.

The severity or size of an earthquake can be expressed in terms of magnitude or by its intensity. The magnitude of an earthquake can be measured in a number of ways. Magnitude is a quantitative measure of the actual size of the earthquake. Professor Charles Richter noticed that.

(*a*) At the same distance, seismograms of larger earthquakes have bigger wave amplitudes than those of smaller earthquakes.

(*b*) For a given earthquake, seismograms at farther distances have smaller wave amplitudes than those at close distances.

These observations prompted him to propose the new magnitude scale. This scale is called Richter scale or local magnitude scale. This scale is obtained from the seismograms and accounts the dependence of wave form amplitude on the epicentral distance. There are other magnitude scales such as Body Wave Magnitude, Surface Wave Magnitude and Wave Energy Magnitude. These numerical magnitude scales have no lower and upper limits. The magnitude of a very small earthquake may be zero or even negative.

As stated above there can be number of ways to measure a earthquake, but all these methods should have two common factors.

1. All the methods must use a measurement of some particular wave form recorded on a seismogram.
2. They must take into account the distance from the focus of the earthquake to the station that recorded the seismic traces. Seismogram record of 1995 Kobe (Japan) earthquake is shown in Fig. 3.21.

3.17.1. Commonly used magnitude scales

Most commonly used magnitude scales are as follows:

1. Ml scale. It is the Richter's magnitude or local magnitude scale. This scale is based on waves with a period of 0.1 to 0.3 seconds. It is a

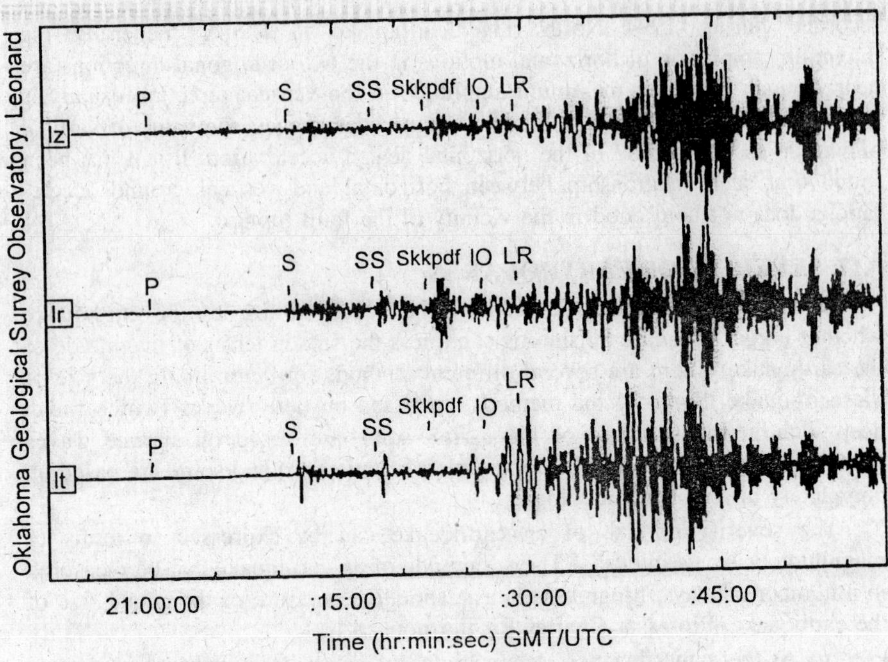

Fig. 3.21. Seismogram Rocord of 1995 Kobe (Japan) Earthquake waves

measure of the amplitude of seismic waves, recorded by seismographic observations on a logarithmic scale so that a magnitude of 8, for example represents 10 times as large as a recording of 7. There is no upper limit to this scale.

2. **Mb scale.** It is the body wave magnitude based on the amplitude of P waves generated by the earthquake.
3. **Ms scale.** It is the surface wave magnitude based on measurements of surface waves with a period of about 20 seconds. This scale is suitable to measure the magnitude of shallow earthquakes.
4. **Mw scale.** It is the moment magnitude scale different from the magnitude scales discussed above. This scale is based on the actual rupture or physical area of the moving fault. Moment magnitude (Mw) represents the total amount of seismic energy released in an earthquake, based on waves with period of about 200 seconds.

This scale generally is used to describe the earthquakes greater than magnitude 7.0 on Richter's scale. This can be established in the following two ways:

1. In the first approach the length and depth of the earthquake fault and the movement of the rock at the fault are measured.
2. In the second approach or method scientists use the data from a

seismograph, a device that records the ground movement. Richter magnitude is based on seismographic data.

3.17.1.1. Advantages of moment magnittude

1. This scale does not saturate as it uses the complete seismogram. Hence it allows the measurement of largest earthquakes.
2. This scale can be determined either from geology or instrumentally. It can be used to determine the size of the old earthquakes and can compare them with the instrumentally recorded events.
3. Estimates obtained by this scale have been found more reliable. Hence a difference of 0.2 in moment magnitude mean some thing.
4. Scientists prefer to describe earthquakes of more than 7.0 magnitude on the moment magnitude scale, as moment magnitude scale describes large earthquakes more accurately than Richter's scale.

The largest earthquake ever recorded on moment magnitude scale measured 9.5. It was an inter plate earthquake that occurred along the pacific coast of Chile in south America in 1960. The known largest intra plate earthquakes that struck in central Asia and in Indian ocean in 1905, 1920 and 1927. These earthquakes had moment magnitudes between 8.0 and 8.3.

3.17.2. Intensity of an earthquake

It is a qualitative measure of the actual shaking at a location during an earthquake. It describes how strong a shock was felt at a particular location during a earthquake. It is a subjective measure.

At a specific location intensity of an earthquake depends upon the following factors:

1. Total amount of energy released from the earthquake.
2. Distance of the specific location from the epicenter of the earthquake.
3. Type of rock and degree of consolidation. In general the extent of destruction and wave amplitude is greater in soft and unconsolidated soils than dense and crystaline rocks.

Though there are many intensity scales but two of them are most common. First of the methods is modified Mercalli (MM) scale, it is a subjective measure, and the other is MSK scale. Both scales are quite similar and range from I to XII. Intensity scales are based on the three features of the shaking:

(*a*) Perception by the people and animals.
(*b*) Performance of structures.
(*c*) Changes to natural surroundings.

3.17.2.1. Intensity based on perception by the people

According to USGS foundation centre, the modified mercalli scale is described as below:

Table 3.1. Showing MMI scale

Intensity	*Observed Effects*
I.	Not felt except by a very few under specially favourable conditions.
II.	Felt only by a few people at rest, specially on upper floors of the buildings. Suspended objects may swing.
III.	Felt noticeably people in door, especially by people on upper floors of the buildings standing automobiles may rock slightly. Vibrations are very weak as that of passing truck. Hence many people do not recognize it as an earthquake.
IV.	Felt by many people in door, but only by a few out door during the day. At night some people awakened. Windows, doors, dishes disturbed, walls making cracking sound. Sensation like heavy truck striking a building. Standing automobiles rocked noticeably.
V.	Felt nearly by every one. Many people awakened. Some dishes and windows broken, unstable objects overturned. Pendulum clocks stopped.
VI.	Felt by all, many of the people frightened. Some heavy furniture moved. Some plaster fallen, damage light.
VII.	Negligible damage in well designed and constructed buildings. Slight to moderate damage in well built ordinary structures. Considerable damage in poorly constructed and badly designed structures. Some chimneys broken.
VIII.	Slight damage in specially designed structures. Considerable damage with partial collapse in ordinary buildings. Great damage in poorly constructed buildings. Heavy furniture overturned, factory stacks, chimneys, columns, monuments and walls etc. fallen.
IX.	Considerable damage in specially designed buildings. Well designed framed structures thrown out of plumb. Great damage in substantial buildings with partial collapse. buildings shifted off from their foundations.
X.	Some well built wooden structures destroyed. Most of the masonry and framed structures destroyed with foundations. Rails bent.
XI.	Hardly any masonry structure remained standing. Bridges destroyed, rails bent greatly.
XII.	Damage total, levels and line of sight distorted objects thrown into the air.

3.17.3. Comparison of Richter magnitude and modified Mercalli intensity scales

This comparison is shown in Table 3.2 below.

Table 3.2.

Intensity by scale	*Mercalli Intensity*	*Description of characteristic effects*	*Richter magnitude corresponding to max. intensity reached*
I.	Measurement instrumentally	It can only be detected by seismographs.	—
II.	Feeble	Could be noticed only by sensitive people.	3.5 to 4.2
III.	Slight	Its effect is as that of passing automobile truck, felt by people at rest, specially on upper floors.	3.5 to 4.2
IV.	Moderate	Felt by people while on a walk. Rocking of loose objects including standing cars and trucks etc.	4.3 to 4.8
V.	Rather strong	It is generally felt by people. Most people awakened at night while sleeping. Heavy furniture over turned.	4.3 to 4.8
VI.	Strong	Felt by all. Heavy furniture moved. Suspended objects and trees swayed. Damage by falling plaster and over turning.	4.9 to 5.4
VII.	Very strong	Walls crack. Considerable damage in poorly built buildings . In one sense it is a general alarm.	5.1 to 6.1
VIII.	Destructive	Fall of chimneys, columns, Masonry fissured, Poorly constructed buildings damaged. Automobile drivers frightened.	6.2 to 6.9
IX.	Ruinous	Considerable damage to specially designed buildings, structures thrown off plumb, structures shifted off from foundations. Pipes break opens.	6.2 to 6.9
X.	Disastrous	Ground cracked badly. Railway lines get bent land slides on steep slopes. Masonry and framed structures destroyed.	7.0 to 7.3
XI.	Very disastrous	Few buildings remain standing. Bridges destroyed, rails got bent greatly. All services such as railways, pipes, cables etc got out of action. Major land slides and flood.	7.4 to 8.1
XII.	Catastrophic	Total destruction. Ground develops wavy form. Objects are thrown in air.	> 8.1 max known value is 8.9

3.17.4. Magnitude of earthquake

The magnitude of an earthquake is a quantitative measure of the actual strength or size of an earthquake.It is more precise a measure of earthquake than intensity. The size of the earthquake is an measure of the amount of strain energy released by the fault rupture. Earthquake magnitudes are based on direct measurement of the size (amplitude) of seismic waves. It is recorded by instruments rather than an subjective destruction caused. The total energy released by the earthquake can be calculated from the amplitude of the waves and the distance from the epicentric.

3.17.4.1. Basic difference between magnitude and intensity

The difference is shown in the tabular form in the Table 3.3.

Table 3.3. Difference between magnitude and intensity

Magnitude	*Intensity*
1. It is a measure of the size of the earthquake. The size is measured by the amount of strain energy released by the fault rupture. Thus the magnitude of earthquakes is a single value for a given earthquake.	1. It is an indicator of severity of shaking generated at a location. The severity of shaking by an earthquake clearly is much higher near the epicenter than farther away at any location
2. At all locations the magnitude of an earthquake remains the same.	From an earthquake of an certain magnitude, different intensity is experienced at different locations.
3. Structures are not designed on the basis of magnitude.	Buildings are designed on the basis of intensity of earthquake at a particular place.
4. They are based on direct measurements of the size of seismic waves.	It is measured in relation to the effect of the earthquake on human life.

3.18. MAGNITUDE AND ENERGY OF AN EARTHQUAKE

Dr. Charles F. Richter recognized that seismic waves radiated by earthquake could provide good estimates of their magnitudes. This concept of Richter is one of the most valuable contribution to the seismology. He collected recordings of seismic waves from a large number of earthquakes occurred since 1935. From the recordings of these earthquakes he prepared diagrams between the peak ground motion and epicentral distance. For the peak amplitudes logarithm scale was adopted on y-axis due to large variation in their values. The epicentral distance was taken in km on x-axis. From the study of these curves, he concluded that the larger the intrinsic energy of the earthquake, larger the amplitude of the ground motion at a given distance. The diagrams are shown in Fig. 3.22.

From the study of these curves, the idea of logarithmic earthquake magnitude scale struck in his mind and suggested the relation between the magnitude and amplitude of ground motion as shown in equation 3.6.

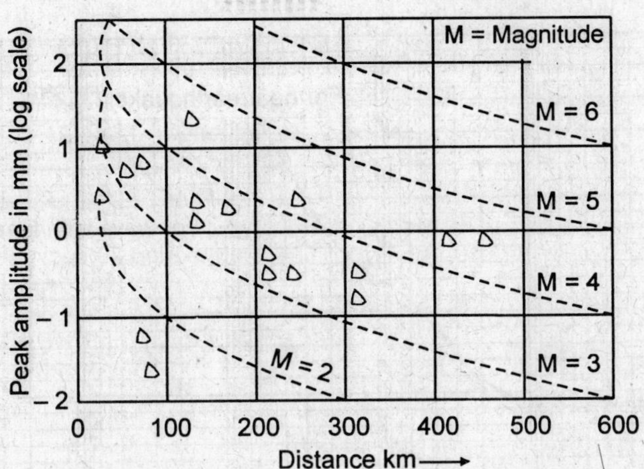

Fig. 3.22. A plot of peak amplitude in mm (Log scale) Versis epicentral distance in km. Recorded in southern California (Different symbols represent different earthquakes)

Thus to estimate the seismic risk at an location Richter suggested that the magnitude of an earthquake can be standardised as the logarithm (to the base of 10) of the maximum amplitude A of the ground motion recorded in micron at a distance of 100 km from the epicenter on a wood-Anderson type Torsion seismograph with 1.25 Hz nodal frequency. The damping of the seismograph should be equal to 80% of the critical, its natural period as 0.8 seconds and magnification of 2800. Thus according to Richter,

$$M = \log_{10} A \qquad \ldots(3.6)$$

As the distance of the instrument from epicenter usually will not be exactly 100 km. Hence the following general equation has been suggested

$$M = \log_{10} A - \log_{10} A_0 \qquad \ldots(3.7)$$

where A is the trace or recorded amplitude in micro metre (μm) as shown in Fig. 3.23 at any station and log A_0 is the distance correction given by the Fig. 3.23. for near as well as for distant earthquakes. In other words A_o is the amplitude for zero magnitude earthquakes at different epicentral distances. The reliability of observations depending upon local conditions or correction according to the instrument is further applied to get true magnitude M. Values of magnitudes obtained at various stations are compared and mean value of magnitude is assigned to the earthquake.

The magnitude of an earthquake may be from 3 to about 9.0, but no shocks smaller the 5 are found to cause appreciable damage. The extent of damage depends upon the depth of focus. The shock of 9.0 will envelop a vast area of the earth. Very shallow shocks can cause damage locally. Usually earthquakes are not found to have focal depth less than 5 km from the earth's surface and maximum focal depth may even be greater than 300 km.

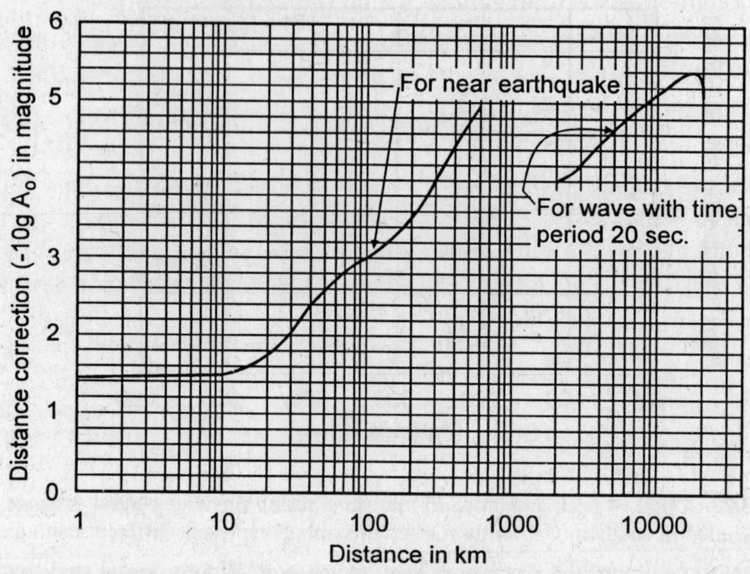

Fig. 3.23. Distance correction for Magnitude derminiw

An earthquake of magnitude 5.0, usually causes damage with in a radius of about 8 km, and that of 7.0 magnitude earthquake may cause damage with in radius of about 80 km. A earthquake of magnitude 8 can cause damage with in a radius 250 km. The effect of above magnitudes 5.0, 7.0 or 8.0 earthquakes have been felt in areas of 150, 400 and 600 km radius. Due to special geological features of the area the felt and damage area of December 1967 earthquake at Koyna (m = 6.5) was about 400 km and 60 km.

3.18.1. General form of Richter Magnitude M

As the magnitude of a earthquake is a measure of the seismic energy released at the fault is proportional to $(A/T)^2$ where A is the ground displacement amplitude and T is the period of the wave considered, the general from of the Richter magnitude M (equation 3.7) can be written as

$$M = \log_{10}\left(\frac{A}{T}\right)_{max} + \sigma(\Delta \cdot h) + C_r + C_s \qquad \ldots(3.8)$$

where,

A = Maximum ground displacement amplitude

T = Time period of the considered wave

$\sigma(\Delta, h)$ = Distance correction factor at epicentral distance Δ, and focal depth h,

C_r = Regional source correction factor

C_s = Station correction factor

3.18.2. Relation between magnitude M, fault length L and slip U

The relation between the magnitude M, fault length *L* and slip *U* at fault are related as follows:

$$M = 0.98 \log_{10} L + 5.65 \qquad ...(3.9)$$

and

$$M = 1.32 \log_{10} U + 4.27 \qquad ...(3.10)$$

Since the original development of Richter's magnitude relationship, much development has taken place in the science of seismology. Now it is a practice in seismology to measure the amplitude of P waves, which is not affected by the focal depth of the source, and thus determines a P wave magnitude called body wave magnitude mb. For shallow earthquakes, a surface wave train is also present. Now it is a common practice to measure the amplitude of the largest swing in the surface wave train that has a period of about 20 seconds. The value of magnitude obtained by surface wave measurement is called surface wave magnitude denoted by M_s. Though neither M_s nor M_b is the Richter magnitude, but each has a significant contribution in describing the size of an earthquake. However M_s correlates much more closely to the general conception of the size of the earthquake than M_b. Hence M_s and M_b can be described. A commonly used relation for computing M_s for shallow focus less than 50 km is given below:

$$M_s = \log_{10}\left(\frac{A_s}{T}\right)_{max} + 1.66 \log_{10} \Delta + 3.3 \qquad ...(3.11)$$

where,

A_s = Amplitude of horizontal ground motion in micro metre (μm).

T = Period (20 ± 2.0)

Δ = Epicentral distance in degrees

$$M_b = \log_{10}\left(\frac{A_s}{T}\right)_{max} + \sigma(\Delta, h) \qquad ...(3.12)$$

where $\sigma(\Delta,h)$= correction factor, this relation holds goods for period range of 0.5 to 12 seconds. It is based on the theoritical amplitude calculations corrected for geometric spreading and attenuation and then adjusted to empirical observations from shallow and deep focus earthquakes. Corrections are applied if distance measured in μM.

3.19. RELATION BETWEEN MAGNITUDE AND ENERGY RELEASED BY AN EARTHQUAKE

The relation between strain energy and magnitude suggested by Richter is given as follows:

$$\log_{10} E = 11.4 + 1.5\, M \qquad ...(3.13)$$

The energy released in earthquakes of different magnitudes is shown in Table 3.4 below.

Table 3.4. Showing magnitude of earthquake and energy released

Richter magnitude M	5.0	6.0	6.5	7.0	7.5	8.0	8.4	8,6
Energy released in Ergs E(10^{20} ergs)	0.08	2.5	14.1	80.0	446.0	2500.0	10000.00	20000.00

Richter and Gutenberg gave correlation between the release of strain energy by an earthquake and surface waves magnitude M_s.

This relation is shown in equation 3.14.

$$\log_{10} E = 4.4 + 1.5\, M_s \qquad \text{...(3.14)}$$

In 1966, Bath suggested for M_s greater the 5.0 equation as

$$\log_{10} E = 5.24 + 1.44\, M_s \text{ where, } E \text{ is in joules} \qquad \text{...(3.15)}$$

More recently Kanamori has suggested a relation between seismic moment and wave energy as $E = \dfrac{\text{Moment}}{20{,}000}$ ...(3.16)

The units of moment is dyne-cm and energy in ergs.

An increase in magnitude given by equation (3.13) by 1.0 implies 10 times higher wave form amplitude and about 31 times higher energy released. For instance energy released by an earthquake of M 7.5 is about 31 times that of released by an earthquake of m 6.5 and about (31 × 31 ≈ 1000) times that released by M 5.5 earthquake.

Most of the energy released is converted into heat energy and some part is utilized in fracturing the rocks. Only a fraction of energy released goes into the seismic waves that travel to large distances causing shaking of the ground in the way and causing damage to the structures. The energy released by M 6.3 earthquake is equivalent to that released by the atomic bomb droped by U.S.A. on Hiroshima (Japan) in 1945.

In 1956, Gutenberg and Richter suggested an approximate relation between the local magnitude M_L of an earthquake and the intensity I_o experienced in epicentral area. This relation is expressed as

$$M_L = \left(\frac{2}{3}\right) I_0 + 1 \qquad \text{...(3.17)}$$

while using equation 3.17, Roman numbers for intensity are replaced with numbers as VIII is written 8.0 or V by 5.0.

Esteva and Rasenblueth suggested a relationship between seismic intensity, magnitude M and a short epicentral distance r. where r is measured in km.

$$I = 8.16 + 1.45\, M - 2.46\, r \qquad \text{...(3.18)}$$

Equation 3.18 cannot be used for cases in which r reaches the same order as the focal region. This is its greatest draw back.

Example. At a certain location a standard torsion seismograph records a trace amplitude as 9.5 mm long in N-S direction and 7.2 mm long in E-W direction. The station correction is + 0.2. Find out the magnitude of the earthquake. The distance of the observation station from the epicenter is found as 150 km.

Solution. From Fig. 3.23, the distance correction is found as 3.2

In N-S direction, $M = \log_{10} 9.5 + 0.2 + 3.2$

$= 0.9777 + 0.2 + 3.2 = 4.32$

In E-W direction, $M = \log_{10} 7.2 + 0.2 + 3.2 = 4.25$

From this single station record, the earthquake may be assigned a magnitude of 4.3. In actual practice average of at least three records from different stations should be taken.

The Richter scale used in southern california for different epicentral distances and at a fixed focal depth of 18 km is given as follows:

$$M = \log_{10} A\,(mm) + \text{distance correction factor } \sigma \qquad \ldots(3.19)$$

The distance correction factor σ is the inverse of zero magnitude amplitude measured in mm at an epicentral distance Δ in km. For different epicentral distances, distance corrections are shown in the following table 3.5. The distance correction factors shown in table 3.5 can not be used in other parts of the world as in the above relation 3.19 a fixed focal depth of 18 km has been used. Now procedures are available to determine the earthquake magnitudes precisely.

Table 3.5. Distance correction factor σ for magnitude M_L (1958)

Distance Δ in km	*Distance correction factor σ in mm*	*Distance Δ in km*	*Distance correction factor σ in mm*	*Distance Δ in km*	*Distance correction factor σ in mm*	*Distance Δ in km*	*Distance correction factor σ in mm*
0	1.4	120	3.1	320	4.1	520	4.8
10	1.5	140	3.2	340	4.2	540	4.8
20	1.7	160	3.3	360	4.3	560	4.9
30	2.1	180	3.4	380	4.4	580	4.9
40	2.4	200	3.5	400	4.5	600	4.9
50	2.6	220	3.65	420	4.5		
60	2.8	240	3.70	440	4.6		
70	2.8	260	3.80	460	4.6		
80	2.9	280	3.90	480	4.7		
90	3.0	300	4.00	500	4.7		
100	3.0						

3.20. LOCAL SITE EFFECTS ON THE DAMAGES OF A EARTHQUAKE

During an earthquake significant difference in structural damage to structures situated in basins and on surrounding rocks or even in the same basin from place to place has been observed. The amplitude of shaking in basin *i.e.*

in soils are found more than 10 times stronger than the surrounding rocks. The other geological conditions which affect amplitude and signal duration are topography (ridge valley and slope variation) and lateral discontinuities. Many researchers worked on the effect of the local site conditions on the damage by earthquakes since 1908.

Wood, Reid and Mac Murdo are some of the workers who worked on these problems. They found that buildings situded on rocks were much less affected than those founded on soil cover as in Kutch (Gujrat) India. Other notable examples of intense effects of local conditions on damage due to earthquake are those of Michoacan earthquake of 1985 which caused heavy damage as far away as 400 km in the Maxico city, where as it caused only moderate damage in the vicinity of its epicentre. Similarly Loma Prieta California earthquake of 1989 caused heavy damage in the city of Francisco and Oakland and damage caused by January 26, 2001 earthquake of Bhuj (India). The classification of local geology in different categories is shown in the following table 3.6.

Table 3.6. Showing classification of local geology in different categories local site effects

Category A *Soil (Basin)*	*Category B* *Topography*	*Category C*
(*a*) Impedance, contrast (*b*) Resonance (*c*) Trapping (*d*) Focussing (*e*) Basin edge (*f*) Damping	(*a*) Ridge (*b*) Valley (*c*) Slope/ slope variation	Strong lateral discontinuities

3.20.1. Soil/(basin) effects

As most of the urbanized areas are generally settled along river valleys over young, soft and superficial soils, the study of different aspects of soil effects on the ground motion is of great importance and needs special attention.

Impedance Constrast. It has been observed that seismic waves travel faster in hard rocks than in softer rocks and sediments. As the seismic waves pass from the hard medium to soft medium, their velocity (celerity) decreases. Thus they must get bigger amplitude to carry the same amount of energy. Leaving the effects of scattering and material damping, the conservation of elastic wave energy requires that the flow of energy (energy flux = $\rho\, V_s \cdot V^2$) from depth to the ground surface must be constant. Thus with the decrease in density ρ, and secondary '*S*' wave velocity V_s of the medium as waves approach the ground surface, the particle velocity '*V*' must increase. Thus shaking tends to be stronger on sites with softer soil layers.

Resonance. When there are resonance of the signal frequency with the fundamental frequency or higher frequencies in the ground, a great increase in the ground motion amplification takes place. Various spectral peaks characterize the resonance pattern. For one layer, one dimensional structure this relation is shown as

$$f_o = V_{s1}/4h \text{ (fundamental mode) and}$$

$$f_n = (2n + 1)\, f_0 \text{ (harmonic mode).}$$

where, V_{s1} is S wave velocity in the surfacial layer of soil and h is the thickness. The amplitudes of these special spectral peaks mainly are related to the impedance (resistance) contrast and sediment damping.

Damping in soil

In mediums in which the collision between neighbouring particles of the medium is not perfectly elastic and a part of the wave energy is lost instead of being transferred through the medium, a lot of energy is absorbed due to inelastic properties of the medium. This type of decrease in the seismic waves energy is called as inelastic damping. The damping of seismic waves is described by a parameter known as *quality factor* 'Q'. This is defined as the fraction loss of energy per cycle.

i.e. $$\frac{2\pi}{Q} = -\frac{\Delta E}{E}$$

where, ΔE is the energy loss per cycle and E is total elastic energy stored in the wave. If the damping of a seismic wave is considered as a function of the distance and the amplitude of the seismic wave then, damping

$$A = A_0 \exp\left(1 - \frac{\pi r}{Q\lambda}\right) = A_0 \exp(-\alpha \cdot r)$$

where, $\alpha = \dfrac{\omega}{2\, Q \cdot V}$ is a absorption coefficient. This relation shows that higher frequencies will be absorbed at a faster rate.

Basin edge

During recent earthquakes due to the generation of strong surface waves near the edge of a basin, intense concentration of damage parallel to the basin edge has been observed. The conclusion that basin edge induces strong surface waves has been drawn based on the studies of (Bard and Bouchan, Hatayama, Kawase, Pitorka and Narayan), by examining the phase and group velocities, polarity and arrival azimuth. Surface waves start generating near the edge of the basin when frequency content in the body wave exceeds the fundamental frequency of the soil and their amplitudes decrease with increase of edge slope.

The major conclusion drawn by the above mentioned researchers are reproduced below:

(*a*) Basin edge induces strong surface waves near the edge.

(*b*) The edge induced surface waves propagate towards the basin normal to the edge.

(*c*) Surface waves start generating near the edge of the basin when frequency content in the body wave exceeds the fundamental frequency of the soil deposit.

(*d*) Surface wave amplitude decreases with increase of edge slope.

(*e*) Damage caused by edge induced surface waves is confined in a narrow zone of width of 2.5 to 3.5 km parallel to the edge at some distance of 0.5 to 1.0 km.

(*f*) Surface wave amplitude increases with the decrease of propagation velocity in soil. Further their characteristics are highly variable with change in propagation velocity and thickness of soil deposit.

(*g*) The characteristics of the edge induced surface waves are also very much dependent on the angle of incidence of body waves.

(*h*) Edge induced surface waves develop significant differential ground. This is the main cause of damage during earthquakes, in addition to amplification and prolongation of the signal.

3.20.2. Basement topography

Seismic waves travelling upwards from depth below may be redirected by negligible (very small) irregularities at geological interfaces, specially the basement topography. The effects of focusing and defocusing are maximum for normal incidence of waves. It decrease with the increase in the angle of incidence. Similarly azimuth also affects the focusing and defocusing effects. This effect shows the importance of considering not only the surfacial soil layer but also the basement topography for seismic microzonation. Thus the focussing and defocussing effects developed due to basement topogrophy are strongly dependent on azimuth and angle of incidence of waves.

Trapping of waves

The trapping and multiple reflections of seismic waves due to the large impedance contrast between soft sediments and underlying bed rock is the fundamental phenomenon responsible for the increase of duration of motion over the soft sediment. Some times when a wave enters a basin through its edge, it can get trapped with in the basin if post critical incidence angle develops, causing total internal reflection at the base of the layer. Waves that are trapped in deep sedimentary basins can thus be potentially very damaging.

Lateral discontinuity effect

There are many consistent large scale seismic observations which show an significant increase in the intensity of damage in narrow areas where a softer material exists or lies besides a more rigid material. The observed damage may be due to the generation of amplification of amplitude and local surface wave in the softer material or medium and development of large differential motion due to shorter wave length of the surface wave. On the basis of theoretical studies of Moczo and bard during 1993) and field observations by Narayan and Rai, 2001) have reported significant increase of damage in the narrow zone located along strong lateral discontinuities *i.e.* in areas where softer medium exists along side the rigid material.

Effect of surface topography

Very often it has been observed that after big or destructive earthquakes in hilly regions, the buildings situated at the hill tops suffered much more damage than those located near the base. 1909 earthquake of France, 1980 earthquake of Italy and 1995 earthquake of Chile are good examples of such observations.

There are also very strong instrumental evidences that surface topography affects considerably the amplitude and frequency contents of the ground motion. The theoretical and numerical model studies have also predicted a systematic amplification of ground motion at ridge crest (Convex part) and de amplification in the valley (Concave part) of the surface topography. These observations have been reported by Kawase and Aki in 1990, Sanchez-Sesma in, 1990 Faccioli in 1991 and Narayan and Rao in 2003.

On the basis of their model studies in 2003 Narayan and Rao, reported surface wave generation near the top of the ridge and their propagation towards the base of the ridge in addition to amplification of ground motion with elevation and slope of the ridge. Narayan also reported strong generation of surface waves for disintegration (weathering) thickness more than 1/8 of wave length. On the basis of simulated results, he reported that damage to the built environment may be maximum on the top of the ridge, if it is not weathered (disintegrated) that is if it is solid. But if the velocity of the disintegrated (weathered) material is very less in comparision to the underlying rock formation, the maximum damage may be more near the base of the ridge, due

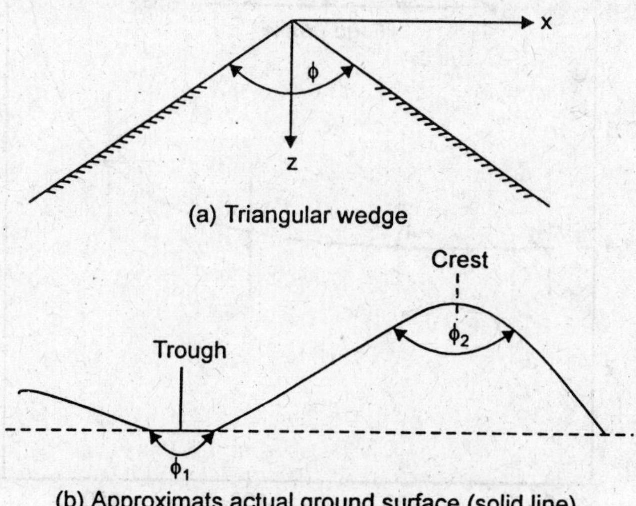

Fig. 3.24. Characteristics of Topographic irregularities

to large amplitude and duration of the generated surface wave. Some of the conclusions drawn on the basis of the above studies are reproduced below:

(*a*) Ground motion amplification increases with the ridge slope *i.e.* more the ridge slope greater is the amplification.

(*b*) Maximum amplification (2 π/ϕ, where ϕ is the crest angle) occurs at the crest of the triangular wedge type topography relative to the base for wave length comparable to the base Fig. 3.24.

(*c*) De amplification (2 π/ϕ) times occurs in the valley relative to the top of the valley.

(*d*) Topographic amplification decreases with the increase of angle of incidence of body waves.

(*e*) Ridge amplification increases with elevation (Fig. 3.25)

(*f*) Surface waves are generated near the top of the topography.

(*g*) The presence of neighbouring ridges accentuates (Makes more noticeable) the topographic effects.

(*h*) The interference between the incident waves and out going diffracted waves produces rapidly varying amplitude and phase, thus causing

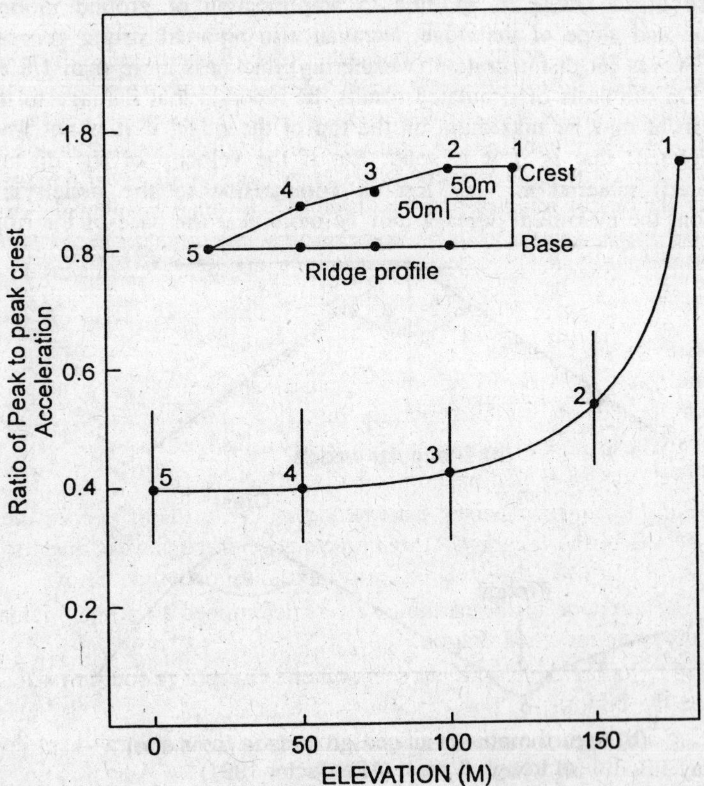

Fig. 3.25. Variation of average amplification factor with elevation (Jibson 1987)

differential ground motion along the slope of the topography.

(*i*) The amplitude of ridge weathering induced surface wave increases towards its base, if the thickness of weathering is more than 1/8 of the wave length.

(*j*) The decrease of weathering velocity increases the amplitude of ridge induced surface waves.

(*k*) Complicated damage pattern occurs on hills with variable slopes. Generally houses built on or near the slope change suffer more damage.

(*l*) In general, theoretical studies predict lower amplification than those obtained by analysis of recorded motion.

3.21. EARTHQUAKE FORECASTING

Earthquakes are one of the deadliest hazards to life on this planet. They have destroyed count less cities and villages on almost all continents. They are one of the most feared natural phenomenon for the human being, as they occur suddenly and cause instantaneous destruction of life and property. Actually the fear of earthquakes is out of proportion of their actual damage as average losses due floods and wind are far in excess than those of earthquakes in most parts of the world. A majority of earthquake fatalities could be checked if ground shocks could be predicted well in a short period. Thousands of lives could be saved if people inhabiting in buildings of suspect construction could be evacuated for some time. Except in cases of land sliding, earthquakes cause death by damaging buildings, dams, bridges and other man made structures. This is the reason, why earthquake prediction is important in the prevention of earthquake related deaths. Thus damage caused by earthquakes is almost entirely associated with man made structures.

3.21.1. Earlier predictions

Some times in A.D. 132 Chinese devised an earthquake weather cock to detect earthquakes and to determine the direction of the epicenter. This weather cock consisted of:

(*a*) Eight dragons holding bronze balls in their mouths.

(*b*) An internal mechanism, activated by a slight tremor opened the mouth of one of the dragons. At this juncture all dragons were made to sound. As it clanked (made sound) into the mouth of a tode below.

(*c*) The direction of the earthquake was determined from the orientation of the open mouthed dragon.

In 1971, Italian developed an seismometer using a pendulum with a brass pointer on the bottom.

During a tremor, the pointer traced grooves in the sand tray kept level in a larger tray filled with water.

In the 19th century mercury filled seismoscope indicated an earthquake, giving its direction and some indication of its size (strength).

Today seismographs may be used to amplify and record earthquake displacement caused by shaking. The seismograph works on the principle of inertia. This instrument records only earth motions. From this seismograph following important informations may be determined:

(*a*) Distance from a specific station of observation upto the epicenter of the earthquake by measuring the difference in time of arrival of P waves and S waves, as these waves travel with different velocities in the earth.

(*b*) Richter's magnitude M of the earthquake can be determined from the maximum amplitude of the seismic trace.

3.21.2. Prediction in 1970's

After the acceptance of plate tectonic theory in 1960, the subject of earthquake prediction has become a serious topic. In early days only astrologers, mystics and religious zealots were considered capable to predict the earthquakes.

Now a days most respected scientists are working on the problem of predicting earthquakes.

Some encouraging leads have been persued, such as strain changes or ground tilts that precede the earthquake and grouping of fore shocks all indicate the same slip direction along a fault plane just before rupture. The changes in physical properties of the ground such as change in porosity, electrical conductivity and elastic velocity in the hypocentral region take place just before faulting. Russian and Chinese geologists have suggested that before a big earthquake, the ground around a fault strains and cracks. Water is leached from under ground uranium deposits. This water seeps upwards into the broken crust. The optimism of earthquake prediction grew brighter in February 1975. Chinese scientists had predicted in February 1975 that a big size earthquake would occur on that day near the city of Haicheng. The population of this city was 90,000. People of the town were advised to go to open air shelters. Movies were arranged in these shelters. These movies helped the people to endure sub freezing temperature. The tremors of magnitude 7.3 at the Richter scale hit the region precisely on scheduled time at 7.36 p.m. 90% structures of the city either were damaged or destroyed. The accurate warning saved thousands of lives.

Chines also suggested some other precursors. According to them before a big size earthquake, a series of small tremors take place, the behaviour of animals change. Frogs start jumping out of ponds and deers start running into the open before the big size earthquake, Tilting of ground. Change in strain of rocks, increase in ground water level, sharp changes in pressure, unusual lights in the sky.

After this February 1975 successful forecast, few predictions came true, but by and large earthquakes continued their annual massacre. After more than a year of this successful forecast, Chinese scientists with all their sophistication failed to predict the 7.8 magnitude earthquake at Tangshan. The official death toll during this earthquake was 25×10^4, but unofficial figure is at least three times that of official figure. The short term clues have been found inconsistent.

3.21.3. Recent attempts

At the beginning of 1980, efforts were made afresh to develop some technique to predict earthquakes. In 1980, David Hill of Geological survey of U.S.A. predicted that a major earthquake would hit California some times before the end of 19th century. Actually instead of one, three earthquakes occurred in california before the end of the 19th century. One earthquake occurred in Lome-Perita in 1986 in San Francisco-Oakland region, Another major earthquake struck california on 17 October 1989. The magnitude of this earthquake was 6.9 on Richter scale. The third major earthquake struck North ridge California on January 1994.

From the various geological records, it is evident that some earthquakes are regularly repeating events. According to Don Anderson former director of California Institute of Technology U.S.A., seismological activity reoccurs roughly in 25 year cycle. San Andreas fault about half way between Los Angeles and San Francisco, the park field section is the most monitored, measured, metered and analysed and thought about fault in the world.

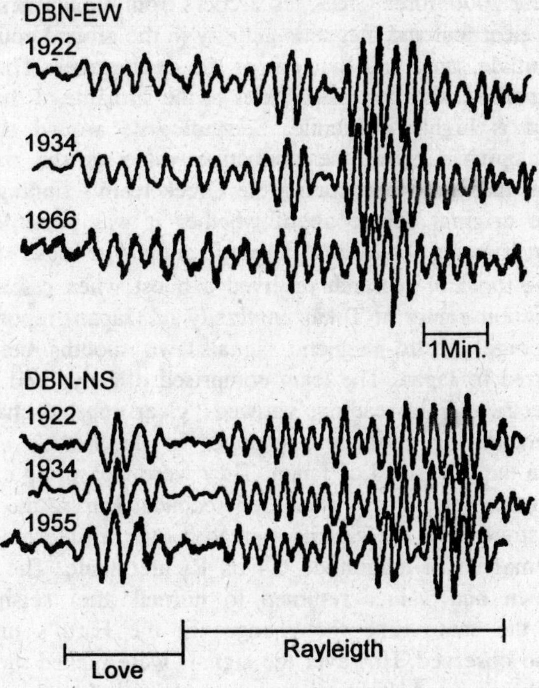

Fig. 3.26.

The seismograms record of three park field earthquakes of 1922, 1934 and 1966 are so similar if they are placed one over the other, they fit perfectly as shown in Fig. 3.26. The park field section of San Andreas fault zone has been characterized by recurring sequence which had an accurate every 22 years period as 1857-1881-1901-1922-1934 and 1966, but 1934 earthquake broke this sequence of 22 years. This shows that park field ruptures just about every 22 years. According to this forecast the next earthquake was due some times in 1988, but it occurred in 1989.

It is worth mentioning that the frequency of occurrence of major earthquakes in the Kutch area of Gujrat (India) is once in a period of 30 years. However the knowledge of cycles is not sufficient clues for forecasting earthquakes. Now geologists are trying hard to provide a few days warning of earthquakes at least for heavily populated areas, but there are many variables. They do not expect to make frequent precise predictions. Much remains to be learnt about the behaviour of plate tectonics which have only been recognised in 1960. Now most of the well known faults in the world are being instrumented to form a part of the global monitoring network. This net work is expected to provide enough data to scientist to be able to forecast earthquakes. Seismic waves even from medium tremors travel large distances, in and around the earth, generating record at the place where seismographs are working.

About the year 2000, three Greek researchers from the university of Athens had claimed that electrical and magnetic activity in the ground could be used to predict the magnitude, time and location of the earthquakes. Their method is known as VAN method after the initial letter of the surname of the researchers. The Van method is highly debatable. Seismologists around the world are divided in their opinion about the predictive value of the method. Other Seismologists are unable in reproducing the Greek team's findings, which did little to help the original debate about whether it was possible to forecast earthquakes by monitoring the electro-magnetic signals of rocks stress.

However this topic of research received a boost when researchers at the Earthquake prediction center at Tokai university of (Japan) reported that they had detected strange electro-magnetic signals two months before a major earthquake occurred in Japan. The team comprised of Seiya and Uyeda's said that their geo-electrical field readings showed "clear unusual changes". They were routinely measuring anomalous changes in the Earth's electrical and magnetic fields in the Izu island of Japan. They were measuring extremely low frequency electro-magnetic waves every ten seconds. During the process they noticed that the strength of the signals increased over a time reaching a peak before first earthmagnet of magnitude 6.4 on Richter scale. The strange field activity died down and values returned to normal after seismic activities increased. Over the same time the changes in the Earth's magnetic field strength were also observed. However the signals were picked up only by two of the antennas being used. The researcher explained that the stress signals could have been propagated along the highly conductive channels, such as faults in the rock that contain pools of water, making them detectable only in certain case only.

With these findings the debate amongst seismologists has again heated up and the Van method once again is under international scrutiny.

Mr. Arun Bapat an Indian scientist is watching indications of occurring earthquake for the last thirty five years. His observations are as follows:

1. A sudden change in radio frequencies takes place before the occurrence of an earthquake. For example if a radio station was available on 1000 kw area, it may go upto 1200 or 1500 Kilo watt area as the earthquake approaches.
2. Wireless frequencies available to police and forest departments are also found distorted to a great extent.
3. Unusual rise in temperature below the ground level has been observed.
4. Animals show disturbed behaviour and refuse any eating.
5. The pat animals such as cow etc. either become too aggressive or too meak. (frightened).

QUESTIONS

1. Discuss the causes of occurrence of earthquakes.
2. Name different types of seismic waves and discuss body waves fully.
3. How the ground motions are measured? Discuss one method in detail.
4. Define a fault and give its classification with neat sketch.
5. How the severity of an earthquake is measured?
6. Differentiate between magnitude and intensity of an earthquake.
7. Write a note on the forecasting of an earthquake.
8. Discuss the composition of earth.
9. The relative movement of the crustal plates gives rise to the formation of
   (*a*) Constructive Margin (Divergence zone)
   (*b*) Destruction margin (Convergence zone)
   (*c*) Conservative margin (Refractive zone)
   (*d*) All the three types
10. Earthquakes of shallow focal depths are generated in
    (*a*) Divergence zones
    (*b*) Convergence zone
    (*c*) Fracture or transform zones
    (*d*) In any of the above zones
11. Most wide spread and intense earthquakes are generated in
    (*a*) Fracture zone
    (*b*) Destructive (sub duction zone)
    (*c*) Divergence zone
    (*d*) In none of the above zones
12. Identify the correct statement/statements
    (*a*) Earthquakes generate only in the upper 700 km depth of the earth

(*b*) Shallow focus earthquakes generally generate upto 70 km depth from the earth surface
(*c*) Intermediate focal depth earthquake occur between 70 to 300 km depth from the surface of the earth
(*d*) Deep focus earthquakes are generated at more than 300 km depth from the surface of earth
(*e*) All are correct

13. Identify the incorrect statement/statements
(*a*) Seismic energy generated decreases as the focal depth increases
(*b*) Seismic energy generated decreases as the focal depth decrease
(*c*) Seismic energy generated at a depth greater than 70 km from the surface of the earth decreases as it reaches the surface
(*d*) Earthquake resistant structures are designed for shallow focus earthquakes

14. Earthquake resistant structures are designed for
(*a*) Shallow focus earthquakes
(*b*) Deep focus earthquakes
(*c*) Intermediate focus earthquakes
(*d*) For all the focus depth earthquakes

15. Seismic waves may be classified as
(*a*) Body waves (*b*) Surface waves
(*c*) Both are true (*d*) Both are untrue

16. P waves are called
(*a*) Primary waves (*b*) Longitudinal waves
(*c*) Compressional waves (*d*) All the three

17. S waves are called
(*a*) Secondary waves (*b*) shear waves
(*c*) Transverse waves (*d*) All the three

18. Identify the correct statement/statements
(*a*) Most earthquakes in the world occur along the boundaries of the tectonic plate
(*b*) Earthquakes generated along the boundaries are known as inter plate earthquake
(*c*) Earthquakes generated away from the boundary with in the plates are called intra earthquakes
(*d*) Slip is generated at the fault during the occurrence of a earthquake
(*e*) All are correct

19. The energy released by an earthquake goes to
(*a*) Mostly to heat generation
(*b*) For fracturing the rocks
(*c*) A fraction of energy goes to seismic waves causing damage to structures
(*d*) In all the three use

20. The average thickness of ground layer is....
(*a*) 33.0 m (*b*) 3.3 m
(*c*) 33 km (*d*) 45 km

21. Temperature under the ground layer is....
    (*a*) 800°C (*b*) 1200°C
    (*c*) 1000°C (*d*) 1350°C
22. The average depth of water over the surface of ground is ....
    (*a*) 3.2 m (*b*) 3.2 km
    (*c*) 11.2 km (*d*) 7.5 km
23. The percentage of oxygen, nitrogen and other gases to gether is ....%
    (*a*) 30% (*b*) 50%
    (*c*) 75% (*d*) 85%
24. Identify the incorrect statement/statements
    (*a*) The thickness of ground layer at all places is constant
    (*b*) The thickness of ground layer varies from 5 km to 56 km
    (*c*) According to scientists our ground is consisted of tectonic plates
    (*d*) These tectonic plates move in all directions with the constant velocity every year
25. Identify the incorrect statement/statements
    (*a*) The point below the focus is called epicenter of the earthquake
    (*b*) The point from which slip starts is called focus of the earthquake
    (*c*) The point over the focus over the ground is called epicenter of the earthquake
    (*d*) The vertical distance between the focus and epicenter is known as focal depth
    (*e*) The distance between the epicenter and place of occurrence of earthquake is called epicenter distance
    (*f*) Earthquakes are generated due to huge deformation in the upper layers of the ground
26. Identify the correct statement/statements
    (*a*) The main seismic waves P move with the highest velocity
    (*b*) The velocity of movement of main waves P is slowest
    (*c*) Secondary seismic waves S travel only in water
    (*d*) The secondary waves move only through solid medium
27. The lowest depth of earthquake focus is...
    (*a*) 1.5 km (*b*) 5.0 km
    (*c*) 3.5 km (*d*) 7.5 km
28. The depth of focus can be more than....
    (*a*) 300 km (*b*) 650 km
    (*c*) 540 km (*d*) 450 km
29. The damage from an earthquake is influenced by
    (*a*) The depth of focus
    (*b*) Condition of soil below the foundation
    (*c*) The distance of the site from the epicenter
    (*d*) All are correct
30. Earthquakes of intensity more than 8.0 M cause damage in a area of .... radius
    (*a*) 100 km (*b*) 150 km
    (*c*) 200 km (*d*) more than 250 km
31. Identify the correct statement/statements

(*a*) Before occurring a earthquake, the water level in wells is lowered
(*b*) During an earthquake the behaviour of animals changes. They either become aggressive or submissive
(*c*) Frogs start jumping out of the tank and Deer start running fast
(*d*) All are correct

32. Seismic waves are of the type....
(*a*) Main or P waves (*b*) Secondary or S waves
(*c*) Surface waves (*d*) All the three types

33. Identify the incorrect statement/statements
(*a*) Thrust faults move the ground in the upward direction
(*b*) Strike slip faults move the ground horizontally
(*c*) Convergence of tectonic plates also cause earthquake
(*d*) Due to submergence of one tectonic plate beneath the neighbouring plate causes a destructive earthquake
(*e*) When fault ruptures, seismic waves are propagated in all directions out warldly.
(*f*) The severity of a earthquake increases with the magnitude of the earthquake and decrease with the increase in epicenter distance
(*g*) All are correct

34. The continental rocks are .... than sea floor
(a) Heavy (b) Light
(c) Equal (d) All are correct

35. Identify the incorrect statement
(*a*) By striking or development of friction between two moving tectonic plates the deformations are developed in the upper layers of ground. When these deformations are more than the bearing capacity of the rocks then these stresses are released through existing faults. This process is called development of earthquake.
(*b*) From the fault point, the plane of rupture expands in all directions
(*c*) This rupture expands unequally on the surface and inside of the earth till the pressure becomes equal
(*d*) Earthquake also occurs by the convergence of tectonic plates
(*e*) All are correct

ANSWERS

9. (*d*)	16. (*d*)	23. (*c*)	30. (*d*)
10. (*a*)	17. (*d*)	24. (*a*)	31. (*d*)
11. (*b*)	18. (*e*)	25. (*a*)	32. (*d*)
12. (*e*)	19. (*d*)	26. (*a, c*)	33. (*g*)
13. (*b*)	20. (*c*)	27. (*b*)	34. (*b*)
14. (*a*)	21. (*c*)	28. (*a*)	35. (*e*)
15. (*c*)	22. (*b*)	29. (*d*)	

4

Vibrations of Single Degree of Freedom System

4.1. INTRODUCTION

Vibrations in structures may be caused by underground blasts, wind, machines, moving loads, flow of water and earthquakes. The pattern of variation of dynamic forces with respect to time consists mainly of two types as follows.

1. **Periodic vibrations.** Periodic vibrations are those, which develop due to unbalanced rotating machine parts, self excited aerodynamic vibrations in chimneys and pipe line structures caused by steady flow etc. These periodical motions can be resolved into Sinusoidally varying components.
2. **Random motions.** These motions have complicated non periodic time history. Vibrations caused by earthquakes and quarry blasts are classified as complicated time history vibrations. For the analysis of events of random type, statistical techniques may be applied. Loads imposed by rough rides in vehicles, and aerodynamic pushing side to side (buffeting) problems. Some loads when applied suddenly cause temporary (transient) motion. Vibrations caused during operation of gates and valves and starting and stopping of large machines are classified as transient or temporary vibrations. Vibrations caused by Nuclear blasts and pile driving are known as transient pulse or a series of few pulses. In order to determine the seismic forces on a structure, it is necessary to study its vibration characteristics on which the effects of earthquake ground motion depend. In this chapter and in the next two chapters methods of determining the characteristics of vibrations are discussed.

4.2. BASIC DEFINITIONS

Mass. The property of a body that describes how an unrestricted body resists the application of an external force is known as *Mass.* It is obtained by dividing the weight of the body by the acceleration of gravity 'g'. Unit of mass is given in kilograms. ($m = W/g$).

Natural Period 'T'. The time of one complete cycle of free vibration is called Natural Period 'T'. It is expressed in seconds.

Natural frequency. The full number of cycles per unit time is known as Natural frequency. When no external force acts on the system after giving it an initial displacement, the body vibrates. These vibrations are known as free vibrations and their frequency is called as natural frequency. It is expressed as radian per second or Hertz.

Stiffness. The force required to produce unit deformation is called *stiffness*. It is an elastic property that describes the level of resisting force that develops when a body undergoes a change in length. The unit of stiffness is Newton per metre (N/m) or N/mm. (1N/mm = 100 N/m).

Amplitude. The maximum deformation or displacement of a vibrating system from its mean position is known as *amplitude*. Usually it is denoted by A.

Free vibration. The vibration which persists in a structure after removal of the force causing the motion in the structure is known as free vibration. It takes place when a system oscillates under the action of forces inherent in the system itself. No external forces act on them. Oscillation of a simple pendulum is a good example of the free vibration.

Forced vibration. The vibration which is maintained in a structure by steady periodic force acting on the structure is called forced vibration. When the excitation is oscillatory, the system is forced to vibrate at the excitation frequency. The behaviour of a system under forced vibration depends upon the type of excitation. Forced vibration may be either deterministic or randum.

Fundamental mode of vibration. The mode having the lowest natural frequency is known as fundamental mode of vibration of a structure.

Damping. The resistance to the motion of a vibrating body is called *damping*. The vibrations of a system associated with this resistance are called as damped vibrations. It is a phenomenon in which the vibrational energy of the system is gradually decreased or amplitude of vibration is gradually reduced. The unit of damping is N/m/s.

Resonance. When the frequency of an external force is equal to the natural frequency of the vibrating system, in such situations the amplitude of the vibration becomes excessively high. This phenomenon is known as *resonance*. The failure of major structures such as bridges and buildings largely is due to resonance.

Simple harmonic motion (S.H.M.). The motion of periodic form is called as harmonic motion. The harmonic motion is represented in terms of circular sine and consine functions. All harmonic motions are periodic in nature, but all the periodic motions are not always harmonic. The to and fro motion of a body about a fixed point is called simple harmonic motion. Following are the characteristics of a S.H.M.

(*a*) The motion is periodic.

(*b*) When displaced from the mean position or the fixed point, a restoring force acts on the particle tending to bring it to the mean position.

(*c*) The restoring force on the particle is directly proportional to its displacement.

A simple harmonic motion may be of the type

$$x = A \sin (\omega t + \phi)$$

or

$$x = A \sin pt + B \cos pt$$

where,

x = Displacement

A = Amplitude

ω = Frequency

p = Angular or circular frequency. It is measured in radians per second

ϕ = Phase angle.

In this text $x = A \sin pt + B \cos pt$ has been used as H.S.M. equation.

4.3. TYPES OF VIBRATIONS

Whatever may be the cause of vibrations, a structure vibrates in one of the following four deformation or a combination of there of. The line diagram of these deformations during vibrations are shown in Fig. 4.1.

(*a*) *Extensional vibrations.* This type of vibrations develop in vertical direction by a rigid block tied with a spring, one end of which is tied with a fixed support as shown in Fig. 4.1 (*a*).

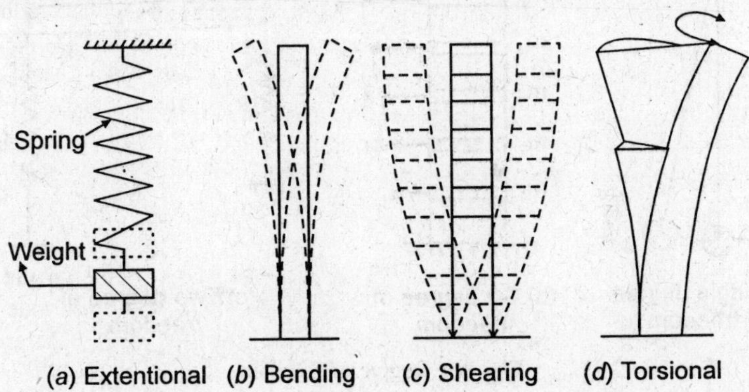

Fig. 4.1. Types of Deformations during vibration

(*b*) *Bending vibrations.* This type of vibrations develop in tall vertical structures as that in a chimney stack as shown in Fig. 4.1 (*b*).

(*c*) *Shear vibrations.* This type of vibrations develop in multistorey buildings having columns stiffened by rigid floor beams at different levels. These vibrations are horizontal vibrations Fig. 4.1 (*c*).

(*d*) *Torsional vibrations.* This type of vibrations develop due to twisting of a building having its supporting parts of different stiffnesses as shown in Fig. 4.1 (*d*).

Generally one type of deformation predominates, though quite often combinations of two types of deformations can be important like that of bending and shear deformations in vibrations of chimneys in higher modes and horizontal and rocking mode vibrations in machine foundations.

The vibration behaviour depends on mass and stiffness distribution and constraints on the system.

4.4. DEGREE OF FREEDOM

The position of a vibrating mass in space with respect to its position of equilibrium can be described by six coordinates, three translational along the three orthogonal axes *x, y, z* and three rotational about the same axes *i.e. x, y* and *z* axes. However a mass may have freedom to move only in certain directions and may be constrained in other directions. The number of independent coordinates required to describe the position of a vibrating mass is known as *degree of freedom* of that mass. For a multi mass discrete (independent from others) system the total *degree of freedom* would be the sum of degree of freedom of individual masses. If a system is represented by a single mass and it is constrained in such a way that its motion is described by a single coordinate, then this system is known as a single degree of freedom system.

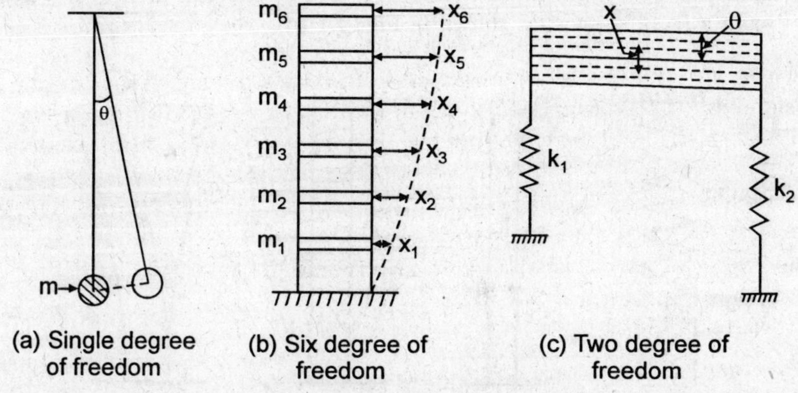

Fig. 4.2. Degree of freedom

Such a system is shown in Fig. 4.2 (*a*) in which θ is the coordinate which defines the position of mass 'm'.

If six masses such as the floor mass of the six storeyed building (the masses are considered to be concentrated at floor levels) vibrate in one plane as shown in Fig. 4.2 (*b*), six displacements for six masses from x_1 to x_6 will describe the deformed position of the structure. This would be known as a structure having six degree of freedom.

If one mass is attached to two springs and is free to vibrate in two independent deformed shapes, it would be known as two degree of freedom structure, since two coordinates will be required to describe the deformed position of the mass Fig. 4.2 (*c*). The two independent coordinates required to define the position of the mass are 'θ and 'x'.

4.5. SPRING ACTION AND DAMPING

Imagine a mass 'm' fixed on the top of a column as shown in Fig. 4.3 (*a*) or a mass resting on rollers and fixed to a spring and a damping device dashpot

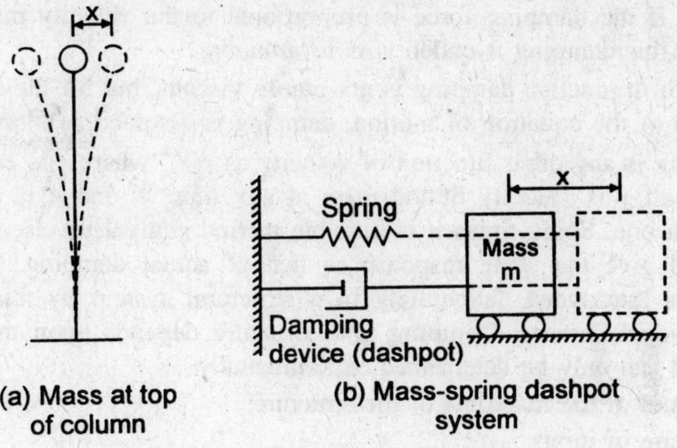

Fig. 4.3. Mass, Spring and Damping

as shown in Fig. 4.3 (*b*). If the mass 'm' is displaced by a distance 'x', the elastic straining of the column in Fig. (*a*) or the stretching of the spring in Fig. (*b*) will tend to bring the mass back to the original position. The force exerted by the column or spring is a function of the displacement 'x' and is known as its *restoring force* or *spring force*. If the displacement 'x' is small, this force could be assumed to be a linear function of 'x'.

This mass 'm' will come back to its original position with a certain

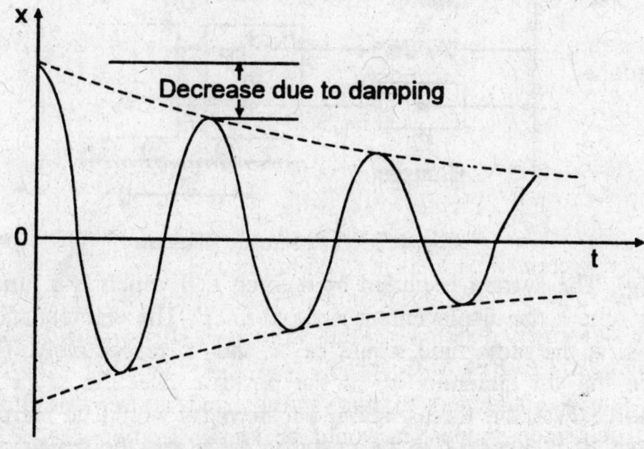

Fig. 4.4. Damped free vibration

velocity and pass to the other side and thus vibrate. In case the system is elastic and there is no loss of energy, the mass will vibrate for ever. But in practice, friction due to air, or friction between the particles of the system or at junctions or due to yielding of the material etc., energy dissipation will take place, so that vibrations will die out in course of time. The forces which cause loss of energy are called as *damping forces* Fig. 4.4 shows the variation of displacement 'x' with time. If the damping force is proportional to the velocity motion of the mass, then this damping is called *viscous damping*.

Though in practice damping is not purely viscous, but for the convenience of solution of the equation of motion, damping is assumed as viscous. In case the damping is any other function of velocity as $c(x)^n$ where c is coefficient of damping and x is velocity of the mass at any time 't' and n is any number higher than one. Some times it is possible to find equivalent viscous damping that would give the same response as that of actual damping. Some times damping is introduced deliberately in a structural system by attaching to it some frictional devices. Damping of a structure depends upon the following factors and can only be determined experimentally.

1. Nature of the materials of the structure.
2. Nature of joints.
3. Quality of construction.
4. Nature and type of foundations.

4.6. EQUATION OF MOTION OF SINGLE DEGREE OF FREEDOM SYSTEM

Consider a mass 'm' attached to a fixed plane AB through a spring as shown in Fig. 4.5 (*a*) or an elastic system such as a portal frame as shown in

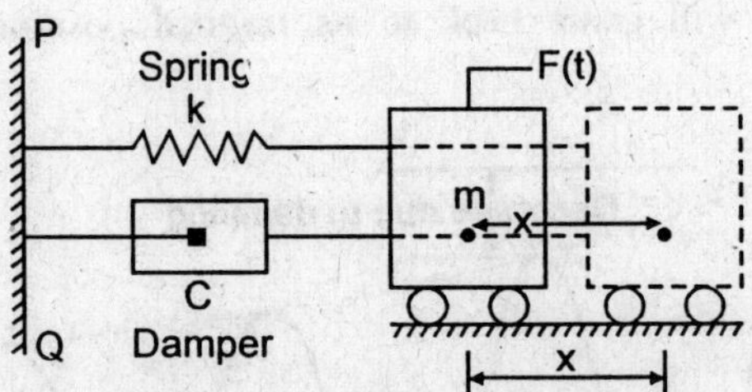

Fig. 4.5. (*a*) Schematic diagram

Fig. 4.5 (*b*). The system is pulled by a force $F(t)$ which is a function of time. Let at any time t, the displacement is equal to 'x'. The velocity and acceleration of the mass at the same time would be '$\dot{x}$' and '$\ddot{x}$' respectively. They are taken positive in the 1st quadrant or on the positive direction of 'x'. Besides the exciting force $F(t)$, the forces acting on the mass would be inertia force ($m\ddot{x}$), spring force ($K.x$) where K is the restoring force that the spring or elasticity of the portal frame exerts per unit displacement and damping force ($C\dot{x}$) where C

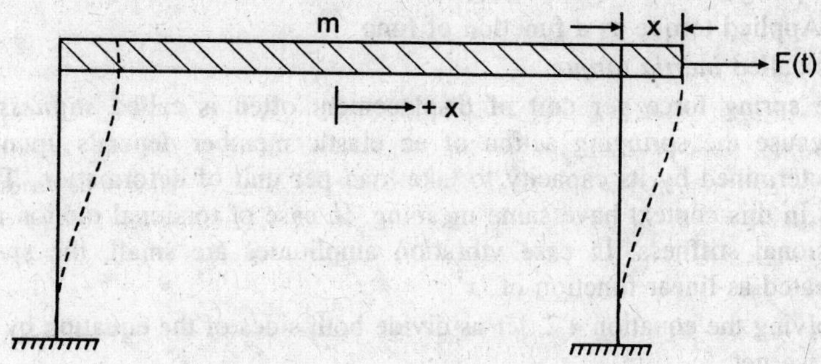

(*b*) Portal frame having same behaviour as mass m in Fig. (*a*)

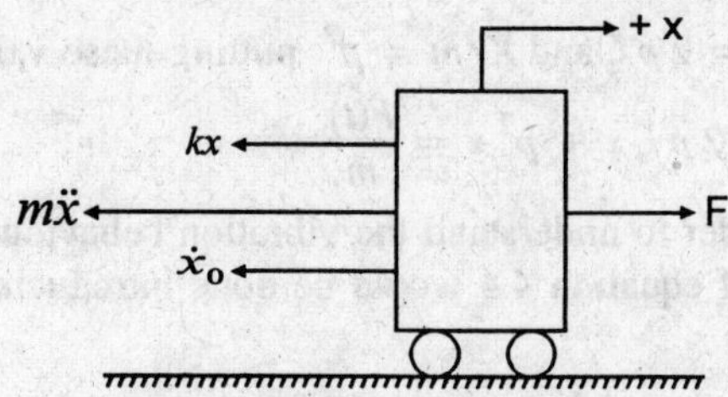

(*c*) Free body diagram

Fig. 4.5. A Single degree of freedom system

is the viscous damping in terms of force per unit velocity. The spring force on the mass is acting towards left and is described by a negative sign. Similarly the damping acts against the direction of the velocity and thus would be acting towards left. Considering the force body of the mass, the forces acting on it are

$$F(t) - Kx - C\dot{x} \quad \ldots(a)$$

According to second law of Newton, these forces are equal to inertia force ($m\ddot{x}$). Thus the relation can be written as

$$m\ddot{x} = F(t) - Kx - C\dot{x} \quad \ldots(4.1)$$

or

$$m\ddot{x} + C\dot{x} + Kx = F(t) \quad \ldots(4.2)$$

Alternatively in stead of second law of Newton, *D′* Alembert's principle may be used. According to *D′* Alembert's principle, if the inertia force $m\ddot{x}$ is applied to the mass as an external force with its direction reversed as shown in Fig. 4.5 (*c*), the system would be in an instantaneous state of equilibrium. Thus we get the same equation as 4.2.

In case of torsional motion, if the angle of torsion of a body having a mass moment of inertia I is θ, the equation of motion can be written as

$$I\ddot{\theta} + \overline{C}\dot{\theta} + \overline{K}\theta = \overline{F}(t) \quad \ldots(4.3)$$

where,

$\overline{c}$ = Damping force per unit of angular velocity

$\overline{K}$ = Spring force per unit of angle of rotation

$\overline{F}(t)$ = Applied torque as a function of time

$I \cdot \ddot{\theta}$ is called *inertia torque*

K, the spring force per unit of displacement often is called *stiffness* of spring, because the springing action of an elastic member depends upon its stiffness determined by its capacity to take load per unit of deformation. Thus both terms in this context have same meaning. In case of torsional motion it is called torsional stiffness. In case vibration amplitudes are small, the spring force is treated as linear function of '*x*'.

For solving the equation 4.2, let us divide both sides of the equation by the mass 'm', we get

$$\ddot{x} + \frac{C}{m}\dot{x} + \frac{K}{m}x = \frac{F(t)}{m}$$

Let us put $c/m = 2p\zeta$ and $K/m = p^2$. putting these values we get

$$\ddot{x} + 2p\zeta\dot{x} + p^2 x = \frac{F(t)}{m} \qquad ...(4.4)$$

To enable the reader to understand the vibration behaviour of the structural system, the solution of equation 4.4 would be done introducing many concepts in the following pages.

4.7. FREE VIBRATIONS OF UN DAMPED SYSTEM HAVING SINGLE DEGREE OF FREEDOM

In case the damping in the structure is very small and the exciting force is withdrawn after initial application, the system would be considered under undamped free vibration having either initial displacement or initial velocity or both, the mass will vibrate freely and its motion will be described by the equation obtained by putting ζ and F equal to zero. Then equation 4.4 reduces to

$$\ddot{x} + p^2 x = 0 \qquad ...(4.5)$$

The solution of equation 4.5 is as

$$x = A\sin pt + B\cos pt \qquad ...(4.6)$$

here, A and B are constants which depend upon the initial conditions of the motion and P is angular or circular frequency of the vibration. The frequency P is measured in radians per second. For determining the value of A and B, Let us assume, that when $t = 0$ we have $x = 0$ and $\dot{x} = \dot{x}_0$. In this case the value of A and B could be obtained from eqaution 4.6 and $\dot{x}$ from its differentiated form.

from equation 4.6, $B = 0$ and $A = \dfrac{\dot{x}_0}{P}$.

Thus equation 4.6 can be written as

$$x = \frac{\dot{x}_0}{P}\sin pt \qquad ...[4.7\ (a)]$$

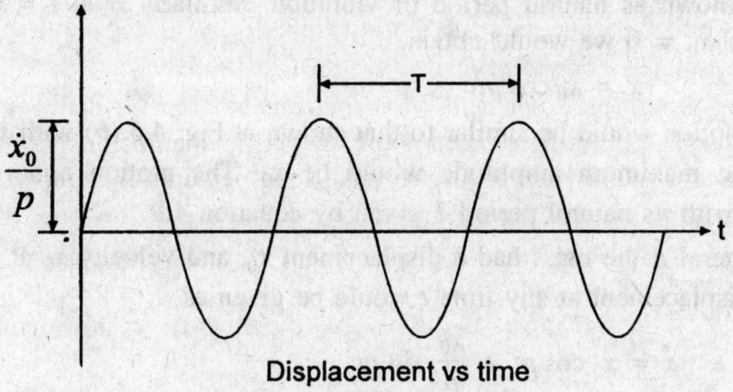

Fig. 4.6 (*a*). Displacement Vs time

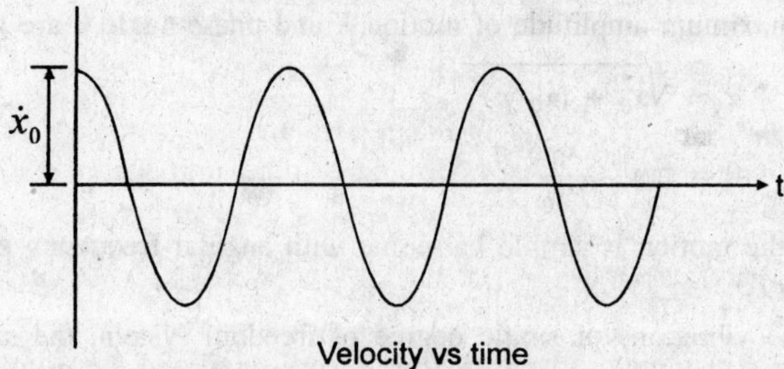

Fig. 4.6 (*b*). Velocity Vs time

The free motion of mass '*m*' is shown in Fig. 4.6 (*a*), which shows the maximum amplitude of vibration as $\dot{x}_0/P$. Differentiating '*x*' with respect to '*t*' in equation 4.7 (*a*) we get velocity equation as

$$\frac{dx}{dt} = \frac{\dot{x}_0}{P} \times P \cos pt$$

or $$\dot{x} = \dot{x}_0 \cos pt \qquad \ldots[4.7(b)]$$

The variation of velocity is plotted against time '*t*' in Fig. 4.6 (*b*). It may be noted that velocity is maximum when the displacement *x* is zero *i.e.* when the mass passes through the equilibrium position.

Equation 4.7 (*a*) relates to simple harmonic motion. The displacements of the system at intervals of one cycle of vibration are equal. In other words if *T* is the time taken by the systems to complete one cycle, then,

$$\frac{\dot{x}_0}{P} \sin Pt = \frac{\dot{x}_0}{P} \sin p\,(t + T)$$

or $$P(t + T) - pt = 2\,\pi$$

or $$T = \frac{2\,\pi}{P} = 2\,\pi\sqrt{m/K} \quad (\text{As } p^2 = \text{k/m}) \qquad \ldots(4.8)$$

T is known as natural period of vibration. Similarly if at $t = 0$, we had $x = x_0$ and $\dot{x}_0 = 0$ we would obtain.

$$x = x_0 \cos pt \qquad \text{...(4.9)}$$

The motion would be similar to that shown in Fig. 4.6 (*b*) with $\dot{x}_0$ replaced by x_0. The maximum amplitude would be x_0. The motion again is simple harmonic with its natural period T given by equation 4.8.

In general if the mass had a displacement x_0, and velocity $\dot{x}_0$ at any time $t = 0$, the displacement at any time t would be given as

$$x = x_0 \cos pt + \frac{\dot{x}_0}{p} \sin pt \qquad \text{...(4.10)}$$

which may alternatively may be written as

$$x = x \cos (Pt - \theta) \qquad \text{...(4.11)}$$

where the maximum amplitude of motion X and phase angle θ are given by

$$x = \sqrt{x_0^2 + (\dot{x}_0/p)^2} \qquad \text{...[4.11 (a)]}$$

and
$$\theta = \tan^{-1} \frac{\dot{x}_0}{Px_0} \qquad \text{...[4.11 (b)]}$$

Again the motion is simple harmonic with angular frequency ρ or natural time period T.

For free vibrations of single degree of freedom system, the same results can be obtained by *Energy method*. If the motion is harmonic, the mass has the maximum kinetic energy when it passes through the position of equilibrium, but the spring is un strained at that moment as the displacement 'x' is zero and stores no energy. Similarly in the position of the maximum amplitude of motion, the strain energy in the spring is maximum and kinetic energy of the mass is zero. As no external work is being done on a free undamped vibrating system and no energy is being dissipated, the amount of energy remains constant through out. The maximum strain energy or potential energy is given by the relation,

$$P \cdot E = \int_0^{x_0} K \cdot x \, dx = \frac{1}{2} K x_0^2 \qquad \text{...(4.12)}$$

Maximum kinetic energy is given as

$$K \cdot E = \frac{1}{2} m \dot{x}_0^2 \qquad \text{...[4.13 (a)]}$$

In harmonic vibration, maximum velocity $\dot{x}_0$ is equal to Px_0 hence,

$$K \cdot E = \frac{1}{2} m p^2 x_0^2 \qquad \text{...[4.13 (b)]}$$

Equating the maximum strain energy (*P.E*) from equation 4.12 to maximum kinetic energy (K.E) from equation 4.13 (*b*) we get

$$\frac{1}{2} K x_0^2 = \frac{1}{2} m p^2 x_0^2$$

or $$K = m p^2$$

or $$T = \frac{2\pi}{P} = 2\pi \sqrt{m/K} \quad \text{as before ...}$$

The natural frequency of vibration in cycles per second is given as

$$f = \frac{1}{T} = \frac{P}{2\pi} = \frac{1}{2\pi} \sqrt{K/m} \qquad \text{...(4.14)}$$

Example 1. Show that the natural period of a light beam of negligible weight with central point load is $2\pi\sqrt{y_0/g}$ where y_0 is the deflection of the beam under load W.

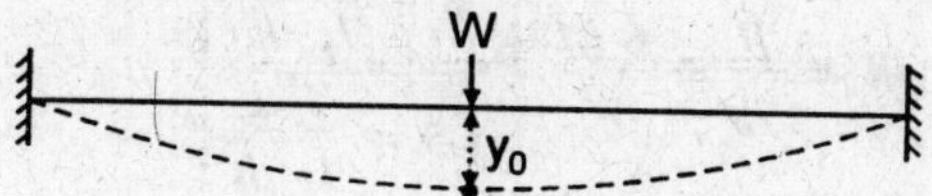

Fig. 4.7. A beam with concentrated load

Solution. The spring force K is the weight or force required for unit deflection.

Thus for this beam $K = \dfrac{W}{y_0}$

If this beam vibrates in the vertical plane. Its natural period of vibration T will be given by equation 4.8 as

$$T = 2\pi \sqrt{\frac{m}{K}} \quad \text{putting the value of } m \text{ and } K \text{ we get.}$$

$$= 2\pi \sqrt{W/g \div W/y_0} = 2\pi \sqrt{W/g \times y_0/W} = 2\pi \sqrt{y_0/g} \quad \text{...(4.15)}$$

Example 2. A portal frame having a weights of its beam and super imposed dead load equal to W is shown in Fig. 4.8. It deforms horizontally by

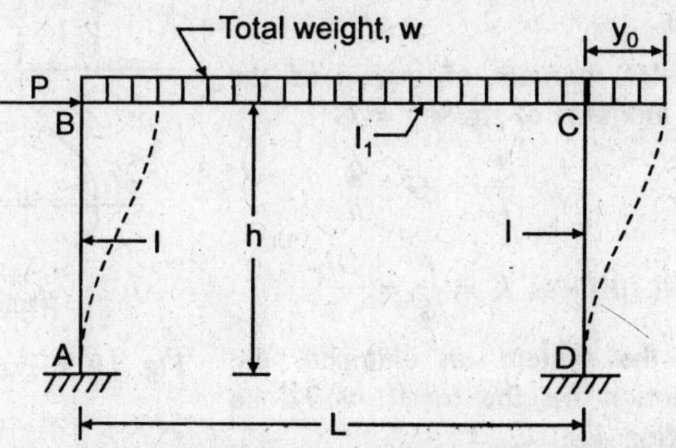

Fig. 4.8. A Portal Frame

y_0 when a horizontal load P acts upon it. Derive the relationship between the deflection y_0 and horizontal load P.

Solution. Taking into account stiffness of individual members and rotation at points B and C. From slope deflection or moment distribution method it can be shown that

$$Y_0 = \frac{P \cdot h^3}{6\,EI}\left\{\frac{1.5 + \dfrac{I \cdot L}{I_1 \cdot h}}{6 + \dfrac{I \cdot L}{I_1 \cdot h}}\right\} \qquad \text{...(4.16)}$$

and the spring stiffness K for horizontal deformation as

$$K = \frac{P}{y_0} = \frac{6\,EI}{h^3}\left\{\frac{6 + \dfrac{I \cdot L}{I_1 \cdot h}}{1.5 + \dfrac{I \cdot L}{I_1 \cdot h}}\right\} \qquad \text{...(4.17)}$$

Natural period of vibration T from equation 4.8, will be

$$T = 2\pi\sqrt{\frac{Wh^3}{6EI \cdot g}\left\{\frac{1.5 + \dfrac{I \cdot L}{I_1 \cdot h}}{6 + \dfrac{I \cdot L}{I_1 \cdot h}}\right\}} \qquad \text{...(4.18)}$$

Example 3. Determine the natural period T of a over head tank mounted on a hollow shaft which is twisted by a torque F as shown in Fig. 4.9.

Solution. Let the tank rotates by an angle ϕ. From this angle and torque F the torsional stiffness is equal to F/ϕ that is torque required for unit rotation.

Let the polar moment of inertia of the shaft = I_P and modulus of rigidity = G

$$\therefore \qquad \frac{F}{I_P} = G \cdot \frac{\phi}{h}$$

$$\therefore \text{ Torsional stiffness } K = \frac{F}{\phi} = \frac{GI_P}{h}$$

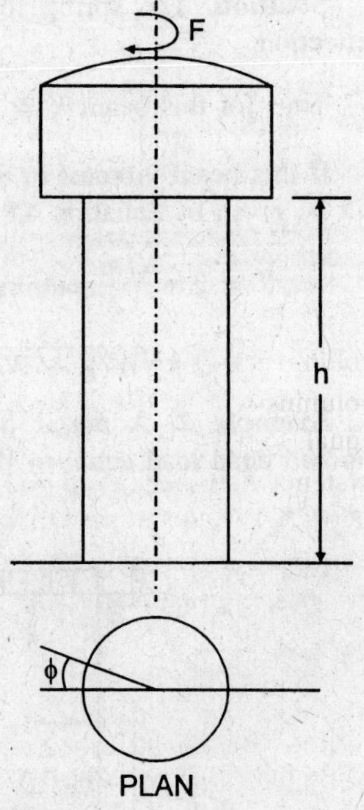

Fig. 4.9. Elevated water tank

Assuming the system un clamped, the equation of motion for the tower would be similar to equation 4.3.

$$I\ddot{\phi} + K\phi = 0$$

where, I is the mass moment of inertia of the tower shaft and K its torsional stiffness.

Putting $\frac{K}{I} = P^2$, we get

$$\ddot{\phi} + P^2 \phi = 0$$

$\therefore$ Natural period of vibration $T = \frac{2\pi}{P} = 2\pi\sqrt{I/K}$

$$= 2\pi\sqrt{\frac{I.h}{G \cdot I_P}}$$

4.8. COMBINATION OF STIFFNESS

Consider a portal frame consisting a beam fixed to the two columns having different moment of inertia as shown in Fig. 4.10 (*a*). The moment of inertia of

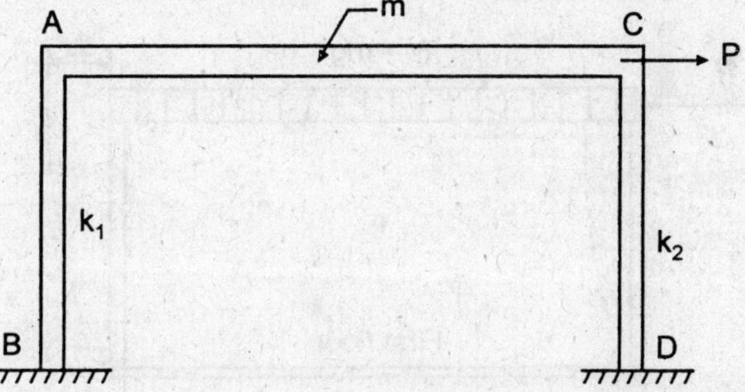

Fig. 4.10. (*a*) Portal frame

column AB is K_1 and that of column CD is K_2. The combined effect of both columns will be that a force required to deform both columns by unity, will be equal to $(K_1 + K_2)$. To determine the period of vibration of the combined system, K in equation 4.2 *i.e.* $m\ddot{x} + c\dot{x} + Kx = F(t)$ has to be replaced by $(K_1 + K_2)$. Such a system of stiffness is said to be *spring in parallel*. The schematic representation of such springs is shown in Fig. 4.10 (*b*) and (*c*). For '*n*' springs in parallel

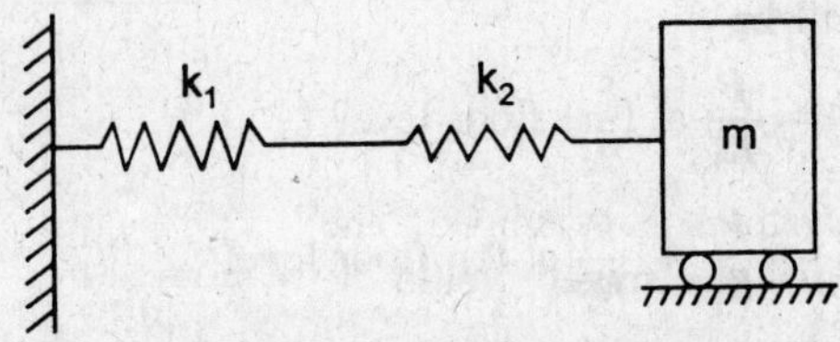

Fig. 4.10. (*b*) Schematic diagram

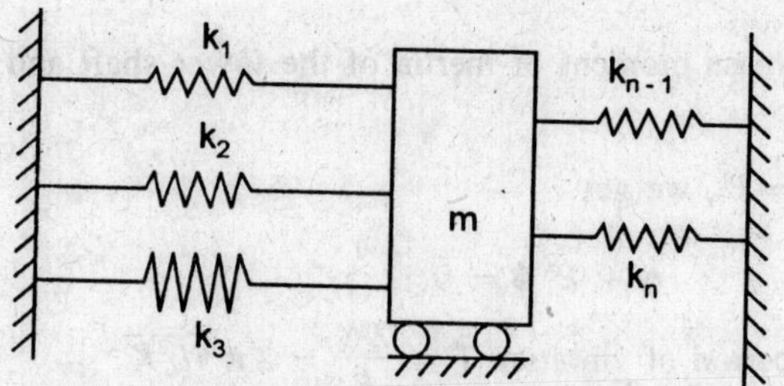

Fig. 4.10. (*c*) Springs in parallel

$$K = K_1 + K_2 + K_3 + \ldots K_n \qquad \ldots(4.19)$$

(*b*) Let us consider a two storeyed frame having beams and columns of a rigid construction and supporting a heavy weight such as a water tank at top, so that the frame can be considered weight less and the whole weight can be considered lumped at its top. Let the individual stiffnesses of the storeys be

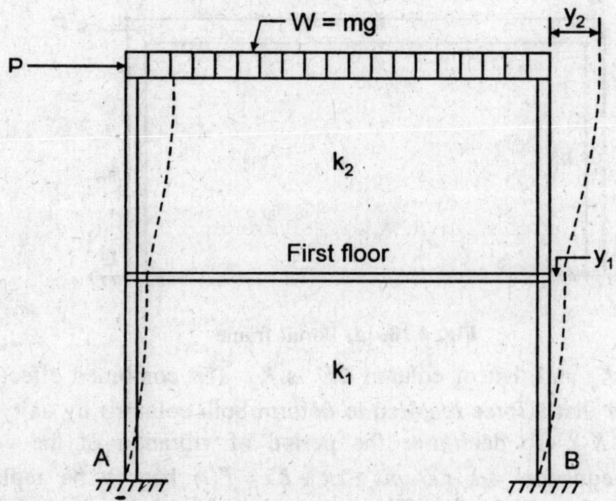

Fig. 4.11. (a) Two storeyed frame

K_1 and k_2 as shown in Fig. 4.11 (*a*). To determine the combined stiffness for deflection at top, let a force P is applied horizontally.

Then deflection will be

$$y_1 = \frac{P}{K_1} \text{ at first floor level}$$

and
$$y_2 = \frac{P}{K_1} + \frac{P}{K_2} \text{ at top floor level}$$

Thus combined stiffness K is given as

$$K = \frac{P}{y_2} = \frac{1}{\dfrac{1}{K_1} + \dfrac{1}{K_2}} = \frac{K_1 K_2}{K_1 + K_2}$$

or ∴
$$\frac{1}{K} = \frac{1}{K_1} + \frac{1}{K_2} \quad \text{...(4.20)}$$

Such a system of stiffness is known as *springs in series* and shown in Fig. 4.11 (*b*). In general the combined stiffness of *n* springs in series will be as

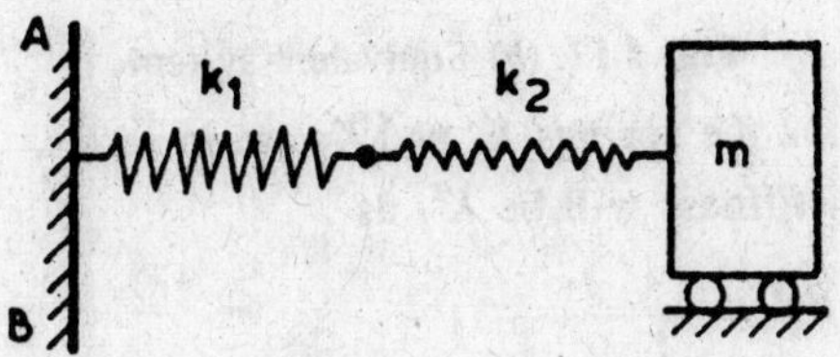

Fig. 4.11. (*b*) Schematic diagram

$$\frac{1}{K} = \frac{1}{K_1} + \frac{1}{K_2} + \frac{1}{K_3} + \ldots \frac{1}{K_n} \quad \text{...(4.21)}$$

Example 4. A mass *m* is connected with the base through five springs as shown in Fig. 4.12. Determine the natural period of the system with the given data:

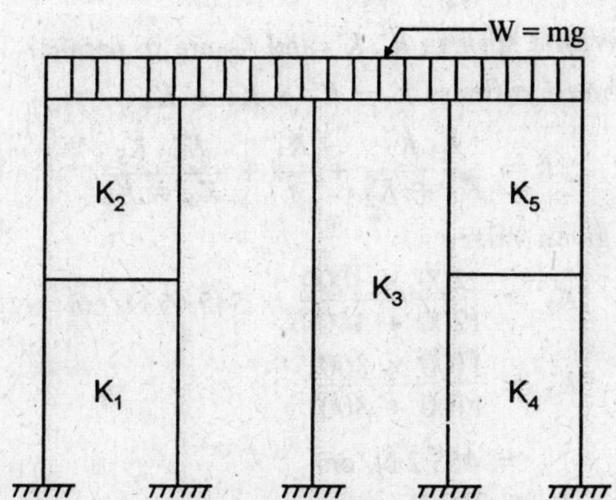

Fig. 4.12. (*a*) Structure

$$K_1 = 1200 \text{ N/cm}, \; K_2 = 1000 \text{ N/cm},$$

$$K_3 = 700 \text{ N/cm}, K_4 = 1100 \text{ N/cm}, \; K_5 = 800 \text{ N/cm}$$

$$m = 2500 \text{ kg}$$

Solution. The structure is shown in Fig. 4.12. To determine the natural period *T*, first equivalent stiffness of the system has to be determined as follows:

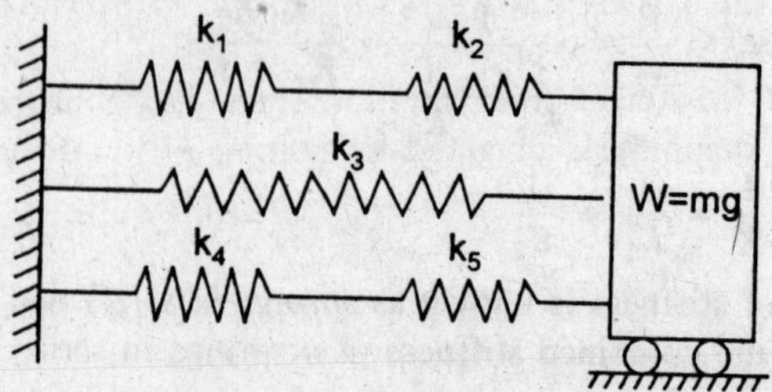

Fig. 4.12. (*b*) Equivalent system

From the Fig. 4.12 the springs K_1 and K_2 are in series. Their combined stiffness will be K'_1 as

$$K_1' = \frac{1}{\frac{1}{K_1} + \frac{1}{K_2}}$$

$$= \frac{K_1 K_2}{K_1 + K_2}$$

Similarly K_4 and K_5 are in series. Their combined stiffness K'_4 will be as

$$K_4' = \frac{K_4 K_5}{K_4 + K_5} \quad \ldots$$

Now the equivalent springs K', K'_4 and K_3 are in parallel.

$\therefore$ Total combined stiffness $K = K' + K_3 + K_4'$

$$\therefore \qquad K = \frac{K_1 K_2}{K_1 + K_2} + \frac{K_3}{1} + \frac{K_4 \cdot K_5}{K_4 + K_5} \qquad \ldots(1)$$

(*b*) From the given values

$$K_1' = \frac{1200 \times 1000}{1200 + 1000} = 545.45 \text{ N/cm}$$

$$K_4' = \frac{1100 \times 800}{1100 + 800}$$

$$= 463.2 \text{ N/cm}$$

$$K_3 = 700 \text{ N/cm}$$

$\therefore$ From equation (1) combined stiffness $K = 545.45 + 463.2 + 700$

$= 1708.65$ N/cm

$\therefore$ Natural period $T = 2\pi\sqrt{\dfrac{2500}{1708.65 \times 10 \times 10}}$

$= 0.76$ sec. **Ans.**

Note: $T = 2\pi\sqrt{m/K}$, $m = w/g$

(value g is taken as $9.81 \approx 10$) and 1 kg = 10 N)

4.9. VIBRATIONS OF DAMPED SYSTEM HAVING SINGLE DEGREE OF FREEDOM

The equation of motion of free vibrations of a single degree of freedom system with viscous damping is obtained by putting $F(t) = 0$ in the following equation (4.4)

$$\ddot{x} + 2P\zeta\dot{x} + p^2 x = \frac{F(t)}{m}$$

By putting $F(t) = 0$, equation reduces to

$$\ddot{x} + 2P\zeta\dot{x} + p^2 x = 0 \qquad ...(4.22)$$

The solution of equation 4.22 is assumed to be of the form as

$$x = Ce^{qt} \qquad ...(4.23)$$

By differenting equation 4.23 with respect to 't' we get velocity ($\dot{x}$) and acceleration ($\ddot{x}$) as follows.

$$\frac{dx}{dt} = \dot{x} = C \cdot q \cdot e^{qt} \qquad ...[4.24\ (a)]$$

$$\frac{d^2 x}{dt^2} = \ddot{x} = C \cdot q^2\, e^{qt} \qquad ...[4.24\ (b)]$$

Putting the values of $\dot{x}$ and $\ddot{x}$ in equation 4.22 we get

$$C\,q^2 e^{qt} + 2P\zeta \cdot C \cdot q \cdot e^{qt} + p^2 \cdot C\,e^{qt} = 0 \qquad ...(i)$$

Dividing the equation (i) by ce^{qt} we get

$$q^2 + 2P\zeta \cdot q + p^2 = 0 \qquad ...(4.25)$$

Equation 4.26 being a quadratic equation will give two values of 'q'

$$q_{1,2} = p\,(\zeta \pm \sqrt{\zeta^2 - 1}) \qquad ...(4.26)$$

The general solution of equation 4.22 will be as

$$x = C_1\, e^{q_1 t} + C_2\, e^{q_2 t} \qquad ...(4.27)$$

where C_1 and C_2 are constants, which are governed by the initial conditions of motion. It would be seen that the form of variation of x will depend on the values of ζ and P.

4.9.1. Effect of the value of ζ

Case 1. Let $\zeta > 1$, then both roots q_1 and q_2 are real and negative. Thus as t increases, x decreases. Such a system does not oscillates as x does not change sign. Hence such a system is known as *over damped system* Fig. 4.13 shows change of x with t for such a system.

If such a system is given an initial displacement or impulse, its mass gets displaced. The spring pulls it back, but the dampers are so strong, that they absorb the energy in the system, before the mass returns to its initial position.

Case 2. When $\zeta = 1$, In this case $q_1 = q_2 = -p\,\zeta$. In such situations the solution would be of the form as

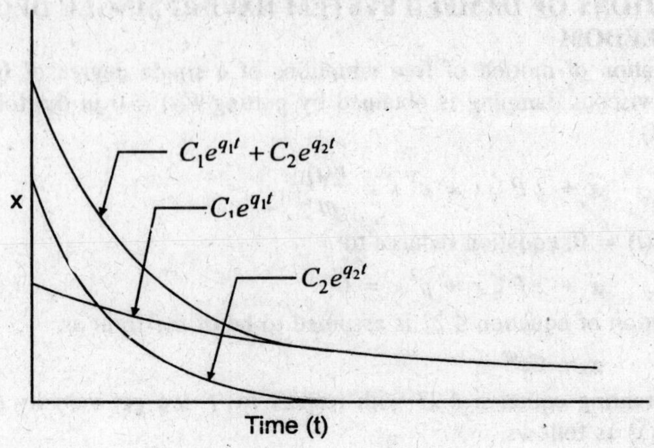

Fig. 4.13. Free motion of an over Damped system

$$x = (C_1 + C_2)\, e^{-p\zeta t} \qquad \ldots(4.28)$$

In this case also as t increases, x decreases, but it never becomes negative. Thus such a system also does not oscillates. Though mass returns to its initial position but it is not left any energy at that time to shoot on the other side. Such systems are called as *critically damped*. This means that for no oscillation in the system, the minimum value of the ζ should be unity.

Case 3. When $\zeta < 1$. In this case the quantity $\sqrt{\zeta^2 - 1}$ becomes negative and it can be written as $i\sqrt{1 - \zeta^2}$. The solution of the equation 4.22 becomes as

$$x = C_1\, e^{pt}\,(-\zeta + i\sqrt{1-\zeta^2}) + C_2\, e^{pt}\,(-\zeta - i\sqrt{1-\zeta^2}) \qquad \ldots(4.29)$$

we known that $e^{\pm i\theta} = \cos\theta \pm \sin\theta$ and if θ is used in place of $p\sqrt{1-\zeta^2} \cdot t$ for convenience, the solution can be written as

$$x = e^{-p\zeta t}\,[C_1 \cdot (\cos\theta + i\sin\theta) + C_2\,(\cos\theta - i\sin\theta)]$$

$$= e^{-p\zeta t}\,[(C_1 + C_2)\cos\theta + i\,(C_1 - C_2)\sin\theta]$$

$$= e^{-p\zeta t}\,[A\cos(p\sqrt{1-\zeta^2})\,t + B\sin(p\sqrt{1-\zeta^2})\,t\,] \qquad \ldots(4.30)$$

where, $A = C_1 + C_2$ and $B = i\,(C_1 - C_2)$

Here the quantity in side the bracket describes a harmonic motion with the natural angular frequency $p\sqrt{1-\zeta^2}$, where as the multiplier $e^{-p\zeta t}$ acts as a damper of the amplitude of the motion, as t increases the quantity $e^{-p\zeta t}$ decreases. The resulting motion is shown in Fig. 4.14, when it starts from a displacement x_0 and with zero velocity at initial time $t = 0$.

Case 4. When $\zeta = 0$, By putting $\zeta = 0$, the solution of equation 4.30 becomes.

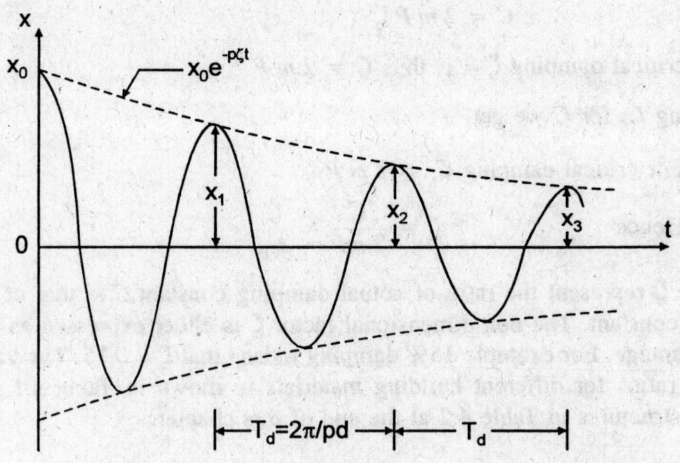

Fig. 4.14. Free vibration of an under damped system

$$x = A \cos pt + B \sin pt \qquad \text{...(4.31)}$$

The natural period of vibration of an un damped harmonic system is $T = \frac{2\pi}{p}$. Calling the damped angular frequency as *Pd*, the natural period *Td* for the damped system would be given by

$$Td = \frac{2\pi}{P\sqrt{1-\zeta^2}} = \frac{2\pi}{Pd} \qquad \text{...(4.32)}$$

where $$Pd = P\sqrt{(1-\zeta^2)} \qquad \text{...(4.33)}$$

Suppose at time *t*, the maximum amplitude is x_1 and at time $(t + Td)$ it becomes x_2, then

$$x_2 = e^{-p\zeta(t+Td)}\,[A \cos Pd\,(t+Td) + B \sin Pd\,(t+Td)] \qquad \text{...}(a)$$

$$x_1 = e^{-p\zeta t}\,[A \cos Pd + B \sin Pd \cdot t] \qquad \text{...}(b)$$

Putting $Td = \frac{2\pi}{Pd}$ and simplifying equations (*a*) and (*b*), we get

$$\frac{x_1}{x_2} = e^{2\pi p\zeta/Pd} \qquad \text{...(4.34)}$$

By increasing the value of damping ζ the value of $\frac{x_2}{x_1}$ will be lower

4.9.2. Critical damping

When the damping is critical, Let the damping constant *C* be denoted by C_c.

We know that $\frac{C}{m} = 2P\zeta$

or $$C = 2\,m\,P\,\zeta$$

For critical damping $\zeta = 1$, thus $C = 2\,m\,P$

Putting C_c for C we get

For critical damping $C_c = 2\,m\,P$

Hence $$\zeta = \frac{C}{2\,mP} = \frac{C}{C_c} \qquad \text{...(4.35)}$$

Thus ζ represent the ratio of actual damping constant C to that of critical damping constant. The non dimensional factor ζ is either expressed as ratio or as a percentage. For example 15% damping means that $\zeta = 0.15$. The values of damping ratios for different building materials is shown in Table 4.1 and for different structures in Table 4.2 at the end of this chapter.

4.9.3. Logarithmic Decrement

From relation of equation 4.34 *i.e.*

$\dfrac{x_1}{x_2} = e^{2\pi P \zeta / Pd}$, we can write taking log at the base e

$$\log_e \frac{x_1}{x_2} = 2\,\pi\,\zeta / Pd \qquad \text{...(4.36)}$$

Using equations 4.32 and 4.33, equation 4.36, can be written as

$$\log_e \frac{x_1}{x_2} = \frac{2\,\pi\,\zeta}{\sqrt{1-\zeta^2}} = \delta \text{ say} \qquad \text{...(4.37)}$$

The logarithm of the ratio of two successive amplitudes is known as logarithmic decrement and is denoted by δ.

As ζ usually is very small in comparison with 1, δ can be written as

$$\delta \approx 2\,\pi\,\zeta \qquad \text{...(4.38)}$$

If we write $x_1 = x_2 + \Delta\,x_1$ then we have

$$\delta = \log_e \frac{x_2 + \Delta\,x}{x_2} = \log_e \left(1 + \frac{\Delta x}{x} \right)$$

$$\approx \frac{\Delta x}{x} - \frac{1}{2}\left(\frac{\Delta x}{2}\right)^2$$

$$\approx \frac{\Delta\,x}{x} \qquad \text{...(4.39)}$$

Thus δ is known as logarithmic decrement as it is approximately equal to fractional decrease of the amplitude.

Some useful relations can be derived by considering the energy relationship during damped free vibrations. Total energy of the system at each peak value x_1, x_2 etc. will be potential energy in the form of strain energy in spring, as the velocity of the mass will be zero. Let w_1 and w_2 represent strain energy at peak amplitude x_1 and x_2 respectively, then

$$w_1 = \frac{1}{2} K x_1^2 = \frac{1}{2} K (x_2 + \Delta x)^2$$

and $$w_2 = \frac{1}{2} K x_2^2 \qquad \ldots(4.40)$$

The loss of energy Δw per cycle between any two successive peak amplitudes $(x + \Delta x)$ and x is given by

$$\Delta w = w_1 - w_2 = \frac{1}{2} K (x + \Delta x)^2 - \frac{1}{2} K x^2$$

$$= K \cdot x \cdot \Delta x + \frac{1}{2} K (\Delta x)^2 \qquad \ldots(4.41)$$

Fractional decrease in energy $$\frac{\Delta w}{w} = \frac{K \cdot x \cdot \Delta x + \frac{1}{2} k (\Delta x)^2}{\frac{1}{2} K x^2}$$

$$\frac{\Delta x}{w} = \frac{2 \Delta x}{x} + \left(\frac{\Delta x}{x}\right)^2 \qquad \ldots(4.42)$$

For small damping $\frac{\Delta x}{x} << 1.$

Thus $$\frac{\Delta w}{w} \approx \frac{2 \Delta x}{x} \approx 2\delta \qquad \ldots(4.43)$$

Often $\frac{\Delta w}{w}$ is called the *specific energy loss* or specific damping capacity.

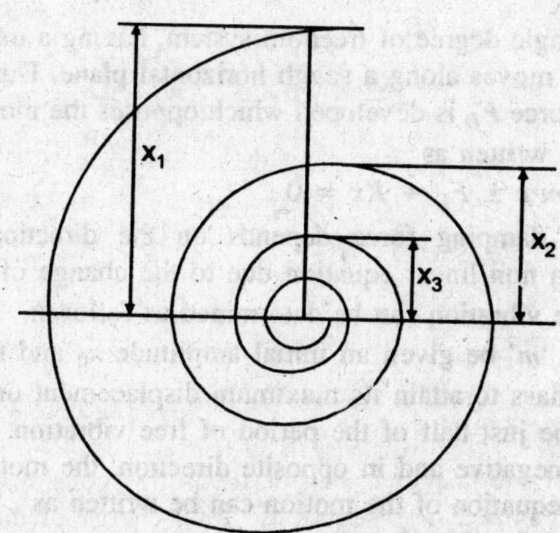

Fig. 4.15. Damped free vibrations recorded as a logarithimic spiral

The variation of x can also be represented by a logarithmic spiral as shown in Fig. 4.15.

4.10. DRY FRICTION DAMPING

Another fairly common type of daming is dry friction type which result due to rubbing together of non lubricated surfaces like that of rivetted joints.

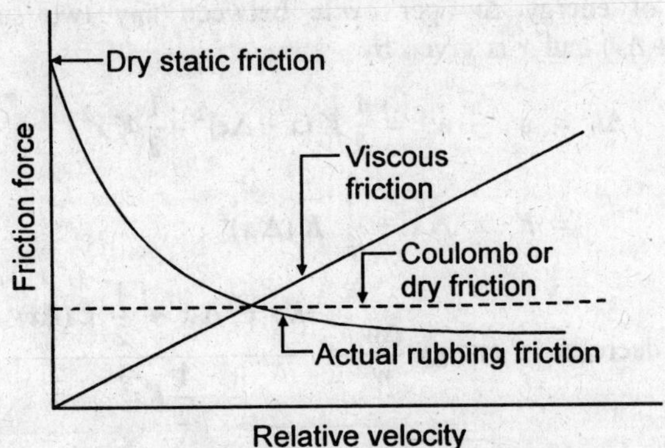

Fig. 4.16. Frictional force verses relative velocity

Fig. 4.16 shows a possible variation of frictional force depending upon relative velocity.

The value of static friction usually is high compared to dynamic friction, which decreases rapidly for small relative rubbing velocities. Such damping force can be approximated by assuming it to be constant, that is, it is independent of velocity. This damping is known as *Coulomb damping*. The shape and values of friction force are influenced by the kind of materials and surface conditions.

Consider a single degree of freedom system, having a mass 'm' and spring stiffness K. Let it moves along a rough horizontal plane. During the motion, a constant friction force F_D is developed which opposes the motion. The equation of motion may be written as

$$m\ddot{x} \pm F_D + Kx = 0 \qquad \ldots(4.44)$$

The sign of damping force depends on the direction of the motion. Equation 4.44 is a non linear equation due to the change of sign of force F_D. The period of free vibration can be determined as follows:

Let the mass 'm' be given an initial amplitude x_0 and released. The time required for the mass to attain its maximum displacement on the other side of equilibrium will be just half of the period of free vibration. During this phase when velocity is negative and in opposite direction, the motion is in the same direction and the equation of the motion can be written as

$$m\ddot{x} + Kx = F_D \text{ for } \dot{x} < 0 \qquad \ldots(4.45)$$

The solution of equation 4.45, is valid for $\dot{x} < 0$

$$x = A\cos pt + B\sin pt + F_D/K \quad \ldots(4.46)$$

where, $P^2 = K/m$.

With the initial conditions, namely for $t = 0$, $x = x_0$ and velocity $\dot{x} = 0$, then

$$A = x_0 - F_D/K \text{ and } B = 0$$

Putting values of A and B in equation 4.46, we get

$$x = (x_0 - F_D/K)\cos pt + F_D/K \quad \ldots(4.47)$$

and $\dot{x} = -(x_0 - F_D/K)\sin pt$ ...[4.47 (*a*)]

At the extreme position on the opposite side, the velocity will again be zero, and the time required for this half cycle will be obtained by putting

$$\sin pt = 0 \text{ or } pt = \pi\text{. This gives } t = \pi/P$$

The period of full cycle or free vibration will be twice of the above value

Hence $T = 2t = 2\pi/p$ ...(4.48)

Thus the coulomb damping does not change the period of free vibration and it remains the same as in undamped case.

The rate of decay of free vibrations with coulomb damping can be calculated from energy considerations. Consider Fig. 4.17.

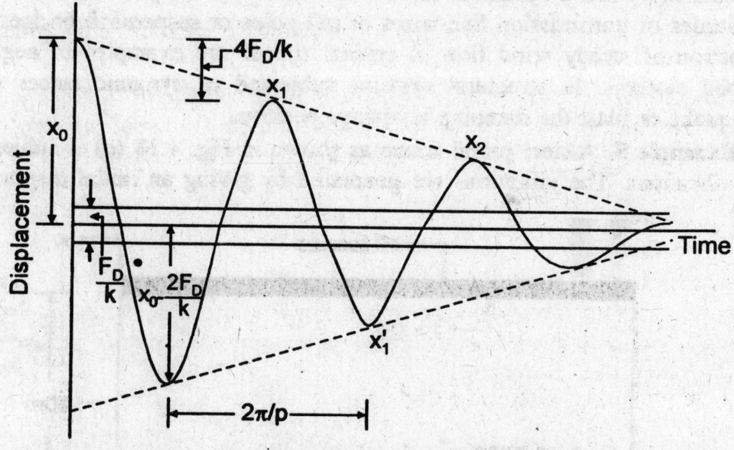

Fig. 4.17. Free vibrations of a Coulomb damped system

At x_1 total energy of the system is the potential (strain) energy of the spring equal to $1/2\ Kx_1^2$. At an other point x_1' it is $1/2\ Kx'^2_1$.

During the half cycle, loss of energy from x_1 to x_1' will be equal to the work done by the damping force.

Work done by damping force $F_D(x_1 + x_1')$

i.e. loss of energy during half cycle $= \frac{1}{2}Kx_1^2 - \frac{1}{2}Kx_1'^2 = F_D(x_1 + x_1')$

$$\therefore \qquad \frac{1}{2} K(x_1 + x_1')(x_1 - x_1') = F_D(x_1 + x_1')$$

$$\text{or} \qquad (x_1 - x_1') = \frac{2F_D}{K}$$

A similar loss would occur from x_1 to x_2. Thus the total loss of amplitude in one cycle from x_1 to x_2 would be $\frac{4F_D}{K}$. ...(4.49)

Since the amplitude decrease per cycle is constant and the period is also constant, the envelop of the decay curve will be a straight line. The mass will come to rest in an extreme position as soon as the displacement in such a position is less than F_D/K. The number of cycles is always an integral number of half cycles. Thus unless the initial displacement is a multiple of $2F_D/K$, the position of rest always will be away from the equilibrium position.

4.11. NEGATIVE DAMPING

Generally damping is positive, hence energy is always absorbed from the system by the damping devices. If the system draws energy from some source or supplied energy, the amplitude would increase in successive cycles leading to instability. Such a system is known as *negatively damped.* The build up of amplitudes of transmission line wires or tall poles or suspension bridges under the action of steady wind flow at critical speeds are examples of negatively damped systems. In structural systems subjected to dynamic forces due to earthquake or blast the damping is always positive.

Example 5. A steel portal frame as shown in Fig. 4.18 (*a*) is subjected to free vibrations. The vibrations are generated by giving an initial displacement

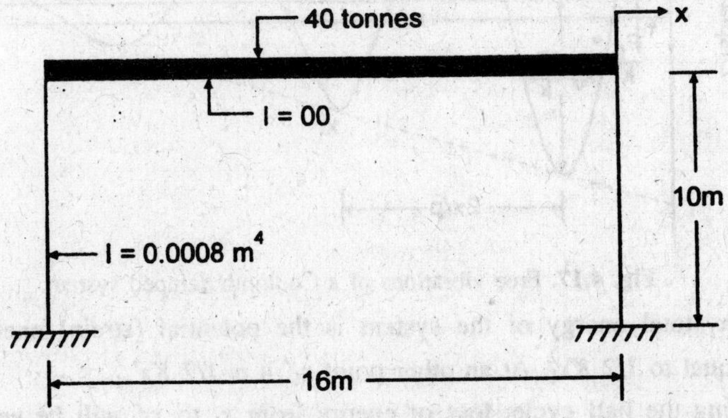

Fig. 4.18 (*a*). Portal frame

with out velocity. The total mass of 40 tonnes is lumped at roof level. The height of columns is 10 m, and their horizontal distance is 16 m. Assuming the columns weight less and the damping as 4% of the critical damping, determine

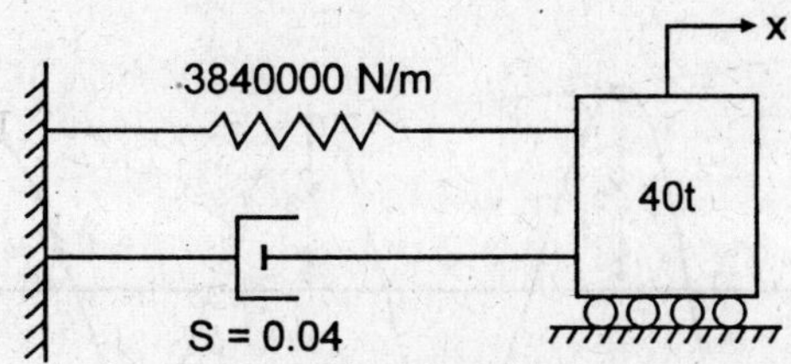

Equivalent S.D.F. system

Fig. 4.18 (*b*). Portal frame subjected to initial displacement

the characteristics of the motion. Take the value of $E = 2.1 \times 10^{11}$ N/m^2 and moment of inertia I of each column as 0.0008 m^4.

Solution. Let the portal be equivalent to a single degree system with mass 'm', stiffness K and damping ratio $\zeta = 0.04$, where

$$K = \frac{24\,EI}{h^3} = \frac{24 \times 2.1 \times 10^{11} \times 0.0008}{(10)^3}$$

$$= 40320000 \text{ N/m}$$

or $\quad 4032000$ kg/m

Weight $\quad m = 40{,}000$ kg

$$\therefore \quad p^2 = \frac{K}{m} = \frac{4032000}{40000} = \frac{403.2}{4} = 100.8$$

$\therefore$ Undamped natural frequency $p = \sqrt{100.8}$

$$= 10.04 \text{ radian/sec}$$

The given value of $\zeta = 0.04$ is much less than 1.0. Thus the given problem is a case of under damping. The solution of the equation of motion will be as under

$x = e^{p\zeta t}(A \cos Pd \cdot t + B \sin Pd \cdot t)$. (1) It is same as equation 4.30,

where, Pd = damped natural frequency, whose value is $Pd = P\sqrt{1-\zeta^2}$

Putting the value P and ζ we get.

$$Pd = 10.04\sqrt{1-(0.04)^2} = 10.04\sqrt{0.9984}$$

$$= 10.04 \times 0.999$$

$$= 10.03 \text{ radian/sec}$$

Now at $t = 0$, $x = x_0$ and $\dot{x} = 0$, substituting these values in equation (1) and solving it we get

$$x = x_0\, e^{-p\zeta t} \cos Pt \cdot t \qquad (P = 10.4, \zeta = 0.04)$$

$$= x_0\, e^{-0.416\,t} \cos 10.03\, t \qquad (\therefore\ P \cdot \zeta = 0.416)$$

The motion of this problem is shown in Fig. 4.19.

(*b*) The solution of the above problem by logarithmic decrement method can be found as follows:

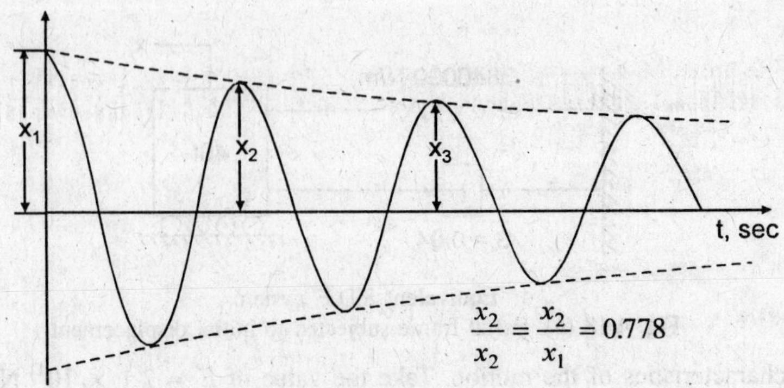

Fig. 4.19. Damped free vibration record

From equation 4.38 logarithmic decrement

$$\delta = 2\,\pi\,\zeta$$
$$= 2 \times 3.142 \times 0.04$$
$$= 0.25136 \approx 0.251$$

$$\log_e \frac{x_1}{x_2} = P\,\zeta\,Td$$

or $$\frac{x_1}{x_2} = e^{\delta} = e^{0.2514}$$

Taking Neprian log $e^{0.2514} = 1.286$

Thus every maximum amplitude will be 1.286 times the succeding maximum amplitude. Inversely each succeding amplitude will be 1/1.826 = 0.778 times the just preceding maximum amplitude. The time interval between consecutive maximum amplitudes is the damped value of time period given by the relation as

$$Td = \frac{2\,\pi}{Pd} = \frac{2\,\pi}{10.03} = \frac{6.284}{10.03} = 0.605 \text{ sec.}$$
$$\approx 0.61 \text{ sec.}$$

Thus in a time interval of 0.61 seconds or after one complete cycle the maximum amplitude reduces by (1 – 0.778) = 0.222 times. After n cycles the maximum amplitude will become as given by the relation.

$$x_{n+1} = x_1\, e^{-n\,\delta} \qquad \text{...(4.50)}$$

Example 6. In an experiment of free vibrations, it is observed that the maximum amplitude has reduced to 0.5 times of its original value in 4 complete cycles. Determine the damping of the system.

Solution. Let the first amplitude be x_1 and that 5th amplitude x_5.

then $x_5 = 0.5\, x_1$ as per given condition.

then from equation 4.50, $x_5 = e^{-4\,\delta}$

$$\therefore \qquad e^{-4\delta} = 0.5$$

The value of δ can be calculated by taking log of both sides

$$\log e^{-4\delta} = 2.303 \log_{10} (0.5)$$

$$\therefore \qquad -4\,\delta \times 1 \text{ (as } \log_e = 1) = 2.303 \log_{10} \left(\frac{5}{10}\right)$$

$$\text{or} \qquad -4\,\delta = 2.303 (\log_{10} 5 - \log_{10} (10))$$

$$\text{or} \qquad -4\,\delta = 2.303 (0.6990 - 1.0)$$

$$= 2.303 \times (-0.3010)$$

$$= -0.6932$$

$$\therefore \qquad \delta = \frac{-0.6932}{-4}$$

$$= 0.1733$$

$$\text{Also} \qquad \delta = 2\,\pi\,\zeta$$

$$\therefore \qquad \zeta = \frac{0.1733}{2\,\pi}$$

$$= 0.02755$$

Thus actual damping is 2.755% of the critical damping.

Example 4.7. Determine the ratio of damped natural frequency to undamped natural frequency for various values of damping ratio of ζ.

Given ζ = 0.02, 0.05, 0.1, 0.2, 0.4, 0.5

Solution. Given ζ = 0.02, 0.05, 0.1, 0.2, 0.4, 0.5

$$\text{To determine} \qquad \frac{Pd}{P} = \sqrt{1 - \zeta^2}$$

$$\therefore (i) \qquad \zeta = 0.02, \frac{Pd}{P} = \sqrt{1 - (0.02)^2} = 0.996$$

$$(ii) \qquad \zeta = 0.05, \frac{Pd}{P} = \sqrt{1 - (0.05)^2} = 0.9987$$

$$(iii) \qquad \zeta = 0.1, \frac{Pd}{P} = \sqrt{1 - (0.1)^2} = 0.995$$

$$(iv) \qquad \zeta = 0.2, \frac{Pd}{P} = \sqrt{1 - (0.2)^2} = 0.98$$

$$(v) \qquad \zeta = 0.4, \frac{Pd}{P} = \sqrt{1 - (0.4)^2} = 0.916$$

$$(vi) \qquad \zeta = 0.5, \frac{Pd}{P} = \sqrt{1 - (0.5)^2} = 0.886$$

From the above results, it will be seen that upto the damping ratio of 0.2, there is little difference between damped natural frequency and undamped values of frequency. Thus for all practical purposes of design, the undamped frequency may be used in computations.

2.12. FORCED VIBRATIONS OF A DAMPED SYSTEM

So far solutions of equation 4.2 have been worked on the basis that no external force was exciting the system except that of the initial force used to initiate the motion. Now it is proposed to examine the equation 4.2 when the system is excited by a periodic force. To begin with let the force be a sinusoidal in form.

Though an earthquake force is an irregular wave form, but it could be assumed as composed of sine waves of different frequencies and amplitudes. Hence a solution of harmonic excitation may be used for obtaining the response of an earthquake type excitations. Other dynamic forces like that caused by vibrations of machines or running water can be solved in a similar manner.

Let the equation of motion be a follows:

$$m\ddot{x} + c\dot{x} + Kx = F(t) \qquad \ldots(4.51)$$

The solution of the equation (4.51) can be expressed as

$$x = e^{-p\zeta t}\,(C_1 \cos Pd \cdot t + C_2 \sin Pd \cdot t) + x\,(t) \qquad \ldots(4.52)$$

The first part of the solution relates to transient state (temporary state) due to initial conditions (displacement and velocity of the system) and is the same as that for free vibration solution. The second part corresponds to vibrations resulting from the exciting force. This part will last as long as the exciting force lasts. In the initial stages the two parts will be super imposed on each other but later (due to damping, transients become negligibly small in few cycles). the second part alone will describe the motion of the vibrating mass.

Let the exciting force is of the form as

$$F(t) = F_0 \sin \omega t \qquad \ldots(4.53)$$

where, F_0 is the maximum amplitude of the force and ω is its angular frequency. The mass will pass through a transient state and settle down to a steady state motion with the same frequency as that of exciting force. Thus the steady state part of the solution could be represented as

$$x(t) = A \sin(\omega t - \phi) \qquad \ldots(4.54)$$

where, A is maximum displacement amplitude and ϕ the phase difference between the displacement and exiting force. Differentiating successively with respect to 't' the relation 4.54 we get.

$$\frac{dx}{dt} = \dot{x} = A\,\omega \cos(\omega t - \phi) \qquad \ldots(4.55)$$

$$\frac{d^2x}{dt^2} = \ddot{x} = -A\,\omega^2 \sin(\omega t - \phi) \qquad \ldots(4.56)$$

Putting the values of $\dot{x}$ and $\ddot{x}$ in equation 4.51 we get

$$m\ddot{x} + C\dot{x} + Kx = F(t)$$

$$-m A \omega^2 \sin(\omega t - \phi) + C A \omega \cos(\omega t - \phi) + KA \sin(\omega t - \phi) = F_0 \sin \omega t \quad \text{...(4.57)}$$

From trigonometry we know that

$$\sin(A - B) = \sin A \cos B - \cos A \sin B$$

$$\cos(A - B) = \cos A \cos B + \sin A \sin B$$

In equation 4.57, expanding the term $\sin(\omega t - \phi)$ and $\cos(\omega t - \phi)$ as above we get.

$$-m A \omega^2 \sin(\omega t - \phi) + C A \omega \cos(\omega t - \phi) + KA \sin(\omega t - \phi) = F_0 \sin \omega t$$

$$= -m A \omega^2 [\sin \omega t \cos \phi - \cos \omega t \sin \phi] + C A \omega [\cos \omega t \cos \phi + \sin \omega t \sin \phi] + KA \sin \omega t \cos \phi - K A \cos \omega t \sin \phi = F_0 \sin \omega t$$

or
$$-\sin \omega t (m A\omega^2 \cos \phi + C A \omega \sin \phi) - KA \cos \phi) + \cos \omega t (m A \omega^2 \sin \phi + CA \omega \cos \phi - KA \sin \phi)$$

Equating the coefficients of $\sin \omega t$ and $\cos \omega t$ we get.

$$A(k - m\omega^2) \cos \phi + A(C\omega) \sin \phi = F_0$$

and
$$-A(K - m\omega^2) \sin \phi + A(C\omega) \cos \phi = 0$$

Expanding sine and cosine functions and equating coefficients of sine and cosine terms on both sides of the equation 4.57 we get

$$A(K - m\omega^2) \cos \phi + A(C\omega) \sin \phi = F_0 \quad \text{...}(a)$$

and
$$-A(K - m\omega^2) \sin \phi + A(C\omega) \cos \phi = 0 \quad \text{...}(b)$$

Squaring and adding the equations (*a*) and (*b*) we get.

$$A^2 (K - m\omega^2)^2 + A^2 (C\omega) = F_0^2$$

or
$$A = \frac{F_0}{[(K - m\omega^2)^2 + (C\omega)^2]^{1\ 2}} \quad \text{...(4.58)}$$

and
$$\tan \phi = \frac{C\omega}{(K - m\omega^2)} \quad \text{...(4.59)}$$

Let η be equal to frequency ratio ω/P, $C/m = 2P\zeta$

$$P^2 = K/m, \; C = 2P\zeta m, \; \omega = P\eta$$

then
$$\frac{C\omega}{K} = \frac{2P\zeta m \cdot P\eta}{K} = \frac{2P^2 \eta \zeta m}{K} = 2\eta\zeta$$

Putting these values in equation in 4.58 and 4.59 we get

$$A = \frac{F_0/K}{\sqrt{(1 - \eta^2)^2 + (2\eta\zeta)^2}} \quad \text{...(4.60)}$$

and $$\phi = \tan^{-1} \cdot \frac{2\eta\zeta}{1-\eta^2} \qquad \text{...(4.61)}$$

Thus complete solution of the equation is

$$x = e^{-p\zeta t}(C_1 \cos Pd \cdot t + C_2 \sin Pd \cdot t) + \frac{F_0/K(\sin \omega t - \phi)}{\sqrt{(1-\eta^2)+(2\eta\zeta)^2}}$$

The two parts of the solution are shown in Fig. 4.20.

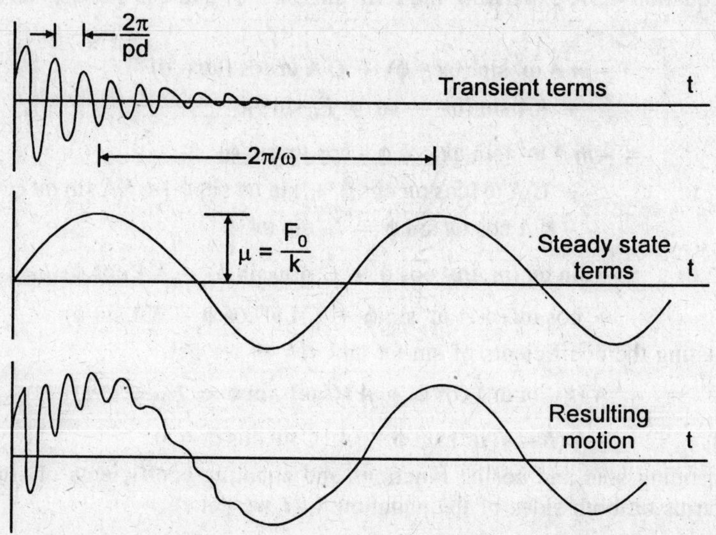

Fig. 4.20. Forced vibration record of a single degree of freedom system

Since F_0/K is the static displacement of the mass and A is the maximum amplitude of the dynamic motion, the dynamic magnification 'μ' of the displacement is given as

$$\mu = \frac{A}{F_0/K} = \frac{1}{\sqrt{(1-\eta^2)^2 + (2\eta\zeta)^2}} \qquad \text{...(4.63)}$$

The value of magnification μ can be determined by equating the differential of μ with respect to η equal to zero, thus

$$\eta^2 + 2\zeta^2 - 1 = 0$$

or $$\eta = \sqrt{1-2\zeta^2)} \qquad \text{...(4.64)}$$

Since ζ^2 is a very small quantity, μ is maximum when $\eta \approx 1.0$. This is the condition of resonance.

Considering the effect of ζ also, it is seen that μ is maximum for η less than 1.0, that is, the maximum magnification occurs for frequency ω slightly less than undamped natural frequency '*P*' of the system.

The values of μ can be determined for different values of η and ζ from the resonance curves shown in Fig. 4.21.

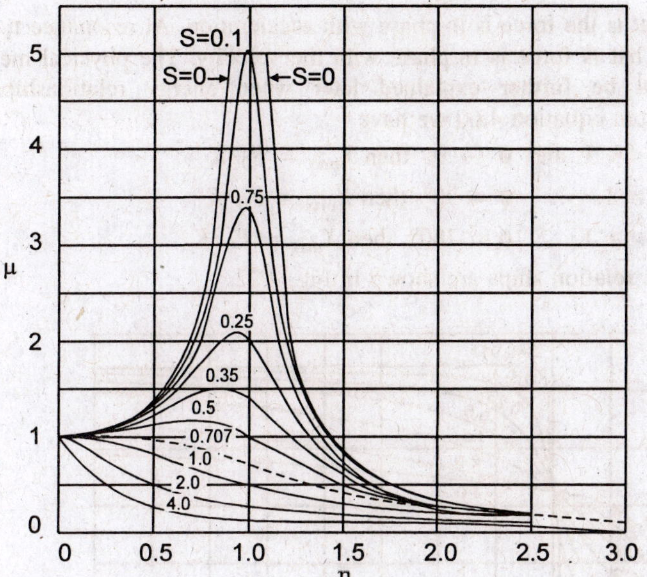

Fig. 4.21. Dynamic amplification factor versus frequency ratio

when $\eta = 1$, then from eqaution (4.63)

$$\mu = \frac{1}{2\zeta} \qquad \ldots(4.65)$$

For steel structures where damping is about 2% of the critical *i.e.* $\zeta = \frac{1}{50}$ the magnification $\mu = 25$. In brick work or concrete structures damping is about 5 to 10% of the critical *i.e.* $\zeta = \frac{1}{20}$ to $\frac{1}{10}$, the magnifications can be 10 to 15.

An earthquake force is not sinusoidal and also the amplitudes are not constant as in the above analysis. The magnification of displacement would also not be as high as determined from equation 4.65. However, it can be taken as 1/4 to 1/3 of the above values.

4.12.1. Phase relationship

Phase relationship between displacement of mass, and force applied on it, would be useful to explain the behaviour of the system physically. The Phase angle ϕ is given by equation 4.61.

$$\phi = \tan^{-1} \frac{2\eta\zeta}{1-\eta^2} \qquad \ldots(4.66)$$

For low frequencies of excitation $\eta << 1$ and ϕ tending to zero, and the motions are in phase as would be expected physically. For large frequencies $\eta < 1.0$ and ϕ tending to 180°, the force and motion are always in opposite directions. That is the force is in phase with acceleration. At resonance $\eta = 1.0$ and $\phi = 90°$. That is force is in phase with the velocity. The physical meaning of this would be further explained later when energy relationships are considered. From equation 4.60 we have

$$\eta << 1, \text{ and } \phi \to 0, \text{ then } X_{max} \approx F_0/K$$
$$\eta = 1, \quad \phi = 90°, \text{ then } \dot{X}_{max} \approx F_0/K$$
$$\eta >> 1, \quad \phi = 180°, \text{ then } \ddot{X}_{max} \approx F_0/K$$

The phase relation ships are shown in Fig. 4.22.

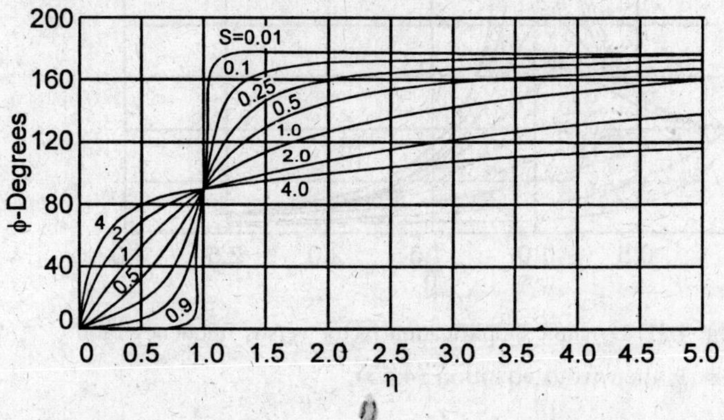

Fig. 4.22. Phase angle versus frequency ratio

4.12.2. Damping

If dynamic magnification factor μ is known then damping ζ can be determined form equation 4.65. An other way to obtain damping is to use

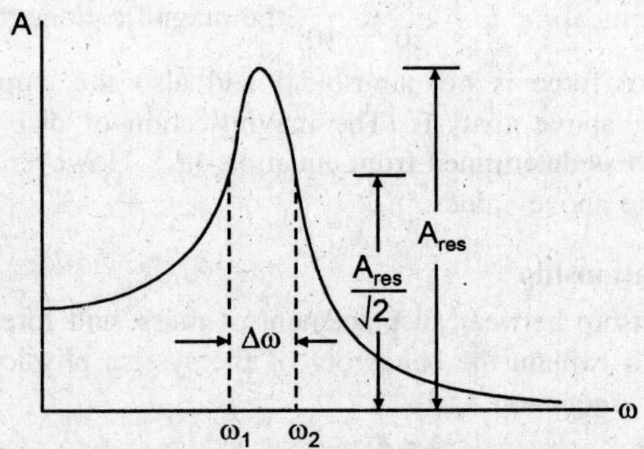

Fig. 4.23. Derminotion of damping from resonance

resonance curve. In this method the resonance curve peak with $\Delta\omega$ is to be measured at an amplitude of (Areas/$\sqrt{2}$) as shown in Fig. 4.23. The (Areas) is the resonant amplitude.

To determine the values of η where the amplitude in Fig. 4.23 is equal to $\frac{Ares}{\sqrt{2}}$ we get from equation 4.60.

$$\frac{F_0/K}{\sqrt{2}\cdot(2\,\eta\,\zeta)} = \frac{F_0/K}{\sqrt{(1-\eta^2)^2 + (2\,\eta\,\zeta)^2}}$$

or $$(1-\eta^2)^2 + (2\,\eta\,\zeta)^2 = 2\,(2\,\eta\,\zeta)^2$$

or $$1 - \eta^2 = \pm\, 2\,\eta\,\zeta$$

or $$1 - \eta_1^2 = 2\,\eta\,\zeta \qquad \ldots(i)$$

or $$1 - \eta_2^2 = -2\,\eta\,\zeta \qquad \ldots(ii)$$

Subtracting equation (*i*) from equation (*ii*) we get

$$\eta_2^2 - \eta_1^2 = 2\,\zeta\,(\eta_1 + \eta_2)$$

or $$(\eta_2 - \eta_2) = 2\,\zeta$$

or $$\frac{\omega_2 - \omega_1)}{P} = 2\,\zeta$$

or $$\frac{\Delta\,\omega}{P} = 2\,\zeta$$

or $$\zeta = \frac{\Delta\,\omega}{2\,P} \qquad \ldots(4.67)$$

4.12.3. Energy relationship

For steady state sinusoidal vibrations the work done W per cycle is given as

$$W = \int F\cdot dx = \int_0^{2\pi/\omega} F\,\dot{x}\,dt \qquad \ldots(4.68)$$

If $$F = F_0 \sin \omega\, t$$

and $$x = A \sin(\omega\, t - \phi)$$

and velocity $$\frac{dx}{dt} = \dot{x} = A\,\omega \cos(\omega t - \phi) \qquad \ldots(4.69)$$

The input work W_i can be given as

$$W_i = \int_0^{2\pi/\omega} (F_0 \sin \omega t)\, A\,\omega \cos(\omega\, t - \phi)\, dt$$

$$= \pi\, A \cdot F_0 \sin \phi \qquad \ldots(4.70)$$

The value of maximum input of energy to the system would be when the value of sin ϕ is maximum, which is at phase angle 90°. In this condition the force and velocity are just in phase. Hence the maximum amount of work can be done on the system causing resonant phenomenon.

The energy dissipated by damping per cycle of vibration can be obtained by putting force $F = c\dot{x}$,

$\therefore$ Energy dissipated $W_d = \int_0^{2\pi/\omega} F(\dot{x})\, dt$ ...(i)

Putting $\dot{x} = A\,\omega \cos(\omega t - \phi)\, dt$

$$\therefore \quad W_d = \int_0^{2\pi/\omega} c\,\dot{x}(\dot{x})\, dt$$

$$= \int_0^{2\pi/\omega} c\,[A\,\omega \cos(\omega t - \phi)]^2\, dt$$

$$= c \cdot A^2\, \pi \cdot \omega \qquad \text{...(4.71)}$$

The balance between the energy input and energy dissipated must be represented by the steady state vibration. The value of amplitude of steady state vibration can be obtained by equating the energy input and energy dissipated. Thus $w_i = w_d$.

$$\therefore \quad \pi A\, F_0 \sin\phi = C \cdot A^2 \cdot \pi \cdot \omega.$$

$$\therefore \quad A = \frac{F_0 \sin\phi}{C \cdot \omega} \qquad \text{...(4.72)}$$

4.13. EQUIVALENT VISCOUS DAMPING

The above relation of equation 4.72 can form the basis of a useful approximate method for solving problems in which damping is other than viscous. The equivalent viscous damping C_{eq} is defined as the work dissipated by actual friction is equal to that of equivalent viscous friction. Thus from equation 4.71, $C_{eq} = C$

$$\text{or} \quad C_{eq} = C = \frac{W_d}{\pi \cdot A^2 \cdot \omega} \qquad \text{...(4.73)}$$

Let the damping force F be proportional to the cube of velocity '$\dot{x}$'

i.e. $F = b\,(\dot{x})^3$

$$\text{then} \quad W_d = \int_0^{2\pi/\omega} b\,(\dot{x})^3 \cdot (\dot{x})\, dt$$

$$= \int_0^{2\pi/\omega} b\,(\dot{x})^4\, dt,$$

using eqatuion 4.69,

$$W_d = \int_0^{2\pi/\omega} b\,[C A \cos(\omega t - \phi)]^4\, dt$$

$$= \frac{3}{4}\, b \cdot \pi \cdot A^4\, \omega^3$$

$$\therefore \quad C_{eq} = \frac{W_d}{\pi\,\omega\, A^2} = \frac{3\, b \cdot A^2\, \omega^2}{4} \qquad \text{...(4.74)}$$

This shows that in this case damping is dependent upon the magnitude and frequency. This could be expected as damping is non linear.

As another example, Let us consider coulomb damping. The energy lost or dissipated per cycle by a frictional force F_D is given by using equation 4.49.

$$W_d = \frac{4\,F_D}{K}$$

This is so because the system has a steady state constant peak amplitude of A and due to a constant frictional force F_D, the work dissipated in quarter cycle is

$$F_D \times A \text{ or } W_D = 4\,F_D\,A$$

$$\therefore \qquad C_{eq} = \frac{4 \cdot F_D \cdot A}{\pi A^2 \cdot \omega} = \frac{4\,F_D}{\pi\,\omega\,A} \qquad \ldots(4.76)$$

Using the relation of 4.76, the equivalent viscous damping, an approximate expression can be derived for the steady state amplitude in case of coulomb damped system. From 4.60, the Amplitude A is given

$$A = \frac{F_0/K}{[(1-\eta^2)^2 + (2\,\eta\,\zeta)^2]^{1/2}} \qquad \ldots(a)$$

In equation (*a*) putting $\zeta = \dfrac{C}{2\,mP}$ and $\eta = \dfrac{\omega}{P}$ we get

$$A = \frac{F_0/K}{\left[(1-\eta^2]^2 + \left\{\dfrac{2\,\omega}{P}\left(\dfrac{4\,F_D}{\pi\,\omega\,A}\right)\left(\dfrac{1}{2\,mP}\right)\right\}^2\right]^{1/2}} \qquad \ldots(4.77)$$

Squaring both sides of equation 4.77 we get

$$\text{or} \qquad A^2 = \frac{(F_0/K)^2}{(1-\eta^2]^2 + \left\{\dfrac{2\,\omega}{P}\left(\dfrac{4\,F_D}{\pi\,\omega\,A}\right)\left(\dfrac{1}{2\,mP}\right)\right\}^2}$$

$$\text{or} \qquad \left(\frac{F_0}{A.K}\right)^2 = (1-\eta^2)^2 + \left\{\frac{2\,\omega}{P}\left(\frac{4\,F_D}{\pi\,\omega\,A}\right)\left(\frac{1}{2\,mP}\right)\right\}^2$$

$$= (1-\eta^2)^2 + \left(\frac{4\,F_D}{A\,\pi\,m\,P^2}\right)^2$$

$$\text{or} \qquad \left(\frac{F_0}{AK}\right)^2 - \left(\frac{4\,F_D}{A\,\pi\,m\,P^2}\right)^2 = (1-\eta^2)^2$$

$$\text{Writing} \qquad \left(\frac{4\,F_D}{A\,\pi\,mp^2}\right)^2 = \frac{4\,F_D \times 4\,F_D}{A^2\,\pi^2\,m^2\,p^4}$$

$$= \frac{4\,F_D}{\pi^2} \times \frac{4\,F_D}{A^2\,m^2\,K^2/m^2} \quad \text{as } (P^2 = K/m)$$

$$= \frac{4\,F_D}{\pi^2} \times \frac{4\,F_D}{A^2\,K^2}$$

($4\,F_D = \pi\,F_0$ from coulomb damping F_0 is max. amplitude of the force, F_D damping force)

$$= \frac{4\,F_D}{\pi^2} \cdot \frac{\pi\,F_0}{AK} \times \frac{1}{AK} \qquad \ldots(b)$$

Multiply by F_0 in the numerator and denominator of equation (*b*), we get

$$= \frac{4\,F_D}{\pi^2}\,\frac{\pi \cdot F_0^2}{A^2K^2}\,\frac{1}{F_0}$$

$$= \frac{4\,F_D}{\pi\,F_0}\left(\frac{F_0}{AK}\right)^2$$

$$\therefore \quad \left(\frac{F_0}{AK}\right)^2 - \left[\left(\frac{4\,F_D}{\pi\,F_0}\right)\left(\frac{F_0}{AK}\right)^2\right] = (1-\eta^2)^2$$

or
$$\left(\frac{F_0}{AK}\right)^2\left(1 - \frac{4\,F_D}{\pi\,F_0}\right) = (1-\eta^2)^2$$

or
$$\left(\frac{A}{F_0/K}\right)^2 = \frac{\left(1 - \frac{4\,F_D}{\pi\,F_0}\right)}{(1-\eta^2)^2}$$

or
$$\frac{A}{F_0/K} = \frac{\sqrt{1 - 4\,F_D/\pi\,F_0}}{(1-\eta^2)} \qquad \ldots(4.80)$$

It can be noted that at resonance, the behaviour is altogether of different character than that for viscous damping. At resonance ($\eta = 1$), the amplitude will be infinite irrespective of the value of coulomb damping provided that $4F_d < \pi F_0$. If $4F_D > \pi F_0$ the friction force will be so large that no vibration would take place.

4.14. VIBRATION ISOLATION

When machines run, they cause vibrations. Thus it is necessary to reduce vibrations by isolating the machines. Some times a sensitive equipment is to be isolated from vibrations, which may damage the equipment. Here such cases are discussed.

A common source of causing vibrations is an unbalanced rotating

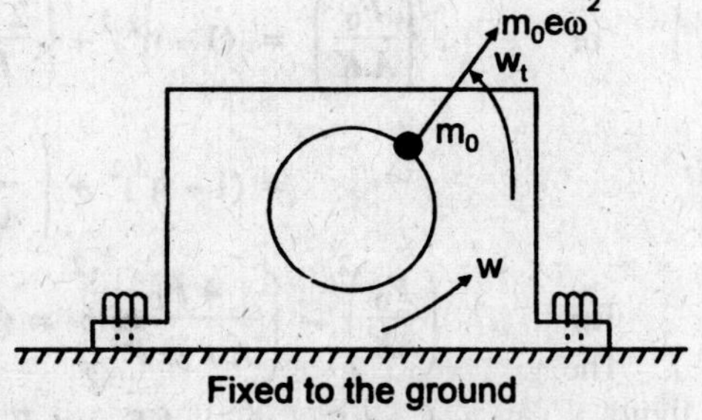

Fig. 4.24 (*a*) Fixed to the ground

machine as shown in Fig. 4.24 (*a*). The machine rotates with a constant speed and has an unbalanced mass m_0 at a distance '*e*' say from its axis of rotation. A rotating radial (centrifugal) force given by the relation $F = m_0 \cdot e \cdot \omega^2$ ...(*i*) acts on the machine. In case the machine is rigidly bolted with its foundation, there will be a vertical component of this force acting on the floor.

This force may cause vibrations. These vibrations may be reduced by mounting the machine on a spring dash pot system as shown in Fig. 4.25 (*b*). Let us assume that machine is constrained to move vertically and the actual motions of the floor are small as compared to the vertical motion of the machine. If the vertical absolute displacement of the machine is '*x*', then the force acting on the floor, which will be transmitted through the spring and dash pot will be as

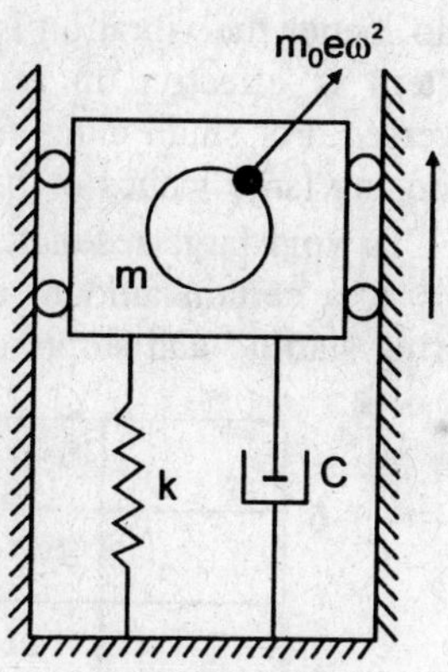

Spring mounted
Fig. 4.24 (*b*) An unbalanced rotating machine

$$F_f = K \cdot x + C\dot{x} \qquad \text{...(4.79)}$$

The equation of the motion of the system will be similar as given by the equation, $m\ddot{x} + c\dot{x} + Kx = F_{(t)}$ where $F_{(t)} = m_0\, e\, \omega^2 \sin \cdot \omega t$

The amplitude *x* by analogy with equation 4.60 will be

$$x = \frac{(m_0\, e\, \omega^2/K) \sin(\omega t - \phi)}{\sqrt{(1 - n^2)^2 + (2\eta\zeta)^2}} \qquad \text{...(4.80)}$$

Thus equation 4.79 can be written as

$$F_f = (m_0\, e\, \omega^2)\, \mu\, [\sin(\omega t - \phi) + c\omega/K \cos(\omega t - \phi)]$$

where, $\mu = [(1 - \eta)^2 + (2\eta\zeta)^2]^{-1/2}$

or $$\frac{F_f}{m_0\, e \cdot \omega^2} = \mu \sqrt{1 + (C\,\omega/K)^2} \cdot [\sin(\omega t - \phi)]$$

Writing F_F as the maximum value of F_f, and $\dfrac{C\omega}{K} = 2\eta\zeta$, the force ratio is given by

$$\frac{F_F}{m_0\, e \cdot \omega^2} = \frac{K}{\sqrt{1 + (2\eta\zeta)^2}} \qquad \text{...(4.81)}$$

This force ratio is called as *transmissibility* of the vibration isolation system.

The graphical relation of equation 4.81 is shown in Fig. 4.25. From the figure it can be seen that the undamped curve is the same as that of Fig. 4.21, but the damped curve differs. All curves intersect at $\eta = \sqrt{2}$. At $\eta > \sqrt{2}$ the damped curve approach η axis asymptotically, so that higher the frequency ratio, better the vibration isolation. For the whole region ($\eta > \sqrt{2}$) in which the system is effective in reducing vibrations the effect of damping is found reversed. For small damping this effect is not large and can be compensated by choosing large values of η.

To void large resonate vibrations especially if the system is operated near $\eta = 1$, a certain amount of damping is always desirable. This could happen during starting and stopping of the machine.

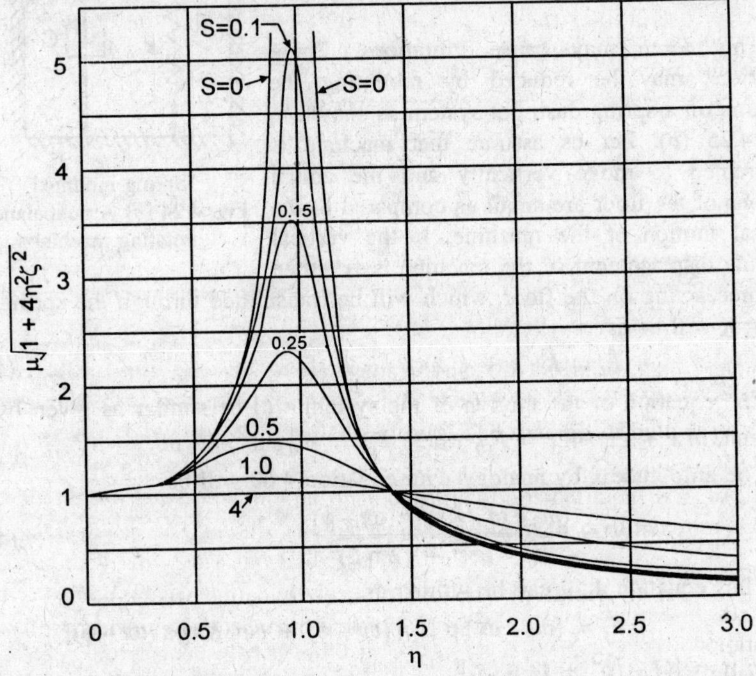

Fig. 4.25. Transmissibility Factors V/S Frequency Ratio

An other example of vibration isolation may be that of an instrument as shown in Fig. 4.26 (*a*). In the Fig. 4.26 (*a*) the equipment is placed on a

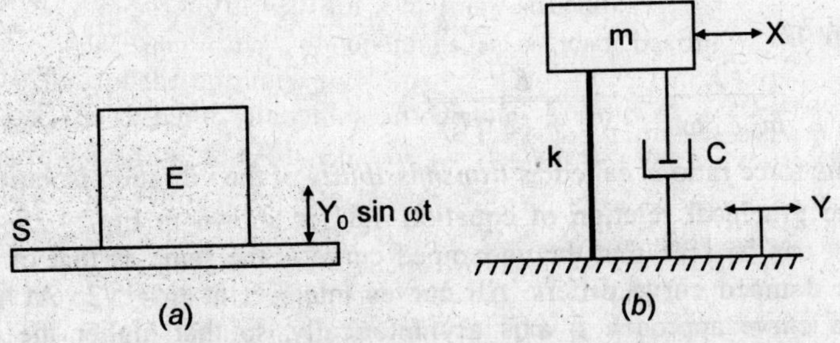

Fig. 4.26. Mounting of an equipment

surface, which has a vertical steady state vibration described by the displacement $y = y_0 \sin \omega t$. In case the equipment is attached rigidly with the surface, it would be subjected to the such motion which might cause damage to the functioning of the equipment. To isolate the equipment,a spring and dash pot may be introduced between it and the surface as shown in Fig. 4.26 (*b*). If x is the absolute vertical motion of mass '*m*' the equation of motion is given by the relation as

$$m\ddot{x} = -K(x-y) - C(\dot{x}-\dot{y})$$

or $$m\ddot{x} + C\dot{x} + Kx = Ky + C\dot{y} \quad \text{...(4.82)}$$

as $y = y_0 \sin(\omega t - \phi)$, equation 4.82 can be written as

$$m\ddot{x} + c\dot{x} + Kx = y_0\sqrt{K^2 + (C\omega)^2} \cdot \sin(\omega t - \phi) \quad \text{...(4.83)}$$

The solution of equation 4.83 is given as

$$x = y_0 \sqrt{1 + \frac{(C\omega)^2}{K}} \cdot \mu \sin(\omega t - \phi) \quad \text{...(4.84)}$$

If x_0 is the maximum value of x, and $\frac{C\omega}{K} = 2\eta\zeta$, then amplitude ratio will be

$$\frac{x_0}{y_0} = \mu\sqrt{1 + (2\eta\zeta)^2} \quad \text{...(4.85)}$$

Equations 4.81 and 4.85 are identical and $\frac{x_0}{y_0}$ can be called transmissibility of the system. The conclusions drawn earlier based on response curves of Fig. 4.25 are also applicable to this system. That is, the amplitude of the mass will be less than that of the support, for frequency ratio greater than $\sqrt{2}$.

In practice it is difficult to isolate the system against low frequency vibrations as in this case. The natural frequency of the isolating system will have to be very low and the supporting system or spring would have to be soft. Thus the static deflection of the system would be rather large.

Example 8. For a system, the transmissibility required is 0.12 and its forcing frequency is 15 cycles per second. Assuming small damping, determine the static deflection

Solution. $\frac{x_0}{y_0}$ transmissibility ratio = 0.12 given

$\therefore$ From equation 4.85, $0.12 = \mu\sqrt{1 + (2\eta\zeta)^2}$

or $$0.12 \approx -\frac{1}{1-\eta^2} \text{ for vary small damping}$$

$$0.12(1-\eta^2) = -1$$

$$0.12 - 0.12\eta^2 = -1$$

or $$\eta^2 = -\frac{1 - 0.12}{0.2}$$

$$\eta^2 = \frac{1 - 12}{0.12} = 9.33$$

or $$\eta = 3.05$$

$$P = \frac{15}{3.05} 2\,\pi \text{ rad/sec}$$

$$P = \frac{2\,\pi \times 15}{3.05} = \frac{94.26}{3.05} = 30.91 = 31.0 \text{ rad/sec.}$$

$$P = \sqrt{\frac{K}{m}} = \sqrt{\frac{K.g}{m.g}} = \sqrt{\frac{g}{\delta_{st}}}$$

where δ_{st} = static deflection.

$$\therefore \text{ Static deflection } \delta_{st} = \frac{g}{P^2} = \frac{981}{(31)^2} = \frac{981}{961}$$

$$= 1.02 \text{ cm}$$

In practice if a system is mounted on a soft spring, it will be difficult to provide stability in different directions. Further machines may have connections of various kinds as pining etc. and these connections must be very flexible if they are not to interfere with the vibration isolation properties of the suspension system.

4.15. VIBRATION MEASURING INSTRUMENTS

Suppose, it is required to measure the motion of a vibrating surface. The quantities of interest to measure may be either displacement, velocity or acceleration. If a fixed reference point is available, then it would be possible to measure the displacement of the vibrating surface from it. However in general a fixed reference may not be available in situations like earthquakes or in measurement of fast moving objects like an aeroplane or an automobile. In such cases a spring mass dash pot system is used where in relative motion between the mass and the supporting frame could be measured as a function of this support motion. Usually this principle is employed for measurement of ground motion and hence such pickups are called seismic pickups.

An idealised system used for measurement is shown in Fig. 4.27. The quantity measured is the relative motion between the mass 'm' and the vibrating surface 'S' (known as ground) and this is related either to ground displacement, velocity, or acceleration depending on the frequency range involved in measurement.

The equation of motion of the mass is given by

$$m\ddot{x} + C(\dot{x} - \dot{y}) + K(x - y) = 0 \qquad \ldots(4.86)$$

Let z denotes the relative displacement $(x - y)$, so that equation 4.86 may be written as

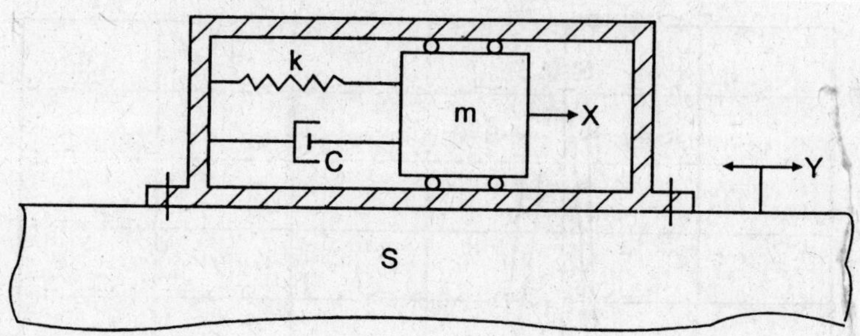

Fig. 4.27. An Idealised vibration measuring instrument

$$m\ddot{z} + C\dot{z} + Kz = -m\ddot{y} \qquad \text{...(4.87)}$$

(as $z = (x - y)$ or $m\ddot{x} = m\ddot{z} - m\ddot{y}$)

Let the harmonic motion of the ground is represented by $y = y_0 \sin \omega t$.

Putting this value in equation 4.87 we get

$$m\ddot{z} + C\dot{z} + Kz = m\omega^2 y_0 \sin \omega t \qquad \text{...[4.87 (b)]}$$

The solution of equation 4.87 (*b*) is given as below as discussed in section 4.11.

$$z = \mu y_0 \frac{m\omega^2}{K} \sin(\omega t - \phi) \qquad \text{...(4.88)}$$

where
$$\mu = \frac{1}{\sqrt{(1-\eta^2)^2 + (2\eta\zeta)^2}} \qquad \text{...(4.89)}$$

and
$$\phi = \tan^{-1} \frac{2\eta\zeta}{1-\eta^2}$$

Denoting Z_n as the maximum value of z and

$$\frac{m\omega^2}{K} = \frac{\omega^2}{P^2} = \eta^2, \text{ we have}$$

$$\frac{Z_m}{y_0} = \eta^2 \cdot \mu \qquad \text{...(4.90)}$$

Curves plotted between $\eta^2\mu$ as ordinate and η as abscissa for various values of ζ are shown in Fig. 4.28. From the figure it can be seen that for $\eta >> 1$, $\eta^2\mu$ tends to unity and the phase angle ϕ tends to 180° as shown in Fig. 4.22, that is

$$z = -y \cdot \sin \omega t \qquad \text{...(4.91)}$$

and the relative motion z measures directly the absolute motion y of the ground. Physically the effect of the soft spring (as discussed earlier for $\eta > 1$, the spring has to be soft) is to leave the mass approximately stationary in the space as reference point. In the frequency range, where excitation frequency is large

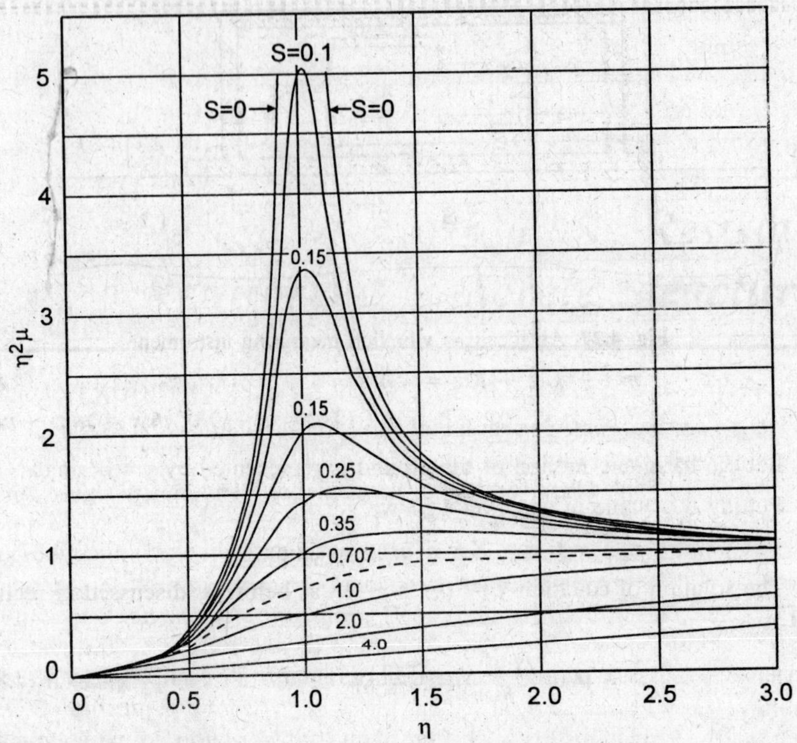

Fig. 4.28. Frequency responses of a displacement pickup

than the natural frequency of the pick up (say $\omega > 3\ P$), the instrument acts a *displacement* pickup. As soft springs are used, hence these instruments are sensitive and delicate.

Case II. Let the frequency is small *i.e.* $\eta << 1$. In this case the natural frequency of the instrument is larger than the excitation frequency and the spring would be very stiff and the equation 4.88 can be written as follows:

$$z = \frac{\mu}{p^2}\,[(y_0\,\omega^2)\,\sin\,(\omega\,t - \phi)] \qquad \ldots(4.92)$$

The acceleration $\ddot{y}$ of the ground is $(-y_0\omega^2)\sin\omega t$ and for $\eta << 1$, ϕ tends to zero as shown in Fig. 4.22 and μ tends to unity from Fig. 4.21.

Thus $$\frac{z}{\ddot{y}} = \left(-\frac{1}{p^2}\right) \qquad \ldots(4.93)$$

and the relative displacement z is proportional to the acceleration of the ground. Such a system is known as acceleration pickup. The maximum operative range of frequency is given by the damping of the order of 0.6 to 0.7 as the value of μ is very near to unity upto $\eta = 0.75$. However as $z/\ddot{y}$ is proportional to $1/P^2$

and P is large for $\eta << 1.0$, the instrument would be relatively insensitive and would require some amplification of the signal for recording. At the same time, as the spring is stiff, the instrument is robust (strong) and ideal for measurement of strong motions. Thus acceleration devices are used for measuring severe earthquakes.

It may also be seen that for $\eta = 1.0$, $\phi = 90°$, z is given by the relation,

$$z = \frac{1}{P\zeta} \cdot \omega\, y_0 \cos \omega t \qquad \ldots(4.94)$$

relation 4.94 shows that the relative displacement is proportional to ground velocity as velocity $\dot{y}$ is equal to $\omega y_0 \cos \omega t$. Since the frequency range is very limited, this principle is not useful for velocity measurements. How ever if the relative velocity $\dot{z}$ measured then from equation 4.88, we have

$$\dot{z} = \eta^2\, \mu\, \omega\, y_0 \cos(\omega t - \phi) \qquad \ldots(4.95)$$

and in frequency range $\eta >> 1.0$ $\dot{z}$ is proportional to ground velocity $\dot{y}$ such instruments are called velocity pickup.

The mechanical characteristics of velocity and displacement pickups are identical, but in one case relative velocity is measured and in the other relative displacement. These instruments are relatively more sensitive and seismographs are designed on this principle.

4.16. SYSTEM SUBJECTED TO TRANSIENT FORCES

The sources of vibrations in a structure are known as transient or temporary forces. These vibrations may be caused by earthquakes, blasts, impact due to sudden dropping or lifting the loads. In many problems of this nature, the maximum motions will develop with in a relatively short time after the application of the load or force, before energy dissipators get time to reduce the amplitudes of motion substantially. For this reason, damping may be of secondary importance for many such transient problems such as suddenly applied loads and single pulse loads. However response due to earthquakes is influenced by damping as it is consisted of a series of pulses. Some cases of this nature are discussed in the following sections.

Case 1. Suddenly applied load

An undamped single degree freedom oscillator consisting of a mass 'm' and spring stiffness K is shown in Fig. 4.29. Let a constant force F_0 is applied suddenly to the mass 'm'.

The equation of motion of mass 'm' can be written as

$$m\ddot{x} + Kx = F_0 \qquad \ldots(4.96)$$

The solution of equation 4.96 is given as

$$x = A \cos Pt + B \sin Pt + F_0/K \qquad \ldots(4.97)$$

The arbitrary constant A and B can be evaluated from the initial conditions *i.e.* at $t = 0$, $x = 0$ and $\dot{x} = 0$, which gives

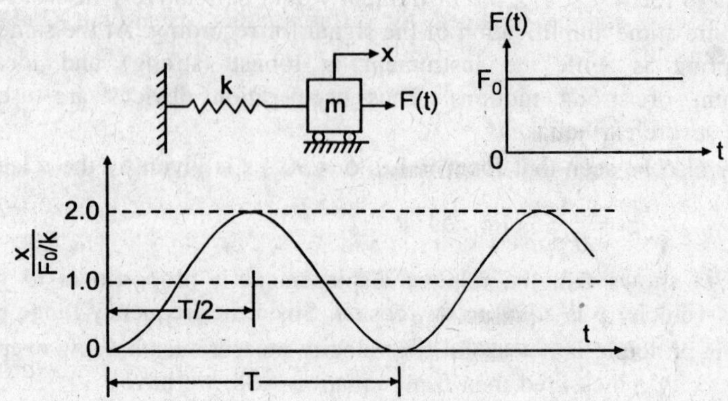

Fig. 4.29. Dynamic Application Factor Due to Suddenly Applied Load

$$A = -\frac{F_0}{K} \text{ and } B = 0$$

Thus equation 4.97 becomes

$$x = \frac{F_0}{K}\,(1 - \cos Pt) \qquad \text{...(4.98)}$$

In case the force F_0 was applied gradually, the static deflection would have been F_0/K. Thus the factor $(1 - \cos Pt)$ represents the magnification due to the load being applied suddenly. Thus a *dynamic amplification* factor μ can be defined as

$$\mu = \frac{x}{F_0/K} = 1 - \cos pt \qquad \text{...(4.99)}$$

The dynamic amplification factor μ is a function of time as shown in Fig. 4.29.

The maximum value of μ is 2.0, when $\cos pt = -1$. Thus maximum dynamic deflection is equal to twice the static deflection F_0/K. The first peak will reach when $pt = \pi$ or $t = T/2$, where T is the natural period of vibration of the system.

Case II. Square Pulse of finite duration

Consider a mass 'm' which is subjected to a force (pulse) of uniform intensity for a given duration τ as shown in Fig. 4.30. When $t < \tau$, the equation of motion of mass 'm' may written as

$$m\ddot{x} + Kx = F_0 \qquad \text{...(4.100)}$$

Equation 4.100 and (4.96) are similar. The solution of equation 4.100 is given as in case 1. as

$$x = \frac{F_0}{K}\,(1 - \cos pt) \qquad \text{...(4.101)}$$

The velocity can be obtained by differentiating equation (4.101) with respect to time 't'

$$\therefore \quad x = \frac{dx}{dt} = \dot{x} = \frac{F_0 \cdot P}{K} \sin pt) \qquad \text{...(4.102)}$$

At $t = \tau$, displacement, x_τ and velocity $\dot{x}_\tau$ can be obtained from equation (4.101) and (4.102) respectively. These values become the initial conditions for the vibrations after the pulse (force) ceases to act *i.e.* for $t > \tau$. In this stage vibrations are free vibrations described by

$$x = A' \cos pt' + B' \sin pt' \qquad \text{...(4.103)}$$

Here t' refers time beyond τ. A' andB' can be determined from the initial condition that at $t' = 0$, $x = x_\tau$ and velocity $\dot{x} = \dot{x}_\tau$ as explained above.

Thus from these conditions, $A' = \frac{F_0}{K}(1 - \cos p\tau)$ and $B' = \frac{F_0}{K} \sin p\tau$

and $$x = \frac{F_0}{K}(1 - \cos p\tau) \cos pt' + \frac{F_0}{K} \sin p\tau \sin pt' \qquad \text{...(4.104)}$$

or $$x = \frac{F_0}{K} \sqrt{(1 - \cos p\tau)^2 + \sin^2 p\tau} \cdot \sin(pt' - \phi) \qquad \text{...(4.105)}$$

where ϕ is the phase difference

simplifying equation (4.105) we get

$$x = \frac{F_0}{K} \sqrt{2(1 - \cos p\tau)} \cdot \sin(pt' - \phi)$$

or $$x = \frac{F_0}{K}(2 \sin p\tau/2) \sin(pt' - \phi) \qquad \text{...(4.106)}$$

Thus the dynamic amplification factor μ for the free vibrations region ($t > \tau$) is given as

$$\mu = \frac{x_m}{F_0/K} = \frac{2 \sin p\tau}{2} = 2 \sin \frac{\pi\tau}{T} \qquad \text{...(4.107)}$$

The maximum value of dynamic amplification factor μ shall depend on the ratio of τ/T and shall be given either from equation (4.101) or equation (4.107).

When τ/T is $< 1/2$, equation 4.107 governs and the maximum value of response occurs during the free vibration phase commencing at the end of the pulse. However when $\tau/T \geq \frac{1}{2}$ equation 4.101 governs and the maximum response μ is obtained during the period or duration of the pulse itself and its value is 2.0. The relationship of τ/T and dynamic magnification factor is shown in Fig. 4.30.

If in equation 4.107, we consider the limiting case, where τ/T is very

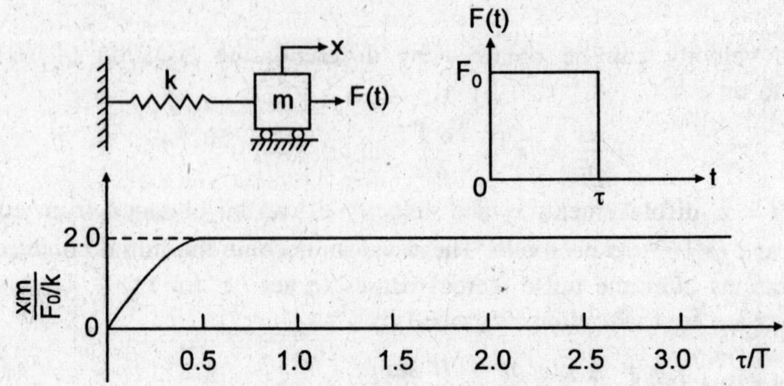

Fig. 4.30. Dynamic Magnification Factor Dur to a Square Pulse Load

small, *i.e.* $\sin \frac{x_\tau}{T} \approx \frac{x_\tau}{T}$ and realising that $T = \frac{2\pi}{P}$ and $p^2 = K/m, x_m$ can be obtained as

$$x_m = \frac{F_0 \tau}{m.p} \qquad \text{...(4.108)}$$

If $F_0\tau$ is the impulse I applied (area under the pulse)

$$x_m = \frac{I}{m\,p} \qquad \text{...(4.109)}$$

Thus in one extreme, when $\frac{\tau}{T} > \frac{1}{2}$, square pulse tends to be a step function (case I) and in the other extreme when $\frac{\tau}{T} << 1.0$ its effect tends to be that of an impulse.

Case III. Half sine pulse

When $t < \tau$, the equation of motion of mass 'm' subjected to half sine pulse loading as shown in Fig. 4.31 is given by the relation as

$$m\ddot{x} + Kx = F_0 \sin \omega t \qquad \text{...(4.110)}$$

where $\omega = \pi/\tau$

The solution of equation 4.110 is given as

$$x = A \cos pt + B \sin pt + \frac{F_0/K}{(1-\omega/p)^2} \cdot \sin \omega t \qquad \text{...(4.11)}$$

Equation (4.111) and (4.62) are same, when damping is zero, From initial condition *i.e.* when $t = 0$, $x = 0$ and velocity $\dot{x}$ also zero, the values of A and B are

$$A = 0 \text{ and } B = \frac{(F_0/K)\,(\omega/p)}{1-(\omega/p)^2}$$

Thus the solution becomes.

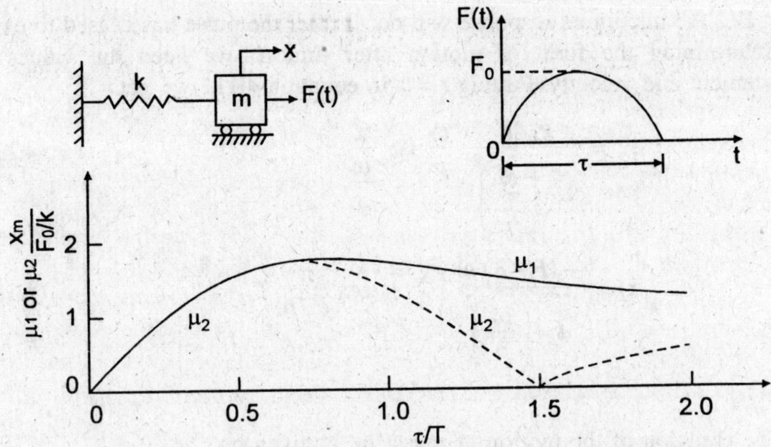

Fig. 4.31. Dynamic Magnification Due to a Half Sine Pulse Load

$$x = \frac{(F_0/K)}{1-\left(\frac{\omega}{p}\right)^2}\left[\sin \omega t - \left(\frac{\omega}{p}\right)\sin pt\right] \qquad \ldots(4.112)$$

For x to be maximum in this range the differential of x with time 't' or velocity must be zero

or
$$\dot{x} = \frac{(F_0/K)\,\omega}{1-\left(\frac{\omega}{p}\right)^2}(\cos \omega t - \cos pt) = 0 \qquad \ldots(4.113)$$

Thus either $\omega = p$ or $t = \dfrac{2\pi}{(\omega + p)}$. Ignoring the condition of resonance *i.e.* $\omega = P$, we get

$$x_{max} = \frac{(F_0/K)}{1-\left(\frac{\omega}{p}\right)^2}\left[\frac{\sin 2\pi\omega}{(\omega+p)} - \frac{\omega}{p}\frac{\sin 2\pi p}{(\omega+p)}\right] \qquad \ldots(4.114)$$

The dynamic amplification factor μ in the range $(t < \tau)$ is given by

$$\mu_1 = \frac{x_m}{F_0/K} = \frac{1}{1-\left(\frac{\omega}{p}\right)^2}\left[\sin\frac{2\pi\omega}{(\omega+p)} - \left(\frac{\omega}{p}\right)\sin\frac{2\pi p}{(\omega+p)}\right] \qquad \ldots(4.115)$$

The equation 4.115 applies only if time of maximum response is less than τ that is
$$\frac{2\pi}{\omega + p} \le \tau \qquad \ldots(4.116)$$

As $\omega = \pi/\tau$ and $p = 2\pi/T$, equation 4.116 reduces to $\tau/T \ge 1/2$. For

$\tau/T < 1/2$ the maximum response will occur after the pulse has ceased to exist. For determining the form of motion after time τ, we need the values of displacement and velocity. Putting $t = \tau$ in equation 4.112 we get

$$x_\tau = \frac{F_0/K}{1-\left(\frac{\omega}{p}\right)^2}\cdot\frac{\omega}{p}\sin\frac{\pi}{\frac{\omega}{p}} \qquad \text{...(4.117)}$$

$$\dot{x}_\tau = \frac{-(F_0/K)\,\omega}{1-\left(\frac{\omega}{p}\right)^2}\left[1+\cos\frac{\pi}{\omega/p}\right] \qquad \text{...(4.118)}$$

For $t > \tau$

The equation of the motion of mass 'm' is given by

$$x = x_\tau \cos pt' + \left(\frac{\dot{x}_\tau}{p}\right)\sin pt' \qquad \text{...(4.119)}$$

In this case t' is counted from the end of the pulse.

Substituting the values of x_τ and $\dot{x}_\tau$ from equations of 4.117 and 4.118 the maximum amplitude of vibration is given by

$$x_{max} = \frac{(F_0/K}{1-\left(\frac{\omega}{p}\right)^2}\left[\left(\frac{\omega}{p}\right)^2 \sin^2\frac{\pi}{\frac{\omega}{p}} + \left(\frac{\omega}{p}\right)^2\left\{1+\cos\left(\frac{\pi}{\omega/p}\right)^2\right\}\right]^{1/2} \qquad \text{...(4.120)}$$

The dynamic amplitude factor μ in this range $(t > \tau)$ is given by

$$\mu_2 = \frac{x_m}{(F_0/K)} = \frac{(\omega/p)}{\left[1-\left(\frac{\omega}{p}\right)^2\right]}\times\left[2\cos\frac{\pi p}{2\omega}\right]$$

$$= \frac{\cos\pi(\tau/T)}{\tau/T\left\{1-\frac{1}{4\left(\frac{\tau}{T}\right)^2}\right\}} \qquad \text{...(4.121)}$$

The variation of magnification factors μ_1 and μ_2 with $\left(\frac{\tau}{T}\right)$ is shown in Fig. 4.31. From the figure, it will be seen that as the maximum force in the pulse takes time to develop, the magnification does not reach the level of 2.0, as it did in the case of square pulse where the force was assumed to be applied suddenly.

Case IV. Impulse load

If the duration of the pulse is very small in comparison to the natural period of the system, it reduces to an impulse.

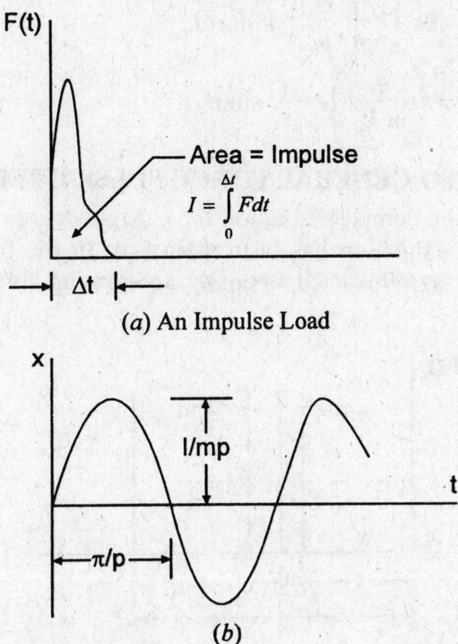

(*a*) An Impulse Load

(*b*)

Fig. 4.32. Amplitude Rcsponse Due to an Impulse Load

Let us assume that an impulse I as shown in Fig. 4.32 (*a*) is applied to an un damped single degree of freedom system. The effect of the impulse applied to the mass will be to give an velocity to the mass.

This velocity can be determined from the impulse momentum relationship

$$I = \int_0^{\Delta t} F(t)\, dt \approx mv_0 \qquad \ldots(4.122)$$

where, V_0 is the velocity given to the mass by the impulse. If time is measured from the end of the impulse and assuming that the mass has not acquired any appreciable displacement during the short time Δt. This problem can be treated as of free vibrations with an initial velocity. The vibrations would be described by

$$x = \frac{V_0}{p} \sin pt \qquad \ldots(4.123)$$

or $$x = \frac{I}{mp} \sin pt \qquad \ldots(4.124)$$

The effect of the impulse is to start a sinusoidal vibration at the natural frequency of the system with an amplitude (I/mp) as shown in Fig. 4.32 (*b*).

In case the system has viscous damping and is subjected to an impulse, then the vibrations would be described by

$$x = e^{-p\zeta t}\left(\frac{V_0}{p}\right)\sin P_d \cdot t \quad \text{...(4.125)}$$

or

$$x = \left(\frac{I}{m\,P_d}\right)e^{-p\zeta t}\sin P_d\, t \quad \text{...(4.126)}$$

4.17. RESPONSE TO GENERAL FORCE PULSE-GREEN'S FUNCTION

In this section the complete solution for a single degree of freedom system subjected to forced excitation has been described. In the first instance, let us assume un damped system acted upon by an exciting force of any form as shown in Fig. 4.33.

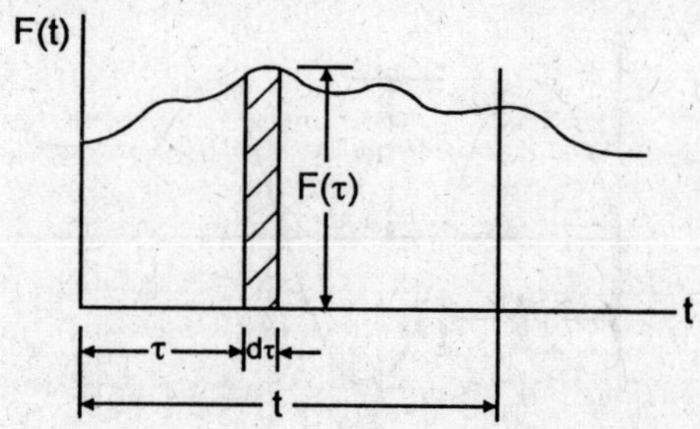

Fig. 4.33. A General Forcing Function

Let the force diagram be divided into a large number of rectangular slices as shown by shaded part in Fig. 4.33. The response of a system acted upon by a single impulse such as $F(\tau)dt$ is given by equation (4.124) and by summing up the contribution from all the impulses, the complete response of the system can be determined.

In Fig. 4.33, τ defines the time at which a typical impulse acts and t defines the time at which the response x to this impulse is determined. The contribution to x of this impulse I, which is $F(\tau)dt$. can be determined by equation 4.124 as

$$\delta x = \frac{I}{mp}\sin p\,(t-\tau) = \frac{F\,(\tau)\,d\tau}{mp}\sin p\,(t-\tau) \quad \text{...(4.127)}$$

The response of all the impulses over a total time t is given by

$$x = \frac{I}{mp}\int_0^t F(\tau)\sin p\,(t-\tau)\,d\tau \quad \text{...(4.128)}$$

The integral of equation 4.128 will give the complete solution transient as well as forced with the constants of integration. The constants of integration can be evaluated for the initial conditions $t = 0$, $x = \dot{x} = 0$.

If $F(t)$ is given in a simple analytical from, it may be possible to integrate the equation 4.128 analytically. In case the $F(t)$ is very complicated or can not be expressed in an analytical form, equation 4.128 can not be evaluated numerically.

If the initial conditions namely x_0 or $\dot{x}_0$ are not zero, then the result would be as follows:

$$x = x_0 \cos pt + \left(\frac{\dot{x}_0}{p}\right) \sin pt + \frac{1}{pm}\int_0^t F(\tau) \sin pt\,(t-\tau)\, d\tau \quad \text{...(4.129)}$$

If in the system there is viscous damping and if it is starting from the rest, the complete response can be obtained by the use of equation 4.130, given below:

$$x = \frac{I}{mP_d}\int_0^t F(\tau)\, e^{-p\zeta(t-\tau)} \times \sin P_d\,(t-\tau)\, d\tau \quad \text{...(4.130)}$$

SOLVED EXAMPLES

1. Derive the equation of motion of a cantilever beam with the following data. This beam carries a suspended weight of 35 kg at its free end as shown in Fig. 4.34.
   1. Length of the beam = 3.5 m
   2. Moment of inertia of the beam $I = 1.5 \times 10^{-4}\ \text{m}^4$
   3. Modulus of elasticity of the material of the beam $E = 2.4 \times 10^4$ MPa
   4. Coefficient of stiffness of spring $K = 40$ kN/m
   5. Suspended weight $W = 35$ kN

   Neglect the weight of the beam and the spring.

Solution. The sketch of the beam at different stages is shown in Fig. 4.34 (*a*) to (*d*).

Fig. 4.34 (*b*) shows the deformed position of the free end of the beam, mass and spring. The displacement *x* of mass 'm', is measured from its original

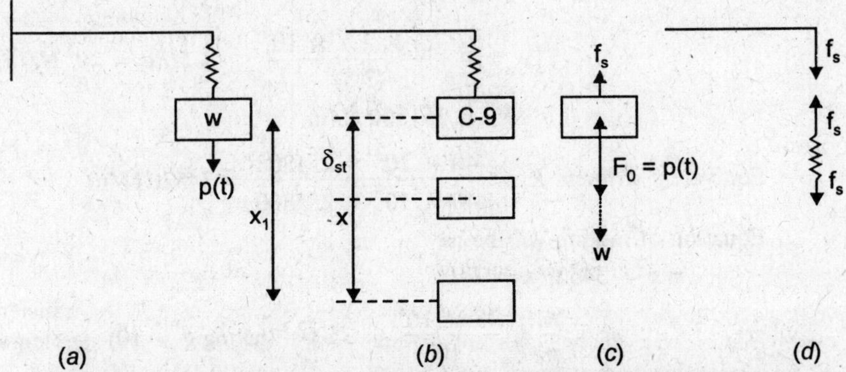

Fig. 4.34. (*a*) System with beam and load, (*b*) Underformed, deformed and static equilibrium positions, (*c*) Free body state, (*d*) Forces of beam and spring

position with respect to beam and spring in their original un deformed position. The equilibrium of the forces is shown in Fig. 4.34 (*c*). The equation of motion of the system can be written as

$$m\ddot{x} + K_e \cdot x_1 = W + p(t) \quad \text{...(4.131)}$$

K_c is the effective stiffness of the system. The displacement x_1 can be expressed as $x_1 = x + \delta_{st}$ where δ_{st} is static displacement due to weight *W*. The static deflection δ_{st} does not vary with time. Hence $\ddot{x}_1 = \ddot{x}$

Thus $K_e \times \delta_{st} = W$ (weight applied)

Hence the equation of motion (4.131) reduces to

$$m\ddot{x} + K_e(\delta_{st} + x) = W + p(t)$$

or $$m\ddot{x} + K_e x = p(t) \quad (\text{As } K_e\,\delta_{xt} = W) \quad \text{...(4.132)}$$

The effective stiffness (K_c) of the system can be determined by equating the displacement x_1 and displacement of beam and spring together *i.e.*

$$x_1 = \delta_{\text{beam}} + \delta_{\text{spring}} \quad \text{...(4.134)}$$

where δ_{beam} is the deflection of right end of the beam and δ_{spring} is the deformation of the spring. From Fig. 4.34, the total force in beam and spring is equal

$$\therefore \quad f_s = K\,\delta_{\text{spring}} = K_{\text{beam}} \times \delta_{\text{bem}} \quad \text{...(4.135)}$$

Equation 4.135 can be written as

$$\frac{f_s}{K_e} = \frac{f_s}{K} + \frac{f_s}{K_{\text{beam}}}$$

or $$\frac{1}{K_e} = \frac{1}{K} + \frac{1}{K_{\text{beam}}} = \frac{K_{\text{beam}} + K}{K \times K_{\text{beam}}}$$

or $$K_e = \frac{K \times K_{\text{beam}}}{K + K_{\text{beam}}}$$

$$K_{\text{beam}} \text{ (stiffness of beam)} = \frac{3\,EI}{(L)^3} = \frac{3 \times 2.4 \times 10^4 \times 1.5 \times 10^{-4} \times 10^5}{(3.5)^3}$$

$$= \frac{7.2 \times 1.5 \times 10^6}{(3.5)^3} \quad (1\,MPa = 10^5\,\text{N/m}^2)$$

$$K_e = 251800\ \text{N/m}$$

$$\therefore \text{ Equivalent stiffness } K_e = \frac{40 \times 10^3 \times 251800}{40 \times 10^3 + 251800} = 34520\ \text{N/m}$$

∴ Equation of motion will be as

$$m\ddot{x} + 34520\,x = P(t)$$

where $$m = \frac{w}{g} = \frac{35 \times 10^3}{10} = 3500 \quad (\text{taking } g \approx 10)$$

Thus equation of motion is $3500\ddot{x} + 34520\,x = p(t)$ **Ans.**

Example 12. From the data of solved example 1, determined the natural circular frequency, natural period of vibration and the natural frequency of weight.

Solution. Natural frequency of weight $P = \frac{1}{2\pi}\sqrt{K/m}$

$$= \frac{1}{2\pi}\sqrt{\frac{K.g}{m.g}} = \frac{1}{2\pi}\sqrt{\frac{g}{\delta_{st}}}$$

$$\delta_{st} = \frac{W}{K_e} = \frac{35000}{34520} = \frac{35}{34.5} \approx 1.014 \text{ m}$$

$\therefore$ Natural frequency $P = \frac{1}{2 \times 3.142}\sqrt{\frac{10}{1.014}} = \frac{1}{6.284} \times \sqrt{\frac{10000}{1014}}$

$\frac{3.140}{6.284} = 0.5$ cps

$\therefore$ Time period $T = \frac{1}{P} = \frac{1}{0.5} = 2.0$ sec.

$\therefore$ Natural circular frequency $\omega = \frac{2\pi}{T}$

$$= \frac{2 \times 3.142}{2.0} = 3.142 \text{ radian/sec.}$$ **Ans.**

Example 3. An elevated tank is mounted on a hollow shaft. The tank is pulled by a horizontal force of 36 kN. The tank is pulled horizontally by 6 cm and the cable is cut suddenly to enable the tank to vibrate freely. The free vibrations are recorded. At the end of 10 complete cycles the time was recorded as 4 seconds and amplitude as 1.5 cm. From this data determine the followings:

(*i*) Damping ratio
(*ii*) Natural period of un damped vibration
(*iii*) Effective stiffness
(*iv*) Effective weight
(*v*) Damping coefficient.

Solution. Damping ratio

Damping ratio $= \log_e \frac{x_1}{x_2} = \frac{2\pi\zeta}{\sqrt{1-\zeta^2}}$

Taking ζ less than 1.0, damping ratio becomes $= 2\pi\zeta$

$\therefore$ The damping ration can also be calculated as

$$\text{Damping ratio} = \frac{1}{2\pi \times \text{1st amplitude}} \times \log_{10} \frac{\text{1st amplitude}}{\text{2nd amplitude}}$$

$$\therefore \text{Damping ratio} = \frac{1}{2 \times 3.142 \times 6} \times \log_e \frac{6.0}{1.5}$$

$\frac{1}{37.68} \log_e \frac{6.0}{1.5} = 0.0368$ $(\log_e x = 2.303 \log_{10} x)$

∴ Damping factor $\zeta = 0.0368 \times 100$

$= 3.68\%$

∴ Natural period of un damped vibrations is given by the relation

$$T_n = T_D \sqrt{1 - \zeta^2}$$

where T_D is damped period.

Hence $T_D = \dfrac{4}{10} = 0.4$ (As time of 10 cycles is 4 sec.)

∴ Natural period of vibration $= 0.4\sqrt{1 - (0.0368)^2}$

$= 0.4\sqrt{1.0 - 0.0014} \approx 0.4$ sec.

∴ Effective stiffness of tank $K = \dfrac{\text{Force}}{\text{displacement}}$

$= \dfrac{36}{0.06} = 600$ kN/m

Angular frequency of vibration $\omega = \dfrac{2\pi}{T}$

$= \dfrac{2 \times 3.14}{0.4} = 15.7$ radians

Mass m is given by the relation $\omega^2 = \dfrac{K}{m}$

or $m = \dfrac{K}{\omega^2}$

∴ $m = \dfrac{600}{(15.7)^2} = 2.444$ kN/m

∴ Effective weight $w = m \times g = 2.444 \times 10$

$= 24.44$ kN

Damping coefficient $c = \zeta\,(2\sqrt{km})$

$= 0.0368 \times 2\sqrt{600 \times 2.444}$

$= 0.0368 \times 2 \times 38.3$

$= 2.32$ kN–s/m **Ans.**

Example 4. The maximum velocity of a simple harmonic motion is 8 m/s and its frequency is 16 cycles per second. Determine the followings:

(*i*) Its amplitude A.

(*ii*) Its period T.

(*iii*) Its maximum acceleration.

Solution. Given

Maximum velocity $\dot{x}_{max} = 8$ m/s

Frequency $f = 16$ cps

We known that $f = \frac{1}{T} = \frac{P}{2\pi}$

$\therefore \quad 16 = \frac{P}{2\pi}$

$\therefore$ Angular frequency $P = 32\pi$

$= 32 \times 3.142$

$= 100.544$ radians/sec.

$\therefore$ Time period $T = \frac{2\pi}{P} = \frac{1}{16}$

$= 0.06025$ sec. ≈ 0.06 sec.

Maximum velocity $8 = A.P.$

$= A\,(100.544)$

$\therefore$ Amplitude $A = \frac{8}{100.544} = 0.0795$ m

$= 79.5$ mm

$\therefore$ Maximum acceleration $= A.P^2$

$= 79.5 \times (100.544)^2$

$= 803 \times 10^3$ mm/sec^2

Example 5. The time period of SHM was found as 0.3 seconds and amplitude A as 0.5 cms. Determine the maximum velocity and its acceleration.

Solution. Given

$T = 0.3$ sec.

$A = 0.5$ cms or 5 mm

Angular frequency $P = \frac{2\pi}{T}$

$= \frac{2 \times 3.142}{0.3} = \frac{6.284}{0.3} = \frac{62.84}{3}$

$= 20.95$ rad/sec.

Max. velocity $= A.P. = 0.5 \times 20.95$

$= 104.75 = 10.475$ cms/sec^2

Max. acceleration $= AP^2 = 0.5 \times (20.95)^2$

$= 219.5$ cm/sec^2

Example 6. A mass of 2 kg is suspended by a spring whose stiffness K is 1000 N/m. The mass is displaced downwards from its equilibrium position by a distance of 1.0 cms. For the given data, determine.

(*i*) Write the equation of motion of the system.

(*ii*) Natural frequency of the system.

(*iii*) The response of the system as a function of time.

(*iv*) Total energy of the system.

Solution. Given

$$m = 2 \text{ kg}$$

$$K = 1000 \text{ N/m}$$

$$\text{displacement } \delta_{st} = 1 \text{ cms} = 0.01 \text{ m}$$

(*i*) The equation of motion of SHM is given as

$$m\ddot{x} + Kx = 0$$

Here it becomes $2\ddot{x} + 1000\,x = 0$

or $\ddot{x} + 500\,x = 0$

(*ii*) Natural angular frequency P is given as $P = \sqrt{\dfrac{K}{m}} = \sqrt{\dfrac{1000}{2}}$

$$= 22.36 \text{ rad/s}$$

$$f = \frac{P}{2\pi}$$

$$= \frac{22.36}{2 \times 3.142} = 3.56 \; cps$$

(*iii*) The response of system (displacement) x can be written as

$$x = A \sin(pt + \phi)$$

where,

A = Amplitude

ϕ = Phase angle.

$$\therefore \quad A = \sqrt{x_0^2 + \left(\frac{\dot{x}_0}{P}\right)^2} = \sqrt{0.01)^2} \text{ given}$$

$$\therefore \quad A = 0.01 \text{ m}$$

$$\text{Phase angle} \quad \phi = \tan^{-1}\left(\frac{x_0 P}{\dot{x}_0}\right)$$

$$= \left(\frac{0.01 \times 22.36}{0}\right) = \tan \infty$$

$$\therefore \quad \phi = \frac{\pi}{2}$$

$$\therefore \text{ Response} \quad x = 0.01 \sin\left(22.36\,t + \frac{\pi}{2}\right)$$

(*iv*) Total energy of the system is the sum of the kinetic energy and potential energy.

$$\text{Potential energy } P.E. = \frac{1}{2} Kx^2$$

$$= \frac{1}{2} \times 1000 \times (0.01)^2 = 0.05 \text{ N/m}$$

Kinetic energy $K.E. = \frac{1}{2} mv^2$

$$= \frac{1}{2} m \ (AP)^2$$

$$= \frac{1}{2} \times 2.0 \ (0.1 \times 22.36)^2$$

$$= 0.05 \text{ N/m}$$

$$K.E. = P.E = \text{Constant}$$

∴ Total energy $= 0.05$ N/m **Ans.**

Example 7. A system vibrating with a natural frequency of 8 cycles per second starts with an initial amplitude (x_0) of 3 cms and inlial velocity of 40 cm/second. Find out the following:

(*i*) Natural period T
(*ii*) Amplitude A
(*iii*) Maximum velocity
(*iv*) Maximum acceleration
(*v*) Phase angle ϕ
(*vi*) Static deflection δ_{xt}

Solution. Given $f = 8$ cycles/s or Hz

$$x_0 = 3.0 \text{ cm}$$

$$\dot{x}_0 = 40 \text{ cm}$$

(*i*) Natural period $T = \frac{1}{f} = \frac{1}{8} = 0.125$ seconds.

$$P = 2\pi f = 2 \times 3.142 \times 8$$

$$= 50.272 \text{ rad/s}$$

(*ii*) Amplitude $A = \sqrt{x_0^2 + \left(\frac{\dot{x}_0}{P}\right)^2}$

$$\therefore \quad = \sqrt{(3.0)^2 + \left(\frac{40}{50.272}\right)^2}$$

$$= \sqrt{9.0 + 0.632} = \sqrt{9.632}$$

Amplitude $A = 3.104 \approx 3.1$ cms

Maximum velocity $\dot{x}_{max} = A.P$

$$= 3.1 \times 50.27$$

$$= 155.827 \text{ cm/s}$$

Maximum acceleration of the system $\ddot{x}_{max} = AP^2$

$= 3.1 \times (50.27)^2$

$= 7833.0 \text{ cm/s}^2$

$= 78.33 \text{ m/s}^2$

Phase angle $\phi = \tan^{-1}\left(\dfrac{x_0 \cdot P}{\dot{x}_0}\right)$

$= \left(\dfrac{3.0 \times 50.27}{155.827}\right) = \left(\dfrac{150.81}{155.827}\right)$

$\tan^{-1} = 0.968$

$\phi = 44.04$ degree

or $(44° - 2' - 24'')$

(1 radian = 57.3°)

$\therefore \quad \phi = \dfrac{44.04}{57.3°} = 0.679$ radians

Static deflection $\delta_{xt} = \dfrac{g}{p^2} = \dfrac{9810}{(50.27)\,2}$ mm

$= \dfrac{9810}{2526} = 3.88$ mm

Equation of motion is $x = A \sin (Pt + \phi)$

$= 3.1 \sin (50.27\,t + 0.679)$ **Ans.**

Example 8. A vertical cable is 3.5 m long, whose cross sectional areas is 5 cm^2. It supports a weight of 45 kN at its lower end. Determine the natural period T and natural frequency of the system. $E = 2.45 \times 10^6 \text{ kg/cm}^2$

Solution. Given

Area of cross section of the cable = 5 cm^2

Length of the cable = 3.5 m

Weight W = 45 kN

$\therefore \quad m = \dfrac{W}{g} = \dfrac{45 \times 1000}{9.81} = 4586$ kg.

$E = 2.45 \times 10^6 \text{ kg/cm}^2$

Stiffness $K = \dfrac{A.E}{L}$

$= \dfrac{5 \times 2.45 \times 10^6}{350}$

$= \dfrac{5 \times 245 \times 10^3}{35} = 35 \times 10^3$ kg/m

or $K = 35000 \times 981 = 3.433500 \times 10^6$ N/m

$$\text{Natural frequency } p = \sqrt{\frac{K}{m}}$$

$$\sqrt{\frac{3.4335 \times 10^6}{4586}} = 27.36 \text{ radians}$$

$$T = \frac{2\pi}{P} = \frac{2 \times 3.142}{27.361}$$

$$= \frac{6.282}{27.36} = 0.273$$

$$f = \frac{1}{T} = \frac{1}{0.273} = 3.66 \text{ cps}$$

Example 9.. A cantilever beam 3.5 m long supports a mass of 450 kg at its upper end. Determine its natural frequency and natural period of vibration $E = 2.4 \times 10^6$ kg/cm^2 and moment of inertia I = 1400 cm^4.

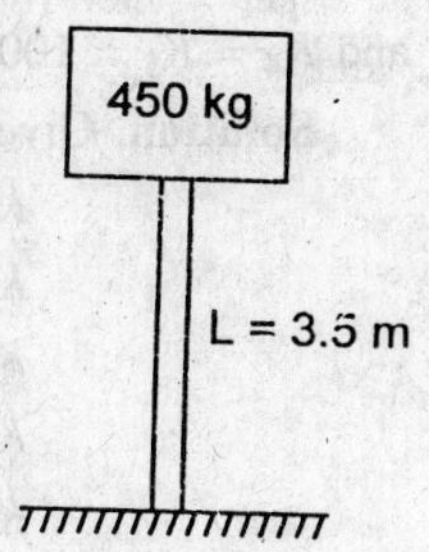

Fig. 4.35.

Solution. Consider the cantilever beam as shown in Fig. 4.35.

Given

Length of cantilever beam = 3.5

Weight at upper end W = 450 kg

Modulus of elasticity $E = 2.45 \times 10^6$ kg/cm^2

Moment of inertia I = 1400 cm^4

$$\text{Flexural stiffness of the cantilever } K = \frac{3\,EI}{L^3}$$

$$\therefore \quad K = \frac{3 \times 2.45 \times 10^6 \times 1400}{(350)^3}$$

$$= \frac{3 \times 245 \times 1400 \times 10^4}{350 \times 350 \times 350}$$

$$= 240 \text{ kg/cm}$$

or $\quad 240 \times 981 \text{ N/cm} = 2.3544 \times 10^5 \text{ N/cm}$

$$\text{Natural frequency } P = \sqrt{\frac{K}{m}}$$

$$= \sqrt{\frac{2.3544 \times 10^5}{450}}$$

$$= 22.87 \text{ radians/sec.}$$

$$f = \frac{P}{2\pi} = \frac{22.87}{6.284}$$

$$= 3.64 \text{ cycles per sec.}$$

$$\text{Natural period } T = \frac{1}{f} = \frac{1}{3.64} = \frac{2\pi}{P}$$

$$= \frac{6.284}{22.87} = 0.275 \text{ seconds } \textbf{Ans.}$$

Example 10. A system is consisted of five springs as shown in Fig. 4.36 below. Find the mass of the system if the natural frequency f of the system is 6. The stiffness of the springs is given as follows.

$K_1 = 1500$ N/m, $K_2 = 3000$ N/m, $K_3 = 2000$ N/m and $K_4 = K_5 = 1000$ N/m.

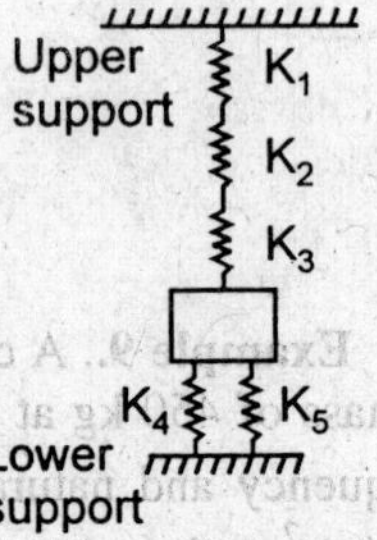

Fig. 4.36.

Solution. Given data

$$K_1 = 1500 \text{ N}/m$$
$$K_2 = 3000 \text{ N}/m$$
$$K_3 = 2000 \text{ N}/m$$
$$K_4 = 1000 \text{ N}/m$$
$$K_5 = 1000 \text{ N}/m$$
$$f = 6 \text{ cycles per second}$$

The springs K_1, K_2, and K_3 are in series. Their equivalent stiffness K_{e1} will be as

$$\frac{1}{K_{c1}} = \frac{1}{K_1} + \frac{1}{K_2} + \frac{1}{K_3}$$

$$= \frac{1}{1500} + \frac{1}{3000} + \frac{1}{2000} = \frac{4+2+3}{6000} = \frac{9}{6000}$$

or $$K_{c1} = \frac{6000}{9} = 666.67 \text{ N/m}$$

The lower springs K_4 and K_5 are in parallel. Their equivalent stiffness K_{e2} will be as

$$K_{c2} = K_4 + K_5$$
$$= 1000 + 1000 = 2000 \text{ N/m}$$

These two equivalent springs K_{c1} and K_{c2} are in parallel

Hence final stiffness $K_c = K_{c1} + K_{c2}$

$\therefore$ $$K_c = 666.67 + 2000 = 2666.67 \text{ N/m}$$

Frequency $$f = \frac{P}{2\pi}$$

or $$P = 2\pi f = 2 \times 3.142 \times 6 = 37.7$$
$$= 37.7 \text{ rad/s}$$

Also $$P^2 = \frac{K}{m}$$

$$\therefore \quad m = \frac{K_c}{P^2} = \frac{2666.67}{(37.7)^2}$$

$$= 1.877 \text{ kg}$$

Example 11. A iron flat 15 cm wide and 4 cm thick is used as a simply supported beam over a span of 2 m. At its mid span it is connected by a spring of stiffness of 200 kg/cm and a mass of 400 kg is attached at the lower end of the spring. Determine the natural frequency of the system. $E = 2.45 \text{ kg/cm}^2$.

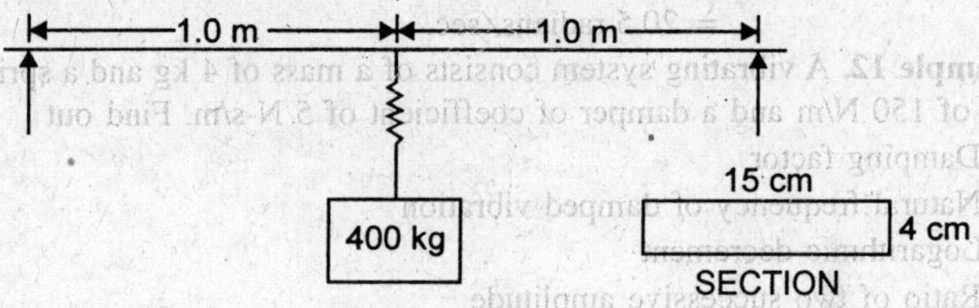

Fig. 4.37.

Solution.

Weight = 400 kg

Stiffness of spring K = 200 kg/cm

The stiffness of simply supported beam $K_b = \dfrac{48\,EI}{L^3}$

$$I = \frac{bd^3}{12}$$

Width of beam b = 15 cm

Depth of beam d = 4 cms

$\therefore$ Moment of inertia of the flat $I = \dfrac{15 \times 4 \times 4 \times 4}{12}$

$$= 80 \text{ cm}^4$$

$\therefore$ Stiffness of flat as simply supported beam

$$K_b = \frac{48 \times 2.45 \times 10^6 \times 80}{200 \times 200 \times 200}$$

$$= 48 \times 24.5 = 1176 \text{ kg/cm}$$

The two springs one flat as beam and the other spring are in series. Hence their equivalent stiffness will be as

$$\frac{1}{K_c} = \frac{1}{K_f} + \frac{1}{K_s} = \frac{1}{1176} + \frac{1}{200}$$

$$= \frac{200 + 1176}{235200} = \frac{1376}{235200}$$

or $$K_c = \frac{235200}{1376} = 171.0 \text{ kg/cm}$$

$$= 171 \times 981 = 1.67751 \times 10^5 \text{ N/cm}$$

Natural frequency $P = \sqrt{\frac{K}{m}}$

$$= \sqrt{\frac{1.67751 \times 10^5}{400}}$$

$$= 20.5 \text{ radians/sec.}$$

Example 12. A vibrating system consists of a mass of 4 kg and a spring of stiffness of 150 N/m and a damper of coefficient of 5 N-s/m. Find out

(*a*) Damping factor

(*b*) Natural frequency of damped vibration

(*c*) Logarithmic decrement

(*d*) Ratio of two successive amplitude

(*e*) No. of cycles after which the initial amplitude is reduced to 25%.

Solution. Given data

$$m = 4 \text{ kg}$$
$$K = 150 \text{ N/m}$$
$$C = 5 \text{ N–s/m}$$

$$P = \sqrt{\frac{K}{m}} = \sqrt{\frac{150}{4}} = 6.123 \text{ radians}$$

Critical damping coefficient $c_c = 2\,mp = 2\,m\sqrt{\frac{K}{m}}$

$$= 2\sqrt{Km}$$
$$= 2\sqrt{150 \times 4} = 2\sqrt{600}$$
$$= 2 \times 10 \times 2.449$$
$$= 48.98 \approx 49.0 \text{ N–s/m}$$

(*a*) Ratio of actual damping and critical damping = ζ = damping factor

$$\therefore \quad \zeta = \frac{5}{49} = 0.102$$

(*b*) Natural damped frequency $= P\sqrt{1-\zeta^2}$

$$= 6.123\sqrt{1-(0.102)^2}$$
$$= 5.80 \text{ radians}$$

(*c*) Logarithmic decrement $\delta = \frac{2\pi\zeta}{\sqrt{1-\zeta^2}} = \frac{2\pi \times 0.102}{\sqrt{1-(0.102)^2}}$

$$= \frac{0.642}{0.947} = 0.678$$

$$\approx 0.68$$

Approximately $\delta \approx 2\pi\zeta = 2 \times 3.142 \times 0.102 = 0.641$

There is not much difference.

(*e*) The ratio between the two consecutive amplitude say $= \frac{x_1}{x_2}$

$$\therefore \qquad e^{\delta} = \frac{x_1}{x_2}$$

δ we calculated in step (*d*) as 0.68 or approximate value is 0.64. We take the calculated value of δ as 0.68.

$$\therefore \qquad e^{0.68} = \frac{x_1}{x_2}$$

By extrapolating it from log table value we get

$$e^{0.68} = \frac{1.9755}{1} = \frac{x_1}{x_2}$$

or $\qquad x_1 = 1.9755\, x_2$

$$x_1 \approx 2.0\, x_2$$

(*e*) Number of cycles after the reduction of 25%.

$$e^{n\delta} = \log 4.0$$

Taking log on base *e* of both sides

$$n\,\delta = 2.303 \log_{10}(4.0) \qquad [\text{As } \log_c = 1]$$

$$n \times 0.68 = 2.30 \times 0.6021$$

$$= 1.385$$

$$\therefore \qquad n = \frac{1.385}{0.68} = \frac{138.5}{68} = 2.05$$

$$\therefore \qquad n = 2.0 \text{ cycles}$$

In case the value of δ is taken as 0.64, then $n = 2.166$ cycles

≈ 2.0 cycles **Ans.**

Example 13. A single degree of freedom system has a mass of 3.0 kg. It is set into motion with a viscous damping and allowed to oscillate freely. The frequency of oscillation is found 21.0 cycles per second. The amplitude of two successive vibrations was found as 7 and 6 mm. Determine viscous damping coefficient.

Solution. Given data

$$m = 3.0 \text{ kg}$$

$$f_d = 21 \text{ cps}$$

$$x_1 = 7 \text{ mm}$$
$$x_2 = 6 \text{ mm}$$

Logarithmic decrement δ is given by the relation

$$e^{\delta} = \log \frac{x_1}{x_2}$$

Taking log on base *e* of both sides we get

$$\delta \log e = 2.303 [\log x_1 - \log x_2]$$
$$\delta \times 1 = 2.303 [\log_{10} 7.0 - \log_{10} 6.0]$$

or
$$\delta = 2.303 [0.8451 - 0.7782] = 2.303 [0.0669]$$
$$= 0.1541$$

For small values of damping ζ, the logarithmic decrement δ is given as

$$\delta = 2\pi\zeta$$

∴
$$\zeta = \frac{\delta}{2\pi} = \frac{0.1541}{2 \times 3.142} = \frac{0.1541}{6.284}$$
$$= 0.0245$$

Damped frequency $P_d = 2\pi f_d = 2 \times 3.142 \times 21$

$$= 131.964 \text{ radians}$$

Also damped frequency $P_d = P\sqrt{1-\zeta^2}$

or
$$P = \frac{P_d}{\sqrt{1-\zeta^2}} = \frac{131.964}{\sqrt{1-(0.0245)^2}}$$
$$= \frac{131.964}{[1-(0.0006)]} = \frac{131.964}{0.9994} \approx 131.964$$
$$\approx 132.0$$

For small values of ζ, $P_d = P$

∴
$$P = \sqrt{\frac{K}{m}}$$

or
$$\frac{P^2}{1} = \frac{K}{m}$$

or
$$K = m \cdot P^2$$
$$= 3.0 \times (132)^2$$
$$= 0.52272 \times 10^5 \text{ N/m}$$
$$\zeta = \frac{c}{c_c} = \frac{C}{2\sqrt{K.m}}$$

or
$$C = c_c \cdot \zeta = 2 \times \zeta \times \sqrt{km}$$
$$= 2 \times 0.0245 \times \sqrt{1.56816 \times 10^5}$$
$$0.049 \times 396 = 19.4 \text{ N–S/m}$$ **Ans.**

Example 14. A damper offers resistance 0.09 N at a constant velocity of 6 cm/sec (0.06 m/s). The damper is used with a spring of stiffness of 15 N/m. Find out the damping ratio and frequency of the system. The mass of the system is given as 300 gram.

Solution. Given data

Damping force $F = c\dot{x} = 0.09$ *where* c is damping coefficient.

$$\dot{x} = 0.06$$

$$K = 15 \text{ N/m}$$

$$m = 0.3 \text{ kg}$$

As $c\dot{x} = 0.09$

$$\therefore \quad c = \frac{0.09}{0.06} = 1.5 \text{ N–s/m}$$

Critical damping coefficient $C_c = 2\sqrt{K.m}$

$$= 2\sqrt{15 \times 0.3} = 2 \times 2.122$$

$$= 4.244 \text{ N–s/m}$$

$$\therefore \quad \zeta = \frac{c}{c_c} = \frac{1.5}{4.224} = 0.355 < 1.0$$

Hence the system is under damped.

Natural frequency $P = \sqrt{\dfrac{K}{m}} = \sqrt{\dfrac{15}{0.3}} = \sqrt{50.0} = 7.07$ rad/s

Damped frequency $Pd = P\sqrt{1-\zeta^2} = 7.07\sqrt{1-(0.355)^2}$

$$= 7.07 \times 0.942$$

$$= 6.66 \text{ rad/sec. } \textbf{Ans.}$$

Example 15. To determine the dynamic properties of a single storey building, a damped free vibration is conducted. The mass of the building is 12 tonnes. The initial displacement of the building is 0.75 cm. Maximum displacement on the first cycle is 0.55 cm and period of this displacement cycle is 1.6 sec. Determine (*i*) Un damped frequency, (*ii*) Effective weight of the system, (*iii*) Logarithmic decrement, (*iv*) Damping coefficient, (*v*) Damped frequency, (*vi*) Amplitude after 6 cycles.

Solution. Given data:

Mass of building $m = 12000$ kg

Period of vibration $T = 1.6$ seconds

Initial displacement $x_0 = 0.75$ cm

$$n = 6.0$$

Undamped frequency $P = \dfrac{2\pi}{T} = \dfrac{2 \times 3.142}{1.6} = 3.93$ rad/s

Also undamped frequency $P = \sqrt{\frac{K}{m}}$

$\therefore \quad 3.93 = \sqrt{\frac{K}{12000}}$

or $\quad \frac{K}{12000} = (3.93)^2$

or
$$K = (3.93)^2 \times 12000$$
$$= 15.45 \times 12000$$
$$= 1.8 \times 10^5 \text{ N/m}$$

Time of vibration of building $T = 2\pi\sqrt{\frac{W}{g.K}}$

or $\quad T^2 = \frac{4\pi^2 \times W}{g.k}$

$$W = \frac{g.K.T^2}{4\pi^2}$$
$$= \frac{9.81 \times 1.8 \times 10^5 \times 1.6 \times 1.6}{4 \times 3.142 \times 3.142}$$
$$= \frac{48.085 \times 10^5}{39.5} = 121.8 \text{ kN}$$

(*iii*) Logarithmic derement δ is given as $e^\delta = \log_e x_1/x_2$

$\therefore \quad e^\delta = \log_e \frac{0.75}{0.55}$

Taking log of both sides we get

$$\delta \log_e = 2.303\,[\log_{10} 75 - \log_{10} 55]$$
$$\delta \times 1 = 2.303\,[1.8751 - 1.7404]$$
$$= 2.303\,[0.135]$$
$$= 0.31$$

$\therefore$ Damping $\quad \zeta = \frac{\delta}{2\pi} = \frac{0.31}{2 \times 3.142}$

$$= \frac{0.31}{6.284} = 0.049$$

Also $\quad \zeta = \frac{c}{c_c} = \frac{c}{2\sqrt{Km}}$

$\therefore \quad c = \zeta \times 2\sqrt{Km}$

$$= 0.049 \times 2\sqrt{1.8 \times 10^5 \times 12000}$$
$$= 0.049 \times 2\sqrt{1.8 \times 10^4 \times 1.3 \times 10^4}$$

$$= 0.098 \times 4.65 \times 10^4 = 0.4555 \times 10^4$$

$$= 4555 \text{ N–s/m}$$

Damped frequency $P_d = P\sqrt{1-\zeta^2}$

$$= 3.93\sqrt{1-(0.049)^2} = 3.92 \text{ rad/s}$$

$$x_n = x_0 e^{-6\delta} = 0.75 e^{-6(0.31)}$$

$$x_n = x_0 e^{-0.186}$$

$$= 0.75 \times 0.1559 = 0.1169 \text{ cm}$$

(**Note:** Calculations by log table)

Example 16. A mass spring system is provided with the coulomb damping system. To this system a mass of 12 kg is attached. The stiffness of the spring is 1500 N/m. The coefficient of friction of the system is 0.05. Determine

(*i*) Frequency of the vibration

(*ii*) No of cycles corresponding to 50% reduction in the amplitude if the initial amplitude is 8 cm.

(*iii*) Time taken in this 50% reduction.

Solution. Given data

$$m = 12 \text{ kg}$$

$$\mu = 0.05$$

$$K = 1500 \text{ N/m}$$

Frictional force $F = \mu m g$

$$= 0.05 \times 12 \times 9.81 = 5.886 \text{ N}$$

Natural frequency $P = \sqrt{\frac{K}{m}} = \sqrt{\frac{1500}{12}} = \sqrt{125}$

$$= 11.18 \text{ rad/s}$$

$$\approx 11.2 \text{ rad/s}$$

Frequency $f = \frac{P}{2\pi}$

$$= \frac{11.2}{2 \times 3.142} = 1.78 \text{ cycles/per sec.}$$

(*ii*) Amplitude after 50% reduction of the initial amplitude = 4.0 cm

Reduction in amplitude per cycle

$$= \frac{4F}{K}$$

$$= \frac{4 \times 5.886}{1500} = \frac{23.544}{1500}$$

$$= 1.57 \times 10^{-2} \text{ m} = 0.0157 \text{ m} = \approx 15.7 \text{ mm}$$

Cycles to be completed in 50% reduction in amplitude

$$= \frac{0.04}{1.57 \times 10^{-2}}$$

$$= \frac{4}{1.57} = 2.6 \text{ cycles}$$

$$\approx 3.0 \text{ cycles}$$

(*iii*) Time taken in achieving 50% reduction

$$= 3\,T = 3 \times \frac{2\,\pi}{P}$$

$$= 3 \times \frac{2\,\pi}{11.18} = \frac{6 \times 3.142}{11.18}$$

$$= 1.7 \text{ seconds } \textbf{Ans.}$$

Table 4.1. Damping ratio for various building materials

Material	*Damping ratio* ζ
Brick	5 to 7%
Concrete	5%
Clay	8 to 10%
Wood	12%
Steel	< 2%

Table 4.2. Damping ratios for structures

Type of structure	*Damping ratio* (ζ)
Timber shear wall construction	15%
Masonry or concrete shear wall construction	10%
Concrete frames with concrete or masonry shear walls	10%
Concrete frames with stiff cladding with all internal walls flexible	7%
Concrete frames with all walls flexible	5%
Steel frames welded or bolted with concrete shear walls	7%
Steel frames welded or bolted with stiff cladding and all internal walls flexible	5%
Steel frames, welded with all the walls of flexible materials	2%

Note:

1. Frames indicate beam and column bending structures distinct from shear structures.
2. Concrete includes R.C.C. and prestressed concrete in buildings.

QUESTIONS

1. Discuss the types of vibrations, which can be developed in a structure.
2. Discuss the degree of freedom of vibrations of a building.
3. Write an essay on Damping. How many kinds of damping you know explain fully. Also write the factors which influence the damping.
4. What do you understand by the term degree of freedom? Explain.
5. During an experiment of free vibration, it has been observed that maximum amplitude has reduced 0.4 times its original value in 3 complete cycles. Determine the value of the damping of the system. [$\zeta = 4.87\%$]
6. Vibrations in buildings can be developed
   (*a*) By working of machines (*b*) By blasting
   (*c*) Flowing water (*d*) By earthquake
   (*e*) By all the above actions
7. The vibrations developed in houses are of the type
   (*a*) Extensional (*b*) Bending
   (*c*) Shear (*d*) Torsional
   (*e*) All are correct
8. The forces which cause loss of energy are called......
   (*a*) Exciting forces (*b*) Amplification forces
   (*c*) Damping forces (*d*) All are correct
9. Damping may be of the of type......
   (*a*) Dry friction damping (*b*) Viscous damping
   (*c*) Negative damping (*d*) All are correct
10. Damping of a structure depends upon......
    (*a*) Nature of the material of the structure
    (*b*) Quality of construction
    (*c*) Nature of joints
    (*d*) Type of foundation and its nature
    (*e*) All are correct.
11. A mass of 100 kg is attached to a horizontal cantilever beam through a linear spring K_2. The thickness of the cantilever beam is 0.8 cm and width 1.2 cm. Take
    $E = 2.1 \times 10^6$ kg/cm^2
    $L = 20$ cms and stiffness of spring $K = 10$ kg/cm.
    Determine the natural frequency and natural period of the system.
    [Ans. $P = 9.2$ rad/sec., $T = 0.68$ sec.]
12. A vibrating system has the following data
    (*i*) Stiffness of spring $K = 160$ N/m
    (*ii*) Damping coefficient $C = 5$ N-s/m
    (*iii*) Mass $m = 2$ kg.
    (*a*) Calculate the decrease in amplitude from its initial value after 3 complete vibrations.
    (*b*) Frequency of vibration P. **[Ans.** (*a*) 0.48 cm, $P = 8.85$ cps]
13. The weight of a building is 200 kN. It is set to vibrate freely by releasing it ($t = 0$) from a displacement of 12 cms. If the maximum displacement of the

return swing is 8.0 cm at time 0.64 seconds. Determine

(*a*) Spring stiffness K

(*b*) Damping ratio

(*c*) Damping coefficient

[**Ans.** K = 19.5 10^5 N/m, Damping ratio = 0.064, Damping coefficient C = 25.68 kN-s/m]

14. A structure's model oscillates as a damped structure. The stiffness of the structure K is 5 kN/m, and undamped natural frequency P is 25 rad/s. A force of 1 N applied to the model is found to produce a relative velocity of 10 cm/s in the damping elements. Determine

(*i*) Damping ratio

(*ii*) Damped period

(*iii*) Logarimathic decrement

(*iv*) The ratio between two consecutive amplitude.

[**Ans.** (*i*) Damping ratio = 0.025, (*ii*) Damping time Td = 0.254, (*iii*) δ = 0.157, (*iv*) x_1/x_2 = 1.17]

ANSWERS

6. (*e*)
7. (*e*)
8. (*c*)
9. (*d*)
10. (*e*)

5

Vibrations of Multiple Degree of Freedom System

5.1. INTRODUCTION

In the previous chapter, vibrations of a systems which can be approximated as having a single mass constrained to move in one direction (translational or rotational) only were considered. In some systems though masses are approximated as a single mass, but the mass may have more than one degree of freedom. The machine foundation is a good example of such a system. The foundation of a machine is approximated as a single mass having translational and rotational freedom. In systems where a large number of masses are connected with each other and each mass is constrained to have only one direction of freedom, the system as a whole has as may degrees of freedom as there are masses. In general, the number of degree of freedom of the system will be equal to the sum of the degree of each discrete mass into which the system has been lumped. For studying the seismic effects on actual structures, the analysis of the behaviour of multimass system is necessary.

5.2. BEHAVIOUR OF MULTIMASS SYSTEM

For analysing the behaviour of multimass system, consider frame work of a five storeyed building shown in Fig. 5.1 (*a*). In the analysis of multi storey buildings, usually the masses are assumed to be lumped (acting) at the floor levels. The value of lumped mass is assumed to be corresponding to the weight of the floor, part of the supporting system (columns) above and below the floor and effective live load. The restoring forces (spring effect) are provided by the supporting system. Such an idealism is shown in Fig. 5.1 (*b*). In case the horizontal vibrations in the plane of the frame are considered, each mass would have one degree of freedom. The entire system would have five degree of freedom. Let the system is set to vibrate in such a way that all masses attain maximum amplitude simultaneously and also all masses pass through the position of equilibrium simultaneously. In such a condition the system is said to vibrate in its *natural* or *normal* or *Principal mode of vibration.*

If there is no damping in the system, then the response in such a mode of vibration would be harmonic and correspond to one of the unique frequencies of the system called as *natural* or *principal frequency*. In the further discussion

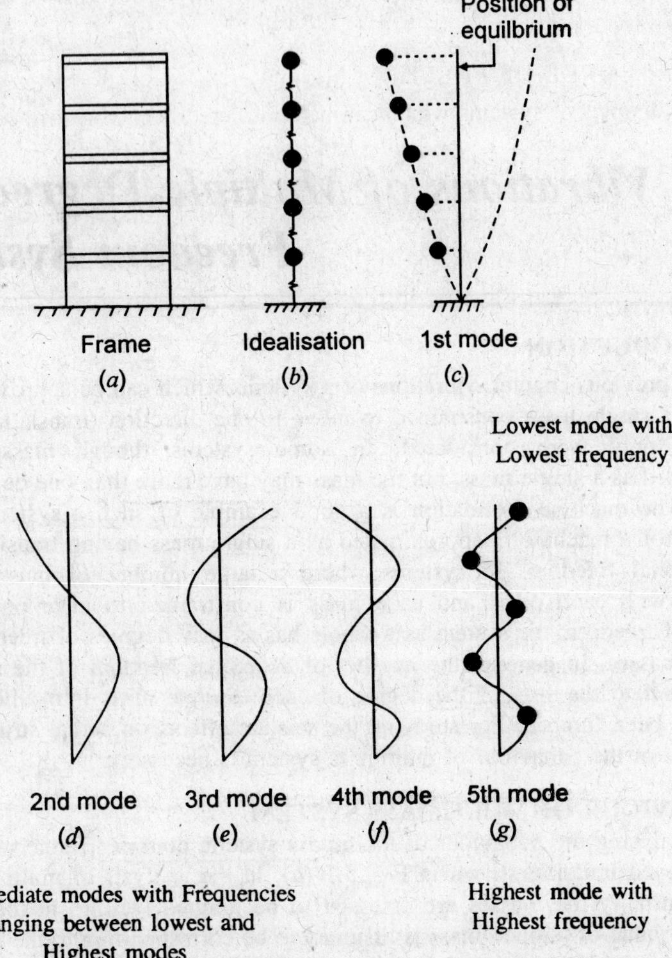

Fig. 5.1. A Five Storeyed Frame-Idealisation and Mode Shapes

of the mode of the frequency the term mode of vibration would imply natural or principal frequency. The various modes for five degree of freedom system are shown in Fig. 5.1 (*c*) to (*g*).

If all the masses vibrate in phase, the mode is known a *first* or *lowest* or *fundamental mode of vibration* and the frequency of the mode would be lowest in magnitude compared to other frequencies. In this case all the masses will have the same sign of amplitude at any particular instant of time as shown in Fig. 5.1 (*c*).

In case all adjacent masses vibrate out of phase with each other, the mode is known as highest mode of vibration and the frequency in the mode would be highest in magnitude compared to other modes. In this case the adjacent masses will have opposite sign of magnitude at any particular instant of time as shown in Fig. 5.1 (*g*).

5.3. TWO DEGREE OF FREEDOM

The examples of systems which can be considered as having two degree of freedom are as follows:

1. Two storeyed structures
2. Two single storeyed structures connected by a flexible link
3. A rigid foundation block subjected to translation and rocking motions
4. Vibration absorbers. The line diagram of all these systems are shown in Fig. 5.2.

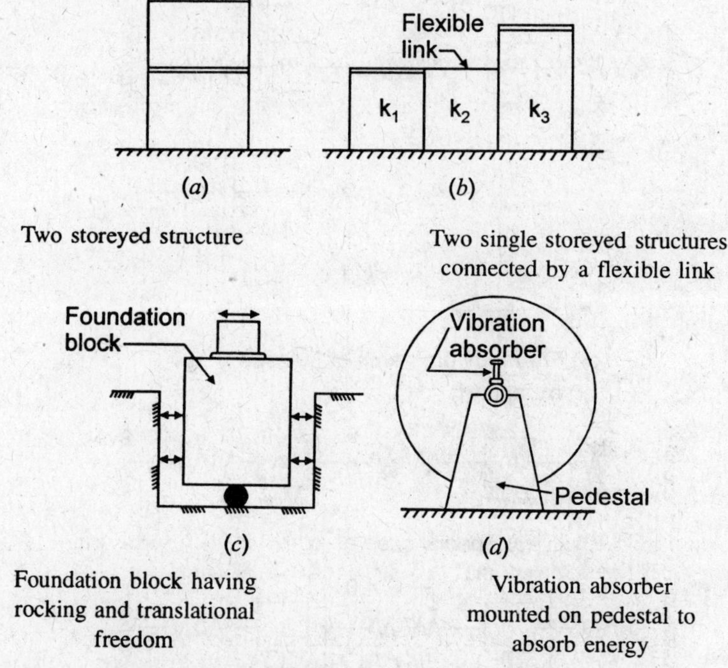

Fig. 5.2. Example of Two-Degree Freedom Systems

5.3.1. Un damped free vibrations

The system shown in Fig. 5.2 (*b*) can be considered as that of two single degree of freedom system coupled with an elastic connection having a spring constant K_2 as shown in Fig. 5.3 (*a*). Consider the free body diagram of the masses m_1 and m_2 as shown in Fig. 5.3 (*b*). Then from Newton's law we get

1. For mass m_1, $m_1 \ddot{x}_1 = -k_1 x_1 - k_2 (x_1 - x_2)$ ...[5.1 (*a*)]
2. For mass m_2, $m_2 \ddot{x}_2 = -k_3 x_2 - k_2 (x_2 - x_1)$ ...[5.1 (*b*)]

Re arranging equation 5.1 (*a*) and 5.1 (*b*) we get.

$$m_1 \ddot{x}_1 + (k_1 + k_2) x_1 - k_2 x_2 = 0 \quad \ldots[5.2\ (a)]$$

$$m_2 \ddot{x}_2 + (k_2 + k_3) x_2 - k_2 x_1 = 0 \quad \ldots[5.2\ (b)]$$

Assuming that the system vibrates in its natural mode with circular natural frequency '*P*' the motion can be described as

$$x_1 = A_1 \sin pt \ \ldots[5.3\ (a)]$$

$$x_2 = A_2 \sin pt \ \ldots[5.3\ (b)]$$

$$\left[\therefore \quad \frac{dx}{dt} = \dot{x} = Ap \cos pt \qquad \frac{d^2 x}{dt^2} = \ddot{x} = -Ap^2 \sin pt \right.$$

In equation 5.3 (*a*) and (*b*) A_1 and A_2 denote the maximum amplitude of

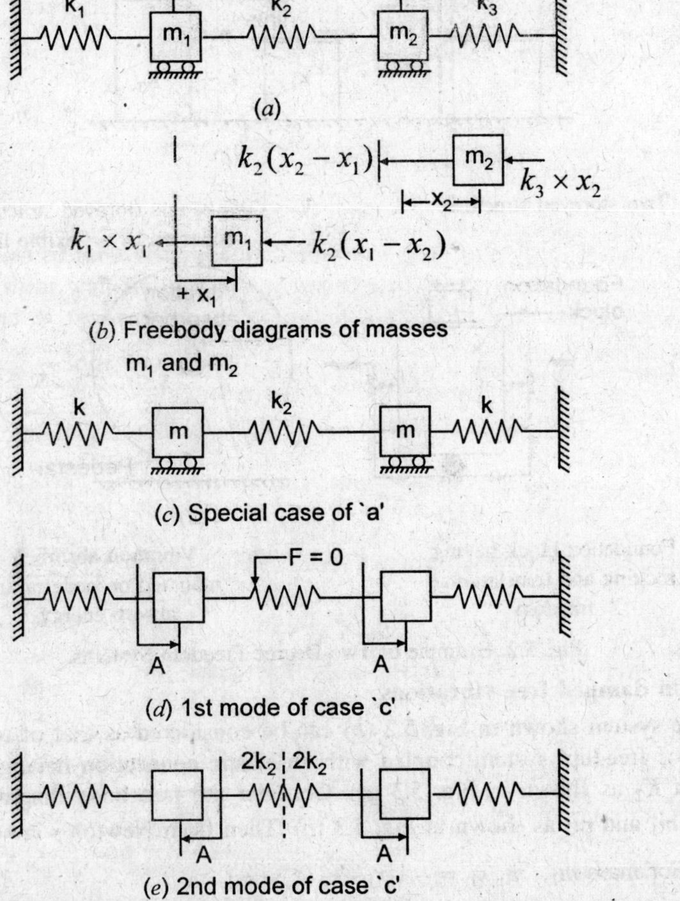

Fig. 5.3. A Two Degree of Freedom System with an Intermediate coupling spring

mass m_1 and m_2 respectively.

Substituting values of x_1 and x_2 from equation 5.3 (*a*) and (*b*) in equation 5.2 (*a*) and (*b*).

$$\therefore \quad -m_1 A_1 p^2 \sin pt + (K_1 + K_2) A_1 \sin pt - K_2 A_2 \sin pt = 0 \quad \text{...[5.4 (a)]}$$

Similarly

$$-m_2 A_2 p^2 \sin pt + (K_2 + K_3) A_2 \sin \omega t - K_2 A_2 \sin pt = 0 \quad \text{...[5.4 (b)]}$$

as sin *pt* is common in all terms, dividing both equation by sin *Pt* and rearranging we get,

$$(K_1 + K_2 - m_1 p^2) A_1 - K_2 A_2 = 0 \quad \text{...[5.5 (a)]}$$

$$(K_2 + K_3 - m_2 p^2) A_2 - K_2 A_1 \quad \text{...[5.5 (b)]}$$

$$\therefore \quad \text{From equation 5.5 (a)} \quad \frac{A_1}{A_2} = \frac{K_2}{(K_1 + K_2 - m_1 p^2)} \quad \text{...[5.6 (a)]}$$

$$\text{From eqaution 5.5 (b)} \quad \frac{A_1}{A_2} = \frac{K_2 + K_3 - m_2 p^2}{K_2} \quad \text{...[5.6 (b)]}$$

equating the ratio of $\frac{A_1}{A_2}$ we get.

$$\frac{K_2}{(K_1 + K_1 - m_1 p^2)} = \frac{K_2 + K_3 - m_2 p^2}{K_2} \quad \text{...(5.7)}$$

or $$(K_1 + K_2 - m_1 p_1^2)(K_2 + K_3 - m_2 p^2) - K_2^2 = 0 \quad \text{...(5.8)}$$

In equation 5.8 all quantities except the frequency term *P* are known. Hence this equation is known as *frequency equation*. The frequency equation can also be obtained by solving equation 5.5 (*a*) and 5.5 (*b*) by putting the determinant of the coefficients equal to zero as

$$\begin{vmatrix} K_1 + K_2 - m_1 p^2 & -K_2 \\ -K_2 & K_2 + K_3 - m_2 p^2 \end{vmatrix} = 0 \quad \text{...(5.8 a)}$$

Equation 5.9 is called frequency determinant.

Solving equation 5.8 we get.

$$p^4 - p^2 \left[\frac{k_1 + k_2}{m_1} + \frac{k_2 + k_3}{m_2} \right] + \frac{k_1 k_2 + k_2 k_3 + k_1 k_3}{m_1 m_2} = 0 \quad \text{...(5.9)}$$

As the last term is always positive, hence the solution of equation 5.9 will always give two positive roots P_1^2 and P_2^2. The two real roots P_1 and P_2 give the two natural frequencies of the system.

Let us consider a special case, when the two masses m_1 and m_2 are equal. Also the spring stiffness are equal *i.e.*

$$m_1 = m_2 = m \text{ and } k_1 = k_2 = k_3 = k, \text{ then equation 5.9 reduce to}$$

$$p^4 - \frac{4k}{m}p^2 + \frac{3k^2}{m^2} = 0 \quad \ldots(5.10) \qquad \left\{ \begin{aligned} & ax^2 + bx + c = 0 \\ & x = \frac{-b \pm \sqrt{4b^2 - 4ac}}{2a} \end{aligned} \right.$$

The roots of equation 5.10 will be as

$$p^2 = \frac{-4K/m \pm \sqrt{(4K/m)^2 - 4 \times 3K/m^2}}{2}$$

$$= \frac{-4K/m \pm \sqrt{16K^2/m^2 - 12K^2/m^2}}{2}$$

$$= \frac{-4K/m \pm 2K/m}{2}$$

$\therefore$ $\qquad p_1^2 = -K/m$

or $\qquad p_2^2 = -3K/m$

p_2^2 can be written as $\dfrac{K + 2K_2}{m}$ as $(K_1 = K_2 = K_3 = K)$

$\therefore$ Roots of the equation 5.10 are $p_1^2 = \dfrac{K}{m}$

and $\qquad p_2^2 = \dfrac{K + 2K_2}{m} \qquad \ldots(5.11)$

From equation 5.5 (*a*) $A_1^{(1)} = \dfrac{K_2}{K_1 + K_2 - m p_1^2} A_2^{(1)} = A_2^{(1)} \qquad \ldots[5.12\ (a)]$

and $\qquad A_1^{(2)} = \dfrac{K_2}{K_1 + K_2 - m p_1^2} A_2^{(2)} = -A_2^{(2)} \ldots[5.12\ (b)]$

The superscript (upper value) denote the mode of vibration and the subscript (lower value) denote the serial number of the mass.

The two frequencies correspond to distinct configuration of the system. Fig. 5.3 (*d*) and 5.3 (*e*). In the first mode, the two masses have the same amplitude and direction. Hence the force in the connecting spring is zero and the system behaves as two independent single degree of freedom systems. The value of frequency is given as P^2 = k/m. In the second mode, the amplitudes are equal but opposite in direction, hence a node is created at the middle of the spring K_2.

With a mode at the middle, the length of the connecting spring is equivalent to half of its actual length. The spring constant K is inversely proportional to its length. The equivalent spring constant would be $2K_2$. The equivalent single degree of freedom system is shown in Fig. 5.3 (*e*) which gives a frequency of $p^2 = \dfrac{K + 2K_2}{m}$.

Similar to sine solution as given in equation 5.3 (*a*) and 5.3 (*b*), there may also be a cosine solution to equation 5.2. The complete solution of equation 5.2 is gives as

$$x_1 = A_1^{(1)} \sin p_1 t + B_1^{(1)} \cos p_1 t + A_1^{(2)} \sin p_2 t + B_1^2 \cos p_2 t \quad ...[5.13\ (a)]$$

$$x_2 = A_2^{(1)} \sin p_1 t + B_2^{(1)} \cos p_1 t + A_2^{(2)} \sin p_2 t + B_2^{(2)} \cos p_2 t \quad ...[5.13\ (b)]$$

From equations 5.4 and 5.6, it can be seen that the ratio of amplitudes A_1 and A_2 of two masses in any one mode is constant. Also if in equation 5.3, the relation written in terms of cosine instead sine as

$$x_1 = A_1 \cos pt$$

and

$$x_2 = A_2 \cos pt$$

even then the frequency relation of equation 5.6 will be the same. Let (*a*) and (*b*) denote the ratios of amplitude of the two masses in the two modes for sine and cosine then

$$\frac{A_1^{(1)}}{A_2^{(1)}} = a = \frac{B_1^{(1)}}{B_2^{(1)}} \quad ...[5.14\ (a)]$$

and

$$\frac{A_1^{(2)}}{A_2^{(2)}} = b = \frac{B_1^{(2)}}{B_2^{(2)}} \quad ...[5.14\ (b)]$$

Thus the amplitudes constants A and B can be determined from the initial condition at $t = 0$ of the displacements and velocities of the masses.

Let x_{10} and x_{20} be the initial displacements and $\dot{x}_{10}$ and $\dot{x}_{20}$ be the initial velocities. Then from equations 5.13 and 5.14 we have,

$$x_{10} = aB_2^{(1)} + b\,B_2^{(2)} \quad ...[5.15\ (a)]$$

$$x_{20} = B_2^{(1)} + B_1^{(2)} \quad ...[5.15\ (b)]$$

Multiplying equation 5.15 (*b*) by (*b*) and subtrating equation 5.15 (*a*) from 5.15 (*b*) we get

$$bx_{20} = b\,B_2^{(1)} + b\,B_1^{(2)}$$

$$x_{10} = a\,B_2^{(1)} + b\,B_2^{(2)}$$

$$- \qquad - \qquad -$$

$$bx_{20} - x_{10} = b\,B_2^{(1)} - a\,B_2^{(1)}$$

or

$$bx_{20} - x_{10} = B_2^{(1)}(b - a)$$

$$\therefore \quad B_2^{(1)} = \frac{bx_{20} - x_{10}}{(b-a)}$$

and

$$B_2^{(2)} = \frac{ax_{20} - x_{10}}{a - b} \quad ...5.16)$$

By differentiating equation 5.13 (*a*) and 5.13 (*b*) once with respect to time *t*., we get

$$\frac{dx_{10}}{dt} = \dot{x}_{10} = A_1^{(1)} p_1 \cos p_1 t - B_1^{(1)} p_1 \sin p_1 t$$

$$+ A_1^{(2)} p_2 \cos p_2 t - B_1^{(2)} p_2 \sin p_2 t = 0$$

$$\frac{dx_{20}}{dt} = x_{20} = A_2^{(1)} p_1 \cos p_1 t - B_2^{(1)} p_1 \sin p_1 t$$

$$+ A_2^{(2)} p_2 \cos p_2 t - B_2^{(2)} p_2 \sin p_2 t = 0$$

Putting $t = 0$, $\sin 0 = 0$ and $\cos 0 = 1$, we get.

$$\dot{x}_{10} = A_1^{(1)} p_1 + A_1^{(2)} p_2 \quad \text{...[5.17 (a)]}$$

$$\dot{x}_{20} = A_2^{(1)} p_1 + A_2^{(2)} p_2 \quad \text{...[5.17 (b)]}$$

From equation 5.14 (*a*) and (*b*) $A_1^{(1)} = a = \dfrac{B_2^{(1)}}{B_2^{(2)}}$

and $$\frac{A_1^{(2)}}{A_2^{(2)}} = b = \frac{B_1^2}{B_2^2} \quad \text{...(5.18)}$$

$$\dot{x}_{10} = p_1\, a\, A_2^{(1)} + p_2 A_2^{(2)}\, b \quad \text{...[5.19 (a)]}$$

$$\dot{x}_{20} = p_1 A_2^{(1)} + p_2 A_2^{(2)} \quad \text{...[5.19 (b)]}$$

Similar to equation 5.15, we get from 5.19 (*a*) and (*b*)

then $$A_2^{(1)} = \frac{b\,\ddot{x}_{20} - \dot{x}_{10}}{p_1\,(b-a)}$$

and $$A_2^{(2)} = \frac{a\,\ddot{x}_{20} - \dot{x}_{10}}{p_2\,(a-b)} \quad \text{...(5.20)}$$

Example 1. A two storeyed building is shown in Fig. 5.4 (*a*). The building is given free vibrations by giving a initial displacement of 20 cm to the upper storey of the building. With the given data, find out the full solution of the problem.

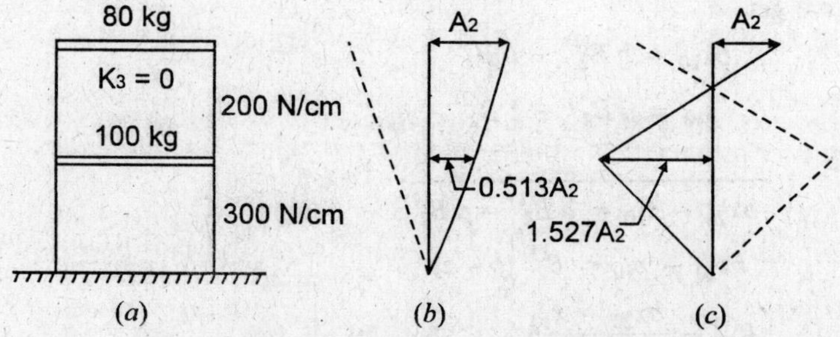

Fig. 5.4. Free Vibration of a Two Storeyed Structure

$$m_1 = 100 \text{ kg}$$

$$m_2 = 80 \text{ kg}$$

$$K_1 = 300 \text{ N/cm}$$

and $$K_2 = 200 \text{ N/cm}$$

$$K_3 = 0$$

Solution. The solution of equation 5.1 is to be determined with the help of given data

The solution is given by the following equation. (Taking K per metre length)

$$p^4 - p^2\left(\frac{K_1 + K_2}{m_1} + \frac{K_2 + K_3}{m_2}\right) + \frac{K_1 K_2 + K_2 K_3 + K_3 K_1}{m_1 m_2} = 0$$

Putting the values of K in metre we get,

$$p^4 - p^2\left[\frac{300 \times 100 + 200 \times 100}{100} + \frac{200 \times 100}{80}\right]$$

$$+ \frac{300 \times 100 + 200 \times 100}{100 \times 80} = 0$$

or $$p^4 - 750\, p^2 + 75000 = 0$$

$$\therefore \quad p^2 = \frac{-(-750) \pm \sqrt{(-750)^2 - 4 \times 1 \times 75000}}{2} = \frac{750 \pm \sqrt{512.3}}{2}$$

$$\therefore \quad p_1^2 = 110 \text{ sec}^{-2},\ p_2^2 = 631.0 \text{ sec}^{-2}$$

From equation 5.5 and 5.14 we have

$$a = \frac{A_1^{(1)}}{A_2^{(2)}} = \frac{B_1^{(1)}}{B_2^{(2)}} = \frac{K_2}{K_1 + K_2 - m_1 p_1^2}$$

$$= \frac{200 \times 100}{100\,(300 + 200) - 100 \times 110}$$

$$= \frac{200}{500 - 110} = \frac{200}{390} = \frac{20}{39} = 0.513$$

$$b = \frac{A_1^{(2)}}{A_2^{(2)}} = \frac{B_1^{(2)}}{B_2^{(2)}} = \frac{K_2}{K_1 + K_2 - m_1 p_2^2}$$

$$= \frac{200 \times 100}{100\,(300 + 200) - 100 \times 631} = \frac{200}{-131}$$

$$b = -1.527$$

The mode shapes are shown in Fig. 5.4 (*b*) and (*c*). The arbitrary constants A and B can be determined from equations 5.16 and 5.20

From initial conditions, $x_{10} = 20$ cm, $x_{20} = 0$ and $\dot{x}_{10} = \dot{x}_2 = a$

$$B_2^{(1)}\ \frac{x_{10}}{a - b} = \frac{20}{0.513 - (-1.527)}$$

$$= \frac{20}{2.042} = 9.8$$

$$B_2^{(2)} = \frac{x_{10}}{b-a} = \frac{20}{-(1.527) - (0.513)}$$

$$= -\frac{20}{2.040} = -9.8$$

$A_2^{(1)} = 0, A_2^{(2)} = 0,$

$$\therefore \quad \frac{a}{1} = \frac{B_1^{(1)}}{B_2^{(2)}}$$

$$\therefore \quad B_1^{(1)} = B_2^{(2)} \times a = 9.8 \times 0.513 = 5.03 \text{ cm}$$

$$B_1^{(2)} = B_2^{(2)} \times b = -9.8 \times (-1.527) = 14.9 \text{ cm}$$

$$A_1^{(1)} = A_2^{(2)} = 0$$

∴ Complete solution is obtained frοm eqation 5.13

$$x_1 = B_1^{(1)} \cos p_1 t + B_1^{(2)} \cos p_2 t \quad \ldots(i)$$

$$x_2 = B_2^{(1)} \cos p_1 t + B_2^{(2)} \cos p_2 t \quad \ldots(ii)$$

In equation (*i*) and (*ii*) putting the values of $B_1^{(1)}, B_2^{(2)}$, we get

$$\left.\begin{aligned} x_1 &= 5.03 \cos p_1 t + 14.9 \cos p_2 t \\ x_2 &= 9.8 \cos p_1 t - 9.8 \cos p_2 t \end{aligned}\right\} \textbf{Ans.}$$

Example 2. Two single storeyed structures of equal mass 80 kg are linked together by a spring. The mass is supposed as lumped at two points linked by a spring as shown in Fig. 5.5 (*a*). Find out the complete solution of the system by the given conditions:

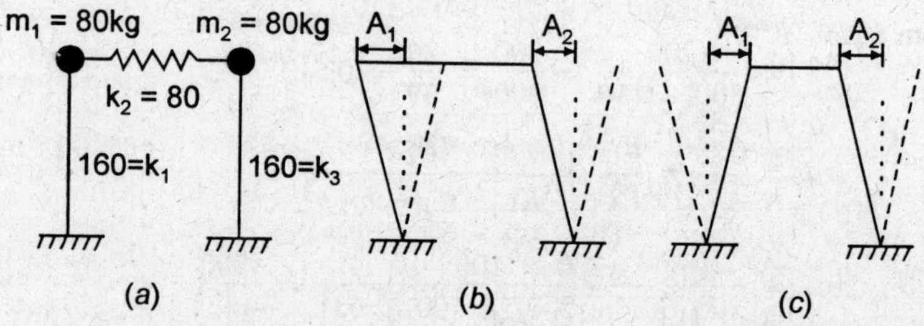

Fig. 5.5. Free Vibration of Another Two Degree of Freedom System

(*i*) The system is given equal initial displacement of 20 cm in phase for both masses.

(*ii*) The system is given equal initial displacement of 20 cm, 180° out of phase for both masses. The value of masses and spring stiffness are shown in the diagram of Fig. 5.5 (*a*) (1 kg = 10 N).

Solution. As per problem $m_1 = m_2 = 80$ kg.

$$K_1 = K_3 = 160 \text{ N/cm} = 16 \text{ kN/m}$$
$$K_2 = 80 \text{ N/cm} = 8 \text{ kN/m}$$

From equation 5.9, we have

$$p^4 - p^2\left[\frac{K_1 + K_2}{m_1} + \frac{K_2 + K_3}{m_2}\right] + \frac{K_1 \times K_2 + K_2 K_3 + K_3 K_1}{m_1 m_2} = 0 \quad \ldots(1)$$

Putting the values of m_1 and m_2 and K_1, K_2 and K_3 etc. in equation (1) we get

$$p^4 - p^2\left[\frac{160 \times 100 + 80 \times 100}{80} + \frac{80 \times 100 + 160 \times 100}{m_1 m_2}\right]$$
$$+ \frac{10^4 [(160 \times 80) + (80 \times 160) + (160 \times 160)]}{80 \times 80}$$
$$= p^4 - p^2\left[\frac{100\,(240)}{80} + \frac{100\,(240)}{80}\right]$$
$$+ \frac{10^4 (12800 + 12800 + 25600)}{80 \times 80} = 0$$

or $$p^4 - 600\,p^2 + 80000 = 0$$

$\therefore$ $$p^2 = \frac{+600 \pm \sqrt{(600)^2 - 320000}}{2} = \frac{600 \pm \sqrt{40000}}{2}$$
$$= \frac{600 \pm 200}{2}$$

or $$p_1^2 = 200 \text{ sec}^{-2} \text{ and } p_2^2 = 400 \text{ sec}^{-2}$$

From equation 5.14

$$a = \frac{A_1^{(1)}}{A_2^{(2)}} = \frac{B_1^{(1)}}{B_2^2} = \frac{K_2}{K_1 + K_2 - m_1 p_1^2}$$
$$= \frac{80 \times 100}{100\,(160 + 80) - 200 \times 80}$$
$$= \frac{80 \times 100}{240 \times 100 - 100\,(160)} = \frac{80}{80} = 1$$

$$b = \frac{A_1^2}{B_2^{(2)}} = \frac{B_1^{(2)}}{B_2^{(2)}} \cdot \frac{K_2}{K_1 + K_2 - m_2 p_2^2}$$
$$= \frac{80 \times 100}{160 \times 100 + 80 \times 100 - 400 \times 80}$$
$$= \frac{80}{240 - 320} = \frac{80}{-80} = -1$$

The mode shape are shown in Fig. 5.5 (*b*) and (*c*). The arbitrary constants A and B can be determined from 5.16 and 5.20.

(*a*) From initial condition $x_{10} = x_{20} = 20$ cm and velocity $\dot{x}_{10} = \dot{x}_{20} = 0$

From equation 5.16

$$B_2^{(1)} = \frac{b\,x_{20} - x_{10}}{b - a}$$

$$= \frac{(-1)(20) - 20}{(-1) - (1)} = -\frac{40}{-2} = 20$$

and $$B_2^{(2)} = \frac{a\,x_{20} - x_{10}}{a - b}$$

$$= \frac{1 \times 20 - 20}{1 - (-1)} = \frac{0}{2} = 0$$

$A_2^{(1)} = 0,\ A_2^{(2)} = 0.$

$$a = \frac{B_1^{(1)}}{B_2^{(1)}} = B_1^{(1)},$$

$$\therefore \quad a \times B_2^{(1)} = 1 \times 20 = 20$$

$$\therefore \quad B_2^{(1)} = 1 \times 20 = 20 = B_1^{(1)}$$

$$b = \frac{B_1^{(2)}}{B_2^{(2)}} = B_1^{(2)}$$

$$\therefore \quad b\,B_2^{(2)} = -1 \times 0 = 0$$

as $$B_2^{(2)} = 0\,B_1^{(2)}$$

$$A_1^2 = 0,\ A_2^2 = 0$$

Thus $$A_1^{(2)} = A_2^{(2)} = 0$$

$$B_2^{(1)} = 20 \text{ and } B_2^{(2)} = 0$$

Hence complete solution is given as

$$\left.\begin{aligned} x_1 &= 20 \cos p_1 t \\ x_2 &= 20 \cos p_1 t \end{aligned}\right\} \textbf{Ans.}$$

(*b*) From initial conditions,

$$x_{10} = 20 = x_{20}$$

$$\dot{x}_{10} = 0 \text{ and } \dot{x}_{20} = 0$$

$$\left(\begin{aligned} x &= \text{displacement} \\ \dot{x} &= \text{velocity } (dx/dt) \end{aligned}\right)$$

$$B_1^{(1)} = \frac{bx_{20} - x_{10}}{b - a}$$

$$= \frac{-(1)(-2.0) - 20}{(-1) - 1} = \frac{0}{-2} = 0$$

$$B_2^{(2)} = \frac{1\,(-20) - 20}{1 + 1} = -20$$

$$A_2^{(1)} = A_2^{(2)} = 0$$

$$B_1^{(1)} = 0,\; B_2^{(2)} = 20$$

$$A_1^{(1)} = A_1^{2} = 0$$

Hence complete solution is

$$\left.\begin{aligned} x_1 &= 20 \cos p_2 t \\ x_2 &= -20 \cos p_2 t \end{aligned}\right\} \textbf{Ans.}$$

5.3.2. Forced vibrations of an undamped system

Consider an system whose one of the masses is subjected to steady state sinusoidal excitation as shown in Fig. 5.6. The equation of motion of the system is given by

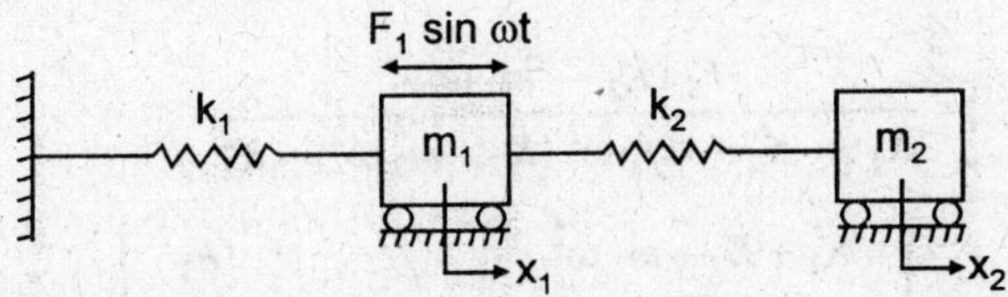

Fig. 5.6. Forced Vibration of a Two Degree of Freedom System

$$m_1 \ddot{x}_1 + K_1 x_1 + K_2 (x_1 - x_2) = F_1 \sin \omega t \qquad \text{...[5.21 (a)]}$$

$$m_2 \ddot{x}_2 + K_2 (x_2 - x_1) = 0 \qquad \text{...[5.21 (b)]}$$

For un damped systems, theoretically the transient (temporary) vibrations would exist indefinitely, but in practice some amount of damping exists and transients die down soon. Then system settles down to vibrate with the same frequency as that of the exciting force.

Assuming a harmonic solution of the motion of the system in terms of time at the same frequency as the forcing function and with the same amplitude of masses. Let the solution be

$$x_1 = A_1 \sin \omega t \qquad \text{...[5.22 (a)]}$$

$$x_2 = A_2 \sin \omega t \qquad \text{...[5.22 (b)]}$$

Differentiating twice equation 5.22 wet.

$$\dot{x}_1 = A_1 \omega \cos (\omega t) \qquad \text{...(i)}$$

$$\ddot{x}_1 = -A_1 \omega^2 \sin \omega t \qquad \text{...(ii)}$$

Similarly for $\dot{x}_2 = A_2 \omega \cos \omega t$ ...(*iii*)

$$\ddot{x}_2 = -A_2 \omega^2 \sin \omega t \qquad \text{...(iv)}$$

Putting the values of $\ddot{x}_1$ and $\ddot{x}_2$ and x_1 and x_2 in equation 5.21 (*a*)&(*b*) we get

$$m_1 (-A_1 \omega^2 \sin \omega t) + K_1 A_1 \sin \omega t + K_2 (A_1 - A_2) \sin \omega t = F_1 \sin \omega t \qquad \text{...[5.23 (a)]}$$

$$m_2 (-A_2 \omega^2 \sin \omega t) + K_2 (A_2 - A_1) \sin \omega t = 0 \qquad \text{...[5.23 (b)]}$$

Equating the coefficients of sin ωt of both sides of both equations we get

$$(K_1 + K_2 - m\,\omega_1^2) A_1 - K_2 A_2 = F_1 \qquad \text{...[5.24 (a)]}$$

$$-K_2 A_1 + (K_2 - m_2 \omega^2) A_2 = 0 \qquad \text{...[5.24 (b)]}$$

The value of A_1 and A_2 can be obtained by solving the determinants of the coefficients of A_1, A_2 as follows.

$$A_1 = \frac{\begin{vmatrix} F_1 & -K_2 \\ 0 & K_2 - m_2 \omega^2 \end{vmatrix}}{\begin{vmatrix} K_1 + K_2 - m_1 \omega^2 & -K_2 \\ -K_2 & K_2 - m_2 \omega^2 \end{vmatrix}}$$

$$= \frac{F_1 (K_2 - m_2 \omega^2)}{K_1 + K_2 - m_1 \omega^2 (K_2 - m_2 \omega^2) - K_2^2} \qquad \text{...[5.25 (a)]}$$

$$A_2 = \frac{\begin{vmatrix} K_1 + K_2 - m_1 \omega^2 & F_1 \\ -K_2 & 0 \end{vmatrix}}{\begin{vmatrix} K_1 + K_2 - m_1 \omega^2 & -K_2 \\ -K_2 & K_2 - m_2 \omega^2 \end{vmatrix}}$$

$$= \frac{F_1 K_2}{(K_1 + K_2 - m_1 \omega^2)(K_2 - m_2 \omega^2) - K_2^2} \qquad \text{...[5.25 (b)]}$$

The denominator of equation 5.25 would vanish if the forcing frequency 'ω' coincides with either of the two natural frequencies P_1 and P_2 of the system

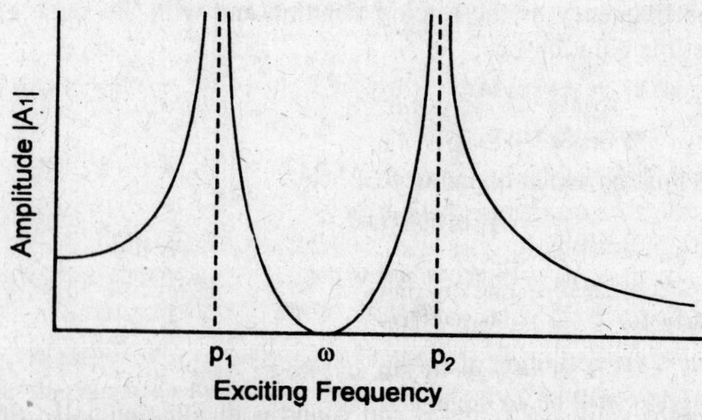

Fig. 5.7. Steady state dynamic response of a two degree of freedom system

(equation 5.8). Hence there would be two resonant peaks if a curve is drawn between the absolute value of amplitude as ordinate and exiting frequency ω as abscissa as shown in Fig. 5.7. From equation 5.25 (*a*), it can be seen that the numerator would be zero if $\omega^2 = \frac{K_2}{m_2}$. That is the amplitude of the mass which is subjected to a exciting force could be zero at a particular frequency. It can be explained physically, if the amplitude of the second mass is examined under these conditions. From equation 4.25 (*b*) for $\omega^2 = K_2/m_2$, we have

$$A_2 = \frac{F_1 K_2}{-K_2^2} = -\frac{F_1}{K_2} \qquad \text{...(5.25)}$$

Here $A_1 = 0$ and the spring force A_2K_2 acting on mass m_1 is equal to $-F_1$ which is equal and opposite to the exciting force. In such a design the second mass spring system is known as *dynamic vibration absorber.*

5.4. MANY DEGREE OF FREEDOM

The aim of solution of *n* degree freedom linear systems subjected to forced excitations is to decompose the system into *n* single degree of freedom systems for which solutions can be obtained easily. For this purpose the frequencies and mode shapes corresponding to undamped vibrations are needed. The methods to obtain these objectives are described in the following pages.

5.4.1. Undamped Vibrations

The equations of motion can be obtained either of the two methods:

1. By considering the equilibrium of forces on each mass.
2. By evaluating the displacement of mass due to forces on all masses.

Consider an multi degree spring mass system as shown in Fig. 5.8.

One of the masses say m_2 is given a unit displacement and all other masses are restrained at their equilibrium position.

Let K_{ij} is called as stiffness coefficients which denote the force on ith mass due to unit displacement at jth mass, while all other masses are held at their equilibrium position.

The force on mass 2 due to unit deflection of spring K_2 at level 2 would be $+K_2$ (This is the definition of spring force itself). There will be an equal and opposite reaction at level (1) and it

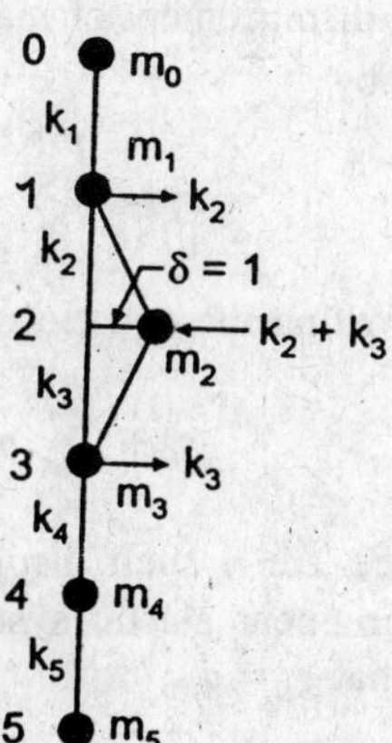

Fig. 5.8. An idealised multiple degree of freedom system with unit displacement applied to one of its mass

would be ($-K_2$). Similarly due to spring K_3 at level 2, the force on mass 2 will be (+ K_3) and at level 3 it would be $-K_3$. Thus the total force at mass 2 due to spring K_2 and K_3 would be $(K_2 + K_3)$.

That is

$$K_{12} = -K_2$$
$$K_{22} = K_2 + K_3$$
$$K_{32} = -K_3$$
$$K_{42} = 0$$

If the displacements of masses are denoted by x_j (where j can take values from 1 to n, then total spring force on mass i, due to displacements x_j of all masses is given as $\sum\limits_{j=1}^{n} K_{ij}\, x_j$ due to the summation of spring forces. Applying Newton's law for ith mass

$$m_i \ddot{x}_i + \sum_{j=1}^{n} K_{ij}\, x_j = 0 \qquad \text{...(5.26)}$$

There are n such equilibrium equations each corresponding to a mass. This procedure is called *stiffness method.* For linear elastic systems, from Maxwell's reciprocal relation $K_{ij} = K_{ji}$ can be shown.

The *second method.* This method is known as *flexibility* method. It is described below.

Let g_{ij} is termed as flexibility coefficient or influence. It represents the deflection at the ith mass due to unit load at *j*th mass. The system can be considered to be in an instantaneous state of static equilibrium under the influence of inertia forces acting on the masses.

The displacement of mass i due to inertia forces $m_j \ddot{x}_j$ action on all j masses is given by

$$x_i = -\sum_{j=1}^{n} (m_j \ddot{x}_j)\, g_{ij} \qquad \text{...[5.27 (a)]}$$

Rewriting the equations 5.27 we get

$$x_i + \sum_{j=1}^{n} m_j \ddot{x}_j\, g_{ij} = 0 \qquad \text{...[5.27 (b)]}$$

There are n such displacement equations each corresponding to a mass. again for linear elastic systems from Maxwell's reciprocal theorem it can be shown that $g_{ij} = g_{ji}$.

5.5. SOLUTION OF EQUATIONS OF MOTION

(a) Stiffness method

Let the system vibrates in one of its principal mode of vibration. Then the motion of the system will be sinusoidal with a frequency say P corresponding to the mode. Let the amplitudes of various masses be as $A_i(i = 1, 2, 3 \ldots n)$. The motion of any mass i can be expressed as

$$x_i = A_i \sin pt \qquad \ldots(5.28)$$

$$\dot{x}_i = A_i p \cos pt \qquad \ldots[5.28\ (a)]$$

$$\ddot{x}_i = -A_i p^2 \sin pt \qquad \ldots[5.28\ (b)]$$

Putting the value of x_i and $\ddot{x}_i$ from equation 5.28 in equation 5.26 we get

$$-m_i A_i p^2 \sin pt + \sum_{j=1}^{n} K_{ij} A_j \sin pt = 0$$

or

$$-m_i p^2 A_i + \sum_{j=1}^{n} K_{ij} A_j = 0 \qquad \ldots(5.29)$$

Putting $\lambda = P^2$, frequency determinant corresponding to equation 5.29 would be as

$$\begin{vmatrix} (K_{11} - m_1 \lambda) & K_{12} & K_{1n} \\ K_{22} & (K_{22} - m_2 \lambda) & K_{2n} \\ \cdots & \cdots & \cdots \\ \cdots & \cdots & \cdots \\ \cdots & \cdots & \cdots \\ K_{n1} & K_{n2} & (K_{nn} - m_n \lambda) \end{vmatrix} = 0 \qquad \ldots(5.30)$$

Expanding the determinant following type of frequency equation in polynomial form would be obtained.

$$A_0 + A_1 \lambda + \ldots A_{n-1} \lambda^{n-1} + (-1)^n (\lambda)^n = 0 \qquad \ldots(5.31)$$

As the coefficient of λ^n is not zero, equation 5.31 will have n roots. The roots would give n different frequencies of vibration namely $P_1, P_2, P_3 \ldots P_n$, corresponding to each value of P say P_r, there would be associated a mode shape with amplitudes which could be obtained by solving equation 5.29. These are identified as principal modes. When a system vibrates in a principal mode, all the masses attain maximum displacement simultaneously and also pass through their position of equilibrium simultaneously.

Taking few equations, the determinant of equation of 5.30 can be written as

$$\begin{vmatrix} (K_{11} - m_1\lambda) & K_{12} & K_{13} \\ K_{21} & (K_{22} - m_2\lambda) & K_{23} \\ K_{31} & K_{32} & K_{33} - m_3\lambda \end{vmatrix} = 0 \qquad \ldots(5.32)$$

Expanding determinant 5.32 we get

$$(K_{11} - \lambda m_1) [(K_{22} - m_2\lambda)(K_{33} - m_3 \lambda)] - K_{32} \times K_{23} - K_{12}$$
$$[K_{21} \times (K_{33} - m_3 \lambda) - K_{31} \times K_{23}]$$

$$+ K_{13} [K_{21} \times K_{32} - K_{31} (K_{22} - m_2 \lambda)] = 0 \qquad ...(5.33)$$

Equation 5.33 is of the form as given below

$$\lambda^2 - X\lambda^2 + C\lambda + m = 0$$

The factor of this equation can be determined. The solution of such a equation is illustrated by the following example.

Polynomial equation. By substracting the multiplication of unit matrix and some scalar quantity from an given matrix we get an polynomial equation. Let the given matrix

$$A = \begin{bmatrix} 3 & 2 & 1 \\ 1 & 2 & 3 \\ 1 & 3 & 2 \end{bmatrix} \text{ and } \lambda \text{ is a scalar quantity.}$$

$$\text{and unit matrix} = \begin{bmatrix} 1 & 0 & 0 \\ 0 & 1 & 0 \\ 0 & 0 & 1 \end{bmatrix}$$

Then characteristic matrix = given matrix A – λ times unit matrix.

Thus the characteristic matrix of given matrix

$$A = \begin{bmatrix} 3 & 2 & 1 \\ 1 & 2 & 3 \\ 1 & 3 & 2 \end{bmatrix} - \lambda \begin{bmatrix} 1 & 0 & 0 \\ 0 & 1 & 0 \\ 0 & 0 & 1 \end{bmatrix}$$

$$= \begin{bmatrix} (3-\lambda) & 2 & 1 \\ 1 & (2-\lambda) & 3 \\ 1 & 3 & (2-\lambda) \end{bmatrix}$$

The determinant of characteristic matrix

$$= \begin{vmatrix} (3-\lambda) & 2 & 1 \\ 1 & (2-\lambda) & 3 \\ 1 & 3 & (2-\lambda) \end{vmatrix} = 0$$

The expansion of the determinant will be

$$(3-\lambda)[(2-\lambda)(2-\lambda) - 3 \times 3] - 2[1 \times (2-\lambda) - 1 \times 3]$$

$$+ 1[1 \times 3 - 1(2-\lambda)]$$

$$= (3-\lambda)[\lambda^2 - 4\lambda - 5] + 2\lambda - 7 - 1 + \lambda = 0$$

$$= \lambda^3 - 7\lambda^2 + 4\lambda + 12 = 0$$

$$= (\lambda - 2)(\lambda - 6)(\lambda + 1) = 0$$

$$\therefore \quad \lambda = -1, 2, 6$$

Example. Consider a three degree of freedom system as shown in Fig. 5.9 (*a*) obtain the solution of free vibration by stiffness coefficient method.

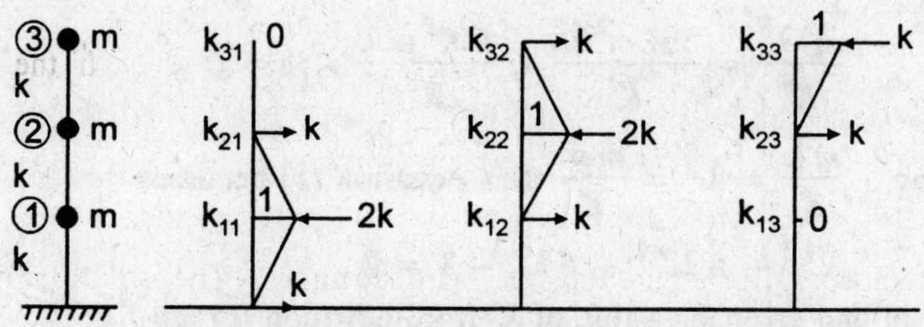

Fig. 5.9. Stiffness coefficient of a three degree of freedom system

Solution. The stiffness coefficients K_{ij} are shown in Fig. 5.9 and are as follows:

$$K_{11} = 2K, \; K_{21} = -K, \; K_{31} = 0$$

$$K_{22} = 2K, \; K_{12} = -K, \; K_{32} = -K$$

$$K_{33} = K, \; K_{23} = -K, \; K_{13} = 0$$

These coefficients are obtained by giving a unit deformation to the mass points successively. When a unit deformation is given to one mass, other mass points are held in their equilibrium position and forces which represent the stiffness coefficients are evaluated at all mass points.

The equation of motion of the system can be written from equation 5.26 as follows:

$$m\ddot{x}_1 + 2Kx_1 - Kx_2 = 0$$

$$m\ddot{x}_2 - Kx_1 + 2Kx_2 - Kx_3 = 0 \qquad \ldots(5.34)$$

$$m\ddot{x}_3 - Kx_2 + Kx_3 = 0$$

The corresponding frequency determinant from equation 5.30 can be written as follows:

$$\begin{vmatrix} (2K - m\lambda) & -K & 0 \\ -K & (2K - m\lambda) & -K \\ 0 & -K & (K - m\lambda) \end{vmatrix} \qquad \ldots(5.35)$$

The frequency equation can be obtained by expanding the determinant of equation 5.35.

$$(2K - m\lambda)[(2K - m\lambda)(K - m\lambda) - (-K)(-K)]$$

$$- [(-K)[(-K)(K - m\lambda) - 0 \times K \times K] + 0$$

$$= (2K - m\lambda)[(2K - m\lambda)(K - m\lambda)] - K^2 (K - m\lambda) - 0[\ldots] = 0$$

$$2K^3 - 7K^2 m\lambda + 5Km^2\lambda^2 - m^3\lambda^3 + K^2 m\lambda - K^3 = 0$$

or $$K^3 - 6K^2 m\lambda + 5Km^2\lambda^2 - m^3\lambda^3 = 0$$

or $$m^3\lambda^3 - 5Km^2\lambda^2 + 6K^2 m\lambda - K^3 = 0 \qquad \ldots[5.36\,(a)]$$

Dividing equation (*a*) by K^3 we get.

$$\frac{m^3 \lambda^3}{K^3} - \frac{5 K m^2 \lambda^2}{K^3} + \frac{6 K^2 m \lambda}{K^3} - 1 = 0 \quad \text{...[5.36 (b)]}$$

Putting $\frac{m \lambda}{K} = \lambda' = \frac{m p^2}{K}$ then equation (*b*) becomes

$$\lambda'^3 - 5\lambda'^2 + 6\lambda' - 1 = 0 \quad \text{...[5.36 (c)]}$$

By trial and error the value of λ' from equation (*c*) are

$$\lambda_1' = 0.198, \; \lambda_2' = 1.555, \; \lambda_3' = 3.247$$

For a single degree of freedom, λ' will be equal to 1.0

Putting $\lambda' = \frac{m p^2}{K}$

$$p_1^2 = 0.198 \text{ K/m}$$

$$p_2^2 = 1.555 \frac{K}{m}$$

and $p_3^2 = 3.247$ K/m

The amplitude coefficients for the three modes of vibrating can be obtained from equation 5.29 or 5.27 (*b*). From equation 5.29 we get the relation as below:

$$-mp^2 A_1 + 2 KA_1 - KA_2 + 0A_3 = 0 \quad \text{...[5.37 (i)]}$$

$$-m p^2 A_2 - KA_1 + 2 KA_2 + KA_3 = 0 \quad \text{...[5.37 (ii)]}$$

$$-m p^2 A_3 - 0 A_1 + KA_2 + KA_3 = 0 \quad \text{...[5.37 (iii)]}$$

Writing $\lambda' = \frac{mp^2}{K}$, the above equations from (*i*) to (*iii*) can be written as

$(-K\lambda' + 2K) A_1 - K A_2 = 0$ Dividing by *K*, we get

$$(2-\lambda') A_1 - A_2 = 0 \quad \text{...[5.37 (iv)]}$$

Similarly other equation will be

$$-A_1 + (2-\lambda') A_2 - A_3 = 0 \quad \text{...[5.37 (v)]}$$

$$-A_2 + (1-\lambda') A_3 = 0 \quad \text{...[5.37 (vi)]}$$

For convenience let us assume arbitratrily that

$$A_3^{(1)} = A_3^{(2)} = A_3^{(3)} = 1.0$$

As it is more convient to work with a simple numerical value than with ratios.

Then from equation 5.37 (*vi*) we get $A_2 = (1 - \lambda') A_3$

and from equation 5.36 (*iv*) we get $A_1 = \frac{A_2}{(2-\lambda')}$

Substituting the values of λ' found from equation 5.36 we get

	1st mode	**2nd mode**	**3rd mode**
A_1	0.445	– 1.247	1.802
A_2	0.802	– 0.555	– 2.247
A_3	1.0	1.0	1.0

The shapes of the mode are shown in Fig. 5.10.

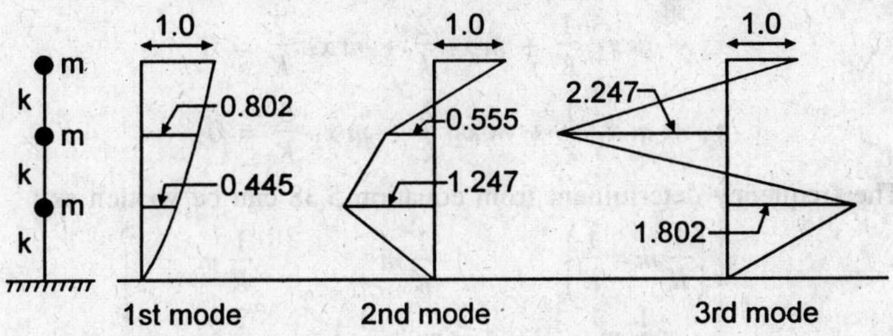

Fig. 5.10. Mode shapes of a three degrees of freedom system

Flexibility method

Proceeding in the similar manner as for stiffness method, the equation 5.27 (*b*) can be written as follows:

$$\begin{vmatrix} (m_1\, g_{11} - 1/\lambda) & m_2\, g_{12} & m_n\, g_{1n} \\ m_1\, g_{21} & (m_2\, g_{22} - 1/\lambda) & m_n\, g_{2n} \\ m_1\, g_{n1} & m_2\, g_{n2} & m_n\, g_{nn} - 1/\lambda \end{vmatrix} \quad \ldots(5.38)$$

Example. Solve the above problem with flexibility method. The influence coefficient g_{ij} are as follows which are shown in Fig. 5.11

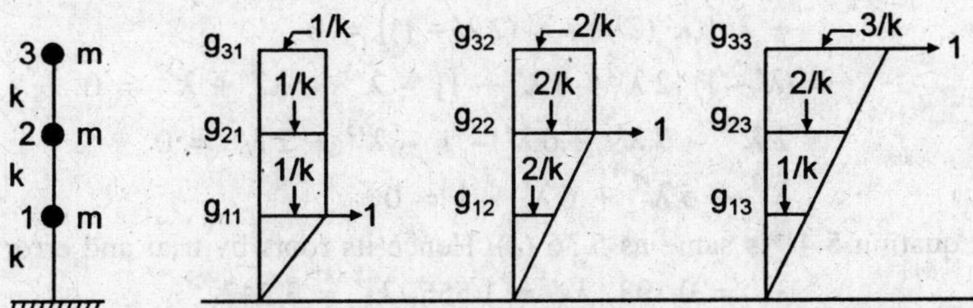

Fig. 5.11. Influence coefficient of a three degree of freedom system

$$g_{11} = \frac{1}{K},\ g_{21} = \frac{1}{K},\ g_{31} = \frac{1}{K}$$

$$g_{22} = \frac{2}{K},\ g_{12} = \frac{1}{K},\ g_{32} = \frac{2}{K}$$

$$g_{33} = \frac{3}{K},\ g_{13} = \frac{1}{K},\ g_{23} = \frac{2}{K}$$

Solution. The above values of flexibility coefficients have been obtained by applying successively a unit load to the mass points. The deflections at various mass points due to a unit load at one mass point corresponding to influence coefficients. The equation of motion of the system from equation 5.27 (*b*) we have as follows:

$$x_1 + m\ddot{x}_1 \frac{1}{K} + m\ddot{x}_2 \frac{1}{K} + m\ddot{x}_3 \frac{1}{k} = 0$$

$$x_2 + m\ddot{x}_1 \frac{1}{K} + m\ddot{x}_2 \frac{2}{k} + m\ddot{x}_3 \frac{2}{K} = 0$$

$$x_3 + m\ddot{x}_1 \frac{1}{k} + m\ddot{x}_2 \frac{2}{k} + m\ddot{x}_3 \frac{3}{K} = 0$$

The frequency determinant from equation 5.38 can be written as

$$\begin{vmatrix} \left(\frac{1}{K}m - \frac{1}{\lambda}\right) & \frac{1}{K}m & \frac{1}{K}m \\ \frac{1}{K}m & \left(\frac{2}{K}m - \frac{1}{\lambda}\right) & \frac{2}{K}m \\ \frac{1}{K}m & \frac{2}{K}m & \left(\frac{3}{K}m - \frac{1}{\lambda}\right) \end{vmatrix} = 0 \quad \text{...(5.39)}$$

Multiplying the above determinant 5.39 by λ and putting $\frac{m\lambda}{K} = \lambda'$ we get

$$\begin{vmatrix} (\lambda' - 1) & \lambda' & \lambda' \\ \lambda' & (2\lambda' - 1) & 2\lambda' \\ \lambda' & 2\lambda' & (3\lambda' - 1) \end{vmatrix} = 0 \quad \text{...(5.40)}$$

Expanding the determinant of equation 5.40 we get.

$$(\lambda' - 1)\,[(2\lambda' - 1)(3\lambda' - 1) - 4\lambda^2] - \lambda'\,[(\lambda')(3\lambda' - 1) - 2\lambda'^2]$$

$$+ \lambda'\,[(\lambda'(2\lambda') - \lambda'(2\lambda' - 1)] = 0$$

$$= (\lambda' - 1)\,[2\lambda'^2 - 5\lambda' + 1] - \lambda'^3 + \lambda'^3 + \lambda'^2 = 0$$

$$2\lambda'^3 - 7\lambda'^2 + 6\lambda' - 1 - \lambda'^3 + 2\lambda'^2 = 0$$

or $$\lambda'^3 - 5\lambda'^2 + 6\lambda' - 1 = 0 \quad \text{...(5.41)}$$

Equation 5.41 is same as 5.36 (*c*). Hence its roots by trial and error are

$$\lambda_1' = 0.198,\ \lambda_2' = 1.555,\ \lambda_3' = 3.247$$

We assume $\lambda' = \frac{m\lambda}{K} = \frac{m p^2}{K}$ as before

$$\therefore \quad p_1^2 = 0.198\,\frac{K}{m}$$

$$p_2^2 = 1.555\,\frac{K}{m}$$

and $$p_3^2 = 3.247\,K/m$$

The amplitude coefficients for the three modes of vibrations will be the same as determined for stiffness method and shown in Fig. 5.10.

Numerical methods

In case the number of degrees of freedom is more than three, the problem of forming frequency equation and solving it for the determination of frequencies and mode shapes becomes difficult. In such cases numerical techniques are invariably used. Here few numerical methods will be discussed.

1. Rayleigh's method. This is an approximate method for the determination of frequency in fundamental mode (lower frequency numerically) of vibration.

Let

m_i = mass of element i

x_i = displacement of mass at any time during the vibration.

$\frac{dx}{dt} = \dot{x}_i$ = velocity of mass.

Then kinetic energy of mass K-E $= \frac{1}{2}\, mv^2 = \frac{1}{2}\, m_i \dot{x}_i^2$

The kinetic energy of the system (all masses) $= \frac{1}{2} \sum_{i=1}^{n} m_i \dot{x}_1^2$

The potential energy of mass $= \frac{1}{2}\, (m_i\, g)\; x_i$

The total potential energy of the system $= \frac{1}{2} \sum_{i=1}^{n} m_i\, g\; x_i$

For an undamped system the total energy of the system (potential + kinetic) energy is constant. For harmonic vibrations (when the system vibrates in pure mode) maximum potential energy during the cycle of vibration is equal to maximum kinetic energy. Hence

$$\frac{1}{2} \sum_{i=1}^{n} (m_i \dot{x}_i^2)_{\max} = \frac{1}{2} \sum_{i=1}^{n} (m_i\, g\, x_i)_{\max} \qquad \ldots(5.42)$$

Assuming $x_i = A_i \sin Pt$

then velocity $\frac{dx_i}{dt} = A_i\, p \cos pt$

The maximum values of x_i and $\dot{x}_i$ in the vibration cycle, would be A_i and PA_i respectively, using these values in equation 5.42,

$$p^2 = \frac{g \sum_{i=1}^{n} m_i A_i}{\sum_{i-1}^{n} m_i A_i^2} \qquad \ldots(5.43)$$

If the shape of the dynamic deflection curve is known, the value of P^2 would be given exactly by equation 5.43. How ever dynamic deflection would not be known till the frequency equation is solved. It has been seen that even if an approximate shape is chosen for the deflection curve, P^2 evaluated from equation 5.43 would be a good approximation to exact value. In particular P^2 evaluated using static deflection curve of the system, under loads acting on it the result would not be over estimated than exact value by more than 2%. The procedure is illustrated by the following example.

Example. On a cantilever beam loads of 3 mg, 2 mg and mg are applied as shown in Fig. 5.12. The value of stiffness also is shown on the Fig. Calculate the frequency of vibration P^2 of the system.

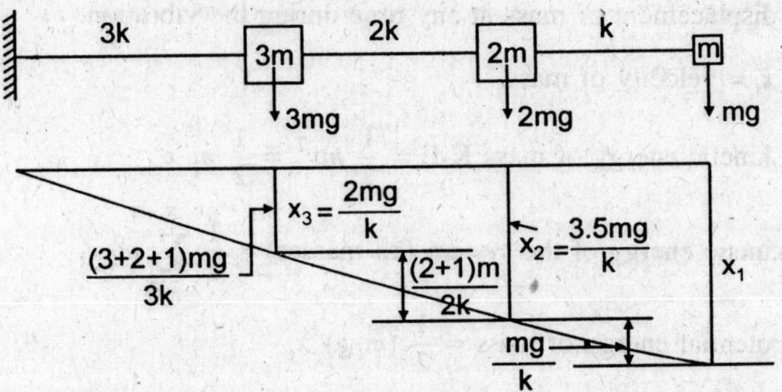

Fig. 5.12. Static Deflections of a three degrees of freedom system

Solution. The deflection under its own weight (static deflection) can be calculated by applying a force equal to the mass times acceleration due to gravity 'g' in the direction of vibration. The loads applied and deflections obtained are shown in the same Fig. 5.12.

$$\text{Deflections, } x_3 = \frac{(3+2+1)\,mg}{3\,K} = \frac{2\,mg}{K}$$

$$x_2 = \frac{2\,mg}{K} + \frac{(2+1)\,mg}{2\,K} = \frac{3.5\,mg}{K}$$

$$x_1 = x_2 + \frac{mg}{K} = \frac{3.5\,mg}{K} + \frac{mg}{K} = \frac{4.5\,mg}{K}$$

$$\therefore \quad p^2 = g\,\frac{(mg/K)}{(mg/K)^2} \times \frac{4.5 \times 1 + 3.5 \times 2 + 2 \times 3}{1 \times (4.5)^2 + 2 \times (3.5)^2 + 3 \times 2^2}$$

$$\text{or} \quad = \frac{K}{m} \times \frac{17.5}{1 \times 20.25 + 12.25 \times 2 + 12.0}$$

$$\text{or} \quad p^2 = \frac{K}{m} \times \frac{17.5}{56.75} = 0.309\,\frac{K}{m} \approx 0.31\,\frac{K}{m} \textbf{ Ans.}$$

Holzer's method

It is a numerical method of solution for problems formulated by stiffness coefficients. This method is applicable for simplified systems such as multi-storeyed shear structures. The procedure of solution for determining the natural periods of vibrations in different modes is discussed below.

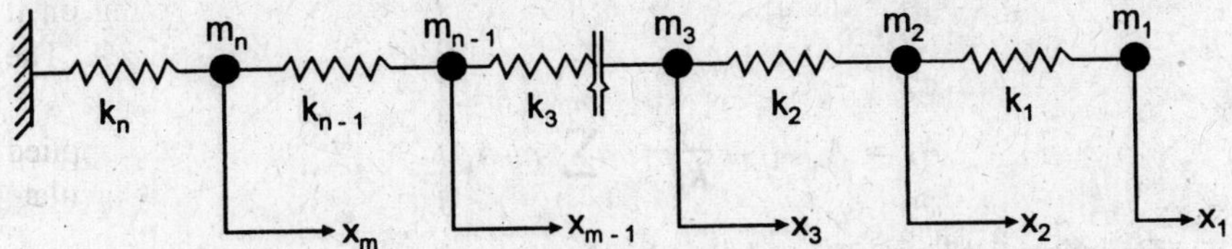

Fig. 5.13. An Idealised Multi-Degree of freedom system

Let the displacements of various masses be denoted by $x_1, x_2, x_3 \ldots x_n$ etc. The masses and their displacements are shown in Fig. 5.13. The equations of motion of the masses may be written as follows:

$$\left.\begin{aligned} m_1 \ddot{x}_1 + K_1 (x_1 - x_2) &= 0 \\ m_2 \ddot{x}_2 + K_1 (x_2 - x_1) + K_2 (x_2 - x_3) &= 0 \\ \vdots \\ m_i \ddot{x}_i + K_{i-1} (x_i - x_{i-1}] + K_i (x_i - x_{i+1}) &= 0 \\ \vdots \\ m \ddot{x}_n + K_{n-1} (x_n - x_{i-1}) + K_n x_n &= 0 \end{aligned}\right\} \qquad \ldots(5.44)$$

Assuming harmonic vibration,

Let $\qquad x_i = A_i \sin pt \qquad \ldots(5.45)$

then $\qquad \dfrac{dx_i}{dt} = \dot{x}_i$

and $\qquad \dfrac{dx_i^2}{dt^2} = \ddot{x}_i$

then from equation 5.45 $\ddot{x}_i = -A_i p^2 \sin pt$ and dividing by $\sin Pt$.

Putting the values of $\ddot{x}_i, x_i$ etc. in equation 5.44, it can be written as

$$\left.\begin{aligned} -m_1 p^2 A_1 + K_1 (A_1 - A_2) &= 0 \\ -m_2 p^2 A_2 + K_1 (A_2 - A_1) + K_2 (A_2 - A_3) &= 0 \\ \ldots \qquad \ldots \qquad \ldots \\ -m_i p^2 A_i + K_i (A_i - A_{i-1}) + K_{i+1} (A_i - A_{i+1}) &= 0 \\ \ldots \qquad \ldots \qquad \ldots \\ m_n p^2 A_n + K_{n-1} (A_n - A_{n-1} + K_n A_n &= 0 \end{aligned}\right\} \qquad \ldots(5.46)$$

From equation 5.46,

$$K_1 (A_1 - A_2) = m_1 A_1 p^2$$

or

$$\left.\begin{aligned} A_2 &= A_1 - m_1 p^2 A_1 \\ &= \frac{A_1 (1 - m_1 p^2)}{K} \\ A_3 &= A_2 - \frac{p^2}{K}(m_1 A_1 + m_2 A_2) \\ &\vdots \\ A_n &= A_{n-1} - \frac{p^2}{K_{n-1}} \sum_{i-1}^{n} m_i A_i \end{aligned}\right\} \quad \text{...(5.47)}$$

Equation 5.47 provides relationship between any two successive amplitude. Starting with any arbitrary value A_1 say 1.0 for simplify, amplitude of all other masses can be determined. Finally (A_{n+1}) should work out zero (due to the fixity of the building at the bases) for certain values of P^2.

A plot between A_{n+1} and P^2 would give the shape as shown in Fig. 5.14. The intersection of the curve with x-axis would give various values of P^2. By

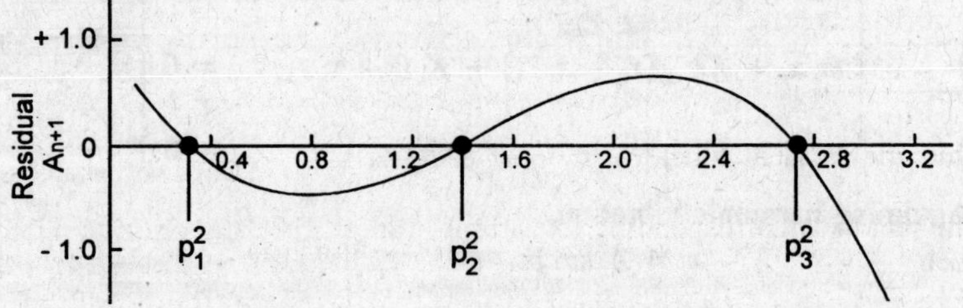

Fig. 5.14. Residual as a Function of frequency in Holzer method

substituting the correct values of P^2 in equation 5.47 the mode shapes would be obtained. The procedure is illustrated with the help of the following example.

Example. For a simple system of few masses as shown in Fig. 5.12 show the use of holzer's method.

Solution. The evaluation of amplitudes 'A' and residual A_{n+1} is carried out in a tabular form.

Usually A_1 is assumed as unity for ease in calculations.

Let $P^2 = 0.3k/m$ as one value of frequency. The calculations in the following table are given for one value of P^2 using equation 5.47.

From equation 5.47, $A_2 = A_1 - \dfrac{p^2 m_1}{K_1} A_1$

We assumed $\quad p^2 = \dfrac{0.3\,K}{m}$, and $A_1 = 1.0$

$$\therefore \quad A_2 = A_1 - \frac{0.3\,K}{m} \cdot \frac{m}{K}$$

$$\therefore \quad A_2 = 1 - 0.3 = 0.7$$

$$\boxed{p^2 = 0.3\,\frac{K}{m},\ A_1 = 1.0}$$

Table 5.1.

Mass No. i	A_i	m_i	m_iA_i	Σm_iA_i	$\frac{1}{K_i}$	$\frac{p^2}{K_i}\ \Sigma\, mA$	$A_{i+1} = A_i - \frac{p^2}{K_i} \sum_{J=1}^{n} m_j A_j$
(1)	(2)	(3)	(4)	(5)	(6)	(7)	(8)
1.	1.0	1.0	1 × 1 = 1.0	1.0	$\frac{1}{K}$	0.3	0.7
2.	0.7	2.0	0.7 × 2 = 1.4	1+1.4 = 2.4	$\frac{1}{2K}$	0.36	0.7 – 0.36 = 0.34
3.	0.34	3.0	0.34 × 3 = 1.02	2.4 + .02 = 3.42	$\frac{1}{3K}$	0.342	– 0.002
	– 0.002						

Thus the residual for $p^2 = 0.3\,\frac{K}{m} = -\,0.002$.

The residuals corresponding to various values of P^2 are given in Table 5.2. below.

Table 5.2.

Frequency parameter α ($p^2 = \alpha\, K/m$)	*Residual* A_{n+1}
0.1	0.5907
0.2	0.2587
0.3	– 0.0020
0.5	– 0.3333
0.8	– 0.4453
1.0	– 0.3333
1.2	– 0.1280
1.4	+ 0.1227
1.7	0.4787
2.0	0.6667
2.3	0.5247
2.6	– 0.1093
3.0	– 2.000

The curve from above values is shown in Fig. 5.14.

The frequency parameter α and mode shapes are shown in Table 5.3.

Table 5.3.

Mode	*Frequency parameter* α	A_1	A_2	A_3
1st mode	0.2987	1.0000	0.7013	0.3425
2nd mode	–1.3041	1.0000	– 0.3401	– 0.5596
3rd mode	2.5655	1.0000	– 1.5556	1.1681

QUESTIONS

1. Name two degree of freedom structures.
2. Name the methods of solving equations of motions.
3. Why the numerical methods of solving equations of motions is preferred?
4. On a two storey building 50 kg and 40 kg weights are placed on 1st and 2nd floor as shown on the sketch no. 5.15. The stiffness of the walls is 150 N/cm and 100 N/cm and zero. The building is given a initial displacement of 10 cms at the top and left. From the given data, determine.

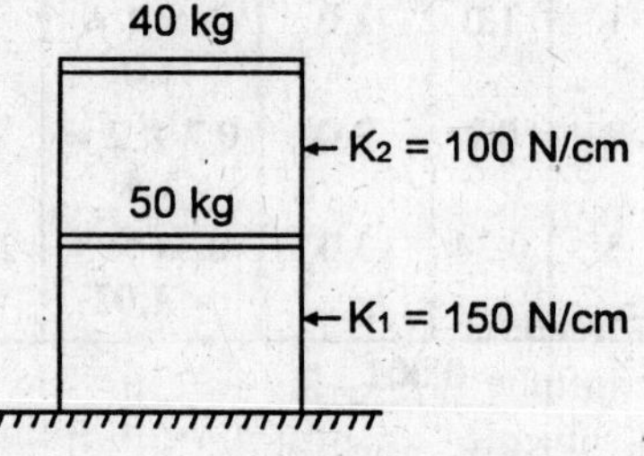

Fig. 5.15.

1. Complete solution of the equation of motion.

(M_1 = 50 kg, M_2 = 40 kg, K_1 = 150 N/cm K_2 = 100 N/cm, K_3 = 0)

$$\left.\begin{aligned} x_1 &= 2.56 \cos p_1 t + 7.44 \cos p_2 t \\ x_2 &= 4.9 \cos p_1 t - 4.9 \cos p_2 t \end{aligned}\right\} \textbf{Ans.}$$

5. A system of masses is said I_0 vibrate in its natural or principal mode if......
   (*a*) If all masses attain their maximum amplitude simultaneously
   (*b*) If all masses pass through the position of equilibrium simultaneously
   (*c*) Both are correct
   (*d*) Both are incorrect
   (*e*) One of the above is correct
6. Identify the correct statement/statements
   (*a*) The Numerical techniques are used if the number of degrees of freedom of the system exceeds three
   (*b*) Rayleigh's numerical method of determination of the fundamental frequency of the system is an approximate method
   (*c*) Holzer's numerical method is applicable for simplified systems as multistoreyed shear structures
   (*d*) Stiffness method for the solution of equations of motions can be used upto three equation
   (*e*) All are correct
   (*f*) All are incorrect

ANSWERS

5. (*c*) 6. (*e*)

6

Continuous Systems

6.1. INTRODUCTION

In many physical systems like beams, bars, plates and shells the mass is distributed uniformly or varying uniformly over their geometry. We have seen in the study of discrete or lumped '*n*' mass systems in which each mass was permitted one degree of freedom, had *n* degree of freedom. In case of continuous system, theoretically the system would have infinite degrees of freedom. In this chapter how ever discussion mainly will be confined to uniform beams having axial shear and bending deformations.

It is assumed that the system is linearly elastic so that the infinite degree of freedom system, each having a single degree of freedom can be assumd as infinite system. Specially the effect of earthquake excitation on beams subjected to shear and bending are discussed.

6.2. FREE VIBRATIONS-FREQUENCIES AND MODE SHAPES

6.2.1. Longitudinal or Axial Vibrations of beams

Consider an element of cross sectional area A, mass density ρ. Let the elastic modulus of elasticity of its material be *E*. The body diagram of the element is shown in Fig. 6.1.

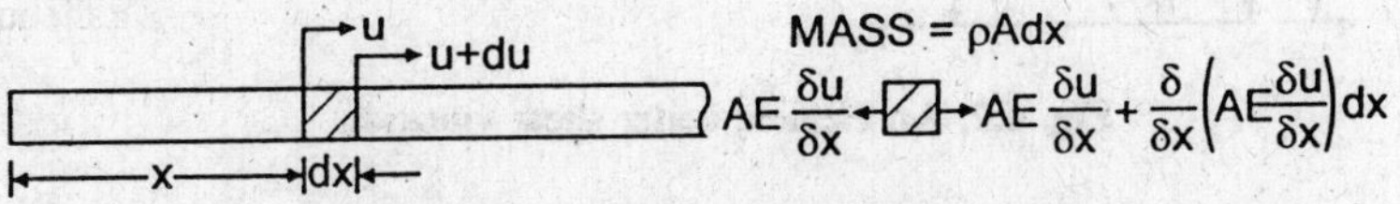

Fig. 6.1. An element under axial vibration

Let u be the axial displacement of the element, then strain would be $\frac{\delta u}{\delta x}$, stress $E \cdot \frac{\delta u}{\delta x}$, and force $AE\frac{\delta u}{\delta x}$. The rate of change of this force would be $\frac{\delta}{\delta x}\left(AE\frac{\delta u}{\delta x}\right)$. According to Newton's law, the net force on the element would be equal to inertia force on the element.

The acceleration of the element would be $\frac{\delta^2 u}{\delta t^2}$

The mass of the element = $\rho \cdot A \cdot dx$.

The equation of equilibrium may be written as

$$\left[\frac{\delta}{\delta x}\left(A.E.\ \frac{\delta u}{\delta x}\right)\right] dx = \left(\rho A \frac{\delta^2 u}{\delta t^2}\right) dx \qquad \ldots(6.1)$$

The differential equation of motion can be written as

$$\frac{\delta}{\delta x}\left(AE \frac{\delta u}{\delta x}\right) = \rho A \left(\frac{\delta^2 u}{\delta t^2}\right) \qquad \ldots(6.2)$$

If the cross section of the beam is uniform and the material is same through out, then equation of motion can be written as

$$\frac{\delta^2 u}{\delta t^2} = (C_L)^2 \frac{\delta^2 u}{\delta x^2} \qquad \ldots(6.3)$$

where, $C_L = \sqrt{E/\rho}$, the velocity of longitudinal wave propagation.

Vertical vibration of a layer of uniform soil resting on bed rock can be simulated by axial vibrations of a beam.

6.2.2. Shear Vibrations of beams

Consider an element shown in Fig. 6.2. Let transverse shear deflection be y_s and $\delta y_s/\delta x$ shear strain

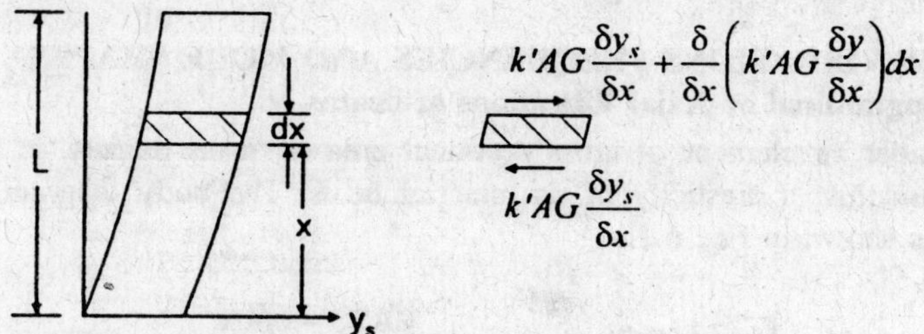

Fig. 6.2. An element under shear vibration

Let

G = Modulus of rigidity

A = Area of cross section of the beam

K' = Shape factor

Then shear force V at any section x would be,

$$V = K' A \cdot G \cdot \frac{\delta y_s}{\delta x} \qquad \ldots(6.4)$$

Here K' represent the ratio of average shear stress on a section to the product of the shear modulus, and the angle of shear at the neutral axis. For a solid rectangular section this has a value of 5/6.

The rate of change of shear force = $\dfrac{\delta v}{\delta x}$

The net force on the element = $\left(\frac{\delta v}{\delta x}\right) dx$

The inertia force on the element = $(\rho A\, dx)\frac{\delta^2 y_s}{\delta t^2}$

Equating the two forces, the equation of motion can be written as

$$\frac{\delta}{\delta x}\left(K' AG \frac{\delta y_s}{\delta x}\right) = \rho A \frac{\delta^2 y_s}{\delta t^2} \quad \ldots(6.5)$$

For a uniform shear beam, equation 6.5 reduces to

$$\frac{\delta^2 y_s}{\delta t^2} = C_s^2 \cdot \frac{\delta^2 y_s}{\delta x^2} \quad \ldots(6.6)$$

where $C_s = \sqrt{K' G/\rho}$, the velocity of shear wave propagation.

The transverse vibrations of earth dams can also be approximately determined by the beams in shear. The equations of motion of shear vibrations of an beam are also analogous to that of a multistorey framed structure whose floors are rigid. The equations of motion of a building, which is usually approximated as multiple degree of freedom system, are a set of ordinary second order differential equations. The equation of motion of a shear beam is a second order, partial differential equation. In case the number of masses is large, the partial differential equation may be regarded as a limiting case for the ordinary differential equation.

6.2.3. Transverse vibrations due to bending of beam

Bending vibrations are predominant in those beams, whose length is long in comparison to their transverse dimensions.

Consider the vibrations in bending of an element of a beam as shown in Fig. 6.3. Let the deflection of the element at a point x from the support be y_b.

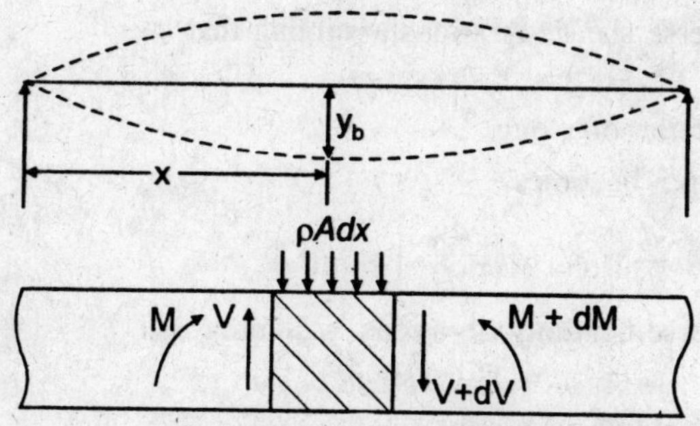

Fig. 6.3. An element under bending vibration

The bending moment of a bending beam $M = -EI\frac{\delta^2 y_b}{\delta x^2}$ ...(6.7)

The shear force of a bending beam $V = \frac{\delta M}{\delta x}$ ...(6.8)

Where, y_b is the transverse displacement.

The rate of change of shear force $= \frac{\delta V}{\delta x}$

Net force on the element $= \left(\frac{\delta V}{\delta x}\right) dx$

The inertia force on the element $= (\rho A\, dx) \frac{\delta^2 y_b}{\delta t^2}$

Equating the net force (Bending force) and inertia force we get

$$\therefore \quad -\frac{\delta^2}{\delta x^2}\left(EI \frac{\delta^2 y_b}{\delta x^2}\right) = \rho A \frac{\delta^2 y_b}{\delta t^2} \quad ...(6.9)$$

For a uniform beam equation 6.9 reduces to

$$-\frac{\delta^2 y_b}{\delta t^2} = \frac{EI}{\rho A} \cdot \frac{\delta^4 y_b}{\delta x^4} \quad ...(6.10)$$

It is seen that in case of continuous systems the equations of motion of (6.2, 6.5 and 6.9) are partial differential equations where as in case of discrete systems they are ordinary differential equations.

Let us assume the solution of equation of motion as harmonic with a circular frequency 'ρ'. Then

(*a*) For longitudinal vibrations, assuming that

$$U(x, t) = U(x) \cdot \sin pt$$

Where, $U(x)$ is a function of x only.

then equation (6.2), becomes

$$\frac{d}{dx}\left(AE \frac{dU}{dx}\right) = -\rho A p^2 U \quad ...(6.11)$$

(*b*) For transverse shear vibrations assuming that

$$Y_s(x, t) = Y_s(x) \sin pt$$

Where, Y_s is a function of x only.

then equation 6.3 becomes

$$\frac{d}{dx}\left(K' \cdot AG \frac{dy_s}{dx}\right) = -\rho A^2 p^2 y_s \quad ...(6.12)$$

(*c*) For transverse bending vibrations, assuming that

$$y_b(x, t) = Y_b(x) \sin pt$$

Where, $Y_b(x)$ is a function of x only.

then equation 6.9 becomes

$$\frac{d^2}{dx^2}\left(EI \frac{d^2 y_b}{dx^2}\right) = \rho A p^2 y_b \quad ...(6.13)$$

The above equations (6.11), (6.12), (6.13) are frequency equations. It will be seen that similar equations for discrete systems were algebraic equations. The explicit solution of frequency equation for continuous system is possible in few cases only. The solutions for uniform shear and bending beams only have been discussed here.

6.3. UNIFORM SHEAR BEAM

For a uniform beam, from equation 6.12, we have

$$\frac{d^2 y_s}{dx^2} = \beta^2 y_s \qquad \text{...[6.14 (a)]}$$

where $$\beta^2 = \frac{\rho p^2}{K' G} \qquad \text{...[6.14 (b)]}$$

The solution of equation 6.14 (*a*) is given by

$$Y_s = C_1 \sin \beta x + C_2 \cos \beta x \qquad \text{...(6.15)}$$

The constants C_1 and C_2 can be determined from boundary conditions.

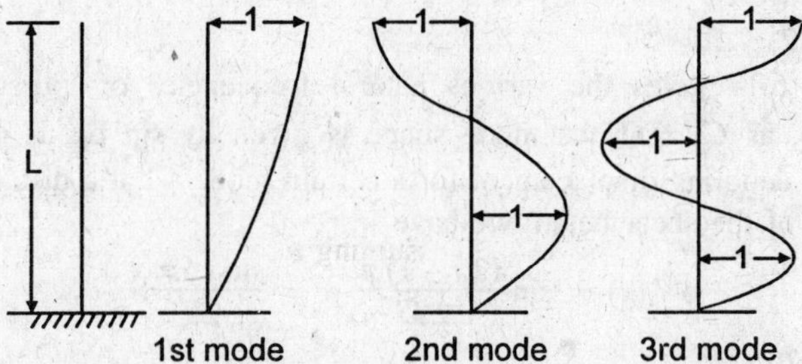

Fig. 6.4. First three mode shapes of a uniform cantilever shear beam

Considering the beam as a cantilever shear beam which is of practical importance (Fig. 6.4). The boundary conditions are as follows:

1. The deflection at fixed end is zero, that is $Y_s = 0$, $x = 0$.
2. At the free end, the shear force is zero, that is shear strain

$$\frac{d\,y_s}{dx} = 0 \text{ at } x = L$$

Applying these conditions to equation 6.15 and if x is measured from the fixed end (origin at fixed end) corresponding to $(Y_s)_{x=0} = 0$.

From condition (1) deflection $Y_s = 0$, when $x = 0$, so $\sin \beta x = 0$, $y_s = 0$, hence $C_2 = 0$ as $\cos \beta x = 1$.

From condition (2) at free end $x = L$, and $\left(\frac{dy_s}{dx}\right)_{x=L} = C_1 \beta \cdot \cos \beta L = 0$

Either C_1 must be zero or $\cos \beta L$ must be zero. In case C_1 is zero, the system will not vibrate. Thus in order to satisfy the boundary conditions, cos βL must be zero, that is the frequency equation for a uniform cantilever shear beam is

$$\cos \beta L = 0 = \cos \frac{(2r-1)\pi}{2} \qquad \text{...[6.16 (a)]}$$

where $\qquad r = 1, 2, 3 \ldots \infty \qquad$ ...[6.16 (b)]

or $$\beta L = \frac{(2r-1)\pi}{2}$$

From equation 6.14 *b*) and equation 16.4 (*b*), we get

From equation 6.14 (*b*) $\beta^2 = \dfrac{\rho p^2}{K' G}$

$$\therefore \qquad p_r^2 = \frac{K' G \beta^2}{\rho}$$

or $$\rho_r = \sqrt{\frac{K' G}{\rho}} \cdot \frac{(2r-1)\pi}{2} \qquad \text{...[6.17 (a)]}$$

or $$p_r = C_s \frac{(2r-1)\pi}{2} \qquad \text{...[6.17 (b)]}$$

where $r = 1, 2, 3 \ldots \infty$

Equation 6.17 gives the various natural frequencies of vibration. From equation 6.15, as $C_2 = 0$, the mode shape is given by sin βx. If $\phi^{(r)}(x)$ is a function of x, denoting displacement for a certain mode 'r' at a distance x from the fixed end of the shear beam, we have,

$$\phi^{(r)}(x) = \sin \frac{(2r-1)\pi}{2L} x = \frac{\sin r' \pi x}{2L} \qquad \text{...(6.18)}$$

where $r' = (2r-1)$.

The first three modes shapes are shown in Fig. 6.4.

6.4. UNIFORM BEAM IN BENDING

For a bending beam, frequency equation may be written as

$$\frac{d^2}{dx^2}\left(\frac{EI\, d^2 y_b}{dx^2}\right) = \rho A p^2 y_b$$

or $$\frac{d^4 y_b}{dx^2} - \frac{\rho A p^2 y_b}{EI} = 0$$

It can be written as

$$\frac{d^4 y_b}{dx^4} - \beta^4 y_b = 0 \qquad \text{...[6.19 (a)]}$$

where $$\beta^4 = \frac{\rho A p^2}{EI} \qquad \text{...[6.19 (b)]}$$

The solution of equation 6.19 (*a*) would be

$$y_b = C_1 \sin \beta x + C_2 \cos \beta x + C_3 \sinh \beta x + C_4 \cosh \beta x \quad ...(6.20)$$

The constants C_1, C_2, C_3 and C_4 can be determined from boundary conditions.

Simply supported beams and cantilever beams are discussed here.

(a) *Pinned End.* Deflection and bending moment are zero.

$$\text{Deflection} \quad y_b = 0 \text{ and } B.M. \frac{d^2 y_b}{dx^2} = 0 \quad ...[6.21\ (a)]$$

(b) *Fixed End.* Deflection and slope are zero.

$$\text{Deflection} \quad y_b = 0 \text{ and slope } \frac{dy_b}{dx} = 0 \quad ...[6.21\ (b)]$$

(c) *Free End.* Bending moment and shear force are zero.

$$B.M., \frac{d^2 y_b}{dx^2} = 0 \text{ and shear force } \frac{d^3 y_b}{dx^3} = 0 \quad ...(6.22)$$

6.4.1. Simply Supported beam

The boundary conditions in case of a simply supported beam are indicated in equation 6.21 (*a*). They are written below as

(*i*) when $x = 0$, at support, deflection $y_b = 0$

(*ii*) when $x = 0$, B.M. $\frac{(d^2 y_b)}{dx^2} = 0$

(*iii*) $x = L$, at other end, deflection $y_b = 0$

(*iv*) when $x = L$, $B.M.$ $\frac{d^2 y_b}{dx^2} = 0$

When condition (*i*) is put in equation 6.20,

$$C_2 + C_4 = 0 \quad ...[6.23\ (a)]$$

When condition (*ii*) is put in equation 6.20,

$$-C_2 + C_4 = 0 \quad ...[6.23\ (b)]$$

$$\therefore \quad C_2 = C_4 = 0$$

From condition (*iii*) when $x = L$, $y_b = 0$, and noting that $C_2 = C_4 = 0$, we get from equation 6.20

$$C_1 \sin \beta L + C_3 \sinh \beta L = 0 \quad ...[6.23\ (c)]$$

From condition (*iv*)

$$-C_1 \sin \beta L + C_3 \sinh \beta L = 0 \quad ...[6.23\ (d)]$$

or $\quad C_1 \sin \beta L = C_3 \sinh \beta L$

or $\quad C_1 \sin \beta_L = 0 \quad ...[6.23\ (e)]$

$$C_3 \sinh \beta_L = 0 \quad ...[6.23\ (f)]$$

From equation 6.24 (*e*)

As C_1 can not zero, (in case $C_1 = 0$, there will be no vibration), hence sin $\beta L = 0$.

Sinh βL is not zero except at $\beta L = 0$, Hence C_3 must be zero.

Hence the frequency equation for a simply supported beam is

$$\sin \beta_L = 0 = \sin r\pi \qquad \text{...[6.24 (a)]}$$

$$\therefore \quad \beta_L = r\pi \qquad \text{...[6.24 (b)]}$$

where $r = 1, 2, 3, \ldots \infty$

Using equation 6.19 and 6.24 (*b*), we get

$$p_r = \frac{r^2 \pi^2}{L^2} \sqrt{\frac{EI}{\rho A}} \qquad \text{...(6.25)}$$

Equation 6.25 gives then various natural frequencies of vibration. From equation 6.20, since $C_2 = C_3 = C_4 = 0$, the mode shape is given by sin βx. For the rth mode, thus the mode shape is obtained by putting βr in place β. or

$$\phi^{(r)}(x) = \sin \beta r(x) = \sin \frac{\pi r \cdot x}{L}$$

where $r = 1, 2, 3, \ldots \delta$

where $\phi^{(r)}(x)$ is the mode shape coefficient at location x and super script '*r*' denotes the mode of vibration. The first three mode shapes are shown in Fig. 6.5.

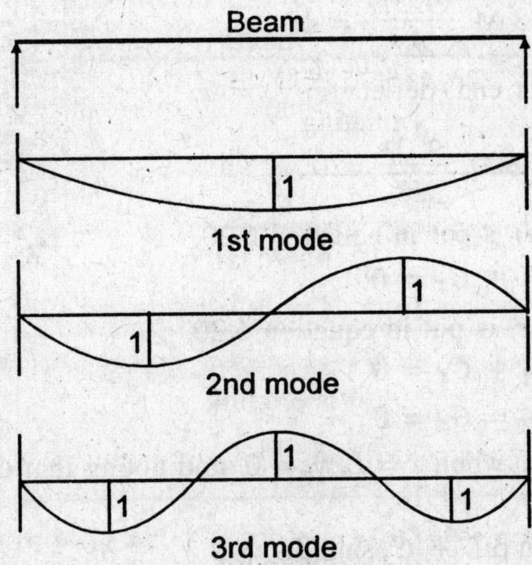

Fig. 6.5. First three mode shapes of a uniform simply supported beam subjected to bending vibrations

6.4.2. Cantilever beam

In the cantilever beam, let $x = 0$ be the built in end.

and $x = L$ free end. For this case the boundary conditions will be as follows:

(*i*) At built in end $x = 0$, deflection $y_b = 0$

(*ii*) At $x = 0$, slope $\frac{dy_b}{dx} = 0$

(*iii*) At $x = L$, *B.M.* $\frac{(d^2 y_b)}{dx^2} = 0$

(*iv*) At $x = L$ shear force $\frac{d^3 y_b}{dx^3} = 0$

Using these conditions in equation 6.20 we get

From condition (*i*)

$$C_2 + C_4 = 0 \qquad \ldots[6.27\ (a)]$$

or $$C_2 = -C_4$$

From (*ii*)

$$C_1 + C_3 = 0 \qquad \ldots[6.27\ (b)]$$

or $$C_1 = -C_3$$

From condition (*iii*)

$$y_b = C_1 \sin \beta x + C_2 \cos \beta x + C_3 \sinh \beta x + C_4 \cosh \beta x = 0$$

$$\frac{\delta^2 y_b}{\delta x^2} = -C_1\, \beta L \sin \beta x + C_2\, \beta L \cos \beta x + C_3\, \beta L \sinh \beta L + C_4\, \beta L \cosh \beta L = 0$$

or $$-C_1 \sin \beta L - C_2 \cos \beta L + C_3 \sinh \beta L + C_4 \cosh \beta L = 0 \ldots[6.27\ (c)]$$

From condition (*iv*), differentiating equation 6.20 3 times, we get

$$-C_1 \cos \beta L + C_2 \sin \beta L + C_3 \sinh \beta L + C_4 \cosh \beta L = 0 \ldots[6.27\ (d)]$$

From these four equations 6.27 (a) to 6.27 (d), the following two eqautions are obtained.

Putting C_3 and C_4 in terms of C_1 and C_2 we get g

$$C_1 (\sin \beta L + \sinh \beta L) + C_2 (\cos \beta L + \cosh \beta L) = 0 \qquad \ldots[6.28\ (a)]$$

$$-C_1 (\cos \beta L + \sinh \beta L) + C_2 [\sin \beta L - \cosh \beta L) = 0 \quad \ldots[6.28\ (b)]$$

By determinant, eliminating C_1 and C_2 we get

$$\begin{vmatrix} (\sin \beta L + \sinh \beta L) & (\cos \beta L + \cosh \beta L) \\ -(\cos \beta L + \sinh \beta L) & (\sin \beta L - \cosh \beta L) \end{vmatrix} = 0$$

Expanding the determinant we have

$$(\sin \beta L + \sinh \beta L)(\sin \beta L - \cosh \beta L)$$
$$+ (\cos \beta L + \sinh \beta L)(\cos \beta L + \cosh \beta L) = 0$$
$$= \sin^2 \beta L + \sin \beta L \sinh \beta L - \sin \beta L \cosh \beta L$$

$$- \sinh \beta L \cosh \beta L + \cos^2 \beta L + \cos \beta L \sinh \beta L$$
$$+ \cos \beta L \cosh \beta L + \sinh \beta L \cosh \beta L = 0$$
$$= \sin^2 \beta L + \cos^2 \beta L + \cos \beta L \cosh \beta L + \sin \beta L (\sinh \beta L$$
$$- \cosh \beta L) + \cos \beta L \sinh \beta L = 0$$
$$= 1 + \cos \beta L \cosh \beta L + \sin \beta L (\sinh \beta L - \cosh \beta l)$$
$$+ \cos \beta L \sinh \beta L = 0 \quad \text{...(6.29)}$$

at fixed end when $L = 0$, then $\sin \beta L = 0$ and $\sinh \beta L = 0$.

$\therefore$ Then equation 6.29 reduces to

$$1 + \cos \beta L \cosh \beta L = 0$$
$$\cos \beta L \cosh \beta L = -1 \quad \text{...(6.30)}$$

Equation (6.30) is a frequency equation. This equation can be solved graphically or numerically. First three values of βL are

$$\beta_1 L = 1.88, \ \beta_2 L = 4.69 \ \text{ and } \ \beta_3 L = 7.85 \quad \text{...(6.31)}$$

The natural frequencies of vibration are given by

$$p_r = C_{pr} \frac{1}{L^2} \sqrt{EI/\rho A} \quad \text{...(6.32)}$$

$\therefore$ where $Cp_1 = 3.516$ $Cp_2 = 22.035$ and $Cp_3 = 61.697$

[From equation $\beta^4 = \dfrac{\rho A}{EI} p^2 = (6.19\ b)$]

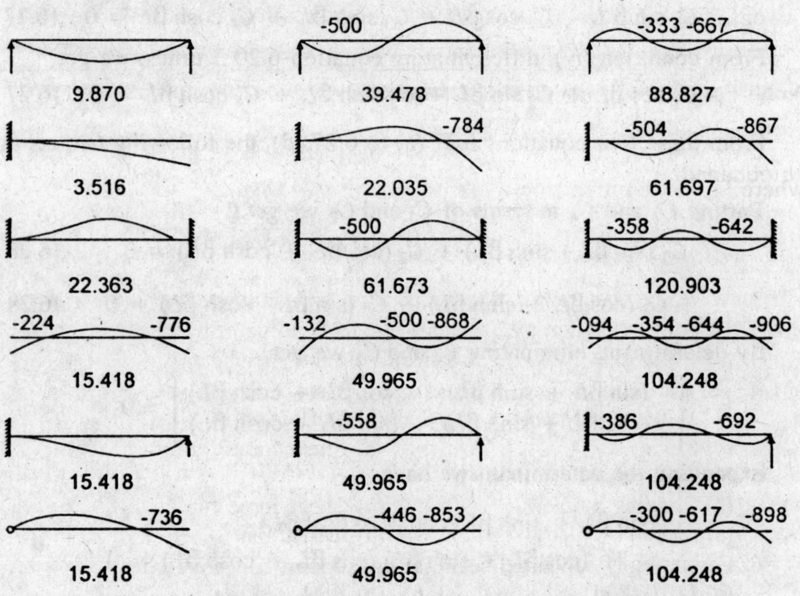

Fig. 6.6. Frequency coefficients C_p for various end conditions

The mode shapes are given by equations 6.20, 6.28 (*c*) and 6.28 (*b*) as

$$\phi^{(r)}(x) = (\sin \beta_r \cdot x - \sinh \beta_r x) - \left(\frac{\sin \beta_r L + \sinh \beta_r L}{\cos \beta_r L + \cosh \beta_r L} \right) \times (\cos \beta_r x - \cosh \beta_r x) \quad \ldots(6.33)$$

It has been seen that even for simple cases of the uniform cantilever beams, the axact analytical expressions for mode shapes is complicated. For the first three modes the mode shape coefficients are given in Table 6.1 below.

The frequencies of vibration for various end conditions of bending beam are shown in Fig. 6.6.

Table 6.6. Mode shape coefficients

x/L	ϕ^1	ϕ^2	ϕ^3
0	0.00000	0.00000	0.00000
0.1	0.03355	0.18526	0.45614
0.2	0.12774	0.60211	1.20901
0.3	0.27297	1.05227	1.51248
0.4	0.45977	1.36694	1.05185
0.5	0.67905	1.42733	0.03937
0.6	0.92227	1.17895	– 0.94753
0.7	1.18175	0.63410	–1.31485
0.8	1.45096	– 0.14007	– 0.78975
0.9	1.72480	– 1.04750	0.45702
1.0	2.00000	– 2.00000	2.00000

Note: For all the modes the shape factor are given by

$$\int_0^L [\phi(x)]^2 \cdot dx = L$$

where '*x*' is measured from built in end.

QUESTIONS

1. Write the equation of velocity of axial and transverse vibrations of a beam.
2. Write the equation of vibrations due to bending of a beam.
3. Draw the sketch of mode shapes of a cantilever beam.
4. For a cantilever beam at fixed end ...... are zero.
   (*a*) Bending moment (*b*) Deflection
   (*c*) Slope (*d*) Shear force
5. For free end of cantilever .... are zero
   (*a*) Bending moment (*b*) Shear force
   (*c*) Slope (*d*) Deflection
6. For a simply supported beam, at the support ...... are zero
   (*a*) Deflection (*b*) B.M.
   (*c*) Shear force (*d*) Slope

7. Identify the correct statement/statements
   (*a*) The vertical vibrations of a layer of uniform soil lying on bed rock can be simulated by axial vibrations of a beam
   (*b*) The transverse vibrations of earth dams can be approximated to those of beams in shear
   (*c*) The equations of motion of the shear vibrations of a beam are analogous to that of a multi-storey framed structures, whose floors are rigid.
   (*d*) The equations of motion of a building of multiple degree of freedom, are of ordinary second order differential equations
   (*e*) All are correct
   (*f*) All are incorrect

ANSWERS:

4. (*b, c*)
5. (*a, b*)
6. (*a, b*)
7. (*e*)

7

Evaluation of Earthquake Resistance of Buildings

7.1. INTRODUCTION

People living in earthquake prone areas have accepted the tremors as a way of life. Even then they are caught suddenly and not ready to face to consequences which bring them only miseries. As explained in chapter 1, world experiences about 800 earthquakes of moderate size (magnitude) of 5.0 to 5.9 on richter scale out of these 800 moderate earthquakes only 18 are of magnitude ranging from 7.0 to 7.9. As earthquakes cannot be predicted, it becomes obligatory for the governments of different countries with earthquake history to ensure that the existing and future buildings and other types of structures strictly comply with earthquake resistant design regulations and by laws of the country. All such countries should be actively involved in preparing seismic zoning maps of their countries using their seismic history and regional geology. Earthquake preparedness for the safety of buildings and infrastructure needs a comprehensive programme of installing and maintaining strong motion recorders in and out side buildings, dams, bridges, and at natural sites. Earthquake preparedness should also include guide lines for people living in seismic areas to educate every individual how to work for safety of self and the neighbourhood.

Although in some seismic affected countries, disaster management committees at government level exist, but often caught off guard when calamities of serious intensity struck the region. Some examples of countries coped with earthquake tragedies are given below.

7.2. PREPAREDNESS TO COPE EARTHQUAKE IN JAPAN AND U.S.A.

For people living in Japan and in greater Los Angeles area earthquakes are a reality for the them. In these regions every body is prepared to face the consequence of a major earthquake. The quality of life and potential for survival has greatly increased by the preparedness. California lies on the top of St. Andrea's fault. This fault is an intricate notwork of more than 1300 km length. Literally in the region about one thousand earthquakes, big and small occur every year. They are not totally predictable. To cope this situation, california has developed an elaborate crisis management system The state government is actively engaged in the task of earthquake disaster management. Government got prepared earthquake risk maps based on the California regional geology and earthquake history.

In order to record the shaking pattern of ground and structures during earthquakes, the strong motion recording instruments have been installed in and out side of buildings, on dams, bridges, and at natural sites. The installing and maintenance is the responsibility of a committee formed by the government. Seismologists and engineers analyse the recorded data and compare it with the behaviour of buildings and ground during the past earthquakes. They also use this information to improve building codes and design for safer buildings. In San Fransisco shock absorbers have been located below the foundations of the buildings to absorb vibrations caused by earthquake. These shock absorbers are containers of layered steel and rubber.

In Japan scientists have created "smart buildings". These buildings are equipped with sensors to detect and counter the earthquake tremors. The sensors installed in basement pickup the tremors and immediately transfer the signal to the computer. Computer actuates a hydraulic power device which promptly shifts the centre of gravity of the building with the help of steel weight.

Under the seismic hazard mapping act in Japan, the state geologist is required to prepare regulatory zones and issue appropriate microzoning seismic hazard maps. Before issuing a development permit, a site specific information is required to determine, whether a significant hazard exists at the site, if so, measures to reduce the risk to an acceptable level are recommended. In addition to above, stringent disclosure norms also have been introduced. When a property located in a seismic hazard zone, state agent must disclose this fact to the potential buyer. Such norms should be introduced in every country for providing protection against earthquakes.

7.3. EARTHQUAKE RESISTANCE PREPAREDNESS IN INDIA

To cope with hazards of future earthquakes some measures exist in India. The national building code of 1983 has clearly identified structural design in terms of earthquakes and cyclones. The union urban development ministry,'s building material and technology promotion council conducted extensive surveys of all natural disaster risk in every part of India and produced two big volumes of vulnerability 'Atlas of India'. The report also includes recommendations for appropriate safety techniques, by laws, practices and regulations for the region.

Though disaster management committee at Government level exists, but often it is caught napping at the time of serious intensity calamities struck the city. In seismic activities prone areas, earthquake preparedness must become a way of life. Every individual must know how to work for safety of self and others whether at work, home or on road.

After Bhuj's disaster of 26th January 2001, one of the reader's letter sent to the editor of Times of India states that over 50,000 people died in earthquake did not die due to natural calamity but actually have been murdered". Had the government authorities been prompt in providing rescue operations and ensured that all recent construction in the earthquake region of the country complied with the country's quake resistant regulations and all builders, had adhered to safety and building by laws and public made aware of earthquake preparedness, the loss of life and property could have been minimized, if not totally prevented. *This reflects on the poor preparedness of India to cope with the major earthquakes.*

7.4. CAPACITY OF STRUCTURES OF DELHI TO SURVIVE A MAJOR EARTHQUAKE

After the 26th January 2001 earthquake of Gujrat, severe shocks were also felt in Delhi for about 30 seconds. The residents of Noida, Mayur Vihar, and Trans Jamuna areas felt the most shaking. The people rushed out of their houses for safety. All these colonies are built on alluvial soil deposits. After this earthquake people of Delhi started to think that whether Delhi could survive a major earthquake as that of Bhuj (Gujrat). Delhi incidentally falls in seismic zone IV of the country, next to the highest seismic activity zone V. According to the survey of some NGO at least 50% of the buildings of Delhi can not resist earthquake.

Perhaps Delhi is the least prepared city for earthquakes for the following reasons.

1. Many high rise buildings have not been designed by qualified and competent professionals and safety by laws have been flouted. No earthquake resistant code and regulations have been adopted in their design and construction.
2. High rise buildings have mushroomed over soft and reclaimed soil and alluvial deposits with high ground water table.
3. Public is not educated about the safety against earthquake.
4. Most of the houses say 80% have been designed by the owners themselves and constructed by unqualified contractors.
5. The DDA apartment owners make adhoc changes with out any consideration of earthquake safety. At the end it can be said that if adequate timely measures are not taken, a major disaster has to be faced in the future earthquake.

7.5. EVALUATION OF EXISTING BUILDINGS

After the Gujrat earthquake of 26th January 2001 earthquake the ministry of Union Urban Development Govt. of India has decided that compliance of the earthquake safety measures in Delhi will be incorporated in the city's building by laws. According to changed laws the builders, architects, structural engineers and even house owners will be punished, if they do not comply with the safety norms. It has also been decided that existing structures in the capital will be checked for their earthquake safety provisions. By laws are not only formed in Delhi, but in all cities of the country by laws will be regulated to ensure safety of the structures during major earthquakes.

To help the evaluation of the adequacy of the existing structures against earthquakes, following steps may be adopted:

1. The doubtful structures may be visually examined and assessment of site condition may be made that is local available geological information of the site may be obtained.
2. If available, examine the "as built" drawings of the buildings. Assess the quality of construction and strength of materials used in different elements by the non destructive testing techniques. For evaluating concrete strength, concrete cores may be obtained from columns, beams and shear walls, where ever it is not possible to cut the reinforcement Fe depth meter may be used to determine the strength of reinforcement. Soil bearing capacity should also be established by testing the soil. The cover to reinforcement may also be measured using Fe depth meter.
3. To ensure the incorporation of sufficient earthquake resistant provision in the design; the original design of the structure may be checked. The design should be checked according to the latest code recommendations with the values of insitue strength of materials obtained in step 2. In case the size of the member and reinforcement are not found sufficient, then the structure needs strengthening and modifications. This job should be entrusted to an expert only.
4. In case "as built" drawings are not available then building plan has to be prepared by taking actual measurements of the dimensions of all structural members by a qualified surveyor' Though it is time consuming job, but it is essential to perform to check the design. Then the building should be designed for both vertical loads and a combination of vertical and lateral loads due to earthquakes. Storey relative deformations and the total drift at the top are computed and compared for the two loading's and verified to comply with the provisions of the code. Comparision, will indicate whether the original structure was designed for earthquake loads. To check the adequacy of the original design the stresses due to over turning moments, shear force and thrust caused by a combination of vertical and lateral loads should be compared with allowable stresses of the materials.
5. In case the existing structure has already suffered cracks or weakening of joints either due to previous earthquake or due to excessive vertical loading or due to change in its functions, the effect of which can not be

estimated directly or otherwise and also it is not certain that the structure will perform satisfactorily during the future earthquake. In that case its over all stiffness can be evaluated by dynamic testing. The parameter selected for Comparision generally is the fundamental period or the fundamental frequency of vibration, which is a function of the over all stiffness of the structure.

The fundamental frequency of an existing structure in a seismic active region can be estimated from its response to micro-tremor excited vibrations.

This method does not require any device or equipment for inducing dynamic loads for small amplitudes. It only requires installation of some sensitive seismic transducers along the height of the building to record its response to micro tremers, occurring constantly on the surface of the earth.

Alternately the natural periods or frequencies on high rise buildings can be obtained with the help of electro mechanical vibration generators. By this method not only natural periods or frequencies, but mode of vibration and damping characteristics for the first 3 or 4 modes of vibration of structures both in elastic and inelastic region of deformation depending upon the size and the power of the vibration generator can be obtained. But this method is very expensive and is recommended only for very special structures. This type of testing is also known as resonance testing of structures by forced vibrations. Such dynamic tests also provide information regarding degradation of stiffness of structures.

6. In case it is found that an existing structure or building has not been designed to resist the earthquake loads (lateral loads) or its design is inadequate to survive a future major earthquake, then it has to be strengthened or rebuilt according to the advice of the expert. Strengthening of structures must be done by experts.

QUESTIONS

1. Discuss how U.S.A. and Japan have coped with earthquakes.
2. Discuss the earthquake resistance preparedness in India.
3. Discuss how to evaluate the earthquake resistance of existing buildings.
4. Identify the incorrect statement/statements:
   (*a*) people living in earthquake prone zones have accepted the tremors as a way of life
   (*b*) Earthquakes come suddenly while people are not ready to face them
   (*c*) Earthquakes only bring miseries for the people
   (*d*) Earthquakes give sufficient warning before they struck
5. Identify the incorrect statement/statements
   (*a*) Japan scientists have developed sensors to detect and counter earthquakes

(*b*) In Japan seismic hazard maps have been developed
(*c*) India is fully prepared to face earthquakes of any magnitude
(*d*) Delhi, Capital of India is least prepared to face major earthquakes

6. Existing buildings can be evaluated to be earthquake resistant by
(*a*) Visual inspection
(*b*) Examining the drawings of the existing buildings
(*c*) The original design of the buildings
(*d*) Any of the above

ANSWERS

4. (*d*) 6. (*d*)
5. (*c*)

8

Causes of Structural Failures and Lessons from Past Earthquakes

8.1. INTRODUCTION

It is not easy to generalize the common causes of failures of structures during the major earthquakes as the construction materials and construction techniques used in different parts of the world are different. But on the basis of study of damaged structures during the past major earthquakes in different parts of the world following common causes have come to light.

8.2. COMMON CAUSES OF FAILURE OF STRUCTURES DURING EARTHQUAKES

From the study of damaged structures, following common causes have been identified:

(*a*) Beam-column joint failure
(*b*) Soft storey effect
(*c*) Poor reinforcement detailing
(*d*) Design deficiency to provide stability against vertical acceleration
(*e*) Design deficiency in low rise masonry structures
(*f*) Liquefaction of soils.

8.2.1. Beam-Column joint failure

After the earthquake, during the damage survey or study very often it has been found that the yielding in columns rather than beams is a contributing factor for the failure of upper storeys of the frames of the buildings. The problem of yielding of columns first has been found more pronounced in structures in which the gravity load effects control proportion and strength, resulting higher flexural strength in beams than columns. This type of situation particularly occurs in buildings having long beam spans in the upper floors of the buildings where design seismic effects are relatively low.

Observation of failures due to yielding in columns gave rise to the design philosophy of weak beam and strong column in which the column strength should be at least equal to the beam strength. Preferably column strength should be some what higher than beam.

The intended aim is that columns form a stiff, unyielding spine over the height of the building and the inelastic action is limited to beams only. Even structures designed on this principle, may have yielding in first storey or ground storey columns due to soft story effect discussed in next sub section. Hence appropriate details should be provided. In buildings where architectural requirements require wide spans needing strong girders, the strong column and weak beam design philosophy may be difficult to implement. In such situations columns should be detailed to sustain inelastic action or provide continuous

Fig. 8.1. A lack of closely spaced ties has led to disintegration of column concrete

structural shear walls to enforce continuity of deformation over the height of the building. Fig. 8.1 shows the failure of the column due to inadequate spacing of ties.

8.2.2. Soft storey effect

The survey of damaged buildings in earthquakes has revealed that most of the buildings collapsed due to the soft storey effect. The bottom or two storeys' had fewer partition walls than the upper storeys. The most common form of vertical discontinuity develops due to unintended effects of non structural elements.

A soft story in a building is a storey usually the first or ground storey which has few or no partition walls or has open exterior walls or having large doors and windows as in garages. This openness makes this storey vulnerable to earthquake damage. Soft storey may also be defined as follows:

A soft storey is characterised by vertical discontinuity in stiffness. When an individual storey in a building is made taller and/or more open in construction is known as soft or weak storey. Some times it is also called flexible storey. Any storey for which the lateral stiffness is less than 60% of that of the storey immediately above it or less than 70% of the average of combined three storeys above it. Some authors have suggested these percentages as 70 and 80% respectively.

The ground storey usually is used for parking and is known as stilt storey.

8.2.3. Poor reinforcement detailing

Poor reinforcement detailing is one of the most important factors that can weaken the structure. Usually it causes structural failure. A large percentage of such failures are due to lack of sufficient stirrups or links and inadequate cover to links or inadequate spacing of strips as shown in Fig. 8.1.

During earthquake, a concrete beam and column joint will oscillate, causing the concrete to crack if it is not restrained properly by stirrups or links

Fig. 8.2. Disintegration of concrete when the links are not anchored in the mid height of a column, Kobe 1995 Earthquake (Courtesy USGS).

as shown in Fig. 8.2. Fig. 8.3 (*a*) and (*b*) show sections of the same column with detailing for static and dynamic conditions respetively. Thus it is obvious that links adequately anchored as shown in Fig. 8.3 (*b*) will stay in place and enable the column to maintain its strength by confining the concrete.

8.2.4. Design deficiency to provide stability against vertical acceleration

The study of damage pattern of buildings during the recent earthquakes has clearly demostrated that the vertical accelerations do cause the additional damage to structures and increase their destruction.

The vertical component of acceleration of ground shaking, which is generally neglected in design has been found to be an other cause of failure of some buildings during earthquakes. In simple words it can be said that vertical ground acceleration enhences the destructive power of the horizontal

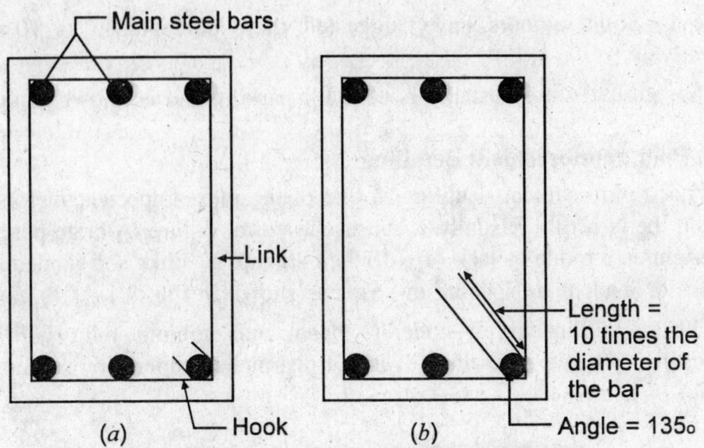

Fig. 8.3. Examples of good column detailing

oscillating movement. Thus it should be accounted for in the design, where ever necessary.

8.2.5. Design deficiency in low rise masonry buildings

Masonry structures have the following two draw backs:

1. Very low tensile strength.
2. Low shear resistance.

Large scale destruction of masonry buildings occurs during earthquake due to the following reasons:

(*a*) Design deficiency to counter act the effect of the above weakness.

(*b*) Damage occurs due to lack of tie beams at lintel and roof levels in brick and stones walls.

(*c*) Absence of strengthening vertical elements at corners which are subjected to torsion effects.

(*d*) Generally no links are provided in heavy roof tiles.

(*e*) The small and medium sized buildings are not constructed according to the seismic regulations.

Similarly earth structures like earthen dams etc. do not have much resistance to seismic stresses. Hence to avoid fatal consequences proper design and detailing of construction is essential. Further use of poor quality materials in the construction increase the damage.

8.3. DETAILING OF STRUCTURAL ELEMENTS

If in selected elements of a building or structure inelastic behaviour is preferred, then design actions and proportions of the elements should be selected to ensure that they could achieve their flexural strengths. Shear failures have been observed to occur in beams and columns during earthquakes as shear forces were determined on the basis of design lateral forces rather than the shear required to neutralize the plastic moment capacity of the member.

Consequently the most modern codes suggest that design shear should be evaluated on the likely plastic hinge locations with appropriate factors of safety applied to the member strength and transverse loading.

Failures have also occurred because bar cutoffs were incosistant with the moment distribution that develops when flexure strengths have reached at member ends. There is uncertaintity in determining these moment distribution. Hence codes have recommended provision of continuous nominal reinforcement on both faces of all structural elements of the buildings or structures.

For reinforced concrete structures to behave in a ductile manner, they should be properly detailed, namely:

1. To prevent the buckling of longitudinal bars and to confine concrete in place in columns, and walls the spacing between stirrups and ties should be less *i.e.* they should be closely spaced.
2. To ensure strength retention during earthquakes, the stirrups and ties should be placed closely spaced in the potential hinge region of the beams.
3. To maintain the integrity of the joints during plastic deformations in the adjacent beam hinge, the detailing of special transverse steel through the beam-column joints in ductile frame should be provided.
4. Careful attention should be paid to connections between all elements on gravity path and earthquake loads or forces.

It has been observed that generally more emphasis in drawings is placed on detailing beam and slab reinforcement at typical sections and very less attention was paid to beam/column joints and columns. It is suggested that this emphasis should be reversed *i.e.* more emphasis should be laid on beam-column joints. During earthquake more damage was found due to widely spaced ties and inadequate detailing of main supporting elements of the structure.

8.4. NON STRUCTURAL ELEMENTS

The performance of buildings during earthquakes and analysis of damage has revealed that many buildings have failed due to the fact that the structural systems were designed neglecting the structure modifications introduced by non structural elements, particularly by the addition of infill panels. Stair cases also usually are considered as non structural components inspite of the fact that mostly they are rigidly connected to the structure of the building, particularly in R.C.C. buildings.

There are following two major aspects to the problem of non structural element response during seismic shaking.

(*a*) The ability of non structural elements to modify or alter the assumed structural response notably in brick or concrete hollow block infilled walls.

(*b*) The tendency of non structural elements to be damaged as the building sways.

The first aspect results in a real danger of building collapse. The second aspect has been found to result more costly damage even in moderate earthquakes. Failure to address the structural implications of non structural elements on the part of engineers and architects has resulted in a major impediment to the improvement of building seismic performance.

Sh. D.V. Mallik based on his studies has suggested that by connecting the infill walls inside the bounding frames through shear connectors, the stiffness of the structure can be increased. Thus by connecting the infill walls through shear connectors in the bounding frames their load carrying capacity can be increased.

During earthquake a common cause of failure of buildings is related to infilled frames. This problem is most severe in structures having relatively flexible lateral load resisting system. In such a case the non structural component may constitute a significant portion of the total stiffness. If properly designed, the infill can improve the performance of the frame due to its stiffening and strengthening action. In a single storey building if infills are omitted, soft storey effect may develop. Even if infills are placed continuously and symmetrically through out the structure, even then soft storey effect may develop if one or more infill panel fail..

Another example of non structural member is that of partial height frame infills. Such constructions are very common. In this form of construction an infill extends from the floor level upto the bottom of the window line, leaving a relatively short portion of the column exposed in the upper portion of the storey as shown in Fig. 8.4. This short length column between floor level and bottom line of window is called *captive column.*

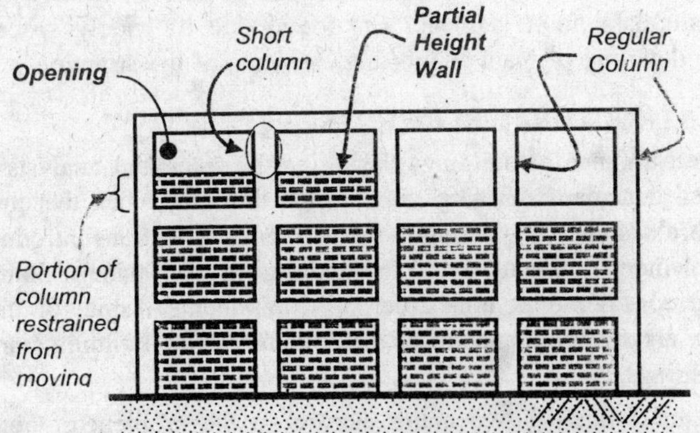

Fig. 8.4. Short columns effect in RC buildings when partial height walls adjoin columns

The shear required to develop flexural yield effectively in the shortened column will be substantially higher than that which would develop for flexural yield of the full length column. If this fact of the in fill has not been taken into account in the design, then shear failure of this captive column may occur even before the flexural yield reaches. Complete collapse of the building may occur if transverse steel is not properly provided to this column. This type of distress is a common cause of damage of buildings and their collapse during earthquakes.

Other non structural members such as slabs on grade can change the structural behaviour. Stair ways and partial infills in frames can also change the member actions. Due to these interactions the shear demand of members can increase substantially and the plastic hinge formation may take place away from regions detailed for ductile action on the basis of intended behaviour.

8.5. CONSTRUCTION AND MAINTENANCE

The analysis of damaged structures after a earthquake and field inspections have shown that building design prepared by following blindly the seismic code regulation does not always guarantee the safety against serious damage or collapse during an earthquake. The damages have been observed due to may uncertainties in assuming the earthquake intensity in the design and the response of soil foundation and super structural system. Further the performance of the system depends on its condition at the time of earthquake. Thus construction and maintenance that includes repair, retro fitting and other modifications must also be considered in addition to the design aspects.

The design and construction of a structure are intimately related and the achievements of good workmanship depend largely on the simplicity of detailing of members, and of their connections and supports. For example detailing of a complex R.C.C. building on paper and even in specimens in the laboratory are easy to realize, but an actual construction in field of such design details may not be economically easily feasible to accomplish. Thus a design is only effective if it can be constructed and maintained in the field.

In many past earthquakes it has been observed that failure of the buildings occurred due to improper anchorage of transverse reinforcement in the columns which could not confine concrete in place properly. Also the improperly executed construction joints in shear walls resulted in movement and damage along the joints.

To ensure that construction is going according to the design details it is necessary that designer and owner or their representatives should be present on the site of construction. Along with construction, the maintenance of buildings should be carried out regularly.

To ensure good performance during the future earthquake timely inspection and repairs are essential.

8.6. BEHAVIOUR OF COLUMNS

A column is a vital element of a building. During a earthquake its response is very important as the failure of even one column may cause substantial damage to the building or even can result in its total collapse. The study of damaged buildings during the past earthquakes has shown that most frequently the cause of structural failures was due to inadequate beam to column and slab to column connection.

8.7. DUCTILITY OF A BUILDING

The ductility of a building can be defined as the ability of the building to dissipate energy and deform with out sudden failure. The sudden failure is known as brittle failure. The term ductile or ductility will be used repeatedly subsequently.

As we know that a concrete column consists of longitudinal steel reinforcing bars. These longitudinal reinforcing bars are tied together either by stirrups called ties or spiral. A spirally confined column basically is more ductile than, a column having stirrups or ties. At the time of earthquake motion the ductility of the column works if the ductility at the connection of the column with beam at the top of column also exists.

For beam and column connection to be ductile, the stirrups at the top of the column should continue either from the column or beam. The spacing between stirrups should not be more than *d*/4 or *D*/4 where *d* is the effective depth of beam and *D* is the least dimension of the column. The spacing should not be less than 75 mm and greater than 100 mm. The details of a ductile and non ductile joint are shown in Fig. 8.5 (*a*) and (*b*) respectively.

In seismic regions, current codes recommend that the ties or stirrups should

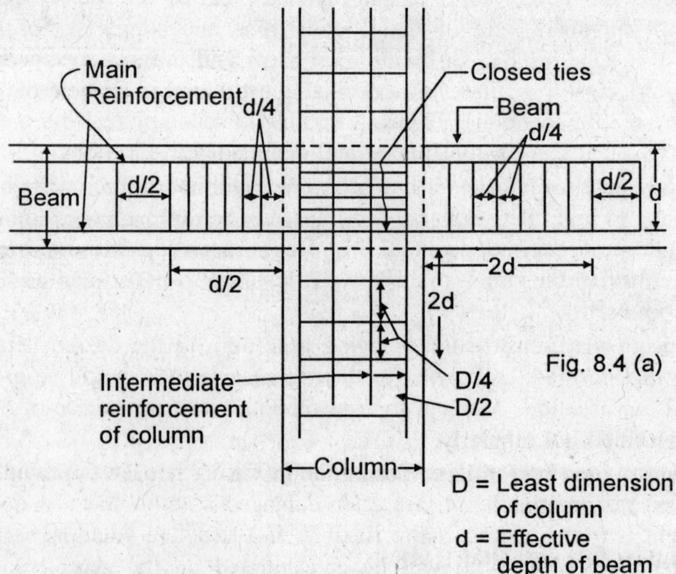

Fig. 8.5. (*a*). Ductile beam to column connection

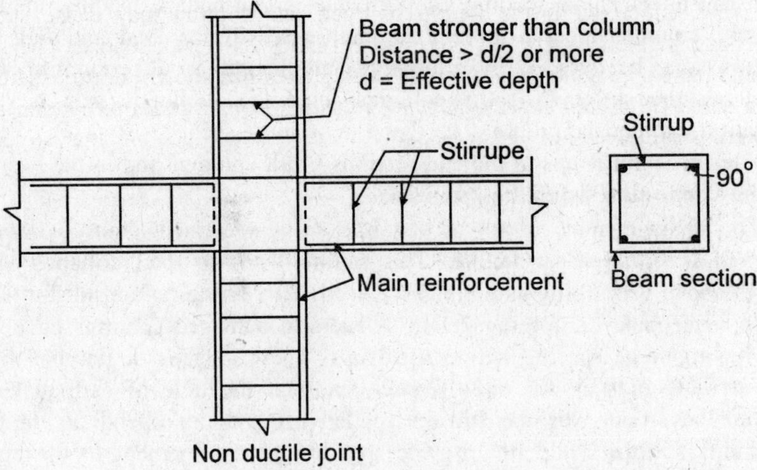

Fig. 8.5. (*b*). Non Ductile beam to column connection

be spaced closely. The spacing should not be less than 75 mm nor greater than 100 mm. In terms of dimension of beam or column it should be as stated above. In terms of diameter of beam reinforcement, spacing should not be more than 8 times the diameter of the beam reinforcement bars. Ties should be of deformed steel bars and they should be bent at an angle of 135° in stead of 90° as in ordinary situation. The length of bent bars should extend upto 10 times the diameter of stirrups and it should not be less than 63 mm. Rectangular ties around the perimeter bars should be supplimented by cross ties. Details of bend are shown in Fig. (*c*).

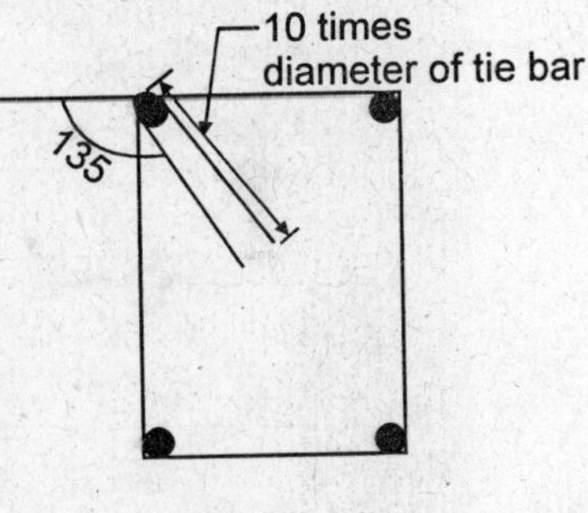

Fig. 8.5. (*c*)

Also the ties must be extended over the joint of the beam and column. The spacing should remain same as stated above. Buildings having these enhanced detailing features are called as ductile moment frames. Designs made on the basis of Japanese code result in stronger column and weak beams where as designs on U.S. codes result weak column and stronger beams.

8.8. SHORT COLUMN EFFECT

During the study of damaged buildings during past earthquakes it has been observed that short columns are often damaged in earthquake. A column twice in height is found 8 times more flexible. If a structure contains both short and long columns, more load will be concentrated on the short columns. Short columns are less prone to buckling, hence are capable of receiving high vertical loads. But under lateral loading *i.e.* horizontal or earthquake loading, the short and stiff columns receive more than their share of the load and fail. This situation may be avoided by adopting same length of all columns. Hence equalizing the stiffness of the columns. Piers and columns may be more resistant to earthquake failure if designed to be more shear resistant. In columns extra ties or spiral wraps in the end sections of all columns and in the beam, to column connection should be provided.

The damage mode (way) of concrete column elements most commonly observed is brittle shear failure. This failure leads to total collapse of the storeys above very easily as a bread is sliced. This brittle failure mostly results due to inadequate reinforcing details. Generally damaged columns have been seen having large spacing between stirrups. These stirrups or ties had hooks bent at their ends at 90° only. Consequently at the time of earthquake the concrete cover out side the stirrups spalled off and ties opend up. In these conditions stirrups could not provide the desired confinement to the central concrete core and complete failure followed quickly.

The failure of columns during the past earthquakes are shown in the following photographs. These photographs have been taken from Geological hazard photo user's Manual by Patricia A Lockridge. Steward D. Racey and Susan JMclean of National Geophysical data Centre U.S.A. Sept. 1997.

Fig. 8.6. Failure of spirally tied column on interstate 5/210 junction, California during the 1971 San Fernando earthquake. Column top is crushed under the impact of the failling upper deck.

Photographs of failure of columns in past earthquakes are shown in Figures 8.6 to 8.12. Authors acknowledge with thanks all these agencies for their reproduction.

Fig. 8.7. Collapsed column of interstate 5/210 interchange, California during 1971 San Fernando earthquake. The bottom part of the column pulled out of the base.

Fig. 8.8. Failure of a column of a hospital building due to the crushing of the concrete during 1971 San Fernando earthquake.

8.9. LESSONS FROM PAST EARTHQUAKES

From the comprehensive study of damage to structures during the past earthquakes, following lessons have been learnt. If these lessons could be implemented in the design of earthquake resistant buildings, sefer and more durable buildings can be obtained:

1. Buildings should be designed for both horizontal as well as vertical

Fig. 8.9. Failure of several spirally tied columns of Freehills Freeway Overpass during 1971 San Fernando earthquake. (Failure may be due to a combination of horizontal and vertical accelerations).

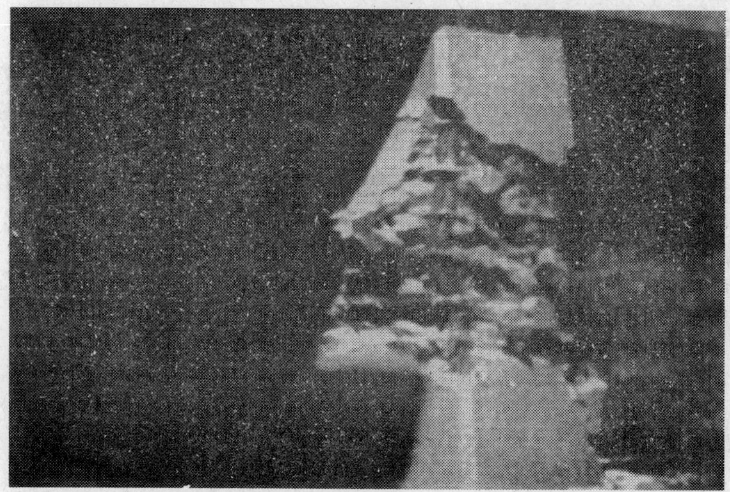

Fig. 8.10. Failed first-storey column in an eleven-storey apartment building after the 1985 mexico City earthquake. (This column failure was induced by a variation in stiffness between the first and other floors of the building, causing concentration of the load in the first story columns. However, column ties appear to be undamaged.)

components of the ground motion.

2. To prevent the total collapse of the R.C.C. buildings, strong column and weak beam concept must be adopted.

Fig. 8.11. Columns supporting the Highway 10 overpass at Venice Boulevard were damaged in the Northridge (California) earthquake of 1994. (The failure was mostly due to lack of spiral ties in the vicinity of the top joint. leading to lack of the necessary column confinement).

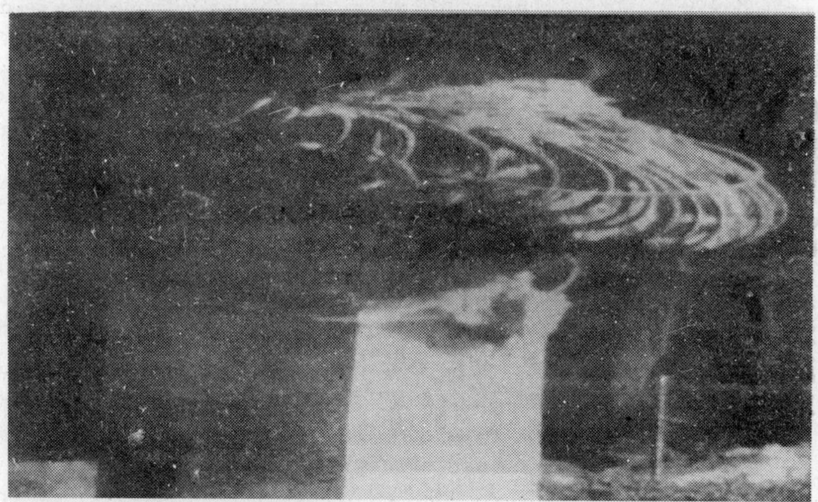

Fig. 8.12. Failed bridge support column supporting Interstate 10 (Santa Monica Freeway) at the La Cienega-Venice overcrossing during 1994 Northridge earthquake.

3. To design the earthquake resistant buildings, special attention to reinforcement detailing must be paid.
4. The mode or pattern of failure of columns suggests that lateral

reinforcement in the form of stirrups or spiral be provided at lesser spacing where the moment is largest. In addition, extra column ties or spiral wraps should be provided in the end sections of all columns and in the beam to column connections.

5. Stiffness in the structure should be well distributed in both horizontal as well as in vertical directions.
6. Infilled frames should be properly anchored to the bounding frames by shear connectors or reinforcement. After proper anchoring only the infilled frames should be considered as structural elements in the design. Random distribution of these infill frames will cause damage due to torsion effects.
7. Mud adobe, stone or brick masonry construction should be planned properly.
8. Structures at lintel and roof level should be tied with the help of R.C.C. bands.
9. To avoid torsion effect corner reinforcement along the height should be provided in masonry structures.
10. Close spacing of expansion joints along the length of the building should be avoided.
11. In order to identify the locations where local geology and sub soil properties are likely to modify the earthquake ground motion, a seismic microzoning survey should be made.
12. No attempt should ever be made to reduce the degree of hyperstaticity of a structure.
13. For very long structures the provision be made so that the seismic movement may not be synchronous.
14. For important structures, proper dynamic analysis be made. For very sensitive and strategic structures models may be tested.
15. New construction techniques developed on the basis of past earthquake damages should be adopted.
16. Continuous updating of country's seismic resistant construction codes should be carried out.
17. Research made upto date in the field of seismic resistant building construction should be included in the up dating of the country,s code of building earthquake resistant structures.
18. In the design the site effects of amplifying the ground shaking should be taken into consideration.
19. The design philosophy that a properly designed structure should resist a moderate earthquake with an acceptable damage and a big earthquake with out collapse has changed. Now clients and their insurer demand that building should simply not collapse but should retain its structural integrity through out the earthquake. Thus new requirements stipulate

that the structure should remain standing in an earthquake and not have to be demolished after the earthquake.

20. The use of asymmetric shapes in plan as well as in elevation and asymmetric distribution of mass and stiffness should be avoided.
21. Soft storeys are recognised universally dangerous and thus should be avoided unless their effect is incorporated in the design.
22. Public should be made aware of earthquake preparedness. Government and non government agencies should always be prepared and trained to deal with the after effects of earthquakes.

QUESTIONS

1. Name common causes of structure failures during an earthquake.
2. Write a detailed note on the failure of the following:
   (*a*) Beam-column joint failure
   (*b*) Soft storey effect
   (*c*) Poor reinforcement detailing
3. What is liquefaction of soil. Discuss its effects on the stability of structures.
4. What are the main defects of masonry structures? Discuss in detail.
5. What are non structural elements in a building or structure. How they affect the stability of the building during earthquake. Discussfully.
6. How construction and maintenance of a building influence its performance during earthquake. Explain.
7. Write a note on the ductility of a column.
8. A captive column is ....
   (*a*) A special type of column made of alloy
   (*b*) A short column built normally between floor and window sill level
   (*c*) A column built between floor and ceiling of the storey
   (*d*) All are correct
9. A column twice in length is 8 times more ....
   (*a*) Flexible (*b*) Stiff
   (*c*) No effect of height (*d*) All are correct
10. If a structure contains both short and long columns, the load will be concentrated more on
    (*a*) Long column (*b*) Short column
    (*c*) Both columns loaded equally (*d*) All are correct
11. The Phenomenon of liquefaction occurs in
    (*a*) Fine and uniform grained sandy soils
    (*b*) Fine grained clayey soils
    (*c*) In rocky soils
    (*d*) Any where
12. Generally the cause of structures failure is except
    (*a*) Provision of lateral reinforcement at relatively more spacing
    (*b*) Provision of lateral reinforcement more closely
    (*c*) Bending of hooks at 90°
    (*d*) All are correct

13. Long columns can bear more load than short columns
    (*a*) Gravity loads (*b*) Lateral loads
    (*c*) Both share equal loads (*d*) All are correct
14. During an earthquake buildings get damaged due to
    (*a*) Failure of masonry
    (*b*) Stone walls
    (*c*) Collapse of heavy roof tiles
    (*d*) Due to absence of tie beams at lintel level and roof level
    (*e*) All the above are correct
15. Identify the correct statement/statements
    (*a*) Widely spaced ties have been found the cause of failures of many columns during an earthquake
    (*b*) Details of column reinforcement should be shown for the full height from the foundation to the roof
    (*c*) To check buckling of longitudinal bars and to confine concrete in place closely spaced stirrups and ties is essential
    (*d*) Cut off reinforcement bars inconsistent with B.M. have led to structural failure
    (*e*) All are correct
16. Identify the incorrect statement/statements
    (*a*) Blindly following the seismic design building code does not always guarantee against serious damage or collapse
    (*b*) The performance of an building during earthquake depends on its state (condition)
    (*c*) Construction and maintenance influence to a great extent the performance of the building during an earthquake
    (*d*) Quality of construction materials does not have any impact on the performance of the building during an earthquake
17. Identify the correct statement/statements
    (*a*) Liquefied soil is a special type of soil
    (*b*) It is a liquid form of soil
    (*c*) In liquefied condition soil looses its shear strength and behaves as a viscous liquid
    (*d*) None of the above
18. Identify the correct statement/statements
    (*a*) Liquefaction of soil occurs when the ground water table is much deeper than the ground level
    (*b*) When the soil becomes saturated due to the ground water table
    (*c*) When the soil becomes air dry
    (*d*) When the soil is over dry.

ANSWERS

8. (*b*)	11. (*a*)	14. (*e*)	17. (*c*)
9. (*a*)	12. (*b*)	15. (*e*)	18. (*b*)
10. (*b*)	13. (*b*)	16. (*d*)	

9

Effect of Soil Properties on Seismic Performance of Structures

9.1. INTRODUCTION

During an seismic or earthquake activity soil mass experiences vibrations of different magnitudes. Actually soil mass experiences vibrations due to many causes such as wave action of water, construction activities, motion of heavy machines, blasting, quarrying and seismic activities.

Vibrations out of all these sources, seismic vibrations are more important from the safety point of view of the structures.

The seismic response of a structure is influenced by the properties of soil on which the structure is standing or founded. Strong and stiff soils transfer less portion of ground motions to the structure, where as weak soils transfer larger portion of the ground motions. Hence response of the structure does not only depends on the properties of the structure and its elements alone, but on the type of soil on which it is founded.

The ground motions that are not influenced by the presence of the structures are called as free field motions.

9.2. INFLUENCE OF SOIL PROPERTIES ON STRUCTURES

The studies of damage during the past earthquakes have revealed that the intensity of ground shaking during earthquakes and the resulting damage to structures are greatly influenced by the local geological and soil conditions. The topography of the site may cause wave amplification, which may cause heavy damage. The damage to structures due to earthquakes may be influenced by the:

(*i*) Maximum acceleration at the site.

(*ii*) Frequency characteristics of the ground motion and its duration.

(*iii*) Dynamic characteristics of the site of the affected area and the structure in terms of its natural period (time of vibration) and its duration.

The effect of soil conditions on the structures is due to the influence they exert on the intensity of ground motion or shaking and the resulting damages of the structures, which they suffer even though the soil under lying a building may remain perfectly stable during the earthquake. It has been observed that loose and unstable soils cause heavy damage, where as buildings founded on hard soils and rock have suffered less damage.

Scientists have observed that the prominant periods of ground vibrations during earthquakes are the periods of natural vibrations of bedded soil layer characteristics of a given locality. Smaller periods are found for firmer soils and larger periods for soft soils. Though the maximum acceleration produced at a particular site is a very important parameter in the seismic resistant design, but it alone does not determine the damage caused to a building. It has been observed that a very high acceleration acting for a very short duration as well as ground motions of very small amplitudes have caused very little damage to many types of structures.

The type of soil also influences the amplitudes of its vibrations. Vibrations of rocks have been found to have very little amplitude of the order of 2 to 5 mm, clays upto 30 mm and slimy and filled soils upto 100 mm or more. The acceleration of soil vibration is found to decrease appreciably with the increase in its density and solidity. Further the increase in the acceleration is caused by the presence of high ground water level, which is most substantial in loose soils. The influence of ground water level in rocks on the vibration acceleration is very small.

9.3. STRESS CONDITION OF SOIL ELEMENT

Soil dynamic problems usually can be divided into the following two categories:

(*a*) Small strain amplitude response

(*b*) Large strain amplitude response

Problems dominated by wave propagation effect usually induce strains of small amplitude in the soil. However for problems involving the stability of soil masses, large amplitude strains are induced. However under the influence of earthquake loading soil element may be subjected either of the following two conditions:

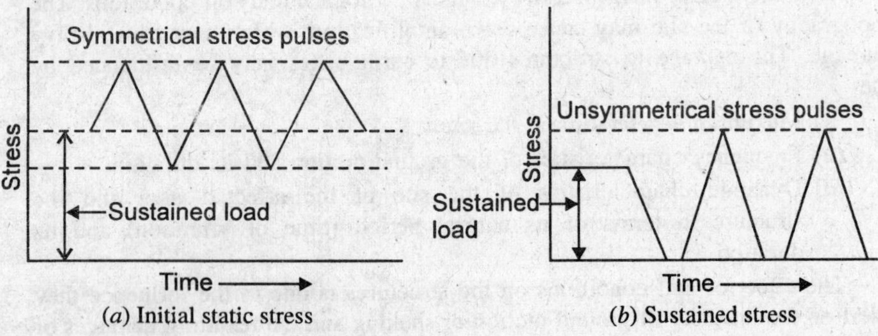

(*a*) Initial static stress (*b*) Sustained stress

Fig. 9.1.

1. The initial static stress is large and additional stresses induced by earthquake are small. Thus a symmetrical pulsating stress system is super imposed on a initial sustained stress. Fig. 9.1 (*a*)
2. The sustained stress is small and the pulsating stress is large. The combined effect is shown in Fig. 9.1 (*b*).

It has been observed that due to an earthquake, a footing resting on a soil does not experience an negative stress and the stresses under the footing acts in one direction only Fig. 9.2 (*a*), where as in the case of an embankment, the soil elements encounter shear stresses in either direction. The stress pattern is shown in Fig. 9.3 (*b*) and (*c*).

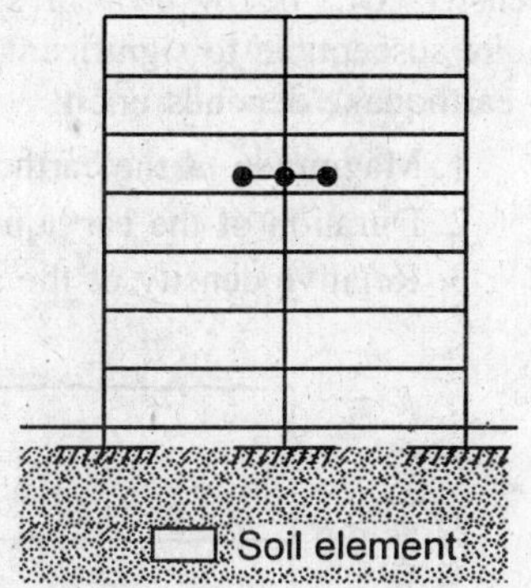

Fig. 9.2.

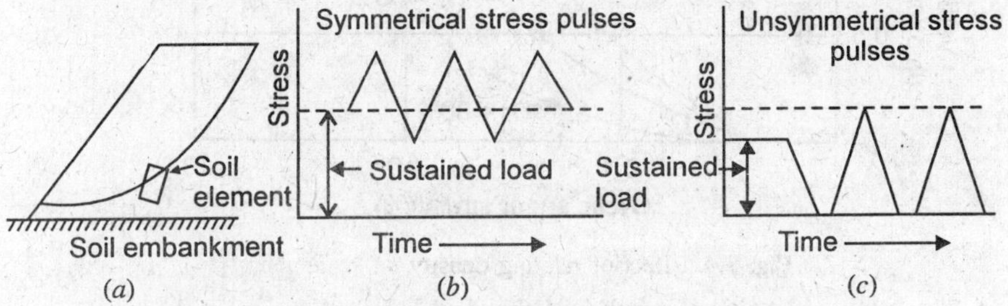

Fig. 9.3. Two dimensional loading on soil during earthquake

9.4. SOIL BEHAVIOUR UNDER VIBRATIONS

(Dynamic behaviour of soil)

The behaviour of soil under dynamic loading has been found to depend upon the following factors:

(*a*) On the magnitude of strain developed.

(*b*) On the rate of development of strain.

(*c*) On the number of loading cycles.

The strength of certain soils such as dry sands increases under rapid cycles of loading, where as the saturated soils and sensitive clays have been found to lose strength due to vibrations. The behaviour of different kinds of soils under earthquake has been discussed in subsequent sections.

9.4.1. Settlement of dry sands

Loose dry sands get compacted under vibrations. During earthquake such sands under go settlement. This is important to assess the extent or degree of settlement of loose sand deposits. Tough it is very difficult to predict the settlement with accuracy. However it has been observed that sands with relative density (Dr.) below 60% or standard penetration resistance 'N' below 15 are quite susceptible to significant settlement. The amount of compaction given by a earthquake depends upon:

1. Magnitude of the earthquake
2. Duration of the earthquake
3. Relative density of the soil

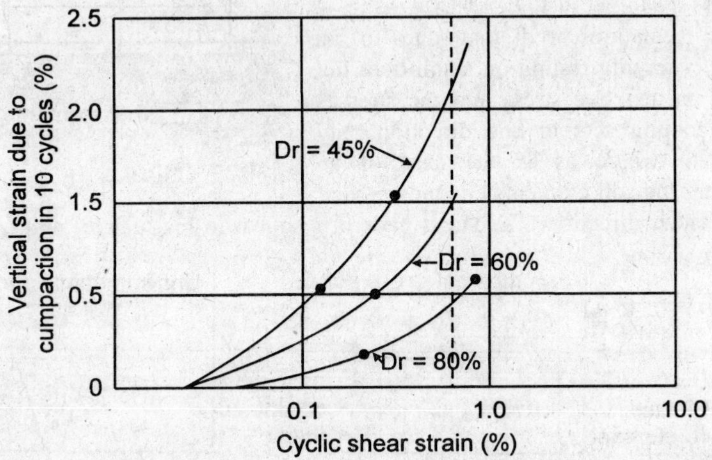

Fig. 9.4. Effect of relating density on settlement

The relative density of a soil is defined as

$$Dr = \frac{e_{max} - e}{e_{max} - e_{min}} \times 100 \qquad \ldots(9.1)$$

where,

e_{max} = Maximum void ratio of the soil in the looset condition

e_{min} = Minimum void ratio of the soil in the denset condition

e = Void ratio of the soil in the natural state.

The relative density of a soil has been found to give a more clear idea of the density of the soil than the void ratio. Two types of sands having the same void ratio may have totally different state of denseness and engineering properties. On the other hand if two sands have the same relative density, they usually behave in identical manner. According to relative density a soil may be divided into the following five categories:

Table 9.1. Denseness of soil

Denseness of soil	*Very loose*	*Loose*	*Medium dense*	*Dense*	*Very dense*
Dr (%)	< 15	15 to 35	35 to 65	65 to 85	85 to 100

In terms of dry unit weights in looset, denset and natural condition of soil, the dry density of soil may be expressed as follows:

$$D_r = \frac{\gamma_{max}}{\gamma_d}\left(\frac{\gamma_d - \gamma_{min}}{\gamma_{max} - \gamma_{min}}\right) \qquad \text{...(9.2)}$$

2. Prediction of settlement

Soil settlement may be evaluated by the following relations:

(*a*)
$$\Delta H = \frac{\Delta_e}{1 + e} \cdot H \qquad \text{...(9.3)}$$

where,

Δ_H = Settlement or change in height of soil deposit

Δ_e = Change in void ratio

e = Void ratio

H = Original height of soil layer or deposit.

(*b*)
$$\Delta_H = \frac{C_c \cdot H}{(1 + e_o)} \log_{10} \frac{P_0 + \Delta_p}{P_0} \qquad \text{...(9.4)}$$

where,

Δ_H = Amount of settlement

P_o = Original load on soil

Δ_p = Increase in load on soil

e_0 = Void ratio of soil

c_c = Compression index of soil.

(*c*) Some authors have suggested the settlement relation between critical void ratio of soil and natural void ratio as follows:

Settlement
$$\Delta_H = \frac{e_{cr} - e}{1 - e} \cdot H \qquad \text{...(9.5)}$$

where,

Δ_H = Settlement

e_{cr} = Critical void ratio above which the granular soil deposit will compact on being vibrated

e = Natural void ratio of the soil deposit

H = Height of soil deposit

The value of critical void ratio e_{cr} can be calculated by the relation as

$$e_{cr} = e_{min} + (e_{max} - e_{min})\ Exp\ (-0.75\ a/g)$$

where,

a = amplitude of applied acceleration

g = acceleration due to gravity.

Example 1. At a site the thickness of a soil deposit is found as 3.6 m. The dry unit weight of the deposit is 16 kN/m^3. Determine the settlement of this deposit with the following given data. The critical void ratio of the soil is 72% and specific gravity G as 2.72.

Solution. Given data

$$\text{Thickness } H = 3.6 \text{ m}$$
$$G = 2.72$$
$$e_{cr} = 72\% \text{ or } 0.72$$
$$\gamma_d = 16 \text{ kN/m}^3$$

The void ratio of a soil in terms of dry weight is given by the relation

$$e = \frac{G \cdot \gamma_w}{\gamma_d} - 1$$

$$= \frac{2.72 \times 10}{16} - 1 \qquad \text{(Here } \gamma_w = 10 \text{ N} = 1 \text{ kg)}$$

$$= 1.7 - 1.0 = 0.7 = 70\%$$

The natural void ratio = 0.7

Critical void ratio = 0.72

Then settlement from equation (9.5)

$$\Delta_H = \frac{c_{cr} - e}{1 - e} \times H$$

$$= \frac{0.72 - 0.70}{1 - 0.7} \times 3.6$$

$$= \frac{0.02 \times 3.6}{-0.03} = 0.24 \text{ m}$$

or settlement = 24 cm **Ans.**

Example 2. At a site the thickness of a sand deposit is 6 m. The natural void ratio of the sand is found as 1.05. After the construction of a building on the site the void ratio is found as 0.95. Determine the settlement of the deposit.

Solution.

Initial void ratio $e_0 = 1.05$

After construction void ratio $e_1 = 0.95$

Thickness of deposit $H = 6.0$ m

$$\Delta_e = 1.05 - 0.95 = 0.1$$

Then settlement from equation 9.3 is given as

$$\Delta_H = \frac{\Delta_e}{1 + e_0} \times H$$

$$= \frac{0.1}{1 + 1.05} \times 6.0$$

$$= \frac{0.6}{2.05} = 0.2927 \text{ m} = 29.27 \text{ cm } \textbf{Ans.}$$

Example 3. At a site soft clay layer exists at a depth of 8 m from the ground surface. The pressure on the clay due to over burden is found of the order of 3 kg/cm^2. Due to the construction of a new house on this site the pressure on the soil is found 4 kg/cm^2. Determine the settlement of the building with the following data:

(*i*) Soil compression index $C_c = 0.5$

(*ii*) Water content in the soil $w = 45\%$

(*iii*) Sp. gravity of the soil $G = 2.7$

From the equation of settlement;

$$\Delta_H = \frac{C_c \cdot H}{1 + e_0} \log_{10} \frac{P_0 + \Delta_p}{P_0}$$

We know the void ratio $e_0 = w.g = 0.45 \times 2.7$

$= 1.215$

Coefficient of compression $C_c = 0.5$

Initial pressure intensity $P_0 = 3.0$ kg/cm^2

Find pressure $P_0 + \Delta_P = 4.0$ kg/cm^2

$\therefore$ $\Delta_P = 4.0 - 3.0 = 1.0$ kg/cm^2

$$\therefore \quad \Delta_H = \frac{0.5 \times 8 \times 100}{1 + 1.215} \log_{10} \frac{3.0 + 1.0}{3.0}$$

$$= \frac{400}{2.215} \log_{10} \frac{4}{3}$$

$= 180.6 \log 1.333$ cm

$= 22.4$ cm **Ans.**

Example 4. At a site the thickness of the sand deposit is 9 m. The ground water table is 3 m below the ground surface. The unit weight of the soil upto a depth of 3 m from the ground surface is found as 20 kN/m^3 and below 3 m it is found as 18 kN/m^3. During an earthquake the ground water level reaches upto the ground surface. Determine the effective dynamic stress at the bottom of the sand layer.

Solution. The normal effective stress at the bottom of the sand layer before earthquake

$$\overline{\sigma} = (\gamma_1 Z_1 + \gamma_2 Z_2) - \gamma_w Z_2 \quad \ldots(i)$$

$\gamma_1 = 20$ kN/m^3

$\gamma_2 = 18$ kN/m^3

$Z_1 = 3$ m

$Z_2 = (9.0 - 3.0) = 6.0$ m

Putting the value in the relation (*i*) we get

$$\overline{\sigma}_n = (20 \times 3 + 18 \times 6) - 10 \times 6$$

$$= 60 + 108.0 - 60 = 108 \text{ kN/m}^2$$

(*ii*) Effective dynamic stress at the bottom of the sand

$$\overline{\sigma}_{dyn} = \overline{\sigma}_n - \gamma_w \times h_w$$

$$= 108 - 10 \times 3 = 108 - 30 = 78 \text{ kN/m}^2$$

Example 5. At a site the soil deposit is consisted of two layers. The thickness of upper layer is 4 m of sand having a unit weight of 18.5 kN/m^3. The thickness of the lower layer is 2 m of soil having a unit weight of 16.5 kN/m^3. The ground water table is upto the ground level. Determine the effective dynamic stress at 4 m and 6 m depth from the ground surface if the water level rises in a stand pipe upto a height of 2.0 m above ground level.

Solution. The normal stress at 4 m depth with out the effect of earthquake

$$\sigma_{n_1} = \gamma_1 Z_1 - \gamma_w \times Z_1$$

$$= 18.5 \times 4 - 10 \times 4 = 34 \text{ kN/m}^2$$

After earthquake, the water rises 2 m above the ground level.

$\therefore$ Effective dynamic stress $= \sigma_n - \gamma_w Z$

Alternatively effective dynamic stress $\gamma_1 Z_1 - \gamma_w (Z_1 + 2)$

$$= 34 - 10 \times 2 = 14 \text{ kN/m}^2$$

or $$= 18.5 \times 4 - 10 \times 6 = 74 - 60$$

$$= 14 \text{ kN/m}^2$$

(*ii*) At 6 m depth

Normal stress in second layer $\sigma_{n_2} = 2 \times 16.5 - 2 \times 10 = 13$

$\therefore$ Total stress at 6 m depth $= \sigma_{n_1} + \sigma_{n_2} = 34 + 13 = 47$

$\therefore$ Effective dynamic stress $=$ Total stress – Pore water pressure

$$= 47 - 2 \times 10 = 27 \text{ kN/m}^2$$

Alternatively dynamic effective stress

$$= \gamma_1 Z_1 + \gamma_2 Z_2 - \gamma_w (Z_1 + Z_2 + 2)$$

$$= 18.5 \times 4 + 2 \times 16.5 - 10 \times 8$$

$$= 74.0 + 33 - 80$$

$$= 107 - 80 = 27 \text{ kN/m}^2$$

$\therefore$ Dynamic effective stress at 4 m depth $= 14$ kN/m^2

Dynamic effective stress at 6 m depth $= 27$ kN/m^2 **Ans.**

9.5. LIQUEFACTION OF SOILS

From the survey of damaged buildings in recent earthquakes it has been observed that the liquefaction of cohesion less sandy soils due to earthquake ground motion presents or poses a great threat to the safety of all kinds of structures. Major land slide, lateral movements of bridge supports, settling and tilting of buildings, with out structural damage and failure of water retaining structures have been observed to occur in recent earthquakes due to liquefaction of soils. Now efforts have been intensified to evaluate the liquefaction potential of soil deposits.

Liquefaction of soils may be defined as a phenomenon in which the cohesion less soils loose their strength during an earthquake and become a viscous liquid which acquires a degree of mobility sufficient to allow movement ranging from several metres to thousands of metres.

According to soil scientist (R.B. Seed) the phenomenon of liquefaction can be defined as follows:

When a saturated sandy soil is subjected to ground motions (vibrations) due to either natural phenomenon as earthquake or due to artificial vibrations developed due to blasts etc., the soil tends to compact and decreases in volume. If there is no provision of drainage of water from the soil, the decrease in volume of soil results in increase of pore water pressure. When the pore water pressure becomes equal to the pressure or weight of over burden, the effective stress becomes zero and the cohesion less soil or sandy soil loses its strength Completely. This state is known s liquefied condition. Per unit area stress on soil is known as effective stress. The liquefaction of soil is also called as quick sand condition. Quick sand is not a kind of sand, but condition of soil when its effective stress zero. The theory of liquefaction is explained as below:

We know that the strength of non cohesive soils depends entirely on the internal friction of the soil as the cohesion intercept C is zero. In case of saturated condition the strength may be expressed as:

$$S = (\sigma_n - u) \tan \phi \qquad \text{...(9.6)}$$

where,

S = Shear strength

σ_n = Normal stress on any plane at a depth z as shown in Fig. 9.5

u = Pore water pressure = $\gamma_w \cdot h$

ϕ = Angle of internal friction of soil

Consider the stress on a plane of soil at a depth z below the ground level.

Then normal stress on the soil at a depth z is given by

$$\sigma_n = \gamma_{sat} \times z \qquad \text{...(9.7)}$$

$$\sigma_n = \overline{\sigma} + u$$

where, $\overline{\sigma}$ is effective stress.

or $\quad \overline{\sigma} = (\sigma_n - u) = (\sigma_n - \gamma_w \cdot h)$

or effective stress $\overline{\sigma} = (\gamma_{sat} - \gamma_w \cdot z) = \gamma_b \cdot z$

where, γ_b is submerged weight of soil.

$\therefore \quad S = \gamma_b \, z \tan \phi$

If the sand deposit is shaken due to an earthquake or any other oscillatory

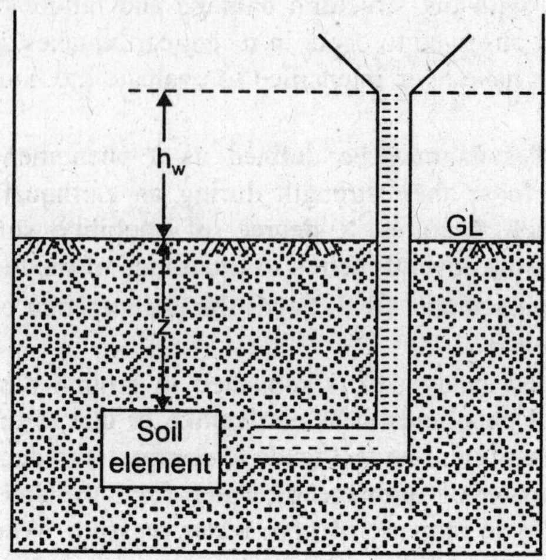

Fig. 9.5.

load or force, extra pore water pressure u will develop and the strength equation can be written as

$$S = (\gamma_b z - u) \tan \phi \qquad ...(9.8)$$

or $$S = (\gamma_b z - \gamma_w h) \tan \phi = \gamma_b \cdot \overline{\sigma} \tan \phi$$

As stated earlier also, as pore water pressure increases, shear strength of sand decreases; and a stage reach when all shear strength of soil is lost. In this condition

$$\gamma_b z - \gamma_w h = 0$$

or $$\frac{h}{z} = \frac{\gamma_b}{\gamma_w} \qquad ...(9.9)$$

Putting equation (9.9) in terms of critical gradient. We get

$$\frac{h}{z} = i_r = \frac{(G-1)\,\gamma_w}{1+e} \cdot \frac{1}{\gamma_w} = \left(\frac{G-1}{1+e}\right)$$

where

G = Specific gravity of soil solids

e = Void ratio of the soil

i_r = Critical hydraulic gradient.

When the value of critical hydraulic gradient is more than unity, the soil particles start to flow along with water and the structures founded on such soils fail. In practice in the design a factor of safety is provided and the value of critical hydraulic gradient is limited to 1/5 to 1/6.

Example 6. The properties of soil at a site are found as follows. Examine the possibility of developing liquefaction of the soil.

Data:

(*i*) The value of specific gravity $G = 2.67$

(*ii*) Void ratio of soil $e = 0.67$

Solution. Critical hydraulic gradient $i_r = \frac{h}{z} = \frac{G-1}{1+e}$

$$= \frac{2.67 - 1}{(1+0.67)} = 1.0$$

As the value of critical hydraulic gradient is 1.0, there is a possibility of occurring liquefaction at the site. For no liquefaction to occur the value of critical hydraulic gradient should be much less than 1.0.

The loss of soil strength occurs due to the transfer of inter granular stress from grains to the pore water. Thus if this transfer is complete, then there is a complete loss of strength. In case the transfer of stress from the grains is partial to the pore water, then only a partial loss of strength will take place.

As the stress condition is cyclic, a momentary transfer of all initial effective confining pressure to the pore water may not be of great importance from the engineering point of view. In case complete transfer of initial effective stress to the pore water is maintained for some time, the soil behaves as a viscous fluid.

The decrease in effective stress indicates reduction in rigidity, resulting in greater strain or settlement. Thus the initiation of partial transfer of stress indicates the possible surface as well as structures settlement founded on such soils. Structures founded on liquefied soils will start sinking in it. The rate of sinking depends upon the duration for which the soil remains liquefied.

9.5.1. Eavourable conditions for occuring liquefaction of soil

Liquefaction is likely to be affected by the following factors:

1. Type of soil. Mostly liquefaction occurs in non cohesive soil, such as coarse grained sandy soils. On the other hand liquefaction does not occur in cohesive soils such as clays.
2. Void ratio and relative density of soils.
3. Initial confining pressure.
4. Characteristics of the earthquake. (Magnitude and ground acceleration = 025g)
5. In case the sandy layer exists within 15 to 20 m from the ground level and is not subjected to high over burden pressure.
6. The sand particles are of uniform medium size 0.04 mm to 5.0 mm Fig. 9.6.
7. The sand layer exists below the ground water level *i.e.* the sand layer is saturated.
8. The standard penetration test value is below a certain level (10 – 21) Fig. 9.7.

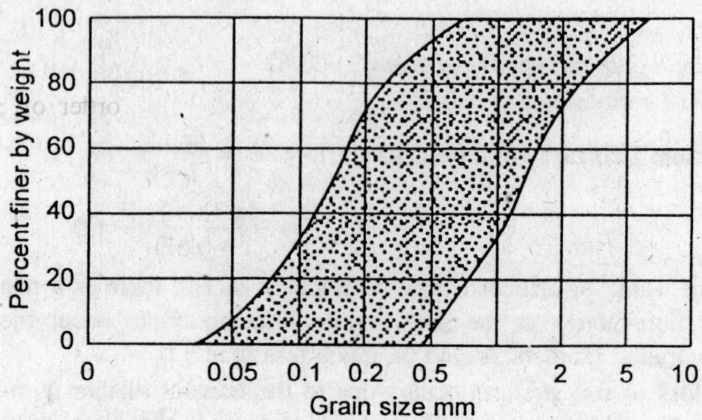

Fig. 9.6. Critical zones for grain size distribution curve (Ohasaki–1970)

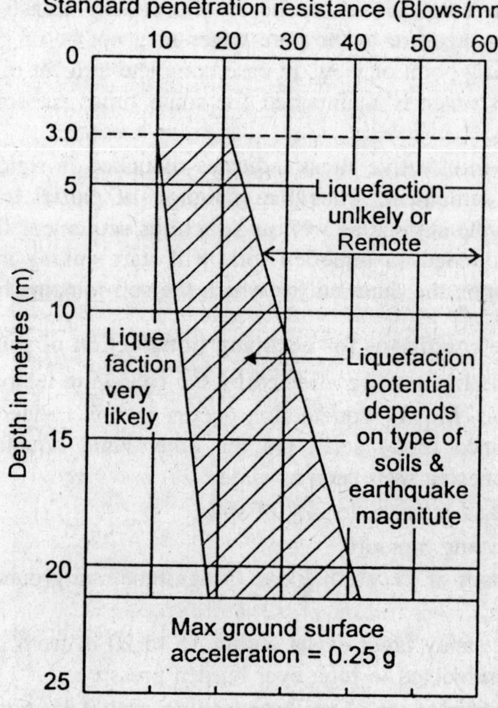

Fig. 9.7. Liquefaction potential evaluation chart courty Prof. R.B. Seed

9.5.2. Effect of liquefaction on structures

In liquefied state of soil, the structures can settle or tilt or ripped (get apart) as the ground spreads laterally or flows. Thus liquefaction allows heavy structures to settle or tip and light/weight structures buried under soil rise above

Fig. 9.8. The Building Sank 1 m evenly due to soil liquefaction the displaced soil caused a bulge on the road

the ground due to buoyancy. Cracking in structures may develop from the movement along the faults due to differential compaction of the soil or land slides. During strong ground shaking the loose cohesionless soils get compressed or compacted causing differential settlements of buildings ranging from 5 cms to more than 1.0 m. The settlement of a building about 1 m is shown in Fig. 9.8. A tilted building is shown in Fig. 9.9.

Fig. 9.9. This building tilted as a rigid body as the raft foundation rose above ground

In liquefied condition of soil building overturn easily. A unevenly sinking building is shown in Fig. 9.10.

Fig. 9.10. Building sank unevenly and leaned against the neighbouring building

Overturning of building in Taiwan during 1999 earthquake is shown in Fig. 9.11. The destruction of a building in Nigata during earthquake of 1964 is

Fig. 9.11. Buildings destroyed from liquefaction in Wufeng, Taiwan, September 1999

shown in Fig. 9.12 due to liquefaction. Liquefaction induced foundation settlement during earthquake continues to be a major cause of damage to all types of structures including buildings, bridges, roads, dikes, sea walls and levees etc.

During Bhuj earthquake of 2001, the mass destruction in the region occurred due to the liquefaction of the soil of the region. Hydrologist and villagers have reported the liquefaction of soil in some cases was sufficient to activate rivers of the desert, that were dry for more than a century. Wide spread liquefaction was confirmed by SPOT imagery and field observations. Many

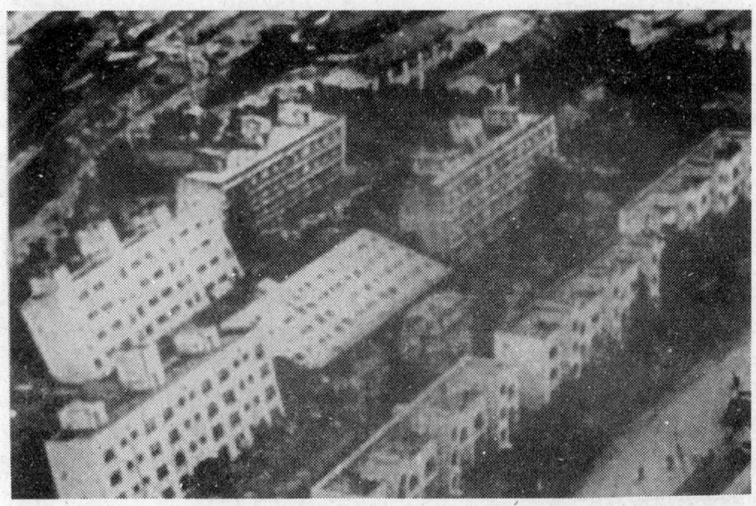

Fig. 9.12. Damage due to liquefaction caused by 1964 Nigata, Japan earthquake of magnitude 7.4.

mud volcanoes in the Rann of Kutch have dimensions of hundreds of metres. One volcano covers a 5 km diameter stretch of the southern Rann with a dark sand and mud as shown in Fig. 9.13. Numerous ancient river channels have

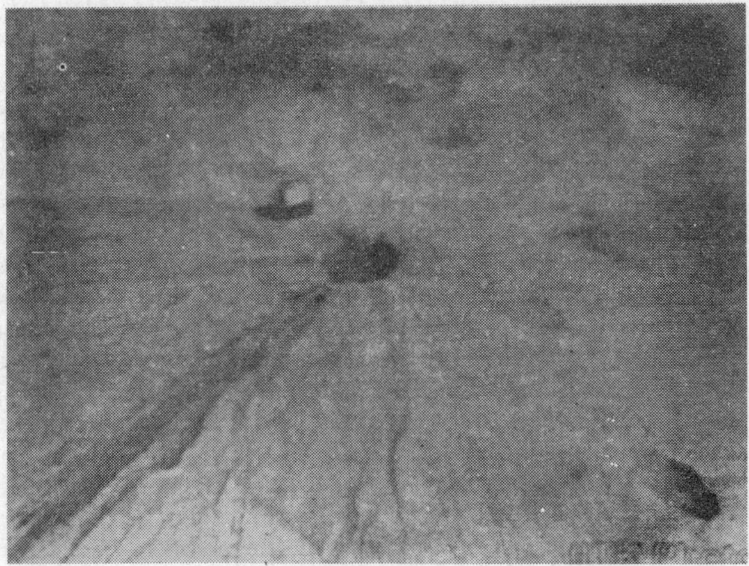

Fig. 9.13. Liquefaction leading to mud spread during Bhuj Earthquake (Courtesy—IIT Kanpur)

been illuminated by a Pock Mark Pattern of sand vents and some have clearly flowed, and breached their old channels.

Similarly the most intense damage during 17 October 1989 Loma Prieta earthquake was confined to areas where buildings and other structures were built over the top of loosely consolidated water saturated soils, as loosely consolidated soils tend to amplify shaking and increase structural damage. Water saturated soils compound the problem due to their susceptibility to liquefaction and corresponding loss of bearing strength.

9.6. MEASURES TO MINIMISE THE EFFECTS OF LIQUEFACTION

Following measures have been found effective to reduce the effects of liquefaction:

1. To increase the relative density of the sands by compaction.
2. Replace the sand by soil which has less likely hood of liquefaction.
3. Lower the ground water table by draining out ground water by suitable equipments.
4. Driving piles into a layer less likely to be liable to liquefaction.

9.7. FACTORS AFFECTING LIQUEFACTION CHARACTERISTICS

The characteristics of liquefaction of sands have been found affected by the following factors:

1. **Grain size distribution of sand.** Under identical conditions fine and uniform size grained sands are found more prone to liquefaction than coarse grained sands. Sands having grain size between 0.04 mm 0.5 mm are found more susceptible to liquefaction.
2. **Initial relative density.** For controlling the liquefaction of the soil (sands), initial relative density is one of the most important factors. With the increase of initial relative density, settlement and pore pressure both are reduced considerably during the period of vibrations. The slope of the stress-strain curve for loose sand is a measure of the rigidity of the soil. It is less for dense sand. Thus under identical stress conditions, sands having smaller initial relative density will experience larger strain and thus will under go greater settlements than those having greater initial relative density. Hence the chances of liquefaction and excessive settlement are considerably reduced with the increase in initial relative density.
3. **Vibration characteristics.** Liquefaction and settlement of soil depends upon the nature, magnitude and type of dynamic loading. Under shock loading, the whole stratum may be liquefied at once, where as in a steady state loading (vibrations) the liquefaction may start from the top and proceed down wards. Under steady state vibrations, the maximum pore pressure develops only after a certain number of cycles of vibrations have been imparted to the deposit. Further in general, it has been observed that horizontal vibrations in dry sand cause larger

settlements than vertical vibrations. Similar behaviour is anticipated in saturated sands.

The stress conditions created by an earthquake are more severe than one directional stress conditions. Thus pore water pressure develops faster under seismic vibrations than unidirectional stresses. The stress ratio required for a peak cyclic pore pressure ratio of 100%, under seismic vibration conditions is about 10% less than that required for unidirectional vibration conditions.

4. **Dimensions of deposits and location of drainage.** Generally non cohessive soils as sands are more pervious or porous than cohessive fine grained soils as clay. In case if a pervious deposit has large dimensions, then the drainage length of water from large soil deposits will be more. During an earthquake under the rapid vibrations, the deposit may behave as if it is undrained. Thus the chances of liquefaction of the deposit increase. To stabilize a potentially liquefiable sand deposit, gravel drains may be introduced. The drains are found fully effective if the materials of the drain is about 200 times more permeable than the material of the deposit *i.e.* the material held by the drain. The drainage path is reduced by the introduction of drains with in the large deposits.
5. **Magnitude and nature of super imposed loads.** On a sample the initial effective stress is isotropic. To transfer large initial effective stress to the pore water, either the intensity of vibrations or number of particular stress cycles must be large. Thus the large effective stress has been found to reduce the possibility of liquefaction of the deposit.
6. **Method of soil formation.** Generally sands do not show the characteristic structure as do the fine grained soils such as clays. Recent research has indicated that the liquefaction characteristics of saturated sands under cyclic loading are significantly influenced by the method of preparing sample and soil structure.
7. **Period under sustained load.** The age of a sand deposit may significantly influence the liquefaction characteristics of the deposit. A study of liquefaction of undisturbed sand dune and its freshly prepared sample has shown that liquefaction resistance of undisturbed sand was found 75% more than the fresh sample. The increase in resistance may be due to some type of cementation at the contact points of sand particles and might be associated with secondary compression of the soil.
8. **Traped air.** A fraction of the pore pressure developed in the deposit might get consumed or dissipated in the compression of traped air in the water. Hence traped air has been found to reduce the possibility of liquefaction of sand.
9. **Previous strain history of sand.** Sand might have been subjected to previous earthquakes. This might have been induced some strain in the sand, which may influence the liquefaction characteristics of the sand.

9.8. DESIGN PARAMETERS OF SOILS

The basic parameters of soil used in the design of dynamic response analysis of soil are shear modulus and damping. These parameters are discussed below.

9.8.1. Shear modulus or modulus of elasticity

Shear modulus of a soil for small strains may be taken as the average slope of the stress-strain curve. But at large strains, the stress-strain curve does not remain liner and markedly becomes non linear. Hence the shear modulus does not remain constant, but still remains dependent on the magnitude of shear strain. For sand and clay the shear modulus decreases as the strain increases. Fig. 9.14. The shear modulus measured from the wave velocity corresponds to

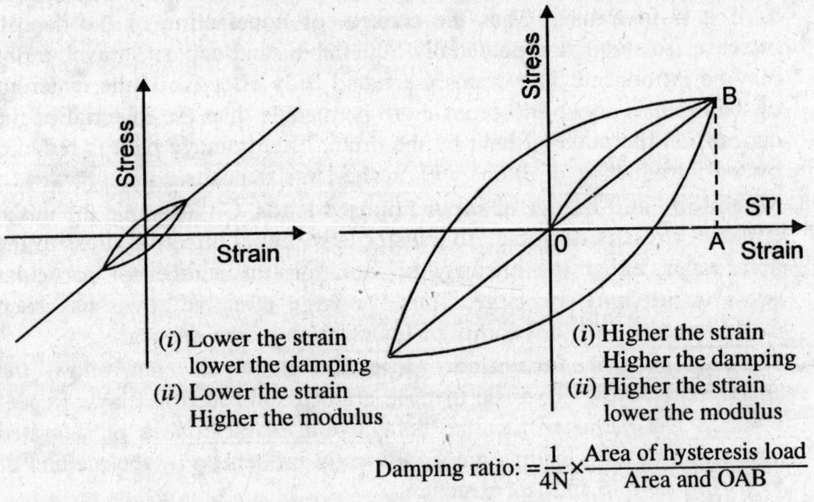

Fig. 9.14. Effect of shear strain on damping and shear modulus

10^{-5} to 10^{-4} of the strain. The relation between shear modulus and shear wave velocity is given by the following equation

$$G = \rho \cdot V_s^2 \qquad \ldots(9.10)$$

where,

G = Shear modulus of soil

V_s = Shear wave velocity

ρ = Mass density of soil.

The modulus of elasticity of soil can be determined in the laboratory by conducting a triaxial compression test. The stress strain curve is drawn between the deviator stress $(\sigma_1 - \sigma_3)$ on y-axis and strain τ_1 on the x-axis. Usually for non cohesive soils (sands) a drained consolidated (C-D) test is conducted. The value of the modulus of elasticity generally is obtained by secant modulus at

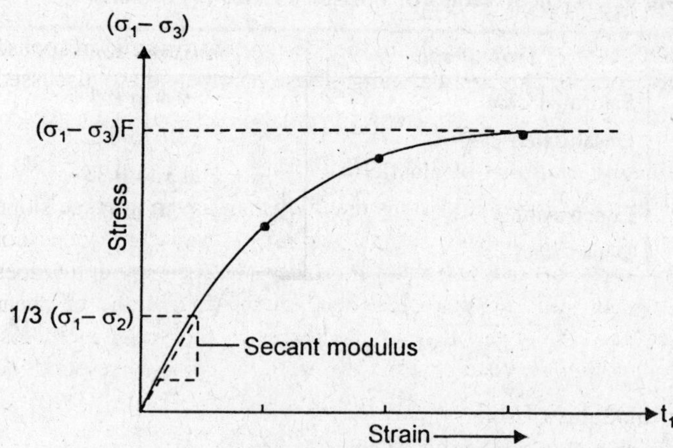

Fig. 9.15. Shear Modulus

1/3rd or 1/2 (half) of the peak stress as shown in Fig. 9.15. It may also be obtained by initial tangent modulus or tangent modulus at 1/2 to 1/3 of the peak stress. σ_1 is major principal stress and σ_3 major minor stress $\sigma_1 - \sigma_3$ is called deviator stress. Some typical values of modulus of elasticity of soils is given in Table 9.2.

Table 9.2. Typical values of E.

S. No.	*Type of soil*	*E*	
		Kg/cm²	*kN/m²*
1.	Soft clay	15 – 40	1500 – 4000
2.	Hard clay	60 – 150	6000 – 15000
3.	Silty sand	60 – 200	6000 – 20000
4.	Loose sand	100 – 250	10000 – 25000
5.	Dense sand	400 – 800	40000 – 80000
6.	Dense gravel	1000 – 2000	10×10^5 to 2×10^5
7.	Sand stone	upto 5 kg/m²	upto 500
8.	Lims stone	2.5 – 10	250 – 1000
9.	Baslt	1.5 – 10	150 – 1000

For an elastic material the value of Poisson's ratio varies from 0.0 to 0.5 as shown in Table 9.3.

From the value of elastic modulus E and Poisson's ratio, ν, the value of shear modulus *G* can be determined as shown in equation (9.11)

Typical values of poisson's ratio of soils are shown in Table 9.3 below.

Table 9.3. Typical values of Poisson's ratios (ν) of soils

S. No.	*Type of soil*	*Poisson's ratio ν*
1.	Saturated clay	0.4 to 0.5
2.	Unsaturated clay	0.1 to 0.3
3.	Silt	0.3 to 0.35
4.	Loose sand	0.30 to 0.5
5.	Dense sand	0.2 to 0.3

$$G = \frac{E}{2(1+\nu)} \quad \text{...(9.11)}$$

where,

G = Shear modulus of soil

E = Elastic or young's modulus of soil

ν = Poisson's ratio of soil.

In the absence of any given data, the values of E and ν can be used as given in Tables 9.2 and 9.3 above.

The average relationship between shear modulus G and strain for sand and clay is shown in Fig. 9.16. During an earthquake the shear strain may increase

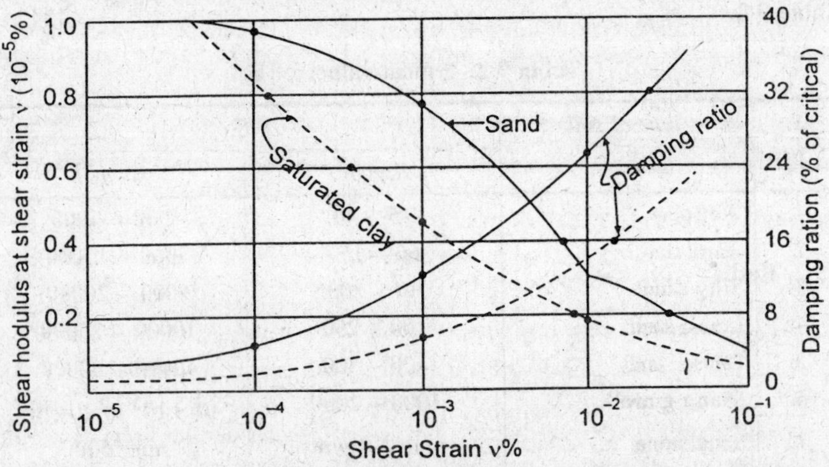

Fig. 9.16. Average relationship between shear modulus and shear strain of sand and saturated clays

by about 10^{-3}% during low magnitude earthquake and by 0.1% or 10^{-1}% during high magnitude earthquakes. The magnitude of maximum strain will be found different in each cycle. For earthquake resistant design purpose the two third value of the shear modulus measured at the maximum strain developed should be used *i.e.* for design purposes the value of shear modulus G = 2/3 of its maximum value observed.

9.9. DAMPING

Damping is a source of energy dissipation in a vibrating structure. Thus damping plays a very important role in limiting the displacement of a structure near resonance. If there was no damping, it was quite possible that almost any structure would have suffered damage in a earthquake due to resonance, as an actual earthquake movement generally consists of a large range of frequencies. When a building resonates in response to ground motion, its acceleration is amplified. However buildings are prevented from resonating as they are damped. The extent of damping in a building depends on its connections, non structural elements and constructional materials. Here we shall discuss following two types of damping.

9.9.1. (1) Material damping

When a vibrating wave passes through soil, it experiences internal or material damping. As stated above daming is a source of dissipating energy. Hence material damping can be considered as a measure of loss of vibration energy due to mainly hysteresis in the soil. Hysteresis can be expressed as a phenomenon where in the energy loss per cycle is related to the internal friction under repeating loading and unloading as shown in Fig. 9.14. Hysteretic action has been found to increase the over all damping of the system and reduction in the deformation of the structure. Damping can be conveniently expressed as a fraction of critical damping, hence it is referred as a damping ratio. The damping ratio ca be defined as

$$\text{Damping ratio} = \frac{1}{4\pi} \frac{\text{Area of Hysteresis}}{\text{Area of triangle OAB}} \qquad \text{(See Fig. 9.14)}$$

In most cases the strain level experienced during earthquakes ranges from 10^{-5} to 10^{-1}. Thus maximum damping for sands may be assumed as 16% and for clay as 10% during an earthquake.

9.9.2. Radiation damping

It is a measure of the loss of energy from a structure through the radiation of the waves away from the footing. Thus it is purely a geometrical effect. There is no convenient method to measure radiation damping of soil in the field.

When damping is introduced, the general shape of the response curve remains the same, but the magnitudes are greatly reduced. Theoretically though damping is considered as variable, but in practice it is not generally regarded as a design variable.

9.10. SOIL-STRUCTURE INTERACTION

The soil-structure interaction may be defined as the interdepdent response relation ship between a structure and the supporting soil. Recent studies on earthquakes have revealved that for determining the seismic response of a structure it is extremely important to understand the relationship between the period of vibration of the structure and the period of vibration of the supporting soil. The structural damage during an earthquake has been found directly related to (*i*) depth of soil deposit overlying the bed rock and, (*ii*) to the period of vibration of soil.

In order to determine the seismic performance of a structure at a given location or site, the dynamic properties of the combined soil and structure system must be evaluated. The nature of sub soil may influence the response of a structure in the following ways.

1. An amplification phenomenon of the sub soil may take place. In this phenomenon the seismic excitation at the bed rock level may get modified during the transmission of vibrations through the overlying soil deposit. This may cause in reduction in the excitation.
2. The fixed base dynamic properties of the structure may be modified significantly due to the presence of the overlying deposit on the bed rock. This includes change in period of vibration and change in the mode shape.
3. A significant part of the vibration of flexibly supported structure may be dissipated by material and radiation damping in the supporting medium.

Studies on earthquakes have shown that the behaviour of the structure depends partly on the nature of the supporting soil and similarly the behaviour of the stratum (soil) is modified by the presence of the structure. Thus it follows that the amplification of the soil is also influenced by the presence of the structure. The soil-structure interaction creates a difference between the motion at the base of the structure and the free field motion which would have taken place at the same point in the absence of the structure. However this factor is seldom taken into account during determining the amplification of soil due to difficulties in its evaluation.

If shear waves are travelling vertically though a soil layer, of thickness *H*, the period of horizontal vibration of the soil can be determined by the following relation. The horizontal vibrations are more pronounced and dangerous than vertical components.

$$T_h = \frac{4H}{(2n-1)V_s} \qquad \text{...(9.14)}$$

where,

T_h = Horizontal period of vibration

H = Thickness of soil deposit

V_s = Shear wave velocity

n = An integer.

9.11. SUMMERY OF DAMAGE DUE TO THE NATURE OF THE SOIL

The effect of soil conditions on the damage of structures may be summarized as follows:

1. Structures founded on loose and unstable soils suffered heavy damage during earthquakes.
2. Structures founded on rocks suffered least damage.
3. During an earthquake the predominant periods of ground vibrations are the periods of natural vibrations of beded layer of soil of a given locality.
4. Smaller periods are observed for firmer soils and larger periods for soft soils.
5. Type of soil also influence the amplitude of its vibration.
6. Amplitudes of different soils have been found as follows:
   (*a*) Rocks 2 to 5 mm
   (*b*) Clay upto 30 mm
   (*c*) Filled and loose soil upto 100 mm or more
7. Increase in acceleration of vibration is influenced or caused by the presence of high ground water levels, which is more pronounced in loose soils.

QUESTIONS

1. Discuss the factors which influence the behaviour of soil under dynamic loading.
2. Define liquefaction of soil. Also discuss the factors which affect the liquefaction of soil.
3. Discuss the conditions under which soil liquefaction takes place.
4. Discuss the measures under taken to reduce the soil liquefaction.
5. The most susceptible soil to liquefaction is......
   (*a*) Clayey soil
   (*b*) Silt
   (*c*) Fine to medium sized uniform grained sized soils
   (*d*) Coarse grained soils and gravel
6. The least susceptible soil to liquefaction is......
   (*a*) Gravel and coarse grained sized soil
   (*b*) Uniform fine to medium sized soils
   (*c*) Silt
   (*d*) Clay
7. The amount of compaction developed in soil by a earthquake depends
   (*a*) Magnitude of earthquake (*b*) Duration of earthquake
   (*c*) Relative density of soil (*d*) All are correct
8. Quick sand is.......
   (*a*) A special type of sand
   (*b*) A condition of cohesionless soil when effective stress of the soil becomes zero
   (*c*) A condition of cohesion less soil when total stress of the soil becomes zero
   (*d*) All are correct

9. The value of critical hydraulic gradient when soil particles start flowing with water is
   (*a*) 1.0 (*b*) 3.5
   (*c*) 7.5 (*d*) 10.0
10. Liquefaction of soil ...... damages of the buildingss
    (*a*) Lowers (*b*) Increases
    (*c*) No effect on damage (*d*) None is correct
11. The presence of high ground water level......acceleration of vibrations
    (*a*) Decreases (*b*) Increases
    (*c*) No effect (*d*) All are correct
12. A sand deposit consists of two layers. The top layer is 4 m and the bottom layer is 6 m. The natural void ratios for the two layers are 63% and 75% white the their critical void ratios are 70% and 76% respectively. Determine the total settlement of both the layers. **[Ans.** $\Delta H = 1.0$m]
13. At a site the soil deposit consists of two layers. The thickness of top layer is 6 m of unit weight 18.0 kN/m^3, and the bottom layer is 4 m thick having unit weight as 16 kN/m^3. In the initial condition the soil is saturated upto the ground surface. After an earthquake, it was found that water in the stand pipe rose to a height of 2.0 m about the ground surface. Find out the dynamic effective stress at 6 m and 10 m depths.
    [Ans. Dynamic effective stress at 6 m depth = 28 kN/m^2
    Dynamic effective stress at 10 m depth = 52 kN/m^2]
14. At a place the soil deposit is of two types of soils. The thickness of the top layer is 6 m and that of the bottom layer is 4 m. The natural void ratio of the top and bottom layers is 67% and75% respectively. Their critical void ratios are found as 72% and 77% respectively. Find out the total settlement of the deposit. **[Ans.** ΔH = 1.23 m]

ANSWERS

5. (*c*) 7. (*d*) 9. (*a*) 11. (*b*)
6. (*d*) 8. (*b*) 10. (*b*)

10

Earthquake Motion and Response

10.1. INTRODUCTION

In chapters from 4 to 6 we have seen that linear systems of any complexity can be split into a combination of single degree freedom system. In this chapter the behaviour of single degree of freedom systems subjected to earthquake excitation would be examined. The response characteristics due to some of the recorded strong earthquakes shall be discussed here. During a severe earthquake invariably structures undergo plastic deformations as it would be uneconomical to design all elements of a structure to remain elastic. Hence the behaviour of non linear single degree of freedom system is also included in this chapter. A numerical method for the evaluation of responses applicable to linear as well as non linear systems is also discussed here.

10.2. STRONG MOTION EARTHQUAKE

In India the first major record of a earthquake was done in 1967 at Koyna (Maharastra) as shown in Fig. 10.1. How ever in the world mostly in western U.S.A. and Japan data on a number of earthquakes have been recorded. Among the recorded data, the record of May 18, 1940 earthquake at EL centro, California (U.S.A.) has been extensively used for analysis and design. This record is shown in Fig. 10.2. Fig. 10.3 shows a record of a typical short duration earthquake.

In case there is a layer of soil overlying the base rock, and if the motion of the earthquake is recorded simultaneously at the rock as well as at the surface of the soil, it is expected that the amplitudes of surface motion at frequencies corresponding to the predominant frequencies of the overburden soil would be magnified as compared to the record on the rock. From the study of these accelerograms following general conclusions can be drawn.

1. Near the epicentre, the acceleration amplitudes exhibit high frequency content of the order of 10 to 15 cycles per second.
2. The peak acceleration may have the values of the order of 40 to 70% g and even higher in exceptional circumstances.
3. Away from the epicentre both the acceleration amplitude and frequencies decrease.
4. About 50 km away from the epicentre the predominant frequencies have been observed of the order of 3 to 6 cycle per second.

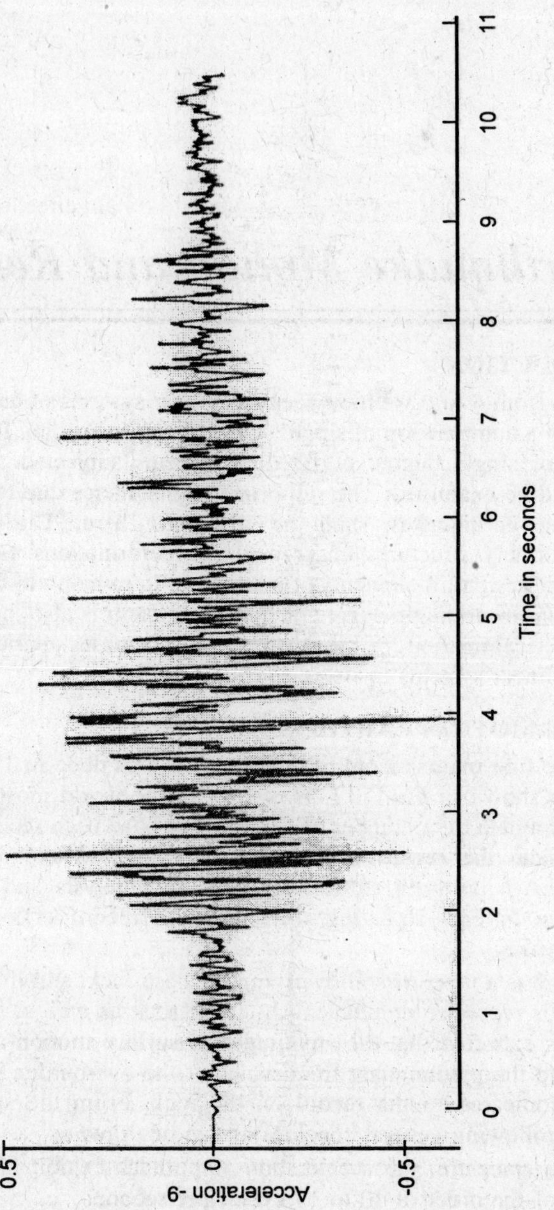

Fig. 10.1. Accelerogram of Koyana Earthquake

5. At epicentre the peak acceleration does not increase directly in proportion to the magnitude of the earthquake.
6. With the increase in magnitude, the rate of decrease of acceleration with distance has been found less.

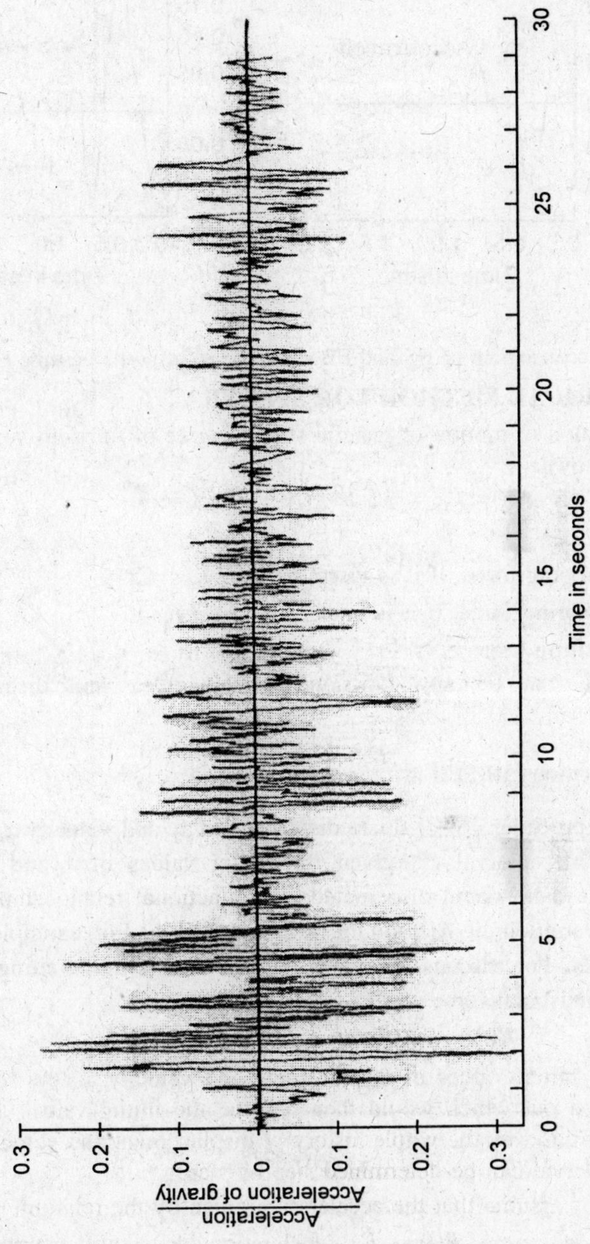

Fig. 10.2. Accelerogram of Elcentro Earthquake

7. Other conditions being equal, motion on a harder ground have been found to exhibit higher accelerations at higher frequencies compared to that on softer ground.

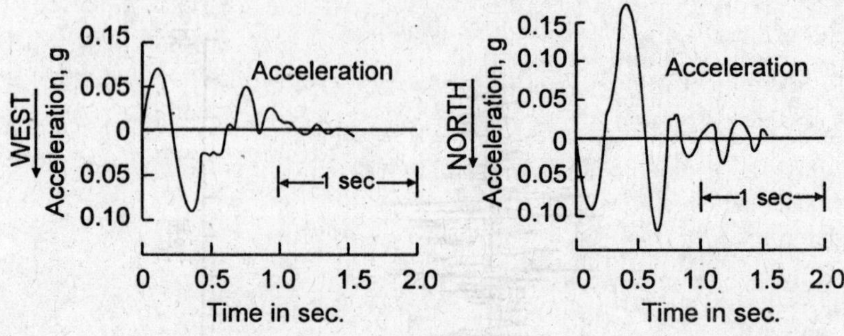

Fig. 10.3. Accelerogram of NS and EW components of port Hueneme Earthquake

10.3. NUMERICAL METHOD FOR SPECTRA

The equation of motion of general single degree of freedom system can be written as follows:

$$m\ddot{x} + F_D + F_R = R(t) \qquad \ldots(10.1)$$

where,

F_D = Damping force. If it is viscous then $F_D = C\dot{x}$

F_R = Restoring force, if it is linear, then $F_R = K \cdot x$

$R(t)$ = Exciting force.

F_D and F_R can be any function of velocity $\dot{x}$ and displacement x respectively.

From equation (10.1), $$\ddot{x} = \frac{R(t) - F_D - F_R}{m} \qquad \ldots(10.2)$$

Now the procedure to evaluate displacement x_e and velocity $\dot{x}_e$ at the end of a small time interval 'h' given the initial values of x_0 and $\dot{x}_0$ shall be discussed. The data would also include the functional relationship of F_R and F_D and the variation of $R(t)$ in the time interval h. For example, in linear system $F_R = Kx$. For viscous damping $F_D = C\dot{x}$ and if the exciting force is a steady state sinusoidal force,

$$R(t) = F_0 \sin \omega t$$

From the initial values of displacement and velocity a new set of values will be worked out which would then become the initial values for the next 'time' step. In this way the whole history of displacement and velocity over the entire time interval can be determined step by step.

Now let us assume that the acceleration given by the relation

$$\ddot{x} = \frac{R(t) - F_D - F_R}{m}$$

varies linearly in the interval h. If h is small, this assumption is reasonable. Usually the value of h is taken equal to or less than $T/20$, where T is the natural period of the system. This method is known as linear Acceleration method due to the assumed shape of acceleration variation shown in Fig. 10.4.

Integrating the equation for acceleration the value of velocity and displacement would be determined as follows:

Velocity $\dot{x} = \int \ddot{x}(t)\, dt + C_1$ ...[10.3 (a)]

and displacement

$$x = \int \dot{x}(t)\, dt + C_2 \quad \text{...[10.3 (b)]}$$

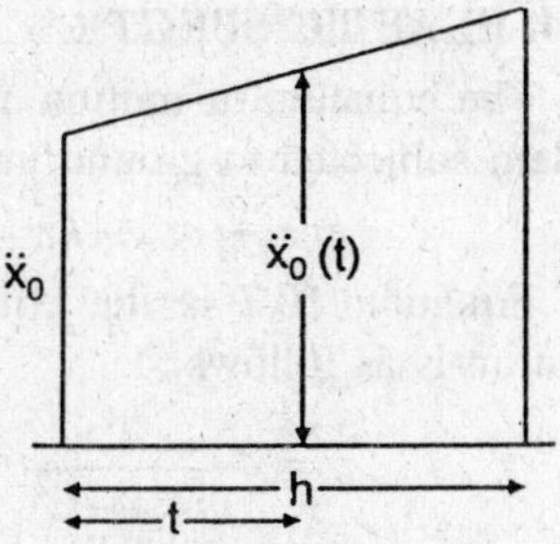

$\ddot{x}_0$ $\ddot{x}_0$ (t) $\ddot{x}_c$ h t

Fig. 10.4. A Trapezoidal Acceleration pulse

From Fig. 10.4 we have acceleration

$$\ddot{x}(t) = \ddot{x}_0 + \frac{\ddot{x}_c + \ddot{x}_0}{h}\, t \quad \text{...(10.4)}$$

Subscripts *e* and *o* denote end and beginning respectively.

Substituting equation 10.4 in equation 10.3 and evaluating the values at the end of the time interval *h* we have

$$\dot{x} = \ddot{x}_0\, t + \frac{\ddot{x}_e - \ddot{x}_0}{h} \times \frac{t^2}{2} + c_1 \quad \text{...[10.5 (a)]}$$

when $t = 0$, $\dot{x} = \dot{x}_0$ Hence $C_1 = \dot{x}_0$

This gives $\dot{x}_e = \dot{x}_0 + \frac{h}{2}(\ddot{x}_0 + \ddot{x}_e)$ ...[10.5 (b)]

From equation [10.3 (*a*)] and [10.5 (*a*)] we get

$$x = \frac{\ddot{x}_0\, t^2}{2} + \frac{\ddot{x}_e - \ddot{x}_o}{h} \times \frac{t^3}{6} + \dot{x}_0\, t + c_2 \quad \text{...[10.6 (a)]}$$

when $t = 0$, $x = x_0$, Hence $C_2 = x_0$.

$$\therefore \quad x_e = x_0 + \dot{x}_0\, h + \frac{h^2}{6}(2\,\ddot{x}_o + \ddot{x}_e) \quad \text{...[10.6 (b)]}$$

If $\ddot{x}_e$ is known, then equation [10.5 (*b*)] and [10.6 (*b*)] can be solved. x_0 and $\dot{x}_0$, are given as initial conditions, and $\ddot{x}_0$ can be determined by substitution in equation 10.2.

To evaluate $\ddot{x}_e$ an iterative procedure is adopted as discussed below. To start with let us assume $\ddot{x}_e = \ddot{x}_0$.

With the assumed value of $\ddot{x}_e$, values of $\dot{x}_e$ and x_e can be determined by substituting new values in equation 10.2. The new values of $\dot{x}_e$ and x_e, we will give new value of $\ddot{x}_e$. The process is repeated till the assumed value and calculated value of $\ddot{x}_e$ are close to each other with in desired accuracy. This procedure can be applied to both linear as well as non linear systems.

10.4. ELASTIC SPECTRA

The equation of motion and solution of a single degree of freedom elastic system subjected to ground motion is given as

$$m\ddot{z} + c\dot{z} + kz = -m\ddot{y} \qquad \text{...(10.7)}$$

Equation 10.7 is the equation of motion of mass m in z direction. Its solution is as follows

$$z = -\frac{1}{p\sqrt{1-\zeta^2}} \int \ddot{y}(\tau)\, e^{-p\zeta\cdot(t-\tau)} \sin p\sqrt{(1-\zeta^2)}\,(t-\tau)\, d_\tau \qquad \text{...(10.8)}$$

The maximum value of z denoted by S_d is known as displacement spectra. Generally it increases with period T. In Fig. 10.5 displacement response spectra of Koyana earthquake (longitudinal components) and EL centro earthquake (NS component is shown.

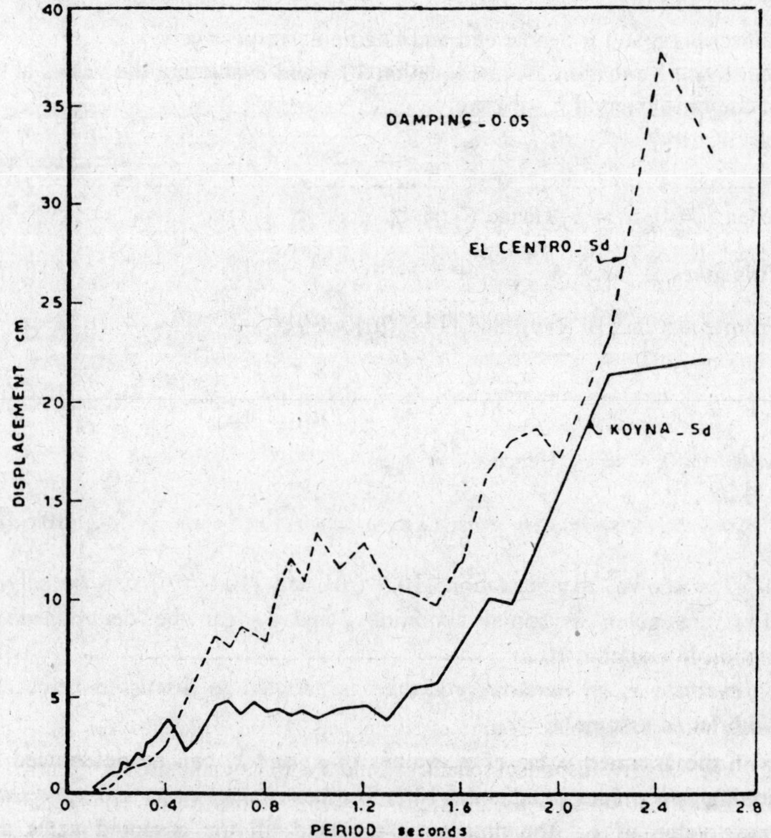

Fig. 10.5. Displacement response spectra of Koyna earthquake (Longitudinal component) and EI Centro Earthquake (NS component)

It is more usual to plot pS_d which has a unit of velocity and denoted by $\overline{S}_v$. The curve is more or less parallel to the abscissa (that is axis of period) for most part and it is easier to read the values.

Another representation, which is convenient for design, is a plot between $p^2 \cdot S_d/g$ and period. $p^2 S_d/g$ is written as $\overline{S}_a/g$ as a function of period. As $K.z$ is the shear force on the system, the maximum shear force V_{max} is given as

$$V_{max} = KZ_{max} = (K \cdot Z_{max}/mg) \times mg = \frac{p^2 S_d}{g} \cdot W = \alpha_s \cdot W$$

where W is weight = mass × acceleration due to gravity and Z_m is the max value of Z.

As seismic coefficient is used to obtain shear as a fraction of the weight of the system it is seen that the exact value of α_s is equal to $\overline{S}_a/g$. It is customary to plot response in terms of either α_s (*i.e.* $\overline{S}_a/g$) or $\overline{S}_v$. In either case S_d can be evaluated easily.

The maximum value of $\dot{z}$, denoted by S_v is called as velocity spectra. The maximum value of $\ddot{x} = (\ddot{z} - \ddot{y})$, denoted by S_a is called acceleration spectra. For small values of damping $S_v \approx \overline{S}_v$ and $S_a = \overline{S}_a$.

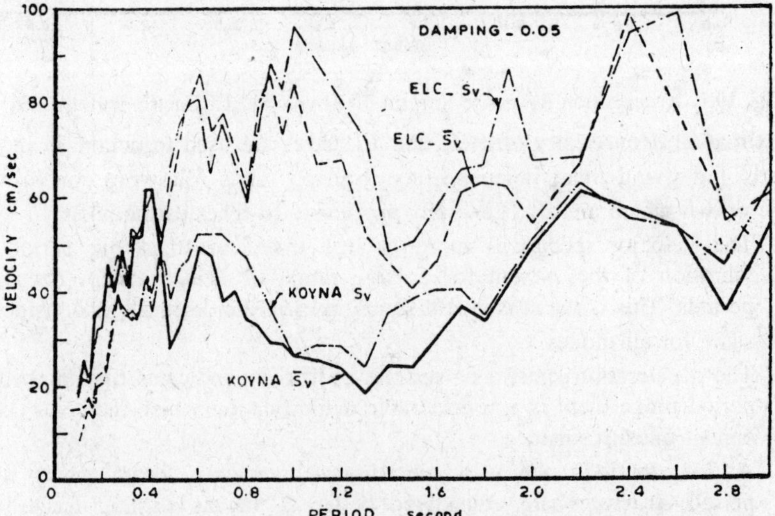

Fig. 9.6. Velocity Response Spectra of Koyna and El Centro Earthquakes

In Fig. 9.6 velocity response spectra S_v and $\overline{S}_v$ of Koyna and EL Centro earthquakes corresponding to 5% damping is shown. From the Fig. 10.6 it can be seen that for a number of values of period S_v is more or less equal to $\overline{S}_v$ ($S_v \approx \overline{S}_v$). Fig. 10.7 shows the acceleration spectra S_a/g. The scale adopted for plotting S_a/g almost coincides with $\overline{S}_a/g$. Generally $S_a \approx \overline{S}_a$ is a very good

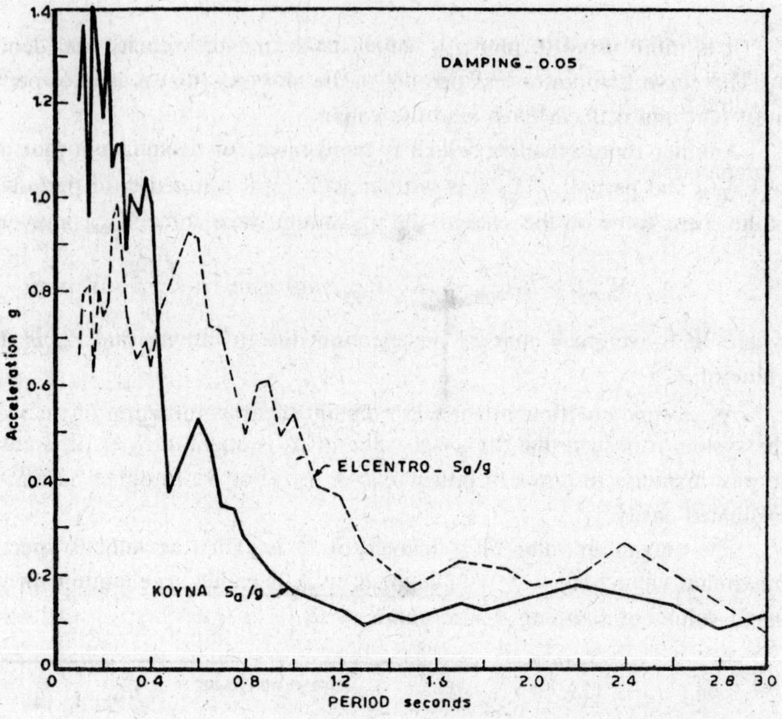

Fig. 10.7. Acceleration Response Spectra of Koyna and El Centro Earthquakes

approximation. Hence very often S_v and S_a curves are used to obtain $\overline{S}_v$ and $\overline{S}_a$ instead of deriving them independently from S_d. Thus following conclusions can be drawn which are also generally applicable to other earthquakes.

1. The velocity spectra is more or less independent of the period of vibration of the system for a large range of values except for short periods. This is the reason that some times in the design S_v is considered same for all modes.
2. The acceleration spectra or seismic coefficient indicates that in a short period range there is a considerable magnification which indicates some sort of quasi resonance.
3. At long periods, the value decreases appreciably. That is why long period structures are considered better as far as seismic forces are concerned.

10.5. COMPARISON OF DIFFERENT EARTHQUAKES

Different earthquakes can be compared by normalising them to the same scale. One such method of normalising is to keep the area under velocity spectrum curve to be the same.

For example, let D_1 and D_2 be the areas under velocity spectrum curve for two different accelerogram. If the ordinates of the second accelerogram are multiplied by D_1/D_2, then the modified second and the original first record would have been normalized.

Based on four different earthquakes in western U.S.A. Housner has prepared average velocity and acceleration spectra as shown in Fig. 9.8 and 9.9,

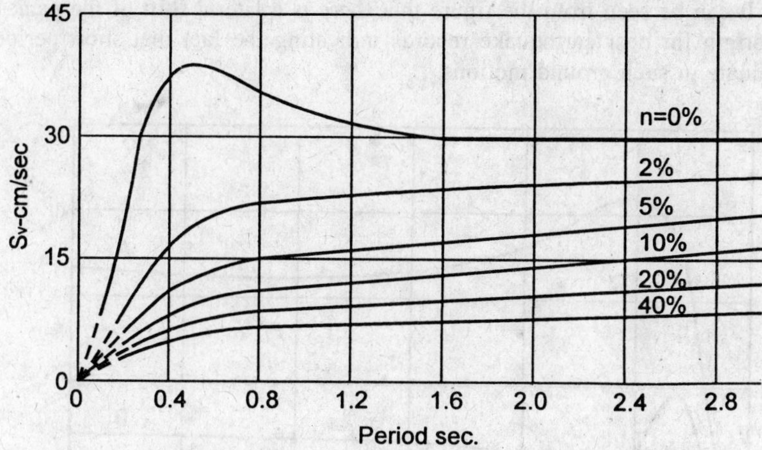

Fig. 10.8. Average velocity spectra (Due to Housner)

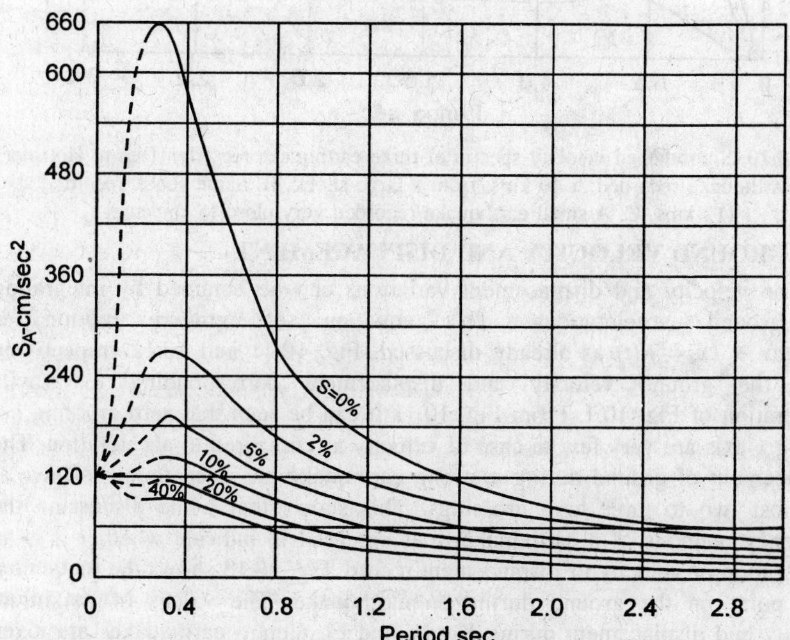

Fig. 10.9. Average Acceleration spectra (Due to Housner)

respectively. These average spectra were incorporated in earlier Indian Standard Code IS 1893.

Comparing average spectra of Koyna with those of Housner's spectra, it can be observed that for epicentral records, the peak shifts laterally towards short period range. An other illustration of the above phenomenon is shown in Fig. 10.10, where in the influence of magnitude and distance on the spectra is shown. It can be seen from the figure that there is a lateral shift of the peak to wards origin for near earthquake records indicating the fact that short periods predominate in such ground motions.

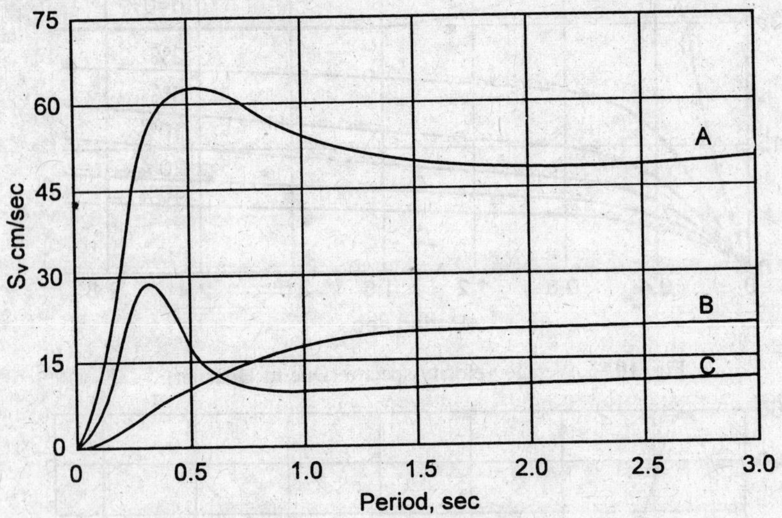

Fig. 10.10. Smoothened velocity spectra of three earthquake records. (Due to Housner) A. Earthquake recorded at 40 kms. from a large shock, B. Same shock recorded at 112 kms. C. A small earthquake recorded very close to epicenter

10.6. GROUND VELOCITY AND DISPLACEMENT

The velocity and displacement variations can be obtained by integrating the ground accelerations. The equation of ground motion is $m\ddot{x} + c\dot{x} + kx = F(t)$ as already discussed. Fig. 10.11 and 10.12 respectively show the ground velocity and displacement corresponding to Koyna acceleration of Fig. 10.1. From Fig. 10.11 it can be seen that zero crossing *i.e.* cutting x-axis are very few in case of velocity as compared to acceleration. The displacement of ground during a strong earthquake has been found to have at the most two to three zero crossings. This shows that while discussing the frequency contents of a earthquake, it is essential to indicate whether it is an acceleration or velocity or displacement record. Fig. 10.13 shows the movement of a point on the ground during an earthquake. The values of maximum velocity and displacement during Koyna and EL Centro earthquakes are given below to give an idea of the order of magnitude of the earthquake.

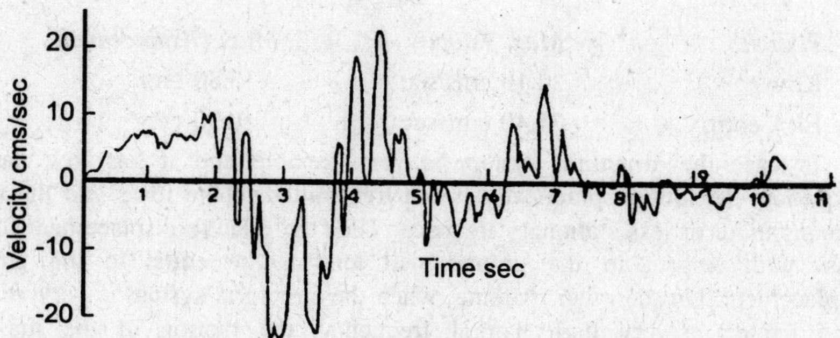

Fig. 10.11. GRound velocity of Koyna earthquake

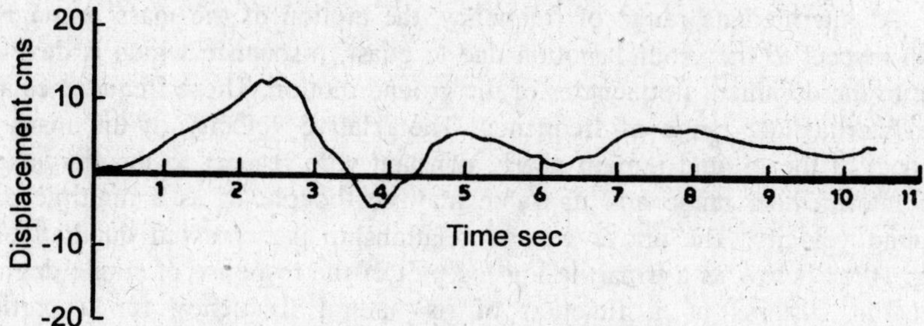

Fig. 10.12. Ground displacement of Koyna earthquake

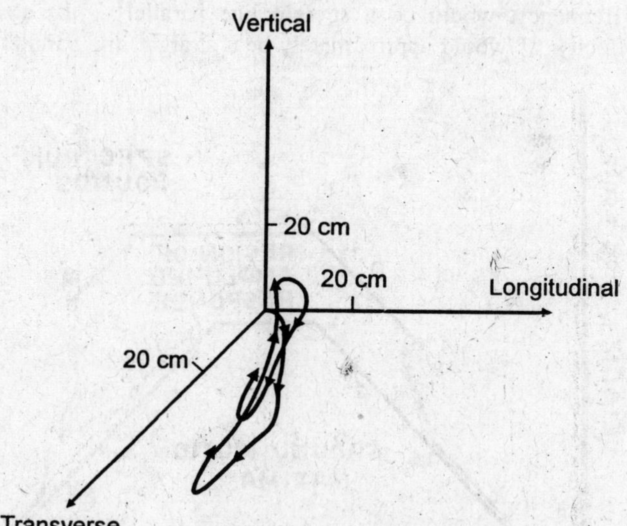

Fig. 10.13. Three dimensional plot of a particle movement during Koyna earthquake

Station	*Max. velocity*	*Max. Displacement*
Koyna	24.19 cms/sec	13.30 cms
EL Centro	33.40 cms/sec	10.90 cms

In case the structural system is very flexible and it has low natural frequency, the motion practically is not transmitted to the mass and the mass remains more or less stationary in space. Thus the relative displacement of the mass with respect to the ground will tend to be equal to the ground displacement. On the other extreme, when the structural system is very stiff or rigid having a very high natural frequency, the motion of the mass is approximately the same as that of the ground and the absolute acceleration of the mass will tend to be equal to the ground acceleration.

At intermediate range of frequency, the motion of the mass is magnified with respect to the ground motion due to quasi- resonance which is developed due to the dominant frequencies of the ground motion. These frequencies are in the intermediate range of frequency. The relative velocity of the mass with respect to the ground remain nearly constant with respect to the frequency in the intermediate range and its value may be thought of as a multiple of the ground velocity. The above general relationship is expressed qualitatively in Fig. 10.14 below as a tripartite log-log plot of the response of single degree of freedom systems as a function of its natural frequency for a particular earthquake. In the figure, the vertical ordinate corresponds to velocity and the abscissa to the natural frequency. The ground velocity '*v*' which is independent of natural frequency, would be a straight line parallel to the abscissa. The response velocity '*V*' would approximately be a straight line parallel to '*v*', but

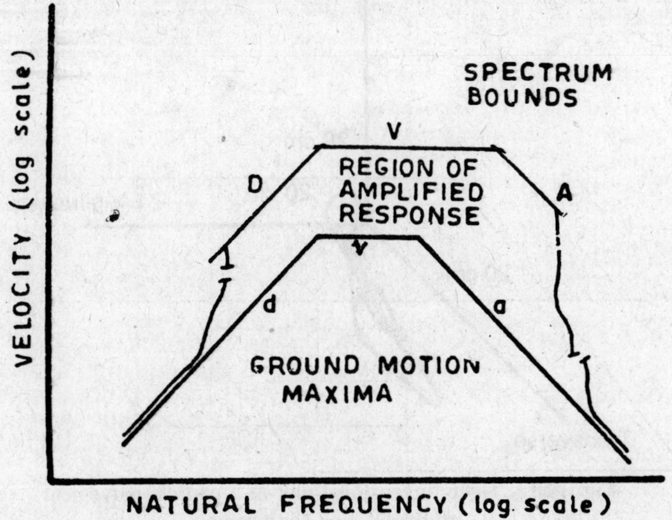

Fig. 10.14. Typical Tripartite logarithmic plot oi response spectrum bounds compared with maximum ground motions

having a larger magnitude.

If the displacement is expressed as velocity divided by '*p*' where '*p*' is the circular natural frequency, then the ground displacement *'d'* which is independent of natural frequency, would appear as an inclined line with a positive slope. The response displacement '*D*' would tend to be equal to that of 'd' at low values of natural frequency. Similarly, if the acceleration is expressed as velocity multiplied by '*p*' then the ground acceleration '*a*', which is independent of natural frequency would appear as an inclined line with a negative slope. The response acceleration 'A' would tend to be equal to that of '*a*' at high values of natural frequency.

10.7. INELASTIC SPECTRA

From the study of acceleration spectra shown in Fig. 10.7, it will be found that for elastic systems, the value of seismic coefficient is very large. To design structures on the basis of elastic system of seismic coefficients whose values are very high would be uneconomial. Hence structures are allowed to under go in elastic deformations in the event of severe earthquakes.

The inelastic behavior of structures usually is approximated by an elasto-plastic behaviour as shown in Fig. 10.15. Under the influence of reversal of ground motion, the system will have an hysteretic behaviour which can be described by Fig. 10.16.

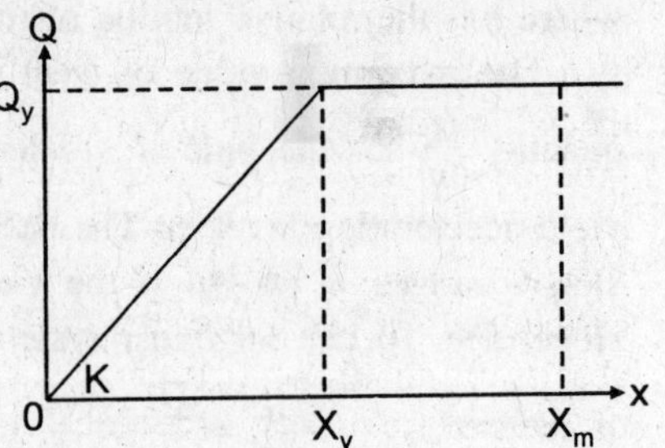

Fig. 10.15. Elasto-Plastic load deflection curve

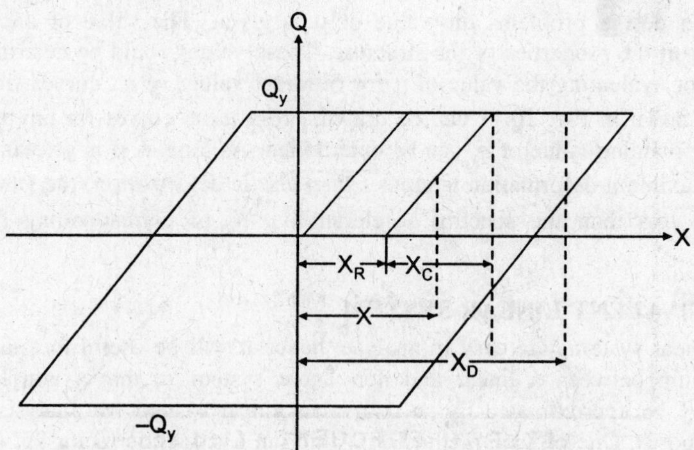

Fig. 10.16. A Hysteretic loop for elasto-plastic system

If the non linearity is due to the restoring force characteristics of the system, the restoring force F_R in equation 10.1 may be represented by the expression $Q(x)$, where $Q(x)$ gives the functional relationship between the load and deflection. For example, in case of elasto plastic systems (Fig. 10.16) we have

$$Q(x) = K(x - x_R) \text{ for } x \leq (x_R + x_c)$$

and $$Q(x) = Q_y \text{ far } x > x_R + x_c$$

where x_R and x_c are shown in Fig. 9.16.

Assuming viscous damping, it is also assumed that the system is excited by a ground motion 'y'. Then the equation of motion would be similar to ground motion equation 10.7.

$$\ddot{z} + 2p\zeta\dot{z} + \frac{Q(x)}{m} = -\ddot{y} \quad \text{...(10.9)}$$

where z is the relative motion of the mass with respect to the base.

The maximum value of $Q(x)$ is the force required to cause yielding. The quantity $\frac{Q}{m}$ has the unit of acceleration and its maximum value is known as yield acceleration level q_y. The deflection corresponding to the point where the slope changes is known as the yield deflection. Its value is Q_y/k where k is slope (Fig. 10.15). for linear system K is equal to the spring constant. Then

$$\frac{Q_y}{k} = \frac{Q_y}{m} \times \frac{m}{k} = \frac{q_y}{p^2} \quad \text{...(10.10)}$$

Usually the maximum deflection is expressed as a ratio of yield deflection. This ratio is also known as ductility factor μ. In the dynamic analysis, for any given value of q_y (For any load-deflection curve) it is possible to evaluate μ. However in design problems the value of μ is given. The value of ductility depends upon the properties of the structure. These values could be determined by tests. For evaluating the value of μ for different values of q_y, curves similar to curves shown in Fig. 10.17 can be drawn. From these curves for any value of μ, corresponding value of q_y can be determined. As long as μ is greater than one (the maximum deformation is greater than elastic deformation) the value of q_y will be less than the spectral acceleration $p^2 S_d$ of corresponding linear system.

10.8. EQUIVALENT LINEAR SYSTEM

As Linear systems are easy to analyse, hence it will be useful to establish a relationship between a linear and non linear system so that a non linear system may be approximated by an equivalent linear system for analysis and design purposes. One of such method is to find out a reduction factor by which the earthquake data should be reduced so that a linear analysis with the modified data indicates a seismic lateral load coefficient which corresponds to

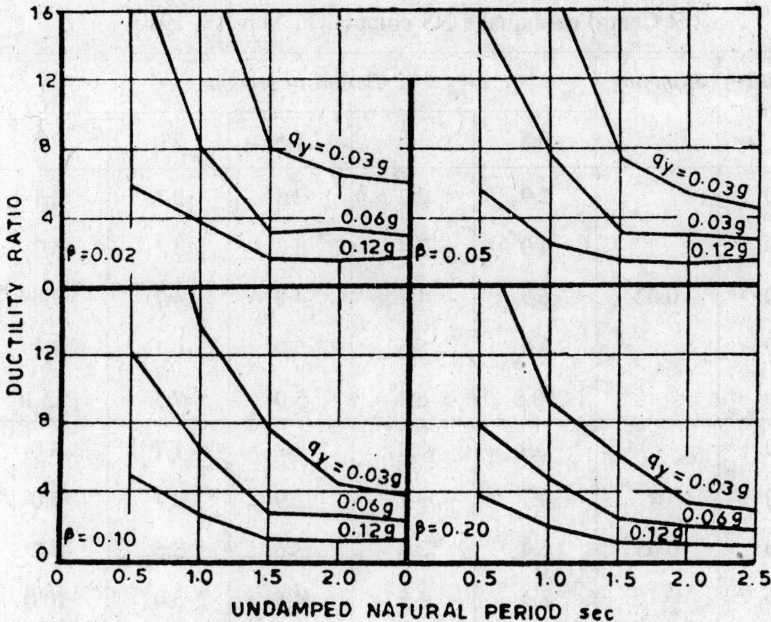

Fig. 10.17. Ductility ratio for different yield levels for elasto- plastic systems subjected to EI Centro earthquake (β represents damping)

that of the yield level of the non linear system.

This shows that the design of a non linear system capable of certain ductility can be based on the knowledge of an equivalent system which is linearly analyzed for the reduced (toned down) earthquake.

The reduction factor R_f is given by the relation.

$$R_f = \frac{p^2 S_d}{q_y} = \frac{p^2 S_d}{g} \times \frac{1}{q_y/g} = \frac{\alpha_s}{\alpha_y}$$

where α_a is the seismic coefficient of the linear system equation.

and α_y = the yield level of non linear system. (q_y/g)

The values of reduction factor R_f for different periods and ductility ratio are given in Table 10.1. As discussed in article 8.7 and chapter11 structures have inherent ductility. Due to this reason the value of seismic coefficient in the design are taken less than large coefficient indicated by elastic analysis.

In case the structure is brittle and has no ductility *i.e.* $\mu = 1$ then the forces on the structure would be corresponding to the full elcentro motion obtained from linear analysis. If the ductility of the structure is 2.0 say then force and yield can be found out from linear analysis corresponding to 1/2.9 times the intensity of the elcentro earthquake motion. From Table 10.1, the reduction factor is 2.9 for the ductility ratio 2.0.

Table 10.1. Reduction factor for various ductility ratio (El Centro earthquake NS component May 18, 1940)

Ductility ratio	*Damping*	*Period in seconds*				
		0.5	1.0	1.5	2.0	2.5
2.0		2.9	2.2	2.3	2.3	3.1
3.0		4.9	3.4	3.3	3.4	5.3
4.0	0.02	6.9	4.7	4.2	4.7	7.4
5.0		8.9	5.6	5.0	6.1	9.7
6.0		10.8	6.4	5.0	7.5	12.3
2.0		2.9	2.3	2.2	1.7	3.0
3.0		4.7	3.1	2.9	2.4	5.0
4.0	0.05	6.4	3.8	3.6	3.6	7.2
5.0		8.4	4.5	4.5	5.0	10.0
6.0		9.3	5.1	5.4	6.2	12.8
2.0		2.7	1.8	1.9	1.8	2.7
3.0		4.2	2.4	2.6	2.6	4.7
4.0	0.1	5.8	3.0	3.5	4.5	6.7
5.0		7.0	3.6	4.5	5.3	8.0
6.0		7.6	4.2	5.4	6.0	9.2
2.0		2.4	1.4	1.6	1.8	2.8
3.0		3.8	2.0	2.2	3.0	4.6
4.0	0.20	4.8	2.6	2.8	4.4	5.8
5.0		5.6	3.2	3.4	5.2	7.0
6.0		6.4	4.2	4.0	6.0	8.4

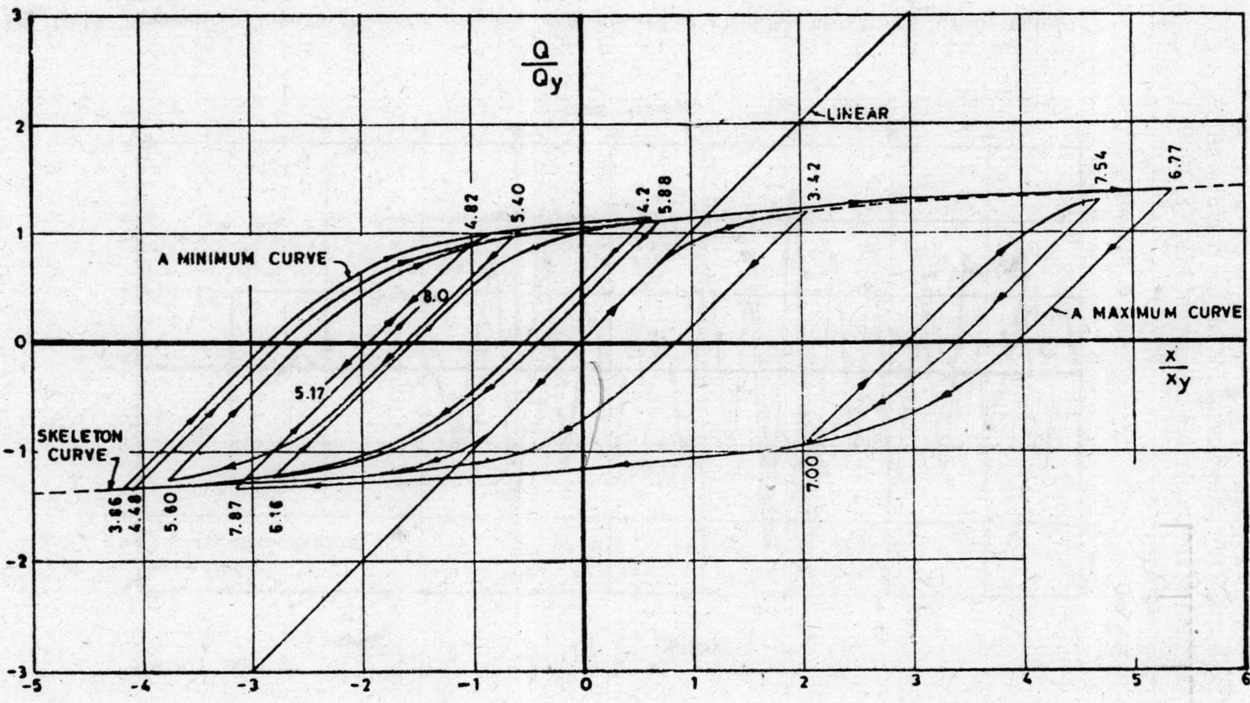

Fig. 10.18. Load deflection curve of a non-linear single degree of freedom system subjected to Taft earthquake of 21.7.1952 T = 0.5 sec, $\zeta = 0.05$, $\alpha_v = 0.06$.

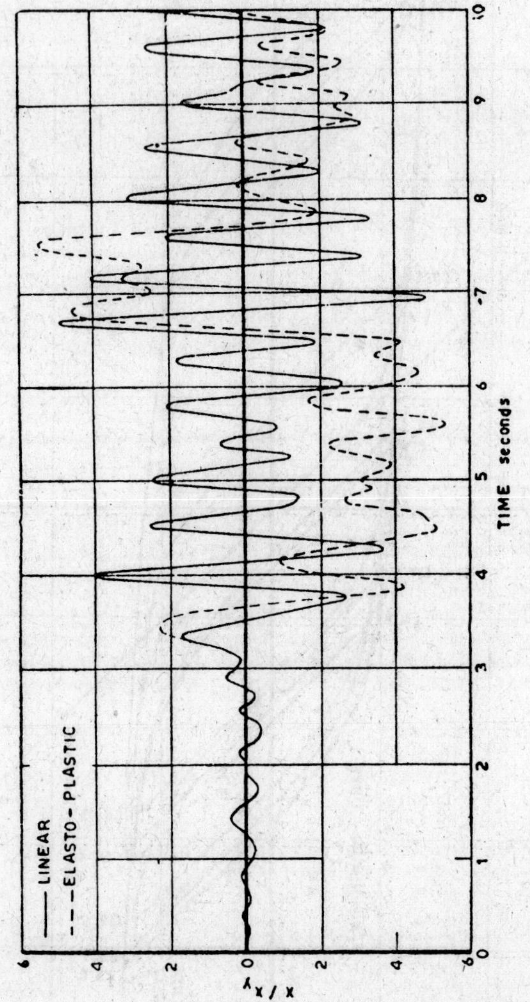

Fig. 10.19. Time-wise relative displacement response 'x' (expressed as a multiple of 'x_y' of a system during Taft earthquake of July 21, 1952 (N 69 W). T = 0.5 sec, $\zeta = 0.05$ and $\alpha_y = 0.06$.

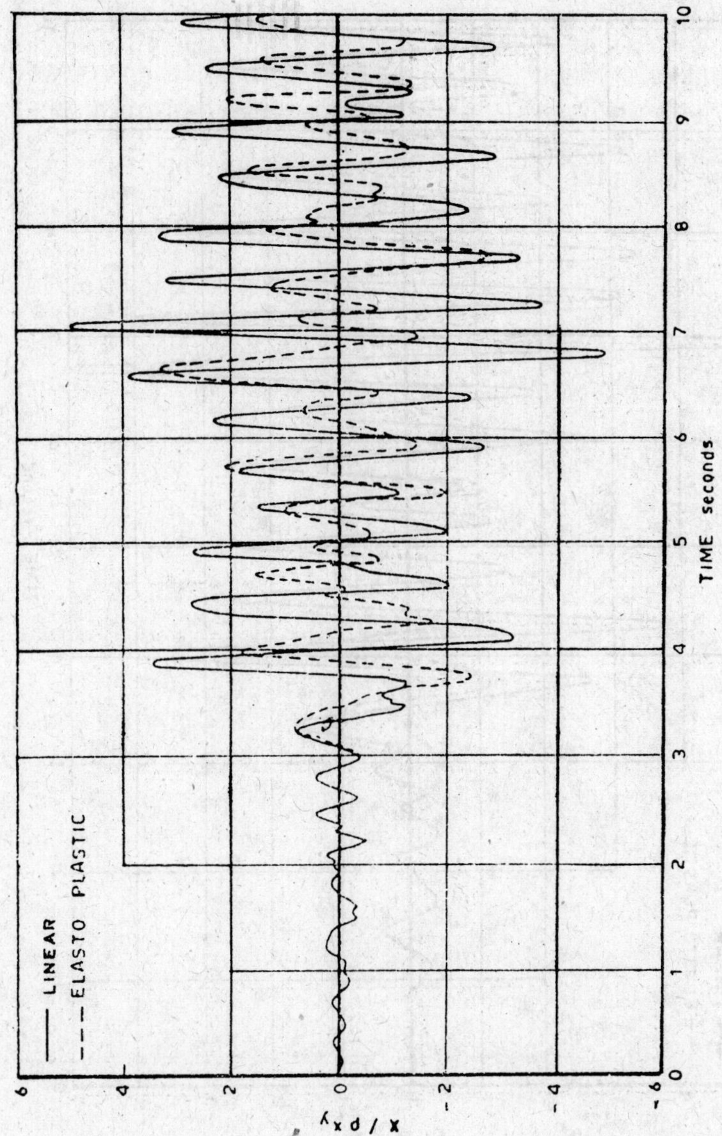

Fig. 10.20. Time-wise relative velocity response '$\dot{x}$' (expressed as a multiple of 'px_y') of the same system in Fig. 10.20

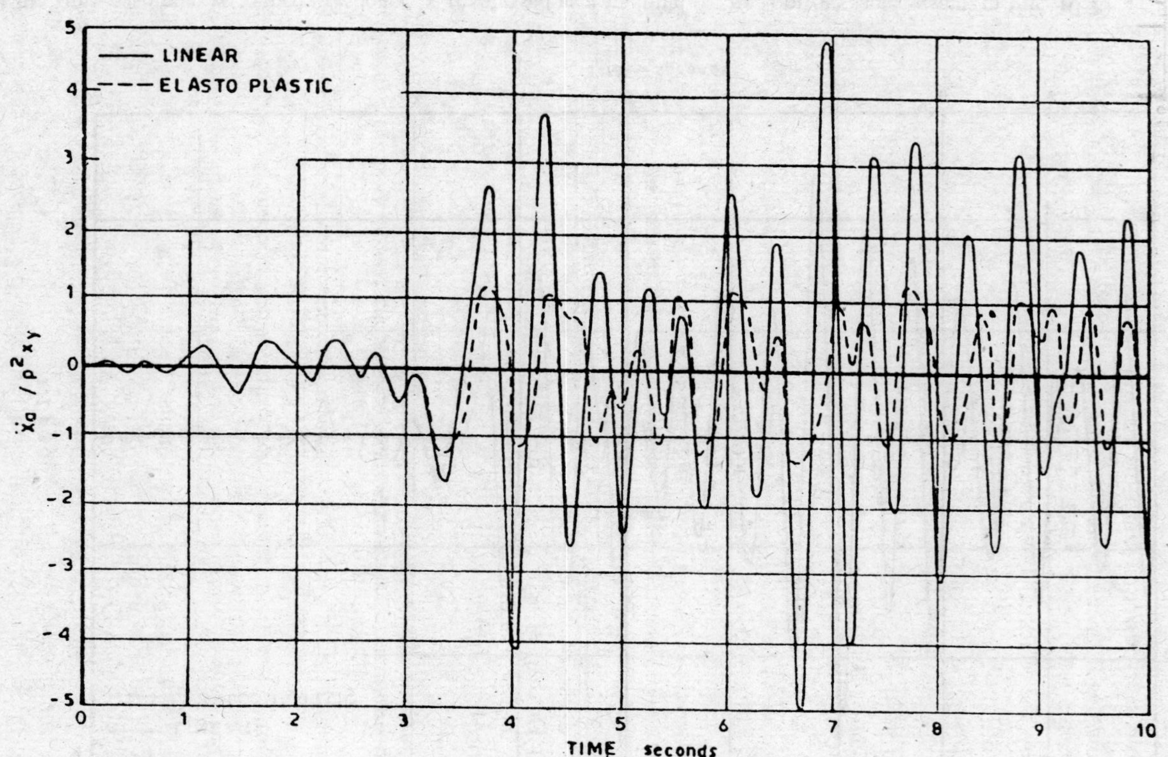

Fig. 10.21. Time-wise absolute acceleration response 'x_a' (expressed as a multiple of '$p^2 x_y$') of the same system in Fig. 10.20

QUESTIONS

1. How the type of soil affect the vibrations of earthquake?
2. How the distance of epicenter from a place affect the earthquake vibrations. Explain fully.
3. How the effects of two earthquakes can be compared.
4. Write short notes on the following:
   (*a*) Non elastic spectra
   (*b*) Ductility factor
   (*c*) Reduction factor
5. Identify the correct statement/statements
   (*a*) The first major record of earthquake was made in India in 1967 at Koyna Mahrastra state.
   (*b*) As there is a layer of soil between the hard rock surface and the foundation, the amplitude of soil surface frequencies would be magnified in comparison to rock surface.
   (*c*) Near the epicenter the amplitude of acceleration is more
   (*d*) At epicenter the peak acceleration does not increase in proportion of the magnitude of the earthquake
   (*e*) With the increase in magnitude, the rate of decay of acceleration with distance would be less
   (*f*) On harder surfaces the motion would exhibit higher acceleration at higher frequencies than on softer soils
   (*g*) All are correct
6. Identify the incorrect statement/statements
   (*a*) While discussing the earthquake record of frequency contents it is not essential to mention, whether it is an acceleration or velocity or displacement record.
   (*b*) In case of very flexible structure having low natural frequency, the motion of the ground practically is not transmitted to the mass
   (*c*) In case of rigid system having a high natural frequency the motion of the mass is nearly equal to that of ground motion
   (*d*) For elastic systems the seismic coefficients are large
7. Identify correct statement/statements
   (*a*) The acceleration of velocity of vibrations developed in buildings founded on hard rocks is more than buildings founded on soft soils
   (*b*) The intensity of earthquake decreases with the increase in distance from the epicenter
   (*c*) In case there is soft soil on a hard rock, the amplitude of the surface motion would be magnified as compared to the rock
   (*d*) With the increase in distance from the epicenter acceleration amplitude as well as frequencies decrease
   (*e*) All are correct
8. Identify the incorrect statement/statements
   (*a*) The amplitude of vibration in clayey soils is 30 mm

(*b*) The amplitude of vibration in clayey soils is 100 mm

(*c*) In fill or un consolidated soils the amplitude of vibration is upto 100 mm

(*d*) In hard soils or rocks the amplitude of vibrations is 25 mm

(*e*) The amplitude of vibration in rocks is 2 to 5 mm.

ANSWERS

5. (*g*)
6. (*a*)
7. (*e*)
8. (*b, d*)

11

Factors Affecting Seismic Resistant Design of Structures

11.1. INTRODUCTION

While planing a construction project in a seismic zone or region proper thought to the shape, form and material of construction and the intended function of the construction and its cost must be kept in mind to avoid serious damage during an earthquake. Often wonderful and imaginative forms and shape have been conceived by the architects which can create an aesthetic and functionally efficient structure. Each choice of shape and form has a significant bearing on the performance of the structure due to the vulnerability associated with each of the form and shape. Architect and structural engineer must consult each other to conceive a most appropriate and seismically safe structure. A reasonable framing system and a good configuration even can ignore the poor quality construction.

The study of performance of buildings during strong earthquakes has revealed the importance of proper and improper construction of earthquake load resisting systems. An observation that suggests just the beginning of collapse is an important lesson. From such observations lession may be drawn not to follow such faulty construction any more. Good examples of performance serve to follow such desirable structural construction.

The basic factors contributing to the proper seismic behaviour of a building in a rational design of a structural system are as follows:

(*i*) Simplicity of the design
(*ii*) Symmetry of the building
(*iii*) Ductility
(*iv*) Transfer of seismic loads or forces to the ground with out excessive rotation

The behaviour of a building during an earthquake depends mainly on two factors, namely form of the super structure and the way of transfer of seismic forces to the ground. Thus over all form, regular configuration, flow path of seismic forces and the framing system of the building are important from the point of view, of designing earthquake resistant building system.

11.2. DEFINITIONS

Following terms have been used frequently in this text. These terms effect the performance of a structure to a great extent during an earthquake.

1. Strength. The property of an element to resist the effects of a load or force is called its strength. Strengths are of the following two types:

(*a*) **Compressive strength.** The ability of an element to resist the load or force which causes compression on the element till its failure is called its compressive strength. The compressive strength of brick and concrete is quite high.

(*b*) **Tensile strength.** The ability of an element to resist tensile force or load upto just its breaking or failure is known as its tensile strength. The tensile strength of bricks and concrete is very small. The tensile strength of the concrete is taken as 10% of its compressive strength.

2. Stiffness. The ability of an element to resist its displacement is known as its stiffness. The stiffness in vertical as well as in horizontal direction effects the performance of a structure during an earthquake to a great extent.

3. Ductility. The property by virtue of which a metal can be drawn into a wire is called the ductility of metal. In case of structures the property of an element by virtue of which it can undergo sufficient deflection or displacement from its original position under the influence of forces is called is ductility and such an element is known as ductile element. An under reinforced concrete element is a ductile element as it under goes sufficient deflection or elongation before its failure *i.e.* it does not fail abruptly. Copper, steel, silver etc. are good examples of ductile materials.

Brittlness. The property of an material by virtue of which it undergoes very little elongation or deflection under loads or force before breaking and it breaks abruptly. Bricks, glass and concrete are brittle materials.

The stiffness of a structure influences its performance to a great extent during an seismic activity. If two elements of two different stiffness are subjected to deflect by the same amount, the stiffer element will need more force than the other to deflect by the same amount. Thus on the basis of their stiffness structures can be classified as brittle or ductile.

Brittle structure. The stiffness of such structures is more. They attract more seismic force to deflect them, and fail abruptly. Hence brittle structures are less durable during an earthquake.

Ductile structure. These structures are less rigid or stiff. They deflect with relatively less force. Hence such structures perform well *i.e.* they are more stable during an earthquake.

Sudden changes in strength and stiffness between two adjacent storeys of a structure are very common in practice. Such changes are associated with set backs, changes over the height of a structural system, changes in the construction materials, changes in the storey height etc. The most common problem which arises due to such discontinuities is the concentration of inelastic deformation in or around such discontinuities. The sudden change in strength, mass or stiffness of the structure either in vertical or horizontal planes may alter the distribution of the lateral loads or forces and deformations more than anticipated for a uniform structure. The sudden change in lateral stiffness in the vertical plane of a building is not advisable due to the following reasons:

(*a*) It is not possible to assess the seismic stress even with most sophisticated computers.

(*b*) The structural detailing is another practical problem.

It has been observed that drastic changes in vertical configuration results changes in strength and stiffness between adjacent storeys of a structure and should be avoided.

11.3. FUNCTIONAL PLANNING

The functional planning of a building involves the way in which the skeleton of the structure can be accommodated. The vertical divisions of the building create problems to avoid irregularities in stiffness and mass of the building. How ever the service cores and exterior cladding provide an opportunity to accomade shear walls or braced panels. One of the main objectives of preliminary planning is to establish the optimum locations of service cores and establishing stiff structural elements which should be continuous upto the foundation.

11.4. LATERAL LOAD RESISTING SYSTEM

From the point of view of lateral load resisting, the principal categories of building system is shown in the following Table 11.1.

Table 11.1. Lateral load resisting systems

S. No.	*Framing system*	*Description of the system*
1.	Bearing wall system	The walls of the system are load bearing walls. In concrete structures some of the bearing walls may be designed as shear walls. The system is designed to carry gravity loads as well as seismic or lateral loads. Gravity loads act vertically where as seismic loads act horizontally. Under lateral loads walls act as cantilevers. The shear distribution is proportional to the moment of inertia of the cross-section of the walls. The relative displacements of the floors result from bending deformation of the walls.
2.	Moment resisting frames	In moment resisting frames, the earthquake forces are resisted by beams, columns and joints in the frame mainly by flexure. These frames when subjected to lateral forces indicate zero moment at mid height of the columns The shear distribution is exhibited proportional to the moment of inertia of the columns

S. No.	*Framing system*	*Description of the system*
		and relative displacements (inter storey drifts) proportional to the shear forces. That is why some times these frames are called as shear systems. The continuity of the frame assists in resisting the gravity loading more efficiently by reducing positive moments in the centre span of girders. Such frames are preferred due to least obstruction in access. Due to the limit of the drift, this system is recommended upto only 30 storeys say upto 95 m height.
3.	Dual system	This system consists of moment resisting frames either with shear walls or braces. The coupling of the above two systems completely changes the shear and moment diagrams of both walls and frames. The characteristic of this combination is that in the lower floors, the walls retain the frame, while in the upper floors the frames prevent or check the large displacement of the walls. Thus frame shows a small variation in storey shear between the first and last floors. The two systems may be designed to resist the total design force in proportion to their lateral stiffness.
4.	Tube system	It is totally a three dimensional system. This system utilizes the entire building perimeter to resist seismic forces (lateral forces or loads). For taller buildings, relatively recently developed framed tube, tube in tube, and bundled tube system are used.

Note. These systems are discussed in chapter 12.

11.5. SEISMIC EFFECT ON STRUCTURES

11.5.1. Inertia forces in structures

Buildings resting on the ground experience shaking due the development of ground motions during an earthquake. In this situation the base or foundation of the building moves with the ground, but the roof has a tendency to remain in its original static position. But walls and columns are connected to the roof, they drag it along with them. This action can be explained with the following example. Consider you have just entered the train at the station and still standing, the train starts of a sudden. At this moment your feet move with the train and the upper body tends to stay back in stationery position, making you fall backwards. This tendency of remaining in the original position is known as *Inertia*. In case of buildings as the walls or columns are flexible, the motion of the roof is different from that of the ground *i.e.* in the opposition direction as shown in Fig. 11.1.

Thus when the ground moves, the building is thrown backwards as explained above, and the roof experiences a force known as inertia force. The

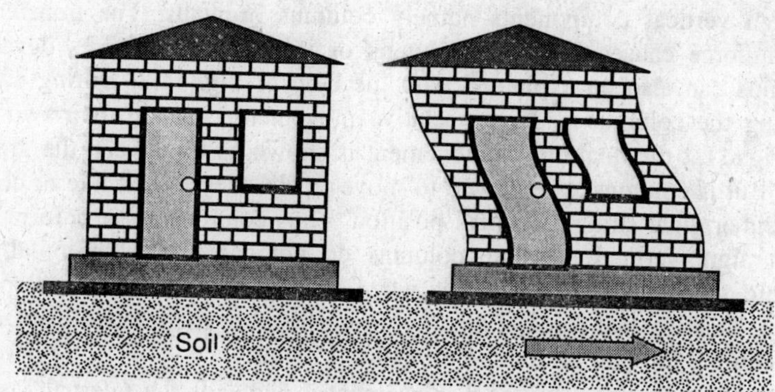

Fig. 11.1. Effect of inertia in a building when shaken at its base. (Courtesy— IITK)

magnitude of the inertia force is equal to mass of the body multiplied by its acceleration. If the mass of the roof is 'M' say and acceleration α, then inertia force developed in the roof $F_i = M\,\alpha$, and its direction is opposite to that of the acceleration.

Hence greater the mass, higher the value of the inertia force. Thus lighter buildings sustain the earthquake shaking better, *i.e.* lighter buildings get less damage during a earthquake.

11.5.2. Effect of deformations in structures

The inertia force experienced by the roof is transferred to the ground below

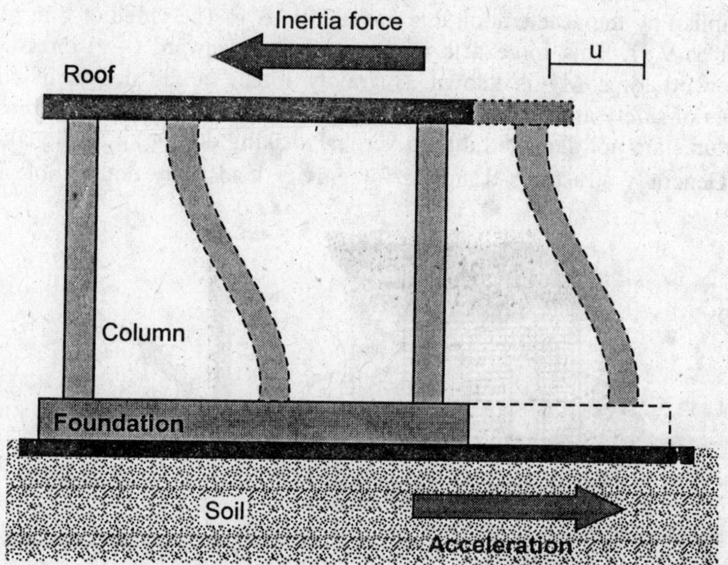

Fig. 11.2. Inertia force and relative motion with in a building (Courtesy— IITK)

through vertical components namely columns or walls. The transfer of this inertia force causes forces in columns or in walls. The forces developed in columns can also be explained with the help of Fig. 11.2. During earthquake shaking the columns under go relative movement between their two ends. In the Fig. 11.2 the quantity of movement is shown as *u* between the ground and roof. But if columns are allowed to move freely, they would like to come back to their original straight vertical position. Thus columns resist deformations. In the straight vertical position, columns do not carry and horizontal force or seismic force through them, but when they are bent, they develop internal forces. This internal force is directly proportional to the relative displacement *u* between the top and bottom of the column. Thus

(*i*) Greater the value of displacement *u*, larger is the internal force of the column.

(*ii*) Stiffer the columns (large size of the column), larger is the internal force.

For this reason, these internal forces are called stiffness forces. Actually the stiffness force in a column is the column stiffness times the relative displacement between its two ends.

11.5.3. Horizontal and vertical shaking

During an earthquake, shaking of ground takes place in all the three directions namely *x*, *y* and *z* directions. Also during earthquakes ground shakes randomly back and forth along all the three directions. Generally all structures are designed to carry the gravity loads *i.e.* (dead load + live load + contents). Thus the gravity force will be equal to the mass due to all the above loads multiplied by the acceleration due to gravity *i.e.* *g*. The value of *g* in M.K.S. is taken as 9.81. This force acts in the vertical downward (– *z*) direction. This downward force Mg is known as gravity force. In the design of structures factors of safety are used to resist the gravity forces or loads, hence most of the structures are not damaged due to vertical shaking during an earthquake.

Generally structures designed for gravity loads may not be able to resist

Fig. 11.3. Principal directions of a building
(Courtesy—IITK)

safely the effect of horizontal shaking during an earthquake. Hence it is necessary to ensure the adequacy of the structure against horizontal earthquake effects. The principal directions of a building are shown in Fig. 11.3.

11.5.4. Flow of inertia forces to the ground

In earthquake resistant design of a building, one of the most fundamental consideration is the provision of a continuous load path. At least one (preferably more) continuous load paths of adequate strength and stiffness should be provided from the origin of development of initial load to the final lateral load resisting system or elements. For good performance of the building under any loading, the selection of the proper load carrying system has been found essential. The proper selection of the structural system, may ignore the relatively small over sights in the proportion, details, analysis and construction etc.

Generally buildings consist of horizontal and vertical components. The horizontal components or elements are usually diaphragms such as floor slabs, beams and horizontal bracing in special floors. The vertical components are shear walls, braced frames, columns, walls and moment resisting frames.

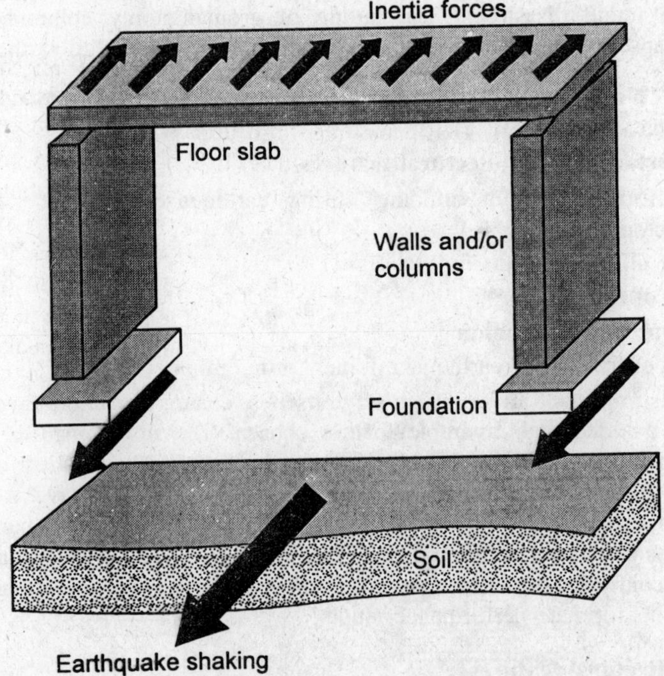

Fig. 11.4. Flow of seismic inertia forces through all structural components.
(Courtesy—IITK)

The horizontal forces developed due to the seismic motion are directly proportional to the mass of building elements and are considered to act at the centers of mass of these elements. The seismic forces developed at different floor level in a building are brought down along the height to the ground through shortest path. Thus the load transfer path is as follows:

The inertia forces generated in a component such as in curtain walls are delivered through a structural connection to horizontal diaphragm (floor slab). The floor slab transfers these forces to walls or columns. These vertical elements transfer the forces to foundation. From foundation, finally these forces are trans- ferred to the ground soil system. Hence all these structural elements (Floor slabs, walls, columns, and foundations) and the connections between them, must be so designed that inertia forces may be safely transferred through them Fig. 11.4.

Walls and columns are the most critical elements in transferring the inertia forces. But in traditional construction more emphasis has been given to floor slabs and beams in design than walls or columns. Walls are relatively thin and generally are made of brittle material like brick or stone masonry. These walls are poor in sustaining horizontal earthquake inertia forces along the direction of their thickness. Failure of masonry walls have been observed in many past earthquakes. Similarly poorly designed and constructed reinforced concrete columns are found disastrous. The failure of ground storey columns have resulted collapse in many buildings during 26th January 2001 Bhuj earthquake.

11.6. EFFECT OF ARCHITECTURAL FEATURES ON BUILDINGS DURING EARTHQUAKES

11.6.1. Importance of architectural features

The performance of a building during earthquakes depends on the following factors:

(*a*) Over all shape of the building

(*b*) Size of the building

(*c*) Geometry of the building

(*d*) Way of transfer of earthquake forces to the ground

Thus it is important at the design stage itself to ensure that the unfavorable features are avoided and favorable feature chosen. The importance of good configuration of a building is quite clear by the words of Late henry Degenkolb, a noted earthquake engineer of U.S.A. "If we have a poor configuration to start with, all the engineer can do is to provide a band-aid improve a basically poor solution as best as he can Conversely, if we start off with a good configuration and reasonable framing system, even a poor engineer cannot harm its ultimate performance much."

11.6.2. Architectural features

In order to create an aesthetic and functionally efficient structure, architects conceive wonderful and imaginative structures. Some times the shape of the structure catches eyes of the visitor. some times the structural system appeals and in some cases both shape and structural system work together to make the structure excellent. However the choices of shapes and structure both have their own significant bearing on the performance of the building during strong earthquakes.

The wide spread damage to buildings in past earthquakes across the world have identified the desirable and non desirable structural configurations. At the time of building planning following points should bc kept in mind:

(*a*) The structure should be simple and symmetrical.

(*b*) The structure should not be elongated in plan or elevation *i.e.* the size of the structure should be moderate.

(*c*) The structure should have a uniform and continuous distribution of strength, mass, and stiffness.

(*d*) The hinges must form in the horizontal members of the structure before the vertical members.

(*e*) There should be sufficient ductility in the structure.

(*f*) Structure should have sufficient stiffness related to sub soil properties.

11.6.3. Simplicity and symmetry

A simple and symmetrical structure as that of a square or circular or other suitable shape as indicated below will have greater chances of survival for the following reasons:

(*a*) The simple and symmetrical form provides better ability to understand the over all behaviour of a structure during an earthquake than for a complex one.

(*b*) The simple and symmetrical form provides better ability to understand the structural details in a better way than a complex one.

Thus it has been observed that buildings regular in plan and elevation with out re entrant corners or discontinuities in transferring the vertical loads to the ground have performed better during earthquakes. It is important that the plan of a building in seismic zone should be symmetrical in both x and y directions. In general, with simple geometry in plan as shown in Fig. 11.5 (*a*) have performed better during earthquakes, where as buildings with re-entrant corners as T, V, U and + sign shapes as shown in Fig. 11.5 (*b*) may sustain sufficient damage during earthquakes.

The desirable and undesirable shapes of Fig. 11.5 (*a*) and (*b*) have been shown in Tabular from in Table 11.2.

11.6.4. Broken Layout Concept

The bad effects of interior corners in the plan can be minimised or checked by breaking the complex plan of L, T, H shape etc. into simple rectangular units with suitable gap at their junctions as shown in Fig. 11.6.

Table 11.2.

Good shapes		Undesirable shapes	
Shape of building	*Remark*		
	Circular form most suitable for buildings, but analysis less easy		Long building. Differential behaviour on opposite ends
	Square form ideal for behaviour, and analysis but suitable for small houses		Asymmetrical effects bad behaviour un predicable.
	Good option, analysis less easy		Though symmetrical, but long wings give problems in behaviour prediction
	Octagonal shape, good symmetry but analysis less easy		Re-entrant corners bad option, poor detailing
	Though symmetrical analysis is not easy		Though symmetrical but projections at end cause problem in analysis and detailing
	Idal for behaviour		
Building Courtyard	Another safe form		Asymmetry will cause torsion problem.

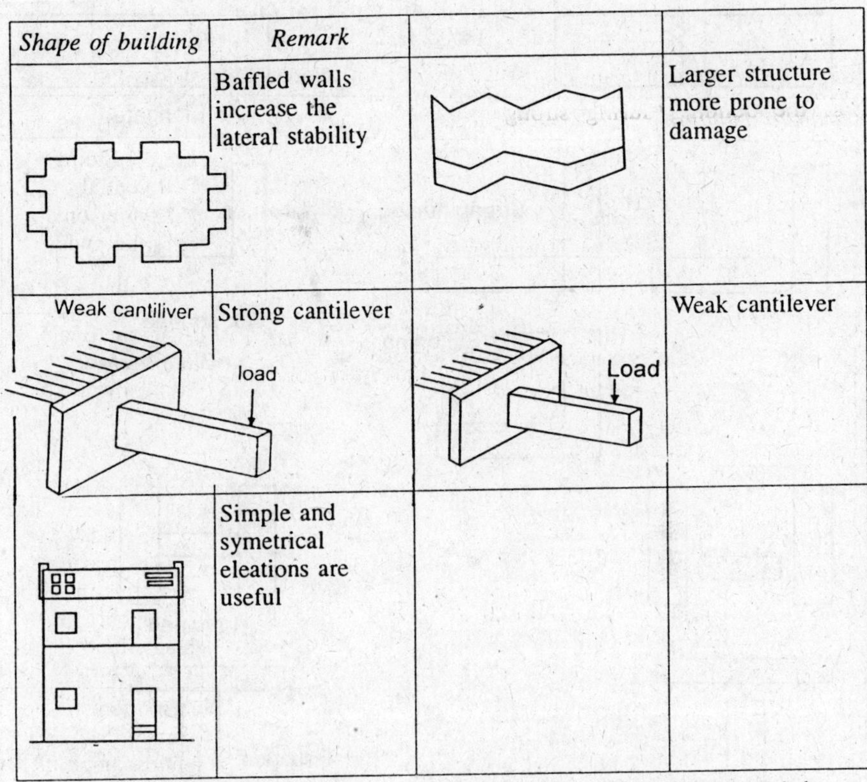

Fig. 11.5 (*a*) Recommended Fig. 11.5 (*b*) Not Recommended

11.6.5. Effect of size of buildings on their performance during earthquakes

In the analysis of the behaviour of buildings during earthquakes, generally following assumptions have been made regarding the ground motion:

1. The ground moves as a rigid mass over the base of the building, which is reasonable for a small area only.
2. The ground is assumed to be elastic.
3. The propagation of seismic waves is not instantaneous.

If different parts of a building are shaken at different times with respect to each other, then incalculable additional stresses will be developed in the building. This effect has been found to increase with size of the building *i.e.* with plan area of the building.

Thus in case of tall buildings having large height to base ratio or slenderness ratio greater than 4 as shown in Fig. 11.7 (*a*) the horizontal movement of the floors during an earthquake is large. For buildings having slenderness ratio less than 4.0, the movement is reasonable. The more slender a building, the worse is the over turning effect during an earthquake. The axial

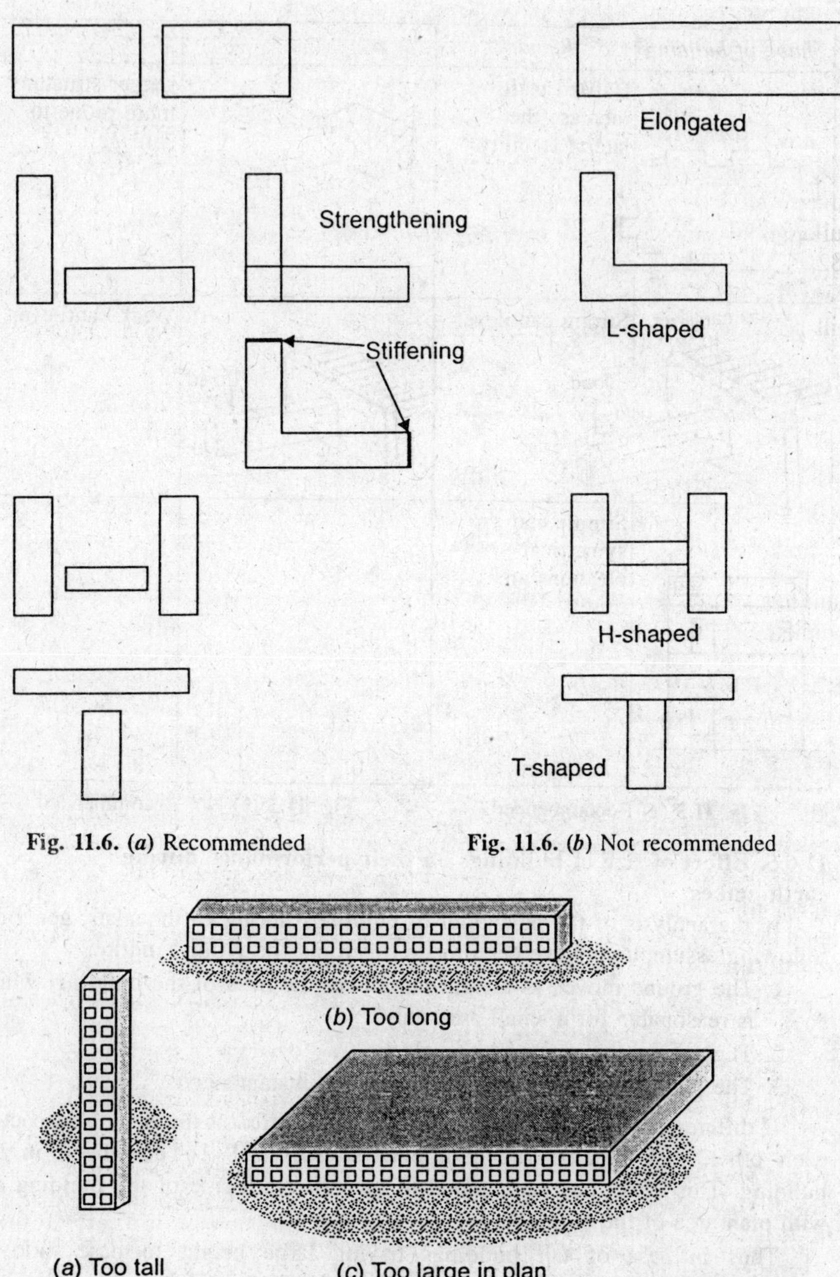

Fig. 11.6. (*a*) Recommended

Fig. 11.6. (*b*) Not recommended

Fig. 11.7. Buildings having one of their overall sizes much larger or much shorter than the other. (Courtesy—IITK)

column load or force due to the over turning moment in such buildings tends to be uncontrollably large. Further the compressive and pull out forces acting on the foundation also increase tremendously.

Case II. In case of buildings that are two long in plan but have short width as shown in Fig. 11.7 (*b*) may be subjected simultaneously at two ends to different movements during an earthquake leading to dangerous results. To avoid adverse effect of earthquake such buildings may be divided into separate square buildings by providing gaps between these parts as shown in Fig. 11.6 (*a*) page 282.

Case III. Buildings having large plan areas such as ware houses 11.7 (*c*) will be subjected to excessive large horizontal seismic forces, that will have to be carried to ground through walls and columns. Such buildings are expected to suffer greater damage during an earthquake. Thus the size of the building should be with in reasonable limits.

11.6.6. Horizontal lay out of buildings

As discussed in section 11.5.3, the simple geometry in plan of buildings have been found to perform well during strong earthquakes. The performance of buildings having re entrant corners like those of U, V, H and + shaped in plan have suffered significant damages. Hence plan should be simple and symmetrical.

11.7. VERTICAL LAYOUT

Earthquake forces developed at different floor levels in a building should be brought down along the height to the ground by the shortest path. Any deviation or discontinuity in this load transfer path results in poor performance of the building. Hence discontinuities as shown in Fig. 11.8 should not be allowed in the buildings. Buildings with vertical set backs as in hotel buildings with few storeys wider than the others as shown in Fig. 11.8 (*a*) cause a great increase in earthquake forces at the level of discontinuity. A large vibrational motion develops in some portions and a large diaphragm action is needed at the border to transmit the inertia forces from the top to the base. The effects of set backs can not be predicted by normal code equivalent static analysis.

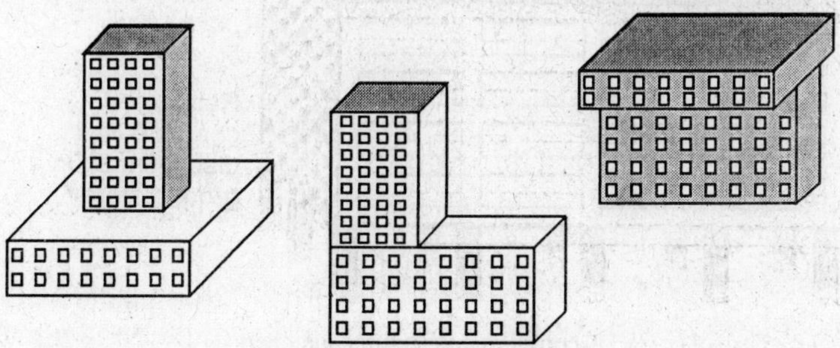

Fig. 11.8. (*a*) Setbacks

Buildings that have fewer columns or walls in a particular storey or that have an unusually tall storey as shown in Fig. 11.8 (*b*) are prone to great damage or collapse.

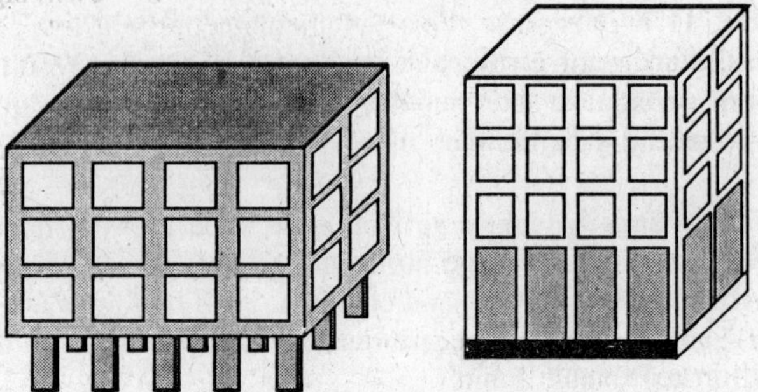

Fig. 11.8. (*b*) Weak or Flexible storey.
(Courtesy—IITK)

One of the most common forms of discontinuity in vertical elements takes place when the shear walls of the upper floors are discontinued in the lower floors. This effect is known as soft storey effect and usually occurs in ground storeys of the buildings. Many buildings with an open ground storey intended for parking purposes collapsed or damaged in Gujrat during 2001 Bhuj earthquake. Fig 11.8 (*b*) shows weak storey.

In seismic regions the soft storey effect usually develops when shear walls are constructed upto the top of ground floor and not taken down upto the foundation. This is one of the most important and common factor which causes discontinuity of the vertical elements. This results in soft storey effect causing concentration of damage to the lower storeys. Fig. 11.8 (*c*) shows a building having shear walls (R.C.C. thin wall for carrying seismic forces) that do not go upto the foundation, but terminated at intermediate storey. It is suggested that in

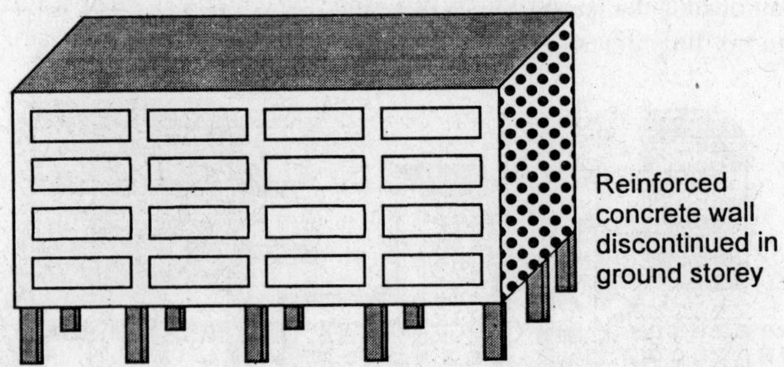

(*c*) Discontinuing structural members

Fig. 11.8. Sudden deviation in load transfer path along the height lead to poor performance. (Courtesy—IITk)

order to reduce the soft storey effect of the lower storey, the stiffness of the lower storey be reduced; so that reduced dynamic force is transmitted to the super structure.

However this argument is based on simple elastic analysis. But when realistic inelastic and geometrical non linear effects are taken into account, the plastic deformations tend to concentrate in soft storey and may cause destruction to the entire building.

11.8. SOFT STOREY

It is also called flexible or weak storey. Soft storey effects are developed in the following situations:

1. Usually soft storey effects are developed in the ground storey where either due to having a show room on the ground or it is used as a parking place for vehicles or as a garage. In case of a floor room, the space between column is filled with glass sheets, so that things inside can be seen from out side also. In case of parking of vehicles either all the four sides are kept open or one or two sides may be provided with masonry in fill walls. In case of a garage large door and windows are provided. All these arrangements cause less stiffness to the storey. Hence it collapse during a earthquake.

2. Soft storey effect may also be developed in any storey of a building in the following situaations:

(*i*) If its height is more than other storeys.

(*ii*) If its lateral stiffness is less than 60% of the storey immediately above it.

(*iii*) If its lateral stiffness is less than 70% of the average stiffness of the three storeys above it.

10.9. EFFECT OF UN EQUAL COLUMNS

Buildings constructed on sloppy ground as shown in Fig. 11.9 (*a*) have columns of unequal height, along the slope which cause vertical discontinuity in the structure. These unequal columns cause twisting in the structure and

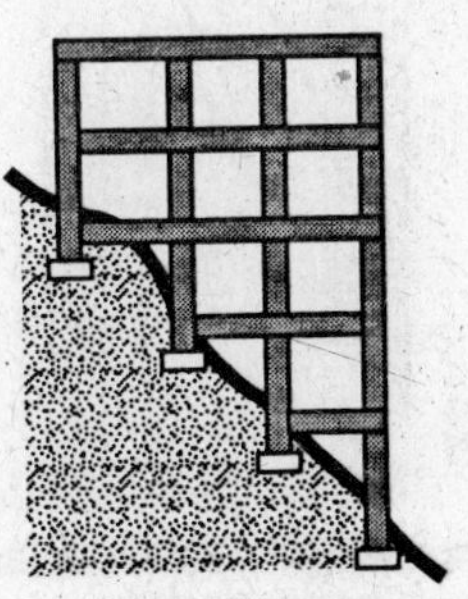

(*a*) Slopy ground

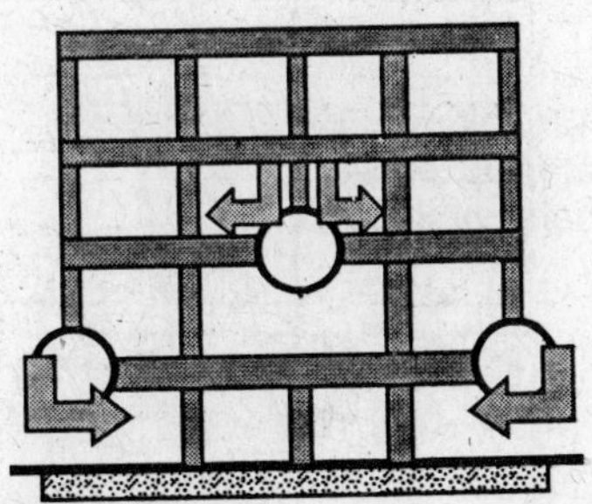

(*b*) Hanging or floaing columns

Fig. 11.9.

damage the short columns of the building. The damage to short columns occurs due to the concentration of shear force in the relatively stiff short columns, which fail before the other long columns. In structural frame system long columns may turn into short columns due to the introduction of spandrel. Buildings whose columns do not go upto the foundation, but are curtailed at intermediate storey beams *i.e.* they float or hang at an intermediate storey beams develop discontinuities in the load transfer path. Fig. 11.9 (*b*).

Short column is not designated by its height, but it is the relative height of the two columns. If a building contains two columns of the same cross-sectional area, but of different heights as shown in Fig. 11.10. The top of the two columns will sway by the same amount say Δx, but smaller column will attract much more force to deflect it than the longer column. During an seismic activity the smaller column attracts may times more load than its share and gets damaged due to its rigidity or stiffness.

A column twice in length (height) is eight times more flexible. If a structure contains both short and long columns, the force or load will be concentrated more on short columns. Short columns are less susceptible to buckling and are capable to bear more vertical loads. But under lateral loading, short columns get more force than their share and fail. This failure occurs in the form of the latter *X*, and is known as shear failure Fig. 11.12. This condition may be avoided by equalizing the height (length of columns), hence equalizing their stiffness. To control shear stress, extra lateral reinforcement in the form of spiral or ties should be provided in the end sections of the columns and beam to column connections.

11.10. SITUATIONS WHERE SHORT COLUMN EFFECTS DEVELOP

Short column effect in a structure develops in the following situations:

(*a*) When a building is constructed on a sloping ground as shown in Fig. 11.9 (*a*). During earth shaking all columns move horizontally by the

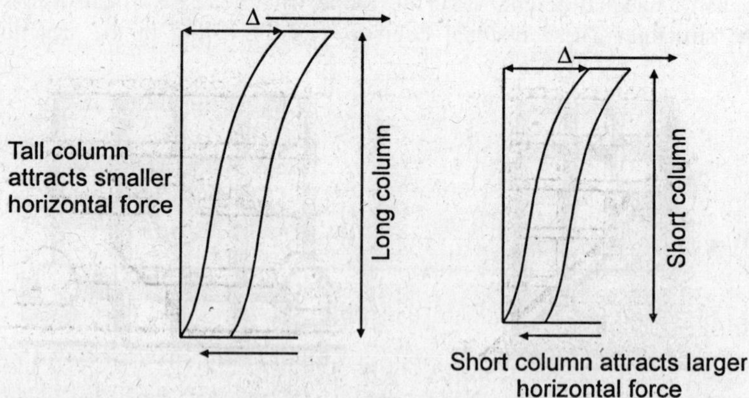

Fig. 11.10

same amount along with the floor slab at a particular level. This phenomenon is known as rigid floor diaphragm action. If there are both types of columns, the short columns will get more loads and suffer greater damage.

(*b*) Short column effect also occurs in columns that support loft slab or menzzinie floors that are added in between two regular floors Fig. 11.11.

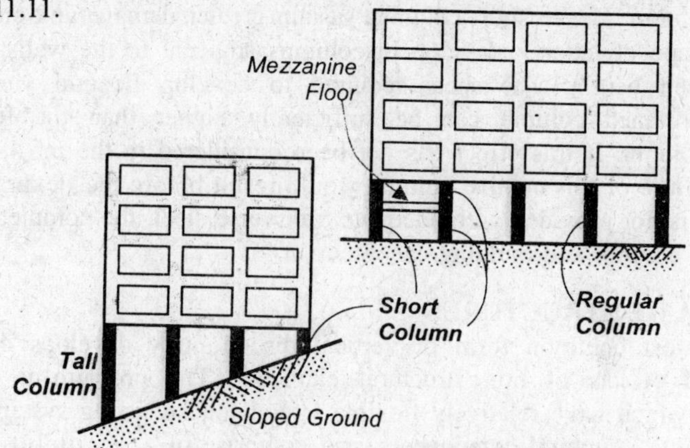

Fig. 11.11 Buildings with short columns
(Courtesy—IITK)

(*c*) Short column effect also occurs in buildings in the following situation.. Consider a building having a masonry or concrete wall of partial height built to fit a window over the remaining height as shown in Fig. 11.12. The adjacent columns of the wall behave as short columns due to the

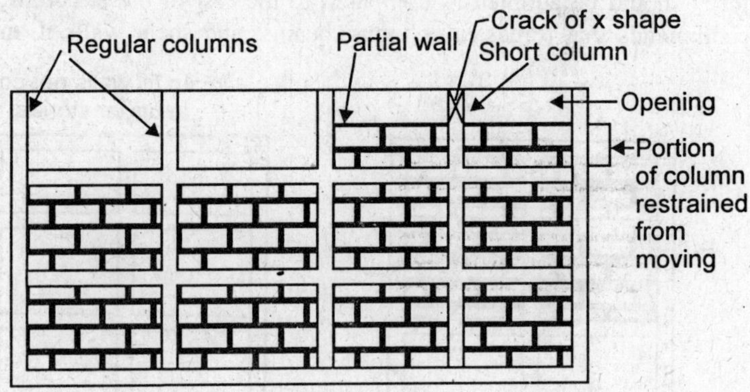

Fig. 11.12

presence of these walls. In many cases in the same story other columns are of the regular (full) height as there are no walls adjoining to them. During an earthquake when the floor slab moves horizontally, the upper ends of these columns undergo the same displacement. How ever the stiff walls restrict the horizontal movement of the lower portion of a short column, and it deforms by the full amount over a short height adjacent to the window opening. Such columns are also known as *captive columns*. On the other hand, regular or full height columns deform over the full height. As the effective height over which a short column can bend freely is small, it offers more resistance to horizontal motion. Thus it attracts larger force or load than regular or full height column. Hence short columns sustain greater damage and crack in the shape of letter × develop in columns adjacent to the walls of partial open height. The shear required to develop flexural yield in the shortened column can be sufficiently higher than the full height Column. If this effect has not been considered in the infill, the shear failure of this captive column would result before the flexural yield. If it is not provided with adequate transverse steel, the complete collapse of column and building can occur.

11.11. FRAME STRUCTURES

The most common form of vertical discontinuity develops due to the unintended effects of non structural elements. The problem is severe in structures which have relatively flexible lateral load resisting system. In such cases the non structural components may comprise of a significant portion of the total stiffness. The common cause of failure has been found, the failure of infilled frames. Such failures are due to the fact that in the design calculations effect of stiff masonry walls is neglected. Thus the inverted pendulum effect is not taken in the design. IS 1893 part 1-2002 has suggested to consider following factors in the design to avoid soft storey effect. After knowing the conditions for developing soft storey effects, higher design forces for soft storey should be adopted as compared to the rest of the structure. Above code recommends that forces in columns, beams, and shear walls if any due to the

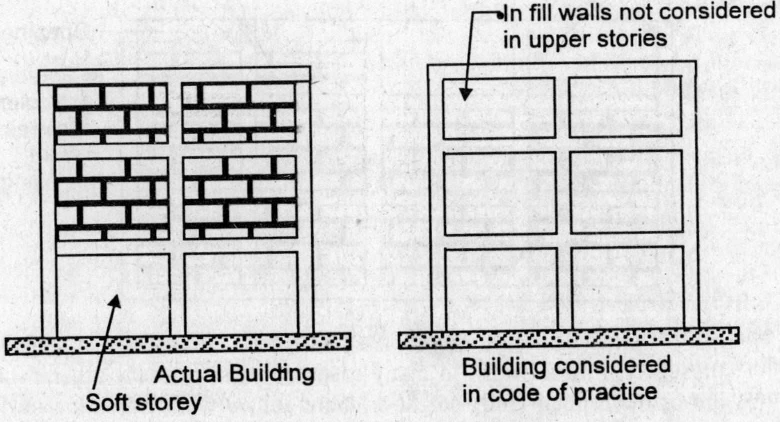

Fig. 11.13

earthquake forces should be calculated considering the bare frame only leaving the infill walls. Fig. 11.13 shows frame with infill walls and bare frame. The columns and beams etc. in the open storey (soft storey) should be designed for 2.5 times the forces obtained from the bare frame analysis.

For all new R.C.C. frames buildings the best option is to avoid sudden and large decrease in stiffness and/strength in any storey. The ideal option would be

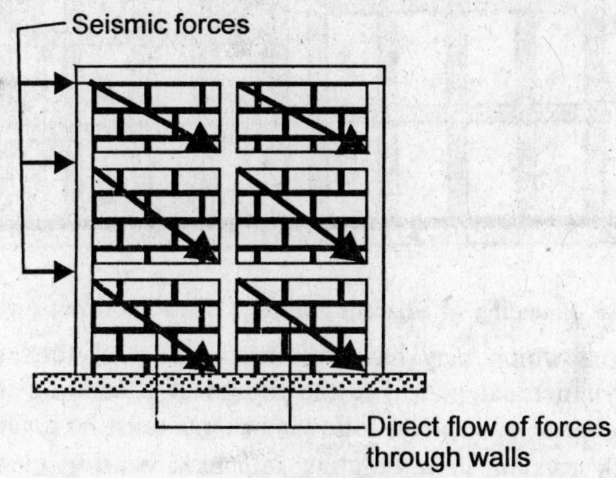

Fig. 11.14

to provide R.C.C. or masonry walls even in the ground storeys. The dangerous effects of flexible and weak ground storeys can be avoided by ensuring that many walls are not discontinued in the ground storeys *i.e.* the drop in stiffness and strength in the ground storey level is not abrupt due to the absence of infill walls as these walls allow direct flow of seismic forces through them to the ground as shown in Fig. 11.14.

11.12. ADJACENCY OF BUILDINGS

The apparent vertical irregularities may occur due to the inadequate separation between the adjoining buildings when they pound against each other during an earthquake. The collision of two buildings becomes a greater problem as the height of the buildings increases. When the height of two buildings is not same, the shorter building may pound against the taller building at the mid point of the column. This situation may be dangerous, hence should be avoided. The separation between the two buildings at least should be 0.004 times the height of the taller building. Fig. 11.15.

11.13. TORSIONAL EFFECTS IN BUILDINGS

The irregular distribution of strength, stiffness and mass in plan can develop significant torsional effects in buildings. Inelastic torsional effect or response can not be rectified with the results obtained by elastic analysis. Techniques for inelastic analysis of a full building system which may include the torsional effect also are cumbersome and unreliable. Thus the best way to

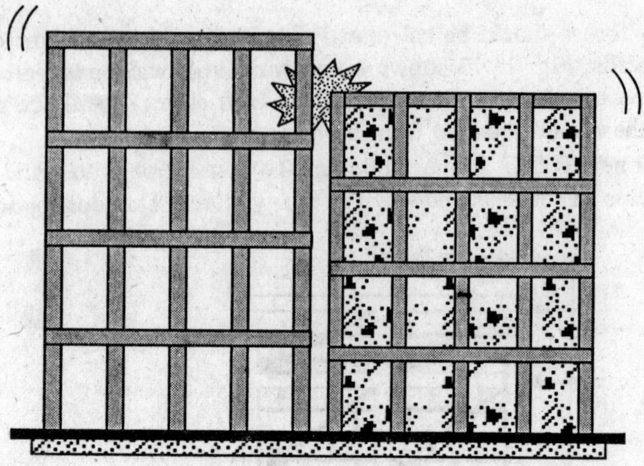

Fig. 11.15. Pounding of adjacent buildings due to horizontal vibrations

design a building which may have minimum effect of torsion is to have a compact and symmetrical plan. For the design of a building to perform well and maximum chance of survival following points must be given due attention.

1. To check torsion in a building, all load bearing elements must be distributed uniformly.
2. The walls and columns should be continuous from foundation to the roof with out any offsets.
3. There should be no off sets in beams.
4. The beams and columns should be coaxial.
5. The width of beams and columns should be equal. This provision helps in good detailing and transfer of moments and shear through the junction of the members concerned.
6. To avoid stress concentration, there should be no abrupt change in the cross section of any member.
7. As far as possible the structure should be continuous (redundant) and monolithic. The seismic resistance of an economically designed structure depends on its capacity to absorb excessive energy input, mainly by repeated plastic deformations of its members.

Thus more continuous and monolithic the structure is, the more plastic hinges, shear and thrust routes are available for energy absorption. Thus the structure should be highly redundant.

11.14. DUCTILITY

The capacity of building materials, structures or their members to under go large inelastic deformation with out significant loss of stiffness or strength is called *ductility*. It is an essential quality of a structure that must response to the strong motions of the ground. Ductility serves in a building as shock absorber, as it reduces the transmitted force to a sustainable magnitude. During strong earthquake action, the survivability of a structure depends on the capacity to deform beyond the elastic range and to dissipate the seismic energy through plastic deformations.

More technically the ductility of a structure or its members may be defined as the ratio of maximum displacement (δ_{max}) at the ultimate strength to displacement at yield or first damage (δ_y). The measure of the structural ductility is the ductility factor, which is written by the letter u. Thus

$$u = \frac{\delta_{max}}{\delta_y}$$

usually displacements are measured at roof level. This is a very important characteristic of a building as it greatly reduces the effect produced by the earthquake in the building.

This is due to the fact that vibrations in the building are set by the energy of the earthquake. The vibrations and the accompanying deflection is reduced as the energy is absorbed by large inelastic deflections of a ductile building. As stated earlier also, some materials as steel, silver and bamboo are inherently ductile, while masonry and plain concrete are brittle materials, which fail suddenly. Building elements constructed with ductile materials have reserve capacity to resist the seismic forces. Thus buildings constructed of ductile materials as steel and adequately reinforced concrete can withstand seismic forces much better than those constructed with brittle materials as brick or plain cement concrete.

11.14.1. Methods of achieving ductility in structural members

Ductility in structural members can be obtained either of the following methods:

1. **Designing elements with known limits.** In reinforced cement concrete members the amount and location of steel should be such that the failure of the member, should occur in steel *i.e.* the steel should reach its tensile strength before concrete reaches its compressive strength. Such a design is known as under reinforced design and the failure is called *ductile failure.*

In R.C.C. buildings the seismic or inertia forces are generated at floor level and transferred to the ground through the various beams, walls and columns. Thus such components which help in transferring seismic forces to the ground must be made ductile. The failure of a beam may cause local damage, where as the failure of a column may damage or collapse the entire building. Thus beams should be made ductile rather than columns. This type of design is called weak beam and strong column design method.

2. **Avoid use of brittle materials.** Ductility of structural members can also be achieved by avoiding the use of brittle materials in the structure. The type of brittle failure is shown in the following Table 11.3.

Table 11.3. Types of brittle failures

S. No.	*Structure*	*Failure (over turning)*
1.	Foundation	Rotational shear failure
2.	Masonry	(*i*) Out of plane bending failure (*ii*) Toppling
3.	Rainforced concrete	(*i*) Anchorage or band failure (*ii*) Member tension failure (*iii*) Member shear failue
4.	Structural steel	(*i*) Member shear failure (*ii*) Member tension failure (*iii*) Tension failure or bolt shear (*iv*) Connection tearing (*v*) Member buckling.

For making entire structural system ductile, following requirement must be met.

(*i*) Brittle type failure modes as over turning must be avoided or adequately safe guarded to ensure ductile failure to occur first.

(*ii*) Any mode of failure should involve maximum possible redundancy.

11.14.2. Factors affecting ductility

Following factors have been found to affect the ductility:

(*a*) Axial load in members reduces the ductility at columns ends. A structure with a weak beam and strong column design improves its ductility.

(*b*) Flexural members exhibit large ductility before collapse, if failure is initiated in steel. Thus ductility can be improved by providing under reinforced flexural members in the structure.

(*c*) Failure of members in diagonal shear should be avoided.

(*d*) Crushing strain in concrete can be improved considerably by confining concrete with the help of closely spaced stirrups.

(*e*) The curvature ductility can be increased by increasing the compression steel.

(*f*) High strength concrete is less ductile. Thus as far as possible very high strength concrete should not be used for earthquake resistant structures.

11.15. FLEXIBLE AND RIGID OR STIFF BUILDINGS

During an earthquake, seismic waves are generated, which flow in all directions from the focus of the earthquake and shake the base or foundation of the structure constructed on the ground. The vibrations of the soil below the foundation are transferred to the building, which cause vibrations in the building. Due to these vibrations the building moves back and forth. The time of one complete cycle of oscillation (one complete back and forth motion) is called *Fundamental Natural Period,* which is denoted by T. The value of T (Fundamental natural period) depends upon the flexibility and mass of the building. The greater the flexibility, longer the value of T, also more the mass, longer the value of T. Thus in general taller buildings are more flexible. Usually the natural fundamental period T for low rise *i.e.* one single storey to 20 storey buildings varies from 0.04 seconds to 20 seconds.

During an earthquake ground shaking contains a group of many sinusodial waves of different frequencies ranging from short to long period (0.03 to 33 secs).

Flexible building. A building whose different elements move differently by the amount of motion of the ground is known as *flexible building.*

Rigid or stiff buildings. A building whose every part moves by the same amount as the ground moves is known as *stiff or rigid building.*

The value of fundamental natural period T depends upon the height and type of the building as shown below in Table 11.4.

Table 11.4. Fundamental period T for different types of buildings

S. No.	*Type of building*	*Value of T in secs.*
1.	General formula for all types of buildings including moment resisting R.C. frame with brick infill walls	$0.09\ H/\sqrt{D}$
2.	Moment resisting R.C. frame buildings with out brick infill walls	$0.075\ H^{0.75}$
3.	Moment resisting steel frame buildings with out brick in fill walls	$0.085\ H^{0.75}$

H = Height of building, D = Dimension along the base.

Theoretically, the construction of structures with moment frames as beam and columns frames is ideal. In such structures masonry infill walls and

Table 11.5.

Item	*Advantages*	*Disadvantages*
1. Flexible structures	(*i*) Flexible structures are suitable for long fundamental natural time period T and for short period sites.	(*i*) The response is high at long period sites.
	(*ii*) Ductility can be achieved easily.	(*ii*) Flexible R.C.C. frames are difficult to reinforce.
	(*iii*) They are more amenable to analysis	(*iii*) Non structural elements may invalidate analysis
	(*iv*) –	(*iv*) Detailing of non structural elements is difficult
2. Stiff structures	(*i*) They are suitable for long period sites.	(*i*) High response on short period sites
	(*ii*) It is easy to reinforce stiff reinforced concrete elements such as shear walls	(*ii*) It is very difficult even to achieve approximate ductility
	(*iii*) The detailing of non structural elements is easy	(*iii*) Less amenable to analysis

partition walls are isolated from the frames movements. This is done to avoid damage in non structural members such as infill and partition walls. This damage is caused due to the extensive lateral deflections developed in the flexible frame structures. In such constructions even shaft walls and lifts also are separated completely. In frame structures these infill and partition walls do not provide extra safety margin as in traditional constructions. But these flexible structures swing when strong winds below. Such swinging of structures causes discomfort to the occupants hence a stiff structure should be provided.

For the construction of flexible structures, materials like masonry are not suitable. For such constructions usually steel is used. For greater stiffness R.C.C. shear wall panels or diagonal braces may be incorporated in steel

Fig. 11.16. Buildings and rope swings both swing back and forth when shaken horizontally. (Courtesy—IITK)

frames. To achieve almost any degree of stiffness, concrete can be readily used. The non structural elements such as partition walls may greatly stiffen a flexible structure. Thus they should be counted in the structural analysis. The comparative advantages and disadvantages of flexible and stiff structures are shown in the Table 11.5.

11.16. TWISTING OF BUILDINGS

During a earthquake ground shaking takes place and buildings built on the ground also swing back and forth along the ground. The swinging of buildings can be explained with the help of an example of an cradle tied with coir ropes to the branch of an old tree or to a steel frame. If the cradle is tied symmetrically with equal ropes, it will swing equally back and forth if one is sitting in the centre. Buildings are just inverted swings. In case of buildings vertical elements as walls and columns act as ropes of the cradle and the floor as cradle it self. Buildings more than one storey behave like rope swings with more than one cradle as shown in Fig. 11.16 on page 294.

11.16.1. Effect of Identical vertical members

If identical vertical members placed uniformly in two horizontal direction are seen from above when shaken at base in a certain direction, they are seen swinging back and forth on the horizontal floor by the same amount in the direction in which they are shaken Fig. 11.17.

Now consider a rope swing tied symmetrically with two equal ropes. In case one sits in the middle of the cradle, the swing will swing back and forth equally in a symmetrical way with out any side ways tilting or swinging. Similarly when a symmetrical building uniformly loaded is shaken or vibrated

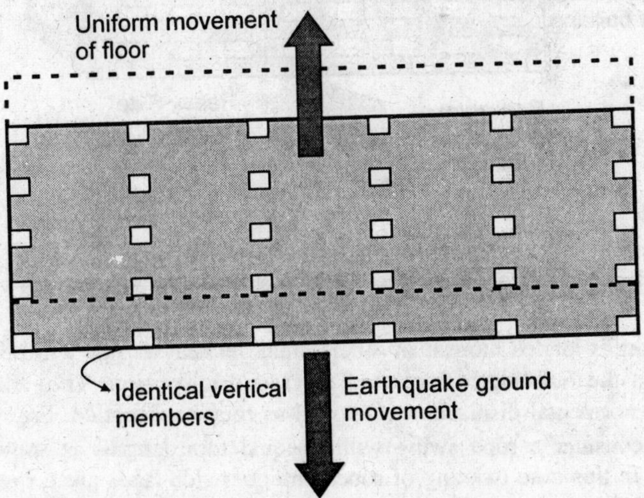

Fig. 11.17. Identical vertical placed members cause all points on the floor to move by some amount

by an earthquake, it will swing back and forth in such a way that all points on the floor move horizontally in the same direction and by the same amount at any given point.

In case if one sits on one side of the cradle of the swing, then it will tilt causing twist in rope as well as in swing Fig. 10.18 (*a*). Similarly if any portion

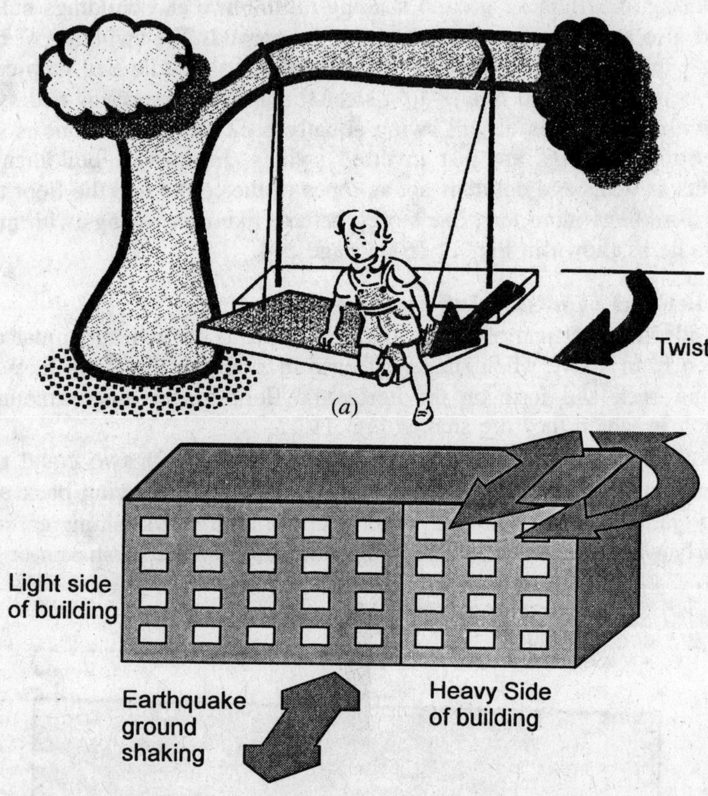

Fig. 11.18. More mass placed on one side causes twists in floors. (Courtesy—IITK)

of a building is loaded more than others, then the heavier side will be displaced more when the building is subjected to ground movement. Thus the building undergoes horizontal displacement as well as rotational motion. Fig. 11.18 (*b*).

Now consider a rope swing with unequal rope lengths as shown in Fig. 11.19 (*a*). In this case twisting of ropes on either side takes place even one sits in the middle of the cradle Fig. 11.19 (a). When a building is located on a sloping ground as showning Fig. 11.19 (*b*). It will have vertical members (wall

(*a*) Swing with unequal ropes

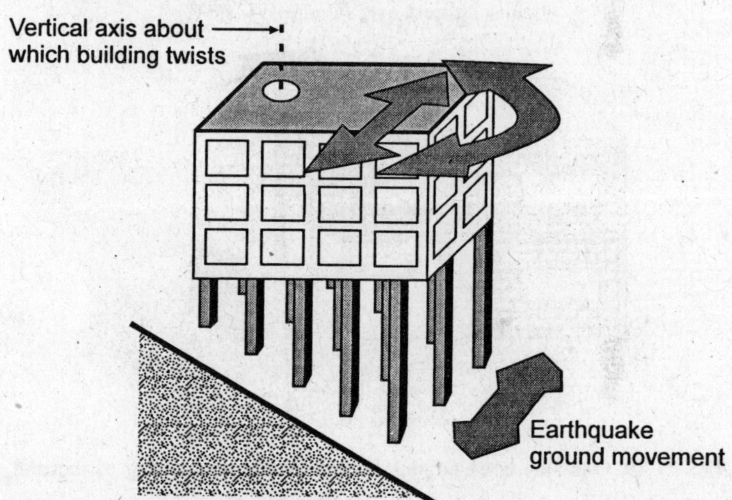

(*b*) Building on slopy ground

Fig. 11.19. Unequal vertical members cause twist in buildings about a vertical axis (Courtesy—IITK)

or column frame etc) of unequal eight. Thus its floors will twist about the vertical axis and displace horizontally. Similarly buildings having walls on one or two sides and flexible frames on the other sides, twist when shaken at ground level as shown in Fig. 11.19 (*c*). Buildings with irregular shapes in plan tend to twist under earthquake shaking. A proped over hanging building is a good example of such a buildings. In this case the over hanging portion swings on the relatively slender column under it Fig. 11.20.

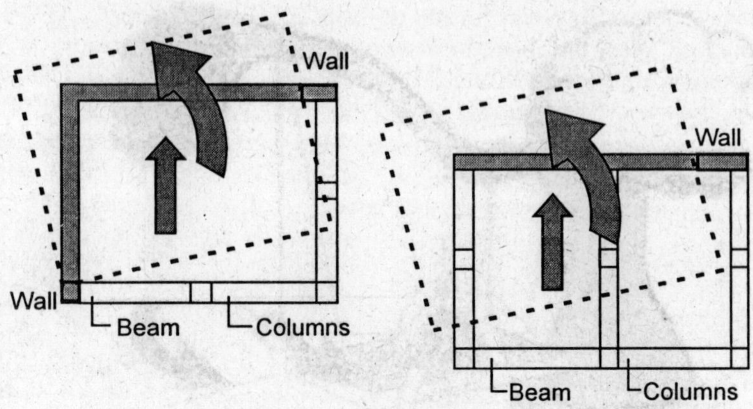

Fig. 11.19 (*c*) Unequal vertical members cause buildings to twist about a vertical axis (Courtesy—IITK)

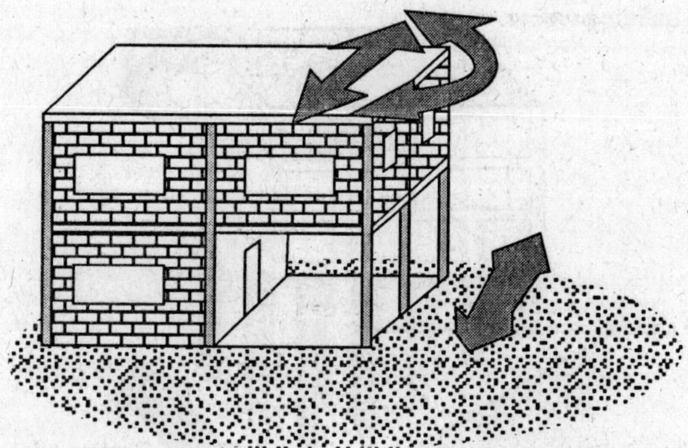

Fig. 11.20. One side open ground story building twist during earthquake

The floor twist and displace horizontally. The best way of minimizing the effect of twist is to ensure that building is symmetrical in plan with respect to vertical members and loads.

11.17. TORSION

Usually torsional forces from ground motion are not of importance, unless the building is inherently of low torsional strength. Twist in buildings causes the different portions of a building at the same floor level to move horizontally by different amounts. This unequal movement causes more damage in the walls or frames on the side on which the movement is more. More damage in frames and walls is caused on the side where movement is more Fig. 11.21. Irregularities of mass, stiffness, and strength in a buildings can cause significant torsional effects. How ever torsion develops due to the eccentric layout of the building *i.e.* when the centre of mass of the building and the centre of rigidity do not coincide with each other. Due to torsion in the building, it will rotate about its centre of rigidity. The twist can be minimised by adopting symmetrical plans of the buildings *i.e.* the mass is distributed uniformly and

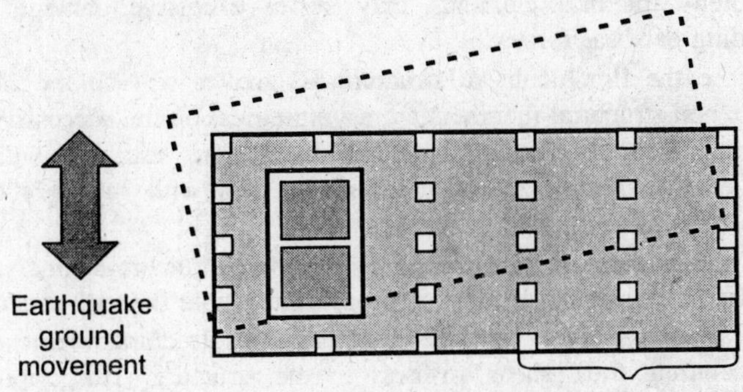

Fig. 11.21. Vertical members which move more horizontally sustain more damage (Courtesy—IITK)

lateral load resisting system also is placed symmetrical as shown in Fig. 11.22. A twisted building will perform poorly during an earthquake.

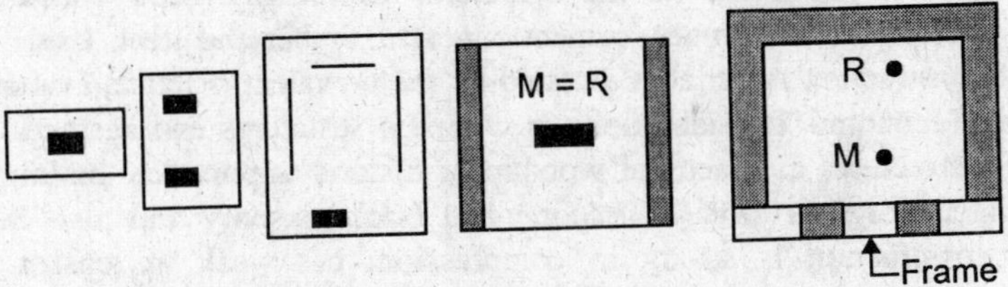

Fig. 11.22.

11.18. EFFECT OF NON STRUCTURAL MEMBERS

Partition walls in buildings, in fill walls in frame structures, claddings, stair cases etc. are non structural elements. In other words, non load bearing members in a building are treated as non structural elements. During an earthquake these, non structural members interfere with the free deformation of the structure and thus become very responsive. In case the structure is made of flexible material, these non structural element will not affect the performance of the structure significantly. However structures usually are made of brittle materials such as bricks and concrete blocks etc., hence the performance of the structure is affected by the non structural members in the following ways.

1. The natural period of vibrations of the structure may be reduced and

may cause change in the intake of seismic energy. Hence seismic stresses of the structure may change.

2. The lateral stiffness of the structure may redistribute. Thus the stress distribution changes.
3. The structure may suffer pre mature failure, usually due to pounding or in shear.
4. The non structural elements may suffer excessive damage due to pounding or shear forces.

Thus more the flexible basic structure is, greater will be the above ill effects. If the non structural members are asymmetrical on the successive floors (*i.e.* the non structural elements are not same), the structure will suffer pronounced effects. There are two methods to deal with such problems in structures as follows:

(*a*) To include these shear elements in the main structure as analysed and to detailed accordingly. This approach is suitable for stiff structures.

(*b*) The other approach is to prevent the non structural elements from contributing their shear stiffness to the structure. This approach is suitable particularly for flexible structures. To achieve this objective, gaps against structures, up the sides and along the top of the element are made, which are later filled with a flexible material.

11.19. CONSTRUCTION MATERIALS

The use of material in the construction affects to a great extent in the determination of the form of the structure. Commonly used construction materials are clay bricks, stones, cement concrete, timber and steel. Usually the choice of construction material is dictated by the prevalent practice, availability of material, economic considerations in common structures and aesthetic look for special structures as places of worship or historic importance buildings in low seismicity regions (zone II). Stone and brick masonry and also cement concrete construction is strong in compression, but weak in tension. The weakness of cement concrete is removed by reinforcing it with mild steel bars. This concrete is known as reinforced cement concrete in which all tensile stresses are born by steel and compressive stresses by concrete. It is quite ductile due to steel.

The reinforced masonry is relatively superior with regard to the strength to weight ratio, deformability, and degradation. It is also economical *i.e.* it is less expensive. R.C.C. material may be placed next economical as well as ductile material.

To make a building ductile, steel is the ultimate choice, but it is quite expensive. R.C.C. structures have been found inferior than steel structures in respect of strength to weight ratio, degradation and deformability. Pre stressing of concrete in case of structures adversely affects the deformability, hence the seismic characteristics of the building. However prestressed concrete can be used for medium to low rise buildings. For high rise or tall buildings steel is most suitable and generally is preferred. For medium rise buildings there is little choice between R.C.C. and steel as long as the structures are well designed and detailed. For low to medium rise buildings usually steel is not used due to its high cost.

The strength to weight ratio of timber is quite high, hence it is quite suitable for building construction, but its fire resistant properties are very low, hence not preferred for the construction of good buildings. The order of suitability of building construction materials is shown in Table 11.6 below. However this order is not fixed. Actually it depends on the qualities of locally available materials, skill of the workers available, prevalent construction methods and quality control exercised.

Table 11.6. Approximate order of suitability of construction materials

Order of suitability	*Type of building*		
	Low rise	*Medium rise*	*High rise*
1.	Steel	Steel	Steel
2.	Insitu R.C.C.	Insitu R.C.C.	Insitu R.C.C.
3.	Pre-stressed concrete	Good Precast concrete	
4.	Good Reinforced masonry	Pre stressed concrete	
5.	Precast concrete	Good reinforced masonry	
6.	Primative reinforced masonry		

However for high seismic activity regions *i.e.* for zones III, IV and V the construction materials should possess the following desirable properties:

1. **High ductility.** The high plastic deformation capacity can enhance the load carrying capacity of the building members.
2. **High strength to weight ratio**. The inertia force is a function of the mass of the structure, hence it will be advantageous to use light and strong materials or structural systems.
3. **Orthotrophy and Homogenecity.** Anisotrophy imperfections in elasticity and in homogeneities modify the effects predicted by simple theories during earthquake. Thus they are un desirable.
4. **Ease in making full strength connections.** The performance of structural elements cannot be evaluated by materials alone. Also at connections the continuity of the structural members is of great significance in evaluating the behaviour of the entire structural system. Hence the ease in making full strength at connections is essential.
5. **Cost.** Often a building plan is rejected due to its high cost despite its superior physical qualities. Thus the cost of the over all structure should be reasonable.

QUESTIONS

1. Discuss the effects of symmetry and elongated shape of the building on the earthquake resistance of the structure.
2. For making a building earthquake resistant, simplicity and symmetry are the key points. Explain the statement with example.
3. A building should exhibit a ductile behaviour in seismic regions. Discuss the measures to make the building stiff.
4. Buildings constructed in seismic zones, the irregularities in the distribution of their mass, stiffness and strength are not desirable. Discuss how these irriguralities are developed and their effects on the building.
5. While planning to construct a building on a sloppy site in a hilly region, discuss the precautions to be adopted to avoid development of twisting in the building.
6. What are non structural elements. Discuss their influence on the behaviour of the building.
7. Discuss the measures to be adopted to increase the followings in a building in earthquake prone area.
   (*a*) Ductility
   (*b*) Period of vibration
   (*c*) Energy dissipation capacity
8. Write short notes on the following:
   (*a*) Strength and stiffness
   (*b*) Symmetry and simplicity
   (*c*) Flexible and stiff building
9. How the inertia forces are transferred from the point of their generation to the ground? Explain fully with the help of a neat sketch.
10. The proper performance of a structure in a seismic zone depends
    (*a*) Symmetry of the building
    (*b*) Simplicity of design
    (*c*) Ductility
    (*d*) Transfer of seismic loads
    (*e*) On all the above factors
11. Identify the correct statement/statements
    (*a*) During an earthquake the foundation of the building moves with the ground motion
    (*b*) The inertia or seismic force experienced by the roof is transferred below to the ground through walls and columns
    (*c*) Circular plan of a building is most suitable, but its analysis is difficult
    (*d*) Though square plan of a building is ideal for behavioural analysis but it is suitable for small buildings
    (*e*) All are correct
12. Short column effects develop in the situations...
    (*a*) When building is constructed on sloping ground
    (*b*) Columns support loft slabs
    (*c*) In buildings having wall of partial height to build a window over it
    (*d*) In all the above situations

13. Captive columns are...
    (*a*) A special type of columns made of pre stressed concrete
    (*b*) Column built near a window opening
    (*c*) Columns made in the ground storey of the building
    (*d*) Columns made of marble as a decorative item
14. For the good performance and maximum survival chances, a building should have...
    (*a*) All load bearing elements must be distributed uniformly
    (*b*) The walls and columns should be continuous from the foundation to the roof with out any off sets
    (*c*) Beams and columns should be coaxial
    (*d*) The width of beam and column should be equal
    (*e*) All are correct
15. Buildings are damaged during earthquakes due to
    (*a*) Soft storey effect
    (*b*) Column-beam joint effect
    (*c*) Faulty reinforcement detailing
    (*d*) Faulty design
    (*e*) Settlement of foundations
    (*f*) Liquefaction of soil
    (*g*) Due to all the above effect
16. In a building storey is called a soft storey if
    (*a*) The roof of the storey rests on columns only and there are no external walls
    (*b*) The building or storey having large doors and windows as in garages
    (*c*) The storey whose height is more than other storeys
    (*d*) The storey whose lateral stiffness is less than 60% of the storey just above it or less than 70% of the combined stiffness of the three storeys above it
    (*e*) All are correct.
17. The soft storey effect can be removed by...
    (*a*) By providing walls in between columns
    (*b*) By providing symmetrical shear walls to the building
    (*c*) By keeping the height of all storeys equal
    (*d*) By reducing the open area in the ground storey
    (*e*) All measures are applicable
18. Identify the incorrect statement/statements
    (*a*) The buildings having height to base ratio more than 4.0 have more horizontal movement of the floor during an earthquake
    (*b*) Buildings having low height but more length are found to suffer more damage during an earthquake
    (*c*) The godowns or ware houses having more plan area, their walls and columns attract more seismic forces than their bearing capacity
    (*d*) During earthquake, buildings having H, U, V or + sign shape suffer less damage during earthquake
19. Identify the correct statement/statements

(*a*) Inertia loads or forces are transferred from roof through walls and columns and foundation to the ground below
(*b*) The design of columns, walls, foundations and their joints should be such that the inertia forces are transferred safely to the ground
(*c*) In the design of buildings, slab is given more importance than columns and walls
(*d*) In the design of a building its configuration is very important
(*e*) All are correct

20. Identify the correct statement/statements
(*a*) The portion of a building which is loaded more, will attract more seismic forces and its displacement also will be more during an earthquake
(*b*) If the height of elements as walls or columns of a building is un equal, then such buildings develop torsion effects and their displacement is also more
(*c*) The buildings having walls on one or two sides and flexible frames on other sides develop torsion during an earthquake
(*d*) The buildings whose plan is unsymmetrical, develop torsion during earthquakes
(*e*) All are correct

21. The frame or walls of a building develop torsion where...
(*a*) In the portion whose displacement is more
(*b*) In the opposite direction of the greatest displacement
(*c*) The portion where displacement is less
(*d*) In all the directions

22. The torsion effect in the buildings can be minimised by
(*a*) By adopting symmetrical plan of the building
(*b*) By the provision of additional shear stresses in the design
(*c*) By distributing the mass of the building uniformly
(*d*) By establishing the transverse load system uniformly
(*e*) All steps are effective

23. To transfer the inertia forces to the ground... element is most important
(*a*) Roof (*b*) Beam
(*c*) Column or walls (*d*) All are equally important

24. During an earthquake the behaviour of a building depends upon
(*a*) Shape of the structure or building
(*b*) size of the building
(*c*) Geometry of the building
(*d*) The process of transferring seismic forces
(*e*) On all factors

25. During an earthquake torsion in a building develops due to...
(*a*) Due to columns of unequal height in a building founded on a sloppy ground
(*b*) Columns being floating (resting on an intermediate floor)
(*c*) No bond between the shear walls and foundation
(*d*) In any storey of a multistorey building, number of columns or walls being less

(*e*) All the above factors cause torsion in a building

26. Identify the correct statement/statements
    (*a*) During an earthquake a building sway to and fro like a pendulum
    (*b*) The walls or columns of the building behave like the rope of a cradle and the floors of the buildings behave like the plank or bottom of the cradle
    (*c*) If heavy material is stored in any portion of the building, that portion will have more displacement and at the same time develops torsion there
    (*d*) In case there are walls on one or two sides of the building in plan, and flexible frames on the other sides, the building will develop torsion
    (*e*) The vertical elements of the building as walls or columns being unequal the building will develop torsion
    (*f*) All are correct

ANSWERS

10. (*e*)	15. (*g*)	20. (*e*)	25. (*e*)
11. (*e*)	16. (*e*)	21. (*a*)	26. (*f*)
12. (*d*)	17. (*e*)	22. (*e*)	
13. (*b*)	18. (*d*)	23. (*d*)	
14. (*e*)	19. (*e*)	24. (*e*)	

12
Framed Structures

12.1. INTRODUCTION

The conventional method of construction of buildings or structures is that of load bearing walls system. This system is the most common system for building low rise structures. However this system has inherent weakness of resisting horizontal or lateral loads (seismic forces). With the increase of population and advancement in building technology high rise buildings have been constructed all over the world. As the conventional load bearing wall method is not suitable for multistoreyed buildings, framed structures have been developed. The frame work of a multi-storey structure consists of a number of horizontal elements known as beam and vertical elements called columns built monolithically forming a network. The ability of multi storey building frame to resist the lateral forces or loads depends on the rigidity of the connections between the beams and columns. When the connections are fully rigid, the structure as a whole is capable of resisting the lateral forces (seismic forces). Thus moment resistant frame is the fundamental structure suitable for multi storeyed buildings.

12.2. TYPES OF FRAMES

Usually frames may be classified into the following three categories:

1. Moment resisting frames

The building frame system consisting of horizontal elements as beams and vertical elements called columns is known as moment resisting frame. These elements together with joints resist the earthquake forces mainly by flexure. Generally the system is preferred by architects as they are relatively un obstructive in comparison to shear walls or braced frames, but they have been found less effective in resisting the seismic effects un less special measures of damage control are adopted. Thus slab-column frames are not recommended as lateral load resisting system.

2. Bearing wall system or building with shear walls

This system supports almost all gravity loads as well as lateral loads. In general this system lacks in redundancy and has a poor inelastic response capacity. Thus this system has comparatively lower value of response reduction factor (R) which is an indicator of the performance of the structure in a earthquake. The low value of R (1.5) is an indication of an extremely earthquake prone building. R = 5.0 indicates an earthquake resistant building.

In severe seismic zones the wall bearing systems are required to be specially detailed as per IS 4326-1993. Thus this system is not much preferred by the architects.

3. Dual system

This system is a combination of moment resisting frame and shear wall or braced frame. This system is designed such that:

(*a*) The moment resisting frames independently resist at least 25% of design seismic base shear.

(*b*) The two systems are designed to resist the total design force in proportion to their lateral stiffness taking into account the interaction of the dual system at all floor levels. In general this system has higher value of *R*. This system is less restrictive architecturally.

12.3. STRENGTHENING OF FRAME SYSTEM

The ability to resist the lateral forces depends on the rigidity of the connections between the beams and the columns. When the connections are fully rigid, the structure as a whole is capable to resist the lateral forces. Thus the moment resisting frame is the fundamental structural system. In case if the stiffness and strength of a frame are not adequate then the frame may be strengthen by introducing load bearing walls, shear walls, the bracing as shown in Fig. 12.1.

Shear walls and bracings are also useful in preventing the failure of non structural components by reducing the drift. Shear walls have large in plane stiffness and can resist effectively lateral loads originated by earthquakes or winds. Thus shear walls are situated in advantageous positions in a building. Shear walls may be made of R.C.C., steel, composite and masonry. However in multi storey buildings mostly R.C.C. shear walls are used. For details refer chapter 19.

For more than forty storey buildings, the effect of lateral forces becomes increasly intense. In such a situation the use of tube system has been found economical. The tube system may be classified as follows:

(*a*) **Framed tube system.** In this system closely spaced columns are tied at each floor level by deep spandrel beams, creating the effect of a hollow tube, perforated by openings for windows. Fig. 12.2 (*a*). This system represents the logical evaluation of the conventional framed structures. These frames possess necessary stiffness and excellent torsional qualities and retain the flexibility of planning.

(*b*) **Trussed tube system.** This system is an improvement over framed tube system. The diagonal members along with girders and columns

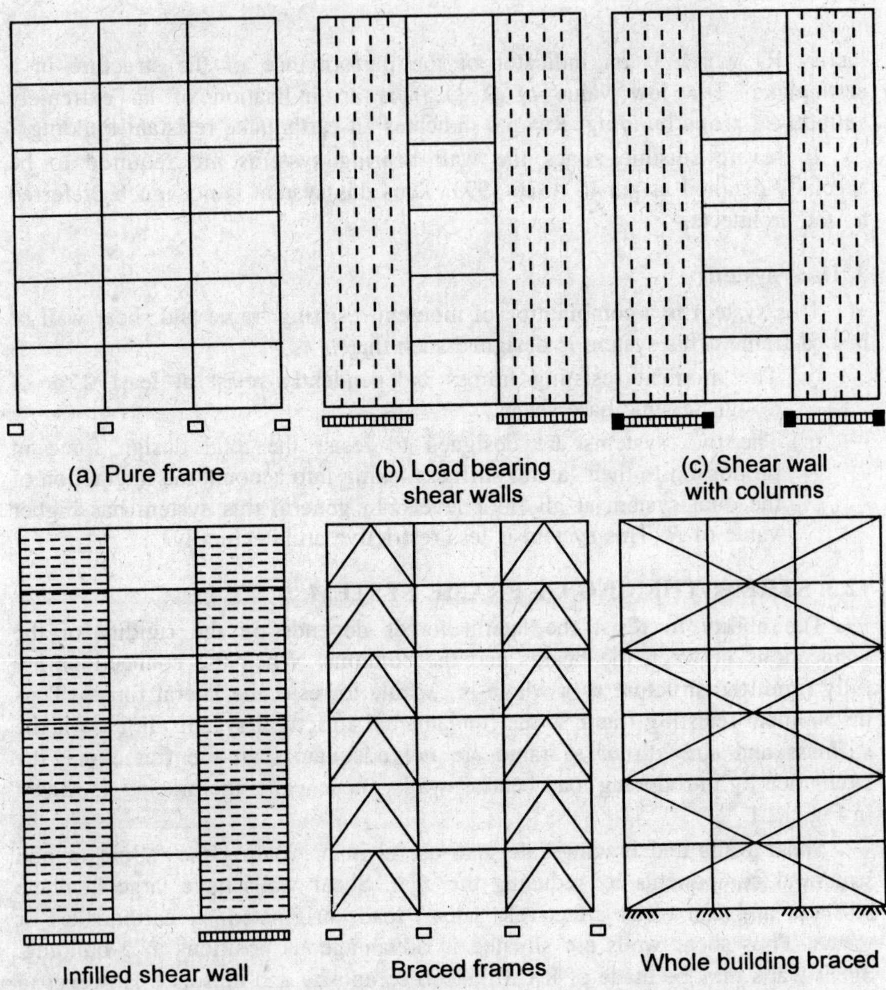

(*d*) Infilled shear wall (*e*) Braced frames (*f*) Whole building braced

Fig. 11.1. Lateral load resisting system

form the truss system. This truss system imparts enormous stiffness to the building. Fig. 12.2 (*b*).

(*c*) **Tube in tube system.** This system consists of an exterior tube. This tube resists the bending moment due to lateral forces and an interior slender tube, which resists the shear produced by the lateral forces Fig. 12.2 (*c*).

(*d*) **Bundle tube system.** This system is made of a number of tubes separated by shear walls. The tubes rise to various heights. In the system each tube is designed independently. Fig. 12.2 (*d*)

The moment resisting frames in a multi storey building along with the

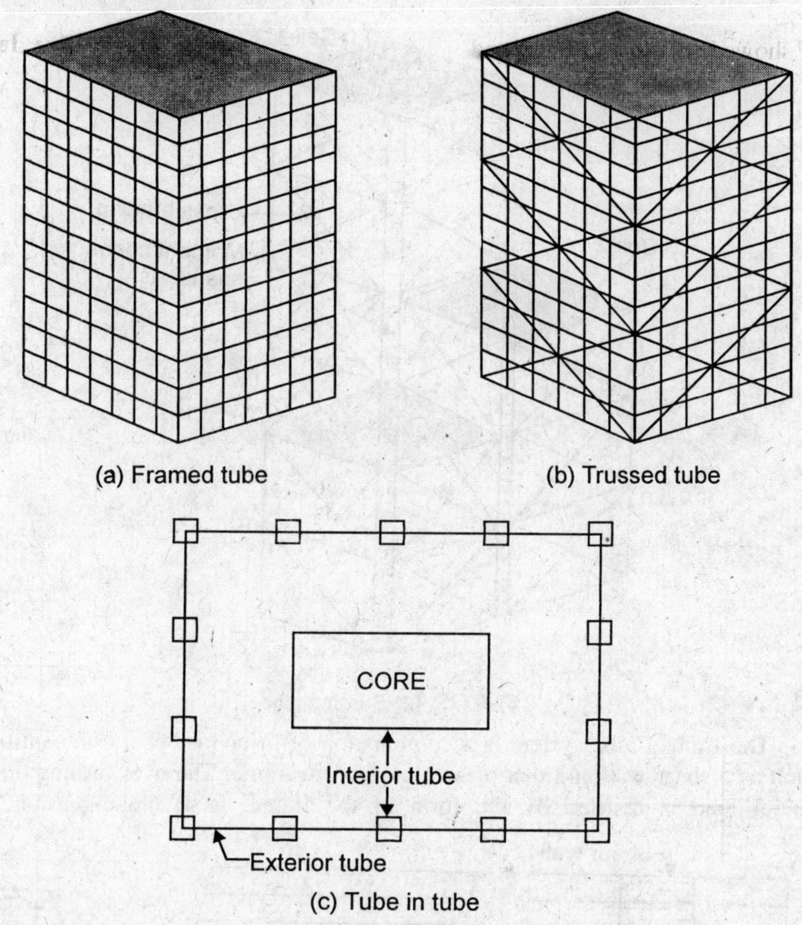

Fig. 12.2 (*c*) Tube in tube

shear walls or bracing resist the lateral forces Fig. 12.3 (*a*). Frames deform predominantly in a shear mode as shown in Fig. 12.2 (*b*), where the relative storey deflection depends on the shear applied at storey level *i.e.* storey floor level). The walls deform essentially in a bending mode as shown in Fig. 12.2 (*c*). A structural frame work with load bearing walls, thus exhibits intermediate form of behaviour as shown in Fig. 12.2 (*d*). In the lower part of the buildings, the walls resist the greater part of the shear force, but gradually shear decreases in higher storeys. If flexure deformation occurs in a load bearing wall, the adjacent boundary beam undergoes a large deflection. Thus it should have adequate ductility. Adjacent columns are also subjected to large axial force. Hence the difficulty arises both in designing the column cross section and in determination of pull out force on the foundation. To avoid this difficulty the building may be provided with shear walls or may be braced as shown in Fig. 12.1.

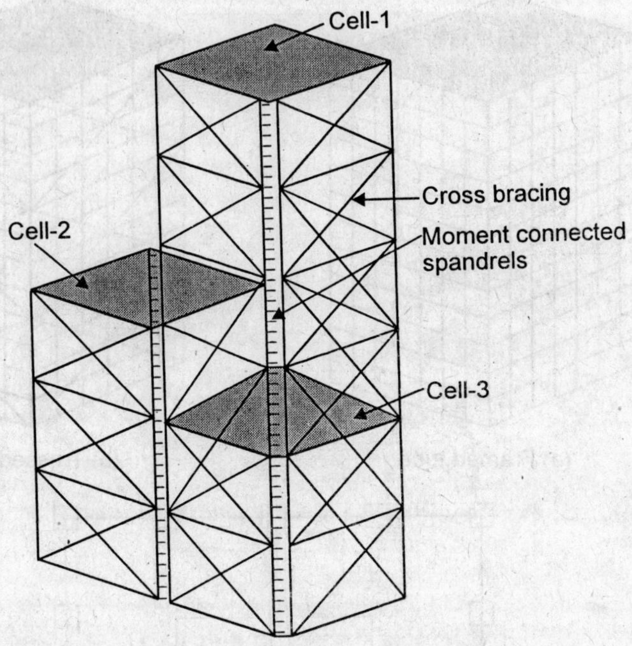

Fig. 12.2 (*d*) Burdled tube

The framed tube system is a combination of behaviour of a true cantilever such as a shear wall and that of a column beam frame. The over turning due to lateral load is resisted by the form of the frame. It develops tension and

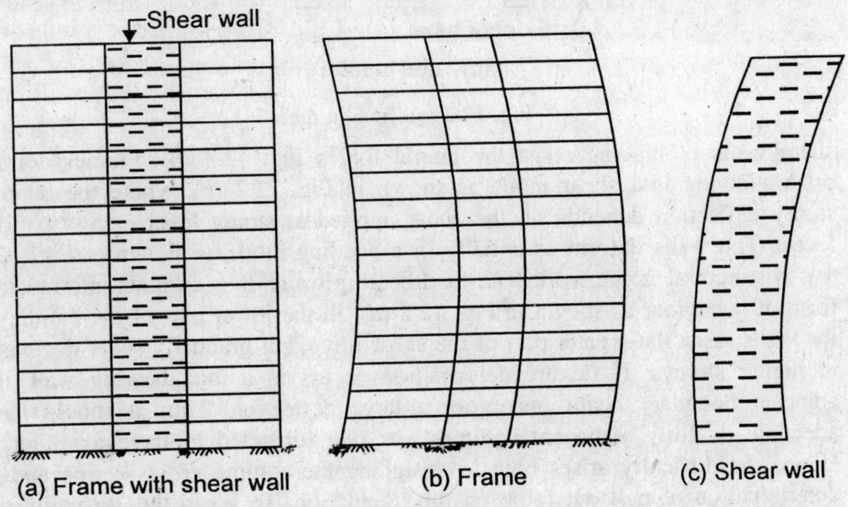

Fig. 12.3 (*a*) (*b*) (*c*)

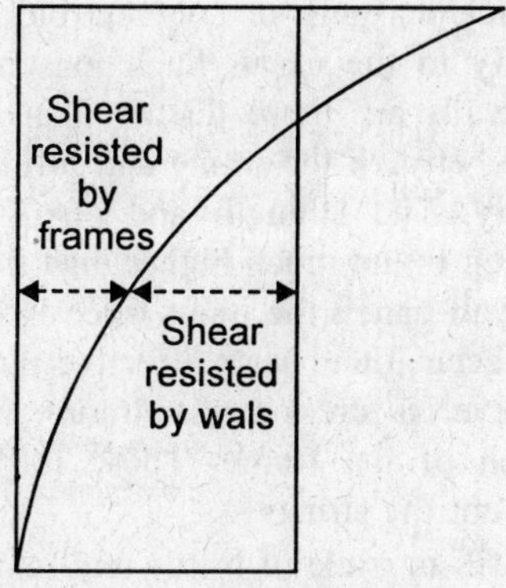

Fig. 12.3. Contribution of frames and shear walls to storey shear

compression in the columns. The shear from the lateral load is resisted by bending in columns and beams primarily in the two sides of the building parallel to the direction of the lateral load.

12.4. IN FILL OF FRAMES

Usually in steel and concrete moment resisting frames infilling of space between columns and ground to under side of ceiling (called bays) is done either with brick masonry or concrete blocks. Infilling of bays with brick masonry is a common practice. Masonry infill usually is specified by the architect as interior or exterior partitions in such a way that they do not contribute to the vertical gravity load bearing capacity of the structure *i.e.* they are treated as non structural members. However due to the tight fill construction with in the structure frame and their large in plane stiffness, infill walls resist wind and seismically induced forces or loads.

Mostly the infills are made of un reinforced non integral brick masonry. Thus the analysis and design of infilled frames considering the composite action are quite complex, hence generally the effect of interaction is ignored. However in seismic areas ignoring this interaction is not always safe, as this action can dramatically change the stiffness and ductility characteristics of the structure.

Improper use of infill panels often has resulted in undesirable response during earthquakes causing damage not only to the infill but also inducing brittle shear failures in the frame members, especially in columns. According to Mr. D.V. Mallik the damage to structures during an earthquake due to infill masonry walls failure can be minimized by connecting these walls inside the bounding frames through shear connectors.

12.5. BEHAVIOUR OF IN FILL WALLS

Usually in framed structures the frames are infilled with stiff construction elements such as brick masonry or concrete block masonry to form enclosure and to provide safety to the users. Such masonry walls are known as *infill walls.* These infill walls are more ductile than isolated walls. There will be structural interaction between the frame and infill panels unless separated from the frame adequately. The strength and energy dissipating capacity of an infilled frame has been found much higher than that of a bare frame. Though in a frame with infill wall panel, the input force is much higher due to its higher stiffness, but it has been found very effective during an earthquake. However these infill walls develop stress concentration in particular members and/or torsional deformation of the frame. These infill walls also alter the shear distribution through out the structure.

Generally the infill is made of brittle and relatively weak material. Thus in severe earthquakes the response of structures having such in fills will be greatly

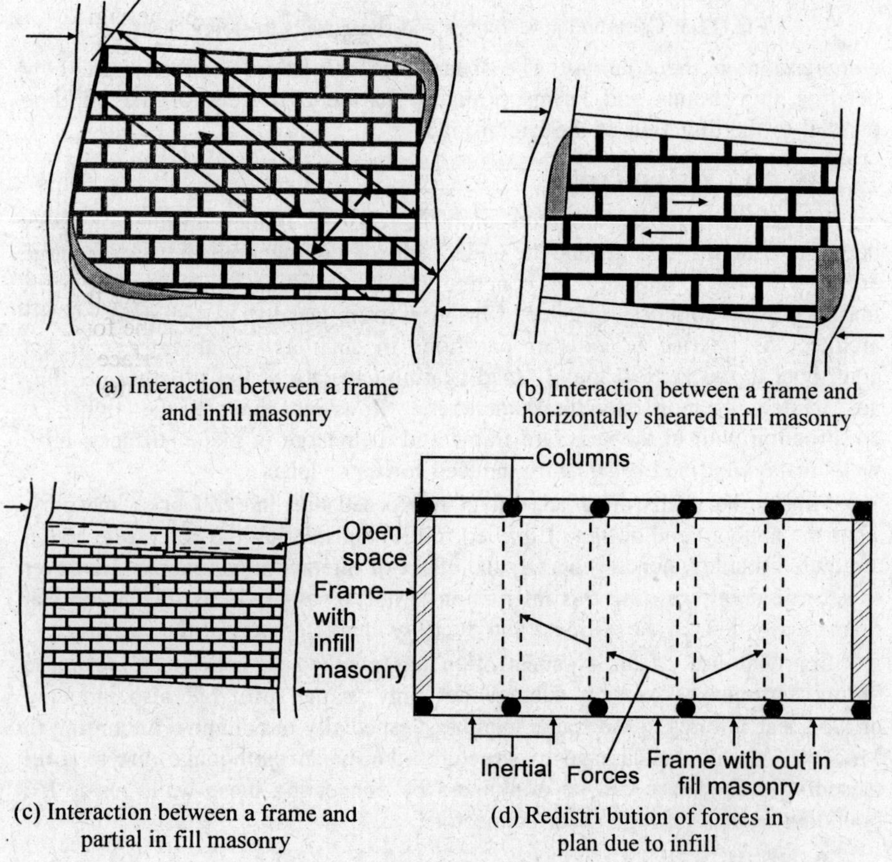

(a) Interaction between a frame and infll masonry

(b) Interaction between a frame and horizontally sheared infll masonry

(c) Interaction between a frame and partial in fill masonry

(d) Redistri bution of forces in plan due to infill

Fig. 12.4. Interaction between a frame and infill massonry and redistribution of forces in plan due to infill.

influenced by the damage sustained by the infill and its stiffness-degradation characteristics. The implications of the frame infill masonry are complex and it is very difficult to account for fully in practice. However for a designer it is essential to have an understanding of these effects to achieve a properly conceived and detailed building.

It has been observed that, a masonry wall surrounded by a frame, when subjected to shear, the wall panel separates from the frame at a load equal to 50 to 70% of the maximum load bearing capacity. In this condition the wall acts as a compression strut or brace as shown in Fig. 12.4 (*a*) resulting in substantial stiffening of the frame and redistribution of bending moment and shear in the frame. When the sliding resistance is smaller than the strength of the diagonal strut, the wall panel may fail by sliding as shown in Fig. 12.4 (*b*).

Once the panel has sheared, the effect of the diagonal compression is lost. In this situation the resistance to the external shear will be provided by the columns only as the friction at the sliding surface becomes negligible. The interaction of a frame and partial infill masonry is shown in Fig. 12.4 (*c*)

The redistribution of forces in plan due to the stiffening effect of infill masonry is shown in Fig. 12.4 (*d*). The whole of the lateral force is resisted by the two end frames. This situation continues till the masonry panels retain their strength. In case the masonry of one of the end frame is damaged, then high torsional effects will develop.

The infill masonry of the frame, increases its stiffness, which reduces the natural period of vibration of the frame, resulting in increase of the effective lateral force. The local effect of stiffening of the frame is to redistribute the forces on the stiffened frames, producing undesirable eccentricity. Thus the forces on a frame increase many folds. The contact at the frame masonry interface modifies the redistribution of the frame forces. This phenomenon reduces the effective length of a column/beam, hence the ratio of shear to bending force is increased.

$$\text{B.M. in column } M = \frac{6\,E.I.x}{l^2}$$

$$\text{Shear force in column } V = \frac{2M}{l}$$

$$\therefore \quad \text{Shear force } V = \frac{12\,EI \cdot x}{l^3}$$

Where,

I = Moment of inertia

E = Modulus of elasticity of material

l = Length of the column

x = Inter storey displacement.

12.6. DESIGN OF MASONRY INFILLED FRAMES

The masonry infilled frames can be designed based on either of the two following approaches:

1. Qualitative design approach

In this approach heavy reinforcement is used both in masonry and the frame. However this provides the following advantage during an severe earthquake.

(*i*) The frame takes full advantage of the additional stiffness provided by providing extra reinforcement in the frame.

(*ii*) The reinforcement provided in the masonry absorbs the energy.

2. Providing full separation of joints

In this case a gap or separation at the joint of masonry and frame is provided at the top and at the end as shown in Fig. 12.5. The out of plane failure may be tackled by the reinforced masonry acting as vertical cantilever as shown in Fig. 12.5 or by providing reinforcement in every layer of massonry.

Brick being cheaper and easily available has been used in building construction. But it has poor shear and tensile strength. It also have brittle

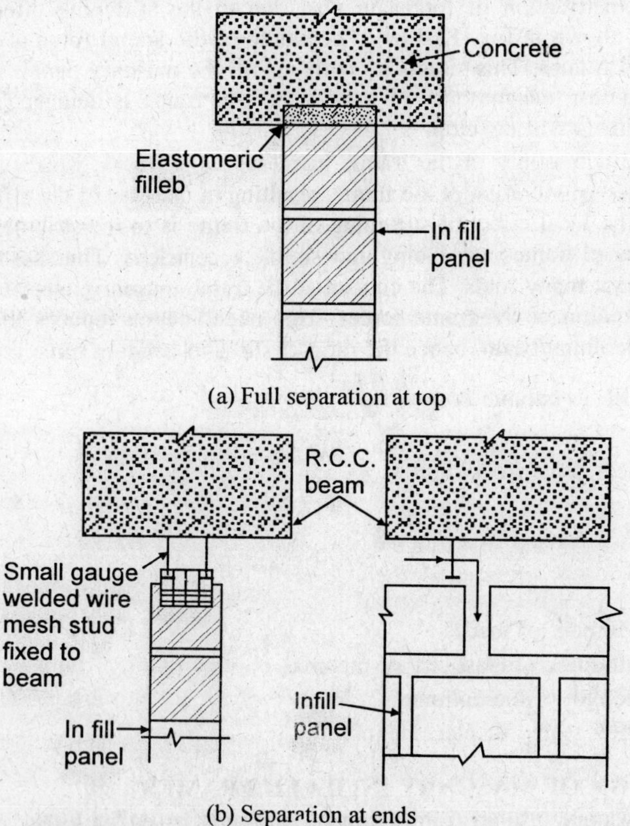

Fig. 12.5. Lateral restraint details due to a 'free' infill panel

characteristics. Due to these causes past studies showed that the stiffness and ductility of the infilled frames were reduced due to strong column-beam joints and corner crushing of brick masonry infill. To over come these draw backs, now a days autoclaved aerated concrete blocks have been tried in place of brick as infill in frames. The use of autoclaved aerated concrete blocks has been found useful due to the following reasons:

(*a*) They are light weight and have unique size.

(*b*) Less mortar is required with the use of these blocks.

(*c*) They have better thermal insulation and ease in handling.

(*d*) They give better speed of construction.

On the basis of the experimental studies Prof. S. Prabavathy and team have found the following effects of the use of aerated autoclaved concrete blocks.

1. The initial and final stiffness of R.C.C. frames with aerated autoclaved concrete blocks are found higher than bare frames.
2. The cumulative ductility of the reinforced aerated autoclaved concrete blocks masonry infilled frame has been found 1.75 times more than that of bare frames.
3. The cumulative energy dissipation for infilled frames has been found 3 times more than that of bare frames.

QUESTIONS

1. Why the necessity of frame structures felt now? Explain
2. How many types of frames can be used in the construction industry?
3. Discuss the advantages and disadvantages of frames and conventional building construction.
4. What are the draw backs of frame structures? How can they be mitigated?
5. Discuss the behaviour of brick masonry infill framed structures.

13

General Principles of Earthquake Resistant Design of Structures

13.1. INTRODUCTION

During an earthquake seismic waves are created. When these waves arrive at a certain location, they produce acceleration in the soil particles there. These accelerations are transferred to the buildings/structures standing on the ground. There is a time lag between the ground motions and the upper levels motion due to inertia. Due to the vibrations in the upper levels the buildings sway and collapse if no earthquake resistant measures have been taken in the design and construction of the buildings/structures.

13.2. FACTORS AFFECTING THE BUILDING DURING A EARTHQUAKE

Following factors affect the influence of earthquake on buildings:

1. The distance between the focus and the site of the building.
2. The nature and layout of terrain between the focus and the buildings.
3. The morphology (Form and structure) of the site.
4. Nature and intensity of the earthquake at the focus.
5. The dynamic characteristics (period of vibration and damping) of the building.
6. State (condition) of the building

These days technology exists to design houses to withstand earthquake magnitude more than 8.0. How ever till now due to practical point of view, it was thought that seismic resistant design should be such that a properly designed and constructed structure should resist the "moderate" earthquake with a damage which can be repaired and in strong earthquakes without collapse, but with a acceptable damage. The criterion of acceptable damage was introduced to limit the increase in the cost of a earthquake resistant building structure. However now it is demanded that a building simply not only collapse but retain its structural integrity through out the earthquake. In an earthquake the ground moves in a random fashion in all directions. The ground motion consists total six components, three of which are liner in x, y, and z direction and the three are rotational.

13.3. GROUND ACCELERATIONS

When the disturbance of seismic nature arrives at a given location, it causes accelerations in the soil particles, which are transferred to the buildings and make them shake. It is believed that only the horizontal accelerations are most destructive. Hence the effect of vertical accelerations is neglected in the design. The study of damage of buildings during the past earthquakes has shown that vertical accelerations also do cause additional damage to structures and enhence the destruction. The vertical component has the impact of vertical expansion and contraction against which usual static calculations provide a safety margin, which in most cases seems to be satisfactory. But whenever vertical component of the acceleration is found much stronger, then its effect should not be neglected.

13.4. INFLUENCE OF SOIL ON STRUCTURES DURING EARTH-QUAKE

The analysis of damage of buildings during the past earthquakes has shown that the intensity of ground shaking during an earthquake and the associated damage to structures, are greatly affected by the soil condition and local geology of the area. The topography of a site may cause wave amplification. At certain frequency levels these amplifications can be considerable. Following factors have been found to influence the damage to structures during a earthquake.

1. Maximum acceleration at the site.
2. The frequency characteristics of the ground motion and its duration.
3. The dynamic characteristics of the site.
4. The dynamic characteristics of the structure (time period and damping)

13.5. EFFECT OF SOIL CONDITIONS

The nature of the soil has a great influence on the intensity of ground shaking, which causes structural damage. These damages have been found to occur even when the soil underlying a building may remain perfectly stable during the earthquake.

(*a*) *Nature of sub soil.* It has been observed that loose and unstable soils coincide with heavy damage *i.e.* building situated on loose and unstable soils suffer heavy damage. On the other hand buildings situated on rocks are damaged very less.

(*b*) It has been found that prominent periods of ground vibrations during earthquakes are the periods of natural vibrations of bedded soil layer characteristics of a given locality. Soft soils are found to have large periods where as firm soils have smaller periods.

(*c*) The type of soil also has been found to influence the amplitude of its vibrations. Vibration amplitudes of different soils have been found as follows:

Type soil	*Amount of amplitude*
(*i*) Rock	2 to 5 mm
(*ii*) Clay	30 mm
(*iii*) Filled and slimy	100 mm or more

(*d*) Accelerations of soil vibrations decrease appreciably with the increase in its density and solidity.

(*e*) The presence of high ground water level increases the acceleration of vibrations which is more pronounced in loose soils. The influence of ground water in rocks on the vibration acceleration is very small.

The influence of actual soil conditions on the seismic hazards can be established by the special studies of local conditions according to their seismic risk potential. This procedure is called micro zoing. From micro zoning it will be revealed that cities situated on loose soil are likely to suffer greater destruction as loose soils amplify the earthquake vibrations. On the other hand cities situated on hard rock would suffer less destruction. Thus micro zoning will help to prepare detailed seismic maps of a city according to density of population and seismic risk. On this basis construction of big structures on weak soil may be avoided.

Liquefaction

The phenomenon of liquefaction and its effects have been fully discussed in chapter 9.

13.6. EARTHQUAKE RESISTANT DESIGN

Since ancient times human being has sought the mitigation of the devastating effects of earthquake, which is one of the most destructive natural force. The studies of the destruction of structures during the past earthquakes have made it possible to establish regulations for increasing the earthquake resistance of structures. The experimental and theoretical studies carried out in U.S.A., Japan, Russia and other earthquake prone countries have prepared the basis for increasing the seismic resistance to structures. Studies have shown that structures built according to seismic codes have suffered minimum damage though could not be eliminated the damage fully.

13.6.1. Masonry structures

Masonry structures are in use since time immemorial due to ease in construc- tion, good heat insulation, good finish and being cheap. Masonry work can be built with stone, bricks, adobe and unburnt mud earth bricks. From the study of damaged buildings during the past earthquakes, it has been observed that mostly buildings made of bricks and rubble stones collapsed during the earthquake due to their low tensile strength and low resistance to shear. The stresses developed due to the earthquake vibrations easily led to their collapse. Generally these buildings are not built according to the regulations of seismic design. Thus they suffered heavy damages during earthquakes. The failure of many such buildings in many countries in past earthquakes have been discussed in chapter 2.

In most cases masonry buildings are small or medium size buildings. Heavy damage systematically occurs due to the following reasons:

(*a*) Inadequate bond between walls and foundation.

(*b*) Inadequate bond between adjacent walls.

(*c*) In adequate bond between walls and roof.

(*d*) Absence of any band of R.C.C. or tie beams at lintel or roof level.

Thus to build strong and stable structures or buildings it is advisable to adopt the following measures.

1. To make the various parts of the building in such a way so that they behave as one single unit as a box. To achieve this objective good R.C.C. bands or beams should be provided at (*i*) plinth level, (*ii*) Lintel level, (*iii*) At roof level. The provision of band at lintel level is more important to bind walls together.
2. Walls should be tied together at corners of the building by providing skillfully vertical reinforcing bars. The provision of corner bars increases the torsion resistance of the building.
3. Roofs should be provided conforming the local climatic conditions and should be as light as possible. A hipped roof has been found best in distributing the roof load.
4. Roof trusses should be well braced against winds and supported on top of R.C.C. bands or ring beams anchored in walls.

13.7. BEHAVIOUR OF BRICK MASONRY WALLS DURING AN EARTHQUAKE

The brick masonry buildings are brittle structures. They are one of the most vulnerable type of buildings of all the types during strong earthquake shaking. This statement is corroborated by large number of deaths in such constructions during the past major earthquakes in India. Thus it is essential to improve the performance of brick masonry buildings during the earthquake. To achieve this objective a number of earthquake resistant features may be introduced.

During an earthquake, ground vibrations cause inertia forces at locations of mass in the building. These forces travel through the roof and walls to the foundation. The main emphasis should be focused to ensure that these forces reach the ground with out causing major damage or total collapse of the building. Following three components of a brick masonry building are most vulnerable to the damage caused by horizontal forces developed in a earthquake. These basic components of a building are shown in Fig. 13.1 (*a*) namely walls, roof and foundation.

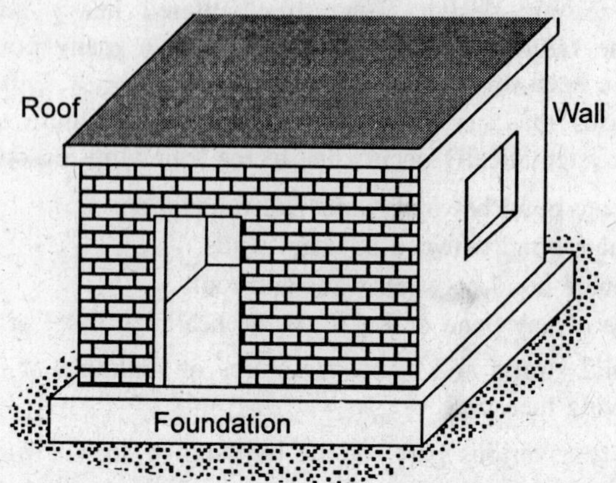

Fig. 13.1. (*a*). Basic components of a masonry building

Walls. The walls topples down easily if pushed horizontally at the top in a direction perpendicular to the weak plane, but offers much resistance if pushed along the length known as strong plane or direction Fig. 13.1 (*b*).

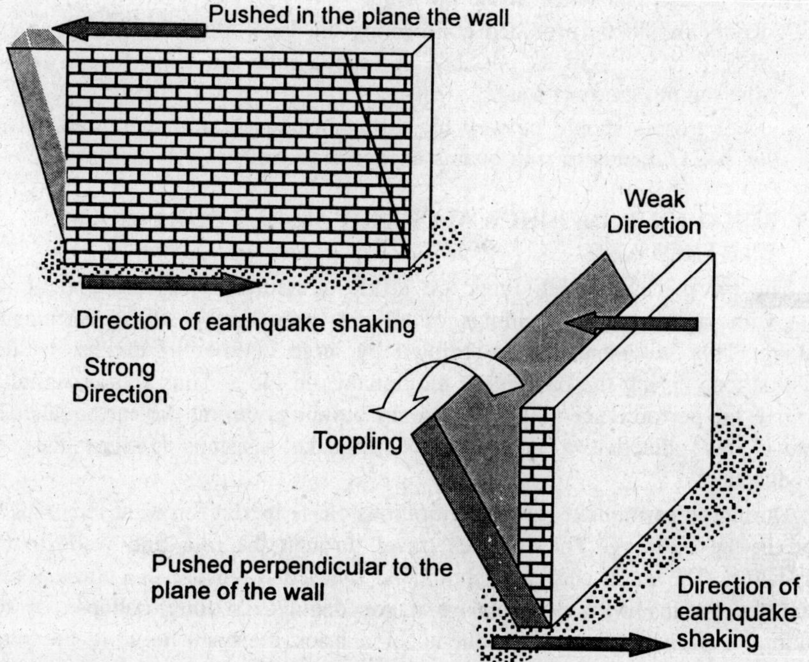

Fig. 13.1. (*b*). Direction of force on a wall critically determines its earthquake performance (Courtesy—IITK)

The ground shakes simultaneously in *x, y,* and *z* directions during an earthquake. For normal masonry buildings, the horizontal vibrations are considered most damaging. The inertia forces developed at roof level are transferred to the walls acting either in the weak direction or strong direction. If all the walls are not tied together to act as one unit like a box, then the walls loaded in their weak direction will tend to topple Fig. 13.2 (*a*).

To ensure good seismic performance, all walls must be joined properly to the adjacent walls.

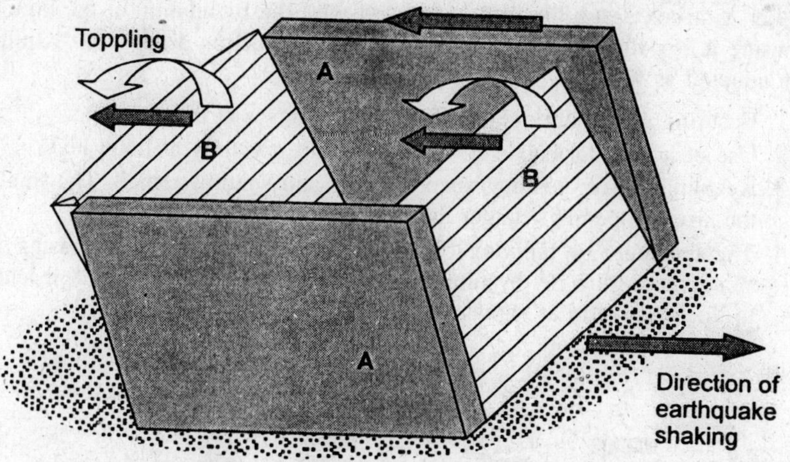

Fig. 13.2. (*a*). For the direction of earthquake shaking shown wall B tends to fail

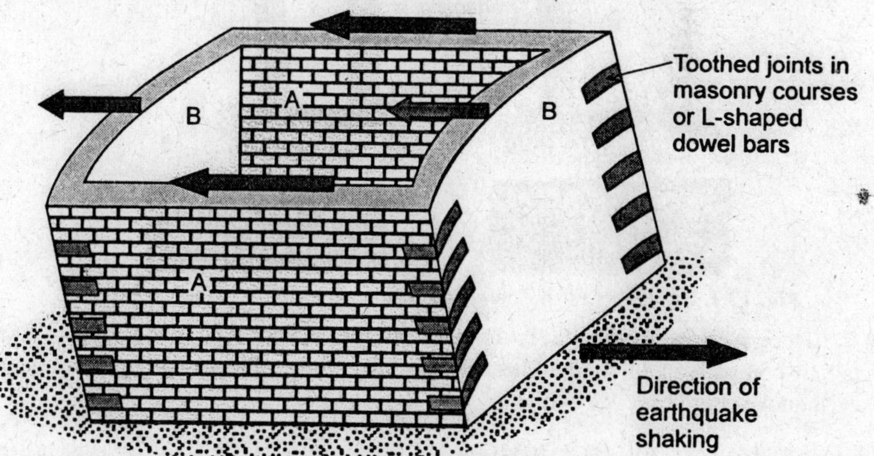

Fig. 13.2. (*b*). Wall B properly connected to wall A (note: roof is not shown) Walls A (loaded in strong direction) support walls B (Loaded in week direction) (Courtesy—IITK)

In this way walls loaded in their weak direction can take help of the good lateral resistance offered by walls in their strong direction as shown in Fig. 13.2 (*b*). Further walls should also be tied to the roof and foundation to maintain their over all integrity.

13.7.1. Measures to improve behaviour of masonry walls

Usually masonry walls are slender due to their small thickness in comparison of their height and length. A simple way of improving the seismic performance of such walls during an earthquake is by making them to act together as a box along the roof at top and with the foundation at the bottom. To ensure a box like action to develop many construction aspects are required to be adopted as follows:

1. Ensuring good interlocking of masonry courses at the junctions.
2. Use of horizontal bands at different levels, specially at lintel level.
3. Keeping size of openings such as doors and windows small. The smaller the size of openings, larger the resistance offered by walls.
4. The tendency of toppling of walls can be reduced by decreasing the slenderness ratio *i.e.* by limiting the height to thickness ratio and length to thickness ratio as shown in Fig. 13.3.

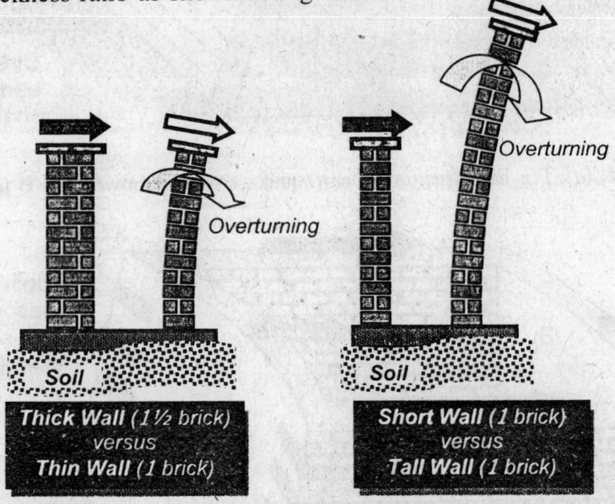

Fig. 13.3. (*a*). Effect of thickness and height on stability (Courtesy—IITK)

Design codes specify limits for these ratios. A wall that is too long or too tall in comparison to its thickness is specially vulnerable to damage during a earthquake. Fig. 13.3 (*a*) and (*b*).

13.7.2. Choice and quality of building material

Earthquake performance of a masonry wall is very sensitive to the properties of its constituents as masonry units and mortar etc. The properties of

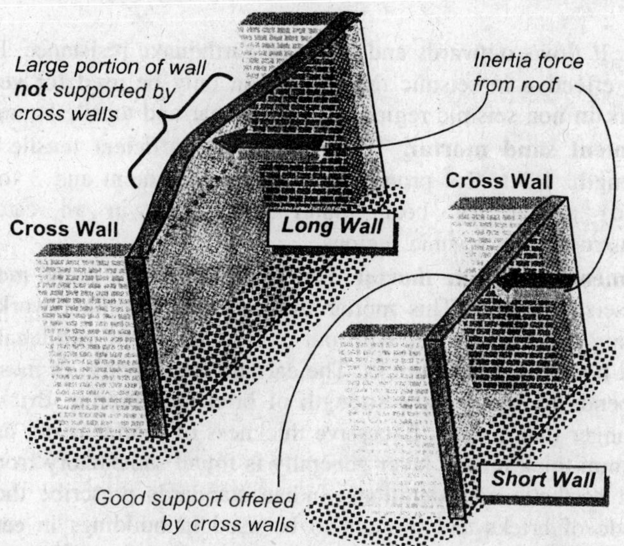

Fig. 13.3. (*b*). Slender walls are vulnerable-height and length to be kept within limits (Courtesy—IITK)

these materials vary from place to place due to the variation in raw material and construction methods used.

The variety of masonry units used in the country are as follows:

(*i*) Clay bricks burnt or unburnt.

(*ii*) Concrete blocks solid or hollow.

(*iii*) Stone blocks.

Most commonly in masonry buildings burnt clay bricks are used. These bricks are inherently porous and absorb much water. Excessive porosity of bricks is determinental to good behaviour of brick masonry as they absorb or suck much water from the mortar used in the masonry to produce good bond between different construction units *i.e.* bricks. The excessive absorption of water from the mortar results in poor bond between the mortar and bricks. It also poses difficulty in positioning masonry units. Thus to increase the performance of brick masonry the use of low porosity bricks must be adopted in the masonry. Thus before use, the bricks must be soaked in water for about 30 minutes or water is sprayed over the bricks. This will minimise the absorption of water by bricks from the mortar and help to retain the strength of the mortar.

13.7.3. Types of mortars used

Various types of mortars can be used as follows:

(*a*) Mud mortar

(*b*) Cement sand mortar

(*c*) Cement sand and lime mortar

(*a*) **Mud mortar.** It is the weakest type of mortar. It crushes easily when dry. It flows outwards and has least earthquake resistance. Hence it is not effective in seismic regions. It can only be used for very inferior work in non seismic regions. It lacks shear and tensile strength.

(*b*) **Cement sand mortar.** This mortar has sufficient tensile and shear strength. 1:3 to 1:4 proportion *i.e.* (1 part cement and 3 to 4 part of sand) mortar has been found satisfactory in all categories of construction in seismic regions.

(*c*) **Cement sand, lime mortar.** This mortar has been found most suitable in seismic zones. This mortar mix provides excellent workability for laying bricks, stretches with out crumbling at low earthquake shaking and bonds well with bricks. The earthquake response of masonry walls depends on the relative strength of brick and mortar. Bricks must be stronger than mortar. Excessive thickness of mortar is not desirable. A 10 mm thick mortar layer generally is found satisfactory from practical and aesthetic considerations. Indian standards prescribe the type and grade of bricks and mortars to be used in buildings in each seismic zone. Following mortars have been suggested for different categories of construction in seismic zones.

Table 13.1. Recommended mortars mixes

Category of construction	*Proportion of cement lime and sand*
1.	Cement sand 1:4 or cement lime-sand 1:1:6 or richer
2.	Cement lime-sand 1:2:9 or richer
3.	Cement sand 1:6 or richer
4.	Cement sand 1:4 or lime cinder 1:3 or richer.

Note. Categories of construction are defined as follows.

Table 13.2. Categories of buildings

Category of construction	*Combinations of conditions for the category*
1.	Important buildings on soft soil in zone A
2.	Important buildings on firm soil in zone A Important buildings on soft soil in zone B Ordinary buildings on soft soil on zone A
3.	Important buildings on firm soil in zone B Important buildings on soft soil in zone A Ordinary buildings on firm soil in zone A Important buildings on soft soil in zone B
4.	Important buildings on firm soil in zone C Ordinary buildings on firm soil zone B Ordinary buildings on firm soil in zone C Ordinary buildings on soft soil in zone C

Note.

1. Firm soil refers to those soils having safe bearing capacity value more than 10 tonnes per metre square and soft soils, those having bearing capacity less than 10 t/m^2.
2. Weak soils are liable to compaction and liquefaction under earthquake conditions. These are not covered here.

Table 13.3. Classification of seismic zones

Zone	*Area risk*	*Magnitude or intensity*
A.	Risk of wide spread collapse and destruction	IX or above
B.	Risk of collapse and heavy damage	VIII or so
C.	Risk of damage as that magnitude VIII.	do
D.	Risk of miner damage	VI

13.8. BOX ACTION OF MASONRY BUILDINGS

Brick masonry structures/buildings have large mass. Due to their large mass they attract large horizontal forces during earthquake shaking. The masonry buildings develop numerous cracks due to tensile as well as compressive forces developed due to earthquake shaking. The stress or focus of earthquake resistant masonry building construction is to ensure that these cracks are sustained with out major damage or collapse. To achieve this goal, an appropriate choice of structural configuration is essential.

The structural configuration of masonry building includes the following aspects.

(*i*) Over all shape and size of the building.

(*ii*) Distribution of mass and lateral load resisting elements across the building. These have been discussed in chapter 11. Large, tall, long and unsymmetrical buildings have been found performing poorly during earthquakes. In order to make all the elements of the buildings earthquake resistant, it is essential to ensure a good box action between them *i.e.* between foundation, walls and roof as shown in Fig. 13.4. Loose connected roof or unduly slender walls are not likely to have a good seismic behaviour. As explained earlier also provision of a horizontal band at the lintel level will tie walls together and help them to behave as a single unit.

13.9. EFFECT OR INFLUENCE OF OPENINGS

Openings in buildings are functional requirements or necessities. The location and size of openings in walls assume significance in deciding the performance of masonry buildings during earthquakes. To understand this fact consider a four wall system of a single storey masonry building as shown in

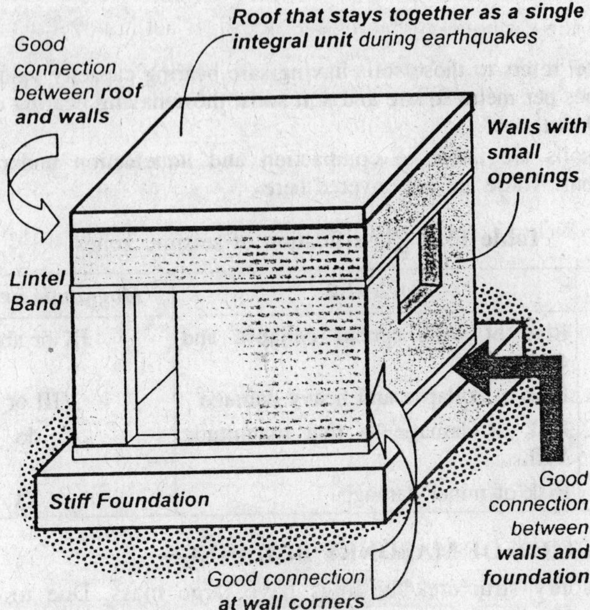

Fig. 13.4. Essential requirements to ensure box action in a masonry building (Courtesy—IITK)

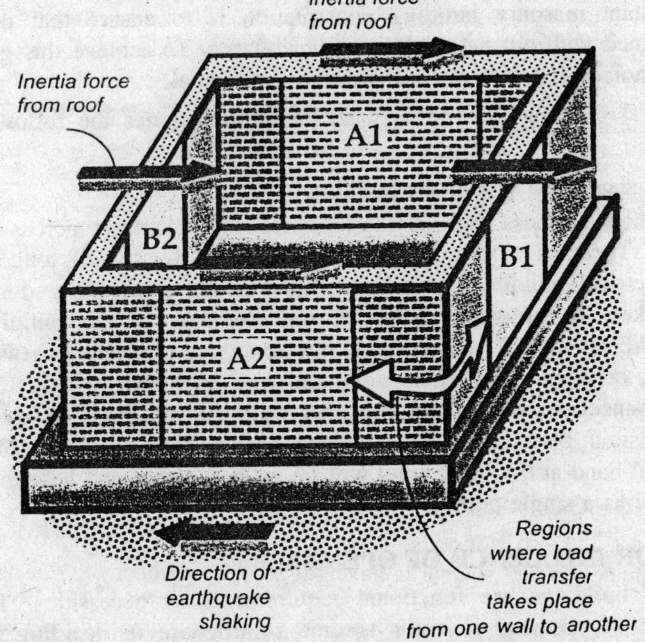

Fig. 13.5. Regions of force transfer from weak walls to strong walls in a masonry building (Courtesy—IITK)

Fig. 13.5. During earthquake shaking inertia forces act in the strong direction of some walls, and in the weak direction of the other. Walls shaken in weak direction take support from other walls. Walls B_1 and B_2 being in weak direction seek support from walls A_1 and A_2 being in strong direction during shaking as shown by thick arrows in Fig. 13.5. More specifically wall B_1 pulls walls A_1 and A_2 while wall B_2 pushes against them. In the event when the direction of shaking changes to the perpendicular direction of the previous direction, then roll of walls changes. In this condition walls B_1 and B_2 become strong one and A_1 and A_2 weak.

Thus walls transfer their loads to each other at their junctions and through roofs and lintel bands. Thus the masonry courses from the walls meeting at corners must have good interlocking. For this reason, the openings near the corners of the walls are detrimental to the good seismic performance. Openings too close to wall corner hamper the flow of seismic forces from one wall to another as shown in Fig. 13.6. Further large openings weaken walls for carrying

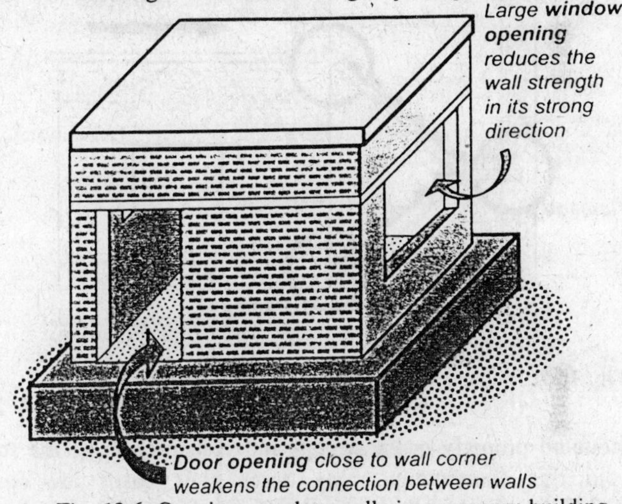

Fig. 13.6. Openings weaken walls in a masonry building (Courtesy—IITK)

the inertia forces in their own plane. Thus to safeguard against these draw backs, it is best to keep all openings as small as possible and as far away from the corners as possible. Further details are given in chapter 16.

13.10. EARTHQUAKE-RESISTANT FEATURES

To develop good box action in masonry buildings and to improve their seismic performance Indian standards have suggested a number of measures as follows:

1. Building plans in shapes of L, T, E and Y should be separated into simple rectangular blocks in plan. (Refer Chapter 11). During earthquake

these separate blocks can oscillate independently and even hammer each other, if they are too close to each other. Thus they should be separated adequately from each other. If the horizontal projections are of the order of 15 to 20% of the length of the building in that direction then provision of gap is not essential.

2. In masonry buildings inclined stair case slab as shown in Fig. 13.7 offers another cause of worry. Such a inclined slab stair case connected integrally acts like a cross brace between floors and transfers large horizontal forces at roof and lower levels shown by circles in the Fig. 13.7. These areas are potential damage spots in the masonry buildings if

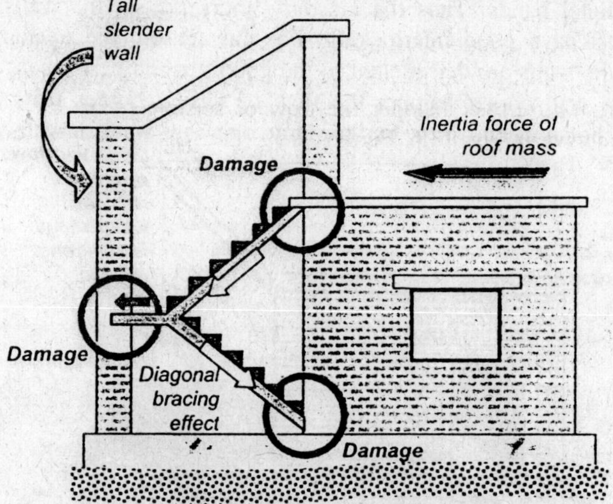

Fig. 13.7. Damage in building with rigidly built-in staircase (Courtesy—IITK)

not accounted properly in the design and construction of the stair case. To avoid this shortcomig, some times stair cases are completely separated from the buildings as shown in Fig. 13.8 and built on a separate R.C.C. structure. Adequate gap should be provided between the stair case tower and the masonry building to ensure that they do not pound each other during strong earthquake.

13.11. ROLE OF HORIZONTAL BANDS

In masonry buildings the horizontal bands have been found most effective and important earthquake resistant features. These bands are provided to hold the masonry building as a single unit by tieing all the walls together. These bands work similar to a closed belt tied around the card board boxes to hold them together.

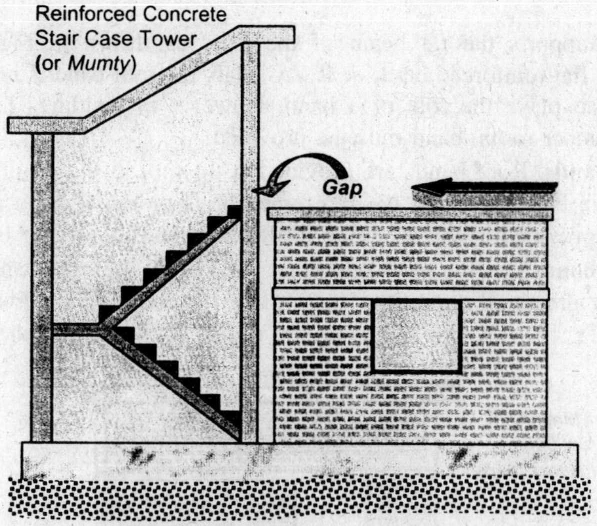

Fig. 13.8. Building with separated staircase
(Courtesy—IITK)

13.11.1. Types of horizontal bands

The horizontal bands may be classified into the following four categories:

1. Gable band. Gable bands are provided only in buildings having pitched or sloped roofs. It is very important band in sloped roofs. The roof band in

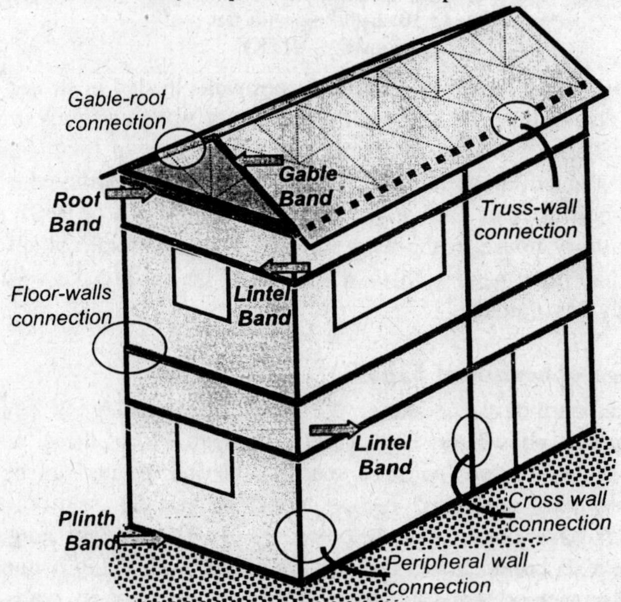

Fig. 13.9. Two storey building with pitched roof with horizontal bands
(Courtesy—IITK)

sloped roofs supports the tie beam of the truss as shown in Fig. 13.9. In buildings with flat reinforced brick or R.C.C. slab, the roof band is not required as the roof slab plays the role of a band. However in buildings having G-1 sheet or flat timber roofs, band must be provided.

2. Roof bands. Roof bands are provided at the roof level to hold the walls together. But in buildings with flat reinforced brick or R.C.C. slab roofs, roof bands are not provided as the roof slab itself plays the role of roof band.

3. Lintel band. It is the most important band of all the bands and needs to be provided in almost all buildings. It is provided at door and window top level as shown in Fig. 13.10. Lintel bands tie the walls together and create a support

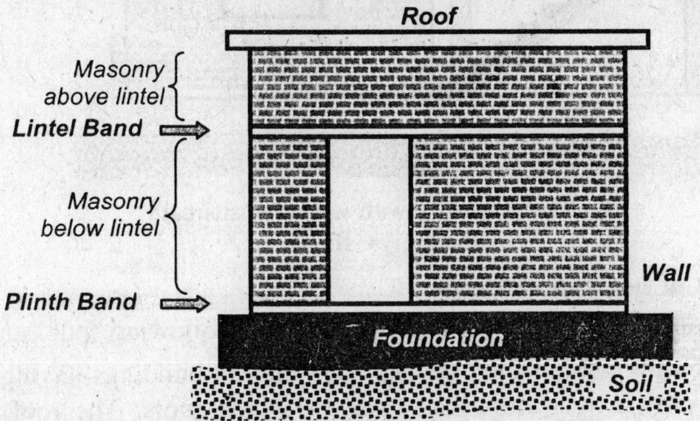

Fig. 13.10. Building with flat roof
(Courtesy—IITK)

for walls loaded along the weak direction from walls loaded in strong direction. These bands also reduce the unsupported height of walls and thus improve the stability of walls in the weak direction. The importance of lintel band can be illustrated by the building damages during Latur 1993 earthquake in killari village of Mahrastra. This earthquake was of magnitude IX on MSK scale and almost all masonry house in the area suffered partial or total collapse, but the house which had lintel band withstood shaking of the earthquake very well and suffered hardly any damage.

13.11.2. Design of horizontal bands

During an earthquake shaking, the lintel band undergoes bending and pulling action as shown in Fig. 13.11. Thus to resist these actions the construction of lintel bands requires special attention. Bands can be made of wood, Bamboo and reinforced cement concrete, but the reinforced cement concrete bands have been found best Fig. 13.11. The straight lengths of the band must be well connected at the corners of the walls. This connection will help the band to support walls loaded in their weak direction by walls loaded in their strong direction. Spacers are used to make the steel bars or straight lengths of wooden runners to act together. The spacers are a small length of wood piece

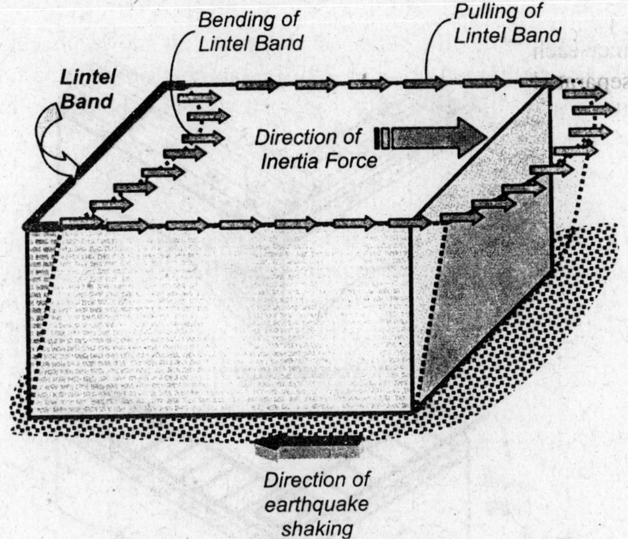

Fig. 13.11. Bending and pulling in lintel bands
(Courtesy—IITK)

in case of wooden runners and steel piece in case of steel bars. In case of wooden bands proper nailing of straight length with spacers is essential. Similarly in R.C.C. bands anchoring of steel stirrups or links with steel bars is essential. Fig. 13.12 shows cross sections of lintel links.

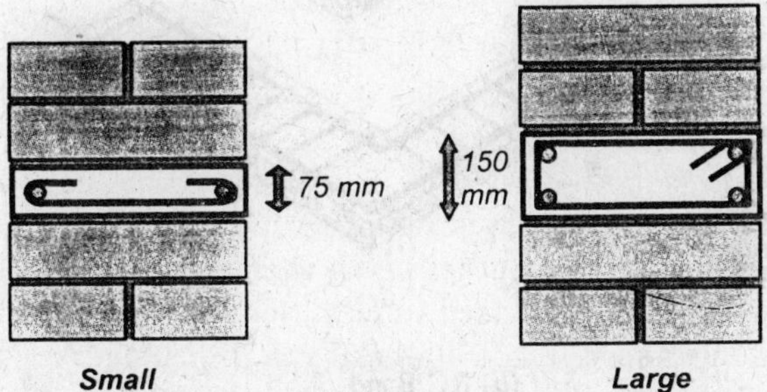

Fig. 13.12. Details of cross links of bands

13.11.3. Details and size of bands

Indian standards 4326-1993 and 13828-1993 recommend the sizes and details of bands. In case of wooden bands the cross section of the runners should be at least 75 mm × 38 mm and for spacers minimum 50 mm × 30 mm. For R.C.C. bands the minimum thickness should be 75 mm. At least two bars of 8 mm diameter should be used as longitudinal reinforcement. The diameter of stirrups or tie bars should be 6 mm and their spacing should be 150 mm centre to centre. Different types of horizontal bands used in masonry buildings are shown in Fig. 13.13.

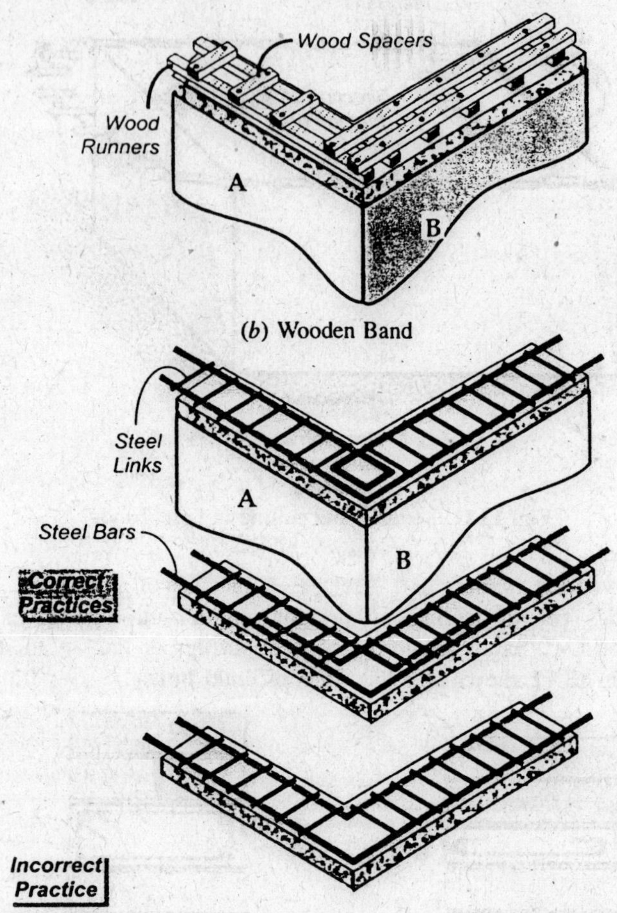

(*b*) Wooden Band

(*b*) RC Band

Fig. 13.12. Horizontal bands in masonry buildings (Courtesy—IITK)

The details of horizontal reinforcement is shown in Table 13.1.

Table 13.1. Longitudinal reinforcement in R.C.C. bands

Spaning m	*Category I*		*Category II*		*Category III*		*Category IV*	
	No of bars	*Dia in mm*	*No of bars*	*Dia in mm*	*No of bars*	*Dia in mm*	*No of bars*	*Dia in mm*
≤ 5	2	12	2	10	2	10	2	10
6	2	16	2	12	2	10	2	10

Spaning m	*Category I*		*Category II*		*Category III*		*Category IV*	
	No of bars	*Dia in mm*	*No of bars*	*Dia in mm*	*No of bars*	*Dia in mm*	*No of bars*	*Dia in mm*
7	2	16	2	16	2	12	2	10
8	4	16	2	16	2	16	2	12
9	4	16	4	12	2	16	2	12

Note:

1. The width of the RC band will be equal to the thickness of wall at least 20 cm. A cover of 2.5 cm from the face of the wall must be maintained. For thicker walls, the quantity of steel need not be increased.
2. The minimum vertical thickness of the RC band should not be less than 7.5 cm where two bars are specified and 15 cm where four bars are specified.
3. The concrete must have crushing strength 20 MPa *i.e.* 200 kg/cm^2 at 28 days.
4. The longitudinal bars should be held in position by links of 8 mm ϕ at 15 cm apart.
5. The bar diameters suggested are for mild steel. If high strength deformed bars are used, the equivalent diameter may be chosen.

13.12. DESIGN OF FOUNDATIONS

The design of foundation depends upon the type of soil on which the building is to be founded. Soils having bearing capacity less than 1.0 kg/cm^2 are known as soft soils. Such soils are liable to liquefaction and unequal settlements during an earthquake. Liquefaction is a major source of large scale damage of buildings. The other causes of heavy damage to buildings during an earthquake are as follows:

1. In case the same structure is located upon two formations of different geological nature.
2. When the buildings are founded on non uniform slope.
3. When building is founded on two different types of foundations.

Thus the foundations may be divided into two categories as follows:

1. Shallow foundations
2. Deep foundations

13.12.1. Shallow Foundations

In high seismic activity zones III, IV and V, where foundations are likely to develop significant unequal settlement should be avoided.

The shallow foundations should be proportioned in such a way that the maximum bearing pressure due to the over turning moment and gravity loads remains with in the safe seismic bearing pressure limit. The horizontal seismic stresses due to soil-structure or foundation interaction are trouble some and complex. Very little literature is available on the subject. Usually the distribution of horizontal and vertical stress is arbitrary. It is customary to assume more horizontal stress between the soil and the foundation than vertical stress.

It is assumed that most of the shear resistance to the base shear is provided by the friction between the soil and under surfaces of the foundation. The total resistance R_f to the lateral moment of the structure may be assumed as

$$R_f = D_f \cdot \phi_s$$

where,

R_f = Total resistance to the lateral movement

D_f = Dead load of the element under consideration

ϕ_s = Coefficient of sliding friction.

In case there is possibility of developing passive soil pressure against the sub surface element, then horizontal resistant should be taken into account or considered. In such cases back fill against the sides of the footing should be compacted adequately. As shallow foundations are most vulnerable to damage, hence it is a common practice to tie the independent column footing with the beams, even for very low structures founded on soft soils.

Deep foundations

Sufficient literature is not available on the seismic design of deep foundations. Usually these foundations are designed on normal structural static design techniques taking into account seismically enhanced soil pressures.

13.12.2. Pile foundations

The design of pile foundations is based on the following factors:

1. Structural stability of the foundation
2. Horizontal stresses
3. Vertical stresses

The base shear is resisted by the lateral bearing on the pile foundations. The vertical seismic force (load) on individual pile may vary significantly depending on their position in relation to the rest of pile group and the super structure. Piles at the edge or corners of the pile system may have to bear large tensile as well as compressive forces during an earthquake.

It must be ensured fully that the strata is contiguous around and below the piles and have sufficient bearing, shear and adhesive strength during seismic activities.

Between piles and pile caps sufficient continuity reinforcement must be provided. Piles themselves must be able to develop the required bending, compressive and tensile strengths. Suitable confinement reinforcement must be provided to take care of development of plastic hinges in the top and bottom of the reinforcement of the R.C.C. piles

The seismic design of lateral strength of piles is the most difficult part as very little knowledge is available of the stress deformations involved in the soil-pile interaction during earthquakes. Thus the design of foundations may be summarized as follows:

1. In highly seismic zone, the bearing capacity of soils should not be less than 1 kg/cm^2. If it is not so, the bearing power should be improved by soil compaction, soil stabilization or by any suitable method.
2. In seismic zones III, IV and V sites where foundations are likely to undergo significant differential settlement, shallow foundations should be avoided.
3. In highly seismic zones the height of masonry buildings should be limited to 2 to 3 storey height and RCC buildings upto 4 to 5 storey height.
4. In seismic zones III, IV and V individual spread footings or pile caps should be inter connected with foundation beams or ties except when the spread footings are directly founded on rock.
5. All ties should be capable to bear the tension and compression forces and an axial force equal to 0.25 A_h times the larger of the pile cap load or column load in addition to other wise computed forces.
6. Foundations should be designed as continuous (raft or mat) to avoid relative horizontal displacement.
7. Parts of building foundations resting an different types of soils or having differential settlements should be designed as separate units. In such cases super structures should also be independent units.
8. In case the different parts of a building are structurally independent due to the shape of their ground plans, their foundations also should be independent.

QUESTIONS

1. Discuss the factors which affect buildings performance during an earthquake.
2. Discuss behaviour of masonry walls during earthquake.
3. Give the proportion of mortar used in different categories of masonry.
4. Discuss the effects of opening on the performance of a building during an earthquake.
5. Discuss the role of horizontal beams on the performance of buildings during the earthquake.
6. Identify the incorrect statement/statements
   (*a*) The distance between the focus and the place of occurring earthquake has no influence on the performance of the building during the earthquake.
   (*b*) The form and structure of the site of earthquake has a great influence on the performance of the building during the earthquake.
   (*c*) Intensity and nature of earthquake at focus has a marked influence on the performance of the buildings.
   (*d*) Dynamic characteristics of the building influence its performance during earthquake

7. The damage to structures during an earthquake is influenced by
   (*a*) Maximum acceleration at the site
   (*b*) Duration of ground motion and characteristics of frequency at the site
   (*c*) Dynamic characteristics of the site
   (*d*) Dynamic characteristics of the building
   (*e*) By all the above factors
8. Hard soils or rocks have amplitude ...... than soft soils
   (*a*) Larger amplitude
   (*b*) Smaller amplitude
   (*c*) Equal amplitude
   (*d*) All are correct
9. Soft soils have amplitudes...... than rockes
   (*a*) Equal
   (*b*) Smaller
   (*c*) Larger
   (*d*) None of the above
10. For all categories of construction in seismic regions. The proportion of cement mortar has been found satisfactory
    (*a*) 1:6 (*b*) 1:2
    (*c*) 1:3 to 1:4 (*d*) 1:7.5
11. The most important and effective band......is
    (*a*) Plinth level band
    (*b*) Roof band
    (*c*) Lintel band
    (*d*) All are equally effective
12. The horizontal band made of...... is most suitable
    (*a*) Timber
    (*b*) Bamboo
    (*c*) R.C.C.
    (*d*) All are equally effective
13. Identify the correct statement/statements
    (*a*) Horizontal bands have no roll in the design of earthquake resistant structures
    (*b*) Building plans in the shape of L and y have shown good performance during earthquakes
    (*c*) In masonry buildings inclined stair case have no cause of worry
    (*d*) The size and location of windows in walls have no influence on the performance of building during the earthquake
    (*e*) Non is correct
    (*f*) All are correct
14. Factor/factors affect the performance of a structure during an earthquake
    (*a*) Distance of the structure from the epicenter of the earthquake
    (*b*) Characteristics of soil below the foundation of the soil
    (*c*) Characteristics of the soil of land between the building and epicentre of the earthquake
    (*d*) Topography of the site of the building

(*e*) Intensity of the earthquake and its nature
(*f*) Dynamic characteristics of the building and its condition
(*g*) All are correct

15. For a building to work as a box it should have......
(*a*) A strong and rigid foundation
(*b*) Good bond between the walls and foundation
(*c*) Less open space in walls
(*d*) Provision of horizontal bands at lintel, roof and plinth level
(*e*) All are correct

16. In highly seismic zones the best mortar is ......
(*a*) Mud mortar (*b*) Lime-Cinder mortar
(*c*) Cement-Sand mortar (*d*) Cement-Lime-Sand mortar

17. The minimum thickness of mortar is sufficient ......
(*a*) 10 cm (*b*) 7.5 cm
(*c*) 12 cm (*d*) 15 cm

18. The minimum bearing capacity of foundation soil should be ......
(*a*) 0.7 kg/cm^2 (*b*) 1.0 kg/cm^2
(*c*) 1.5 kg/cm^2 (*d*) 2.0 kg/cm^2

ANSWERS

6. (*a*)	9. (*c*)	12. (*c*)	15. (*e*)	18. (*b*)
7. (*e*)	10. (*c*)	13. (*e*)	16. (*d*)	
8. (*b*)	11. (*c*)	14. (*g*)	17. (*a*)	

14

Effects of Earthquake on Concrete Structures

14.1. INTRODUCTION

After world war II, the use of concrete has increased in all walks of life all over the world. Initially concrete was used as a cover to steel members to protect them from rusting. Gradually its use spread to all kinds of structures. Now a days it is widely used for the construction of dwellings also due to ease in moulding in any shape when the concrete is green.

Concrete is a mixture of cement, fine and coarse aggregate in appropriate ratio and a measured quantity of water. The compressive strength of concrete is sufficiently high, but its tensile strength is very poor. The tensile strength of concrete is about 10% of its compressive strength. Though due to the advancement in technology, concrete upto 500 kg/cm^2 strength can be produced in factories, but its tensile strength could not be increased in the same proportion. Hence to increase the tensile strength of concrete, steel is used along with concrete in concrete structures. The design of the structure is based on the assumption that compression will be borne by concrete and tension by steel. The compressive and shear strengths as laid down in IS Code 456-2000 are reproduced below in Table 14.1 to 14.3.

The study of R.C.C. damaged buildings during the past earthquakes has revealed that these buildings damaged due to low strength of concrete, errors in placing and splicing of reinforcement, inadequate number of stirrups in columns and more spacing than required. If R.C.C. structures are designed properly according to the recommendations of Indian codes of practice for earthquake resistance, then they will have the ductility and strength to resist major earthquakes. To achieve ductility following points are important in the design of reinforced cement concrete structures.

(*a*) To make the transverse or shear strength of the member greater than its ultimate flexure strength. Adequate shear or transverse reinforcement must be used.

(*b*) In order to increase the energy absorption capacity of the member, the tensile or compression steel be limited.

(*c*) To increase the ductility of columns under combined axial load and bending at critical sections of stress concentration spirals or hoops should be used for the confinement of concrete.

(*d*) Special attention should be paid to details such as splices in reinforcement and avoidance of planes of weakness that might be developed by bending or curtailing all reinforcement bars at the same section.

Table 14.1. The grades of concrete as per (IS 456-2000)

Grades	*Grade designation*	*Specified characterestic compressive strength of 150 mm cube at 28 days in N/mm²*	*Remark*
Ordinary concrete	M10	10 (100 kg/cm²)	1 N/mm² = 10 kg/cm²
	M15	15 (150 kg/cm²)	1 Pa (pascal) = 1N/10⁶mm²
	M20	20 (200 kg/cm²)	1 MPa (Mega pascal) = 10⁶ × N/10⁶ mm²
Standard concrete	M25	25 (250 kg/cm²)	∴ 1 MPa = 1 N/mm²
	M30	30 (300 kg/cm²)	∴ 1 MPa = 10 kg/cm²
	M35	35 (350 kg/cm²)	
	M40	40 (400 kg/cm²)	
	M45	45 (450 kg/cm²)	
	M50	50 (500 kg/cm²)	
	M55	55 (550 kg/cm²)	
High strength concrete	M60	60 (600 kg/cm²)	
	M65	65 (650 kg/cm²)	
	M70	70 (700 kg/cm²)	
	M75	75 (750 kg/cm²)	
	M80	80 (800 kg/cm²)	

Table 14.2. Permissible stresses in concrete. All values in N/mm² (IS 456-2000)

Grade of concrete	*Permissible stress*	*In compression Direct*	*Average permissible bond stress for plain bars in tension*
M10	3.0	2.5	—
M15	5.0	4.0	0.6
M20	7.0	5.0	0.8
M25	8.5	6.0	0.9
M30	10.0	8.0	1.0
M35	11.5	9.0	1.1
M40	13.0	10.0	1.2

Grade of concrete	*Permissible stress*	*In compression Direct*	*Average permissible bond stress for plain bars in tension*
M45	14.5	11.0	1.3
M50	16.0	12.0	1.4

Table 14.3. Permissible shear stress in concrete as per (IS 456-2000)

$\frac{100 \times A_s}{b.d}$	*Permissible shear stress in concrete N/mm² in different grades of concrete*					
	M15	M20	M25	M30	M35	M40
(1)	(2)	(3)	(4)	(5)	(6)	(7)
≤ 0.15	0.18	0.18	0.19	0.20	0.20	0.20
0.25	0.22	0.22	0.23	0.23	0.23	0.23
0.50	0.29	0.30	0.31	0.31	0.31	0.32
0.75	0.34	0.35	0.36	0.37	0.37	0.38
1.00	0.37	0.39	0.40	0.41	0.42	0.42
1.25	0.40	0.42	0.44	0.45	0.45	0.46
1.50	0.42	0.45	0.46	0.48	0.49	0.49
1.75	0.44	0.47	0.49	0.50	0.52	0.52
2.00	0.44	0.49	0.51	0.53	0.54	0.55
2.25	0.44	0.51	0.53	0.55	0.56	0.57
2.50	0.44	0.51	0.55	0.57	0.58	0.60
2.75	0.44	0.51	0.56	0.58	0.60	0.62
3.0 and above	0.44	0.51	0.57	0.60	0.62	0.63

14.2. CONFIGURATION OF R.C. BUILDINGS

A typical reinforced concrete building is consisted of the following type of members:

1. **Horizontal members.** Floor slabs and beams are classified as horizontal members or components of a building. Beams resist loads and slabs facilitate the functional use of the building.
2. **Vertical members.** Walls and columns are classified as vertical members, which resist the loads of the building. These members are supported by foundations that rest on ground.

The system comprising of R.C. columns and connecting beams is known as R.C. frame. The R.C. frame takes part in resisting the seismic forces. The seismic forces are inertia forces and generated due to the shaking of the ground. The inertia forces are proportional to the mass of the building. The mass of the building is assumed to concentrate at the floor level, hence earthquake induced inertia forces also primarily develop at the floor levels. As discussed in chapter

11 and shown in Fig. 11.4, these forces travel down wards through slab, beams, columns, walls and then to the foundation. From foundation these forces are dispersed to the ground. As inertia forces accumulate down wards from top of the building, the higher forces are experienced by the columns and walls at the lower storeys as shown in Fig. 14.1.

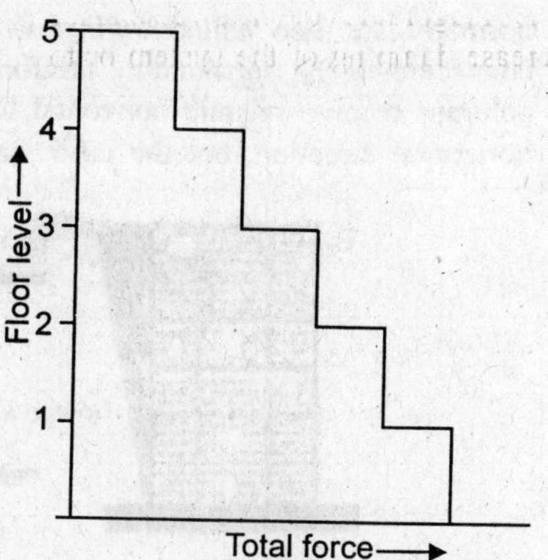

Fig. 14.1. Total horizontal earthquake force in a building increase downward along its height

14.2.1. Behaviour of floor slabs and walls

Floor slabs of a building are horizontal elements and facilitate the functional use of the building. At a storey level usually beams and slabs are cast monolithicelly *i.e.* together. In residential multi storeyed buildings the thickness of slabs is kept about 10 to 15 cms, where as the thickness of beams is much more at least 3 times the thickness of slab. When during an earthquake, beams bend in the vertical direction, the thin slabs also bend along with them as shown in Fig. 14.2 (*a*). When beams move along with columns in the horizontal direction, the slab usually forces the beams to move along with it. In most of the buildings, the geometric distortion of the slab is very small in the horizontal plane. This behaviour of slabs is known as the rigid diaphragm action. Fig. 14.2 (*b*). This fact should be kept in mind at the time of design of earthquake resistant R.C.C. buildings.

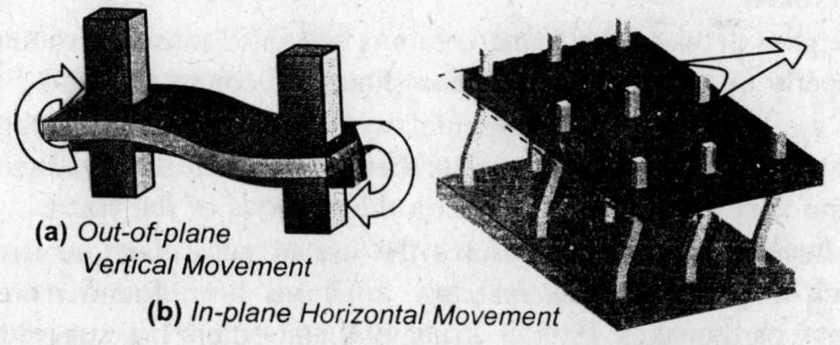

Fig. 14.2. Floor bends with the beam but moves all columns at that level together (Courtesy—IITK)

14.2.2. Behaviour of frames

After casting columns and floors in a reinforced concrete building, when the concrete hardness, the vertical spaces between columns and floors are usually filled in with brick masonry walls. These masonry walls are provided to demarcate the floor area into functional spaces (rooms). These masonry walls normally are also called *infilled walls.* These infill masonry walls are not connected to the surrounding reinforced concrete columns and beams. When columns receive seismic horizontal forces at floor levels, they try to move in horizontal direction, but the infill walls tend to resist this movement. Due to

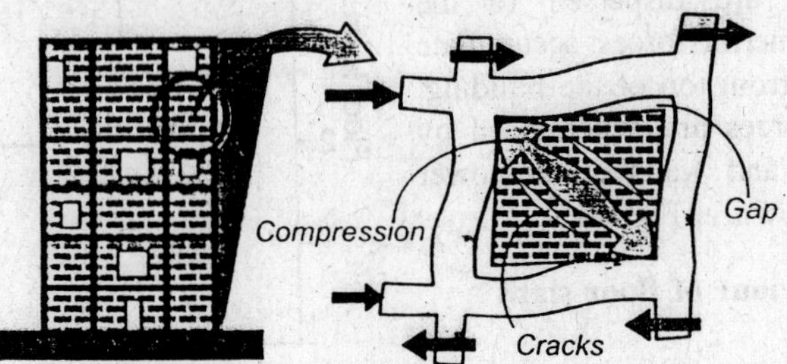

Fig. 14.3. Infill walls move together with the columns under earthquake shaking (Courtesy—IITK)

their more thickness and higher weights these infill walls attract rather large horizontal forces as shown in Fig. 14.3.

As the masonry is a brittle material, these brick infill walls develop cracks as soon as the horizontal forces exceed their resisting capacity. Though these infill walls develop cracks under severe ground shaking, but they help in sharing the load between the beams and columns untill they crack.

14.3. MEASURES TO IMPROVE PERFORMANCE OF INFILL WALLS

The performance of infill wall panels can be improved by the following measures:

1. Mortar in the masonry should be used of high strength.
2. Masonry courses should be of uniform height and vertical bonds should be broken.
3. The gaps between the frame columns and infill masonry should be filled properly *i.e.* the in fill and frame should be connected well.
4. On the basis of his experimental work D.V. Mallik has suggested that the provision of shear connector between the infill and frame has been found very effective in increasing the stiffness of the frame.

   Besides the above measures the use of auto clave aerated concrete block in place of brick masonry infill has been found more effective during earthquakes. Prof. S. Prabavthy and others has suggested that.

5. The use of one 6 mm dia bar as horizontal reinforcement in the bed mortar in each course in auto claved aerated concrete block infill masonry in R.C. frames has proved very effective in strengthening the frames against lateral forces.
6. The load carrying capacity of R.C. frames using auto claved aerated concrete blocks masonry infill has been found 1.88 times more than that of bare frame.

7. The initial and final stiffness of R.C. frame with auto clave aerated concrete blocks masonry infill are higher than that of a bare frame.
8. The cumulative ductility for reinforced autoclved aerated concrete block masonry infill frames is found 1.75 times more than that of bare frame.
9. The cumulative energy dissipation for infilled frame is 3 times greater than that of bare frames.

How ever an unduly tall or long in fill wall in comparison to its thickness can fall out of plane *i.e.* along the thin direction, which can prove fatal. Also irregularly placed masonry infills in the building causes ill effects like torsion and short column effects. These effects have been discussed separately in chapter 11.

14.4. LOADING SYSTEM ON BUILDINGS

Normally buildings are loaded with vertical loads but during an earthquake or due to wind pressures buildings are also loaded with lateral or horizontal forces. These loads are discussed as follows:

14.4.1. Vertical loading

The dead load or self load of the building and the weight of contents in the building are vertical loads. These loads are also called gravity loads. When these loads act on the buildings cause reinforced concrete frames to bend resulting in shortening and stretching at various locations. The surfaces which stretch develop tension and surfaces which shorten develop compression. Under

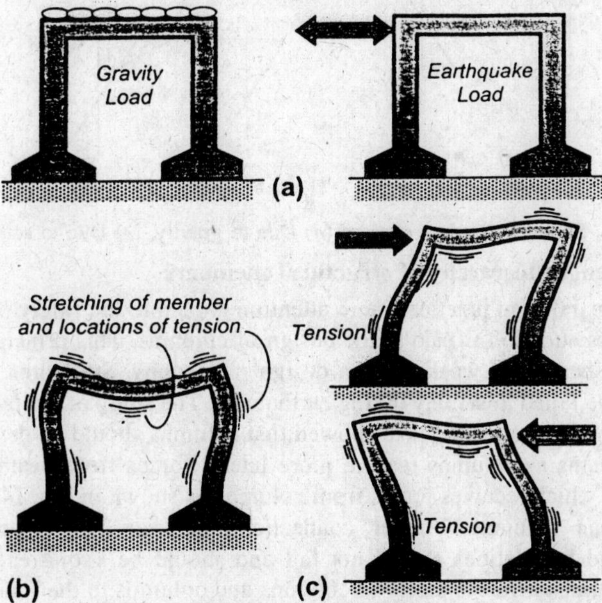

Fig. 14.4. Loads on members (*a*) Gravity and earthquake load on frame, (*b*) Location of development of tensions, (*c*) Location of development of B.M. due to earthquake loads (Courtesy—IITK)

gravity loads, tension develops at the bottom of the central portion of the beam and at top surface at the ends as shown in Fig. 14.4 (*b*) and B.M. developed is shown in Fig. 14.5 (*d*).

14.4.2. Horizontal or lateral earthquake force or load

The forces due to earthquake or wind act horizontally and are called lateral loads or forces. The earthquake forces develop tension on the beam and column faces at locations different from those under gravity loading as shown in Fig. 14.4 (*a*), (*b*), (*c*). The bending movement generated by gravity and seismic loads are shown in Fig. 14.5 (*d*) and (*e*), respectively. The magnitude of B.M. due to earthquake forces depends upon the severity of shaking. It can exceed than that of gravity loading. Thus under sever earthquake shaking beam ends can develop tension at either of the top or bottom faces. As concrete is weak in tension and can not bear tension, hence reinforcement has to be provided on both faces to resist the reversals of bending moments. Similarly reinforcement is required on all faces of the columns.

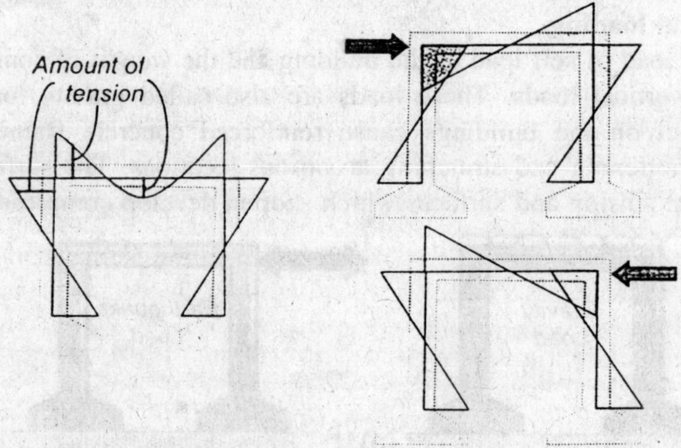

Fig. 14.5. Showing bending stresses (*d*) Due to gravity, (*e*) Due to seismic loads

14.4.3. Strength hierarchy of structural members

In normal design practices more attention is paid to the safety of beams and slab and less attention is paid to the design of columns. This principle is known as a strong beam and weak column design philosophy. Structures designed on this principle failed miserably during earthquake. The study of the failure of buildings during the past earthquake showed that columns should be designed stronger than beams as columns receive more lateral forces from beams and slabs. Foundation which receives forces from columns as shown in Fig. 14.4 should be stronger than columns. Further connections between beams and columns, columns and foundations should not fail and should be strong enough so that beams can transfer forces safely to columns and columns to the foundations.

When this strategy is adopted in the design of R.C.C. structures, the damage first develops in beams. In case the beams are detailed properly to have

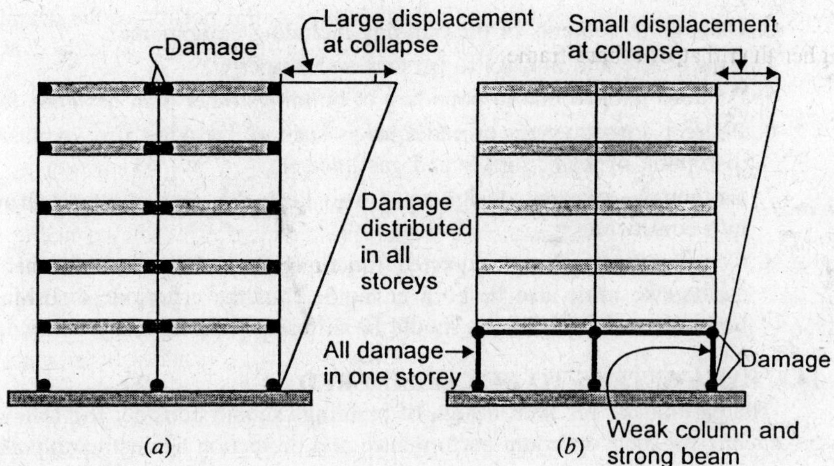

Fig. 14.6. (*a*) Strong columns weak beams, (*b*) Weak columns strong beams (Courtesy—IITK)

large ductility, the building as a whole can deform to large amounts despite progressive damage developed due to the consequences of yielding of beams as shown in Fig. 14.6 (*a*). On the other hand if the columns are made weaker than beams, buildings suffer severe local damage at the top and bottom of a particular storey as shown in Fig. 14.6 (*b*). This localized damage can lead to the collapse of the building, though columns at above storeys remain practically undamaged. Hence structures in seismic zones should be designed as strong columns and weak beams.

14.5. FACTORS GOVERNING THE PERFORMANCE OF BUILDINGS DURING EARTHQUAKE

There are two main aspects of earthquake resistant design that differentiate earthquake engineering from other branches of engineering:

1. The uncertainty or enormous spread in the ground motion.
2. Nature of the ground motion itself.

Due to these uncertantities it is advisable to apply the theory of probability and optimization in the earthquake resistant design more extensively than in other branches of engineering.

14.6. TYPES OF DAMAGES OR FAILURES TO BE CONSIDERED WHILE DESIGNING AN EARTHQUAKE RESISTANT STRUCTURE

Usually following failures or damages are considered while designing earthquake resistant structures:

1. Structural and non structural damage.
2. Collapse

3. Damage to contents of the building including equipments
4. Loss of life and injuries to persons and property.
5. Panic developed due to pounding of buildings other than designed for it.
6. Indirect consequences of earthquakes such as breaking fire, explosions, disruplion of water supply and gas lines etc.
7. Earthquake resistant design must also keep the cost of repair damage into consideration.
8. Considerations of the expected functions from the structure after the earthquake must also be born in mind. Thus the criterion of design for hospitals and fire stations should be different from others.

14.7. PARAMETERS TO BE CONSIDERED

The earthquake resistant design of buildings should consider the following parameters for their optimum performance and protection against earthquakes.

14.7.1. Site location of the structure

The site location of the structure is directly influenced by the intensity of the earthquake. Hence site location of the structure should be given due consideration. The best location of the site will be in the least sloping zone away from the active faults, peaks, spurs and edges of cliffs. The site should not be located on loose alluvium and cohesionless soils as they are more prone to liquefaction and amplify the vibrations of the structure during earthquake.

14.7.2. Dynamic characteristics of the materials

The dynamic characteristics of the materials to be used in the structure must be taken into account during the design stage. The energy absorption capacity and inelastic behaviour of construction materials is very important to accommodate their ductility capacity or certain ductility factors.

14.7.3. Dynamic characteristics of buildings

For the design of earthquake resistant structures following two dynamic characteristics of the buildings must be taken into consideration:

(*a*) Periods of vibrations of the structures.

(*b*) Damping of the structures

The trend of construction of tall buildings and decrease in factor of safety have increased the importance of resonant vibrations in the modern designs. In many buildings, it is highly desirable that the amplitudes of near resonant vibrations experienced in service be decreased. Thus to check resonance in buildings there can be two approaches as follows.

To control the magnitude of the exciting force caused by an earthquake or to change its frequency to avoid the resonant conditions. But both these factors are out of our control during earthquakes. On the other hand ground motion during an earthquake is not simple or prescribed. It is random and chaotic. Two disturbances are never identical.

Thus in such conditions to reduce the magnitude of near resonance vibrations, it becomes necessary either to increase damping of the system or to make the structure more vibration resistant.

14.7.4. Natural period of vibration

An earthquake does not damage a structure by impact or externally applied pressure by wind or other agency. An earthquake causes ground motion which impart vibrations to the buildings. These vibrations generate inertia forces internally due to the mass of the building.

The fundamental period of vibration of a structure is a function of its mass and stiffness of the structure. It is an important parameter for determining the lateral design forces according to modern codes of designing earthquake resistant structures. The natural period of different structures may be as shown in Table 14.4 below.

Table 14.4. Fundamental periods of structures

S. No.	*Type of structure*	*Natural period in seconds*
1.	One storey simple bent or frame	0.05 to 0.1
2.	Low rise buildings upto 4 storeys	0.4 to 0.5
3.	High rise buildings upto 15 storeys	1.0 seconds
4.	Buildings between 10 to 20 storeys	1 to 2 seconds
5.	R.C.C. chimneys	2.0 seconds
6.	Elevated water tanks	4 seconds
7.	Large concrete gravity dams	0.8 seconds
8.	Suspension bridges	6.0 seconds
9.	Natural soil usually it varies	0.5 to 1.0 seconds

Hence it is possible that both building as well as soil may have the same fundamental periods. Thus there is a high probability that a partial resonance may develope.

Hence in the design of an earthquake resistant structure it is desirable to estimate the fundamental periods of both of the building and the site, to check the possibility of developing partial resonance. In general it has been found that a more flexible and longer period design experiences lesser forces proportionately than stiffer building if the site is composed of bed rock which will transmit short period vibrations efficiently and filter out longer period motions. On the other hand for a soft layer of alluvium soil at hundreds of metres depth, it will be difficult to vibrate rapidly, though the input motion from the bed rock beneath it may be of high frequency. A stiffer building may have much less response than a flexible building with a longer period.

14.7.5. General importance of flexibility

During an earthquake, the ground shaking contains a mixture of many sinusoidal waves of different periods as shown in Fig. 14.7. The time taken by

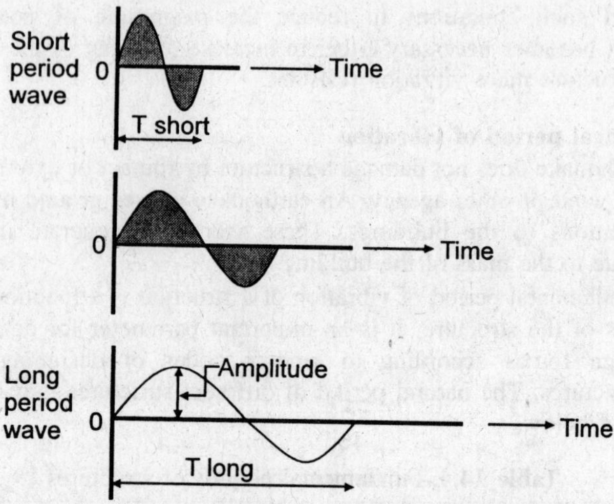

Fig. 14.7. Strong earthquake ground motion is transmitted by waves of different periods (Courtesy—IITK)

the wave to complete one cycle of motion is called period of the earthquake wave. The earthquake shaking wave period has been found to vary from 0.03 to 33 seconds. The intensity of waves at a particular building location depends upon the following factors.

(*a*) Magnitude of the earthquake

(*b*) Distance from the epicentre

(*c*) Type of ground soil through which the earthquake wave has travelled.

14.7.6. Effect of the thickness of soil under the building.

Thus depending upon the value of natural period 'T' of the building and the characteristics of the earthquake ground motion *i.e.* period and amplitude of the earthquake, some buildings will be shaken more than the others.

During the 1967 earthquake of Caraces in south America, the response of buildings was found to depend upon the thickness of the soil layer under the buildings. From the study it was found that the damage intensity to 3 to 5 storeyed tall building was higher in areas where the underlying soil layer was between 40 to 60 m, but minimal damage intensity was found in areas having the under neath soil layer thickness more than 80 m as shown in Fig. 14.8. On the other hand the damage intensity was just the reverse in case of 10 to 14 storey buildings, the damage intensity was higher where the soil cover was in the range of 150 to 300 m and small for lesser soil cover as shown in the same Fig. 14.8. Thus the soil layer under the buildings acts as a filtre, allowing some ground waves to pass through and filtering the rest.

Hence flexible buildings under go higher relative horizontal displacements

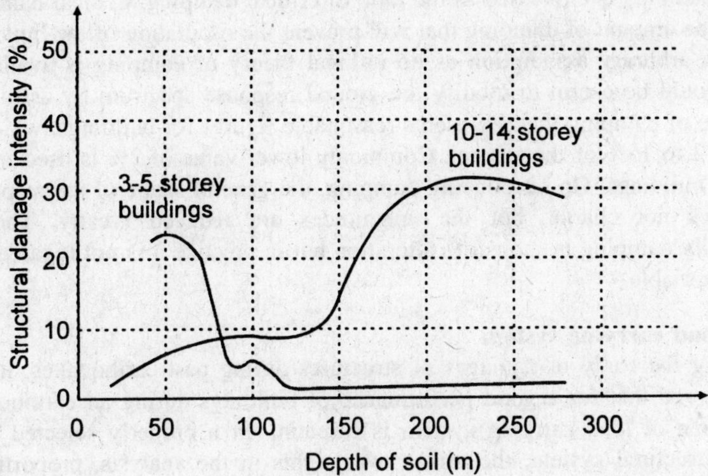

Fig. 14.8. Intensity of damage depends on the thickness of underlying soil layer (Courtesy—IITK)

resulting damage to various non structural elements and the contents of the building.

Item like glass of windows and other items which can not take large laterat movement suffer severe damage or get crushed. Un secured shelves at upper storeys may topple, especially at upper storeys of multi storey buildings. These damages may not affect the safety of the buildings but cause economic losses, injuries and panic in peoples.

14.7.7. Damping

Damping is a device used to decrease the vibrations of a structure. Damping plays a very important role in limiting the displacement of a vibrating structure near resonance. If there was no source of energy dissipation or damping in a vibrating structure, then possibly all structures would have suffered damage in an earthquake due to resonance as an earthquake movement consists generally of large range of frequencies. When a building resonates due to ground motion, its acceleration is amplified similar to the response of certain type of soils which amplify ground motion which results large forces in building and destroy it. However buildings are prevented from vibrating as they have certain damping in them.

In a structural system actually there are many types of energy dissipation and damping sources. The extent of damping in a structure depends upon the following factors:

(*a*) Non structural members in the building.

(*b*) Connections in the building.

(*c*) Kind of construction material used in the building.

The damping is expressed as the ratio of critical damping. Critical damping refers to the amount of damping that will prevent the oscillation of the building. This is an arbitrary assumption as no rational theory of damping is available. Thus it would be useful to modify the ground response spectrum by assuming percentage of damping that represents reasonable figures for buildings, which is generally 2 to 15% of the critical. Commonly lower value of 2% is used in the design of buildings. On introducing damping, the general shape of the response curve does not charge, but the magnitudes are reduced greatly. Though theoretically damping is subject to alteration but in practice it is not regarded as a design variable.

14.7.8. Load carrying system

During the study of damages of structures during past earthquakes, it has been observed that for a good performance of buildings during an earthquake, the selection of load carrying system is essential. In a properly selected load carrying structural system, the minor over sights in the analysis, proportions, details and construction may be ignored *i.e.* their ill effects may be neglected. On the other hand extra attention to the analysis and details etc. are not likely to enhence the performance significantly of a poorly conceived structural system.

Buildings having simple, regular and compact layouts incorporating a continuous and redundant lateral force resisting system has been found to perform well and are desirable. Complex structural systems that introduce uncertaintities in the analysis and detailing can cause un anticipated and un desirable structural behaviour. It has been discussed in detail in chapter 11. An essential characteristic of any lateral load resisting system is that it must provide a continuous load path to the foundation. The inertia forces or loads that develop due to accelerations of individual elements must be transferred from the individual reactive elements to floor diaphragms, to vertical elements in the lateral load system and to the foundation and eventually to the ground soil as shown in Fig. 11.4. Failure to provide adequate strength and toughness of individual elements in the system can result in complete collapse of the system. Thus structural and non structural elements must be tied adequately to the structural system. Failure due to discontinuity of vertical elements of the lateral load resisting system are most spectacular or impressive. One of the most common discontinuity of this type occurs when the shear walls are present only in upper floors or storeys, but discontinued in the lower floors. This results in soft storey effect and causes damage to the lower floors.

14.7.9. Geometrical shapes

Proper consideration of geometric shapes in plan must be given at the planning stage by the architects. Square, rectangular and triangular shapes disperse the seismic forces in all directions equally hence are considered safe. Stiffness, mass and strength irregularities in plan can result sufficient torsion response, discussed in chapter 11. Asymmetric lay out of infill panels has been found to contribute to many structural failure. Corner buildings that had in fill panels on the two inner perimeter walls and open frames on the street side perimeter walls suffered high proportion of damage during earthquake. Torsion due to asymmetric failure of in fill panels also have contributed to the failure of buildings. After 1985 Mexico earthquake destruction, torsion has been recognised as one of the most important contributor of failures of buildings during earthquake.

14.7.10. Buildings separation

In case buildings are constructed in close proximity to one another, then damage is possible to buildings due to their pounding. Thus buildings should be located in relation to property lines and constructed in such a way that they could not pound during earthquake. During earthquake buildings sway and can hammer against one another unless separated adequately. In some cases this hammering may cause massive local damage to the buildings. Hence hammering of buildings should be avoided.

The drift is the maximum lateral displacement of the structure with respect to total height of the building or relative inter-storey displacement. The over all drift index is the ratio of the maximum roof displacement to the height of the structure and the inter storey drift is the ratio of maximum difference of lateral displacements at top and bottom of the storey divided by the height of the storey. The story drift in any storey due to minimum specified design lateral force and with partial safety factor unity should not exceed 0.004 times the storey height.

Two adjacent buildings or two adjacent units of the same building with a separation joint in between should be separated by the distance equal to 'R' (Reduction factor) times the calculated storey displacement. When the floor levels of two similar adjacent units or building are at the same elevation levels, in that case R should be replaced by R/2.

From comfort point of view of occupants there is no need of providing limit on drift or deflection as earthquakes happen rarely and frighten every body regardless of drift.

14.7.11. Strength and flexibility of the structure

Strength and flexibility of a structure are two important parameters which influence the performance of a building to a great extent during the earthquake. These parameters play an important role in the design of earthquake resistant buildings. American and Japanese engineers have designed buildings using the above parameters. American engineers designed buildings for less strength and more flexibility where as Japanese engineers designed houses for more strength and less flexibility. The buildings designed on the basis of higher strength and low flexibility performed better in smaller earthquakes, but in high magnitude earthquakes only more flexible buildings could survive. This fact has been proved during 17th October 1989 earthquake when high rise buildings built on American concept *i.e.* less strength and more flexibility bent during earthquake but suffered very less damage though sway of these high rise buildings frightened its occupants (Also refer chapter 11)

14.7.12. Mass of the structure

The excess mass of a structure leads to the following ill effects:

(*a*) Unnecessary increase in lateral inertia forces.

(*b*) Reduced ductility of vertical load resisting elements.

(*c*) Increased tendency to collapse due to P delta effect. (Refer appendix 1)

For these reasons, efforts should be made to achieve a system that is as light weight as possible. After the 1985 Mexico city earthquake it was found that many buildings collapsed due to the presence of excessive vertical load. Irregularity of the mass distribution in vertical and horizontal planes can produce irregular responses and complex dynamics. As far as possible these should be avoided.

14.7.13. Redundancy

It has been observed that structural systems that combine several lateral load resisting sub systems or elements generally perform well during earthquakes. Redundancy in structural system permits redistribution of internal forces in case of failure of main or key elements. With out capacity of redistribution, global structural collapse can take place due to failure of individual members or connections.

Redundancy in structures can be provided in many ways such as a dual system. It is a system of inter connected frames which makes possible redistribution of forces between frames after the yield has taken place in individual frames, and multiple shear walls. Redundancy combined with adequate strength, stiffness, and continuity reduces or lessen the need of excessive ductile detailing. The benefits of redundancy are also clear by comparing the successful performance of bearing wall buildings with the nearby precast frame buildings as reported for the 1988 American earthquake.

14.7.14. Structural arrangement

For the stability and to withstand earthquakes adequately. American experts have suggested the following steps in this regard:

1. The provision of small and symmetrical windows *i.e.* windows should be small in size and be placed symmetrically in the walls.
2. Joints should be properly reinforced and braced.
3. The floors or storeys should be of uniform (equal) height and equal strength.
4. The storeys or floors should be structurally flexible allowing the building to sway horizontally.

5. The walls of the building should be thicker so that they may provide more stability to the building.
6. For high rise towers several constructions can be used as cross bracing. Cross braces absorb lateral forces.
7. Shear walls can be provided in high rise towers because the vertical wall of concrete resists most of the earthquake forces.
8. The tube in tube concept of shear walls in high rise buildings can be used to resist lateral loads (seismic forces) and to provide stability during earthquake.
9. Moment frames have been found effective where beams and columns bend with force.
10. Isolation bearings containing layered steel and rubber can be used as shock absorbers as in automobiles to separate the building from the moving ground. It helps to transfer reduced vibrations to the super structure.

14.7.15. Structural solution

In the design of earthquake resistant buildings proper choice of structural solution also is very important. The optimum structural solution is dictated by functional and architectural and economic considerations. Mainly it depends on the seismicity of the location of the site. The design of very slender and high buildings should not only conform to the seismic design code but also should be based on special studies of structural dynamics. The response calculations must be done by experts irrespective of the materials used.

14.7.16. Foundations

Foundations is a vital element of any building or structure. It should be designed properly. Generally it has been found that foundation should rest on stiff soil. The bearing power of the soil should be at least 10 tonn/m^2 or 1.0 kg/cm^2. Further it has been observed that heavier damages occur when the same structure is founded on two formations of different geological nature or when the foundation slope is not uniform or the foundations are of different types.

Plastic soils as black cotton soil have been found to be more dangerous and destructive than the rigid soils and rocks. For structures founded on soft soils, the soil structure interaction is an very important factor. This inter action can be considered in the dynamic analysis of the building. According to new techniques "Seismic isolators" have been used in foundations. They have been discussed fully in chapter 18.

14.7.17. Earthquake resistant design philosophy

So far the philosophy of earthquake resistant design of structures was based on the concept that a properly designed and constructed structure should resist a 'moderate' earthquake with a damage that can be repaired and during an major or strong earthquake it should not collapse but can suffer a damage with an acceptable limit. The criterion of acceptable limit of damage was introduced to limit the increase in the cost of building the earthquake resistant structures. But this concept has been changing for the past few years. Now the demand is that building should not only collapse but retain its structural integrity through out the earthquake. Serviceability and ultimate limit state define these two types of design.

The older design requirements were that in an earthquake the building should maintain enough structural integrity to remain standing. This meant that if serviceability limit state is passed the structure would have to be demolished as it would not be safe to use it. Though this concept provides safe escape from the buildings, but there is nothing to check the huge expenditure needed for demolishing and rebuilding the damaged structures. Thus the new concept of ultimate state limit stipulates that building should remain standing in an earthquake and it should not have to be demolished after the earthquake.

14.7.18. Ductility Consideration

Ductility of a material is its property by virtue of which it can elongate or drawn into wires with out breaking or sudden failure. Thus silver, steel, copper etc. are ductile materials. On the other hand materials which break suddenly with out undergoing any elongation or deflection are known as brittle materials such as bricks, stones, cement concrete etc. are brittle material.

Thus ductile structures are those structures which have the ability to dissipate energy and deform with out, brittle or sudden failure.

It has been found by the analysis of damaged structures in past earthquakes that in spite of avoiding resonance and constructing the structures well damped, the seismic forces developed in the structures were much in excess than those for which they were designed under the building code. By the use of code's equivalent static force formula, the design lateral force will be developed about 5% to 20% of the building mass in high seismic zones *i.e.* the acceleration of the building will be 5% to 20% of gravity (0.05 to 0.2g). However real earthquakes produce much higher accelerations than the amount mentioned above, but our structures bear these higher accelerations due to their ductility as defined above. As stated above the act of deformation of buildings absorbs energy and defers absolute damage or failure of the structure.

For seismic effects resistant design, the ductility of the structures is an extremely important factor or consideration. It is important due to the fact that in the case of severe earthquake to enable a structure to survive with out collapse, reliance can only be placed on the availability of sufficient ductility after yielding. The large deflections at near the maximum force or load give ample warning of failure and by preserving the load carrying capacity total collapse may be prevented and precious lives may be saved. Due to the ductile behaviour of members, the bending moment B.M. distribution principle can be used in the design.

To ensure ductile behaviour of a building, special attention should be paid to the following details.

(*i*) Longitudinal reinforcement contents.

(*ii*) Anchorage of reinforcement.

(*iii*) Proper confinement of concrete in compression.

The reserve capacity and ductility are closely related after a point at which loads cause permanent deformations. At this stage, ductile materials can take further loading before completely rupturing. The reserve capacity is the ability of a complete or full structure to resist overload. The reserve capacity is dependent on the ductility of its individual members. The ductility of a building or structure is influenced by

(*i*) Members proportions

(*ii*) Connection details

(*iii*) End condition

The only reason for not providing for ductility is to provide so much resistance that members may not exceed elastic limit.

14.7.19. Members Proportioning and detailing

To enable redistribution of seismic forces, reduction in internal actions and dissipation of seismic energy, conventional earthquake resistant design of buildings relies on ductility of the members. But observations have revealved the necessity of paying attention to proportioning and detailing. Proportioning is essential to ensure that an inelastic action only should occur in a desired appropriate location, where as detailing is essential to ensure adequate ductility in those locations that yield.

Structures should be so proportioned that they yield in locations that are most capable to sustain inelastic deformations. In case of R.C.C. frame buildings efforts should be made to minimize the yielding in columns due to the fact that detailing for ductility in the presence of high axial loads is difficult and due to the possibility that yielding of columns may collapse the storey due to increase in storey sway mechanism. The failures due to column weakness and limited ductility have been discussed in chapter 2 and 8.

The problem of yielding in columns rather than beams is more pronounced in structures where the gravity load effects control the proportions and strength, resulting more flexural strength in beams by some factor of the column flexural strength. This situation occurs in structures which require long beam spans and in upper floors of buildings where design seismic effects are relatively low. The failure in upper storeys of framed buildings has been found more due to the later situation mentioned above.

The failures of buildings due to the yielding of columns gave birth to the strong column and weak beam design philosophy in which the column strength is made at least equal to beam strength. The result of this philosophy is that columns form a stiff and unyielding spine over the full height of the building with inelastic action limited mainly to beams. Even in structures so designed yielding in 1st storey columns should be anticipated and appropriate details should be provided. In situations where long span beams are a architectural necessity, in such cases columns should be detailed to sustain inelastic action or continuous structural walls should be provided to enforce continuity of deformation over height.

Generally the coupled wall systems are proportioned in such a way that a considerable portion of the inelastic energy dissipation takes place in the coupling beams. The performance of such systems generally has been found good, though damage to coupling beams and slabs is not uncommon. In coupled beams system special reinforcement details or provision of closely spaced transverse reinforcement is recommended.

The structures should be proportioned and detailed in such a manner that is consistant with the expected inelastic deformation mode. If in selected members inelastic flexure is preferred, then design actions and appropriate proportioned should be selected to ensure that the selected elements can achieve the flexural strength.

The shear failures for beams and columns have occurred as the design shear forces were determined on the basis of design lateral forces rather than shear required for equalization for the plastic moment capacities of the members. Thus most modern codes suggest that design shears should be evaluated on the basis of likely plastic hinge locations with appropriate factor of safety applied to the member strength and transverse loading.

Failures of structures also have occurred due to inconsistent reinforcement bars cut off with respect to moment distribution that developed when the flexural strengths have reached at members ends. This moment distribution is quite uncertain. Hence due to the uncertaintities in determining this moment distribution, most of the codes have recommended that nominal reinforcement be carried continuously on both faces of all structural elements.

As discussed earlier also, non structural components also have been found to alter the structural behaviour. For example slabs on slope can change the assumed fixidity conditions. Similarly stair ways and partial infill in frames can alter the member actions. These interactions can cause increased member shear demand and formation of plastic hinges away from the pre determined locations detailed for ductility action. This type of damage emphasize the need for realistic assessment of the member behaviour.

Corner columns have been found to suffer greater damage rate than other columns in moment resisting frames. The cause of this high rate of damage seems to be the combined effect of actions from perimeter frames oriented perpendicular to one another and connecting at the corner columns.

Thus extra care should be taken in the selection of design actions considering the orthogonal effects and in detailing and construction of corner columns.

14.7.20. Joint design and detailing

For resisting earthquake induced forces, a proper design and detailing of various joints in a reinforced cement concrete structural system is very important similar to member proportioning and detailing. For the satisfactory performance of a joint in a R.C.C. structure park and paulay have suggested the following requirements of the joints.

(*a*) The service load performance of a joint should be equal in quality to that of the members it joins *i.e.* the members which join at the joint.

(*b*) The strength of the joint should be at least equal to that corresponds to the most adverse load combinations that the adjoining members could sustain, several times if necessary.

(*c*) The strength of the structure normally should not be governed by the strength of the joint, and the behaviour of the joint should not stop or delay in the development of the full strength of the adjoining member.

(*d*) In case of seismic design, the design of the joint will not only be governed by its strength, but also by the ductility of the adjoining members. Due to the possible degradation of concrete strength, a large amount of joint reinforcement will be required.

(*e*) Other points of importance in the design of joint and detailing are ease of construction and access to the joint for pouring concrete and its compaction.

(*i*) In concrete members such as beam, columns and beam-column connections and in reinforced walls generous amount and appropriate placement of transverse reinforcement has proved very beneficial. Such reinforcement has been found usefull for confinement of concrete, resistance to shear, restraint to buckling of longitudinal reinforcement and providing improved anchorage. The failure of providing adequate transverse reinforcement at the ends of the members where plastic hinges are anticipated to develop, results in reduced flexural strength and ductility and degradation of shear resistance as well.

(*ii*) Closely spaced transverse reinforcement is specially recommended for the un restrained length of captive columns where inelastic flexure is combined with shear force.

(*iii*) The boundary elements of walls where significant inelastic action is anticipated should be well confined to provide ductility under axial compression.

(*iv*) Columns supporting continuous walls should be confined over their entire height.

(*v*) Inadequate confinement of joints has been found to cause total collapse of many buildings.

(*vi*) Many failures have been observed where heavy spiral or rectilinear confinements in columns below and above of a joint was discontinued at a joint. In general the confinement in columns should be continued through the connection region.

Effective confinement of concrete can be obtained using either spiral or rectilinear tie reinforcement. Generally spiral reinforcement has been found more effective form of confining reinforcement. To be more effective transverse reinforcement must be coupled with properly distributed longitudinal reinforcement. During past earthquakes it has been observed that poorly spaced and bundled column reinforcement bars caused many structural collapse. In addition, the transverse reinforcement must be anchored properly, so that it may remain effective even when the concrete cover starts to spall. Perimeter hoops with out hook anchorage into the core of concrete have been found ineffective during many past earthquake.

The toughness and strength must not only develop with in members themselves but in connections between members also. Continuity between members and joint is also essential.

Under the action of cyclic (seismic conditions) inelastic load reversals proper anchorage of reinforcement is essential. Further there must be sufficient transverse reinforcement and concrete must surround each bar. Improper anchorage of transverse reinforcement has resulted confinement failure in columns during almost all earthquakes. The improperly executed construction joints in shear walls have resulted in movements and damage along the joint. There are numerous examples where poor construction and poor quality materials have contributed failures to many buildings.

14.8. EFFECTS OF AFTER SHOCKS

Basically after shocks are minor earthquakes that occur at random timings after the first shock. Usually the effects of these shocks are not taken into consideration. Generally these shocks have no effect on the undamaged buildings, but on already damaged buildings they can inflict heavy damage as much of the resisting power of the buildings was lost in the first shock. These shocks cause total collapse and disturb rescue operations. In the assessment of building damage after the earthquake, the effect of energy from an after shock must also be taken into consideration.

14.9. ECONOMIC, SOCIAL AND ENVIRONMENTAL EFFECTS

In order to achieve the best solution of earthquake resistant building design following factors must be linked with the engineering design:

(*a*) Economic aspects

(*b*) Social and environmental parameters

(*c*) Safety factor

The inclusion of these factors has been found good where a safe building design is required for all types of earthquakes, but it does not fit the design description or details. For example a design 'safe' for all types of earthquake is quite expensive and is not economically viable to design buildings in zone 1 and 2 of the Indian zoning maps as chances of occurring a major earthquake there are very remote.

Thus the behaviour of a building during the earthquake must be given due consideration in the design rather following design codes blindly.

QUESTIONS

1. Discuss the influence of ground accelerations on buildings.
2. Explain the influence of soil on structures during earthquake.
3. Write a brief note on the design of a masonry earthquake resistant structure.
4. Name the factors which influence the design of concrete earthquake resistant structures.
5. In severe seismic activity regions the buildings designed for more flexibility and less strength cause.....
   (*a*) More damage (*b*) Less damage
   (*c*) No effect on damage (*d*) All are correct
6. In less seismic regions buildings designed on the basis of more strength and less flexibility cause......
   (*a*) Less damage (*b*) More damage
   (*c*) No effect on damage (*d*) All are correct
7. Excess mass of a building causes...... except
   (*a*) Increase in lateral inertial forces
   (*b*) Decrease in the lateral inertial forces
   (*c*) Reduction in ductility of vertical load resisting system
   (*d*) Increases the tendency towards total collapse
8. To ensure better performance during earthquakes, structures should have......
   (*a*) Small and symmetrical windows
   (*b*) Braced and reinforced joints
   (*c*) Floors or storeys of uniform height and strength
   (*d*) Building should be quite flexible to enable it to sway horizontal
   (*e*) All are correct (*f*) None is correct
9. Geometric shapes like square, rectangle or triangle disperse the seismic forces.....
   (*a*) Only in horizontal direction (*b*) Only in vertical direction
   (*c*) In all directions (*d*) All are correct
10. In an seismic zone a more flexible and of longer natural period structure is prone to......
    (*a*) More damage (*b*) Less damage
    (*c*) Equal damage (*d*) All are true
11. In seismic zones the tie rods should be bent at angle......
    (*a*) 100 degree (*b*) 120 degree
    (*c*) 135 degree (*d*) 90 degree
12. The length of stirrups or tie rod beyond bend should be...... of the diameter of the tie rod
    (*a*) 5% (*b*) 10%
    (*c*) 15% (*d*) 20%
13. Identify the incorrect statements/statements
    (*a*) In the design of earthquake resistant buildings the vertical and horizontal components of ground motion should be considered

(*b*) In the design of earthquake resistant buildings the provision of horizontal component of ground motion is sufficient
(*c*) The rigidity of the structure should be well distributed in both vertical and horizontal direction.
(*d*) Boundary frames filled with masonry in fill should be tied firmly by shear connectors.

14. Total collapse of a structure can be avoided by adopting......
(*a*) Weak beam and strong column concept
(*b*) Weak column and strong beam
(*c*) Column and beam should be of equal strength
(*d*) None is correct

15. In strong seismic zones, the reinforcement of columns should be of the from
(*a*) Circular (*b*) Rectangular
(*c*) Spiral (*d*) Any shape

16. Identify the incorrect statement/statements
(*a*) The natural period 'T' of vibration of any building is influenced by its flexibility
(*b*) The natural period 'T' of vibration of a building depends upon its rigidity
(*c*) More flexible a building is, more will be its natural period of vibrations
(*d*) Greater the máss of the building, more is its natural period of vibrations
(*e*) More the rigidity of the building, higher is its natural period of vibrations
(*f*) Higher the height of the building, greater is its natural period of vibration

17. Identify the incorrect statement/statements
(*a*) During an earthquake the response of a building depends upon the thickness of soil layer beneath the foundation
(*b*) The thickness of soil layer beneath the foundation has no effect on the natural period of vibration of the building
(*c*) The characteristics of soil beneath the foundation influence the damages of structures to a great extent
(*d*) The soil beneath the foundations works as a filter
(*e*) All are correct

18. During an earthquake...... most unsafe element is
(*a*) Walls (*b*) columns
(*c*) Foundations (*d*) All the three

19. By increasing the number of floors in a multi-storey building its natural period of vibrations......
(*a*) Increases (*b*) Decreases
(*c*) No effect (*d*) All are correct

ANSWERS

5. (*b*)	9. (*c*)	13. (*b*)	17. (*b*)
6. (*a*)	10. (*b*)	14. (*a*)	18. (*d*)
7. (*b*)	11. (*c*)	15. (*c*)	19. (*a*)
8. (*e*)	12. (*b*)	16. (*b, e*)	

15

Seismic Resistant Building Design as per I.S. Codes

15.1. INTRODUCTION

An earthquake generates motions in the ground in all directions. When a structure standing on the ground encounters such ground motions, it vibrates in all the three directions. The predominant direction of shaking or vibrating is horizontal. All structures primarily are designed for gravity loads (mass times gravity in the vertical direction). Usually a factor of safety is used in the design specifications, hence most of the structures remain adequately protected against vertical shaking. Generally the inertia forces generated by the horizontal components of ground motions need greater attention in the seismic design. The vertical inertia forces generated by the earthquake must also be considered in the design unless checked and proved to be insignificant.

Generally buildings are not susceptible to vertical ground motion, but its effect should be taken into account in the design of R.C.C. columns, steel column connections and prestressed concrete beams. Vertical accelerations should also be taken into account in the design of structures of large span. In general, structures designed only for vertical accelerations may not be able to safely sustain the effects of horizontal shaking. Hence it is essential to ensure the adequate resistance of the structure to the horizontal seismic shaking.

During an earthquake the horizontal component of the ground motion mainly causes the damages to the structures. Structures get damaged due to the fact that they (structures) do not move along with the ground motion, but react or appose (response) it. Thus stresses and strains are induced in the structures.

15.2. STEPS INVOLVED IN THE EARTHQUAKE RESISTANT DESIGN

Following steps are involved in the design of an earthquake resistant building or structure:

(*a*) Selection of a workable over all structural concept.

(*b*) Establishing proper sizes of the members.

(*c*) Performing structural analysis of the members to verify that the stress and displacement requirements are satisfied.

(*d*) Providing structural and non structural details so that the building may accommodate all stresses and distortions likely to be developed.

15.3. STRUCTURAL RESPONSES (Reactions)

The response (reaction) of the structure depends upon the following factors:

(*a*) Acceleration to which the structure is subjected. The acceleration depends upon the frequency of vibration or time period of vibration and damping etc.

(*b*) Materials, form, size and mode of construction of the structure.

(*c*) Soil-structure interaction.

(*d*) Post yield behaviour of the structure.

15.4. BASIC ASSUMPTIONS

In the analysis of seismic resistant design of structures usually following assumptions are made:

1. The ground motions caused by an earthquake are impulsive. These motions are complex and irregular in character. The character of ground motions changes with the change of period and amplitude of the vibrations. Thus resonance visualized under steady state sinusodial excitations will not occur, as it needs time to build up such amplitudes. But in exceptional cases resonance like conditions have been seen occurring between long distance waves and tall structures built on deep soft soils.
2. An earthquake is not likely to occur simultaneously with powerful floods and sea waves or strong wind. The probability of occurrence of severe earthquake motion along with maximum sea waves and/or strong winds is very low. Thus it is justified to assume that these hazárdous events are not occurring at the same time.
3. The value of elastic modulus of materials whereever required may be used as for static analysis, unless a more suitable value is available for such conditions.

It may be noted that values of modulus of elasticity for various construction materials vary to a great extent.

15.5. DESIGN EARTHQUAKE LOADS

The random ground motion caused by an earthquake generates inertia forces in a structure in all the three (*x, y, z*) directions.

The design earthquake loads and their combinations are discussed below.

15.5.1. Design horizontal seismic load

When designing lateral load resistant elements oriented along the orthogonal horizontal directions, the structure should be designed in such a way that the effects due to full design seismic load act in one horizontal direction at a time. In case the lateral load resisting elements are not oriented along the orthogonal horizontal direction, then the structure should be designed for the effects for the full design seismic load in one horizontal direction and 30% seismic design load on the other direction. For example a building may be designed as ($\pm$ EL_x – 0.30 EL_y) or as [$\pm$ 0.30 EL_x + EL_y] where x and y are two orthogonal horizontal direction and EL is the seismic design load adopted for design.

15.5.2. Design vertical seismic load

During an earthquake usually all structures experience a constant vertical acceleration (down ward) that may be additive or subtractive to the gravity depending upon the direction of ground motion of that instant. Factor of safety applied for gravity loads usually is sufficient to take care of the earthquake induced vertical acceleration. In case it is desired to design for vertical acceleration, then the value of vertical acceleration may be assumed as 67% of the horizontal acceleration.

How ever this approach should not be adopted for sensitive structures.

15.6. BASIC LOAD COMBINATIONS

The load combinations of gravity and lateral loads with appropriate load factors as suggested by the codes are given below. The structure is analysed and designed for the combination that gives the most critical results. For plastic design of steel structures following load combinations may be adopted. Here the numerical value of 1.7 and 1.3 are partial factors of safety.

(*a*) 1.7 (DL + IL)

(*b*) 1.7 (DL ± EL)

(*c*) 1.3 (DL + IL ± EL)

Here DL, IL and EL represent response quantities due to dead load, imposed load and designed earthquake (seismic) load respectively. For the limit state design of prestressed concrete structures, following load combinations may be adopted. Numerical values represent partial factors of safety as above.

(*a*) 1.5 (DL + IL)

(*b*) 1.2 (DL + IL ± EL)

(*c*) 1.5 (DL ± EL0)

(*d*) 0.9 (DL ± 1.5 EL)

15.7. permissible stresses

Permissible stresses on soils subjected to static loading for the design of structures are specified by the codes. The increase has been recommended considering the factor of safety to take care of the transient effects.

When seismic forces are considered along with other normal design forces, the permissible stresses in the material may be increased by 33% in case of

Table 15.1. Permissible increase in allowable bearing pressure of soils

Type of soil mainly constructing the foundation	*Permissible increase in allowable bearing pressure in soils in percent*					
	Pile passing through any soil but resting on soil type I	*Pile not covered under column 2*	*Raft foundation*	*Combined or isolated R.C.C. footing with tie beams*	*Isolated R.C.C. footing with out tie beams or un reinforced strip foundation*	*Well foundation*
(1)	(2)	(3)	(4)	(5)	(6)	(7)
Type I. Rock or hard soils. Well graded gravels and sand, gravel mixture with or with out clay binder, any clayay sands, poorly graded sand or sand clay mixtures (GB, CW, SW, SC)$^{+}$ having N* above 30, where *N* is the standard penetration value.	50	—	50	50	50	50
Type II. Medium soils. All soils with N between 10 and 30 and poorly graded sands or gravely sands with little or no fines (SP^{+}) with N > 15.	50	25	50	25	25	25
Type III. Soft soils. All soils other than (SP^{+}) with N < 10	50	25	50	25	0	25

+ IS 1948 Classification and identification of soils for general engineering purposes.
* IS 231 Method of standard penetration test for soils.

elastic method of design. How ever for steel with a definite yield point, the stress may be limited to 80% of the ultimate strength or 0.2% of proof stress, which ever is smaller. For prestressed concrete members, the tensile stress in the extreme fibres of the concrete may be permitted to limit these stresses not to exceed the 2/3 times of modulus of rupture of the concrete.

The allowable bearing pressure in soils is increased as suggested in Table 15.1, depending upon the type of foundation of the structure and type of soil below it.

Note:

1. The allowable bearing pressure shall be determined in accordance with IS 6403+ or IS 1888++.
2. If any increase in bearing pressure has already been permitted for forces other than seismic forces, the total increase in allowable bearing pressure when seismic force is also included may not exceed the limits specified above.
3. In submerged loose sands and soils falling under classification SP with standard penetration values less than the values specified in note 5 below, the vibrations caused by earthquakes may cause liquefaction or excessive total and differential settlements. In important projects this aspect of the problem need be investigated and appropriate methods of compaction or stabilization adopted to achieve suitable value of N. Alternatively deep pile foundation may be provided and taken well down into layers which are not likely to liquefy.
4. The pile should be designed for lateral loads neglecting lateral resistance of soil layer liable to liquefy.
5. Desirable field values of N are as follows shown in Table 15.2.

Table 15.2.

Zone	*Depth in m*	*N values*	*Remark*
III, IV and V	5 m 10 m	15 25	For values between 5 to 10 m linear interpolation is recommended
I and II (For important structures only)	5 m 10 m	10 20	

+ IS 6403. Determination of allowable bearing pressure for soils for shallow foundations.

++ 1888. Method of load test on soil.

15.8. METHOD OF SEISMIC ANALYSIS

The method of seismic analysis can be performed as shown in the following linear diagram.

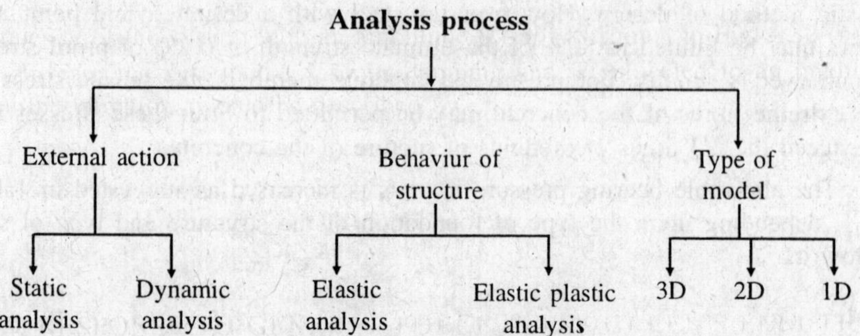

Line diagram of method of analysis

Based on the external action and behaviour of structure the analysis can further be classified as linear static analysis, linear dynamic analysis, non linear static analysis or non linear dynamic analysis.

The linear static or equivalent static analysis can be used for regular structures with low to medium heights. The linear dynamic analysis can be performed in two ways as

1. Response spectrum method
2. By the elastic time history method

The significant difference between linear static and linear dynamic analysis is as follows:

1. Magnitude (Level of forces
2. Distribution of forces along the height of the structure.

Non linear static analysis is an improvement over linear static or dynamic analysis as it allows inelastic behaviour of the structure. This method is simple to use. It provides information regarding strength, deformation and the ductility of the structure. It also provides distribution of demands along the height of the structure.

This method facilitates the identification of the critical members that are likely to attain the limit states during the earthquake. This limit state should be taken into consideration at the time of design and detailing process.

However this method is based on many assumptions, which neglect the effect of variation of loading patterns, higher modes of vibrations, and effect of resonance etc. Inspite of all these shortcomings, this method provides a reasonable estimation of the global deformation capacity, especially for structures which respond according to the first mode.

During an earthquake the actual behaviour of a structure is only described by a non linear dynamic analysis or inelastic time history method. This method is based on direct numerical integration of the differential equations of motion considering the elasto-plastic deformation of the structural elements.

15.8.1. Methods of elastic analysis

The most commonly used methods of elastic analysis are based on the approximations. The effects of yielding can be estimated by linear analysis of the building, using design spectrum for inelastic systems. Forces and displacements due to each horizontal component of the ground motion are determined separately by the analysis of an idealized building of one lateral degree of freedom per floor in the direction of the ground motion component being considered. Such analysis may be carried out by any of the following methods.

(*i*) By equivalent lateral force method (Static method)

(*ii*) By response spectrum analysis method (Dynamic method)

(*iii*) By elastic time history method. It is a refined method of dynamic analysis

Both static or dynamic method lead directly to the lateral forces in the direction of ground motion component. The main differences between the two methods are in the magnitude and distribution of the lateral forces over the height of the building. The static method mainly is suitable for preliminary design of buildings. The preliminary design of the building is then used for dynamic analysis or any other refined method as elastic time history method.

15.8.1.1. Equivalent lateral force method (Seismic Coefficient method)

The seismic analysis of most of the structures is still carried out on the assumption that the lateral force (horizontal force) due to earthquake is equivalent to the actual (dynamic) loading. This method requires only natural period or fundamental period of the building, and periods and shapes of higher modes of vibration are not required. Hence this method is less labourious. The base shear, which is the total horizontal force on the structure is calculated on the basis of mass of the structure, its fundamental period of vibration and corresponding shape. The base end shear is distributed along the height of the structure in terms of lateral forces according to the code formula. The planar models appropriate for each of the two orthogonal (x and y) lateral directions are analysed separately. The results of the two analysis and other effects as that of torsional motions of the structures are combined. This method usually is limited to low to medium height buildings with regular configuration.

15.8.1.2. Response spectrum analysis

This method is also known as mode superimposition or model method. This method is applicable specially to those structures, whose responses are significantly affected by the modes other than fundamental mode. Generally this method is applicable to the analysis of the dynamic response of asymmetrical or having areas of discontinuity or irregular structures in their linear range of behaviour. Particularly this method is applicable to the analysis of forces and deformations in the multi storey buildings due to medium intensity of ground shaking. This ground shaking causes a moderately large but essentially linear response in the structure. This method is based on the fact that for certain form of damping, which are reasonably models for many buildings, the response in each natural mode of vibration can be computed independently of the others.

The total response can be determined by combining the model responses. Each mode responds with its own particular pattern of deformation (mode shape) with its own frequency and with its own model damping. The time history of each model response can be determined by the analysis of single degree of freedom (SDOF) oscillator with properties chosen to be representative of the particular mode and the degree to which it is excited by the earthquake motion. In general the responses should be determined only in the first few modes, as the response to the earthquake mainly is due to lower modes of vibration.

A complete modal analysis provides the history of response, that is history of forces, displacements, and deformation of a structure to a specified ground acceleration history. However for design of structures complete response history is seldom required. For design purposes the maximum response values during the period of earthquake usually are sufficient.

In its most general form this method is applicable to arbitrary three dimensional structural systems. But for the purpose of design of buildings, it can be simplified from the general case by restricting its application to the lateral motion in a plane. The planar models for each of the two orthogonal directions can be analysed separately and the results of the analysis and other effects such as torsional motion of the structure are combined.

15.8.1.3. Comparative study of equivalent lateral force and response spectrum analysis

The main difference is in the magnitude of base shear and distribution of lateral forces. It is shown in tabular form in Table 15.3 below

Table 15.3.

S. No.	*Equivalent lateral force method*	*Response spectrum method*
1.	Both are based on the basic assumptions made	In this method the force calculations are based on compound period and mode shapes of several modes of vibrations.
2.	In this method the force calculations are based on an estimate of the fundamental period	This method can be applied to the analysis of model
3.	The force distribution is based on simple formula apropriate for buildings with regular distribution of mass and stiffness over the height.	It requires more computational efforts in analysis.
4.	This formula usually is used.	It is more complex.

15.8.1.4. Elastic time history method

Though linear time history analysis over comes all disadvantages of model response spectrum analysis provided non linear behaviour is not required, but it is more laborious. This method requires large number of calculations for determining the response at discrete times. In most cases this is not required.

15.9. ASSUMPTIONS MADE IN MODEL ANALYSIS

In the model analysis of a building certain assumption have to be made for simplicity in calculations. In building analysis usually following assumptions are made.

1. In the model of a building, usually the floor is assumed rigid and the columns as flexible.
2. In the model of a building for simplicity usually the floor is assumed infinitely rigid as compared to columns.
3. In multi storeyed buildings the lateral force or load is assumed to act at floor level.
4. In case of R.C.C. structures the effective length of columns is assumed as the distance from the centre to centre of the floors. This assumption is reasonable for buildings having the ratio of moment of inertia per unit length of the beam to that of the column of the order 3 to 8.0.
5. The elastic modulus of R.C.C. column is assumed to be between 0.15 to 0.3×10^{11} N/m^2. The value of elastic modulus is a function of the composition of concrete and its age under stress.
6. The damping of the system usually is chosen arbitrarily. It (damping) varies with strain in material, its nature and details of construction.

The damping is specified in terms of model damping. The percentage damping for various materials increases with strain levels and in the following range:

Material	**Damping**
Concrete	5 to 10%
Steel	2 to 5%
Masonry	5 to 10%
Soil	10 to 30%
Timber	2 to 5%

The model analysis for the estimation of ground motions is adopted for important and special structures only. For routine structures and for preliminary design of special structures empirical coefficients are used. For a rational design these coefficients should be based on detailed dynamic study of a class of typical structures.

15.10. FACTORS GOVERNING THE SEISMIC DESIGN

Following parameters govern the seismic design:

1. Design load
2. Seismic weight

3. Zone factor
4. Importance factor of structure

15.10.1. Design loads

Earthquake is a rare phenomenon, in which a structure mainly is subjected to horizontal forces. The probability of acting seismic as well as wind forces at the same time is very less. Thus load factors specified in codes should be used either for seismic loads or for wind loads. The various load combinations specified in code 1893 for the seismic design are shown in section 15.6. For various load combinations specified in the code, the earthquake force shall be calculated for the full dead load plus a percentage of live load as given in Table 15.4 below. But where the probable loads at the time of earthquake are more accurately estimated, the designer may change the proportions or even replace the imposed load proportions by actual estimated load. In the calculation of lateral design force of earthquake the impact effect from imposed loads will not be taken into consideration.

Table 15.4. Percentage of imposed load to be considered in seismic weight calculations

Imposed uniformly distributed floor load kN/m²	*Percentage of imposed load*
Upto and including 3 kN/m² (2000, 2500, 3000 N/m²)	25%
Above 3 kN/m² (4000, 5000, 7500, 10,000 N/m²)	50%

In using working stress method, the permissible stresses in material shall be increased by 1/3rd, limiting it to yield stress of steel. Depending upon the type of the foundation of the structure and the type of soil, the allowable bearing pressure in soil shall be increased as specified in Table 15.1. The classification of the soil is based on the average shear wave velocity for top 30m of rock/soil layer or based on the average standard penetration test N values for top 30 m given in Table 15.2.

15.10.2. Seismic weight

The seismic force is due to inertia of mass. The imposed load which includes the impact effects does not contribute fully to the seismic load. In addition to this the probability that the building will be loaded to its full design load during an earth is very rare. These facts are taken into consideration and the code incooperates only part of the loads to be taken under earthquake. Since the reduction of load has already been made, no further reduction in the imposed loads shall be made as specified in section 3.2.1.2 of IS 875 (Part 2).

Thus the seismic weight of each floor consists of full dead load plus appropriate amount of imposed load specified in Table 15.4. While computing the seismic weight of each floor the weight of walls and columns in each storey should be equally distributed to floors above and below the storey.

The seismic weight of the whole building is the sum of the seismic weight of all the floors. Any weight supported in between the storeys should be distributed to the floors above and below in inverse proportion to its distance from the floors.

15.10.3. Zone factor

The earthquake severity has been classified into zones on the basis of maximum ground acceleration based on past earthquake data. In 1984 India has been redivided into four zones instead of five zones as divided earlier. The

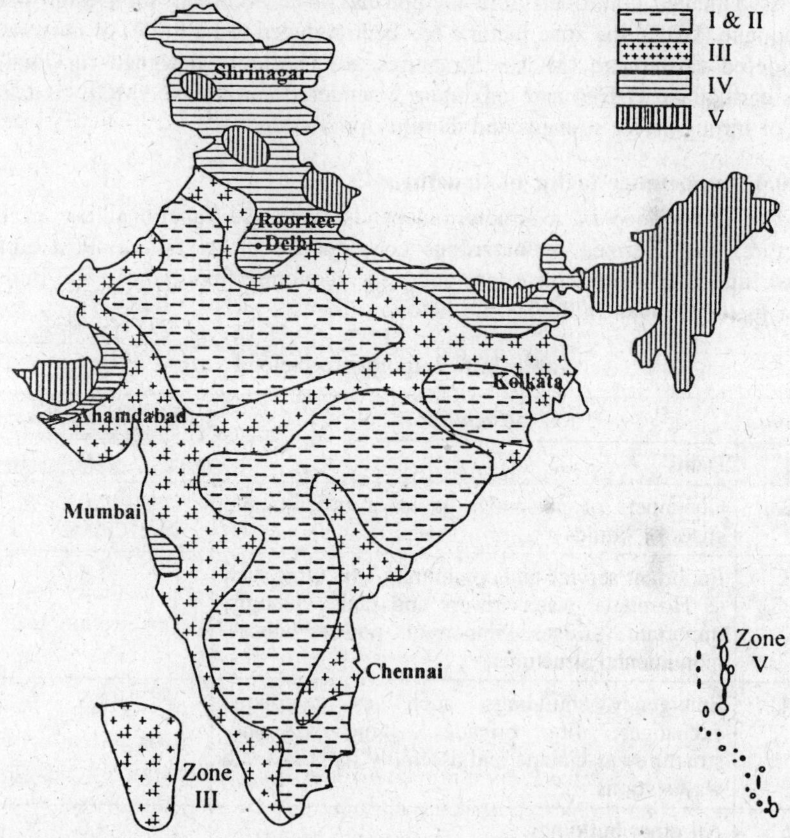

Fig. 15.1. Seismic zone map

1984 division has been shown in Fig. 15.1, while the earlier division is shown in Fig. 1.1. This division is based on the maximum considered earthquake (MCE) and service life of the structure in a zone. The map shown in Fig. 15.1 is based on expected intensity of ground shaking but does not consider the frequency of occurrence of the earthquake. These zone factors are shown in Table 15.5.

Table 13.5. Zone factors value 'Z'

Seismic zone	II	III	IV	V
Seismic intensity	Low	Moderate	Severe	Very severe
Z	0.10	0.16	0.24	0.36

As damaged controlled limit method has been accepted, for Design basis earthquake (DBE), the zone factor *z* has been reduced to half (*z*/2) of maximum considered earthquake (MCE). Structures are explicitly designed for Design basis earthquake (DBE) and maximum considered earthquake (MCE) is taken care of through over strength and ductility provisions.

15.10.4. Importance factor of structure

The importance of a structure depends upon the functional use of the structure, characterized by harzrdous consequence of its failure. Post earthquake functional needs, historical value, or economic importance. The importance factor is given in Table 15.6 below.

Table 15.6. Importance factor I

S. No.	*Structures*	*Importance factor I*
1.	Dams	3.0
2.	Containers of poisonous gases or inflammable gases or liquids	2.0
3.	Important service and community structures such as Hospitals, water towers and tanks, schools, important bridges, important power houses, monumental structures.	1.5
4.	Emergency buildings such as telephone exchanges, fire brigades, large assembly structures as cinema and assembly halls and sub way stations.	1.5
5.	All other buildings.	1.0

Note:

1. The value of importance factor I given above are for guidance. The designer may change it depending upon economy, strategy considerations like multi storey buildings having several residential units.
2. This does not apply to temporary structures like excavation, scaffolding etc. of short duration.

15.10.5. Over strength

The additional strength over the design force incorporated in design codes in called over strength. This is due to ignorance about the actual behaviour of the structure subjected to lateral forces. Following factors contribute to the over strength.

1. Partial safety factors applied on material properties.
2. Load factors used for design forces.
3. The contribution of non structural elements neglected.
4. The reserve strength of redundant members not taken into account.
5. Larger sizes of members and more reinforcement provided than required as per design.

15.10.6. Ductility

The ductility of a structure or its member is the capacity to under go large inelastic deformations with out significant loss of strength or stiffness. Ductility can also be defined as the ratio of maximum displacement (δ_{max}) at ultimate strength to the displacement at yield (d_y). Ductility of a structure is measured by the ductility factor. The ductility factor u is the ratio and given by the relation as

$$u = \frac{\delta_{max}}{\delta_y} \qquad \text{...(15.1)}$$

Usually displacements are measured at roof level.

15.10.6.1. Factors affecting the ductility

These factors are as given below:

1. Axial load in members reduces the ductility at column ends. A structure with a strong column and weak beam improves ductility.
2. Flexure members exhibit large ductility before collapse, if failure is initiated by steel. Thus ductility can be improved by providing under-reinforced flexural members.
3. Avoid failure of a member in diagonal shear.
4. Crushing strain in concrete can be improved considerably by confining the concrete by providing closely spaced stirrups.
5. Curvature ductility increases with increase in compression steel.
6. High strength concrete is less ductile. Thus as far as possible very high strength concrete should not be selected for earthquake resistant structures. Further for ductility detailing see chapter 17.

15.10.7. Response reduction factor R

The response reduction factor takes into account the ductility of the structural system, and over strength so that the structure can be designed to the level of yield force of the structure and rely on the non linear response of the structures in case of severe earthquake. Thus it is obvious that structures having low over strength or low ductility should be designed for higher seismic coefficients. This means that buildings such as steel stacks, over head water tanks etc. should be designed for higher design seismic coefficients than that of buildings.

In case, the importance factor I is taken more than 1.5, and the value of reduction factor 'R' is taken lower, then I/R will give greater value than unity. In such a case the base shear to which the structure will be subjected will be very large. Hence the code restricts the ratio I/R as unity. However for building frame system, the maximum value of I is taken 1.5 as shown in Table 15.6 and the lowest value of *R* is 1.5. Therefore the ratio of I/R will not exceed unity. The response reduction factor is also important from the view point of discouraging the construction of ordinary moment resistanting frames and ordinary R.C.C. shear walls, by considering higher level forces in the design of earthquake resisting structures. The response reduction factors are shown in Table 15.7.

Table 15.7. Response reduction factor R for building frame system

S. No.	*Lateral load resisting system*	*R*
Building frame system:		
1.	Ordinary R.C. Moment-Resisting Frames (OMRF) These frames shall be designed and detailed as per IS 456 or IS 800, but not meeting ductile detailing requirements as per IS 13920 or SP 6(6) respectively.	3.0
2.	Special R.C. Moment Resisting frames (SMRF) These frames shall be detailed to provide ductile behaviour and comply with the requirements as given in IS 4326 or IS 13920or SP 6(6)	5.0
3.	*Steel frames with*	
	(*a*) Concentric braces	4.0
	(*b*) Ecentric braces	5.0
4.	Steel moment resisting frames designed as per SP 6 (6)	5.0
	Building with shear walls. Building with shear walls also include building having shear walls and frames, but where	
	(*a*) Frames are not designed to carry lateral load or	
	(*b*) Frames are designed to carry lateral loads but do not fulfil the requirements of dual systems.	
5.	*Load bearing masonry wall buildings:*	
	(*a*) Un reinforced.	1.5
	(*b*) Reinforced with horizontal R.C. bands	2.5
	(*c*) Reinforced with horizontal R.C. bands and vertical bars at corners of rooms and jambs of door openings.	3.0

S. No.	*Lateral load resisting system*	*R*
6.	*Ordinary reinforced concrete shear walls*	
	Such shear walls are not allowed in zone IV and V	3.0
7.	*Ductile shear walls*	
	Ductile shear walls are those which are designed and detailed as per IS 13920	4.0
	Buildings with dual systems	
	Building with dual systems consist of shear walls (or braced frames) and moment resisting frames such that	
	(*a*) The two systems are designed to resist total design force in proportion to their lateral stiffness considering the interaction of the dual system at all floor levels and	
	(*b*) the moment resisting frames are designed to resist independently at least 25% of the design seismic base shear.	
8.	Ordinary shear wall with ordinary R.C. moment resisting frames (OMRF)	3.0
9.	Ordinary shear wall with special RC moment resisting frames (SMRF)	4.0
10.	Ductile shear wall with ordinary RC moment resisting frame (OMRF)	4.5
11.	Ductile shear wall with special RC moment resisting frame (SMRF)	5.0

Note. The values of response reduction *R* are to be used for lateral load resisting elements and not just for the lateral load resisting elements built in isolation.

15.10.8. Drift

The maximum lateral displacement of the structure with respect to total height or relative inter storey displacement is known as *drift*. The over all drift index is the ratio of maximum roof displacement to the height of the structure. The inter storey drift is the ratio of maximum difference of lateral displacements at top and bottom of the storey divided by the height of the storey.

Non structural elements and structural non seismic members primarily get damaged due to the drift. Higher the lateral stiffness, lesser is the likely damage. The storey drift in any storey due to minimum specified design lateral force, with partial safety factor of unity shall not exceed 0.004 times the storey height.

Separation between adjacent buildings

Two adjacent buildings or two adjacent units of the same building with separation joint in between shall be separated by a distance equal to R times the sum of calculated storey displacements as specified above of each of them, to avoid damaging contact when the two units deflect towards each other. When the floor levels of two similar adjacent units or buildings are at the same elevation levels, factor R in this case be replaced by *R*/2.

15.10.9. Soft storey

The storey in which the lateral stiffness is less than 70% of the storey just above it or less than 80% of the average lateral stiffness of the three storeys above is known as soft storey or flexible storey. Some authors have suggested above percentages as 60% and 70% respectively.

Usually ground storey having large open space as doors and windows as in garages or for show rooms having large space covered with glass sheets or open all sides or having walls on one or two sides used for parking purposes, is known as a soft storey. To increase the lateral stiffness and strength of such soft storeys special arrangements have to be made.

For such buildings dynamic analysis is carried out including the strength and stiffness effects of infills and inelastic deformations in the members, particularly, those in the soft storey and the members designed accordingly. Alternatively following design criteria should be adopted after carrying out the earthquake analysis, neglecting the effect of infill walls in other storeys.

(*a*) The beams and columns of the soft storey should be designed for 2.5 times the storey shear and moments calculated under seismic loads specified in the other relevant clauses, or

(*b*) Besides the columns designed and detailed for calculated storey shears and moments, the shear walls should be placed symmetrically in both directions of the building as far away from the centre of the building as feasible. These shear walls should be designed exclusively for 1.5 times the lateral storey shear calculated as before.

15.10.10. Foundations

The foundations which are vulnerable to significant differential settlement due to ground shaking should be avoided for structures in seismic zones III, IV, V. In seismic zone IV and V individual spread footing or pile caps should be inter connected with ties, except when individual spread footings are directly supported on rock. All ties should be capable of carrying in tension and incompression, an axial force equal to $A_h/4$ times the larger of the column or pile cap load, in addition to the otherwise computed forces. A_h is the design horizontal spectrum value.

15.10.11. Projections

(*a*) **Vertical projections.** Tower, tanks, parapets, smoke stacks and other vertical cantilever projections attached to the buildings and projecting above the roof, should be designed and checked for stability for five times the design horizontal seismic coefficient A_h. In the analysis of the building, the weight of these projecting elements should be combined with the weight of the roof.

(*b*) **Horizontal projections.** All horizontal projections such as balconcies and cornices should be designed and checked for stability for five times the design vertical coefficient equal to 10/3 A_h. The increased designed forces either for vertical projections or horizontal projections are only for designing the projecting parts and their connection with the main structure. Thus for the design of the main structure the increased forces should not be used.

15.10.12. Redundancy

For good performance during a earthquake, redundancy is a fundamental characteristic. To provide a building with a redundant system is a good practice. If there is no redundancy in a building, the failure of single connection or element may adversely affect the lateral stiffness of the structure. The provision of redundancy thus prevents the damage to the lateral stiffness of the structure on the failure of a single connection of the structure. Yielding at one location in the structure does not mean yielding of the whole structure. The load redistribution in the redundant members provides additional safety margin. Some times the additional margin due to redundancy is taken to be included in the term of over strength itself.

Redundancy can be provided by several means such as dual system. It is a system of inter connecting frames. This system enables redistribution of forces among the frames after the yield has started in individual frames, and multiple shear walls. Redundancy combined with stiffness, strength and continuity may eleminate the need for excess in ductile detailing.

15.11. DESIGN RESPONSE SPECTRUM

The design response spectrum is a smooth response spectrum which specifies the level of seismic resistance required for a design. The requirement of seismic analysis is that the design spectrum be specified. IS 1893 (Part 1)-2002 states clearly that a design acceleration spectrum or base shear coefficient is a function of fundamental period of the structure. These coefficients are the ordinates of the acceleration spectrum divided by acceleration due to gravity 'g'. Thus sa/g is a function of natural or fundamental period T. This relation is shown in Table 15.8. This relation ship works well for single degree of freedom systems. The inertia forces are computed by the spectra ordinates shown in Fig. 15.2. Curves of Fig. 15.2 show a relation between the response acceleration coefficients sa/g and natural period T in seconds for 5% damping for hard or rocky soil, medium, and soft

Table 15.8. Values of response acceleration coefficient corresponding to natural period of vibration T for 5% damping

For Rocky or hard soils sites	*Medium soil sites*	*For soft soil sites*
$\frac{S_a}{g} = \begin{cases} 1+15T 0.00 \le T \le 0.10 \\ 2.5, \quad 0.10 \le T \le 0.40 \\ 1.00/T 0.40 \le T \le 4.00 \end{cases}$	$\frac{S_a}{g} = \begin{cases} 1+15\,T, 0.00 \le T \le 0.10 \\ 2.5, \quad 0.10 \le T \le 0.55 \\ 1.36/T, 0.55 \le T \le 4.00 \end{cases}$	$\frac{S_a}{g} = \begin{cases} 1+15\,T, 0.00 \le T \le 0.10 \\ 2.5, \quad 0.10 \le T \le 0.67 \\ 1.67/T, 0.67 \le T \le 4.0 \end{cases}$

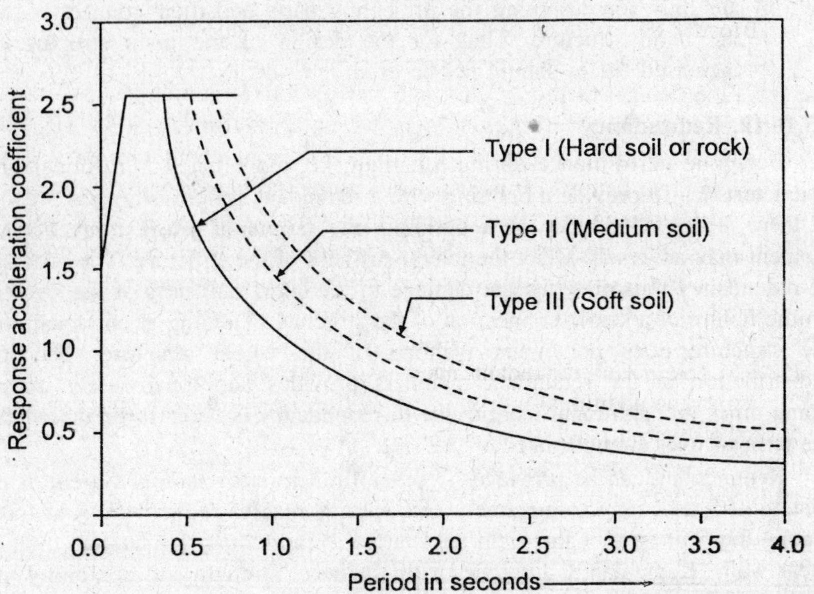

Fig. 15.2. Design response spectrum for rock and soils for 5% damping

soils. The value of spectra for other than 5% damping can be obtained by multiplying the factor given in Table 15.9. Note that (multiplication should not be done for zero period accelerations). The design spectrum ordinates are independent of the amount of damping (multiplication factor of 1.0) and their variation from one material or one structural solution to another.

Table 15.9. Multiplying factor for obtaining spectral values for damping other the 5% damping

Damping %	0	2	5	7	10	15	20	25	30
Multiplying factor	3.2	1.4	1.00	0.90	0.80	0.70	0.60	0.55	0.50

15.12. SEISMIC BASE SHEAR

The design seismic base shear (V_B) along any principal direction or total design lateral force is determined by the relation.

$$V_B = A_h \times W \qquad \text{...(15.2)}$$

where, A_h is the design horizontal acceleration spectrum value, using the natural period T.

$$A_h = \frac{z}{2} \times \frac{I}{R} \times \frac{S_a}{g} \qquad \text{...(15.3)}$$

15.13. METHOD OF ANALYSIS

Broadly the methods of analysis are classified as:

1. Static method. It is also known as equivalent static method or seismic coefficient method. This method is quite simple. It requires less computational efforts. It is based on formulae given in the code of practice. In the design, first base shear is computed for the whole structure and then it is distributed along the height of the structure. Thus the lateral forces at each floor level are obtained and then distributed to individual lateral load resisting member or element. This procedure does not need dynamic analysis.
2. Dynamic method.

15.13.1. Seismic coefficient method

This method is based on static approach normally referred as pseudo static approach using the seismic coefficients.

15.13.1.1. Assumptions made in the method

Following two assumptions have been made in this approach:

(*a*) The fundamental mode of the building is the major contributing factor to the base shear V_B.

(*b*) The total building mass is used in this method where as model mass is used in dynamic method.

The base shear or total design lateral force is determined by the relation

$V_B = A_h \times W$ above equation (15.2)

where A_h = Design horizontal spectrum value using fundamental natural period in the considered direction of vibration.

i.e. $$A_h = \frac{Z}{2} \times \frac{1}{R} \times \frac{S_a}{g} \quad \text{as eqaution ...(15.3)}$$

where,

Z = Zone factor as shown in table 15.5

I = Importance factor table 15.6

R = Response reduction factor table 15.7

Sa/g = Average acceleration response coefficient for approximate natural period of vibration 'T' as shown in Table 15.8.

W = Seismic weight of the building (section 15.10.2)

This method of seismic coefficient does not need the theoretical concept of structural dynamics and model analysis.

15.13.1.2. Vertical distribution of base shear to different floor levels

The design base shear V_B is distributed along the height of the building as given by the following equation.

$$Q_i = V_B \frac{W_i h_i^2}{\sum_{j=1}^{n} W_i h_j^2} \qquad \text{...(15.4)}$$

where,

Q_i = Design lateral force at floor i

W_i = Seismic weight of floor i

h_i = Height of floor measured from the base

n = Number of levels (No. of storeys) at which the masses are located.

15.13.1.3. Fundamental Natural Period 'T'

The approximate fundamental or Natural period of vibration T in seconds for different type of buildings is given as follows:

(*a*) For moment resisting R.C. frame buildings

$$T = 0.075\, h^{0.75} \qquad \text{...(15.5)}$$

(*b*) For moment resisting steel frame buildings

$$T = 0.085\, h^{0.75} \qquad \text{...(15.6)}$$

where h is the height of the building in metres in both cases.

(*c*) For all other buildings including moment resisting frame building with brick in fill panels. The value of fundamental natural period of vibration T in seconds is given by

$$T = 0.09 \frac{h}{\sqrt{d}} \qquad \text{...(15.7)}$$

where,

h = Height of building in m

d = Base dimension of the building at plinth level in metres along the considered direction of the lateral force *i.e.* perpendicular to the direction of seismic force.

15.13.2. Dynamic method

The dynamic analysis is carried by the time history method or response spectrum method.

15.13.2.1. Response spectrum

Response spectrum of any earthquake ground motion is a plot of maximum values of response quantities (displacement, velocity and acceleration) as a function of natural vibration period T or frequency and damping ratio of single degree freedom system (SDOF).

During the ground motion a structure subjected to the maximum stiffness force depends on the maximum displacement response. The maximum displacement is known or called as spectral displacement S_d of the structure. This corresponds to the condition of zero kinetic energy and maximum strain (potential) energy.

The maximum strain (potential) energy

$$E_{max} = \frac{1}{2} K (S_d)^2 \qquad \text{...(15.8)}$$

The maximum velocity response is estimated by multiplying the spectral displacement S_d by circular frequency 'ω'.

$$\therefore \text{ The maximum kinetic energy } E_{max} = \frac{1}{2} m v^2$$

$$= \frac{1}{2} m (\omega S_d)^2 = \frac{1}{2} m S_{pv}^2 \qquad \text{...(15.9)}$$

Equating the strain energy to kinetic energy we get

$$E_{max} = \frac{1}{2} K (S_d)^2 = \frac{1}{2} m (\omega S_d)^2$$

$$= \frac{1}{2} m S_{pv}^2 \qquad \text{...(15.10)}$$

where, $S_{pv} = \omega S_d$ is called Pseudo (artificial) spectral velocity. A plot of S_{pv} with respect to time or ω is called Pseudo velocity response spectrum.

The maximum base shear in single degree of freedom system can be obtained as

$$(Q)_{max} = K \cdot S_d = m\,\omega^2 S_d \text{ (As } K = m\,\omega^2)$$

$$= m (\omega^2 \cdot S_d) = \omega\, S_{pv} \quad \text{is called Pseudo spectral acceleration.}$$

The Pseudo spectrum acceleration has the units of acceleration which when multiplied with the mass gives max base shear.

The spectral values of S_d, S_{pv} and S_{pa} are related as

$$S_{pa} = \omega^2 S_d = \omega (\omega \cdot S_d)$$

$$= \omega\, S_{pv} = \frac{2\pi}{T} \cdot S_{pv} = \left(\frac{2\,\pi}{T}\right)^2 S_d$$

Normally they are plotted on a single graph with log scale on each axis, and called tripartite log plot. The response spectra for a single earthquake record is used for analysis, but they are not suitable for the purpose of design. They are not found suitable for design purposes, because in design response spectra, information regarding the effect of near and distant earthquake is required, which they do not provide. They also do not account for the inherent variability of earthquake motion with respect to both frequency and amplitude at a given station.

15.13.2.2. Response spectrum method

In this method, the maximum model response is estimated for each mode, using response spectrum. The number of modes to be combined in the analysis are such that the sum total of all modes considered is at least 90% of total seismic mass.

Mode shapes

Mode shapes are the displacement shapes of an vibrating system corresponding to the natural frequencies.

Under the undamped free vibrations, multi mode of freedom buildings having N degree of freedom will vibrate in N modes of vibrations. The equation of multi-degree undamped free vibration system can be written as

$$m\ddot{x} + Kx = 0 \qquad \text{...(15.12)}$$

As the mass is assumed to execute the simple harmonic motion. The solution of the equation may be assumed as.

$$x = \phi_n \sin \omega_n t \qquad \text{...(15.13)}$$

then differentiating equation (15.13) w.r.t. twice we get

$$\frac{\delta^2 x}{\delta t^2} = \ddot{x} = -\phi_n \omega_n^2 \sin \omega_n t \qquad \text{...(15.14)}$$

where, ϕ_n represent displaced shapes of vibrating system (*i.e.* mode shapes) which do not change with time 't' but vary only with amplitude. ω_n is circular frequency.

Substituting the value of $\ddot{x}$ in equation (15.12) we get.

$$m(-\phi_n \omega_n^2 \sin \omega_n t) + K\phi_n \sin \omega_n t = 0 \qquad \text{...(15.15)}$$

or $\quad (K - \omega_n^2 m)\phi_n \sin \omega_n t = 0$

If $\quad \sin \omega_n t = 0$

Then $\quad [K\phi_n] = [\omega_n^2 m \cdot \phi_n]$

$\sin \omega_n t$ can not be zero, as in that case x will be zero, which means that there is no motion .

$\therefore \quad (K - \omega_n^2 m)\phi_n = 0$

or $\quad K\phi_n = m\omega_n^2 \phi_n$

Again ϕ_n can not be zero as it leads to trivial (un important) solution implying that $x = 0$.

For more equations or non trivial solution, the determinant of coefficient of x should be zero *i.e.*

$$|K - m\omega_n^2| = 0 \qquad \text{...(15.16)}$$

Equation 15.16 is known as characteristic equation.

The solution of this characteristic equation will give N roots, representing the frequencies of N modes of vibrations.

15.13.3. Time History analysis

It is an analysis of the dynamic response of the structure at each increment of time, when its base is subjected to a specific ground motion. This means that this needs the studies of ground motion of the specific site. However in majority of the cases the time history method is not required.

15.13.4. Selection of the method

In dynamic analysis either time history method or response spectrum method shall be used for the following types of buildings.

(*a*) **Regular buildings.** Buildings having height greater than 40 m in zone IV and V and buildings having height more than 90 m in zone II and III.

(*b*) **Irregular buildings.** All buildings having height more than 12 m in zone IV and V and more than 40 m height in zone II and III, though dynamic analysis is not mandatory, but recommended.

Thus in general the dynamic analysis should be performed for buildings in zone IV and V. For buildings in zone II and III having height less than 40 m seismic coefficient method should be used which is simple to use.

Example 1. A six storeyed R.C. framed building has plan dimensions as shown in Fig. 15.3 (*b*). The size of the exterior columns (7 each on line A and C) are 30 cm × 50 cm and the interior columns (7 on line B) are 30 cm × 60 cm for the bottom three floors and 30 cm × 40 cm and 30 cm × 50 cm respectively for the upper three floors. The height between the floors (storey) is 3.5 m. The dead load per unit area of the floor which consists of floor slab, beam, half of the weight of column above and below the floor, partition walls etc. is assumed to be of intensity 5000 N/m^2. The intensity of normal live load is assumed as 2500 N/m^2. The soil below the foundation is hard. The building is located in seismic zone IV.

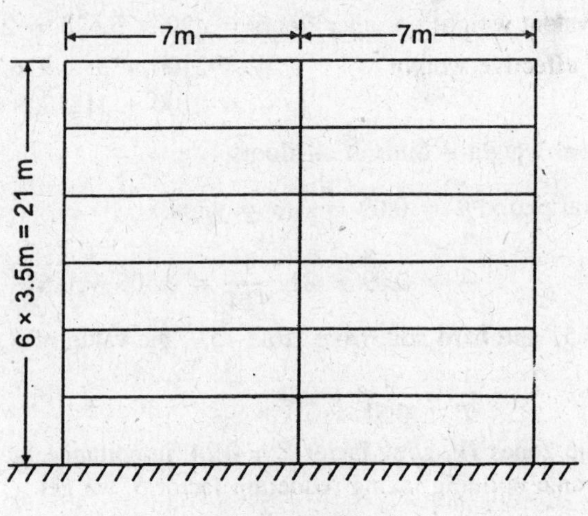

ELEVATION
Fig. 15.3. (*a*)

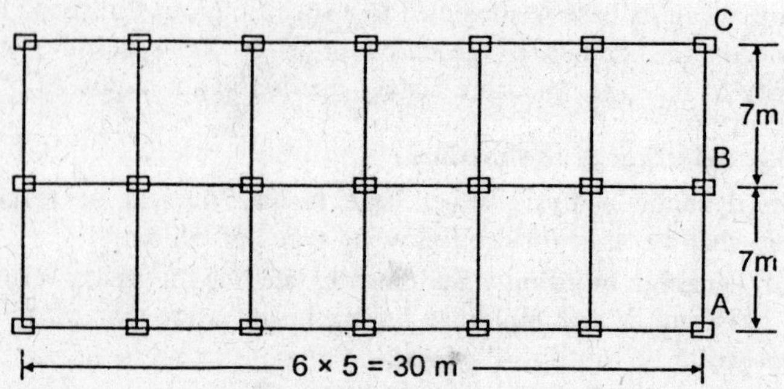

PLAN

Fig. 15.3. (*b*)

Determine the base shear and its distribution along the height of the building.

Solution. The elevation and plan of the building is shown in Fig. 15.3 (*a*) and (*b*).

Equivalent lumped weight at various floors:

For calculating earthquake forces the design live load is taken 25% of the given load as per Table 15.3 No live load will be considered acting on the roof.

Hence effective weight at all floors except roof = 5000 + 0.25 × 2500

$$= 5000 + 625.0 = 5625 \text{ N/m}^2 = 5.625 \text{ kN/m}^2$$

Weight at roof= $5000 \text{ N/m}^2 = 5.0 \text{ kN/m}^2$

The plan area of the building $= 14 \times 30 = 420 \text{ m}^2$

∴ Equivalent weight on roof level $= 420 \times 5 = 2100$ kN

Equivalent weight on other floors $= 420 \times 5.625 = 2362.5$ kN

∴ Total effective weight $W = 2100 + 5 \times 2362.5$

$$= 2100 + 11812.5 = 13912.5$$

(*i.e.* Roof weight + Sum of all floors.)

(*i*) Natural period $T = 0.09 \dfrac{h}{\sqrt{d}}$ (d = width)

$$= 0.09 \times 21 \frac{1}{\sqrt{14}} = 0.505 \approx 0.51$$

For $T = 0.51$ and hard soil, from table 15.7, the value of S_a/g for

$$\frac{1}{T} = \frac{1}{0.51} \approx 2.0$$

For seismic zones *IV*, zone factor $Z = 0.24$, importance factor $I = 1.0$ and for concrete frame building taking reduction factor 5, we get

$$A_h = \frac{Z}{2} \times \frac{I}{R} \times \frac{S_a}{g}$$

$$= \frac{0.24}{2} \times \frac{1}{5} \times 2.0$$

$$= \frac{0.24}{5} = 0.05$$

$\therefore$ Design base shear along x-axis $= A_h \times W$

$$= 0.05 \times 13912.5 = 695.63 \approx 696.0$$

The lateral load at different floors can be determined by the following relation.

$$Q_i = \frac{V_B \times w_i \times h_i^2}{\sum_{i=1}^{n} w_i \times h_1^2}$$

where,

w_i = Weight working at level i

h_i = Height of the floor from the base

V_B = Base shear

i = 1, indicates the height at 1st floor level.

The calculations are shown in the tabular form as below in Table 15.10.

Table 15.10.

Mass No.	W_i *kN*	h_i *in m*	$w_i h_i^2$ *in kN/m*^{2}	$\frac{w_i h_i^2}{\sum_{i=1}^{n} w_i h_i^2}$	Q_i in kN $V_B \times$ *Col. 5*	$V_i = kN$, *sum of col. 6 from top*
1	2	3	4	5	6	7
6.	2100.00	21.0	926100.0	0.3700	257.5	257.5
5.	2362.50	17.5	723515.6	0.2895	201.9	459.4
4.	2362.50	14.0	463050.0	0.1853	129.0	588.4
3.	2362.50	10.5	260465.6	0.1031	71.77	660.17
2.	2362.50	7.0	115762.5	0.0441	30.7	690.87
1.	2362.50	3.5	29531.25	0.0118	8.2	698.87
	Σw_i = 1392.5		$\Sigma w_i h_i^2$ = 2498425.0			

Note. Calculation by log. Difference due to approximation in values.

Example 2. The plan and elevation of a five storey building are shown in Fig. 15.4. Determine the base shear and its distribution along the height with the following given data.

Given data.

Thickness of slab = 13.0 cm

Load due to roof finish = 2 kN/m^2

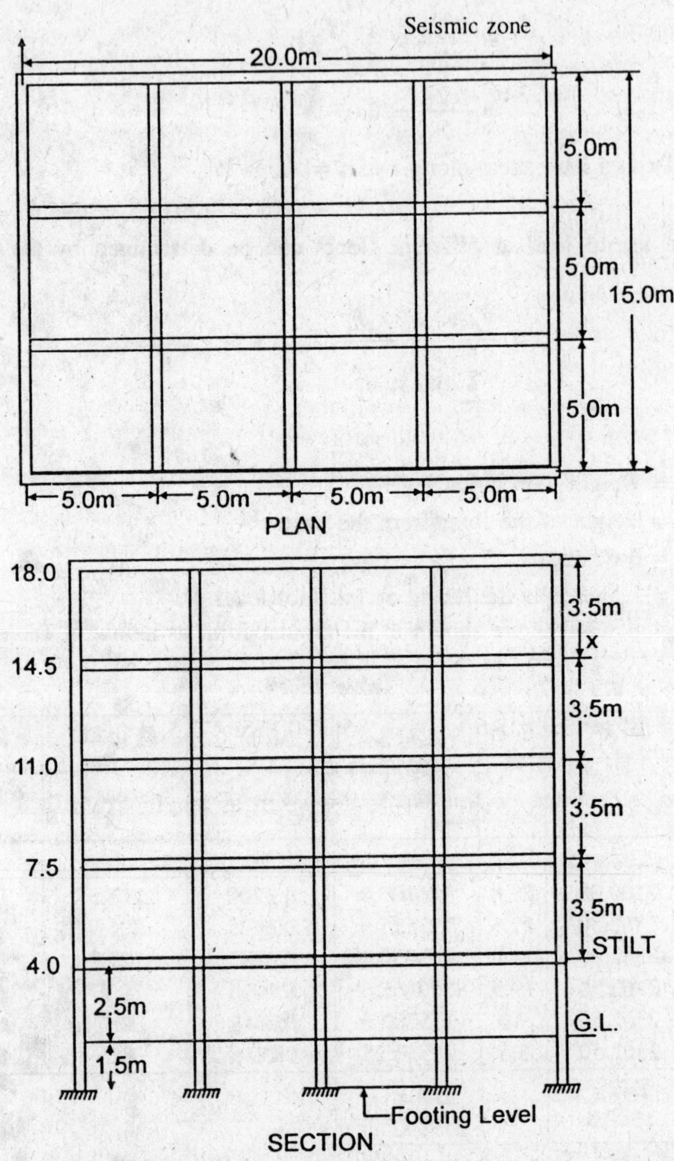

Fig. 15.4.

Load due to floor finish = 1 kN/m^2
Thickness of outer walls with plaster = 30.0 cm
Thickness of inner walls with plaster = 17.5 cm
Density of brick masonry = 20 kN/m^3
Density of concrete = 25 kN/m^3

Imposed load on the structure = 4 kN/m^2
Size of columns at ground level = 30 cm × 40 cm
Type of foundation = Isolated footing
Soil condition under foundation = Hard murum soil available at a depth of 1.5 m from the ground level
Seismic zone = IV

Solution.

Seismic weight

(*i*) Total floor area = 20 × 15 = 300 m^2.

(*ii*) No imposed load to be lumped at roof

The roof load consists of self weight or dead weight of slab + 50% weight due to the weight of wall below the storey.

Weight of wall at each floor level = Total length of outer walls × thickness of wall × storey height × unit weight of masonry

Plus total length of inner walls × thickness × storey height × unit weight of masonry

$= 2\,(20 + 15) \times 0.3 \times 3.5 \times 20 + (2 \times 20 + 3 \times 15) \times 0.175 \times 3.5 \times 20$

$= 70 \times 0.3 \times 3.5 \times 20 + 85 \times 0.175 \times 3.5 \times 20$

$= 1470 + 1041.25 = 2511.25$ kN

Note. The self weight of columns is not taken as length of the wall is taken equal to centre length. The difference in unit weights of concrete and masonry is neglected due to ease in calculations.

Roof load W_4= (Self weight of slab + Finish load) × Area × Half wall load

$$= [0.13 \times 25 + 2.0] \times 300 + \frac{2511.25}{2}$$

$$= (3.25 + 2) \times 300 + \frac{2511.25}{2}$$

$$= 1575.0 + 1255.62 = 2830.62 \text{ kN}$$

At floor level only 50% of the imposed load will be taken into calculation as per table 15.3 as given load is 4 kN.

∴ Floor loads = (Self weight of slab + Finishing load + 50% imposed load) × Area

$= (0.13 \times 25 + 1.0 + 4.0 \times 0.5) \times 300$

$= (3.25 + 1.0 + 2.0) \times 300 = 6.25 \times 300 = 1875.0$ kN

Wall load = 2511.25 kN

∴ The estimated load at floor W_3, W_2, and W_1 = 1875 + 2511.25
= 4386.25 kN

Load at plinth level W_0 = Half wall load + floor load
+ 45 cm masonry and 23 cm concrete weight

$$= \frac{2511.25}{2} + 1875 + (0.23 \times 25 + 0.45 \times 20) \times \frac{4}{2}$$

$$= 1256.62 + 1875 + 29.5 = 3161.26 \text{ kN}$$

∴ Total seismic weight $W = \Sigma w_i$
= Weight at roof + weight at the three floors
+ weight at plinth level
= 2830.62 + (4386.25 × 3) + 3161.62
= 2830.62 + 13158.75 + 31.61.62
= 19151.0

Fundamental natural period $T = 0.09 \dfrac{h}{\sqrt{d}}$

Here as per given data h = 18.0 m
Length of the building along x axis = 20 m

∴ $$T = 0.09 \times \frac{18}{\sqrt{20}} = \frac{1.62}{4.52} = 0.362$$

∴ From table 15.7, for T = 0.362 the value of S_a/g = 2.5

∴ Design horizontal seismic coefficient

$$A_h = \frac{Z}{2} \times \frac{I}{R} \times \frac{S_a}{g} = \frac{0.24}{2} \times \frac{1}{5} \times 2.5$$

$$= 0.12 \times 0.5 = 0.060$$

∴ $A_h = 0.06$

∴ Design seismic base shear along x axis = 0.06 × 19151.0
= 1149.06 = 1149.06 kN

The base shear is distributed along the height as shown in Table 15.11 below.

Table 15.11.

Storey level	*Weight at different level w_i kN*	*Height at different levels h_i in m*	*$w_i \times h_i^2$ in kN*	$\dfrac{w_i h_i^2}{\Sigma w_i h_i^2}$	*Lateral force at ith level*	*Base shear sum of col (6)*
(1)	(2)	(3)	(4)	(5)	(6)	(7)
4	2830.62	18.0	91720.0	0.3382	388.7	388.7
3	4386.25	14.50	922600.0	0.3401	390.8	779.5

Storey level	*Weight at different level w_i kN*	*Height at different levels h_i in m*	*$w_i \times h_i^2$ in kN*	*$\frac{w_i h_i^2}{\Sigma w_i h_i^2}$*	*Lateral force at ith level*	*Base shear sum of col (6)*
(1)	(2)	(3)	(4)	(5)	(6)	(7)
2	4386.25	11.0	530900.0	0.1958	225.0	1004.5
1	4386.25	7.5	290600.0	0.1071	123.2	1127.7
Stilt	3161.12	4.0	05046.0	0.0186	21.4	1149.1

(*ii*) Earthquake load in *y* direction

$$\text{Natural period } T = \frac{0.09 \times 18}{\sqrt{15}} = \frac{1.62}{3.873} \approx 0.42$$

$$\frac{S_a}{g} = \frac{1}{0.42} \approx 2.4$$

Which is very near to 2.5.

Hence the value of A_h remains the same as other factors such *Z*, *I* and *R* the same.

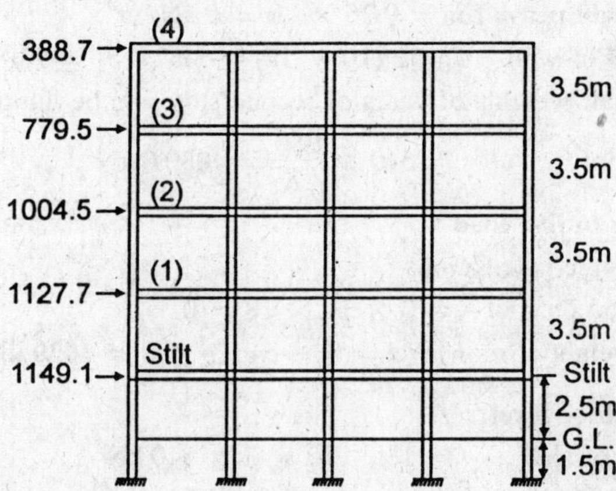

Fig. 15.5. Design seismic force on a building in *x* direction

Hence design seismic force remains same in both direction as shown in Fig. 15.5.

Example 3. A two storeyed building is to be constructed on a 10 m wide and 18 m deep plot. Determine the lateral seismic loads on the building with given data. The height of each storey of the building is 3.5 m.

Data

Thickness of floor and roof slab = 12.0 cm

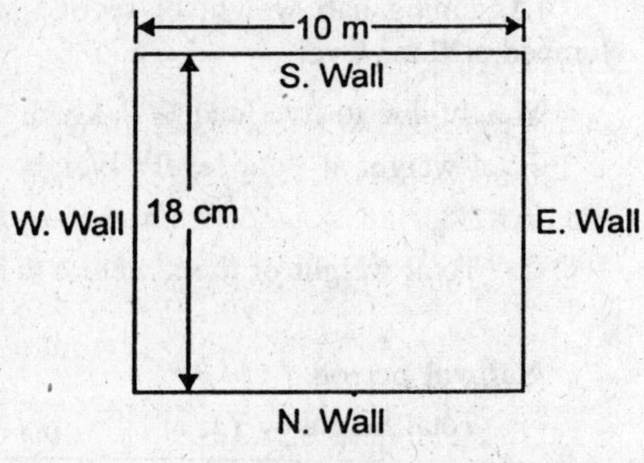

Fig. 15.6.

Thickness of walls = 15 cm
Density of concrete = 25 kN/m^3
Density of masonry = 20 kN/m^3

Live loads

Live load on roof = 0 (for seismic calculation = 0)
Live load on floors = 1 kN/m^2
Seismic zone = V
Zone factor Z = 0.36
Importance factor I = 1.0
Reduction factor R = 3.0

The foundation soil is medium hard.

Solution. Seismic weight calculations

Areas of roof $= 10 \times 18 = 180 \text{ m}^2$

Weight of roof $= (0.12 \times 25 \times 10 \times 18) = 540 \text{ kN}$

Weight of wall per m run $= 0.25 \times 20 = 5 \text{ kN/m}^2$

Total weight of wall $= [2\,(10 + 18) \times 3.5 \times 5] = 980 \text{ kN}$

Assuming half weights of walls of second storey to be lumped at roof.

Weight at roof $= 540 + \dfrac{980}{2} = 1030.0 \text{ kN}$

Weight due to live load

For seismic calculations

Live load on roof $= 0 \times 10 \times 18 = 0$

$\therefore$ Total weight at roof level $= 0 + 540 + 490 = \mathbf{1030\ kN}$

Weight at floor level

Weight of slab $= 18 \times 10 \times 3 = 540 \text{ kN}$

Weight of walls $= 2 \times \dfrac{1}{2}\,[2\,(10 + 18)\,3.5 \times 5] = 980 \text{ kN}$

(Assuming half weight of second storey and half weight of lower storey lumped at floor level.

Weight due to live load @ 1 kN/m^2 $= 1 \times 10 \times 18 = 180 \text{ kN}$

Total weight at floor level= Weight of floor + weight of walls + Live load

$= 540 + 980 + 180 = 1700.0 \text{ kN}$

$\therefore$ Total weight of the structure = Weight of roof + all floors

$= 1030 + 1700 = 2730 \text{ kN}$

Natural period T

Total height = 7.0 m

d = 10 m

$$\therefore \quad T = \frac{0.09 \times 7}{\sqrt{10}} = \frac{0.63}{3.162} \approx 0.2$$

From table 15.8, $\frac{S_a}{g} = 2.5$ as soil is medium hard type.

$\therefore$ Seismic horizontal design coefficient $A_h = \frac{Z}{2} \cdot \frac{I}{R} \times \frac{S_a}{g}$

$$= \frac{0.36}{2} \times \frac{1}{3} \times 2.5 = 0.15$$

$\therefore$ Base shear along x axis $= 0.15 \times 2730 = 409.50 = 409.5$

The base shear distribution along the height is shown in Table 15.12 below.

Table 15.12. $V_b = 409.5$

Storey level	*Weight at different level w_i kN*	*Height at different levels h_i in m*	*$w_i \times h_i^2$ in kN*	*$\frac{w_i h_i^2}{\Sigma w_i h_i^2}$*	*Lateral force at ith level $V_B \times$ col 5*	*Vid. each level*
(1)	(2)	(3)	(4)	(5)	(6)	(7)
2	1030	7.0	50470.0	0.7106	290.75	290.75
1	1700	3.5	20830.0	0.2934	118.75	409.50
	$\Sigma w_i =$ 2730		71300.0			

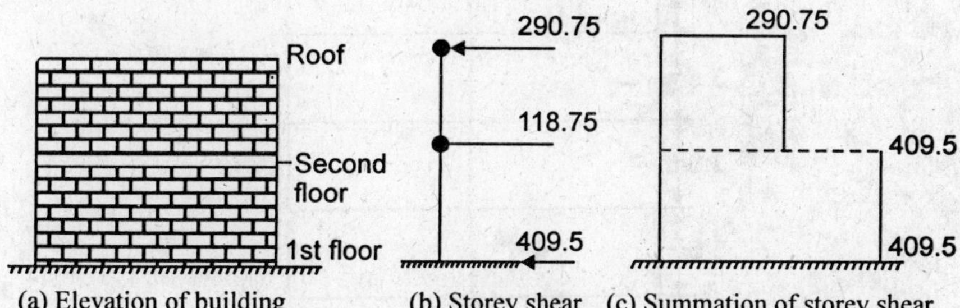

(a) Elevation of building (b) Storey shear (c) Summation of storey shear

Fig. 15.7.

Example 4. A six storey building on a 20 m × 20 m plot is to be constructed in Shimla. The plan and elevation of the building are shown in Fig. 15.8. The height of each storey is 3.5 m. The construction is of ordinary shear walls with special moment resisting frame (SMRF). The loads may be assumed as given below. Determine the seismic forces and shear at different levels.

(*i*) The dead load per unit area of the floor consisting of the floor slab and finishing etc. may be taken as 4 kN/m^2.

(*ii*) Weight of partitions on the floor can be taken as 2 kN/m^2

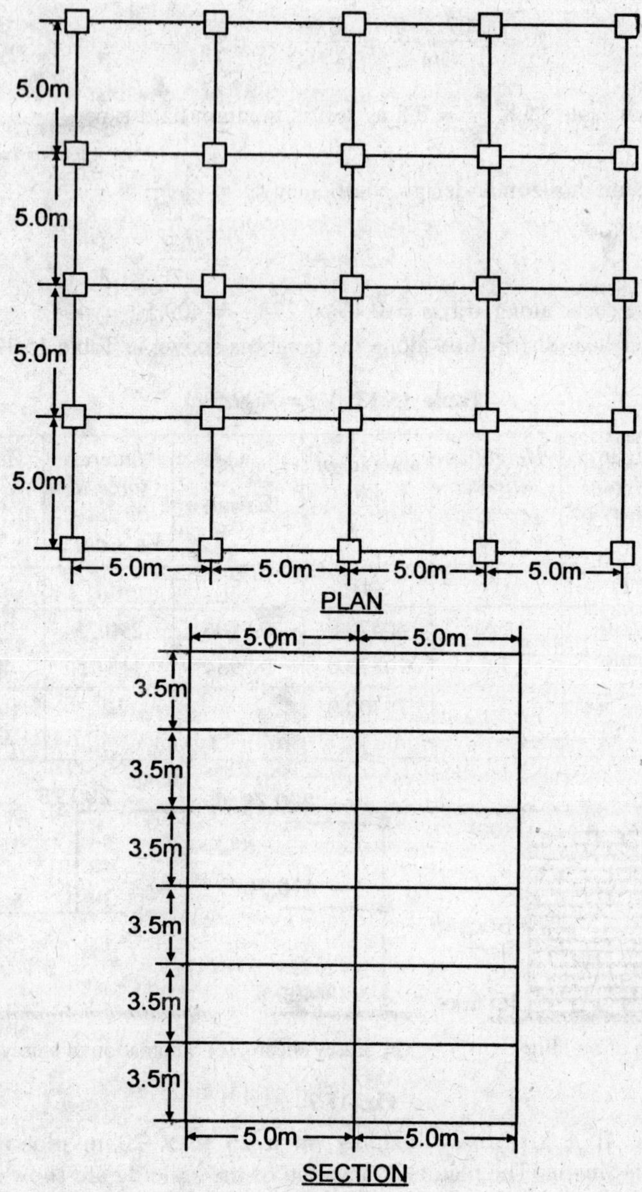

Fig. 15.8.

(*iii*) The intensity of live load on each floor is 3 kN/m^2

(*iv*) The intensity of live load on the roof is 1.5 kN/m^2

The soil below the foundation is hard. The size of beams and columns may be assumed as 30 cm × 60 cm.

Solution. The design parameters are as follows:

The construction area is Shimla, which comes under zone V. Hence zone factor $Z = 0.36$

The importance factor $I = 1.0$

The reduction factor $R = 4.0$

Seismic weights

(*i*) Floor area $= 20 \times 20 = 400 \text{ m}^2$

(*ii*) Dead load given $= 4 \text{ kN/m}^2$

(*iii*) The weight of partition walls $= 2 \text{ kN/m}^2$

(*iv*) Intensity of live load on floor $= 1.5 \text{ kN/m}^2$

(*v*) Live load $= 3 \text{ kN/m}^2$

From Table 15.3, for live load upto and including 3 kN/m^2, only 25% of the live load is considered.

$\therefore$ Total seismic weight on the floors $W = \Sigma w_i$,

where Σw_i is sum of loads from all floors, which include dead loads and appropriate percentage of live loads.

Effective weight at each floor except roof

$$= \text{dead weight} + \text{self weight and finishing weight} + 25\% \text{ live load}$$

$$= 4.0 + 2.0 + 0.25 \times 3 = 6.75 \text{ kN/m}^2$$

Effective weight at roof $= 4.0 \text{ kN/m}^2$

Weight of beam at each floor and roof

$$= 0.3 \times 0.6 \times 25 \times 20 \times 10 = 900 \text{ kN}$$

Weight of column at each floor of 5 columns

$$= 0.3 \times 0.6 \times (3.5 - 0.6) \times 25 \times 25$$

$$= 0.18 \times 2.9 \times 25 \times 25 = 325.25 \text{ kN}$$

Note. The effective height of column = column height – beam depth

$$= (3.5 - 0.6) = 2.9 \text{ m}$$

Weight of columns at the roof = Half the weight of columns

$$= \frac{325.25}{2} = 162.625$$

Equivalent load at roof level $= 4 \times 400 + 900.0 + 162.625$

$$= 1600 + 900 + 162.625 = 2662.625 \text{ kN}$$

Equivalent load at each floor $= 6.75 \times 400 + 900 + 325.25$

$$= 2700 + 900 + 325.25 = 3925.25$$

$\therefore$ Seismic weight of structure = Weight of roof + weight of all floors

$$= 2662.625 + 5 \times 3925.25$$

$$= 2662.625 + 19626.25 = 22288.875$$

$$\approx 22289.0$$

Base shear

Fundamental period of vibration of a moment resisting frame with out in fill

$$T = 0.075\, H^{0.75} = 0.075 \times (21)^{0.75}$$

(As building of 6 storey of 3.5 m height of each storey)

$$= 0.075\ [0.75 \times \log_{10} 21]$$

$$= 0.075\ [0.75\ (1.3222)]$$

$$0.075\ [0.9917] = 0.075 \times 9.81 \quad \text{(Anti log of 0.9917)}$$

$$T = 0.736$$

From Table 15.7, value of $\frac{S_a}{g} = \frac{1.67}{T} = \frac{1.67}{0.736} = 2.27$ sec.

$\therefore$ Design seismic coefficient $A_h = \frac{Z}{2} \times \frac{I}{R} \times \frac{S_a}{g}$

$$= \frac{0.36}{2} \times \frac{1}{4} \times 2.27 = 0.102$$

$\therefore$ Base shear $= A_h \times W = 0.102 \times 22289.0$

$$= 2272.0 \text{ kN}$$

Table 15.13. $V_B = 2272.0$

S. No.	*Weight w_i kN*	*Height h_i in m*	*$w_i \times h_i^2$ in kN m^2*	$\frac{w_i h_i^2}{\Sigma w_i h_i^2}$	*$Q_i = V_B \times$ col. 5*	*V_i sum of col (6) down words ↓*
(1)	(2)	(3)	(4)	(5)	(6)	(7)
6.	21	2663.0	1175.0×10^3	0.3073	699.0	699.0
5.	17.5	3925.0	1202×10^3	0.3148	715.3	1414.3
4.	14.0	3925.0	769.1×10^3	0.2014	457.6	1871.9
3.	10.5	3925.0	432.7×10^3	0.1133	257.5	2128.4
2.	7.0	3925.0	192.3×10^3	0.0536	114.4	2242.8
1.	3.5	3925.0	48.09×10^3	0.0126	28.6	2271.4
			$\Sigma w_i h_i^2 = 3819.2 \times 10^3$			≈ 2272.0

15.14. TORSION

For the seismic resistant designs all Indian codes have assumed that the building is symmetrical in plan and the centre of gravity of the mass and the centre of rigidity of the building are nearly coincident.

The centre of rigidity is the geometric centre of stiffnesses of the various

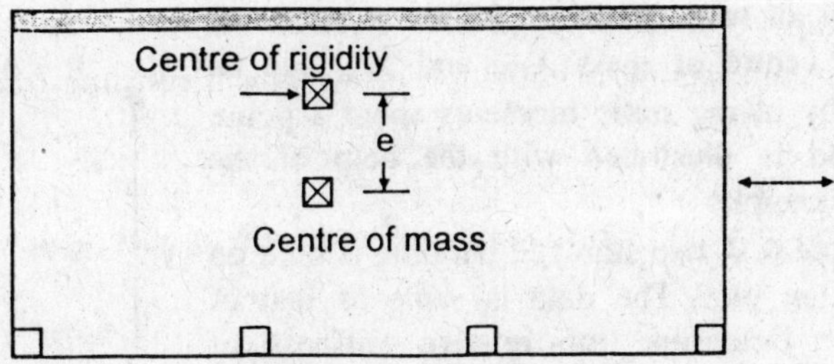

Fig. 15.9. Ecentricity causing torsional vibrations

elements. Consider the plan of a floor shown in Fig. 15.9. The one edge of the floor rests on wall and the other on the columns as shown in the Fig. 15.9.

The wall is stiffer than columns, hence for vibration in the direction parallel to the wall, the centre of rigidity will be nearer to the wall as it is stiffer than columns.

If the mass is contributed predominatly by the floor, then the mass of the floor will be close to the centre of the floor. The distance '*e*' between the centre of mass and centre of rigidity is known as eccentricity, which causes torsion in the building.

Where a building is considerably unsymmetrical, it is essential to investigate the torsional forces properly. Similar situation may arise when buildings of different rigidities are connected rigidly with each other.

In simple cases, the effect of torsional oscillations can be determined. It is difficult to evaluate torsional stresses in buildings statically, even due to torques applied. The dynamic problem is much more complicated due to coupling between translational and torsional oscillations.

The IS code suggests an adhoc provision of an increase in shear resulting from horizontal torsion due to an eccentricity between the centre of mass and centre of rigidity. Negative shears are neglected. The design eccentricity is taken as 1.5 times the computed eccentricity between the centre of mass and centre of rigidity. The method of computation is illustrated by the following examples.

15.14.1. Determinations of torsional forces

For determining the shear forces due to torsion, first the determination of locations of centre of mass and centre of rigidity is essential. The difference between the centre of mass and centre of rigidity is called eccentricity, usually denoted by ***e***.

Thus the moment of rigidity or torsional moment

$$M_T = \text{Base shear} \times \text{Ecentricity}$$

$$= V_B \times e \quad \text{...(15.17)}$$

15.14.2. Location of centre of mass

Though for symmetrical structure, the centre of mass is the same as centre of gravity of the structure. The method of calculating centre of mass $\overline{X}_{CM}$ and $\overline{Y}_{CM}$ can be determine by taking static moments about a point. The method is illustrated with the help of the following example.

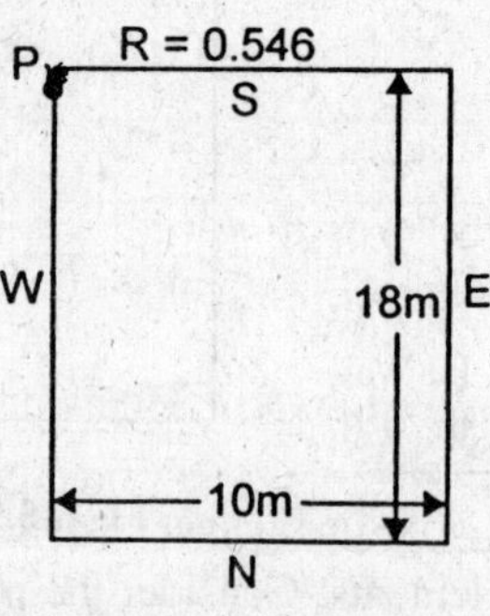

Fig. 15.10.

Example 6. A two storeyed building is built on a 10 × 18 m plot. The data is same as that of example 3. Determine the relative stiffness of walls. Also determine the direct and torsional stresses. The relative rigidity of the walls may be assumed as rigidity for north wall as 0.454 and rigidity for south wall as 0.546.

Solution.

The centre of mass X_{CM} and $\overline{Y}_{CM}$ is estimated by taking moment at a point say at *P* in this case. Point *P* is situated at the corner of south and west wall. The respective weights are used as forces in the summation of moment. The calculations are shown in tabular form in Table 15.14.

Table 15.14. For calculations of centre of mass

Item	*Weight i (kN)*	*X (m)*	*Y (m)*	*w.x (kN-n)*	*w.y (kN-m)*
Roof	$10 \times 18 \times 3 = 540$	5.0	9.0	2700	4860
North wall	$10 \times 3.5 \times 5 = 175$	5.0	18	875	3150
South wall	$10 \times 3.5 \times 5 = 175$	5.0	0	875	0
Eastern wall	$18 \times 3.5 \times 5 = 315$	10.0	9.0	3150	2835
Western wall	$18 \times 3.5 \times 5 = 315$	0	9.0	0	2835
	$\Sigma w = 1520.0$			$\Sigma wx =$ 7600.0	$\Sigma wy =$ 13680.0

$$\therefore \quad \overline{X}_{cm} = \frac{\Sigma w.x}{\Sigma w} = \frac{7600}{1520} = 5.0$$

$$\overline{Y}_{cm} = \frac{\Sigma w.y}{\Sigma w} = \frac{13680}{1520} = 9.0$$

Thus the centre of mass of building will be at the centre of the plan of the building.

15.14.3. Location of centre of rigidity

The centre of rigidity $\overline{X}_{CR}$ and $\overline{Y}_{CR}$ is calculated by taking static moments about a point say at *P*, the corner of south and western wall, using relative stiffnesses of the walls as forces in the summation of moment. In the determination of centre of rigidity, the rigidity of roof is not considered. The calculations are shown in Table 15.15 below.

Table 15.15. Calculations for centre of rigidity

Item	R_x	R_y	$X(m)$	$Y(m)$	$Y R_x$	$X R_y$
N Wall	0.454	—	—	18	8.172	—
S. Wall	0.546	—	—	0	0	—
E. Wall	—	0.5	10	—	—	5.0
W. wall	—	0.5	0	—	—	0
	$\Sigma R_x = 1.0$	$\Sigma R_y = 1.0$			$\Sigma y\, R_x = 1.0$	$\Sigma X R_x = 1.0$

$$\therefore \quad \overline{X}_{CR} = \frac{\Sigma x\, R_y}{\Sigma\, R_y} = \frac{5.0}{1.0} = 5.0 \text{ from W. wall}$$

$$\overline{Y}_{CR} = \frac{\Sigma\, y.R_x}{\Sigma\, R_x} = \frac{8.172}{1.0} = 8.172 \text{ from S. wall}$$

15.14.4. Torsional Eccentricity

Torsional eccentricity in y direction.

Eccentricity between the centre of mass and centre of rigidity

$$e_y = 9.0 - 8.172 = 0.828 \approx 0.83$$

Add minimum 5% as accidental eccentricity = 0.05 × 18 = 0.9

∴ Total eccentricity = 0.83 + 0.90 = 1.73 m

∴ Torsional eccentricity in x direction.

Eccentricity between the centre of mass and centre of rigidity

= 5.0 − 5.0 = 00

Add minimum 5% as accidental = 0.05 × 10 = 0.5 m

∴ Total eccentricity = 0.0 + 0.5 = 0.5 m.

15.14.5. Torsional moment

The torsional moment due to E-W seismic forces rotate the building in y direction, hence

$$MT_x = V_x \cdot e_y = 409.5 \times 1.73 \qquad \text{(Base shear = 409.5)}$$

$$= 708.7 \text{ kN–m}$$

Similarly torsional moment due to N-S forces rotate the building in x direction.

$$\therefore \quad MT_y = V_y \cdot e_x = 409.5 \times 0.5 = 204.75 \text{ kN–m}$$

From Table 15.8, for time period 0.2, which is in between 0.1 and 0.55, the value of say S_a/g is 2.5 is constant.

$$\therefore \quad VB_x = VB_y$$

15.14.6. Distribution of direct shear force and torsional force

As we are considering the seismic forces in E-W direction, the walls in

N-S direction will resist the forces and walls in E-W direction may be neglected.

The distribution of direct shear and torsional shear is shown in Table 15.16.

Table 15.16. Distribution of forces in North and South shear walls

Item	R_x	d_y^* *(n)*	$R_x\,d_y$	$R_x \cdot d_y^2$	*Direct shear force (kN)*	*Torsional shear force** (kN)*	*Total shear shorce (kN)*
N. wall	0.454	(18–8.172) = 9.828	4.432	43.82	290.75	+ 39.1	329.85
S. Wall	0.546	8.172	4.492	36.46	118.75	– 39.62	118.75
				$\Sigma R_x d_y^2$ = 80.29			

Note. *Distance of considered wall from centre of rigidity. (18- 8.172) = 9.828

$$**\text{Torsional force in N wall} = \frac{R_x d_y}{\Sigma R_x d_y^2} \times V_B \cdot e_y$$

$$= \frac{4.432}{80.29} \times 409.5 \times 1.73 = 39.1$$

$$\text{Torsional force in S wall} = \frac{R_x \cdot d_y}{\Sigma\, R_x\, d_y^2} \times V_D \times C_y$$

$$= \frac{4.492}{80.29} \times 409.5 \times 1.72 = 39.62$$

Torsional forces are additive on the North wall and subtractive on the south wall as shown. The code directs that negative torsional shear shall be neglected. Hence the total shear acting on the south wall is simply direct shear only.

The centre of mass, centre of rigidity and forces are shown in Fig. 15.11.

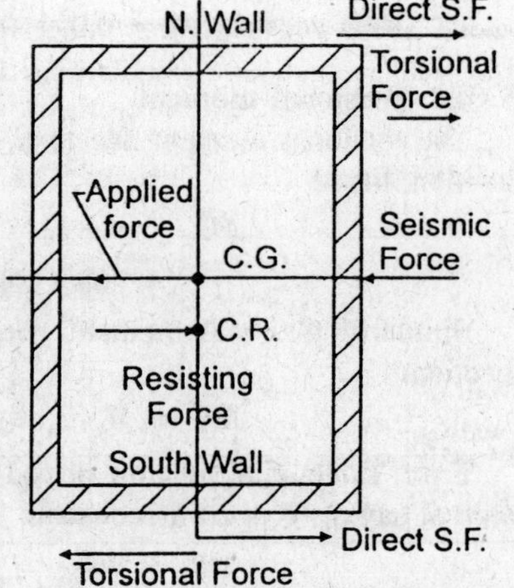

Fig. 15.11

Example 7. Determine the torsional forces in a one storey shear wall masonry structure with a rigid diaphragm roof with the following data. There are four shear walls with relative rigidity. The rigidity of walls are shown on the Fig. 15.12.

Data:

Height of parapet walls = 1 m

Height of walls upto roof level = 4.0 m

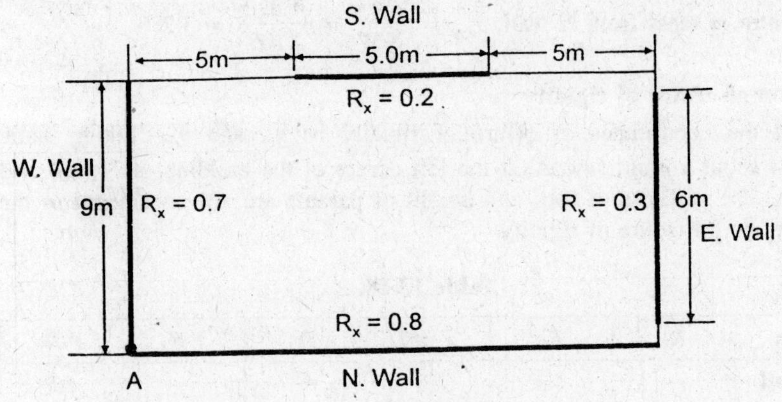

Fig. 15.12

Self weight of roof = 3 kN/m^2
Self weight of walls = 5 kN/m^2
Base shear = 330 kN
Seismic zone of structure is V, *i.e.* Z = 0.36, I = 1.0

$$R = 1.5 \text{ and } \frac{S_a}{g} = 2.5$$

Concrete density = 25 kN/m^3 and masonry density = 20 kN/m^3.

Solution.

(*i*) Location of the centre of mass

Let $\overline{X}_{CM}$ and $\overline{Y}_{CM}$ be the coordinates of the centre of mass. Taking static moments about a point of the building say A, the left corner of building N wall and W wall we get. The calculations are shown in Table 15.17.

Table 15.17. Calculation for centre of gravity

Item	*Weight w in kN*	*X (m)*	*Y (m)*	*W.x (kN.m)*	*W.y (kN.m)*
Roof slab	15 × 9 × 3 = 405.0	7.5	4.5	3037.5	1822.5
E. wall	6 × 4 × 5 = 120	15.0	4.5	1800.0	540.0
W. wall	9 × 4 × 5 = 180	0	4.5	0.00	810.0
S. wall	5 × 4 × 5 = 100.0	7.5	4.5	750	450.0
N. wall	15 × 4 × 5 = 300	7.5	0.00	2250.0	0.00
	ΣW = 1105			ΣWx = 7837.5	ΣWy = 3622.5

$$\text{Centre of mass from W wall, } \overline{X}_{cm} = \frac{\Sigma W.x}{\Sigma W} = \frac{7837.5}{1105} = 7.094$$

$$\approx 7.1 \text{ m}$$

Centre of mass from N wall, $\overline{Y}_{cm} = \dfrac{\Sigma W.y}{\Sigma W} = \dfrac{3622.5}{1105} = 3.278$

Location of centre of rigidity

Let the coordinates of centre of rigidity be $\overline{x}_{cr}$ and $\overline{y}_{cr}$. Taking static moment about a point say 'A' at the left corner of the building of N wall and W wall. The stiffness of roof and height of parapet are not considered in the calculations for centre of rigidity.

Table 13.18.

Item	R_x	R_y	*x (m)*	*y (m)*	$Y R_x$	$X R_y$
E. wall	—	0.3	15	—	—	4.5
W. wall	—	0.7	0	—	—	0.00
S. wall	0.2	—	—	9.0	1.8	—
N. wall	0.8	—	—	0	—	—
	$\Sigma R_x = 1.0$	$\Sigma R_y = 1.0$			$\Sigma xR_x =$ 1.8	$\Sigma xR_y =$ 4.5

$$\overline{X}_{CR} = \frac{x R_y}{\Sigma R_y} = \frac{4.5}{1.0} = 4.5 \text{ m}$$

$$\overline{Y}_{CR} = \frac{\Sigma y R_x}{\Sigma R_x} = \frac{1.8}{1.0} = 1.8 \text{ m}$$

Torsional eccentricity

Torsional eccentricity in x direction $e_x = \overline{X}_{CM} - X_{CR}$

$= 7.1 - 4.5 = 2.6$ m

Accidental eccentricity @ 5% $= 0.05 \times 15 = 0.75$ m

∴ Total eccentricity $= 2.6 + 0.75 = 3.35$ m

Torsional eccentricity $\overline{Y}_{CM} - \overline{Y}_{CR} = 3.278 - 1.8 = 1.478$ m

Accidental eccentricity @ 5% $= 0.05 \times 9 = 0.45$ m

∴ Total eccentricity $= 1.478 + 0.45 \approx 1.93$ m

Torsional moment

The torsional moment due to seismic force in East and West direction will rotate the building in x direction hence

$$MT_x = V_x e_y = 330 \times 1.93 = 636.9 \text{ kN–m}$$

Similarly the seismic force in North-south direction will rotate in the y direction hence

$$MT_y = V_y \cdot e_x = 330 \times 3.35$$

$$= 1105.5 \text{ kN–m}$$

Distribution of direct shear force and torsional shear force

(*i*) If the seismic force is considered only in East and West direction, then the walls in the south and North direction will resist the seismic forces and the walls in East and West direction may be ignored.

(*ii*) If the seismic force is considered in South and North direction the walls in East and West direction will resist the seismic forces and the walls in south and North direction may be ignored. The distribution of forces in the walls will be as follows:

Direct shear force in south wall

$$= \frac{R_x}{\sqrt{\Sigma R_x}} \times V_x$$

= Relative rigidity of the wall concerned × Base shear

$= 0.2 \times 330 = 66$ kN

Direct shear force in the North wall

= Relative rigidity of the wall × Base shear

$= 0.8 \times 330 = 264$ kN

Rigidity shear force in the south wall

$$= \frac{R_x \cdot d_y}{\Sigma R_x \cdot d_y^2} \times V_x \cdot e_y = \frac{1.44}{12.5} \times 636.9 = 70.85 \text{ kN}$$

Rigidity shear force in North wall

$$= \frac{R_x \cdot d_y}{\Sigma R_x \cdot d_y^2} \times V_x \cdot e_y = \frac{1.44}{12.5} \times 636.9 = -70.85 \text{ kN}$$

(It is minus as distance *dy* is (–) as point is down ward the centre of rigidity).

The distribution of forces in south and north shear walls is shown in Table 15.19.

Table 15.19.

Item	R_x	d_y *(m)*	$R_x \cdot d_y$	$R_x \cdot d_y^2$	*Direct shear force kN*	*Torsional shear force kN*	*Total shear force kN*
S. wall	0.2	(9.0-1.8) = 7.2	1.44	10.368	66.0	70.85	136.85 kN
N. wall	0.8	– 1.8	1.44	2.592	264.0	– 70.85	264.0*

*Neglecting negative rigidity shear as per code.

Direct shear in Eastern wall

= Relative rigidity of concerned wall × Base shear

$= 0.3 \times 330 = 99$ kN

Similarly direct shear in western wall $= 0.7 \times 330 = 231$ kN

Rigidity shear in East wall $= \dfrac{R_y\, d_x}{\Sigma R_y\, d_x^2} \times V_y \cdot e_x$

Distance of centre of rigidity from Eastern wall = 15.0 – 4.5 = 10.5 m

Distance of centre of rigidity from Western wall = – 4.5

Note. The direction of centre of rigidity from Eastern wall is in opposite direction, hence negative.

Table 15.20.

Item	R_y	d_x *(m)*	$R_y \cdot d_x$	$R_y \cdot d_x^2$	*Direct shear in kN*	*Torsional shear kN*	*Total shear kN*
E. wall	0.3	15–4.5 = 10.5	3.15	33.075	99.0	73.7	172.7
W. wall	0.7	0 – 4.5 = – 0.45	3.15	14.175	231.0	– 73.7	231.0
				Σ 47.25			

∴ Torsional rigidity in Eastern wall $= \dfrac{R_y\, d_x}{\Sigma R_y\, d_x^2}\, V_y\, e_x$

$$= \frac{3.15}{47.25} \times 330 \times 3.35 = 73.7 \text{ kN}$$

Similarly torsional rigidity in Western wall $= \dfrac{R_y \cdot d_x}{\Sigma R_y\, d_x^2}\, Y_y \cdot e_x$

$$= \frac{3.15}{47.25} \times 330 \times 3.35$$

$$= 73.7 \text{ kN}$$

Results are shown in Table 15.20.

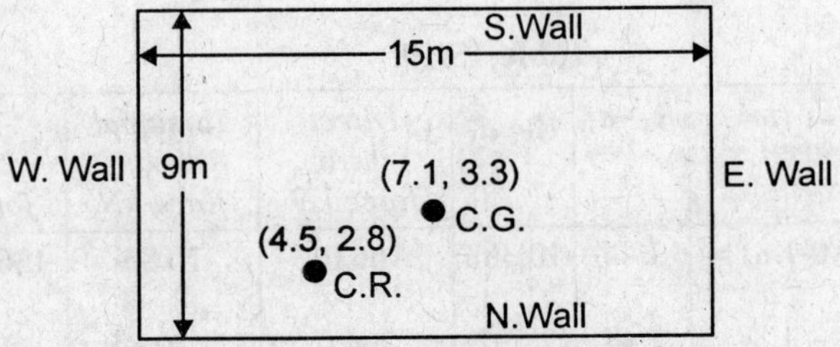

Fig. 15.13. Postion of C.G. and C.R.

QUESTIONS

1. Name the forces which work on a structure.
2. Discuss the factors which influence the motion of an earthquake.
3. Write short notes on the followings.
   (*a*) Determination of base shear

(*b*) Natural or fundamental period of a structure
(*c*) Distribution of seismic forces along the height of the building
(*d*) Drift
(*e*) Torsion
(*d*) Effective weight

4. A two storey building is constructed in seismic zone III on a plot of 18 × 8 m. The height of the building is 3.5 m. Determine the lateral forces on the building with the following given data.
   (*i*) Live load on the building = 1 kN/m^2
   (*ii*) Weight of roof = 3.0 kN/m^2
   (*iii*) Weight of walls = 5.0 kN/m^2
   Zone factor Z = 0.16, Importance factor I = 1.0, Reduction factor R = 1.5.
   The value of S_a/g may be taken as 2.5.

Seismic weight = 2373 kN
Base shear = 316.4
Distribution

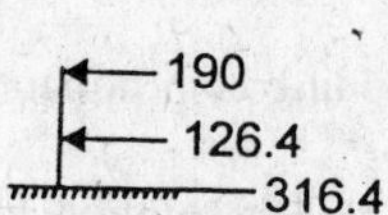

5. A three storeyed building is to be constructed in seismic zone V on a plot of 8 × 8 m. The building is to be designed with special moment resisting frame. Determine the seismic weight and base shear of the building with the following data.
   (*i*) Intensity of dead load on the building = 10 kN/m^2
   (*ii*) Intensity of weight at floor level is = 3 kN/m^2
   (*iii*) Soil of the area is medium hard.
   Zone factor Z = 0.36, I = 1.5, R = 5.0, and S_a/g = 2.5.
   (*iv*) Height of each storey is 3.5 m.

Seismic weight = 2016 kN
Base shear 272.16 kN

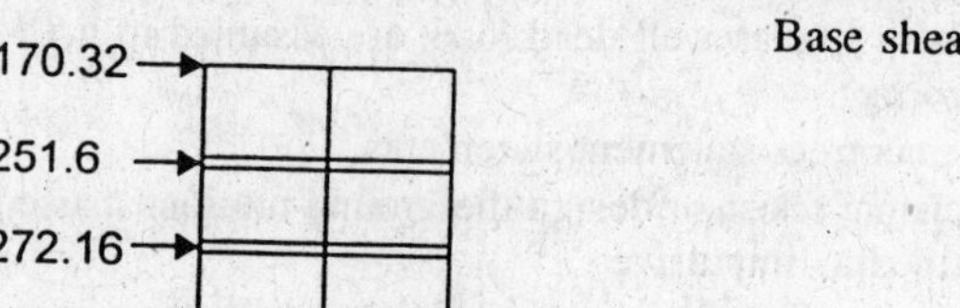

Design seismic base shear

6. Determine the rigidity of shear wall of a structure whose N and S walls are 8 m long and E and W walls 15 m long.
   The height of the storey is 4.0 m
   The design data is as follows:
   Weight of the roof slab = 3 kN/m^2
   Weight of walls = 5 kN/m^2

Zone factor $Z = 0.36$, Importance factor $I = 1.0$, Reduction factor $R = 3.0$ and $S_a/g = 2.5$.

The relative stiffness of north wall is 0.46 and that of south walls is 0.54. The relative rigidity of East and West wall may be assumed equally as 0.5.

[**Ans.** Northern wall: Direct shear = 153.85, Torsional shear = 33.94,
South wall: Direct shear = 179.5, Torsional shear = – 33.94]

7. Seismic design is governed by
   (*a*) Design load (*b*) Seismic load
   (*c*) Response reduction factor (*d*) Zone factor
   (*e*) Importance factor of the building
   (*f*) By all the factors
8. Identify the incorrect statement/statements
   (*a*) The horizontal inertia force at the time of earthquake at any floor is equal to the effective total load above that level multiplied by seismic coefficient.
   (*b*) In the design of a seismic resistant building only horizontal forces are considered
   (*c*) In the design of a seismic resistant building both horizontal as well as vertical components are considered
   (*d*) The safety of multi storeyed buildings is checked on the basis of seismic forces
   (*e*) The safety of multi storeyed buildings is checked on the basis of wind loads
   (*f*) At the time of an earthquake the shear force, Bending moment and seismic forces distribution along the height of the building should be done simultaneously.
   (*g*) The seismic coefficient at top is greatest and zero at bottom
9. In multi-storeyed buildings the seismic coefficient....by increasing the number of storeys
   (*a*) Increases (*b*) Decreases
   (*c*) Remains constant (*d*) All are correct
10. Identify the correct statement/statements
    (*a*) At roof live load is assumed to act
    (*b*) At roof live load is not assumed to act
    (*c*) At roof both live as well dead load, are assumed to act
    (*d*) All are correct
11. Identify the incorrect statement/statements
    (*a*) In the seismic resistant design the ground motions caused by earthquake are assumed as impulsive
    (*b*) The character of ground motion changes with the change in period and amplitude of vibrations
    (*c*) An earthquake takes place simultaneously with floods and winds
    (*d*) The value of elastic modulus of materials is used for static analysis

ANSWERS

7. (*f*) 9. (*b*) 11. (*c*)
8. (*c, d, f*) 10. (*b*)

16

Design of Earthquake Resistant Masonry Structures

16.1. INTRODUCTION

Till early twentieth century mostly masonry construction was in use all over the world. Latter steel and R.C.C. construction became popular due to their inherent characteristics. About 67% area of India lies in sever seismic zones and about 90% population lives in masonry houses. World over also masonry construction is still popular due to the following reasons:

1. Masonry construction is cheaper in first cost.
2. Construction skill and material is easily available locally.
3. Masonry construction has a good finish.
4. Masonry structures are good for thermal insulation.

However it has the following draw backs for earthquake.

1. It is brittle as bricks, stones and concrete blocks are used in its construction. Its strength degrades more severly due to repetition of seismic loads.
2. It has high mass due to thick walls, hence it has high inertial response to the earthquake.
3. Its construction quality is difficult to control.
4. Large stiffness of materials leads to large response to earthquake waves of short natural period.

Mostly masonry is used for wall construction. How ever it is also used for in fill panels, and partitions in framed buildings. In framed structures the masonry walls are subjected to inertia forces and forces from displacement of frames. The interaction of in fill and frames may modify the response of frames and forces working on them. In this chapter construction of masonry structures will be discussed according to the provisions of IS 4326-1993.

16.2. GENERAL REQUIREMENTS

The execution of brick masonry structures should be of very high quality. The brick course all round the building should be strictly level and perfectly vertical. The vertical joints should be staggered and the width of joints should be one to two centimeters. The masonry should be non shrinkable. 1:1:6

(Cement lime sand) proportion mortar is found best for seismic regions. Horizontal and vertical reinforcement bars should be embedded in the mortar at an vertical interval of about 50 cm.

The total areas of the openings as doors and windows should not exceed 15 to 20% of the wall surface. The width of the openings should be limited to 35% of the length of the wall. The width of wall piers between openings should be at least 90 cms. The walls should be connected by horizontal bands as discussed in chapter 13.

16.3. MASONRY CONSTRUCTION

From the study of damages of past earthquakes as discussed in chapter 2, it is obvious that construction of un reinforced brick, composite constructions and adobe houses are not suitable for seismic zones due to large weight and with no lateral strength and ductility.

In order to improve the seismic performance of masonry buildings following parameters should be given due consideration.

1. **Selection of site.** The building construction site should be sufficiently away from the steep slopes and the building should be founded on firm and uniform soils.
2. **Plan uniformity.** The plan of the building should be of simple geometric form as discussed in chapter **13.** Simple plan will avoid torsion to develop in the building.
3. **Avoid pounding.** To avoid pounding during an earthquake a gap of 0.04 × height of the storey or at least 15 mm gap per storey should be provided.
4. **Avoid large over hanging and projèctions.** Large over hanging projections, cantilevers, floating columns and attachment of heavy mass as water tanks on roofs should be avoided.
5. **To ensure good workmanship.** Workmanship of the construction affects the performance of the building to a great extent, hence good workmanship should be ensured.

16.4. SEISMIC INTENSITY SCALES

These scales are as under:

Zone A. Risk of wide spread collapse and destruction (MSK IX or above)

Zone B. Risk of collapse and heavy damage (MSK VIII likely)

Zone C. Risk of damage (MSK VII likely)

Zone D. Risk of minor damage (MSK VI maximum)

16.5. WALLS

In case of masonry buildings, the lateral strength and stiffness mainly is imparted to the buildings by the masonry walls. Thus from the point of view of earthquake resistance, walls should be symmetrical and straight in plan to avoid torsional shears.

16.5.1. Dimensions of walls

Wall thickness. The wall thickness 't' should not be less than 20 cm.

16.5.2. Height of the wall

The height of wall should not be more than 20 times of its thickness t *i.e.* $H = 20 \times t$. Thus height should not be more than 4.0 m where t is the thickness of the wall.

16.5.3. Length of the wall

The length of wall between cross walls should not be more then 40 t. In case longer rooms are required then either the thickness of the wall should be increased or buttresses should be provided. The buttresses should be taken upto the full height of the wall, having thickness at top equal to the width of wall 't' and bottom width should be 1/6 of the height of wall. The maximum spacing of buttress should be less than 20 t.

16.6. MORTAR

For masonry work of different categories of buildings mortar to be used is shown in Table 16.1.

Table 16.1. Recommended mortar mixes

Categories of constructions (Buildings)	*Proportion of cement lime and sand*
I	Cement-sand 1:4 or cement-lime-sand 1:1:6 or richer.
II	Cement-lime-sand 1:2:9 or richer.
III	Cement-sand 1:6 or richer.
IV	Cement-sand 1:6 or lime-cinder 1:3 or richer.

16.7. CLASSIFICATION OF MASONRY STRUCTURES

According to seismic intensity zones, importance of building and foundation soil, masonry buildings have been classified as given in Table 16.2.

Table 16.2.

Category	*Condition for the category of buildings*
I	Important buildings on soft soils in zone A
II	Important buildings on firm soils in zone A
	Important buildings on soft soils in zone B
	Ordinary buildings on soft soils in zone A
III	Important buildings on firm soils in zone B
	Important buildings on soft soils in zone C
	Ordinary buildings on firm soils in zone A

Category	*Condition for the category of buildings*
IV	Important buildings on soft soils in zone B Important buildings on firm soils in zone C Ordinary buildings on firm soils in zone B Ordinary buildings on firm soils in zone C Ordinary buildings on soft soils in zone C

Note:

1. Firm soils means whose bearing strength is more than 10 t/m^2 and soft soil whose bearing strength is less then 10 t/m^2 ($1 kg/cm^2$).
2. Weak soils liable to liquefaction and compaction under earthquake conditions are not covered here.

16.8. DESIGN ASPECTS

16.8.1. Height of masonry walls

Code 4326-1993 recommends that reinforced masonry load bearing walls should not be built more than 15 m in height, subject to a maximum of four storeys, unless rationally designed. However on the basis of experimental studies on un reinforced buildings, researchers have suggested that for ordinary workmanship and quality of building materials, the height of dwellings should not exceed three storeys preferably two, and under no circumstances the total height of dwellings should exceed 11 metres including the height of parapet in seismic zones.

16.8.2. Behaviour of walls

The behaviour of un reinforced masonry walls during earthquake has been

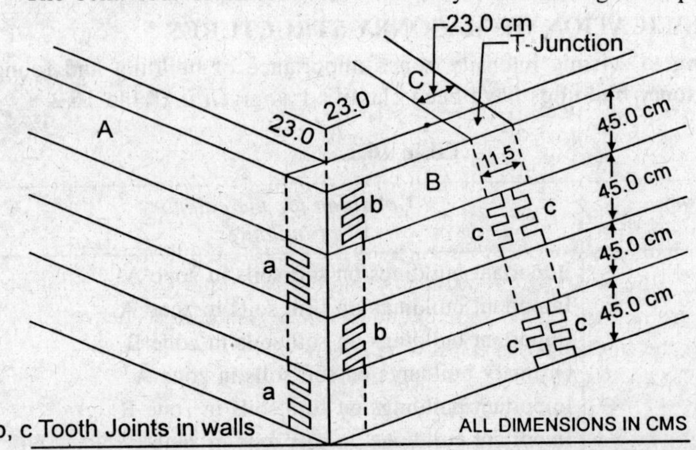

Fig. 16.1. Alternating toothed joints in walls at corners and T junctions

discussed fully in chapter 13. How ever method of increasing bond between walls is suggested as follows:

The joints in the walls should be made sloping *i.e.* stepped joints by making the corners first to a height of 60 cm and then constructing the wall in between them or toothed joints may be made in both walls alternately in lifts of about 45 cm as shown in Fig. 16.1.

16.8.3. Openings in bearing walls

It has been observed that openings in walls, divide them into a series of piers. The strength of these piers determines the strength of the wall element. It has been found by the analysis of openings that sections around the jambs of openings are vulnerable sections and must be safe guarded. Further it has also been observed that:

1. Larger the opening, smaller the strength of the all.
2. The strength of wall depends upon the position (location) of the opening in the wall.
3. More central the location of the opening, higher the strength of the wall.
4. Higher the opening, higher the strength of the wall.

Thus in view of the above findings, the code has recommended certain guide lines about the size and location of openings in load bearing walls.

1. Openings should be located away from the inside corner by a clear distance equal to at least 0.25 times the height of the opening, but not less then 60 cm.
2. The total length of openings should not be more than 50% of the length of the wall between consecutive cross walls in single storey construction, 42% in two storey construction and 33% in three storey buildings.

The horizontal distance (pier width) between two openings should not be less then 50% of the height of the shorter opening, but in no case less than 60 cm as shown in Fig. 16.2.

The vertical distance from an opening to another opening directly above it should not be less than 60 cm, nor it should be less than 50% of the width of the smaller opening Fig. 16.2.

In case the openings do not comply with the requirements as mentioned above, they should be boxed in reinforced concrete all-round the opening or reinforcing bars (minimum one bar of 8 mm diameter) should be provided at the jamb through the masonry Fig. 16.3.

16.8.4. Thickness of walls

For a single storey building the thickness of the load bearing wall should not be less than one brick (20 cm). For buildings upto three storeys, the thickness of wall for bottom storeys should not be less than 1½ brick (30 cm)

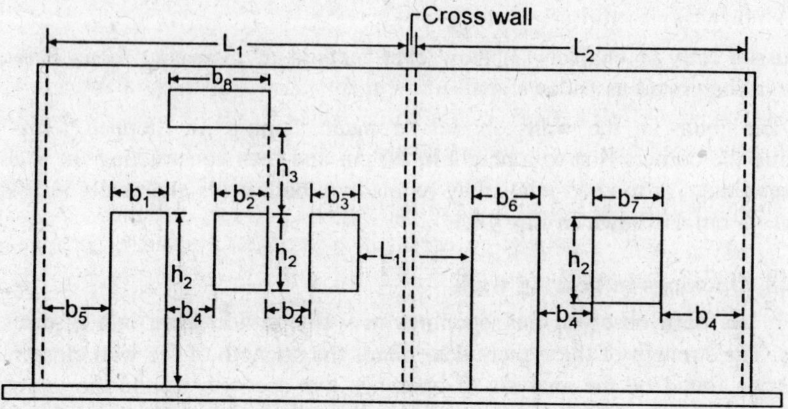

Note:

$b_1+b_2+b_3<0.5L_1$ For one storey, 0.42 L_1 For two storyed, 0.33 L_1 for three storyed.
$b_6+b_7 \leq 0.5\ L_2$ For one storey, 0.42 L_2 Two storyed, 0.33 L_2 For three storyed
$b_4 \geq 0.5\ h_2$, but not less than 60 cms
$b_5 \geq 0.25\ h_1$, but not less than 60 cm
$h_3 > 60$ cm or 0.5 b_2 or b_8, which is ever is more.

Fig. 16.2. Opening in load bearing walls as per code

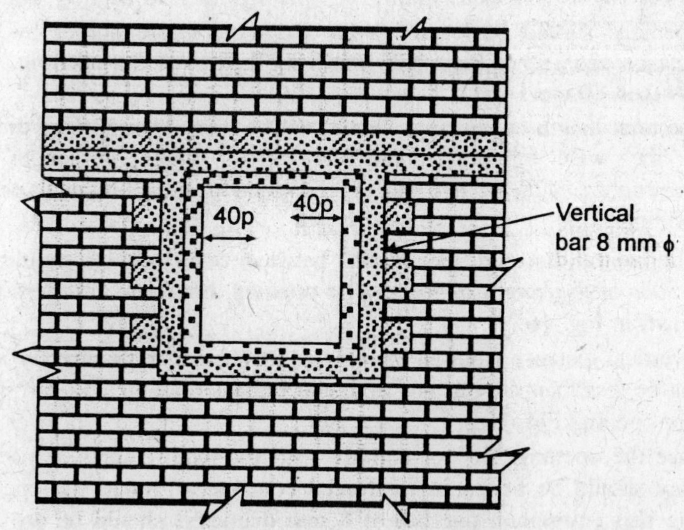

Fig. 16.3. Strengthening masonry with R.C.C. around opening

and for the top storey it should not be less than one brick (20 cm). The thickness of the wall also not be less than 1/6 of the length of the wall between two consecutive perpendicular walls.

16.8.5. Horizontal reinforcement

To strengthen the walls against horizontal inplane bending horizontal reinforcement must be provided in them. This also helps to bind or tie the perpendicular walls together. The provision of bands at various levels and their merits have bean discussed in chapter 13.

16.8.6. Dowels at corners and junctions

Steel dowel bars may be used at corners and T junctions as a supplement to bands to create the box action of walls as shown in Fig. 16.4. Dowels serve to reinforce the wall in horizontal bending near the junction. Generally dowels are placed in every fourth course or at about 50 cm interval and taken into walls to sufficient length so as to provide full bond strength. Alternatively, strengthening of T junctions and corners wire mesh may be used as shown in Fig. 16.5.

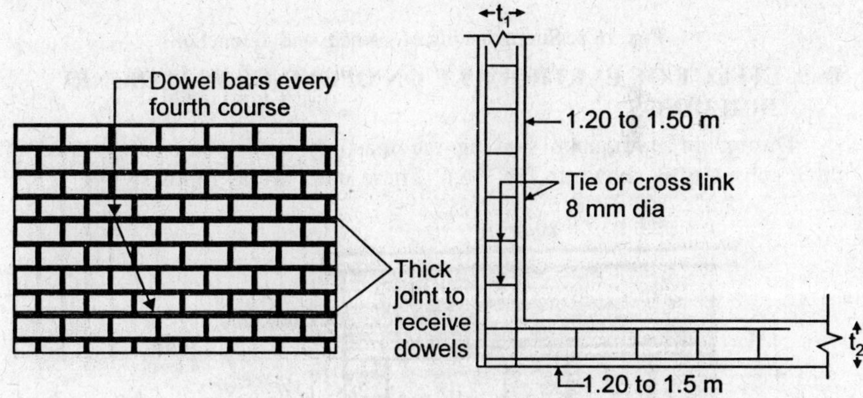

(*a*) Corner strengthening by dowel bars

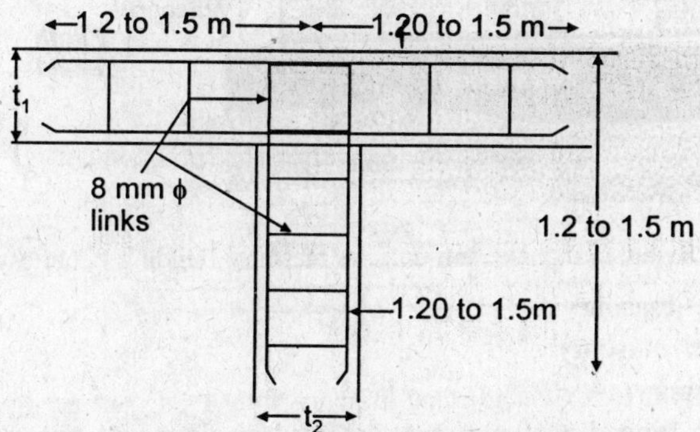

(*b*) T-Junction strengthening by dowels

Fig. 16.4.

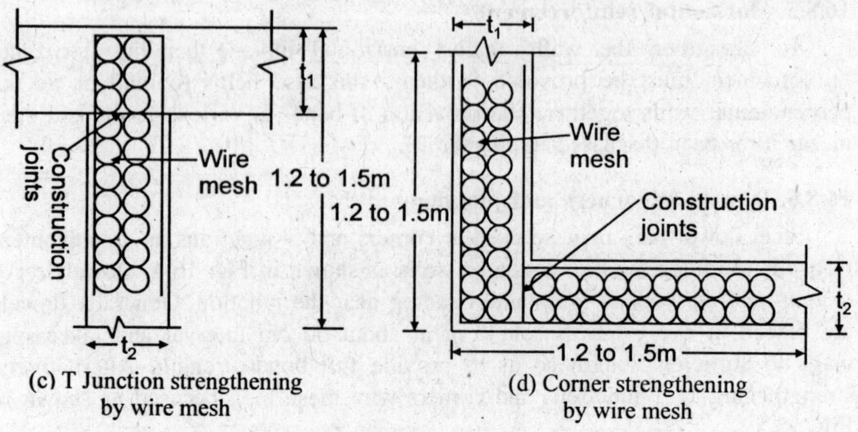

Fig. 16.5. Strengthening of corners and T-Junctions

16.9. EFFECT OF EARTHQUAKE ON OPENINGS IN MASONRY BUILDINGS

During an earthquake shaking, the masonry walls may be grouped into three sub units as shown in Fig. 16.6. These units are as follows:

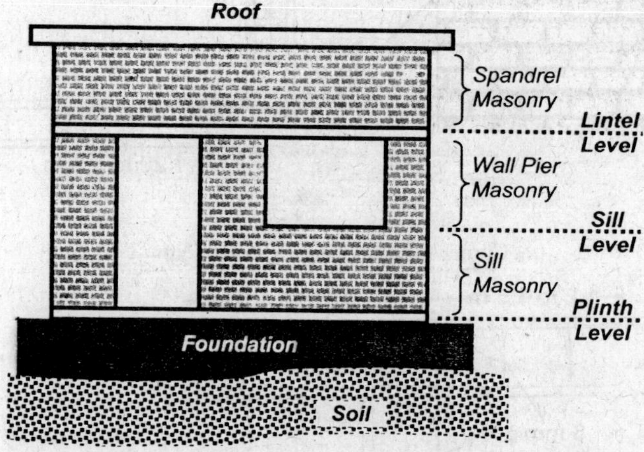

Fig. 16.6. During earthquake sub-units in masonry building (Courtesy—IITK)

1. Spandrel masonry
2. Wall pier masonry
3. Sill masonry

Consider a hipped roof masonry having one door and two windows in a wall as shown in Fig. 16.7 (*a*). This building also has been provided with plinth; lintel and roof band. During the ground shaking, the inertia force disconnects the small sized masonry wall pier at the top and bottom from the

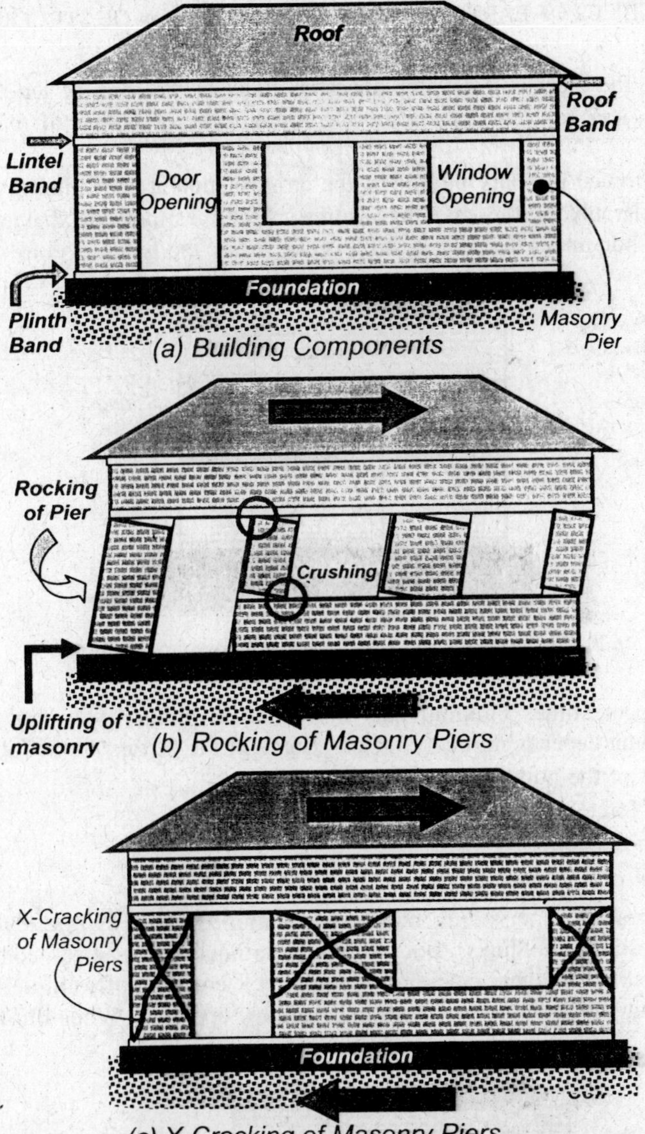

Fig. 16.7. Earthquake response of a hipped roof masonry building (Courtesy—IITK)

masonry. These sub units of masonry rock back and forth, developing contact at the opposite diagonals only as shown in Fig. 16.7 (*b*). Due to the rocking of masonry pier the opposite corners of the masonry can be crushed. During rocking, uplifting of masonry may also take place. Rocking is possible under the following conditions:

(*a*) When the masonry piers are slender

(*b*) When weight of structure above the pier is small

Otherwise the piers will develop shear cracking in the form of letter *X* as shown in Fig. 16.7 (*c*). This is the most common type of failure of masonry structures.

In un reinforced masonry buildings, the cross section area of masonry wall reduces considerably at the opening. During strong earthquake shaking the building may slide under the roof at sill level or below the lintel level as shown

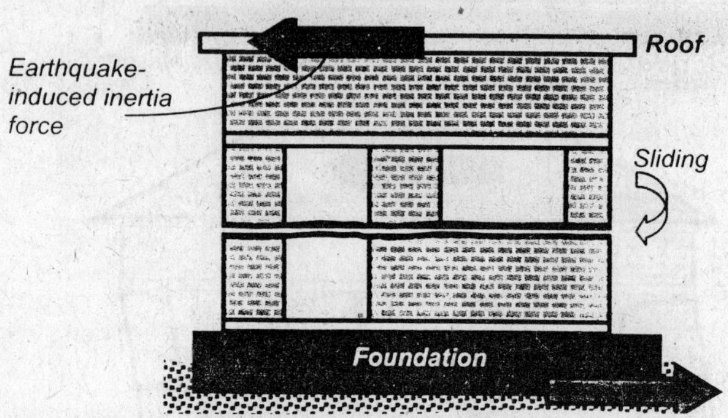

Fig. 16.8. Horizontal sliding at sill level in a masonry building
(Courtesy—IITK)

in Fig. 16.8. some times building may also slide at plinth level. The exact location of sliding depends on many factors. Some of the factors are as follows:

(*a*) Weight of the building

(*b*) Inertia force induced by the earthquake

(*c*) Area of openings

(*d*) Type of door frames used

In actual practice, the sliding failure as mentioned above is rare, even in unconfined masonry buildings. But after an earthquake the most common damage observed is the shear cracking or diagonal × cracking of wall piers and inclined cracking at the corners of door and window openings. When during an

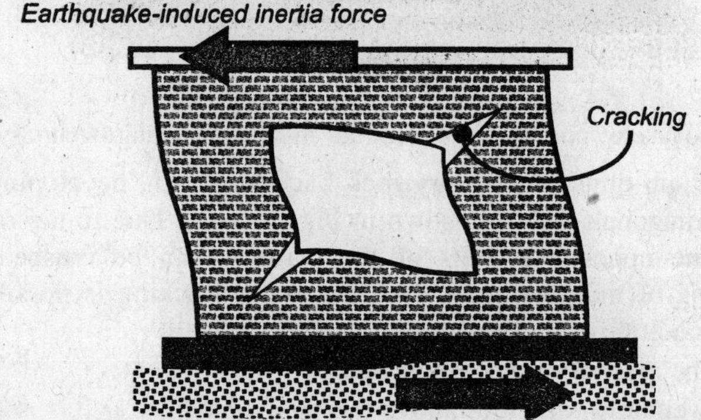

Fig. 16.9. (*a*) Cracking in buildings with no corner reinforcement

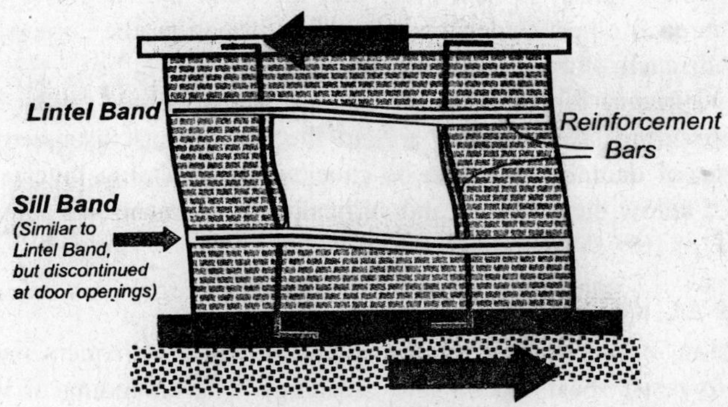

Fig. 16.9. (*b*) No cracks with vertical reinforcement (Courtesy—IITK)

earthquake shaking a wall with an opening deforms, the shape of the opening gets distorted and takes the form of a rhombus. Thus the two opposite corners

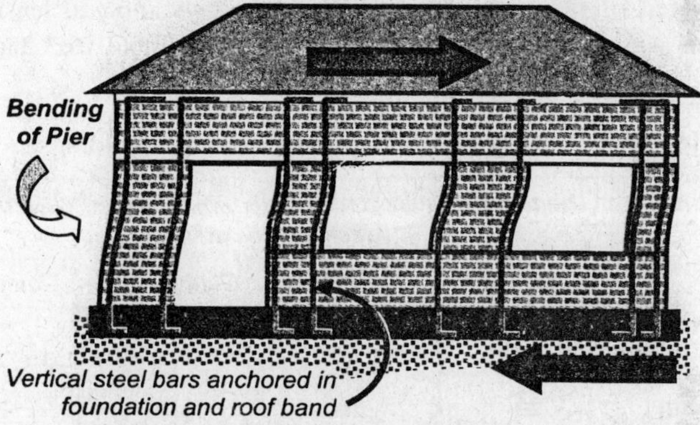

(*a*) Vertical reinforcement causes bending of masonry piers in place of rocking

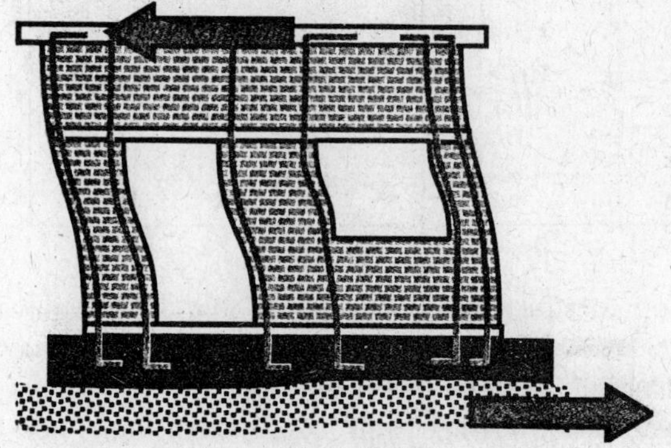

(*b*) Vertical reinforcement prevents sliding in walls

Fig. 16.10. Vertical reinforcement in masonry walls (Courtesy—IITK)

of the opening come closer to each other and the other two opposite corners move away from each other. Under this type of deformation, the corners which come closer with each other develop cracks as shown in Fig. 16.9 (*a*). These cracks are found bigger for large sized opening. These corner cracks can be restricted by providing steel bars all around the opening as discussed under 16.7.3. This type of damage may also be checked by providing lintel and sill bands above and below the openings and vertical reinforcement bars adjacent to vertical edges Fig. 16.9 (*b*).

16.10. VERTICAL REINFORCEMENT

The provision of the vertical reinforcement in wider wall piers increases their capacity to resist shear cracking (*x* cracking). The embeding of vertical reinforcement bars in the edges of wall piers and anchoring them in foundation at the bottom and in the roof bends at top makes the slender wall piers to under go bending instead of rocking as shown in Fig. 16.10 (*a*). The vertical reinforcement also checks the sliding and collapsing in weak direction. Fig. 16.10 (*b*).

Adequate area of the vertical bars prevent their yielding in tension. The area of bars for walls upto 1½ brick thick is shown in Table 16.3 and typical details at corner and T junctions are shown in Fig. 16.11.

Table 16.3. Vertical reinforcement in masonry buildings

No. of storeys	*Storey*	*Diameter of mild steel single bar in mm at each critical section for category*			
		Category I	*Category II*	*Category III*	*Category IV*
One		16	12	12	Nil
Two	Top	16	12	12	Nil
	Bottom	20	16	16	Nil
Three	Top	16	12	12	Nil
	Middle	20	16	12	Nil
	Bottom	20	16	16	Nil
Four	Top	(ii)*	(ii)*	12	12
	Third			12	12
	Second			16	12
	Bottom			16	12

Note:

(*i*)* Category of construction is shown in Table 16.2. Equivalent area of deformed or twisted bars or a number of mild steel bars may be used, but the diameter should not be less than 13 mm.

(*ii*)* Four storyed load bearing wall construction may not be used for category (I) and (II) buildings.

16.11. INCLINED FLIGHTS OF STAIRS

The inclined flights of stair joining the different floors levels will act as a cross brace between various floors. They transfer large horizontal forces at the

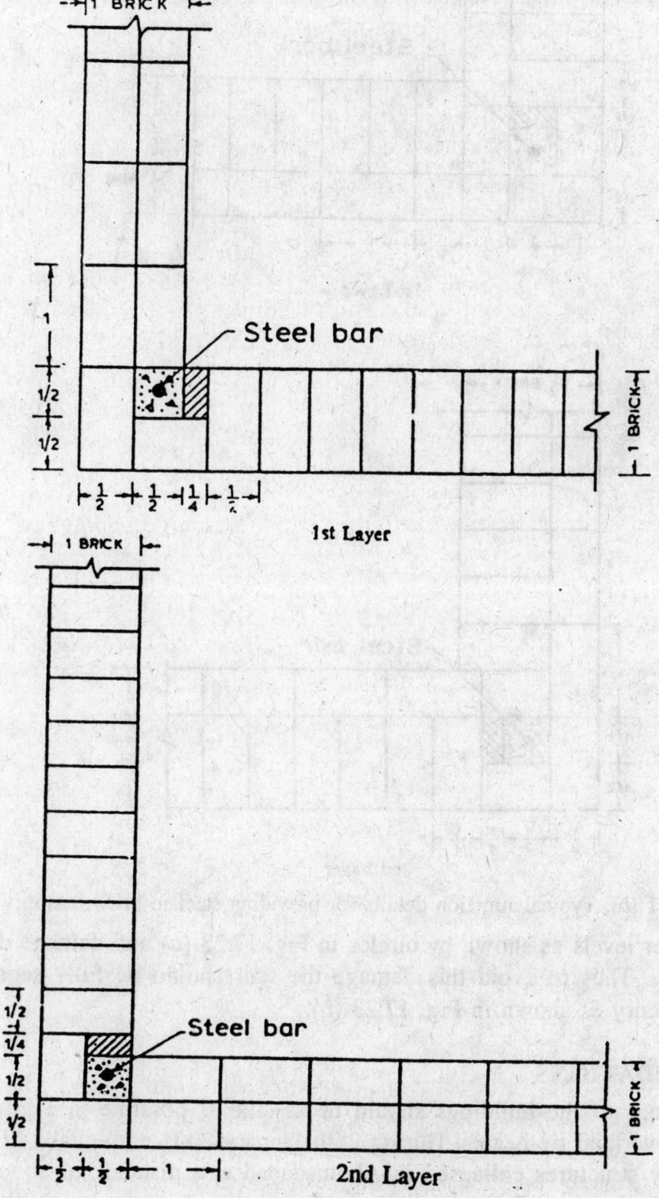

Fig. 16.11. (*a*) Typical Junction details for providing steel in brick masonry

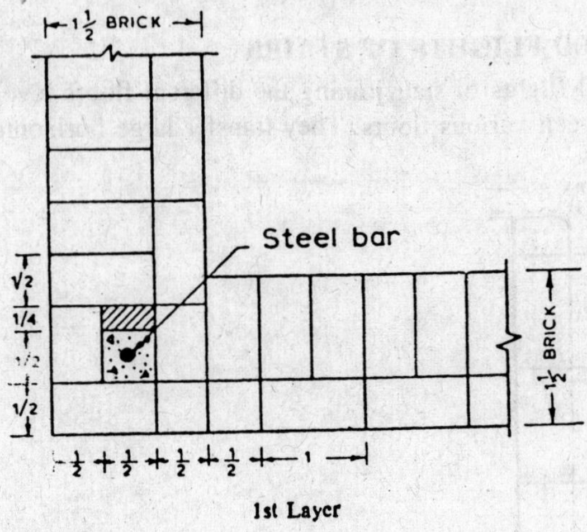

1st Layer

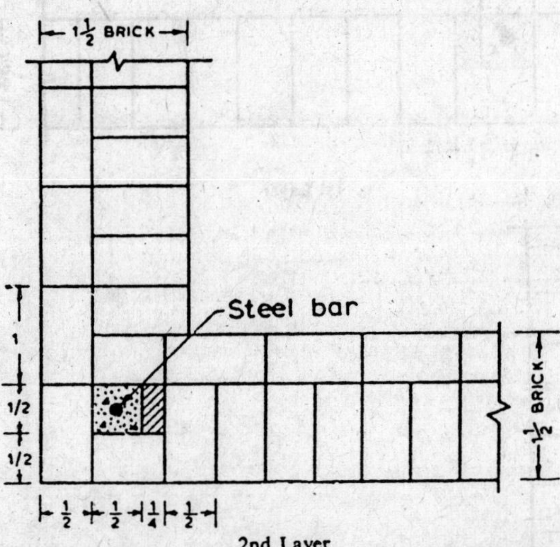

2nd Layer

Fig. 16.11 (*b*). Typical Junction details for providing steel in brick masonry

roof and lower levels as shown by circles in Fig. 17.23 (*a*) and damage during an earthquake. Thus to avoid this damage the stair should be fully separated from the masonry as shown in Fig. 17.23 (*b*).

16.12. FOUNDATIONS

Foundations of the buildings should be as stiff as possible in a grid and linked to the vertical tie beams. During 26th January 2001 earthquake of Bhuj (Gujrat) many structures collapsed in Ahemedabad at a distance of about 250 km from the epicentre. Geologist have attributed this damage due to the soil formation of the region as alluvial soil made by the deposition of flowing silt.

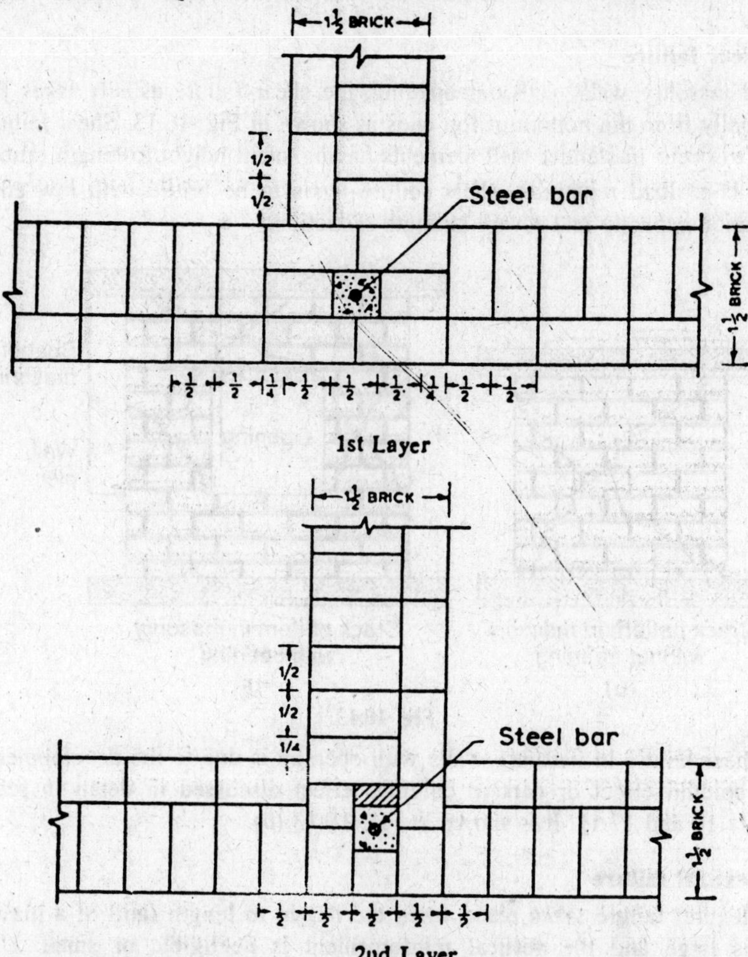

Fig. 16.12. Typical Junction details for providing steel in brick masonry

This soil is uncompacted and loose, which liquefied during earthquake, resulting huge damage to the buildings. The effects of soil liquefaction have been discussed fully in chapter 9

16.13. BEHAVIOUR OF REINFORCED MASONRY WALLS

The reinforced masonry walls are designed and used for lateral out of plane loads and axial loads. Mostly the reinforced masonry walls are designed to span vertically and transfer the lateral loads to the roof, floor or foundation. Generally these walls are designed as simple beams spanning between structural support. The axial loads are transferred directly to the foundation except for eccentric loading which may cause tension in the wall. A reinforced masonry wall may fail either in shear or flexure. These failures are discussed in brief in the following paragraphs.

(*a*) Shear failure

In masonry walls with out opening, the shear failure usually takes place diagonally from the bottom or top ends as shown in Fig. 16.13. Shear failure is likely to occur in slender wall elements having small height to length ratio.

Due to load repetition, shear failure tends to be brittle with low energy dissipation capacity and severe strength reduction.

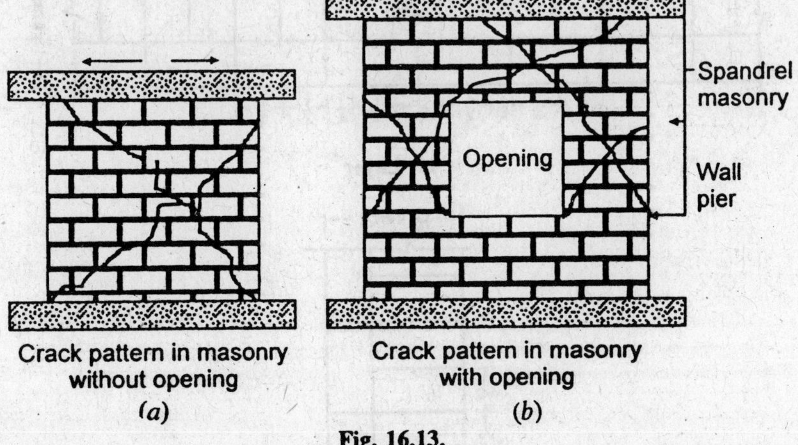

Fig. 16.13.

Shear failure in masonry walls with opening is due to the development of short column effect or captive columns effect discussed in detail in section 11.9, 11.10 and 17.11. It is shown in Fig. 16.13 (*b*).

(*b*) Flexural failure

Flexural failure takes place when the height to length ratio of a masonry wall is large and the vertical reinforcement is negligible or small. Under repeated in plane bending with low axial forces the hysteresis behaviour of such walls is approximately elasto-plastic type. Such walls show high ductility and low strength reduction or degradation. It is not essential that a masonry wall which is subjected to high axial load (force) and fails in flexure is highly ductile and its degration also is severe. The behaviour of reinforced masonry wall subjected to out of plane bending is similar to R.C.C. wall and its ductility is very high.

16.14. FORCE DISPLACEMENT RELATIONSHIP OF A MASONRY WALL

Consider a masonry wall subjected to static lateral force as shown in Fig. 16.14 (*a*). The height of wall is h and base width is 'b'.

The wall behaves elastically upto a point A shown in Fig. 16.14 (*c*). At this point the base cracks and the force immediately fails from F_A to F_B.

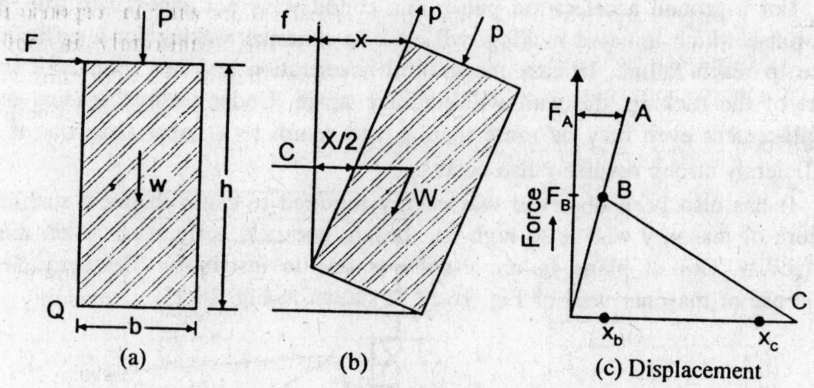

(a) (b) (c) Displacement

Fig. 16.14.

Resolving the static forces at the cracked condition, taking moment at point Q, we get

$$F_B \times h = P \times \frac{b}{2} + W \times \frac{b}{2}$$

$$\therefore \qquad F_B = \frac{(P + W)b}{2\,h} \qquad \text{...(16.1)}$$

The force F reduces to zero at c, where for small rotation,

$$\text{Stabilizing force} = \frac{P \times b}{2} + \frac{W \times b}{2}$$

$$\text{Un stabilizing force} = W \times \frac{x}{2}$$

Equating the two forces we get

$$F \times h + p \cdot x + \frac{W x}{2} = \frac{P \cdot b}{2} + \frac{W \cdot b}{2}$$

$$\text{or} \qquad F \cdot h = P\,(b/2 - x) + W(b/2 - x/2)$$

$$\text{or} \qquad F \cdot h = \frac{P \cdot b}{2} - P_x + \frac{W \cdot b}{2} - \frac{W \cdot x}{2}$$

$$\text{or} \qquad 2\,F \cdot h = p \cdot b - 2\,Px + Wb - W \cdot x$$

$$\text{or} \qquad x\,(2p + W) = Ph + W.h - 2\,F \cdot h$$

$$\text{or} \qquad x = \frac{Ph + W.b - 2\,F.h}{(2\,P + W)} \qquad \text{...(16.2)}$$

$$\text{when } F = 0, \qquad x_c = \frac{pb + Wb}{(2\,p + W)} \qquad \text{...(16.3)}$$

At point A as shown in Fig. 16.14 (*c*) the incremental stiffness of the wall becomes negative, so that for a steady applied force F_A, the collapse of the wall will occur unless the force F_A is not transferred to other stiffer structural element through another alternative load path.

For a ground acceleration pulse, this condition is not necessarily true, as the pulse which initiated rocking will have to continue rocking for a sufficient time to reach failure. In case the ground acceleration reverses soon after the start of the rocking, the wall will stabilize again. Under seismic loading the displacement even may be more than x_c and return to a stable condition if a sufficiently strong reverse pulse occurs.

It has also been observed that energy required to cause in plane·stability failure of masonry wall is so high that failure normally is by shear rather than instability. Out of plane failure usually is due to instability. The simplified response of masonry wall of Fig. 16.14 is shown in Fig. 16.15.

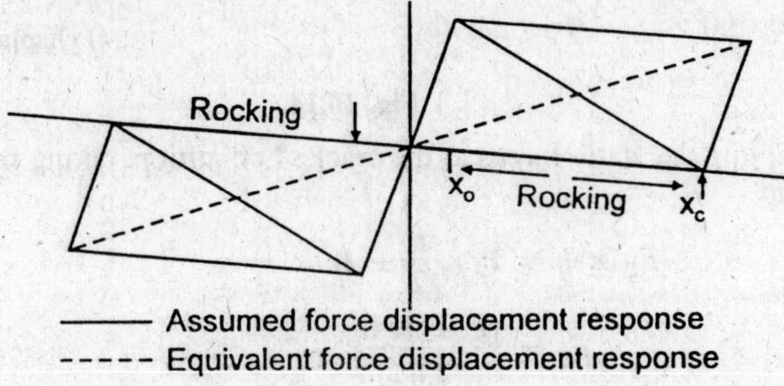

Fig. 16.15.

For simple buildings the ultimate loading can be estimated approximately by replacing the actual wall by an equivalent elastic structure. The response of such a structure is shown by broken line. The energy required to cause failure is approximately equal for the actual and equivalent structure. For practical conditions x_b is much smaller then x_c. The equivalent stiffness can be obtained by the following relation.

$$K_c = \frac{F_B}{x_c} \qquad \ldots(16.4)$$

and the equivalent natural frequency $f_c = \frac{1}{2\pi}\left[\frac{K_c}{W+p}\right]^{1/2}$ ...(16.5)

The maximum displacement can be determined by response spectrum or any suitable method applicable to elastic structure.

Criteria for stability being $x \leq x_c$

The application of equations 16.1 to 16.5 are shown by the following example.

Example 1. Estimate the design seismic coefficient and frequency of vibration for an ordinary masonry shear wall for a public library in Delhi which comes in seismic zone IV with the following data:

1. Load at roof $p = 18$ kN/m
2. Height of the wall $h = 3.5$ m

3. Width of the wall $b = 0.20$ m
4. Unit weight of masonry wall $W = 20$ kN/m^3
5. Soil is medium hard.

Solution. Given data

Height of wall $h = 3.5$ m

Width of base $b = 0.2$ cm

Roof load $p = 18$ kN/m

Self weight of the wall W = height of wall × base of wall × density of masonry

$$= 3.5 \times 0.2 \times 20 = 14.0 \text{ kN/m}$$

From equation (2) $F_B = \dfrac{(p+W)\,b}{2\,h}$

$$= \frac{(18 + 14) \times 0.2}{2 \times 3.5} = \frac{6.4}{7} = 0.914$$

When $x = x_c$, $F = 0$, then from eqaution (16.3).

$$x_c = \frac{P \cdot b + W.b}{2\,p + W}$$

$$= \frac{(18 + 14) \times 0.2}{(36 + 14)} = \frac{6.4}{50} \approx 0.1280$$

From equation 16.4, $K_c = \dfrac{F_B}{x_c} = \dfrac{0.914}{0.128} = 7.1$ kN/m

Equivalent natural frequency

$$f_c = \frac{1}{2\,\pi}\left[\frac{K_c}{(p+W)}\right]^{1/2}$$

$$= \frac{1}{2 \times 3.142}\left[\frac{7.1 \times 9.81}{18 + 14}\right]^{1/2} \qquad (F = M \times g)$$

$$= \frac{1}{6.284}\left[\frac{69.651}{32}\right]^{1/2} = \frac{2.176}{6.284} = 0.345 \text{ Hz or cps}$$

Natural period $T = \dfrac{1}{f}$

$$= \frac{1}{0.345} = 2.90 \text{ seconds}$$

For zone IV, $Z = 0.24$. Importance factor $I = 1.5$, for public use building $R = 1.5$.

Assuming 5% damping coefficient for masonry, the value of S_a/g from table **15.8** for medium hard soil and time period 2.90, the value of S_a/g will be $1.36/T$.

i.e. $\frac{S_a}{g} = \frac{1.36}{2.9} = 0.469$

$\therefore$ Design seismic coefficient $A_h = \frac{Z}{2} \times \frac{I}{R} \times \frac{S_a}{g}$

$$= \frac{0.24}{2} \times \frac{1.5}{1.5} \times 0.469 = 0.12 \times 0.469$$

$$= 0.05628 \approx 0.0563 \textbf{ Ans.}$$

16.15. LOAD COMBINATIONS AND PERMISSIBLE STRESSES

Dead loads of walls, columns, floors, roofs and imposed loads from floor and roofs and wind loads on walls and sloping roofs should be calculated as specified in the IS codes 1911 and 875. Seismic loads should be taken as specified in IS 1893 part (1). For masonry structures following load combinations may be adopted.

1. DL + IL
2. DL + IL + WL or EL
3. DL + WL
4. 0.9 DL + EL.

Where,

DL = Dead load

IL = Imposed load

WL = Wind load and

EL = Seismic load

The permissible stresses may be increased by 33%, when wind or seismic forces are considered along with the normal loads in case of 2, 3, 4.

16.16. DESIGN OF SEISMIC RESISTANT MASONRY WALLS

The provision of IS 4326-1993 are empirical in nature based on past successful application. These provisions do not require any rational analysis. The provisions of IS 4326-1993 can be applied for the design of small buildings upto three storeys. However other important buildings and those located in high seismic zones of IV and V should be designed as per provisions of IS 1893 part (1) and IS 1905.

As per code, masonry bearing walls should be straight and symmetrical in plan. As stated earlier also, the un reinforced masonry walls should not be more than 15 m in height, subject to a maximum of four storeys unless designed on the basis of proper analysis. For reinforced masonry walls, reinforcement should be provided as recommended in Table 16.3.

As per IS 1905, the performance of masonry buildings depends on the performance of shear walls. The walls designed and constructed to resist the lateral forces due to earthquake or wind forces are known as shear walls. The R.C.C. shear walls have a very large in plane stiffness and thus resist lateral loads and control deflection very efficiently. Shear walls also help to ensure development of all available plastic hinges locations through out the structure prior to failure.

16.17. MASONRY SHEAR WALLS

As per IS 1905 code, masonry shear walls are divided into four categories as follows:

1. Ordinary un reinforced masonry shear walls

These shear walls are with out reinforcement and have poor post elastic response. This type of walls can be used only in low seismic zones as zone II and for un important buildings. In the design of such shear walls the response reduction factor *R* should be used as 1.5.

2. Detailed un reinforced masonry shear walls

Though these walls are designed as un reinforced masonry, but contain minimum reinforcement in both horizontal as well as vertical direction. Due to reinforcement, these walls display improved inelastic response and energy dissipation potential. This class of shear walls can be used for low to moderate seismic risk zone II and III.

In the design of these shear walls, the value of response reduction R to be used is 2.25. In such walls a minimum of 100 mm^2 vertical reinforcement should be provided at the centre of wall at a maximum spacing of 3.0 m at the critical section and at corners, within 40 cm of each side of the openings and with in 20 cms of the end of the walls.

(*a*) Horizontal reinforcement

(*i*) At least two bars of 6 mm diameter should be placed not more than 40 cm apart or.

(*ii*) Band beams may be placed at not more than 3.0 m apart. The area of reinforcement in these beams should be at least 100 mm^2.

(*b*) At the bottom and top of the openings the reinforcement should extend upto at least 50 cm beyond the boundary of the opening or 40 times the diameter of the reinforcing bar.

3. Ordinary reinforced masonry shear walls

The steel requirement of these shear walls is same as that detailed un reinforced masonry shear walls discussed above under (2).

The ordinary reinforced masonry walls may be subjected to large inelastic deformation and loss of strength and stability of the system. Thus these shear walls dissipate less energy. These walls are recommended for seismic zones of IV and V. In the design the value of response reduction factor R should be taken as 3.0.

4. Special reinforced masonry shear walls

This category of shear walls is recommended for seismic zones IV and V with an response reduction factor R as 4.0. The masonry should be reinforced uniformly in both horizontal as well as vertical direction. The sum of reinforcement area in both directions should be 0.2% of the gross cross-sectional area of the wall. The minimum area of the reinforcement should not be less than 0.07% of the gross cross-sectional area of the wall. The maximum spacing of the horizontal as well as vertical reinforcement should be lesser of the followings.

1. 1/3rd of the length of the shear wall
2. 1/3rd of the height of the shear wall
3. 1.20 m, which ever is lesser of the three values.

Note: 1. The minimum area of vertical steel should be 1/3rd of shear steel required.

2. The shear steel should be anchored at 135° around the vertical bars or with 180° standard hook.

16.18. SEISMIC DESIGN OF MASONRY BUILDINGS

To improve the performance of masonry buildings when subjected to earthquake, specifications and limit specified in IS 1905 should be applied to the design and construction of such masonry buildings. The provisions of IS 1905 are in addition to general requirements of IS 1893 (Part I). For seismic design of masonry buildings following procedure should be applied.

1. Calculation of lateral loads. The lateral loads should be calculated by static method. This is known as determination of base shear or storey shear. This base shear is distributed along the height of the building. This has been illustrated by examples in chapter 15.

2. In case of rigid diaphragms, the storey shear is distributed to the vertical resisting member or element in direct proportion to their relative rigidities. In case of flexible diaphragms, the exterior vertical resisting elements share half the base shear and the remaining half base shear is shared by the interior vertical resisting elements. As in case of masonry buildings these vertical lateral load resisting elements are masonry shear walls.

Thus it becomes essential to determine the relative rigidity of walls. For the determination of rigidity of shear walls, following assumptions are made:

(*a*) The shear walls are assumed to behave as cantilever.

(*b*) The segments of wall between adjacent openings (door and windows) called piers are assumed fixed at their top and bottom.

(*c*) However wall as well as piers may be assumed as cantilever or fixed depending on the relative rigidities of walls and floor diaphragms.

Let the deflection of the wall or pier fixed at the bottom and free at top *i.e.* (cantilever) be Δ_c, then

$$\Delta_c = \frac{P}{E_m \cdot t}\left[4\left(\frac{h}{d}\right)^3 + 3\left(\frac{h}{d}\right)\right] \qquad \ldots(16.6)$$

and the rigidity R_c of the cantilever pier is given as

$$R_c = \frac{1}{\Delta_c} \quad \text{...(16.7)}$$

where,

P = Lateral force on the pier or wall

E_m = Modulus of elasticity of masonry in compression

h = Height of pier or wall

d = Width of the pier panel

t = Thickness of wall or pier

(*ii*) If deflection of a wall or pier fixed at top and bottom = Δ_f

Then $$\Delta_f = \frac{p}{E_m \cdot t}\left[\left(\frac{h}{d}\right)^3 + 3\left(\frac{h}{d}\right)\right] \quad \text{...(16.8)}$$

and Rigidity $$F_f = \frac{1}{\Delta_f} \quad \text{...(16.9)}$$

(**Note:** Suffix f denotes fixed wall pier at top and bottom and c denotes cantilever).

3. In case the masonry shear wall segments are combined horizontally then combined rigidity is given by the relation

$$R_c = R_{C1} + R_{C2} + R_{C3} + \ldots R_{Cn} \quad \text{...(16.10)}$$

(*a*) In case of vertical combined rigidities, the combined rigidity is given as

$$\frac{1}{R_c} = \frac{1}{R_{C1}} + \frac{1}{R_{C2}} + \frac{1}{R_{C3}} \quad \text{...(16.11)}$$

(as resistance in parallel)

(*b*) Usually the walls have openings as shown in Fig. 16.16.

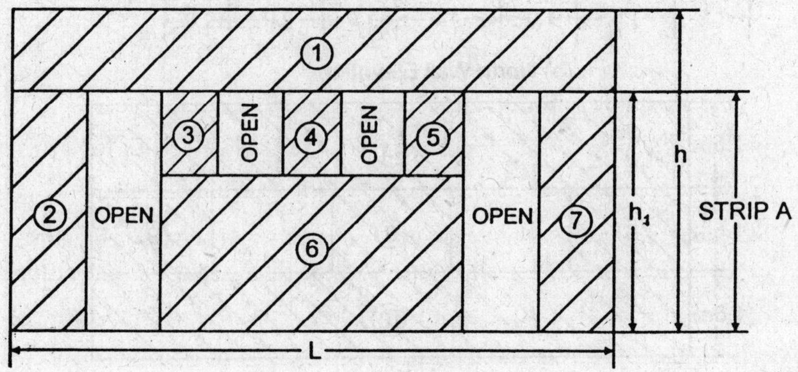

Fig. 16.16.

4. Steps in calculation of deflection and rigidity.

(*i*) The deflection of solid wall of length 'L' and height h is calculated as a cantilever as say Δ_{S_0}.

(*ii*) The opening having a height equal to the height of the largest opening is selected. The deflection of this height of strip say A as shown in figure is calculated. Let it be Δ_{ST}. The size of strip A is $L \times h_1$.

(*iii*) Let deflections (Δ_p) of all piers numbered 2, 3, 4, 5, 6 and 7 is calculated.

Then total deflection of the wall is

$$\Delta = \Delta_{S_0} - \Delta_{ST} + \Delta_P \qquad \text{...(16.12)}$$

and rigidity

$$R = \frac{1}{\Delta} \qquad \text{...(16.13)}$$

The method is illustrated by the following solved example 5...

Example 5. A building is constructed on a 9 × 9 m plot. The height of the storey is 4.0 m. The size and location of door and windows on its north and south walls is shown on the Fig. 16.17. Determine the rigidity of these walls in terms of $E_m \cdot t$, where E_m is modulus of elasticity of masonry in compression and t is the thickness of the wall.

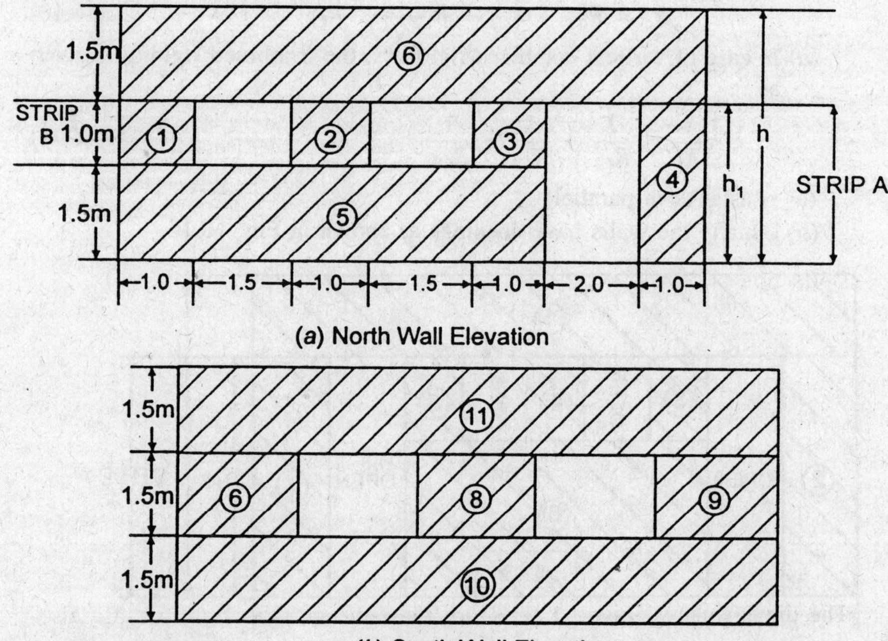

(*a*) North Wall Elevation

(*b*) South Wall Elevation

Fig. 16.17.

Solution. Openings in walls are shown in Fig. 16.17 (*a*) and (*b*) by strips

Let

Deflection of given wall = Δ_{wall}

Deflection of solid wall as cantilever = $\Delta_{\text{solid wall}}$

Deflection of strip A = Δ_{st}

Deflections of solid wall portions as 1, 2, 3, 4, 5

$$\Delta_{\text{WALL}} = \Delta_{SOLID\ \text{WALL}} - \Delta_{st} A + \Delta_{1,2,3,4,5}$$

$$\therefore \quad \Delta_{1,2,3,4,5} = \frac{1}{R_{1,2,3,4,5}}$$

where R is relative rigidity.

But $\quad R_{1,2,3,4,5} = R_4 + R_{1,2,3,5}$

$$R_{1,2,3,5} = \frac{1}{\Delta_{1,2,3,5}}$$

Now deflection of piers 1, 2, 3, 5 as a fixed wall

$$\therefore \quad \Delta_{1,2,3,5} = \Delta_{\text{solid }1,2,3,5} - \Delta_{st\,B} + \Delta_{1,2,3}$$

$$\Delta_{1,2,3} = \frac{1}{R_1 + R_2 + R_3}$$

$$\Delta_{\text{solid}} = \frac{1}{E_m \cdot t}\left[4\left(\frac{h}{d}\right)^3 + 3\left(\frac{h}{d}\right)\right]$$

$$= \frac{1}{E_m \cdot t}\left[\frac{4 \times 4 \times 4 \times 4}{9 \times 9 \times 9} + \frac{3 \times 4}{9}\right]$$

$$= \frac{1}{E_m \cdot t}[0.3512 + 1.333] = \frac{1.6845}{E_m \cdot t}$$

$$\text{Deflection of strip } A = \frac{1}{E_m \cdot t}\left[4\left(\frac{h}{d}\right)^3 + 3\left(\frac{h}{d}\right)\right]$$

$$= \frac{1}{E_m \cdot t}\left[\frac{4 \times 2.5 \times 2.5 \times 2.5}{9 \times 9 \times 9} + \frac{3 \times 2.5}{9}\right]$$

$$= \frac{1}{E_m \cdot t}[0.0375 + 0.8333] = \frac{0.8906}{E_m \cdot t}$$

$$\Delta_{1,2,3,4,5} = \frac{1}{R_{1,2,3,4,5}}$$

The dimensions of piers, 1, 2, 3 are same, hence their rigidities are also same.

i.e. $R_1 = R_2 = R_3 = \dfrac{E_m \cdot t}{\left[\left(\dfrac{h}{d}\right)^3 + 3\left(\dfrac{h}{d}\right)\right]} = \dfrac{E_m \cdot t}{\left(\dfrac{1}{1}\right)^3 + 3\left(\dfrac{1}{1}\right)} = \dfrac{E_m \cdot t}{1 + 3}$

$$= \frac{E_m \cdot t}{4} = 0.25\, E_m \cdot t$$

$\therefore$ $\Delta_{1, 2, 3} = \dfrac{1}{3 \times (0.25\, E_m \cdot t)} = \dfrac{1}{0.75\, E_m \cdot t} = \dfrac{1.333}{E_m \cdot t}$

$$\Delta_{\text{solid } 1, 2, 3, 5} = \frac{1}{E_m \cdot t}\left[\left(\frac{h}{d}\right)^3 + 3\left(\frac{h}{d}\right)\right]$$

$$= \frac{1}{0.75\, E_m \cdot t}\left[\left(\frac{2.5}{6}\right)^3 + 3\left(\frac{2.5}{6}\right)\right]$$

$$= \frac{1}{E_m \cdot t}\,[0.07233 + 1.25] = \frac{1.3223}{E_m \cdot t}$$

$$\Delta_{\text{strip B}} = \frac{1}{E_m \cdot t}\left[\left(\frac{h}{d}\right)^3 + 3\left(\frac{h}{d}\right)\right]$$

$$= \frac{1}{E_m \cdot t}\left[\left(\frac{1}{6}\right)^3 + 3\left(\frac{1}{6}\right)\right]$$

$$= \frac{1}{E_m \cdot t}\left[\frac{1}{216} + \frac{1}{2}\right]$$

$$= \frac{1}{E_m \cdot t}\,[0.00463 + 0.5]$$

$$= \frac{0.50463}{E_m \cdot t}$$

$\therefore$ $\Delta_{1, 2, 3, 5} = \Delta_{\text{solid } 1, 2, 3, 5} - \Delta_{\text{strip B}} + \Delta_{1, 2, 3}$

$$= \frac{1.3223}{E_m \cdot t} - \frac{0.50463}{E_m \cdot t} + \frac{1.3333}{E_m \cdot t} = \frac{2.151}{E_m \cdot t}$$

$\therefore$ Rigidity of piers 1, 2, 3, 5 $= \dfrac{1}{\Delta_{1, 2, 3, 5}} = \dfrac{E_m \cdot t}{2.151} = 0.465\, E_m \cdot t$

Rigidly of pier 4 $= R_4 = \dfrac{E_m \cdot t}{\left(\dfrac{h}{d}\right)^3 + \left(\dfrac{h}{d}\right)} = \dfrac{E_m \cdot t}{\left(\dfrac{2.5}{1}\right)^3 + 3\left(\dfrac{2.5}{1}\right)}$

$$= \frac{E_m \cdot t}{15.625 + 7.5} = \frac{E_m \cdot t}{23.13} = 0.04325\, E_m \cdot t$$

Adding $R_{1,2,3,5} + R_4 = 0.465\, E_m \cdot t + 0.04325\, E_m \cdot t$

$$= 0.5083\, E_m \cdot t$$

∴ Deflection $\Delta_{1,2,3,4,5} = \dfrac{1}{R_{1,2,3,4,5}} = \dfrac{1}{0.5083\, E_m \cdot t}$

$$= \frac{1.967}{E_m \cdot t}$$

Hence deflection of wall $\Delta_{\text{wall}} = \Delta_{solid\,1,2,3,5} - \Delta_{strip\,R} + \Delta_{1,2,3,5}$

$$= \frac{1.6845}{E_m \cdot t} - \frac{0.8906}{E_m \cdot t} + \frac{1.967}{E_m \cdot t}$$

$$= \frac{2.761}{E_m \cdot t}$$

∴ Rigidity of wall $R_{\text{wall}} = \dfrac{1}{\Delta_{wall}} = 0.3622\, E_m \cdot t$

Thus the rigidity of north wall = $0.3622\, E_m \cdot t$.

(*ii*) *Rigidity of south wall*

The deflection of wall $\Delta_{\text{wall}} = \Delta_{solid\ wall} - \Delta_{strip\ B_2} + \Delta_{7,8,9}$

Assuming solid wall as cantilever we get

$$\Delta_{solid} = \frac{1}{E_m \cdot t}\left[4\left(\frac{h}{d}\right)^3 + 3\left(\frac{h}{d}\right)\right]$$

$$= \frac{1}{E_m \cdot t}\left[\frac{4 \times 4 \times 4 \times 4}{9 \times 9 \times 9} + \frac{3 \times 4}{9}\right]$$

$$= \frac{1.6845}{E_m \cdot t}$$

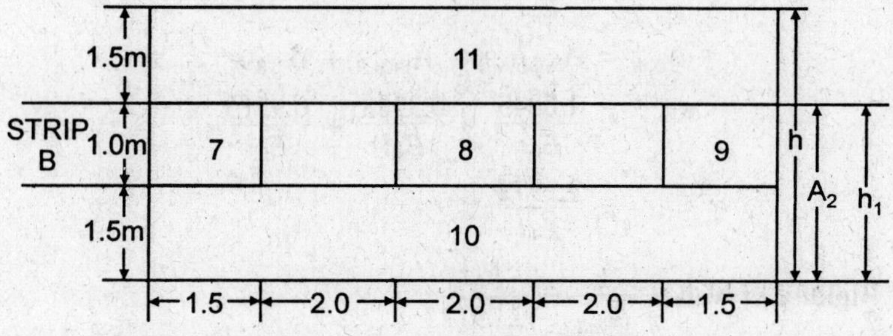

Fig. 14.18

Deflection of strip B $\Delta_{\text{strip B}} = \dfrac{1}{E_m \cdot t}\left[4 \times \left(\dfrac{1}{9}\right)^3 + 3\left(\dfrac{1}{9}\right)\right]$

$$= \frac{1}{E_m t}\,[0.0055 + 0.3333]$$

$$= \frac{0.3388}{E_m t}$$

Deflection of piers 7, 8, 9, $\Delta_{7,8,9} = \dfrac{1}{R_7 + R_8 + R_9}$

$$R_{7,8,9\,(f)} = R_{7(f)} + R_{8(f)} + R_{9(f)}$$

$$R_{7(f)} = R_{(f)} = \frac{E_m t}{\left(\dfrac{1}{1.5}\right)^3 + 3\left(\dfrac{1}{1.5}\right)}$$

$$= \frac{E_m t}{\dfrac{1}{3.375} + \dfrac{3.0}{1.5}}$$

$$= \frac{E_m t}{2.2962} = 0.4355\,E_m t$$

$$R_8 = \frac{E_m t}{\left(\dfrac{1}{2}\right)^3 + 3 \times \left(\dfrac{1}{2}\right)}$$

$$= \frac{E_m t}{1.625} = 0.615\,E_m t$$

$$\therefore \quad R_{7,8,9} = 0.615\,E_m t + 2\,(0.4355)\,E_m t = 1.0505\,E_m t$$

$$R_{7,8,9} = \frac{1}{R_{7,8,9}} = \frac{1}{1.0505\,E_m t}$$

$$= \frac{0.9515}{E_m t}$$

$$\therefore \quad \Delta_{wall} = \Delta_{solid\ wall} - \Delta_{strip\ B} + \Delta_{7,8,9}$$

$$= \frac{1.6845}{E_m t} - \frac{0.3388}{E_m t} + \frac{0.9515}{E_m t}$$

$$= \frac{2.2972}{E_m t}$$

Rigidity of wall $= \dfrac{1}{\Delta_{wall}} = \dfrac{E_m t}{2.2972}$

$$= 0.4353\,E_m t$$

The rigidity of south wall = 0.4353 $E_m t$.

The rigidity of north wall = 0.3622 $E_m t$.

$$\text{The relative rigidity of south wall} = \frac{0.4353}{(0.45353 + 0.3622)}$$

$$= \frac{4353}{0.7925} = 0.546$$

$$\text{The relative rigidity of north wall} = \frac{0.3622}{(0.4353 + 0.3622)}$$

$$= \frac{0.3622}{0.7925} = 0.454$$

Hence relative rigidity of north wall = 0.454

Relative rigidity of south wall = 0.546 **Ans.**

16.19. EARTHQUAKE RESISTANT STONE MASONRY BUILDING

Stone has been used in building construction since ancient times in India and other countries like Iran, Turkey and Greece etc. due to the locally availability of stone at cheap rates. Stone also is durable and strong. There are large number of stone buildings in the country ranging from rural stone houses to temples and royal palaces. The thickness of walls of a typical rural stone house varies from 60 cm to 120 cm. These walls usually are built with round stones obtained from river beds. In rural areas usually mud mortar is

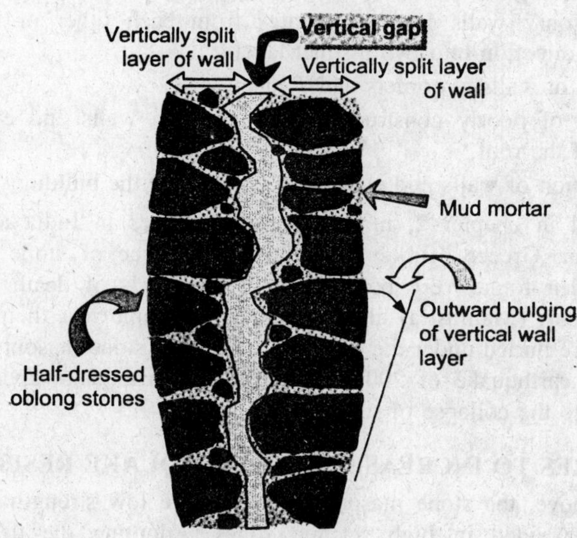

Fig. 16.19. Wall section of a traditional stone house (Courtesy—IITK)

used in the construction of stone masonry houses. The masonry is random rubble masonry as it is constructed by placing stones in a random way. The layers of this type of masonry are not coursed like a brick masonry layer. These un coursed walls have two exterior vertical layers (called Wythes) of large stones. The un filled space is filled with smaller size stones and mud mortar. A typical un coursed stone masonry wall is shown in Fig. 16.19. In most cases these walls support heavy roofs of slate, or timber joist with thick mud overlays etc.

A lay man considers such stone masonry buildings very strong and durable due to the large thickness of walls and robust appearance of the stone buildings. But these buildings are one of the most deficient building system from the point of view of earthquake resistance.

16.19.1. Deficiencies of stone buildings

Following deficiencies have been observed of the stone masonry:

1. The two vertical layers or wythes have no interconnection between them.
2. The thickness of walls is very excessive.
3. In the construction of the walls round stones have been used randombly. No regular shaped layers exist in these walls.

16.20. TYPE OF DAMAGE OF STONE MASONRY

Stone masonry buildings have been found to suffer from the following main disadvantages during an earthquake:

1. Stone masonry walls layers separates from each other or bulge in horizontal direction into two distinct layers.
2. Separation of walls at corners and T junctions.
3. Separation of poorly constructed roof from the walls and eventually collapse of the roof.
4. Disintegration of walls and eventually collapse of the buildings.

As discussed in chapter 2, in the past earthquakes in India and other counties like Iran, Greece, Turkey etc. the performance of stone masonry dwellings has been found very poor resulting thousands of death. In 1993 earthquake of Kilari (Mahrastra) alone about 8000 people lost their lives as most of them were buried under the debris of traditional stone masonry houses. Similarly in the earthquake of 2001, Bhuj (Gujrat) earthquake about 13800 people died due to the collapse of such type of houses.

16.21. MEASURES TO INCREASE THE EARTHQUAKE RESISTANCE

As stated above, the stone masonry buildings are low strength buildings and should be avoided in high seismic zones. Adopting the design and construction features suggested by IS 1382-1993 the earthquake resistance of stone masonry buildings may be increased sufficiently and risk of loss of life may be reduced. However these buildings can not be made totally free from damage and even from collapse in case of a major earthquake.

However, following measures have been found useful to reduce the damage of buildings:

1. To ensure proper construction of wall

The thickness of the wall should not be more than 45.0 cm. The round boulders should not be used in the construction of the wall, instead tooled surface of stones should be used in the construction. Mud mortar should not be used. Cement sand mortar of 1:6 ratio or lime sand mortar of 1:3 or richer should be used.

2. To ensure proper bond in masonry courses

The masonry should not be constructed in height more than 60 cm at a time. As far as possible the through stones should extend over the full width of the wall. If it is not possible, a pair of through stones from each side may be used over lapping each other. A through stone should extend upto 3/4 the

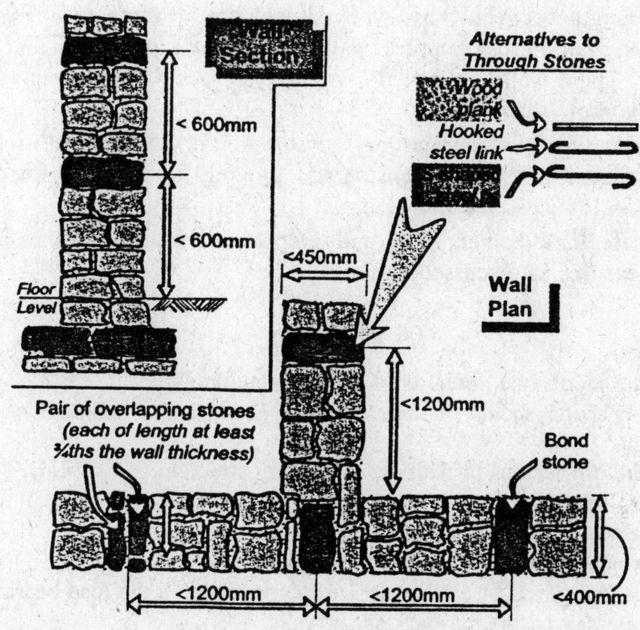

Fig. 16.20. Use of 'through stones' or 'bond stones' in stone masonry walls (Courtesy—IITK)

thickness of the wall, but should not be less than 35 cm for a end stone of thickness of 20 cm and for a 15 cm thickness its length should not be less than 30 cm. The through stone should be placed at every 60 cm along the height and a maximum spacing of 1.2 m along the length as shown in Fig. 16.20. Instead through stone, wood plank, hooked end steel links may be used as shown in Fig. 16.20 (*b*).

3. Provision of horizontal reinforcing elements

The stone masonry buildings also should be provided with horizontal bands at roof, lintel or plinth level as in case of brick masonry discussed in chapter 13. In stone masonry at least one band must be provided, preferably at lintel level.

4. Control on overall dimensions and height of masonry

(*a*) The height of each storey should not be more than 3.0 m.

(*b*) In general the stone masonry buildings should not be more than two storey when built with cement mortar and only one storey if built with lime or mud mortar.

(*c*) The minimum thickness of wall should not be less than 1/6th of its height.

(*d*) The length between cross walls should not be more than 5.0 m. For longer walls, cross support walls should be raised from the ground level. These walls are called *buttress*. The spacing of buttresses should not be more than 4.0 m.

Though this type of stone masonry construction is deficient with regards to earthquake resistance, but its extensive use is likely to continue for years to come due to its low cost and tradition.

But to safeguard human lives and property in future, it is essential to follow the measures as discussed above.

QUESTIONS

1. Give the merits and demerits of masonry buildings.
2. What measures should be taken to make the masonry buildings earthquake resistant.
3. Give the dimensions of wall for a masonry structure.
4. Discuss the significance of openings in a load bearing wall. Suggest dimensions of the openings.
5. Give a neat sketch to strengthen an opening.
6. Discuss the effects of earthquake on the openings in the load bearing walls.
7. Write a essay on the masonry shear walls.
8. Determine the rigidity of North and South shear walls shown in Fig. 16.21 in terms of E.t., where *E* is modulus of elasticity and *t* is thickness of the wall. The East and west walls are 15 m long and North and south wall 8.0m long. The height of the building is 4.0 m.

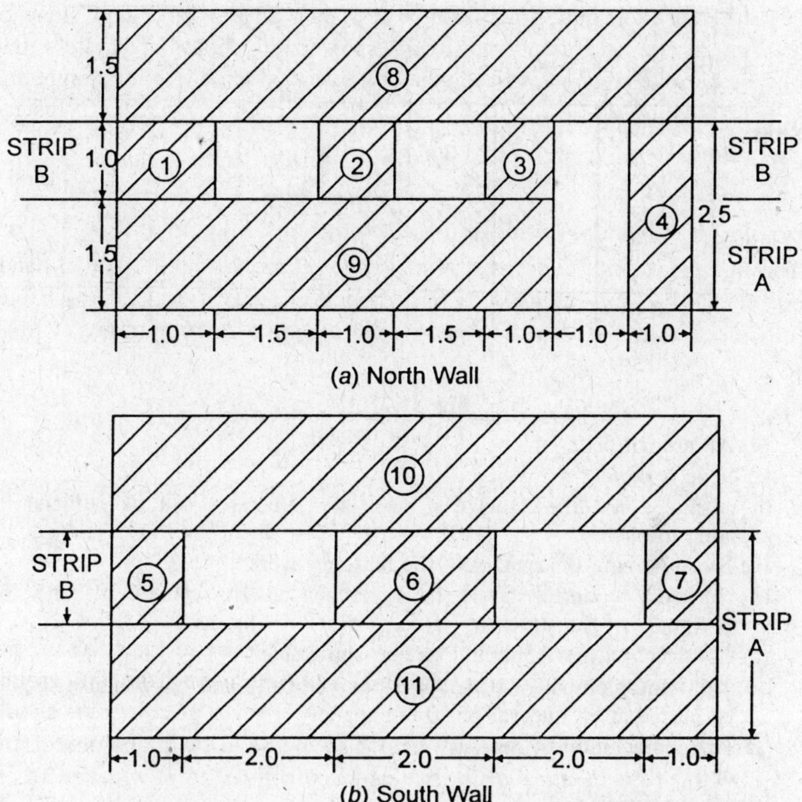

Fig. 16.21

[**Ans.** Rigidity of N wall = 0.345 Et,
Rigidity of South wall = 0.398 Et,
Relative rigidity of N wall = 0.46,
Relative rigidity of S wall = 0.54]

10. Determine the rigidity of the wall shown in the figure 16.22 in terms of E.t. where E is the elastic modulus and t is the thickness of wall [**Ans.** 0.3303 Et]
11. During an earthquake the masonry buildings usually are more damaged due to
    (*a*) Lack of bond between different units of the structures as bricks or stone units
    (*b*) More weights of masonry units
    (*c*) Less tensile strength of masonry buildings
    (*d*) Less shear resistance of masonry buildings
    (*e*) Improper bond between the walls and foundation of the structure
    (*f*) Absence of bonding arrangement between different walls of the building
    (*g*) Absence of proper bond between roof and walls.

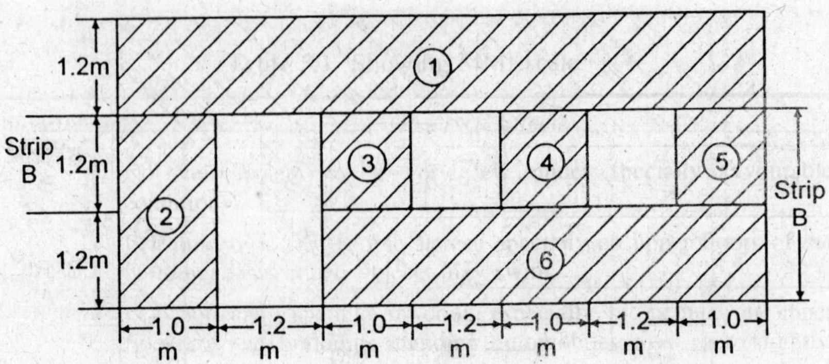

Fig. 16.22

(*h*) All are correct
(*i*) None is correct

12. In seismic zones the damage of masonry structures can be reduced by adopting measures
    (*a*) By improving the quality of the masonry work
    (*b*) Masonry courses should be level and totally vertical alround the periphery of the structure
    (*c*) Construction mortar should be non shrinkable
    (*d*) The reinforcement in both directions vertically and horizontally should be placed at an interval of 50 cm apart
    (*e*) The composition of masonry mortar should be of the proportion of 1:6 or 1:3
    (*f*) All are correct
13. To provide more stability to masonry structures in seismic zones measures can be taken
    (*a*) The open space in walls should not be more than 15% to 20% of the gross area of the wall
    (*b*) The width of open space should not be more than 35% of the length of the wall
    (*c*) The minimum space between two open spaces should not be less than 90 cms
    (*d*) To avoid to develop torsion in the corners, vertical reinforcement should be provided fully
    (*e*) All are correct
14. By adopting..............measures the stability of masonry structures can be improved
    (*a*) As far as possible buildings should be founded on level ground
    (*b*) The location of structures or buildings should be away from active faults, peak of mountains and their series
    (*c*) As far as possible buildings should not be founded on alluvial soils and non cohesive soils
    (*d*) All are effective measures

15. Elements............are included in the configuration of the building
    (*a*) Over all dimension and shape of the building
    (*b*) Distribution of mass of the building
    (*c*) Horizontal and lateral components of the building
    (*d*) All the above
16. In seismic zones the proportion of mortar is most efficient
    (*a*) 1:3 cement sand mortar
    (*b*) 1:1:6 cement lime-sand mortar
    (*c*) 1:2:9 cement lime-sand mortar
    (*d*) Mud mortar
17. In seismic zones IV and V the numbers of stone masonry storey should be limited to
    (*a*) 6 (*b*) 4
    (*c*) 2 (*d*) 5
18. The height of stone masonry storey should be limit to
    (*a*) 4.5 m (*b*) 1.5 m
    (*c*) 3.0 m (*d*) No restriction
19. The minimum thickness of wall should be of its height
    (*a*) 1/10 (*b*) 1/5
    (*c*) 1/2 (*d*) 1/6
20. The thickness of stone masonry wall should not exceed
    (*a*) 75 cm (*b*) 45 cm
    (*c*) 60 cm (*d*) 30 cm
21. Maximum spacing along the height of the through stone or bond stone should not be more than
    (*a*) 90 cm (*b*) 60 cm
    (*c*) 120 cm (*d*) 150 cm

ANSWERS

11 (*h*)	14. (*d*)	17. (*c*)	20. (*b*)
12. (*f*)	15. (*d*)	18. (*c*)	21. (*b*)
13. (*e*)	16. (*b*)	19. (*d*)	

17

Design of Earthquake Resistant Reinforced Concrete Structures

17.1. INTRODUCTION

Concrete is a plastic material in its initial mixing stage and can be moulded into any desired shape without any difficulty. Due to this property of concrete it is used in structural activities all over the world on large scale. The compressive strength of concrete is very good and can be produced of any desired compressive strength, but its tensile strength is only 10% of its compressive strength. Hence to increase its tensile strength, steel is used along with concrete in concrete structures. The design is based on the assumption that all compressive stresses will be borne by concrete and tensile stresses by steel. The study of failure of structures during past earthquakes has revealed that R.C.C. structures properly designed and constructed performed well. By incorporating the provisions of Indian standards on earthquake resistant design of structures, concrete structures can be designed and constructed in any seismic zone to withstand earthquake of any intensity with out collapse. IS 456-2000 has laid down the compressive and shear strength of concrete and tensile strength of steel to be used in earthquake resistant design of R.C.C. structures.

17.2. DAMAGES TO R.C.C. STRUCTURES

Typical damage to R.C.C. structures include:

1. Cracking in tension zone
2. Diagonal cracking in the core
3. Loss of cover to reinforcement
4. Crushing of concrete core by reversal of forces
5. Bursting of stirrups out wards
6. Bulging of main reinforcement bars
7. Bond failure
8. Direct shear failure in case of short elements
9. Shear cracking in beam-column intersection zone is one of the reasons of failures.
10. Shear cracking in the beam and column intersection zone.

11. Diagonal cracking in shear walls.
12. Tearing of slabs at junctions and discontinuities with stiff vertical elements.

In short it can be said that even in well reinforced concrete, the main or root cause of failure of a concrete member is the cracking of the concrete which leads to degradation in the cracked zone. Due to cracking reinforcement gets elongated permanently and cracks do not close and the interlocking of aggregates is destroyed. In joint zones concrete is destroyed completely between the cracks and sliding of reinforcement takes place. The stiffness and energy absorption capacity of the members reduce considerably.

Though most of the ill effect of seismic loading can be eliminated by providing closely spaced stirrups or ties in the zones of plastic hinges. How ever following provisions must be adopted in the case of R.C.C. structure construction.

1. All elements of the frames should be detailed in such a way so that they can with stand the severest earthquake in a ductile manner. The elements which are unable to behave in a ductile manner, should be designed to remain elastic at the severest loading or load conditions.
2. Shear and bond failures of the structures must be avoided. Such failures are known as non ductile modes of failures. To avoid shear and bond failures of the elements, anchorages and splicing of reinforcement bars should not be done in the zones of high stresses and high resistance to shear should be provided.
3. The rigid elements must be attached to the structure by flexible fixtures or fixing.
4. In order to develop more energy absorbing ductility zones before a failure mechanism is developed, a high degree of structural redundancy should be provided. For such a condition to occur in the framed structure, the yielding of beams should occur first and the failure in columns should be avoided. Columns should remain elastic at the maximum design seismic level.
5. At discontinuities joints must be provided with sufficient provision of movement, so that striking or pounding of two faces of the buildings against each other may be avoided.

17.3. PRINCIPLES OF EARTHQUAKE RESISTANT DESIGN OF R.C.C. MEMBERS

The lateral loads or forces produced by earthquakes are unpredictable. Hence to design a structure to be resistant of the severest earthquake will result in very massive elements, whose cost will be exhorbitively very high. Secondly the frequency of severe earthquakes is very low, some times they occur after 500 years or even more. Thus the design philosophy of earthquake resistant structures adopted so far is based on the concept that a properly designed structure resists the moderate earthquake with a damage that can be repaired and strong earthquake with out collapse but with an acceptable damage. The criterion of acceptable damage was introduced to limit the increase in the cost of construction of earthquake resistant structures.

The older design requirements used to insist that in an earthquake serviceability limit state could be passed as long as the building stayed with in its ultimate limit state *i.e.* the building should have enough structural integrity to remain standing.

This meant that if serviceability limit state were passed the structure would have to be demolished, as it is no longer safe to use. Thus the new concept of ultimate limit state stipulates that the structure should remain standing in an earthquake and need not be demolished after the earthquake. By observing the following principles of earthquake resistant design, the collapse of R.C.C. structures can be prevented.

1. The failure of the structure should be ductile rather than brittle. Thus ductility with large energy dissipation capacity (less deterioration in stiffness) must be ensured.
2. Flexure failure should occur or take place before the shear failure.
3. Beams should fail before the columns.
4. The joints or connections should be stronger than the members which join the connections or joints.

17.4. DUCTILITY

The ratio of the displacement at the maximum load to the displacement at yield load is called the ductility of a member.

17.4.1. Ductile Behaviour

The ability of a member to under go large inelastic deformations with the little decrease in its strength is known as ductile behaviour of the member. The available ductility of a member increases with the following factors:

(*a*) The ductility of a member increases with the increase in the compression steel content.

(*b*) It increases with the increase in compressive strength of concrete.

(*c*) It increases with increase in ultimate concrete strain.

However ductility decreases with the following factors:

(*a*) With the increase in tensile steel content,

(*b*) Increase in axial load, and

(*c*) increase in steel yield strength.

Reinforced concrete structures properly designed as per provisions of IS 456-2000 and IS 13920-2002 have desired strength and ductility to withstand the major earthquakes. Following points are important from the point of view of ductility.

(*a*) The confinement of concrete at critical sections of stress concentration by spirals or hoops, increases the ductility of column under combined axial load and bending. The stress concentration section may be as a beam and column connection.

(*b*) Limitations on the use of compression reinforcement, or on the amount of tensile reinforcement or increase in energy absorbing capacity.

(*c*) The confinement of concrete with stirrups or spirals reinforcement increases the ultimate strain of concrete. The confining reinforcement also increases:

(*i*) Shear resistance

(*ii*) It provides additional lateral support to the main reinforcement.

(*iii*) In increases the strength in shear and makes it greater than ultimate flexure strength.

The effect of axial load and confinement on rotational ductile capacity is shown in Fig. 17.1.

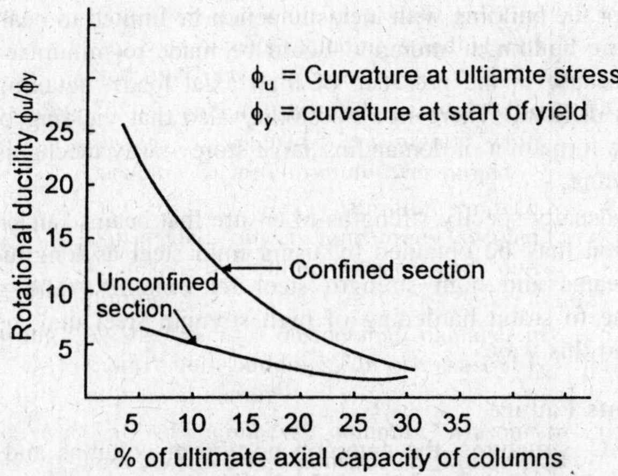

Fig. 17.1. Variation in rotational ductility for tied columns

(*iv*) Detailing of the section must be given special attention, such as splices in reinforcement and avoidance of planes of weakness that might be developed by bending or terminating all bars at the same section.

17.4.2. Flexure failure

The earthquake resistant structures for load deflection characteristics are mainly dependent on the moment curvature relationship of the sections. When in a section the tension steel content is less than the compression steel content, the yield strength in the tension steel reaches first. At this stage for nearly constant B.M. large increase in curvature takes place. This type of failure is called as tensile failure or flexural failure. On the other hand when there is more tension steel and low compression steel, the tension steel does not yield and concrete crushes and section fails in a brittle manner if the concrete is not confined well. This failure of the sections is called as compression failure. Thus beams should be so proportioned as to exhibit the ductile characteristics in a tension failure. Further to check the shear failure taking place before the bending failure the design should be such that tension steel in the member yields, while the shear steel remains at less stress than the yield stress. Thus for beams a conservative approach to ensure safety of beams in shear is to make the shear strength equal to the maximum shear demand (shear developed).

17.4.3. Weak beam-strong column design concept

For locations that are likely to sustain large inelastic deformations the structures should be designed to yield. The observations of the failures of structures due to yielding in columns during past earthquakes has led the concept of weak beam and strong column design, in which the strength of column is made at least equal to that of beams strength. The aim of such design is that strength of columns which form a stiff and unyielding spine over the height of the building with inelastic action be limited to beam strengths. For R.C.C. frame buildings, attempts should be made to minimise the yielding in columns because in the presence of high axial loads, detailing for of ductile response is difficult. There is a possibility also that yielding of columns may result in the formation of demanding large storey-sway mechanism and collapse of the structure.

Codes usually specify strengths to ensure that beams fail prior to columns. This situation may be obtained by using mild steel as longitudinal reinforcement in beams and high strength steel for columns. The greater strength increase due to strain hardening of high strength steel may be utilized to an advantage in this way.

17.4.4. Joints Failure

In R.C.C. structures, the common portion of columns and beams at their inter sections are known as beam column joint. A beam-column joint is shown in Fig. 17.2 (*a*). The strength of beam and column parts at the intersection is limited. Hence the joints also have limited force carrying capacity. When during earthquakes large force than their carrying capacity is applied at joints, they are severely damaged. The joint section having steel bars of beam and column passing through it, is over crowed and has less space for repair. Hence repair of a damaged beam-column joint is difficult. Thus as far as possible damage to beam-column joint must be avoided. Therefore beam-column joint must be designed to resist the seismic forces.

17.4.5. Behaviour of joints during earthquake

During earthquake shaking beams adjoining a joint are subjected to moments in the same direction (clock wise or anti clockwise) as shown in Fig. 17.2 (*a*). Due to these moments the top reinforcement bars in the beam-column joint are pulled in one direction and the bottom reinforcement bars in the opposite direction as shown in Fig. 17.2 (*b*). These forces are balanced by the bond stress developed between concrete and steel in the joint zone. In case the column is not-wide enough or the strength of concrete of the joint is low, the grip of concrete on reinforcement bars is insufficient, resulting slips of steel bars in side the joint region. Thus the load carrying capacity of beams decreases.

Further due to push and pull action of forces at the top and bottom ends, joints under go geometric distortion. One length of the joint diagonal elongates and the other shortens or compresses as shown in Fig. 17.2 (*c*). If the size of the cross-section of the column is insufficient; then concrete in the joint develops diagonal cracks and the structure may be damaged. The failure of the structure may be due to the following reasons.

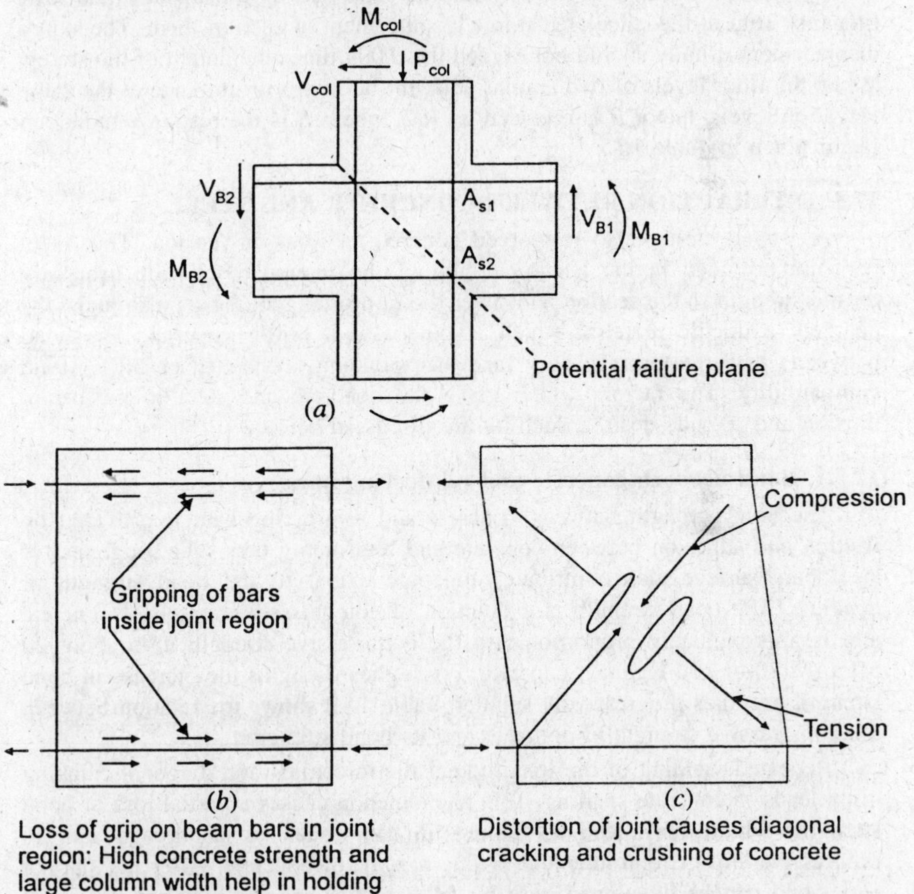

(*b*) Loss of grip on beam bars in joint region: High concrete strength and large column width help in holding the grips of steel bare

(*c*) Distortion of joint causes diagonal cracking and crushing of concrete

Fig. 17.2. Pull-push forces on joints cause two problems (Courtesy—IITK)

1. Anchorage failure of the beam reinforcement in the joint.
2. Development of shear with in the joint.
3. Bond failure of the beam or column reinforcement passing through the joint.

17.4.6. Joints at Discontinuities

To avoid pounding of two adjacent buildings or two adjacent units of the same building, proper joints should be provided at the discontinuities. During earthquake shaking two adjacent building or two adjacent parts of the same building may pound (strike or hit) each other. The pounding of buildings or the two units can alter the dynamic response of the buildings or units. To avoid damaging contacts when the two buildings or units deflect towards each other such pounding buildings or units should be separated by a distance equal to R times the sum of the calculated storey displacement of each of them. The storey displacement usually should not exceed the 0.004 times the height of the storey. When the floor levels of two similar adjacent buildings or units are at the same elevation levels, factor R is replaced by $R/2$, where R is the response reduction factor given in Table 15.7.

17.5. INTERACTION BETWEEN CONCRETE AND STEEL

As stated earlier also reinforced concrete is weak in tension. Thus steel bars are provided in the tension region of the section to provide necessary tensile strength to the section. However the reinforcing steel bars also make the concrete a ductile material which is otherwise a brittle material. The bond between the reinforcing bars and surrounding concrete ensures strain compatibility. The factors which make the concrete and steel to behave in unision and provide desired ductility are discussed below:

17.5.1. Bond between concrete and reinforcing bars

The bond strength between concrete and reinforcing bars is provided by friction and adhesion between concrete and reinforcing bars. The roughness of steel bars surface also contributes to some extent to the bond strength of concrete. The bond strength is a function of compressive strength of concrete and is approximately proportional to the compressive strength upto about 20 MPa (M 20 or 200 Kg/cm^2) concrete. For higher strengths the increase in bond strength becomes progressively smaller. Table 14.2 shows the relation between the compressive strength of concrete and its bond strength.

Repeated yielding of the longitudinal reinforcement and diagonal cracking often leads to concrete spalling. This phenomenon causes a partial loss of bond strength, which may lead to failure in the zones of anchorage due to progressive slip of reinforcement or due to split of concrete. After the start of slip, bond can be developed only by friction. For seismic resistant design of concrete structures use of deformed bars as reinforcement is recommended due to their better bond characteristics. Deformed bars have better bond characteristics than plain bars due to the formation of ribs at their surface.

The bond strength of deformed bars at the initial slip practically is the same as that of plain round bars, but with the progress of the slip resistance increases due to the ribs being wedged into the concrete. When a deformed bar is embedded in concrete which is transversely reinforced against splitting with sufficient cover, concrete between ribs eventually gets crushed and the bar pulls out. Pulling of bar is often accompanied by splitting of the surrounding concrete. The bond strength associated with this type of failure mechanism increases with the increase in the thickness of the concrete cover and increase in the transverse reinforcement.

17.5.2. Confining effects of transverse reinforcement

When the stress in a concrete specimen approaches its compressive strength, internal cracking of the specimen takes place progressively and the concrete expands transversally. If the concrete in the compressive zone is confined by transverse reinforcement as spirals and hoop ties, the ductility of the concrete increases greatly. In case the square hoop ties are provided in the section of the member, then the concrete along the diagonals of the tie is

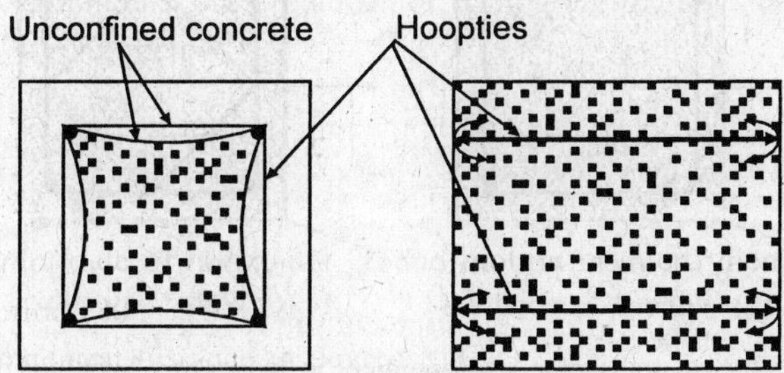

Fig. 17.3. Confinement of concrete by square hoop ties

confined as shown in Fig. 17.3. It has been observed that a square hoop tie generally apply confining pressure near the corners only as the pressure of the concrete tries to push the sides of the tie out wards. However spirals confine concrete more effectively due to its circular shape. The circular shape of the tie provides a continuous confining pressure around the whole circumference.

17.5.3. Buckling of reinforcement bars

The bending of compression steel in columns and beams from its vertical position toward out side is known as buckling of reinforcing bars. In beams and columns the longitudinal reinforcing bars under compression are prevented from bucking by the lateral restraint provided by the concrete. Under cyclic loading that does not cause alternating flexural, the compression steel in straight members ordinarily does not buckle out of concrete even in the absence of restraining stirrups and ties or at high strains. Normally the concrete cover to reinforcement is sufficient to check buckling, but at places where longitudinal

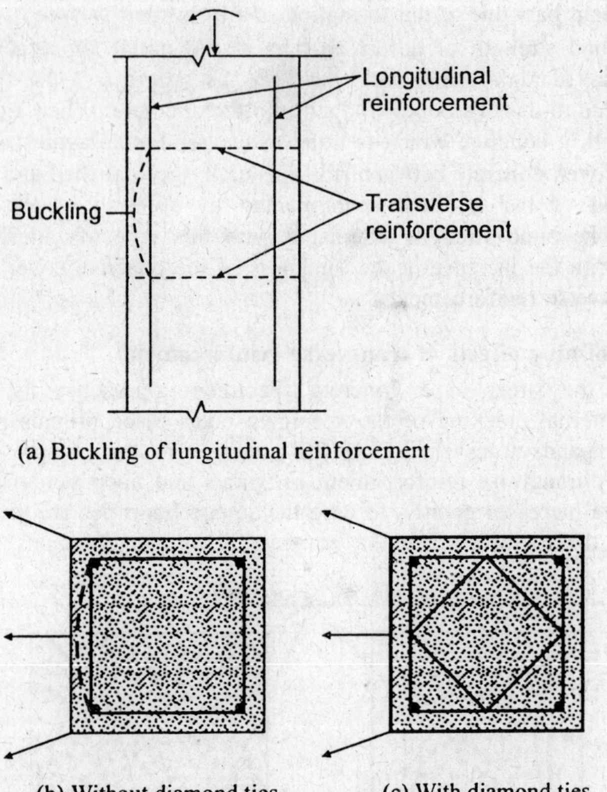

(a) Buckling of longitudinal reinforcement

(b) Without diamond ties (c) With diamond ties

Fig. 17.4. Effect of transverse reinforcement in preventing buckling of main reinforcement

steel bars bend inwards, curvatures are induced. The later phenomenon is not applicable to corner reinforcement, but a moderate number of ties or stirrups are sufficient to check the buckling. Placing of stirrups in beams is shown in Fig. 17.4.

When covering concrete subjected to high compressive stresses become unstable, the restraining effect is reduced and the bars buckle out wards as shown in Fig. 17.4 (*a*) and the axial force carried by the compression steel bar is reduced. Thus the load carrying capacity of the member is reduced. Also in situations where the bending moment changes its sign and reaches values such that the steel yields in tension during one part of the cycle and acts as compression member during another part of the cycle, the reinforcing bars tend to buckle out of the member and need transverse reinforcement for confinement.

In order to minimise the reduction in load carrying capacity of columns and other compressive members and to ensure sufficient ductility Indian codes have put limits on the ratio of the distance between the transverse reinforcement to the diameter of longitudinal reinforcing bars. In case of beams the distance between the ties or stirrups should not be more than 8 times the diameter of the main reinforcing bars or $d/4$ where d is the effective depth of beam (distance between the top of beam and the centre of main reinforcement).

In case of columns spacing of stirrups should not be more than $D/2$ where D is the least dimension of the column. Details are shown on page 216, Fig. 8.5, 17.16.

The transverse reinforcement does not effectively support the longitudinal reinforcing bars placed at intermediate points between the corners as stirrups bend out wards as shown in Fig. 17.4 (*b*). For confining concrete effectively diamond ties as shown in Fig. 17.4 (*c*) are found useful.

17.6. DESIGN LOADS

To work out the maximum member forces following combinations of loads may be used

For design limit state method as per IS-456-2000 following combination

1. 1.5 (DL + LL)
2. 1.2 (DL + LL + EQX)
3. 1.2 (DL + LL + EQZ)
4. 1.2 (DL + LL – EQX)
5. 1.2 (DL + LL – EQZ)
6. 1.5 (DL + EQX)
7. 1.5 (DL + EQZ)
8. 1.5 (DL – EQX)
9. 1.5 (DL – EQZ)
10. 0.9 DL + 1.5 EQX
11. 0.9 DL + 1.5 EQZ
12. 0.9 DL – 1.5 EQX
13. 0.9 DL – 1.5 EQZ

may be adopted.

However IS 1893 part-1-2004 suggests following load combination for the design of seismic resistant structures.

1. DL + IL
2. DL + IL + WL or EL
3. DL + WL
4. 0.9 DL + EL

where, DL = Dead load

IL = Impact load

WL = wind load

EL = Earthquake load

LL = Live load

EQX = Seismic load in X Direction

EQZ = Seismic load in Z Direction

17.7. CONCRETE DETAILING (GENERAL REQUIREMENTS)

As stated above the design, construction and detailing of R.C.C. structures should be done as pr IS-450-2000 except the provisions as suggested below. For satisfactory earthquake resistant performance the following rules must be observed strictly. These details should be satisfactory for the medium and high seismic activity regions. In low risk regions some relaxations may be made in the following requirements, but the principles of lapping, containment, and continuity must be maintained to obtain adequate ductility.

17.7.1. Concrete quality or grade

For structural concrete the minimum recommended characteristics strength should be of 20 N/mm^2 *i.e.* 20 MPa or 200 kg/cm^2. But in regions of IV & V seismic activity, where the height of building is more than 15 m (4 storeys), the minimum grade of concrete may M25 or 25 N/mm^2 or 25 MPa *i.e.* 250 Kg/cm^2 strength concrete. For different elements following grades of concrete may be adopted.

1. For R.C.C. columns in lowest few stories
   M 35 or 35 N/mm^2 or 35 Kg/cm^2
2. For R.C.C. columns in the middle few stories
   M 30 (30 N/mm^2 or 300 kg/cm^2
3. For R.C.C. columns in top few stories — M 25
4. For beams, slabs and stair cases etc. — M 20
5. For Raft foundation — M 20 or M 25
6. Maximum water cement ratio may be adopted as 0.45
7. Minimum cement contents — 300 Kg/m^3 of concrete

Any admixture of approved brand may be used as per design requirements.

17.7.2. Clear cover to reinforcement

Following cover thickness may be adopted:

For foundation R.C.C.

1. Raft — 60 mm
2. Footings — 60 mm
3. For columns — 40 mm
4. For beams — 25 mm or equal to the diameter of the main steel bar which ever is more
5. For slabs — 20 mm

For further details table 16 and 16 (*a*) of IS 456-2000 may be consulted.

17.7.3. Reinforcement quality

For achieving adequate earthquake resistant structures the properties of steel reinforcement must be ensured before use by applying the appropriate tests. While selecting the reinforcing steel for earthquake regions following points should be observed:

1. A minimum adequate yield stress of steel must be ensured. Grades of steel having characteristic strength more than 415 N/mm^2 should not be used. How ever high strength deformed bars manufactured by the thermo-mechanical treatment process of grade Fe 500 and Fe 550 having elongation more than 14.5% may be used as reinforcement. Cold worked

steel is not recommended.

2. Actual yield strength based on tensile test of steel should not exceed the specified yield strength by more than 120 N/mm^2. If the difference is more, then shear or bond failure may occur before the flexural hinge formation. In such conditions the capacity design concept will not work.
3. The minimum ratio of actual ultimate strength to the actual yield strength should be 1.25. To develop an inelastic rotation capacity, a structural member needs an adequate length of yield region along the axis of the member. The length of the yield region is directly proportional to the ratio of ultimate to yield moment *i.e.* larger the ultimate to yield moment ratio, longer the yield region.
4. The elongation test is important, particularly for ensuring adequate steel ductility.
5. For ensuring sufficient ductility of reinforcement, the bend and rebend tests are most important.
6. Welding of reinforcing bars may cause embrittleness in them. Hence as a general rule it should not be allowed in all steels. Welding of reinforcing bars should be allowed for steel of suitable chemical properties and approved welding techniques should be used for the purpose.

Galvanising of reinforcing bars also may cause embrittlement of the bars. Thus it needs special considerations.

Welding steel fabric or mesh is not suitable for seismic resistance due to its potential brittleness.

17.7.4. Splices

In seismic resistant frames the laps of reinforcement must continue to function while joints or members undergo large deformations. The stress transfer takes place through the concrete surrounding the bars. Thus it is essential that to place and compact the concrete well there must be adequate space around the bars in the member. Thus splices should ideally be staggered and located away from the sections of maximum tension. Lapped splices should never be located in potential plastic hing regions. In columns of buildings the splices should be located in the mid height region between the floors.

As far as possible laps should not be located in the high stress zone, such as near the connections of beam and column. The concrete may crack under large deformations affecting adversely the stress transfer by the bond. In high stress regions the laps should be considered as an anchorage problem rather than lap problem. In other words in high stress regions the transfer of stress from one bar to another bar through concrete should not be considered instead reinforcement bars required to resist tension should be extended beyond the zone of expedted high deformations to develop their strength by anchorage.

As the stress transfer primarily takes place through the surrounding concrete, both contact as well as spaced laps perform equally well. Usually the contact laps reduce the congestion and provide better opportunity to get well compacted concrete over and around the bars. As far as possible laps should be staggered, but where it is not practicable and large number of bars are to be lapped at one location as in the case of columns, adequate ties or links should be provided to minimize the possibility of splitting of the concrete. In case of beams and columns when laps have to be provided in even low stress zones, at least two links should be provided.

17.7.5. Anchorage

Now a days the use of plain round mild steel bars is obsolete and in the design it is assumed that deformed steel bars will be used as longitudinal reinforcement. For achieving anchorage, the hooks have been avoided. Thus anchorage is achieved by extending the length of the reinforcing bars or using 90° or 180° bends. However the efficiency of anchorage largely will be governed by the state of stress in the anchorage length. Tensile reinforcement should not be anchored in the regions of high tension. In case it is not possible to avoid it then additional reinforcement in the form of links should be provided to helps to confine the concrete in the anchorage length, specially in the region where high shear exists. Specially it is desirable to avoid anchoring reinforcing bars in the panel zone of beam-column connections.

At any one section large amount of reinforcement should not be curtailed. In a region of tension where anchorage of reinforcement would be required under seismic effects, bars should not be cut off at such points in the span. If the cut off is unavoidable then additional transverse reinforcement should be provided to avoid discontinuity.

17.7.6. Confinement

The strength and ductility of concrete can be greatly increased by confining the compression zone with closely spaced steel links. The rectangular enclosing links are moderately effective for small columns. They are of very little use in case of large columns. In large columns spirals are found much superior for confining the concrete than rectangular links.

17.8. FLEXURAL MEMBERS IN FRAMES

Frame structures consist of horizontal as well as vertical members as beams and columns. To prevent brittle failure of a structure causing partial or complete collapse, ductile detailing as given in code IS-13920 is given in the following paragraphs.

17.8.1. Design of a beam

To ensure good ductility in beams, good design details are necessary as discussed below.

The designed axial stress on the member under seismic loading should not exceed 0.1 f_{CK}. If it exceed 0.1 f_{CK} then the member will be designed for axial as well as for bending as discussed in article 17.9. Though no mention is made of the area on which the stresses should be determined, but ACI has suggested the gross area of the concrete of the member excluding the contribution of the steel reinforcement.

As per IS 456-2000, the flexural strength of concrete is given by the relation,

$$\text{Flexural strength} = 0.7\sqrt{f_{CK}}$$

where f_{CK} is the 28 days crushing strength of the concrete.

17.8.2. Dimensions of the beams

On the dimensions of the beams, following three limitations are imposed:

(*a*) The width b to depth D ratio should be more than 0.3.

i.e. $$\frac{b}{D} > 0.3$$

or $$D < 0.333\, b$$

(*b*) The width b of the beam should not be less than 200 mm *i.e.* for b = 200 mm, the value of D should be less than 660 mm.

(*c*) The depth of the member *i.e.*beam D should not be more than 1/4 of the clear span *i.e.* $D \not> 1/4$ of clear span.

The limits *a* and *b* are to check the difficulties in confining the concrete through stirrups in narrow section of the beam, which exhibits poor performance in comparison to well confined concrete.

The third *i.e.* *c* limit is related with the structural behaviour of the member. For appreciable ratio of total depth of the member to span, it behaves like a deep beam. The behaviour of deep beam under cyclic inelastic deformation is quite different from that of a relatively slender member. Thus design rules for relatively slender members do not apply to members with l/D less than 4, especially with respect to shear strength.

17.8.3. Longitudinal Reinforcement

In order to ensure adequate ductility in reinforced cement concrete beams, the amount of longitudinal reinforcement must be limited in respect to dimensions of beam, quality of concrete, and the yield stress of the reinforcement. In case of seismic resistant design, the critical sections for longitudinal reinforcement in frames occurs at the face of beam to column and girder column connection and at the beam girder connection immediately adjacent to the columns. The distribution of B.M. along the beams or girders framing into the columns may be quite different from that of gravity loads during a severe earthquake. Thus the cut off points of reinforcement bars need special considerations. It is desirable that straight bars should only be used in beams. How ever bent bars may be used in beams which do not frame into columns. The following requirements are for the reinforcement.

(*a*) There should be at least two bars at top as well as at bottom face through out the length of the member.

(*b*) The minimum permissible diameter of the longitudinal bar is 12 mm.

(*c*) The tension steel ratio at any face at any section should not be less than 0.24 $\sqrt{f_{ck}/f_y}$

(*d*) The maximum steel ratio an any face at any section should not be more than 0.25 *i.e.* $P_{t,(max)} \not> 0.25$

The provisions of minimum and maximum steel limit have been derived on the following considerations:

(*i*) The minimum amount of reinforcement is specified in positive and negative moment regions to prevent sudden or brittle failure. In case of small loads on a R.C.C. member, the entire concrete section bears the load. But as the load increases, tensile cracks start to develop in concrete. In this situation concrete transfers the load to reinforcement present in the tension region. In case the reinforcement is not adequate to bear the load transferred to it,then section will fail suddenly causing brittle failure. Thus adequate tensile reinforcement must be there to bear the tensile force that was born by the concrete before cracking.

(*ii*) The maximum steel requirement is intended to avoid steel congestion. This may cause insufficient compaction and poor bond between concrete and reinforcement. Above this limit the ductility also has not been found satisfactory.

(*e*) The positive steel at the joint face must be at least equal to 50% of the negative steel provided at that face.

This provision covers the following two aspects:

(*i*) The seismic moments are reversible. Further the designed seismic load may increase by an considerable amount during an severe

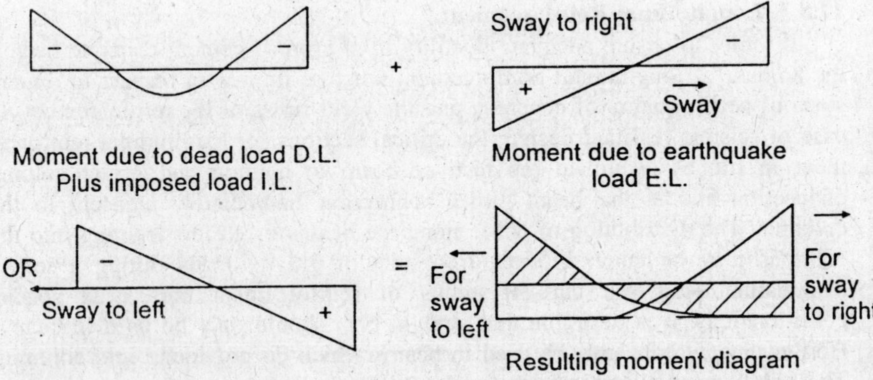

Fig. 17.5. Reversal of moments due to seismic forces

earthquake shaking. Thus substantial sagging moment may develop at the end of the beam during the strong earthquake shaking, which may not be accounted in the analysis. Fig. 17.5.

(*ii*) The compression reinforcement increases ductility. Thus adequate compression reinforcement at the location of potential yielding is, essential. The application of the provision is illustrated in Fig. 17.6.

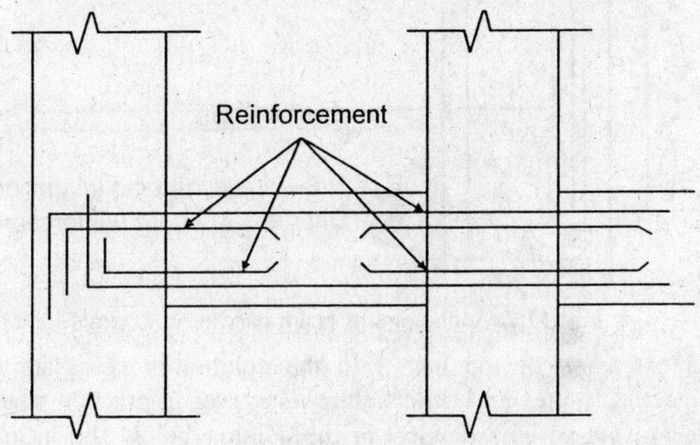

Fig. 17.6. Longitudinal reinforcement at the joins in a beam

(*f*) The steel provided at each of the top and bottom faces of the member at any section along its length at least should be equal to 25% of the maximum negative moment steel provided at the face of the either joint. An example of this is shown in Fig. 17.6. To take care of reversal of loads or unexpected B.M. distribution, sufficient reinforcement should be available at any section along the length of the member. Thus code specifies that steel provided at top and bottom face of the member should be some fraction of the maximum negative moment steel provided at any the face of the either joint.

(*g*) In an external joint, both the top and bottom steel bars of the beam should be provided with the anchorage length beyond the inner face of the column equal to the development length in tension plus 10 times the bar diameter minus the allowance for 90° bends as shown in Fig. 17.7.

In an internal joint both face bars of the beam should be taken continuously through the column.

The zone of inelastic deformation that exists at the ends of a beam, during an earthquake may extend for some distance into the column. Due to this shift, the bond between the concrete and steel in this region becomes ineffective. Thus the development length of the bar in tension is provided beyond a section, which is at a distance of 10 times the diameter of the bar from the inner face of the column.

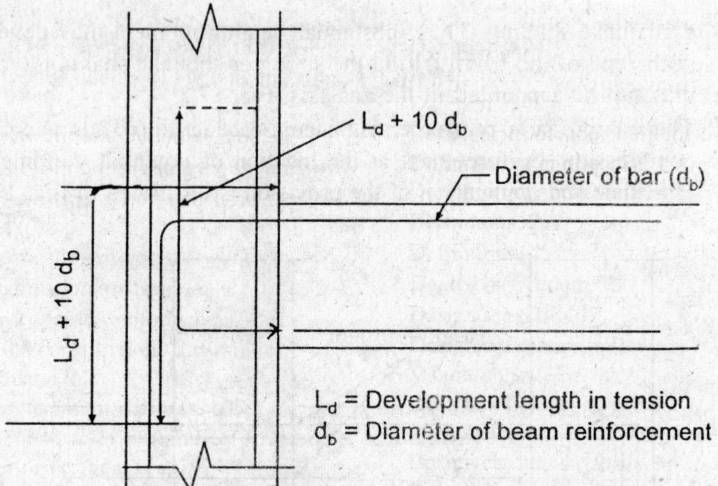

Fig. 17.7. Anchorage of beam bars in an external joint

The extension of top bars into the column is necessary to get proper anchorage and to prevent brittle failure. However in practice when the top bars of the beam are to be extended in the column below the beam sofit, it will cause difficulty in concreting of the column upto the bottom of the beam framing into it. This will leave the part of the column jut below the beam with poor quality concrete. This region is most vulnerable during earthquake. Thus to avoid the above problem either the size of the column along length of the beam may be increased or reduce the diameter of the bar or increase the grade of the concrete of the column.

In an internal joint both face bars of the beam should be taken continuously through the column. The possibility of stress reversal is taken care of by taking face bars continuously through the column at the joint.

17.8.4. Lap splices

Under cyclic inelastic deformations lap splices are not-reliable hence should not be provided in the critical regions. As far as possible the lap splices of main reinforcing bars should be provided in the zones of low stress. These are neither acceptable in the potential plastic hinge zones nor with in the column zones. When the cover concrete spalls off, closely spaced hoop stirrups help to improve the performance of the splice.

(*a*) The longitudinal bars should be spliced only if the hoops are provided over the entire spliced length at a spacing not more than 150 mm Fig. 17.8. In lapping length the spacing of stirrups or ties should not be more than 150 mm. The lap length should not be less than the bar development length in tension. The lap splices should not be provided in any of the following cases:

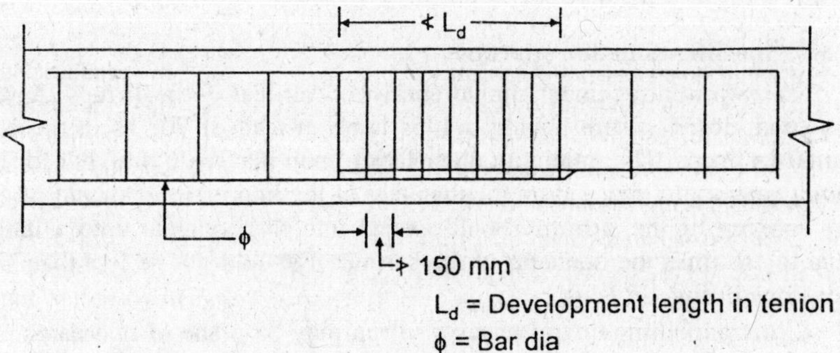

Fig. 17.8. Lap splice in beams

(*i*) With in a joint.

(*ii*) With in a distance of 2d from the face of the joint, where *d* is the effective depth of the beam.

(*iii*) With in the quarter length of the member, where the flexural yielding occurs under the effect of seismic forces.

Note: Not more than 50% bars should be spliced at one section.

17.8.5. Welded splices and Mechanical connections

Welding of ties, stirrups or other similar elements to the longitudinal reinforcing bars may lead to local brittleness of the steel. If welding of these elements to the longitudinal bars is required to facilitate placement of reinforcement or fabrication, the welding should be done on the bars to be added for such purposes. Though a welded splice reduces the dependence on the concrete for stress transfer, but it introduces the discontinuity in the chemical and physical properties of the reinforcement in the weld area and reduces its ductility. Fillet welded splices usually will require adequate transfer reinforcement, where as butt welded splices may be treated as continuous bars.

17.8.6. Web reinforcement

To ensure that the capacity of the beam will be governed by the flexure and not by shear, sufficient transverse reinforcement must be provided in the web of the beam of an earthquake resistant frame. When ever the reinforcing bars are required to under go compression stress, ties must be provided to check the buckling of the reinforcement after the spalling of the concrete cover. Stirrups in concrete elements help in the following three ways.

1. They carry the vertical shear force and thus resist the diagonal shear cracks.
2. They protect the concrete from bulging out wards due to flexure. Thus they confine the concrete.
3. They prevent the buckling of the compression longitudinal bars due to flexure by providing sufficient anchorage.

17.8.7. Specifications for stirrups

The web reinforcement should consist of vertical hoop stirrups. A vertical hoop is a closed stirrup having a 135° hook instead of 90° as in the case of ordinary stirrups. The minimum diameter of hoop may be 6 mm, but for beams having span more than 5.0 m, the diameter of the hoop stirrup should be 8 mm. The hooking of the stirrups should extend into the concrete upto a length of equal to 10 times the diameter of the bar, but it should not be less than 75 mm at each end. Fig. 17.9 (*a*).

2. In compelling circunstences a stirrup may be made of two parts:

(*a*) A *U* stirrup with 135° hook and 10 diameter extension, but not less than 75 mm at each end embedded in the confine core. Fig. 17.9 (*b*)

(*b*) A cross tie as shown in Fig. 17.9 (*c*). The hook shall be engaged in the peripheral longitudinal bars. The consecutive cross ties engaging the same longitudinal bars should have their 90° hooks at the opposite sides of the flexural member. If the longitudinal reinforcement bars secured by cross ties are confined by a slab on only one side of the flexural frame member, the 90° hook of the cross ties should be placed on that side.

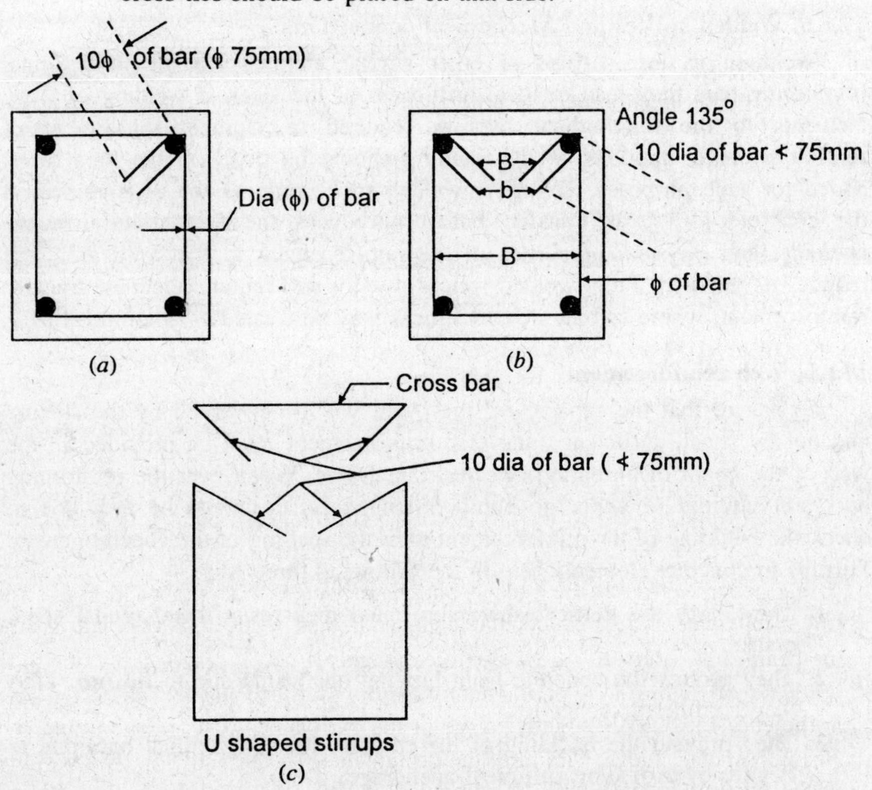

Fig. 17.9. Web reinforcement of beam

In addition to the above, the requirements specified by IS 456-2000 should also be adhered to. They are reproduced as under for ready reference

(*i*) For the design of shear reinforcement, the spacing of stirrups should be

$$S \leq \frac{0.87\ f_y \cdot A_{sv} \cdot d}{V_{usv}}$$

(*ii*) Spacing of stirrups for minimum shear reinforcement should be

$$S \leq \frac{0.87 f_y A_{sv}}{0.4b}$$

(*iii*) Spacing for stirrups should be less than 0.75 *d* or 300 mm which is ever is less.

where,

f_y = steel yield stress

A_{sv} = Area of vertical steel

V_{usv} = Vertical shear stress in reinforcement

3. The shear force to be resisted by the vertical hoops should be the maximum of

(*i*) The calculated designed (factored) shear force as per analysis.

(*ii*) The shear force due to formation of plastic hinges at both ends of the beam, plus the design gravity load on the span. This is given by

For sway to left

$$V_{ua} = V_a^{D+L} + 1.4\left[\frac{M_u^{ha} + M_u^{sb}}{L}\right]$$

$$V_{ub} = V_b^{D+L} - 1.4\left[\frac{M_u^{ha} + M_u^{sb}}{L}\right]$$

For sway to the right

$$V_{ua} = V_a^{D+L} - 1.4\left[\frac{M_u^{sa} + M_u^{hb}}{L}\right]$$

$$V_{ub} = V_a^{D+L} + 1.4\left[\frac{M_u^{sa} + M_u^{hb}}{L}\right]$$

Where $M_u^{ha}, M_u^{hb}, M_u^{hb}, M_u^{sb}$ are the hogging and sagging moments of resistance of the beam section at the ends A and B respectively as shown in Fig. 17.10. These moments should be calculated as per IS 456- 2000. *L* is the clear span of the beam. V_a^{D+L} and V_b^{D+L} are shear fores at ends A and B respectively due to the vertical loads along with partial safety factors of 1.2 of loads. The design shear at the end A should be greater of the of the two values of V_{ua} for left and right sway computed above. Similarly the design shear at the end B should be larger of the two values of V_a and V_b computed above.

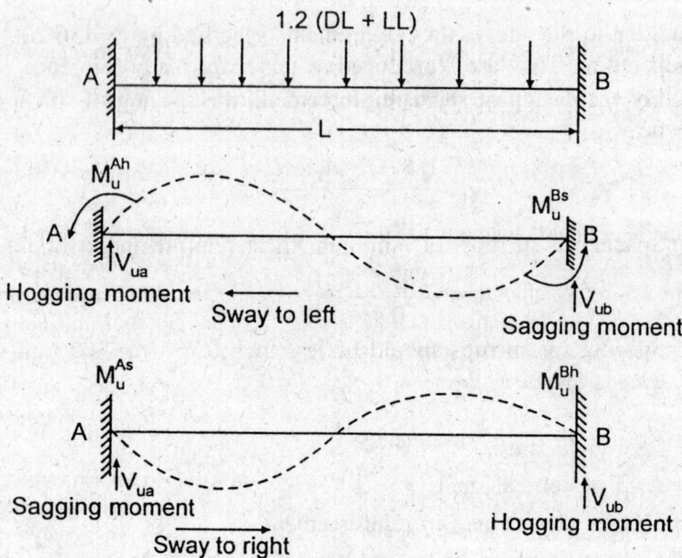

Fig. 17.10..

The above provision ensures that brittle shear failure does not occur before the actual yielding of the beam in flexure. Further this provision simplifies the process of calculating the plastic moment capacity of the section by assuming it to be 1.4 times the calculated moment capacity with the usual partial safety factors. This factor of 1.4 is based on the assumption that the stress in flexural reinforcement is 1.25 f_y instead 0.87 f_y in the calculations of moment capacity.

Note. It is advisable that in beams not much more reinforcement than the required quantity should be provided as it may cause brittle failure. On the other hand to ensure ductile failure, some what less reinforcement should be provided. Further the contribution of bent up bars and the inclined hoops to shear resistance of the section should not be considered. During earthquake, the direction of the shear force may reverse. Bent up bars and inclined stirrups are effective in resisting shear in one direction only. Thus their contribution to shear resistance of the section should not be considered.

To obtain large energy dissipation capacity and better confinement, the closely spaced hoops at the ends of the beam are recommended. At either end over length equal to 2 d the spacing of the hoops should not be more than

(*i*) $d/4$

(*ii*) 8 times the diameter of the smaller longitudinal bar,but it should not be less than 100 mm.

This restriction is required to prevent the occurrence of flexural yielding in the region near the ends of the beams during the earthquake. Further it helps to provide sufficient space for the consolidation of concrete by needle vibrators. In the remaining length ($L - 2 \times 2d$), the spacing of the hoops should not exceed $d/2$.

The first hoop should be at a distance not more than 50 mm from the face of the joint. The vertical hoops at the same spacing as above should also be provided over a length equal to $2d$ on either side of the section where flexural yielding may occur due to earthquake forces. In the remaing part of the beam stirrups should be provided at a spacing of $d/2$. However IS 456 permits 0.75 d spacing as against 0.5 d in the region (L–$4d$). However one should keep in mind that the provision of IS 13920 are over and above those of IS 456. The details are shown in Fig. 17.11

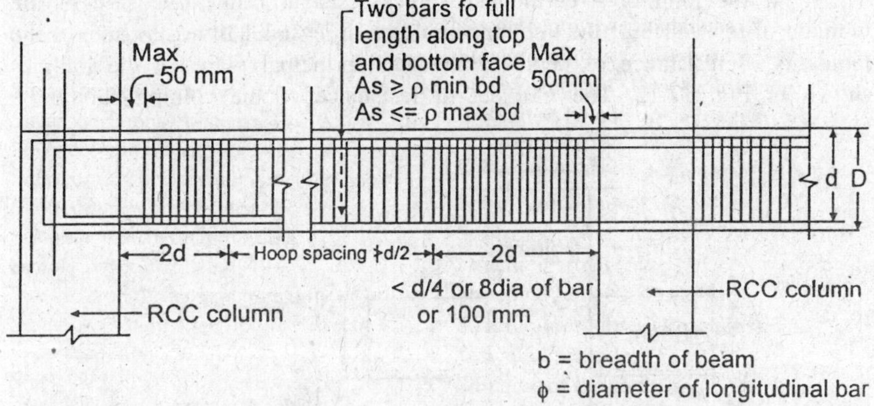

Fig. 17.11. Special confinement of reinforcement required for beams

17.9. FRAMES AND COLUMNS SUBJECTED TO BENDING AND AXIAL LOADING

In earthquake resistant frames the proportioning of columns and their reinforcement detailing must be done with utmost care. These requirements apply to frame members which have to carry the designed axial stresses in excess of 0.1 f_{ck} due to the effect of earthquake. In case the design axial load is less than the specified limit, then the frame members will be treated as flexure members discussed in section 17.8.

17.9.1. Dimensions

The minimum dimensions of the columns should not be less than 300 mm or 15 times the diameter of longitudinal reinforcement bar used in the longest beam passing through the column or anchored into the column joint. A smaller section than the above mentioned dimension of 300 mm may lead to the following two problems.

1. The moment resistant capacity of smaller dimension column will be very low as the lever arm between the compression steel and tensile steel will be too small.

2. The beam reinforcement bars may not be properly anchoraged in the column.

The confinement of concrete relatively has been found better in case of a square column than a column with large width to depth ratio. The ratio of the shortest cross-sectional dimension to its perpendicular dimension preferably should be 0.4 or more.

i.e. $\frac{b}{D} \nless 0.4$

or $b \geq 0.4\,D$

17.9.2. Longitudinal reinforcement

1. At the joint of a earthquake forces resistant frame, the sum of the moment of resistance of the column should be at least 1.1 times the sum of the moments of resistance of beams along each principal plane of the joint as shown in Fig. 17.12. The moment of resistance of the column should be

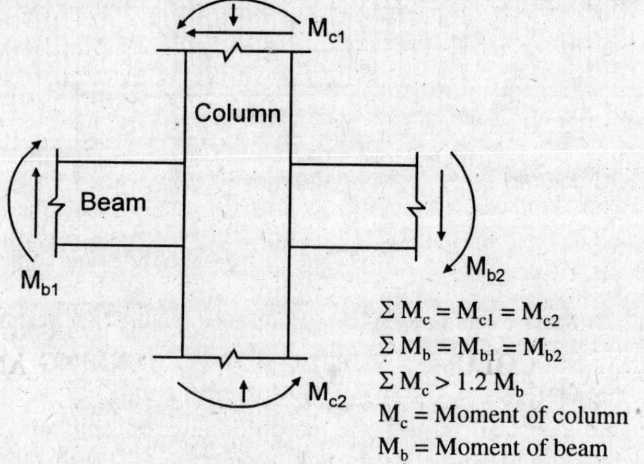

Fig. 17.12. Weak beam and strong column concept

calculated on the basis of the design axial forces on the column. The sum of moment of resistance should be summed in such a way that the column moment oppose the moments of the beam. This condition must be satisfied for the beam moments acting in both directions in the principal planes of the joint under consideration. The columns which do not satisfy this condition should have special confining reinforcements over their full height and not just in the critical end regions.

This requirement is based on the principle of strong column and weak beam. It is meant to fail the building in the beam hinge mechanism (beam yields before the column. If the column yields before beam, the mechanism is known as storey failure mechanism. Storey failure (column failure) always must be avoided as it causes greater damage to the building. Thus in seismic regions columns always should be designed stronger than the beam meeting at a joint.

2. Between corner bars at least one intermediate bar should be provided along each face of the column. This implies that rectangular columns in lateral loads resisting frames should have at least eight bars. Intermediate bars are required to ensure the integrity of the column-beam joint and to increase the confinement to the core of the column.

3. The lap splices in columns should be provided only in the central half of the member length. They should be proportioned as tension splices. In the splice region the centre to centre spacing of stirrups should not be more than 150 mm or $D/2$ where D is the least dimension of the column. At any one section not more than half the bars should be spliced. The other half or 50% bars of a storey may be spliced in the next storey.In case more than 50% bars are spliced at one section, then the length of lap should be 1.3 L_d, where L_d is the development length of the bar in tension as per IS 456-2000.

Actually the length of development depends on the type of reinforcement and concrete. For ordinary situation the lap length should be about 50 times the diameter of the bar. In case of deformed bars Author while working at C.B.R.I., Roorkee (1956-60) found that a lap length of 30 times the diameter of bar was sufficient.

Seismic moments in columns are maximum just below and just above the beam as shown in Fig. 17.12. So No change in reinforcement should be done in these regions. Thus lap splices also should not be provided near the joint.

This provision has very important implication for dowels that are to be left for future extension. Inadequate projected length of the column reinforcement for future extension is a very serious seismic threat. This creates a very weak section in all columns at a single location. Thus at this level all upper storeys are prone to collapse.

During an earthquake columns are likely to develop reversible forces at each face. hence the reinforcement should be provided along all faces, which is sufficient to resist the earthquake forces. All bars are liable to develop tension, hence only tension splices should be provided.

17.9.3. Projection of an column area

In case any area of a column exceeds more than 100 mm beyond the confined core due to architectural requirements should be detailed as follows:

(*a*) In case strength contribution of this area has been considered, then the longitudinal and transverse reinforcement should be provided as per provison of IS 13920-1993.

(*b*) In case this area has been treated as non structural as shown in Fig. 17.13 then the minimum longitudinal and transverse reinforcement should be provided as per IS code 456-2000. Such extended areas even if considered as non structural, even then they contribute to the stiffness of the column. If these extensions are not properly tied to the

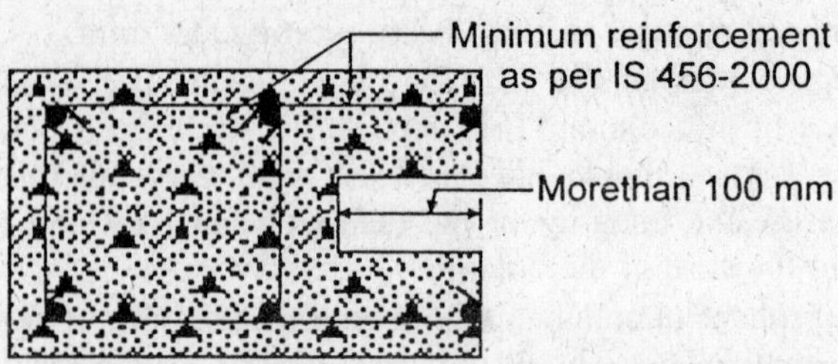

Fig. 17.13. Reinforcement required column projected more than 100 mm

core of the column, a severe shaking many cause spalling of this extended area, resulting a sudden change in the stiffness of the column. Thus code requires that these extensions should be detailed as per IS code 456-2000 requirements for columns.

17.9.4. Transverse Reinforcement (Stirrups)

Transverse reinforcement (stirrups) serves the following purposes:

1. The transverse reinforcement provides the shear resistance to the member.
2. It increases the ductility of the member by confining the concrete core.
3. It provides lateral resistance to the compression reinforcement against buckling.
4. It safeguards the bond strength of vertical bar splices with in the column.

To ensure the required ductility of the beam-column connections, it is essential to confine the concrete fully in the column. The failure to provide transverse reinforcement at the ends, where plastic hinges are expected, results in reduced ductility, flexural strength and degradation of shear resistance.

For the unrestrained length of captive columns where inelastic flexure is combined with the high shear force, closely spaced stirrups or transverse reinforcement is particularly recommended.

To provide ductility under axial compression, the boundary elements of the wall where significant inelastic action is expected should be well confined. Columns supporting discontinuous walls should be confined over the entire height.

17.10. RECOMMENDATIONS FOR TRANSVERSE REINFORCEMENT USING FULLY CONFINED CONCRETE

Using fully confined concrete, following recommendations should be followed for transverse reinforcement:

(*a*) For circular columns, spiral or circular hoops may be used as transverse reinforcement. However use of spiral transverse reinforcement has been found more effective.

(*b*) In rectangular columns rectangular hoops may be used. The rectangular

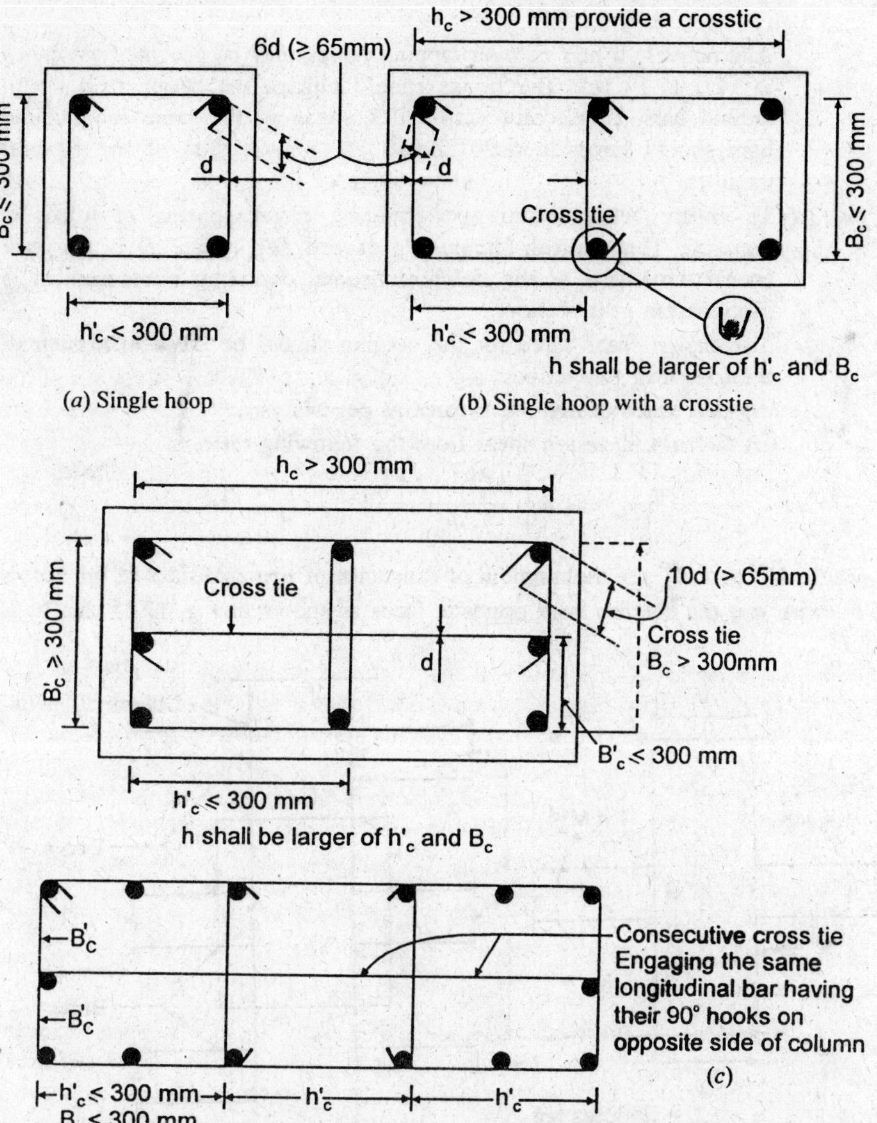

(*a*) Single hoop (b) Single hoop with a crosstie

(*c*)

Fig. 17.14. Transverse reinforcement in column

hoop is a closed stirrup having a 135° hook with a side extension equal to 10 times the diameter of the stirrup, but not less than 65 mm at each end that is embedded in the confined core. Such stirrups do not open during earthquake.

(*c*) The distance between the parallel legs of the rectangular hoop should not be more than 300 mm centre to centre, if this distance exceeds 300 mm, then a cross tie should be provided as shown in Fig. 17.14 (*b*).

Alternatively a pair of over lapping hoops may be provided as shown in Fig. 17.14 (*c*). The hooks should engage the peripherical longitudinal bars. Consecutive cross ties engaging the same longitudinal bars should have their 90° hooks at opposite side of the flexural member.

(*d*) To ensure better seismic performance, closer spacing of hooos is required. This spacing should not exceed *D*/2, where *D* is the least lateral dimension of the column. Special confining reinforcement is discussed in next section.

(*e*) The design shear force for the column should be taken maximum of the following two values:

(*i*) Calculated design-shear force as per analysis.

(*ii*) Calculated design shear from the following relation

$$V_u = 1.4 \left[\frac{M_u^{bL} + M_u^{bR}}{h_{st}} \right]$$

where M_u^{bL} and M_u^{bR} are the moment of resistance of opposite sides of the beams framing into the column from opposite faces as shown in Fig. 17.15 and h_{st} is

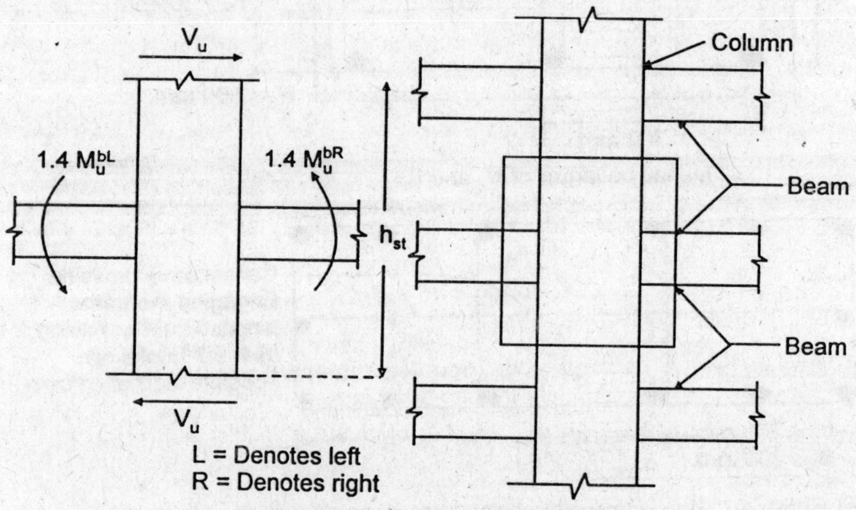

Fig. 17.15.

the storey height. The capacity of beam element should be calculated as per IS 456-2000. This provision is based on the concept of weak beam-strong column.

Here the column shear is calculated based on the beam flexural yielding with the expectation that yielding will occur in beams rather than in columns. The factor of 1.4 is based on the consideration that plastic moment capacity of a section is usually evaluated by assuming that flexural stress of reinforcement is 1.25 f_y against 0.87 f_y assumed in moment capacity evaluation.

Stirrups and extra links in columns are provided to check buckling as shown in Fig. 17.14 (*c*).

17.11. SPECIAL CONFINING REINFORCEMENT

To provide adequate rotational ductility in the potential plastic hinge region of the columns the confinement of concrete is essential. The length of potential plastic hinge region in columns is generally smaller than that of beams as the

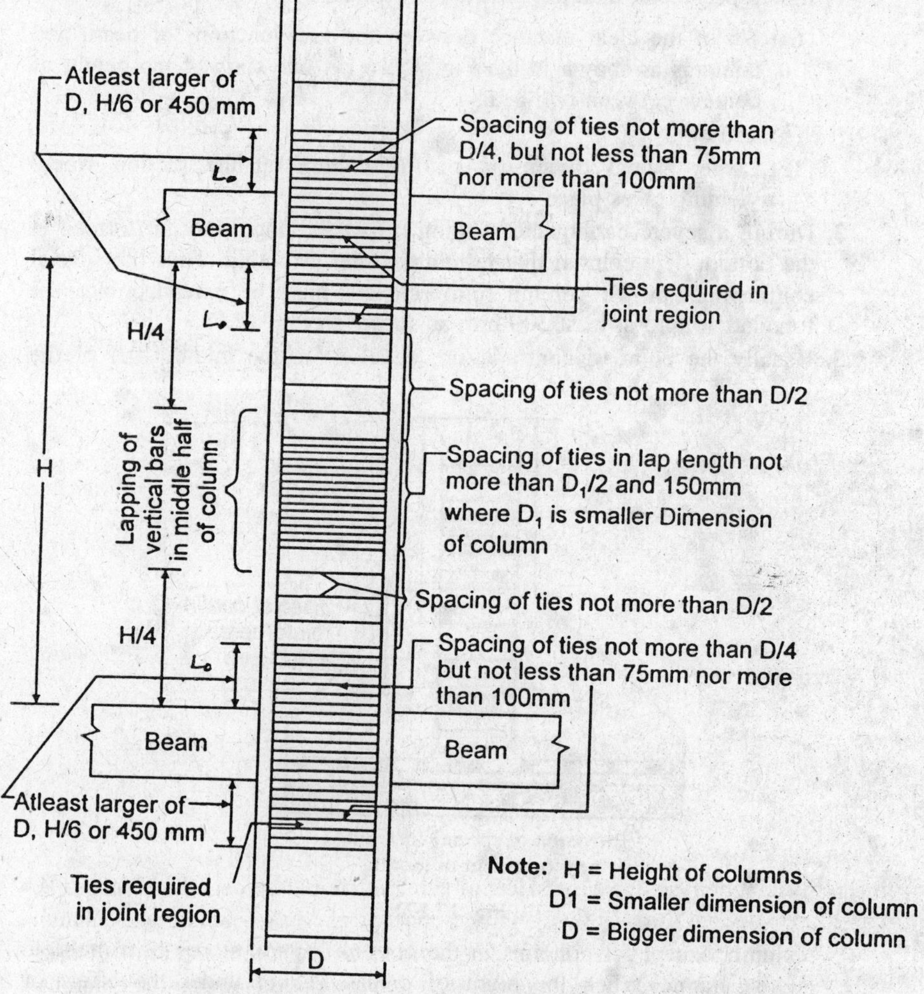

Fig. 17.16. Placing vertical bars and closed ties in columns. Columns ends and lap lengths are to be protected with closely spaced ties

moments in columns vary along the storey height with a comparatively large gradient. Thus the region of a frame column subjected to tension yielding of reinforcement is limited. Unless a large amount of transverse reinforcement is required for shear strength considerations, following arrangements are sufficient.

1. The region of tension yielding of reinforcement is near the junction of beam and column as shown in Fig. 17.16. Thus the special confining of reinforcement should be provided for a length as specified by L_o from each joint face towards the mid span and on any section where flexure may develop due to the forces of earthquake. Thus the value of L_o should be greater than any of the followings:
   (*a*) 1/6 of the clear distance between the two junctions of beam and columns as shown in the Fig. 17.16 *i.e.* one sixth of the height of column between two beams.
   (*b*) 450 mm.
   (*c*) Larger lateral dimension of the column at the section where yielding takes place.
2. During a severe earthquake shaking, a plastic hinge may be formed at the bottom of a column that terminates into a footing. Thus the special confinement of the column reinforcement must be extended into the foundation upto at least 300 mm as shown in Fig. 17.17.
3. Usually the point of contraflexure develops in the middle half of the

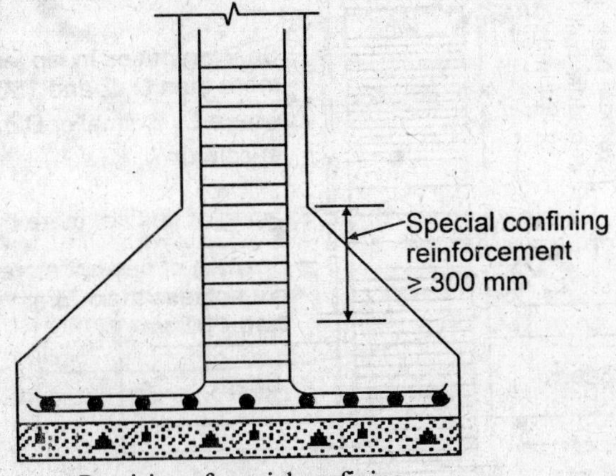

Provision of special confining reinforcement in footing

Fig. 17.17.

column, except for columns in the bottom and top storey of a multiple storey frame. When the point of contra flexure under the effect of earthquake and gravity loads does not develop with in the middle half of the column, in that case the zone of inelastic deformation may extend beyond the region that is provided with closely spaced hoop reinforcement. This needs the provision of the special confining reinforcement over the full height of the columns.

4. The study of the failure of buildings during the past earthquakes has shown that buildings whose walls of the upper storey were terminated on the columns of the lower storey performed very poorly. Thus special confinement of reinforcement must be provided over the full height of such columns. This shows that columns supporting the reactions from discontinued rigid members such as walls should be provided with special confining reinforcement over their full height as shown in Fig. 17.18. This reinforcement must continue over the discontinuity for at least upto development length of the largest diameter longitudinal bar in

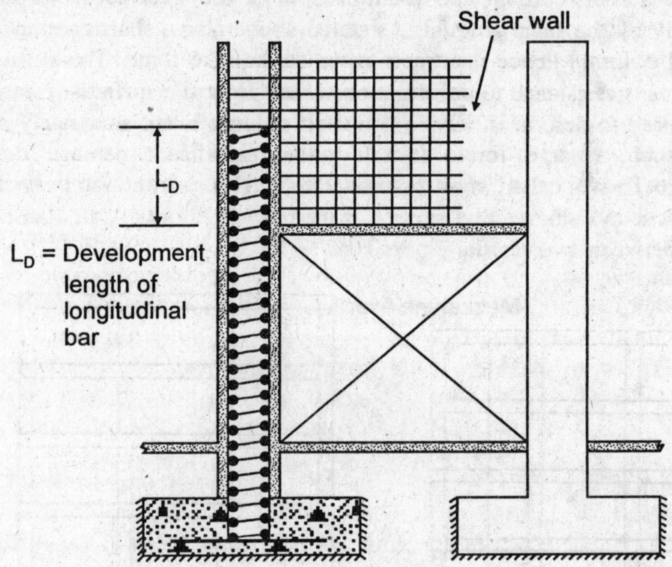

Fig. 17.18.

the column. In place where the column is supported on the wall, the reinforcement should be provided for the full height of the column. This reinforcement must also be carried below the discontinuity upto the same development length.

5. It has been found that the stiffness of the column is inversely proportional to the cube of the height of column *i.e.* shorter the column greater the stiffness. Thus if in any storey of a building, there are columns of different heights, then shorter columns have much higher lateral stiffness and consequently attract much greater seismic shear force. There is a possibility of brittle shear failure taking place in the unsupported regions of such short columns. This length is called captive length. The special confining reinforcement should also the provided over the full height of a column which has significant variation in stiffness along its height due to bracing or RCC wall on either side of the column extending over a part height of the column.

6. **Situations where short column effect may develop.** The short column effect in buildings may occur in the following cases:

When a building is rested on a sloping ground, during earthquake shaking all its columns move horizontally by the same amount along with the floor slab at a particular level. This action is called rigid floor diaphragm action. If short as well large columns exist with in the same storey level, then shorter columns attract several times more earthquake forces than large columns and suffer more damages than taller columns. It happens due to the fact that during an earthquake a short column and a tall column of the same cross section move horizontally by the same amount. As stated above also a short column is stiffer than a tall column, hence it attracts more earthquake force. The stiffness of a column means resistance to deformation. Thus larger the stiffness, greater is the force required to deform it. Hence if a short column is not adequately designed to bear such a large force, it can suffer significant damage during an earthquake. This is called short column effect. The short-column effect is also seen to occur in columns that support a mezzanine floors or loft slabs, that are added in between two regular floors Fig. 17.19.

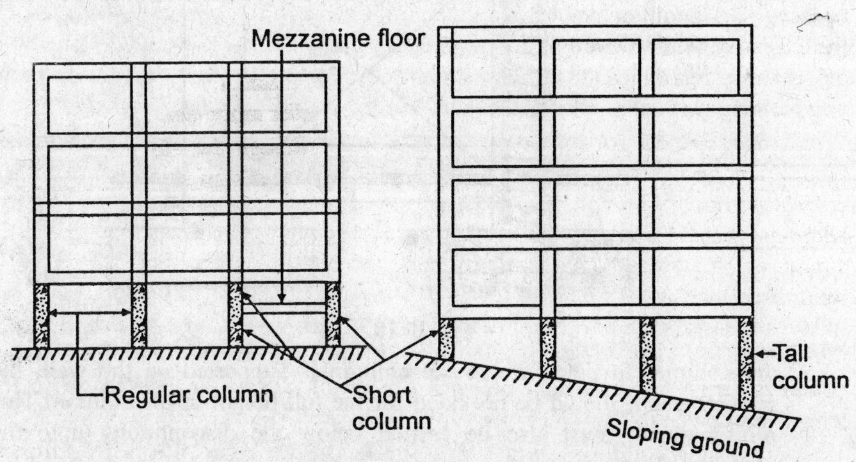

Fig. 17.19.

There is an other special situation in buildings where, short column effect occurs. Consider a R.C.C. or masonry wall of partial height built to fit a window over the remaining height Fig. 17.20. The adjacent columns behave as short column due to the presence of these walls. In many cases other columns in the same storey are of regular height as there are no walls adjoining them. When during an earthquake the floor slab moves horizontally, the upper ends of

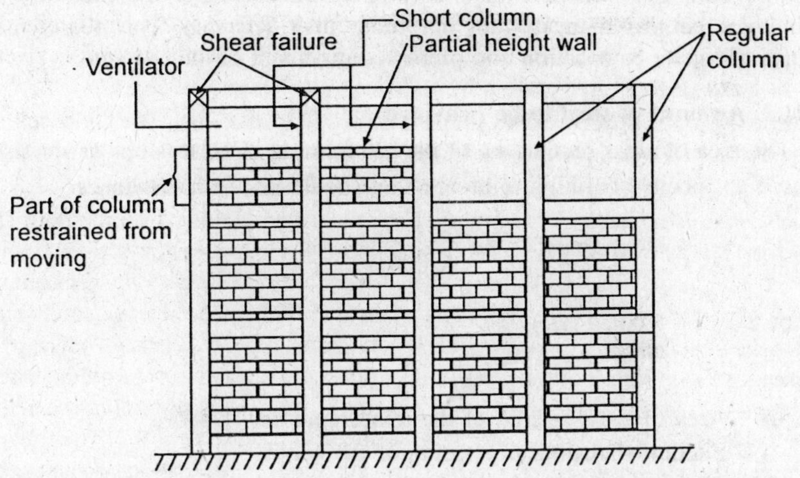

Fig. 17.20. Short column effect in R.C.C. buildings

these columns under go the same displacement. How ever the stiff walls restrict the horizontal movement of the lower portion of the short column, and it deforms by the full amount over the short height adjacent to the window opening. On the other hand, the regular columns deform over the full height. As the effective height over which a short column can bend freely is small, it offers more resistance to horizontal motion and thus attracts a large force in comparison to regular columns. Thus short column suffer more damage.

7. Solution of short column effect. In new buildings the short column effect must be avoided as far as possible at Architectural design stage itself. In case it is not possible to avoid it at the design stage, then it can be rectified by adopting the recommendation of IS 13920-1993 for ductile detailing R.C.C. structures. According to the requirements of IS 13920, the special confining reinforcement should be provi- ded over the full height of the column that are likely to sustain short column effect. The special confining reinforcement (closely spaced closed ties) must be extended beyond the short column into the columns vertically above and below by a certain distance called development length as shown in Fig. 17.16.

In existing buildings short column effects can be rectified by different retrofiting techniques to avoid damage during future earthquakes. In cases where walls of partial height exist, the simplest solution to avoid short column effect is to close the opening by building the wall upto the full height. In case it is not possible to close the opening by building the wall, then short columns must be strengthened by a well established retrofit technique.

17.11.1. Spacing of stirrups

The spacing of hoops used as a special confining reinforcement should not be more than $D/4$, where D is the smallest dimension of the member, but should not be less than 75 mm nor more than 100 mm. This requirement ensures adequate compaction and proper confinement of the concrete.

17.11.2. Amount of steel to be provided

The area of cross section A_{sh} of the bar forming circular hoops or spirals to be used as special confining reinforcement should not be less than *i.e.*

$$A_{sh} = 0.09\, SD_K \frac{f_{ck}}{f_y}\left[\frac{A_g}{A_K} - 1.0\right] \quad \ldots(i)$$

or

$$0.024\; SD_K \frac{f_{ck}}{f_y} \quad \ldots(ii)$$

where

A_{sh} = Area of cross-section of the reinforcing bar $(\pi/4d^2)$

S = Pitch of the spiral or spacing of the hoops.

D_K = Diameter of the core of the member measured upto the out side of the spiral or hoop.

f_{ck} = Characteristic compressive strength of concrete cube at 28 days.

f_y = Yield stress of steel of circular hoop or spiral.

A_g = Gross area of the column cross section.

A_K = Area of concrete core $(\pi/4\, D_K^2)$.

Equation (*i*) gives low values of confining reinforcement.

Equation (*ii*) is used for large sections as those of bridge piers.

For rectangular hoops used for confining reinforcement, its cross sectional area A_{sh} should not be less than

$$A_{Sh} = 0.18\, S \cdot h \frac{f_{ck}}{f_y}\left[\frac{A_g}{A_k} - 1.0\right] \quad \ldots(iii)$$

or

$$0.05\; S \cdot h \frac{f_{ck}}{f_y} \quad \ldots(iv)$$

where,

S = Pitch of the rectangular hoop.

h = Large dimension of the rectangular confining hoop measured upto the outer face of hoop. Its value should not exceed more than 300 mm. Fig. 17.14 (*a*)

Equation (*iii*) is based on the assumption that rectangular hoops are 50% efficient in comparison to spiral.

Equation (*iv*) is applicable to large sections as before.

17.12. FRAME JOINTS

Usually joints are not provided with stirrups due to constriction difficulties.

Similarly in traditional construction bottom reinforcement bars of beams are often not continuous through the joints. The above practices are not acceptable in case buildings have to resist lateral forces or loads. Following points need attention at the joint.

1. **Serviceability.** This means that joint should be durable. Thus joint should not suffer cracks *i.e.* cracks should not occur at joint due to diagonal compression and joint shear.
2. **Strength of joint.** The strength of the joint should be more than the adjacent members *i.e.* joint must be stronger than adjacent members.
3. **Ductility.** Though ductility is not required for gravity loads but it is essential for seismic loads.
4. **Anchorage of bars.** Joints should be capable to provide proper anchorage to the longitudinal bars of the beams.
5. **Ease of construction of joints.** Joints should be easy to construct. Thus there should not be congestion of reinforcement at the joint.

To ensure adequate behaviour of the concrete specially under repeated cyclic or alternating loading, the lateral restraint of the concrete in the joint is essential. Unless the concrete is restraint in the joint it may split under bending moments. A few cycles of loading are sufficient to reduce the capacity of the joint practically to zero. More over large diagonal cracks develop at relatively low stresses.

17.12.1. Anchoring of beam bars

IS 13920-1993 has laid down that in seismic zones III, IV and V, building columns should be at least 300 mm in each direction of the cross-section when they support beams longer than 5 m or when the height of columns between floors is more than 4 m.

1. **Exterior joints.** In exterior joints where beams terminate at columns as

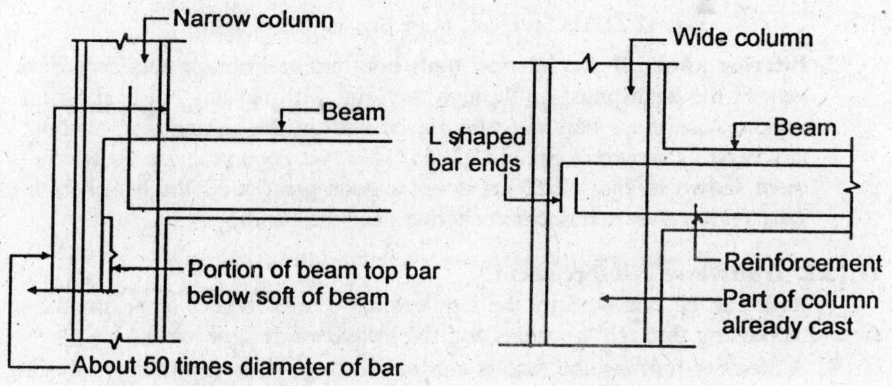

(*a*) Poor (*b*) Good

Fig. 17.21. Enchorage of beam bars in exterior joints

shown in Fig. 17.21 the longitudinal reinforcement bars of the beam are required to be embedded into the column to ensure proper gripping of bars in the joint. The length of anchorage for a bar of grade Fe 415 (characteristic tensile strength of steel Fe 415 is 415 MPa *i.e.* 415 kg/cm^2) is about 50 times of its diameter. This length is measured from the face of the column to the end of the bar anchored into the column. In case the width of the column is small and the diameter of the bars of the beam is large, a portion of the top bars of beam reinforcement is embedded in the column that is cast upto the sofit of the beam, and a part of it over hangs. It is difficult to hold such a over hanging beam top bar in position while casting the column upto the sofit of the beam. More over the vertical distance beyond 90° bend in beam bars is not found very effective in providing anchorage. On the other hand if the column width is large, beam bars may not extend below the sofit of the beam as shown in Fig. 17.21 (*b*). Thus it is preferable to have column of sufficient width. Many codes have recommended it.

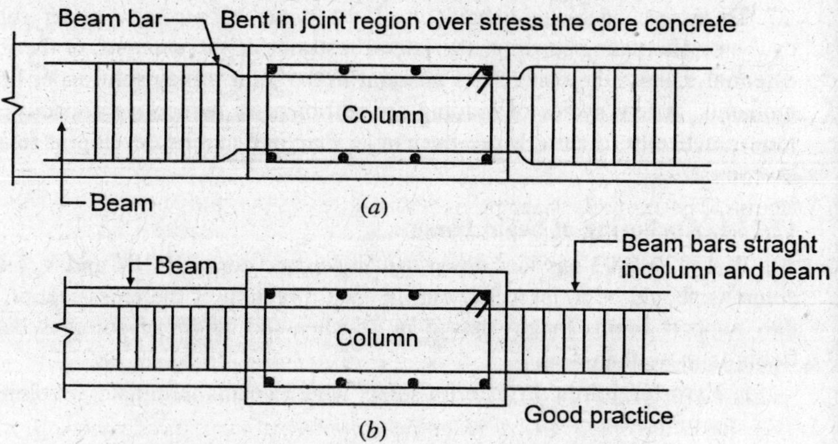

Fig. 17.22. Enchorage of beam bars in interior joint

2. **Interior joints.** In the interior joints both top and bottom reinforcement bars of the beam must go through the joint with out any cut in the joint region. Also these bars must be placed with in the column bars without any bend as shown in Fig. 17.22 (*b*). This is a good practice. Reinforcement shown in Fig. 17.22 (*a*) is not a good practice as the bent bars in joint region over stress core concrete near the bends.

17.12.2. Transverse reinforcement

A joint can be confined by the longitudinal reinforcement of beams/slabs around it passing through the joints and the transverse reinforcement.

1. A member framing the face is considered to provide confinement to the joint if at least 75% face of the joint is covered by the framing member and if such confining member frames into all the four faces of the joint.

2. In a joint which is confined by structural members from all the four sides of the joint, the transverse reinforcement equal to at least 50% of the special confining reinforcement required at the end of the column should be provided with in the depth of the shallowest framing member. The spacing of hooks should not be more than 150 mm. This provision is required in case the beam is wider than column. In that case the beam reinforcement not confined by column reinforcement should be laterally supported either by the girder framing into the same joint or by transverse reinforcement.
3. In case of corner and exterior joints all the 135° hooks of the cross ties should be along the outer face of the column. To confine concrete core, a 135° hook in a cross tie is more effective than 90° hook. As the interior face of the beam column joint is confined by beams, it is preferable to place the cross ties in such a way that all 90° hooks remain on the inner side and 135° hooks at the exterior side of the joint.

17.13. SLABS

Usually the floor slabs which form a part of normal beam and slab system generally are designed for gravity loads as flexural members. Their primary function is to resist the vertical loads. In addition to their primary function, floor slabs also act as seismic forces distributor element to the vertical structural members. This action of floor slabs usually is known as diaphragm action. The in-plane shear produced due to seismic forces acting on the floor is transferred to a stiff seismic resisting element such as shear wall. In most of the building structures the in-plane shear is not significant.

The reinforcement designed for gravity loads in the slabs forming the normal part of beam and slab system generally is sufficient to ensure that the slabs behave satisfactorily as flexural member and as well as horizontal diaphragms transmitting seismic forces. Certain elements such as waffle slabs, flat slabs etc. which may form a part of seismic resisting frame work must be designed and detailed accordingly.

17.13.1. Diaphragm Action

The horizontal seismic forces at roof level or at any floor level are transferred or distributed to the vertical resisting members such as walls and columns, by using the rigidity and strength of the roof or the floor deck to act as a diaphragm. Usually a diaphragm is considered analogous to a plate girder laid in a horizontal plane where the roof or floor deck performs the functions of the plate girder web. The beams function as web stiffeners and peripherals beams or integral reinforcement function as flanges. The fundamental requirements for the chord are the continuity of the chord and connection with the slab. An opening in the floor such as a stair, elevator, or sky light opening may weaken it (floor) just like a hole in the web drilled for a mechanical duct weakens the beam. Similarly a break in the edge of the floor may weaken the diaphragm just a notch in a flange weakens the beam. In each case the diaphragm should be detailed such that all stresses around the opening are developed into the diaphragm.

An other analogy applicable to diaphragms is the rigidity of the diaphragm compared to the walls or frame that provide lateral support and transmit the lateral forces to the ground. A metal deck roof is relatively flexible compared to concrete walls, while a concrete floor is relatively rigid compared to steel moment frames.

Another characteristic of the beam is its continuity over the intermediate supports. For example consider a building which has four bays. In case the diaphragm is relatively rigid, the chords may be designed as the flanges of a beam continuous on the intermediate supports. On the hand if the diaphragm is flexible, it may be designed as a simple beam spanning between walls with out any consideration of continuity. The continuity is neglected. The neglect of continuity may cause some damage at places where adjacent spans meet.

17.13.2. Ductile detailing

1. The minimum content of tension reinforcement in each direction should be 0.15% of the cross section area of concrete for high tensile steel and 0.25% for mild steel. The minimum content of secondary reinforcement should be 0.15%.
2. The minimum diameter of the reinforcement bar should be 10 mm.
3. For cantilever slabs, the bottom steel should be provided to counter act bending tensions which may develop during an earthquake.
4. The holes through the slabs should be framed with extra steel due to diaphragm action of slabs during earthquakes.
5. Basement slabs or for ground floors which are designed for bearing the pressure from ground, special seismic considerations may not exist. Thus it is usual to place one layer of nominal steel in both directions to prevent cracking and shrinkage. This reinforcement usually is placed on top of the slab. The steel between column bases may also be placed in the ground slab in some cases, instead of tie beams in foundations.

17.14. STAIR CASES

In masonry buildings the inclined stair case slabs may be a source of vulnerability to the masonry structures during an earthquake. The integrally connected stair case slab acts as an cross brace between floor and lower levels and transfer large horizontal seismic forces at roof and lower levels as shown in Fig. 17.23 (*a*). These areas are the potential damage areas in the masonry structures if not accounted in the design and construction of the stair cases. To over come this defect stair cases should be designed and constructed in any of the following three types:

1. Separate construction of stair case

In this case a gap is maintained between the building and the stair case. A

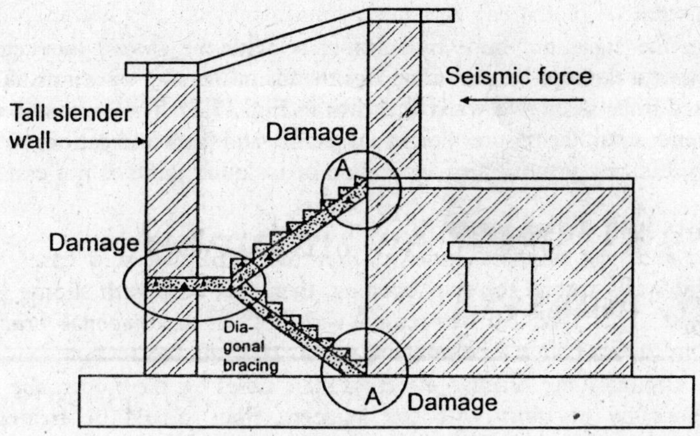

Fig. 17.23 (*a*). Damage in a rigidy built in stair case

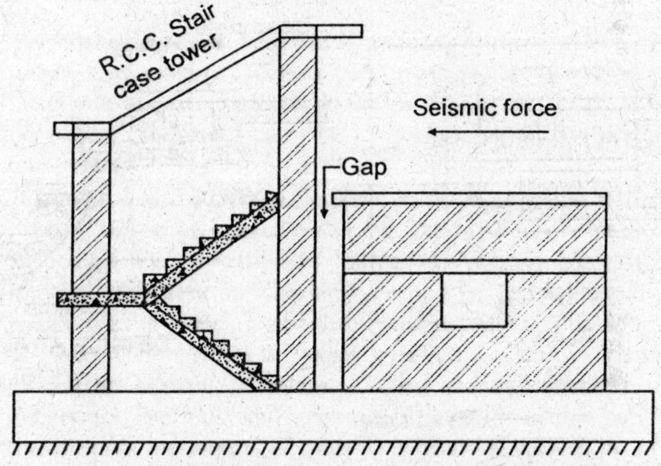

Fig. 17.23 (*b*). Building with seprated stair case

masonry building stair case is shown in Fig. 17.23 (*b*). For a R.C.C. building, one end of the stair case is made to rest on a wall and the other end is carried by beams and columns not connected with the floors. The opening at the vertical joints between the floors and the stair case may be covered either with a tread plate attached to one side of the joint and sliding on the other side or covered with some material of appropriate qualities which could fracture or crumple during an earthquake with out causing any damage to the structure. The supporting members as walls, columns are separated or isolated from the surrounding floors by the use of crumple or separation sections. A separate type masonry building is shown in Fig. 17.24 (*a*) and R.C.C. stair case is shown in Fig. 17.24 (*b*).

2. Built in stair

In case the stairs are built monolithically with the floors, they can be protected against damage by providing rigid walls at the stair openings. A stair case enclosed in between two walls is shown in Fig. 17.25. The enclosing walls should extend upto the entire height of stairs and the foundations of the building. In this case provision of separation or isolation joints is not essential.

3. Stair cases with sliding joints

In case it is not possible either to construct separated stair cases or to provide rigid walls around the stair opening, then stair case with sliding joints may be tried. This type of stair cases will not act as diagonal bracings. Following precautions should be adopted in this type of construction.

(*a*) To eliminate the bracing effect of stair cases on the floors, the inter connection of stairs with the adjacent floor should be treated by providing sliding joints appropriately.

(*b*) Large stair halls should preferably be separated from the rest of the building by either crumple or separation sections.

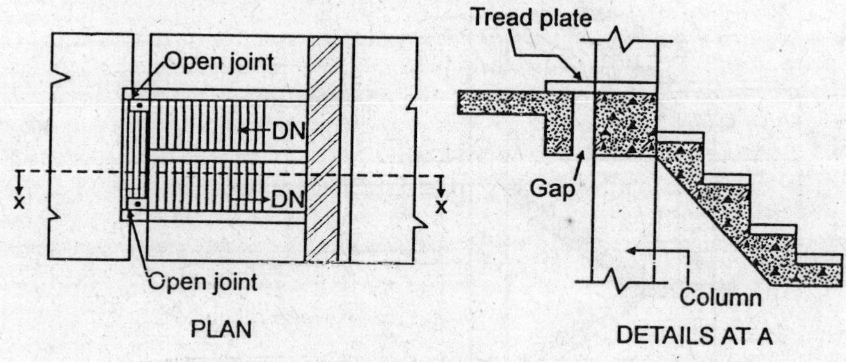

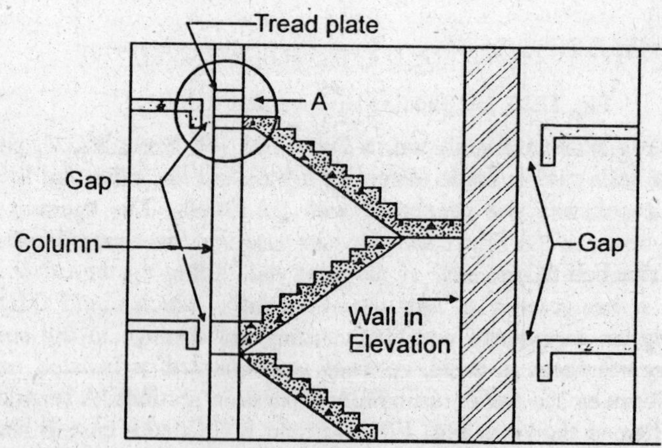

Fig. 17.24 (*b*) Separated stair case

Ductile detailing

1. Generally rules discussed for slabs are applicable to the stair cases also. For bending tension, the top steel should be provided at each landing, which may not be necessary from simple analysis.
2. In case the stairs are a part of horizontal diaphragm (Roof slab and beam system) or the moment resisting frame work, they should be reinforced accordingly. Proper care should be taken to confine the longitudinal reinforcement bar at the point of change in slope.

17.15. PARAPETS AND UPSTAND

parapets and upstands also should be carefully designed against seismic

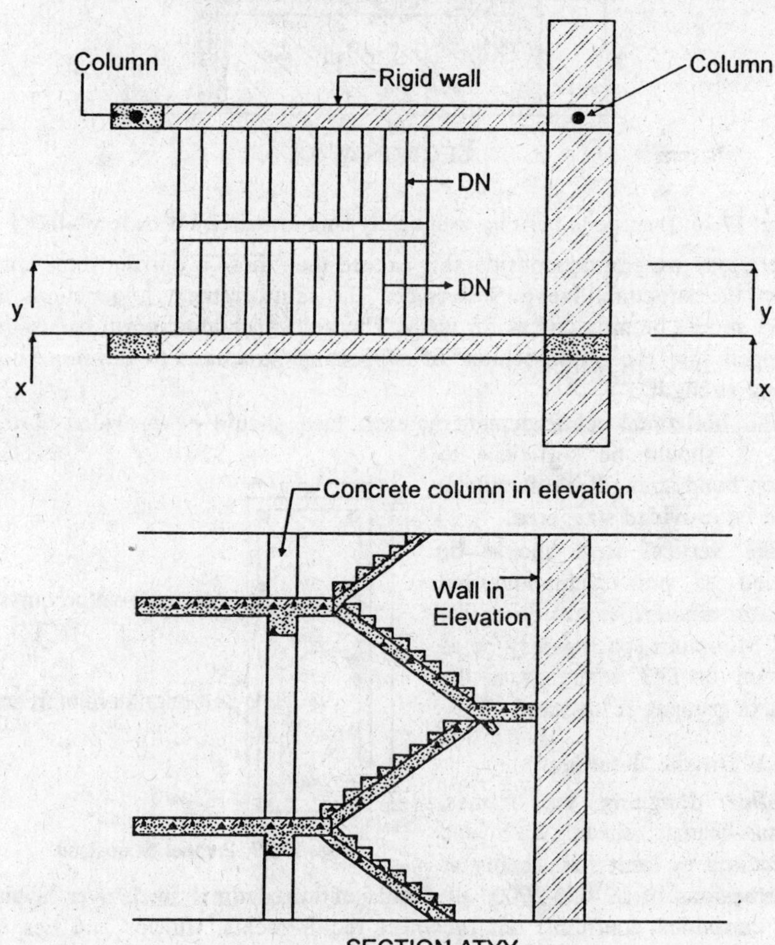

Fig. 17.25.

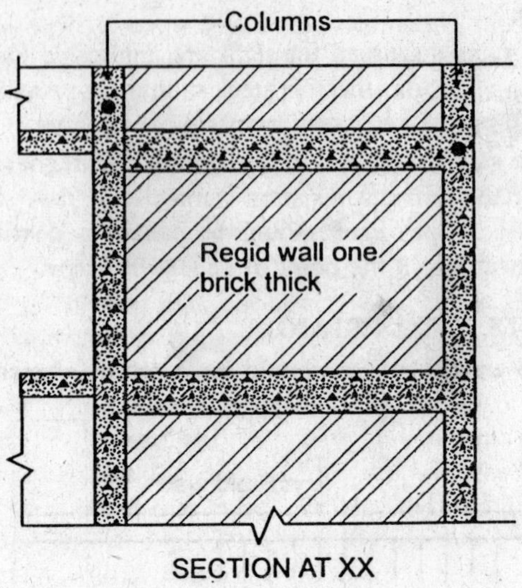

Fig. 17.26. Damage in building with rigidly built-in staircase (Courtesy—IITK)

accelerations which may considerably exceed than those occurring some where else in the structure due to resonance. The reinforcement at junctions and corners should be provided as for walls. The vertical reinforcement bars should be lapped into the reinforcement of supporting structures to develop lateral bonding strength.

The horizontal reinforcement at each face should be provided at least 0.2%. It should be sufficient to develop bond strength. Preferably it should be provided staggered.

The vertical steel should be provided as per calculation, but minimum amount should be as for walls. Minimum spacing may be as 300 mm or *D*/3 where *D* is the height of parapet or up stand.

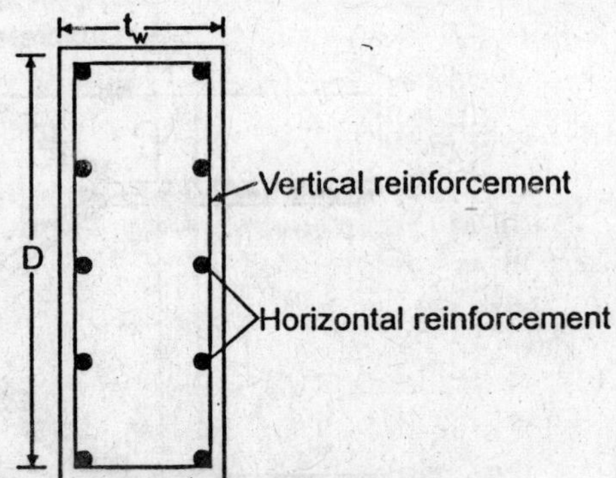

Fig. 17.27. Parapet or upstand

17.15.1. Ductile detailing

After designing the frames, columns-beams, shear wall and foundations by limit state theory as per provisions of IS 456-2000, all details of longitudinal steel, over lapping, shear capacities confining reinforcement requirements, stirrups and ties etc. should be worked out as per provision of IS 13920-1993. All details should be clearly shown on the drawings.

QUESTIONS

1. Enumerate the damages suffered by an concrete structure during an earthquake.
2. What provisions should be adopted while constructing an R.C.C. structure?
3. Define ductility of a structure. How it can be increased?
4. Discuss weak beam and strong column design concept.
5. The distance between ties or stirrups should not be more than... of main steel
   (*a*) 15 times the diameter (*b*) 10 times the diameter
   (*c*) 8 times the diameter (*d*) 12 times the diameter
6. The ductility...... with the increase in compressive strength of concrete,
   (*a*) Increases (*b*) Decreases
   (*c*) No change in ductility (*d*) None of above
7. The collapse of an R.C.C. structure can be prevented by
   (*a*) By ensuring angainst ductile failure
   (*b*) By ensuring flexural failure before the shear failure.
   (*c*) By ensuring failure of beams before the columns
   (*d*) The joint should be stronger than the member joining the connection
   (*e*) All the above
8. In case of weak beam and strong column design concept the minimum strength of column should be
   (*a*) More than beam strength
   (*b*) Equal to beam strength
   (*c*) Less than beam strength
   (*d*) None of the above
9. The bond strength of deformed bars at the initial stage is ...... to plain round bar
   (*a*) Equal (*b*) More
   (*c*) Less (*d*) All are true
10. In the severe seismic activity zones of IV and V the minimum compressive strength of concrete should be
    (*a*) 150 kg/cm^2 (*b*) 200 kg/cm^2
    (*c*) 250 kg/cm^2 (*d*) 300 kg/cm^2
11. In the concrete structures the ratio of width to depth of beam should be
    (*a*) 0.25 (*b*) 0.30
    (*c*) 0.45 (*d*) 0.50
12. During an earthquake concrete structures suffered most of the damages due to
    (*a*) Weak column and strong beam design
    (*b*) Hollow core walls
    (*c*) Walls made of prefabricated units
    (*d*) Orientation of the building being orthogonally to the fault
    (*e*) All are correct
13. Concrete structures can be made more earthquake resistant by......
    (*a*) Adopting symmetrical plan

(*b*) Constructing symmetrical shear walls on both axes of the building
(*c*) Adopting smaller spans of the beams
(*d*) Removing the soft storey effects of the building
(*e*) All are correct

14. R.C.C. Building can be made more earthquake resistant by......
(*a*) Eliminating projections from the buildings
(*b*) Constructing symmetrical windows and doors and keeping the window small
(*c*) Fixing wire net on the joints and junctions of wall
(*d*) Constructing rigid roofs and floors
(*e*) All are correct

15. Identify the correct-statement/statements
(*a*) In R.C.C. structures failure first should take place in reinforcement
(*b*) In R.C.C. structural failure first should take place in concrete
(*c*) In R.C.C. structures failure should take place simultaneously in both steel and concrete
(*d*) All are correct

ANSWERS

5. (*c*)	8. (*b*)	11. (*b*)	14. (*e*)
6. (*a*)	9. (*a*)	12. (*e*)	15. (*a*)
7. (*e*)	10. (*b*)	13. (*e*)	

18

New Techniques in Seismic Resistant Design of Structures

18.1. INTRODUCTION

Man is facing the fury of earthquakes from the very beginning. One earthquake takes place daily throughout the world some where or the other. During the last few decades a series of devastating earthquakes have occurred causing great loss of life and property. This unprecedented damage of property has developed a keen interest in the mind of concerned nations facing the earthquake frequently to develop earthquake resistant design of structures.

The conventional approach to seismic design of structures is based on ductile behaviour of the structural system to dissipate seismic energy through the plastic deformation cycles. The main draw back of this approach is that structures suffer heavy damage during the severe earthquakes, requiring costly repairs and some times buildings have to be demolished. In order to minimise structural damage and to control structural response, the dynamic interaction between the earthquake ground motion and the structure can be modified. The control is based on the following two approaches.

1. Modification of dynamic characteristics of the structure.
2. Modification of the energy absorption capacity of the structures.

As discussed earlier also, earthquakes develop or cause following two effects in the buildings:

(*a*) Earthquakes cause high acceleration in stiff buildings, thus their natural period is large.

(*b*) Earthquakes cause large inter storey drifts in flexible structures. The natural period of such structures or buildings is less.

The possibility of artificially increasing both the period of vibration and energy dissipation capacity of structures is an attractive way of improving the seismic resistance of the buildings.

18.2. DEVICES FOR SEISMIC CONTROL

For this purpose following two types of devices may be adopted:

(*a*) Either to prevent an earthquake force from acting on a structure. This type of device is known as *base isolators.*

(*b*) To absorb a part of he seismic energy. This type of device is known as dampers.

These concepts are discussed as follows:

18.2.1. Seismic Isolation

Base Isolation provide a means of limiting seismic effects entering into the buildings.

In seismic isolation, a gap is created in the fundamental period of vibration of the structure or building and the predominant period of the earthquake induced ground motion, *i.e.* they should not coincide. This will reduce the quantum of forces entered or transmitted into the building by separating or decoupling the base of the building from its super structure. Thus the main feature of the base isolation technology is to introduce flexibility in the building or structure The base isolators have been found most effective for low rise to medium rise relatively stiff (rigid) buildings located on hard grounds with large mass.

It has not been found suitable for use in a high rise building due to large overturning moments. However base isolation technology is costly and complex.

18.2.2. Need for base isolation

The need of base isolation has been found essential in the following situations:

1. When the building is to be located in highly seismic activity prone areas.
2. In essential services buildings as hospital, water tanks etc, which are essential to be operational even after the earthquake.
3. In the construction of precast or masonry constructions.
4. In case the existing structures are found un safe during earthquakes, such buildings can be safeguarded against earthquake by providing base isolation devices.
5. To minimise the damage to primary and secondry structural members.
6. To minimise the cost of repair and strengthening structures after the earthquake.

18.2.3. Energy absorption or dissipation concept

This concept allows the seismic energy into the building by incorporating damping mechanism into the lateral load resisting system of the structure. The seismic energy of the structure is dissipated as the structure moves back and forth due to earthquake loading or forces. The essential concepts of both techniques are appropriate and logical.

The energy dissipation concept helps in the over all reduction in the displacement of the building. This technique has been found most effective in structures that are relatively flexible and also have some inelastic deformation capacity. Though this technique also is complex but less costly than base isolation techniques.

18.3. MODERN APPROACH

The modern approach to seismic design is based upon the inelastic response of structural members and systems to dissipate the energy imparted to structures by means of base isolation and energy dissipation devices.

The concept of base isolation is quite different from the practice of conventional seismic design. In the normal seismic resistant design full structure is designed to withstand the disastrous shaking resulted from the earthquake, where as in base isolation concept the upper portion from the base is isolated from the destructive vibrations of the earthquake by confining the severe distortions to a specially designed portion at the base. Thus building is isolated from the ground vibrations in such a way that only a fraction of the seismic ground motions are transmitted to the building. In other words it can be said that ground under neath the building vibrates violently, but the building itself will get a fraction of vibrations and will remain practically stable. This results significant reduction in floor acceleration and inter storey drift, providing protection to building components and contents. In practice isolation is limited to horizontal forces which are most destructive to buildings.

In a more simple way it can be explained by the following example.

Consider a building resting on friction less smooth rollers as shown in Fig. 18.1. When the ground vibrates or shakes, the rollers move freely and the building above remains unaffected *i.e.* building does not move. Thus no force is

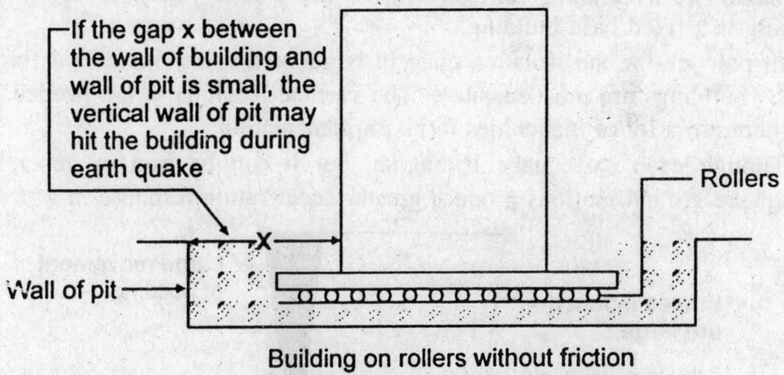

Fig. 18.1. (*a*) Hypothatical building

not transmitted to the building due to the vibrations of the ground due to the earthquake. If the same building is rested on flexible pads that offer resistance to horizontal movement, then some effect of ground motion will be transferred to the building above Fig. 18.2. In case the flexible pads are chosen properly, then a fraction of seismic forces can be transmitted to the building above in

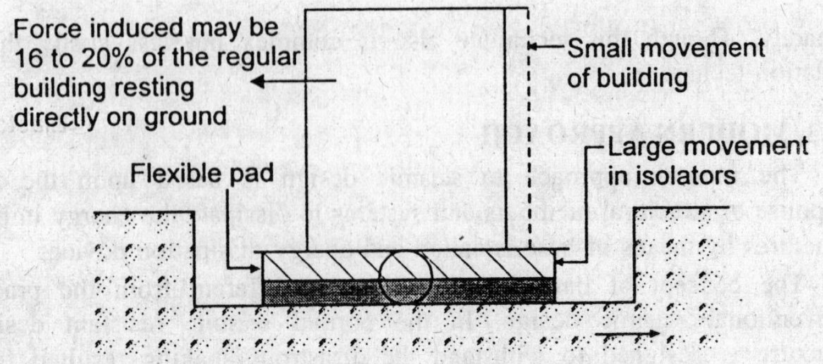

Fig. 18.1. (*b*)

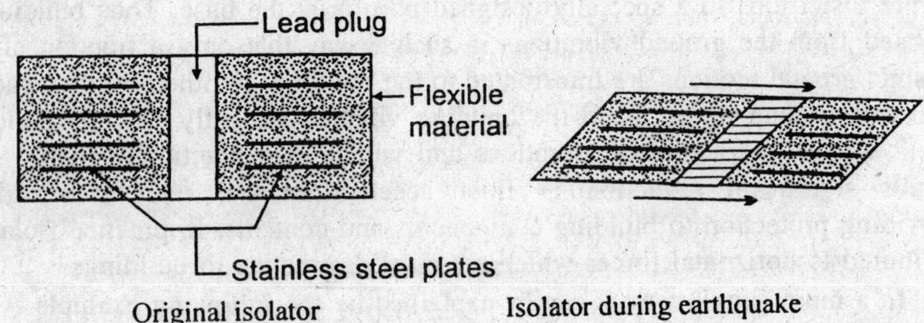

Fig. 18.2. Building on flexible pads connected to building and foundation

comparison to a building built directly on the ground Fig. 18.3 *i.e.* as if the building is a fixed base building.

In practice the the isolation concept is adopted to the horizontal forces to which buildings are most sensitive. The vertical isolation is not needed much and there are a lot of difficulties in its implementation.

Though each earthquake is unique, but it can be said in general that earthquake ground motions produce greater acceleration response in a structure

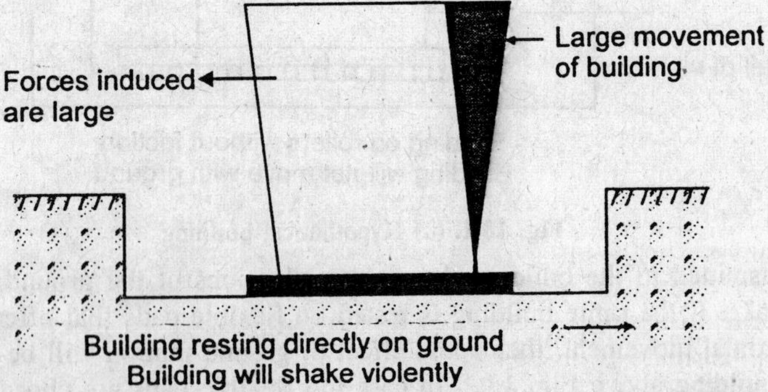

Fig. 18.3. Building resting directly on ground will shake violently

of shorter periods than structures of longer periods (rigid structures). A seismic isolation system utilizes this fundamental principle by changing the fundamental or natural periods of the buildings of shorter periods which are more force vulnerable to the longer periods buildings which are less force vulnerable. Thus the principle of seismic isolation is to introduce flexibility in the horizontal plane of the basic structure and at the same time adding damping elements to restrict the resulting motion. A practical base isolation system should consist the following components.

1. To increase the period of vibration of the building sufficiently and to reduce the transmission of seismic forces to the building above, the base isolation system should have a flexible mounting.
2. To reduce the relative deflections between the building and the ground to a practical level, the base isolation system must have a damper or dissipator.
3. There must be a procedure or method to provide the rigidly to control the behaviour during minor earthquakes and wind loads.

At the base of the building, flexibility can be introduced by using many devices such as sliding plates, Elastomeric pads, rollers, cable suspension sleeved piles, rocking foundations etc. The substantial reduction in the acceleration of the building with the increase in its natural period and consequent reduction in the base shear are possible. But the degree of reduction depends on the initial fixed base period and shape of the response curve. However the flexibility introduced at the base will develop large relative displacements across the flexible mount. Thus the necessity of providing additional damping arises at the isolators level. The additional damping can be provided by mechanical devices which use plastic deformtion of lead or mild steel to achieve high damping through hysteretic energy dissipation.

18.4. PROPERTIES OF ISOLATION SYSTEM

An isolation system should possess the following properties:

(*a*) The isolation system should be strong enough to support the structure.

(*b*) It should be able to provide additional horizontal flexibility and dissipation of energy.

(*c*) Under the maximum wind load this isolation system should have adequate stiffness and essentially exhibit the linear elastic behaviour.

(*d*) When subjected to earthquake forces it should yield slightly greater than maximum wind load.

Thus by allowing the isolation system at the base of a structure to yield at a predetermined lateral load, the structure above the base, can be effectively isolated from the seismic forces which can cause inelastic deformation in it. Thus the structure should be designed for vertical and wind loads with special attention for seismic resistance focused only on the isolation mechanism at the base of the structure. An effective isolation system not only keeps the structure above it in inelastic condition during an severe earthquake, but also protects the non structural elements from extensive destruction. It has been observed that in a typical multistorey structures, the cost of non structural elements is about 80% of the total building cost. Thus significant amount of money can be saved in repair and replacement of broken items by providing base isolation system.

18.5. BASE ISOLATORS

The flexible pads are called base isolators and the structures protected by them are called base isolated buildings. The main feature of the isolation pads is to introduce flexibility in the structure with respect to horizontal forces. They serve the following purpose:

(*a*) They increase the period of fundamental mode.

(*b*) They concentrate practically all the masses in the mass of fundamental mode and thus reduce the higher mode responses to a insignificant limit or value. Hence they reduce input energy drastically.

18.5.1. Types of seismic base isolation system

The seismic base isolation system can be classified into the following two classes:

1. Decoupling system
2. Sliding system

1. Decoupling system. This is the most widely adopted system. In this approach the building or the structure is decoupled from the horizontal components of the seismic ground motion by interposing a layer with low horizontal stiffness between the structure and its foundation. This layer gives much lower fundamental frequency to the structure than its fixed base frequency and also much lower than predominent frequencies of the ground motion.

The most widely used base isolators are made of laminated rubber pads similar to the bridge bearings. These pads are consisted of thin layers of natural rubber that are vulcanized and bonded to steel plates as shown in Fig. 18.4. Vulcanization is the process of treating natural rubber with sulpher to make it stronger. These pads are very flexible in horizontal direction due to the shear stress of rubber.

On the other hand in the vertical direction these pads are very stiff due to the presence of steel plates, which result in relatively high bearing capacity. This kind of pads show a substantial linear response. These responses are governed by the properties of the rubber. The rubber pads may be made of natural rubber or artificial elastomers. The choice of rubber composition is extremely important to maintain the properties of the pads. These properties are as follows:

(*a*) The pads should have large load bearing capacity.

(*b*) The pads should have low degrability with time.

(*c*) The pads should have good mechanical properties which concern the

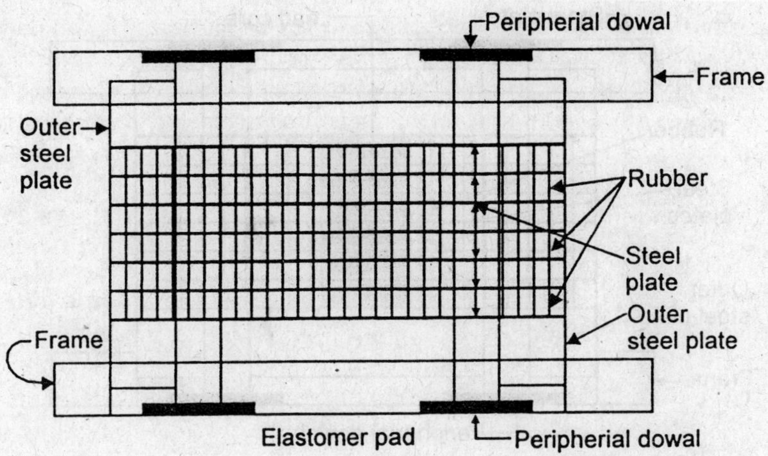

Fig. 18.4. Structure of an elastomer pad

dynamic behaviour such as low shear strain modulus, high damping capacity and resistance to large strain.

The above properties may be obtained by the adjustment of fillers in the rubber.

The pad damping provided by the viscous behaviour is very low upto about 5% only. The damping can be increased for certain rubber compositions using ferrite filler upto 20%. Damping upto about 30% may be obtained by incorporating lead core in the central part of the pad. The energy absorption is obtained by the yielding of the lead which remain confined by the rubber, as shown in Fig. 18.5.

The lead core under high seismic forces behaves as viscous liquid with out loosing its basic properties and after the release of seismic forces it again becomes solid with out loosing any of its basic properties. Structures built on

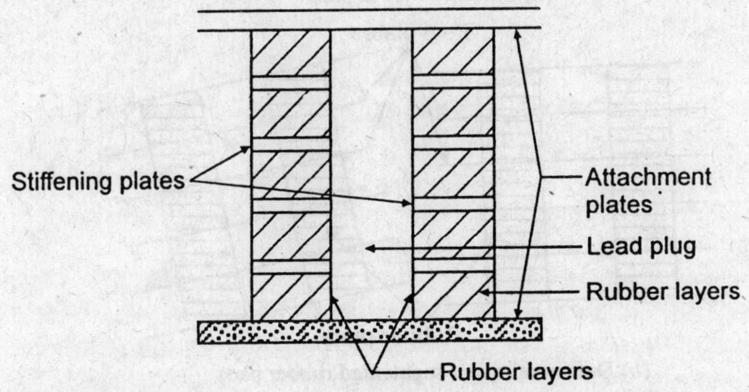

Fig. 18.5. (*a*) Section of pad

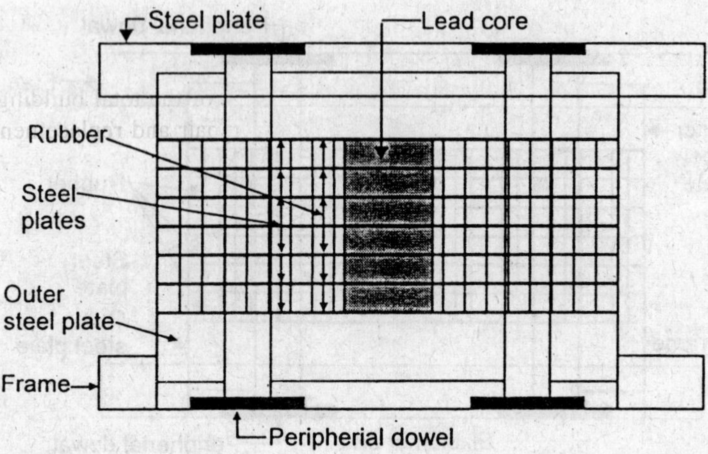

Fig. 18.5. (*b*) Elastomer pad with lead core

such pads can sway upto 35 cm in any direction. Section of the pad is shown in Fig. 18.5 (*a*). Fig. 18.5 (*b*) shows elastomer padwith lead core.

The seismic displacement of the rubber pads as discussed above is about one half of the dimensions of the pad in plan. The allowable displacement can be increased by segmenting the pad and providing stablilizing plates, which

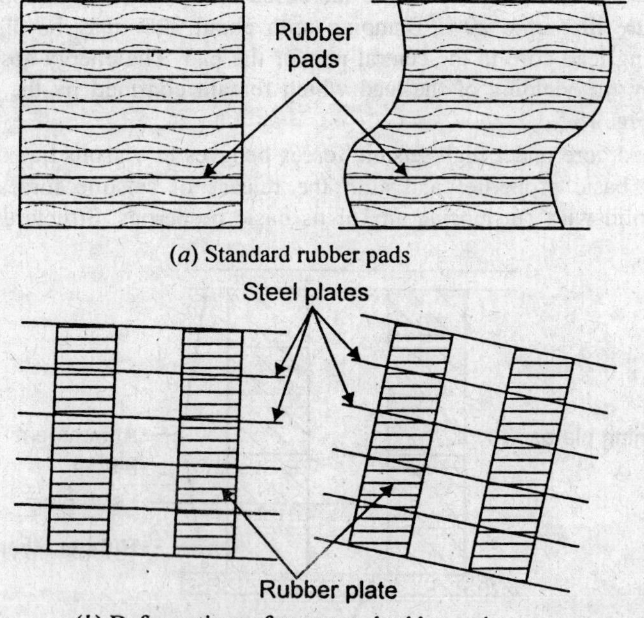

(*a*) Standard rubber pads

(*b*) Deformations of segmented rubber pads

Fig. 18.6. Deformation of standard and segmented rubber pads

may increase the height of the pad. Usually the height of the pad is limited by its buckling. By using multistage rubber bearing shown in Fig. 18.6 the height of the pad can be increased and also its stability can be maintained. The intermediate plates prevent the rotation of the rubber bearings under horizontal displacement, thus they maintain the stability of the bearings against buckling.

18.5.2. Load Limiter

It is a torsional or flexural member with various configuration. One such configuration is shown in Fig. 18.7. It resists movement due to small horizontal loads. It is made of steel, lead and other materials such as rubber or artificial elastomer. In the figure the horizontal mounting and load limiter are built as one piece. The limiter is central cylinder which resists flexure. The horizontal flexible mounting is a combination of sand wiched rubber and steel plates. These laminated piates have very high vertical stiffness. The load limiter works elastically upto a certain load and at higher loads than this limit, it exhibits plastic deformation, which allows horizontal movement of the building. At plastic deformed stage it works as a damper to minimise the response and limit the amount of horizontal movement of the building.

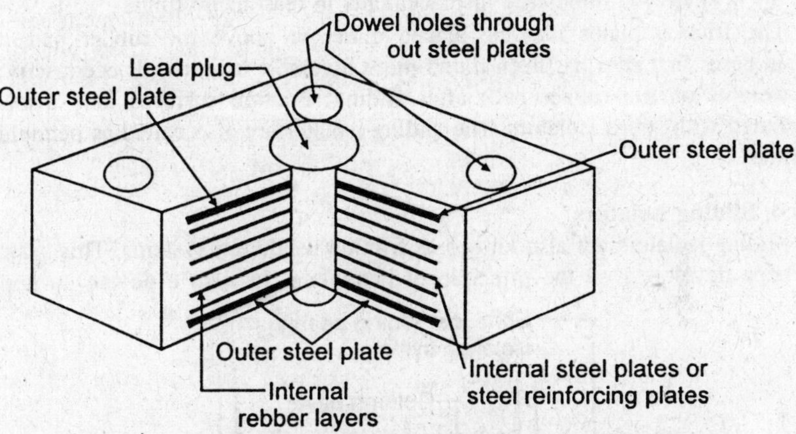

Fig. 18.7. Lead rubber laminated pads

18.5.3. Devices based on dry friction

A simplest system based on dry friction is shown in Fig. 18.8. The system consists of friction plates installed above a rubber pad. The upper plate is made of stainless steel and is fixed to the super structure. The lower plate is made of bronze and lead and is fixed above a special rubber pad. That is one part slide with respect to the other.

Advantages of the system

Following advantages have been observed of this system:

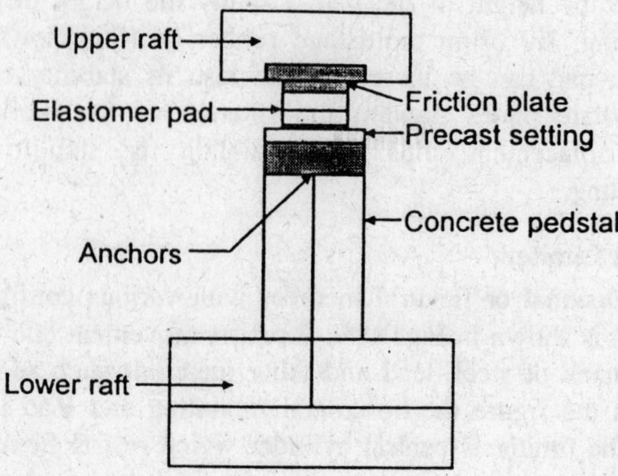

Fig. 18.8. Sliding plate with a delaminated elastomer pad

(*a*) It avoids the self sizing of the two plates.

(*b*) It provides for a suitable friction factor.

(*c*) The friction factor induces a reasonable acceleration.

(*d*) It keeps the remaining displacements in reasonable limits.

The friction plates may be placed under or above the rubber pads. In certain cases first case has been found more favorable as it avoids ecentricity of the weights on the rubber pads after sliding. Friction surfaces may also be associated with slides isolators. The sliding isolator are also called as pendulum bearings.

18.5.4. Sliding isolators

Sliding isolators are also known as friction pendulum systems. This system has been developed on the principle of pendulum. In such a device an upper

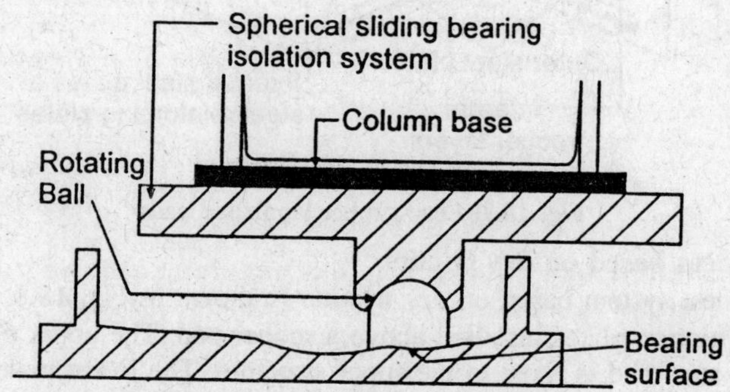

Fig. 18.9. Sliding bearing isolation system

rotating ball or an articulated slider (Articulated means a body composed of several parts) moves on a concave surface as shown in Fig. 18.9.

At the time of any movement (during an earthquake motion) any horizontal movement would cause an up lift of the super structure. The stiffness to lateral force, period of natural vibration and range of vertical load capacity are of the same order of magnitude as those of lead rubber pads of similar size.

It has been found that all types of base isolators are not useful for all types of structures. Hence a careful study should be made to select the suitable base isolator for a structure. The type of base isolators discussed so far are useful to low to moderate rise buildings made of masonry and concrete and rested on hard soils under neath. Base isolators have not been found suitable for high rise buildings or buildings rested on soft soils.

This system is based on the principle of limiting the transfer of shear across the isolation interface. This system is simple in principle or concept. A layer with a defined coefficient of friction limits the acceleration to its value (eqaul to coefficient of friction) and the forces will be transmitted limiting to coefficient of friction times the weight.

18.6. RESPONSE OF BUILDINGS

During an earthquake ground under neath all buildings starts to vibrate and may move in any direction depending upon the direction of waves. The response of the buildings is shown in the following Fig. 18.10. Let the earth

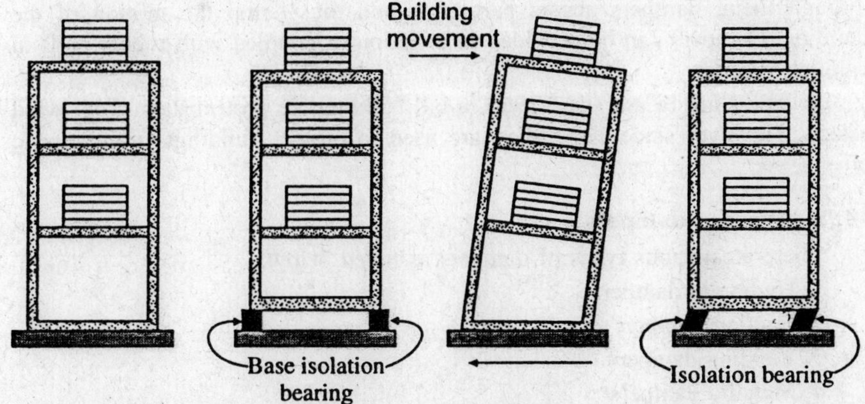

(*a*) Fixed base building (*b*) Isolated building (*c*) Ground movement (*b*) Isolated building

Fig. 18.10. Response of buildings

moves towards left. Building responds to this movement and starts to move in the opposite direction *i.e.* towards right due to inertia. The inertial forces are most important and destructive than all those forces acting on a building. But buildings which are provided with base isolators do not move during an earthquake as no inertia force is transferred to the building due to ground shaking. The inertia force acting on the buildings has been reduced and acceleration decreased due to the insertion of base isolation system. Thus the period of vibration or natural period of the building has been increased. The inertia forces experienced by buildings during an earthquake are proportional to the acceleration of the building during the ground motion. In general structures having longer periods of vibrations tend to reduce the acceleration while those with short periods of vibration tend to increase or amplify the acceleration.

18.7. SEISMIC DAMPERS

The artificial device introduced in structures to improve their seismic performance and to control seismic damage is called dampers. These dampers are installed in place of structural elements such as diagonal bracing. These dampers absorb seismic energy during an earthquake. These dampers are not used to support the structures. The dampers shift the natural period of structures from the noticeable or main period of earthquake, where as passive energy dissipaters (bracing etc.) allow earthquake energy to enter into the building. To intercept the seismic energy it is directed through the appropriate configulation of the lateral resisting system to wards the energy dissipation devices located in the system. The energy dissipator device (dampers) transform seismic energy into heat which is dissipated into the structure. The dampers work like hydraulic shock absorbers in automobiles. Most of the sudden Jerks are absorbed in hydraulic fluids and only a fraction of the Jerks are transmitted above to the chassis of the automobile. When seismic energy is transmitted through them, dampers absors part of it and thus damp the motion of the building. Dampers can be provided in isolation or coupled with rubber pads in parallel or series.

Dampers are in use since 1960 in tall buildings to protect them from wind effects. However since 1990, they are used to protect buildings from seismic effects.

18.7.1. Types of dampers

There are various types of dampers as noted below:

1. Hydraulic dampers
2. Friction dampers
3. Yielding dampers
4. Metallic dampers
5. Steel dampers
6. Lead extrusion dampers

1. Hydraulic dampers. These dampers are used to achieve the following objectives:

(*a*) To allow the slow development of displacements of the buildings due to thermal movements.

(*b*) To limit the response under dynamic actions.

This system dissipates energy by forcing a silicone based fluid through an orifice similar to shock absorbers of automobiles as shown in Fig. 18.11 (*a*). The oil and very high molecular weight polymers may also be used as fluid.

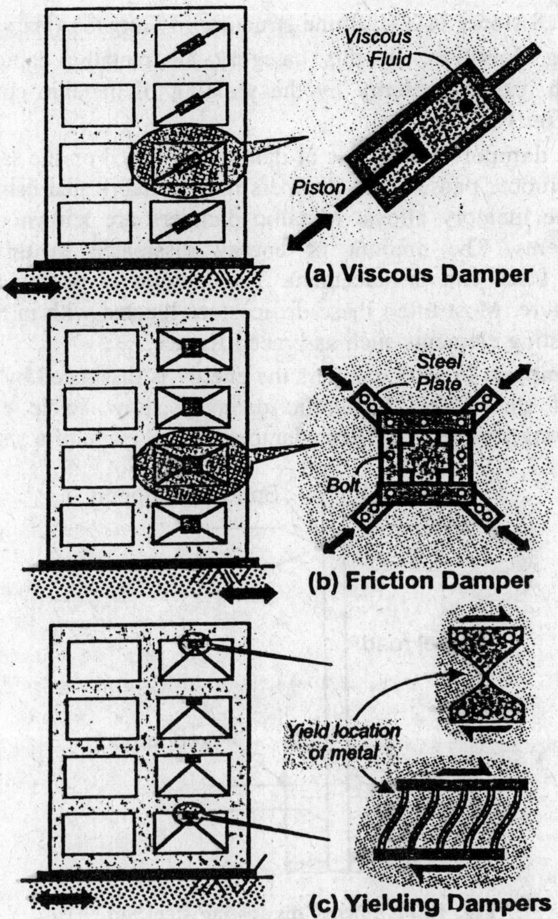

Fig. 18.11. Seismic energy dissipation devices (Courtesy—IITK)

The system may constitute a piston moving axially in a polymer inside a cylinder.

The system also may be comprised of a piston which can move in all directions in very viscous elastomers like bitumen or silicone. Usually oil dampers are not recommended as they need frequent repair and maintenance.

2. Friction dampers. In this system the friction surfaces or plates are connected by prestrssing bolts as shown in Fig. 18.11 (*b*). This system is known as displacement dependent system as the amount of energy dissipated is proportional to displacement. In this system almost a perfect rectangular hystreretic behaviours is exhibited. This is the main characteristic feature of this system. In this system the contact surfaces used are lead-bronze against stainless steel or teflon against stainless steel. In India friction dampers have been used in a 18 storey R.C.C. frame structure in Gurgaon (Haryana).

3. Yielding dampers. In this category all metallic dampers can be classified which dissipate energy by the yielding of metallic components as steel dampers Fig. 18.11 (*c*).

4. Metallic dampers. This class of dampers is based on the same principle as lead core in rubber pads. These dampers may be fabricated using steel, lead or special shape memory alloys. Metallic dampers are known as amplitude dependent systems. The amount of energy dissipated in this system is proportional to force and displacement. The amount of energy dissipated is hysteretic in nature. Most often these devices are located with in the structural lateral load resisting elements such as braced frames.

5. Steel dampers. In steel dampers the energy is dissipated by softening or plastification of steel. Steel hysteretic dampers show stable elastic-plastic behaviour and long fatigue life. These damper can be made of a simple bar and

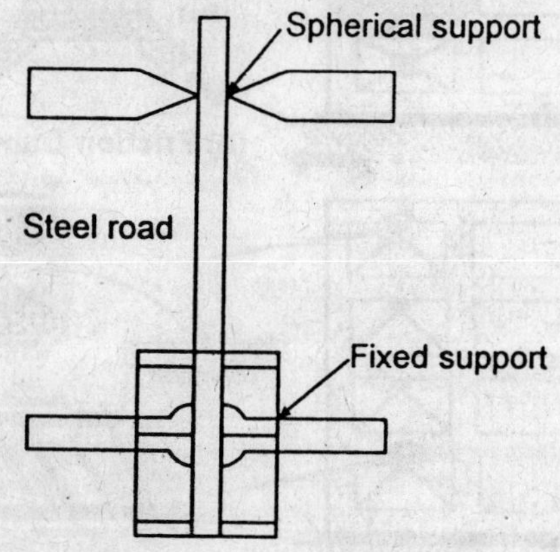

Fig. 18.12. Energy dissipating steel rod

a plate. A typical steel damper is shown in Fig. 18.12. In the most common steel dampers plastic flexural or torsional deformations of steel are utilized. Such dampers can be inserted in the bracing of the building or at wall to wall joints or at the borders of a wall and a surrounding frame Fig. 18.13 (*a*). Isolation coupled with energy absorbing damping is shown in Fig. 18.13 (*b*).

6. Lead extrusion dampers

In this process energy dissipation takes place due to the yielding *i.e.* softening of the metal. In this system the lead is forced to pass through an orifice. During the process of pushing the lead through the orifice, the cross-section of the lead reduces and plastic deformations take place in the lead with significant development of surface friction and heat generation. If the temperature increases, the extrusion force and the heat generated decreases. At the end of dynamic process, lead passes through the cycle of physical recovery, re crystallization and development of grain. Thus lead returns to its original form.

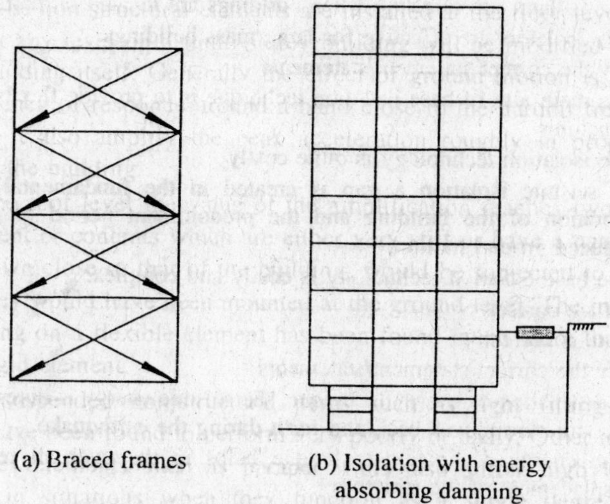

(a) Braced frames (b) Isolation with energy absorbing damping

Fig. 12.13. Structural configuration with energy absorbing dampers

18.8. USE OF BASE ISOLATION IN BUILDINGS IN INDIA

Though base isolation has been used in thousands of buildings in counties like Japan, Italy, U.S.A. Newzealand. Base isolation also has been used for retrofitting important buildings as Hospitals and monumental buildings.

In India for the first time base isolation technique was used after the 1993 Killari (Mahrastra) earthquake. In killary after this earthquake two single storey buildings one school building and the other shopping complex building were built using rubber base isolators. These buildings were founded on hard ground. Both buildings were brick masonry with R.C.C. roof. Both these buildings remained unaffected while whole village buildings were collapsed. After 2001 Bhuj earthquakes the Bhuj Hospital also has been built with base isolation technique. It is hoped that this hospital will be able to work in severest earthquake.

Thus the behaviour of a building during an earthquake must be given due consideration in the design rather following the design codes blindly.

QUESTIONS

1. Explain the seismic response of a building.
2. What is the modern approach to seismic design of structure? Explain.
3. Explain base isolator and energy dissipation concepts.
4. What is the necessity of using base isolator.
5. Discuss the response of a building during an earthquake with neat sketch.
6. Identify the incorrect statement/statements
   (*a*) Base isolators are found most useful for high rise buildings
   (*b*) Base isolators are most useful for low to medium rise buildings

(*c*) Base isolator are effective when buildings are located on hard grounds
(*d*) Base isolators are effective for large mass buildings

7. Identify the correct statement/statements
(*a*) The main aim of base isolation technique is to provide flexibility to the structures
(*b*) The isolation technology is quite costly
(*c*) In seismic isolation a gap is created in the fundamental period of vibration of the building and the predominant period of earthquake induced ground motion.
(*d*) The base isolation technology is costly and complex.
(*e*) All are correct
(*f*) None is correct

8. Identify the correct statement/statements
(*a*) In dissipation of energy technique, the seismic energy is dissipated when the structure moves back and forth during the earthquake
(*b*) The energy dissipation technique helps in the over all reduction of displacement of the structure
(*c*) Energy dissipation technique has been found more effective relatively in flexible structures
(*d*) This technique is less costly than base isolation technique
(*e*) All are correct

9. Identify the correct statement/statements
(*a*) The base isolation concept is adopted to deal the horizontal forces to which the structures are more sensitive
(*b*) Vertical components of seismic forces are not dealt in base isolation concept
(*c*) In base isolators the lead core behaves as a viscous liquid under the high seismic forces
(*d*) Structures built on such pads can sway upto 35 cm in any direction
(*e*) All are correct

10. Identify the incorrect statement/statements
(*a*) In base isolators under high seismic forces the lead core changes its basic properties after the release of seismic forces
(*b*) The displacement of rubber pad under seismic forces may go upto 50% of the dimension of the pad in the plan
(*c*) In case of a sliding isolator the seismic force is transmitted equal to coefficient of friction of the layer times the weight of the member
(*d*) In sliding isolators the acceleration of the structures is limited by the layer upto its coefficient of friction
(*e*) After the earthquake the lead core regains its original shape with out losing its intrinsic properties

ANSWERS

6. (*a*)	8. (*e*)	10. (*a*)
7. (*e*)	9. (*e*)	

19

Shear Walls and Their Design

19.1. INTRODUCTION

In seismic zones structures have to resist large horizontal forces called seismic forces. Hence structures in seismic zones need special protection to safe guard them from damage. Thus to provide safety against earthquake damage R.C.C. structures in seismic regions are provided with R.C.C. vertical plate like walls in addition to normal slabs, beams and columns. These plate like walls are like vertical oriented wide beams that carry the earthquake forces or loads down wards to the foundation. These walls generally start from the foundation level and made continuous through out the height of the structure. The minimum and maximum thickness of these walls may be 150 mm and 400 mm respectively. These walls are called shear walls. Usually shear walls are provided both along length and width of the building.

19.2. DEFINITION OF SHEAR WALL

The walls constructed in structures to resist the lateral load or forces developed due to wind or earthquake are known or called as shear walls. Shear walls have a very large in plane stiffness and thus resist-lateral load and control deflection very efficiently. Shear walls being flexible in the perpendicular plane, they can transfer the lateral forces in their own plane by developing movement and shear resistance. Shear walls also help to ensure development of all available plastic hinge locations through out the structure prior to failure. Usually shear walls resist a large portion of the lateral loads on a building as well as the shear force developed due the above loads. To resist the horizontal forces either R.C.C. shear walls are constructed for this purpose or concrete walls enclosing stair ways, elevated shaft or utility cores may serve as shear wall.

To control the inter storey deflection of high rise buildings caused by the lateral forces (seismic forces), the use of shear walls or their equivalent has become essential. Well designed shear walls not only provide adequate safety, but also give a great measure of protection against costly non structural damages during moderate earthquakes.

Actually for high rise buildings, the term shear wall is a misnomer as a slender shear wall when subjected to lateral forces has predominantly moment deflections and only very insignificant shear distortions. The high rise structures are becoming taller and more slender, hence with this trend the analysis of shear walls may become a critical design element.

19.3. ARCHITECTURAL ASPECTS OF SHEAR WALLS

As stated earlier also shear walls resist large horizontal seismic forces, they have more over turning effect on them. Thus the design of their foundations needs special attention. Shear walls preferably should be provided along both length and width of the building. How ever if they are provided along only one direction, in that case a proper grid of beams and columns in the vertical plane (called a moment resistant frame) must be provided along the other direction to resist storey earthquake effects.

If doors and windows are provided in the shear walls then their size should be small to ensure least interruption to forces flowing through the walls. More over the openings should be symmetrically located. To ensure that the cross-

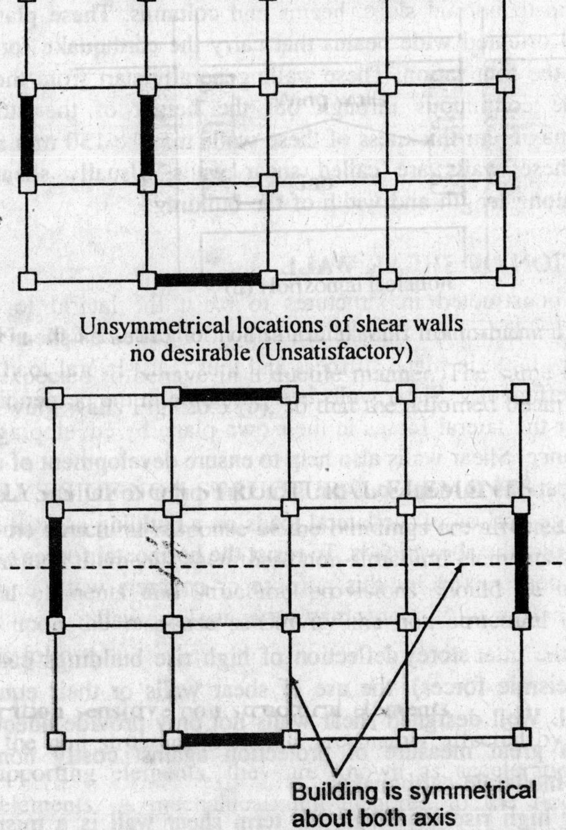

Fig. 19.1. Shear walls must be symmetric in plan layout (Courtesy—IITK)

sectional area at the opening is sufficient to carry the horizontal seismic forces, special design checks are necessary.

Shear walls in buildings must be symmetrically located in plan to minimize the ill effects of twist of building. They could be placed symmetrically along one or both directions in plan. Shear walls are found more effective when located along the exterior perimeter of the building. Such a layout increases the resistance of the building to the twisting. Fig. 19.1.

Shear walls having door and windows are called coupled shear walls. These walls on both sides of the openings are inter connected by short deep beams forming part of the wall or floor slab or both of these. In this chapter shear walls with out any openings have been discussed. The building with lateral force acting on the edge of each floor or roof is shown in Fig. 19.2 (*a*).

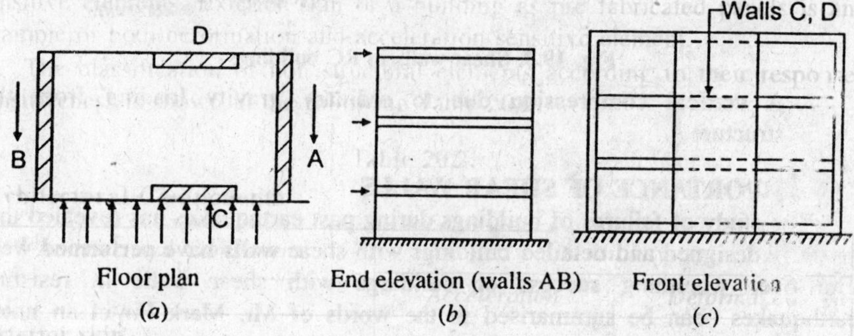

Fig. 19.2. Building subjected to horizontal forces with shear walls

The horizontal surfaces act as deep beams to transfer these loads to vertical resisting elements– the shear walls A and B Fig. 19.2 (*b*). These walls in turn act as cantilevers fixed at their base and transfer loads to the foundation below. Additional shear walls C and D are provided to resist lateral loads that may act in perpendicular direction. Fig. 19.2 (*c*). The plan is shown in Fig. 19.2 (*a*)

19.4. SHAPE OF SHEAR WALLS

The cross section of the shear wall is oblong, *i.e.* one dimension of the cross-section is much larger than the other. The rectangular cross section of the shear wall is common. How ever cross sections of *C, L* shape are also used (Fig. 19.3). The thin walled hollow R.C. shafts around the elevator core of buildings also act as shear walls. The advantages of such structures should be taken to resist seismic forces.

19.5. LOADS ON SHEAR WALLS

Shear walls are subjected to the following loads:

1. A variable shear force whose maximum value is at the base.
2. A bending moment. This B.M. causes vertical tension near the loaded edge and compression at the far edge.

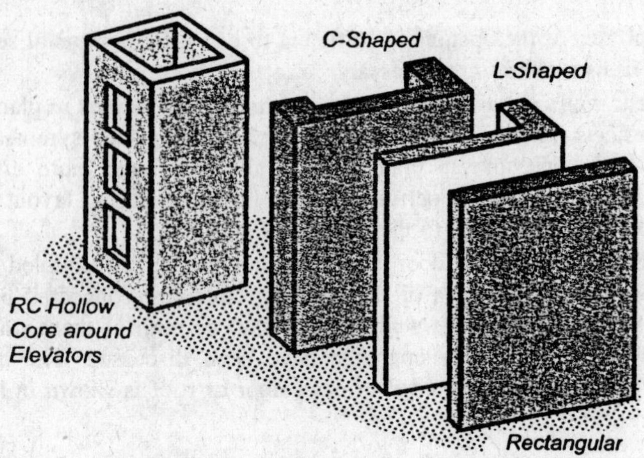

Fig. 19.3. Shear walls in RC buildings

3. A vertical compression due to ordinary gravity loading from the structure.

19.6. IMPORTANCE OF SHEAR WALLS

The study of failures of buildings during past earthquakes has revealed that properly designed and detailed buildings with shear walls have performed well. The over whelming success of buildings with shear walls in resisting earthquakes can be summarised in the words of Mr. Mark Fintel an noted American Consulting engineer.

"We can not afford to build concrete buildings meant to resist severe earthquakes with out shear walls."

In high seismic regions shear walls need special detailing. However in past earthquakes buildings even with sufficient amount of walls which were not specially detailed for seismic performance but had enough well distributed reinforcement withstood the fury of the earthquakes well *i.e.* they stood safe. In many seismic prone countries like U.S.A., Chile and New Zealand shear wall buildings are a popular choice.

Shear walls are easy to construct, due to the detailing of walls reinforcement relatively is straight forward and thus easy to implement at site. Shear walls are efficient in terms of construction cost as well as in effectiveness in minimizing the seismic damage in structural and non structural elements such as glass windows and building contents.

To reduce the ill effects of twist in buildings, the shear walls should be located symmetrically as shown in the Fig. 19.1. Shear walls are more effective when located along exterior perimeter of the building. Such a layout increases the resistance of the building to twisting.

19.7. CLASSIFICATION OF SHEAR WALLS

Shear walls may be classified in the following two categories:

1. Squat shear walls
2. High rise shear walls

19.7.1. Squat shear walls

They are also called low shear walls. The ratio of their height to base or depth or length is less than unity. In this case the height of the shear wall is less than its depth. Thus low shear walls or squat shear walls fail in shear just like deep beams. Thus shear is critical for low height to length ratio shear walls.

Though the behaviour of low shear walls is assumed to be similar or analogous to deep beams, but there is a difference between the two. In deep beams arch action prevails or dominates due to type of loading system. In such beams the stirrups crossing the main diagonal cracks which develop between the load points and the support are not found effective in resisting the shear as no compression struts can be formed between stirrups anchorages. In shear walls the load is introduced along the joint between floor slabs and walls as a live load. Thus no arch action develops with this kind of loading.

Normally low shear walls carry only very small gravity loads. Thus the beneficial effect of gravity loads in shear walls is absent *i.e.* the shear strength of shear walls is very small. How ever the large internal lever arm provides for a small flexural steel demand. Hence it is more practical to distribute the vertical *i.e.* flexural reinforcement uniformly over the full length of the wall, allowing a nominal increase at the vertical edges. Also loss of ductility for seismic loading is not likely to be of great importance.

The crack pattern of shear wall shown in Fig. 19.4 (*a*) shows the formation of diagonal struts. The formation of diagonal struts indicates the necessity of providing stirrups as shown in Fig. 8.4 (*b*). After the diagonal cracking, the horizontal shear is developed at the top of the squats shear wall. This shear force is required to be resolved into diagonal compression and vertical tensile forces. The vertical flexural distributed reinforcement will enable the shear to

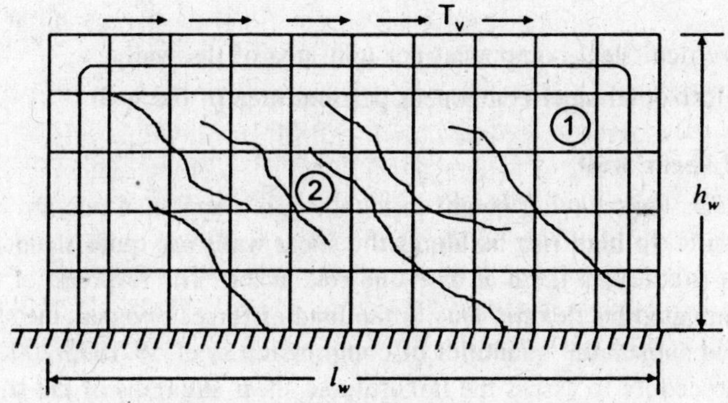

Fig. 19.4 (*a*)

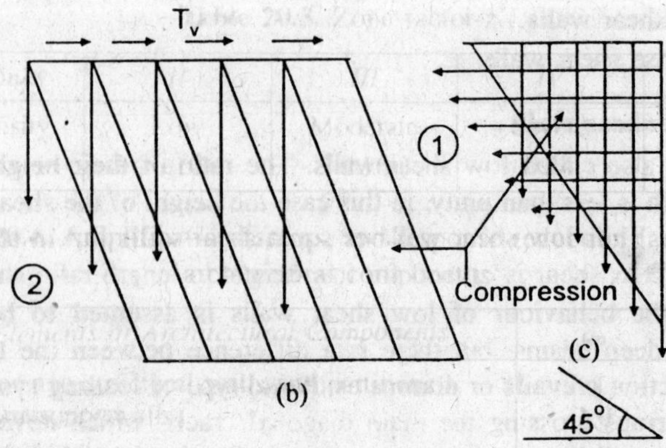

Fig. 19.4. Shear restence of low rise shear walls (Courtesy: Prof. Duggal)

be transmitted to the foundation. This condition is shown in the free body diagram marked as 2 in Fig. 8.4 (*b*). The horizontal component as shown in free body diagram Fig. 19.4 (*c*) marked by (1) does not find any support at foundation level. Thus this component needs an equal amount of horizontal shear reinforcement. In the absence of external vertical compression, the horizontal and vertical steel must be equal to generate a 45° compression diagonal.

In the free body diagram Fig. 19.4 (*b*) only vertical forces equal to the shear intensity is required to be developed to create the necessary diagonal compression. This steel is called shear reinforcement though its main purpose is to resist the moment that tends to over turn the free body shown in Fig. 19.4 (*b*). For squat shear walls the shear reinforcement for height to length ratio between 0.5 to 2.5 is given by the following equation 19.1.

$$\rho_v = 0.0025 + 0.5\left(2.5 - \frac{h_w}{l_w}\right)(\rho_h - 0.0025) \quad \ldots(19.1)$$

where,

ρ_v = Vertical steel component per unit area of the wall.

ρ_h = Horizontal steel component per unit area of the wall.

19.7.2. Tall shear wall

The shear walls having height to length ratio more than one are known as tall shear walls. In high rise buildings the shear walls are quite slender and are idealized as cantilevers fixed at base and free at top. The response of tall shear walls is dominated by flexure. Due to the load or forces reversal, the shear wall sections need substantial quantities of compression steel. IS 1893-2002 has laid down the procedure to assess the flexural and shear strengths of tall shear walls which are discussed in the subsequent paras.

19.8. FLEXURAL STRENGTH

In non seismic areas the flexural steel requirement in shear walls is not much. However there is a traditional practice to provide about 0.25% reinforcement uniformly in both directions over the entire depth as shown in Fig. 19.5 (*a*). Such an arrangement does not utilize the steel efficiently at the ultimate moment as many bars operate on a relatively small lever arm. More over the ultimate curvature and curvature ductility is considerably reduced by

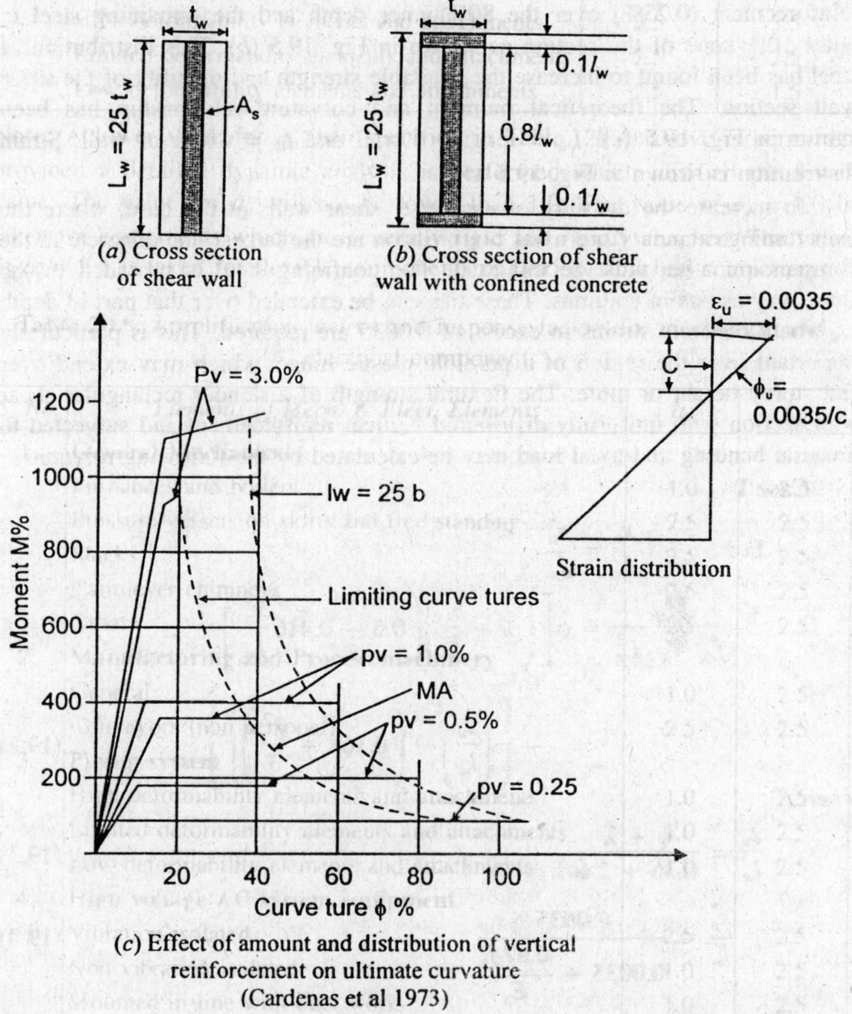

Fig. 19.5. Effect of amount and distribution of vertical reinforcement on ultimate curvatures (Carden as at al 1973)

this arrangement of reinforcement. This arrangement of reinforcement also has been found uneconomical.

For a shear wall section subjected to considerable moments, the efficient arrangement of placing flexural reinforcement will be to place the flexural reinforcement near the tensile edge. Due to the moment reversal produced by lateral loads normally equal amount of reinforcement is placed at both extremities as shown in Fig. 19.5 (*b*). Hence a considerable part of the bending moment (B.M.) can be resisted by the internal steel couple. This will also enhance the ductility properties. The practice is to provide minimum reinforcement (0.25%) over the 80% inner depth and the remaining steel to outer 10% zone of the section as shown in Fig. 19.5 (*b*). This distribution of steel has been found to increase the available strength and ductility of the shear wall section. The theoretical moment and curvature relationship has been shown in Fig. 19.5 (*c*). L_w = length of wall and t_w = width of wall. Strain distribution is shown in Fig. 19.5 (*d*)

To increase the ductility of cantilever shear walls at the base, where the over turning moments and axial compression are the largest, the concrete in the compression zone must be confined. The confining steel is provided in the same way as ties in columns. These ties can be extended over that part of depth t_w, where concrete strains in excess of 0.0035 are required. This is particularly important over the region of a possible plastic hinge, which may extend over full storey height or more. The flexural strength of a slender rectangular shear wall section with uniformly distributed vertical reinforcement and subjected to uniaxial bending and axial load may be calculated by the following relations.

Case I

For $$\frac{x_u}{l_w} = \frac{x_u^*}{l_w}$$

$$\frac{M_{ux}}{f_{ck} \cdot t_w \cdot L_w^2} = \phi \left[\left(1 + \frac{\lambda}{\phi} \right) \left(0.5 - 0.416 \frac{x_u}{l_w} \right) - \left\{ \left(\frac{x_u}{l_w} \right)^2 \left(0.168 + \frac{\beta^2}{3} \right) \right\} \right] \quad \ldots(19.2)$$

where,

$$\frac{x_u}{l_w} = \frac{\phi + \lambda}{0.36 + 2\phi} \quad \ldots(19.3)$$

$$\frac{x_u^*}{l_w} = \frac{0.0035}{0.0035 + \dfrac{0.87 f_y}{E_s}} \quad \ldots(19.4)$$

$$\phi = \frac{0.87 f_y \rho}{f_{ck}}$$

$$\lambda = \frac{P_u}{f_{ck} \cdot t_w \cdot l_w}$$

$$\rho = \frac{A_{st}}{t_w \cdot l_w}$$

$$\beta = \frac{0.87 f_y}{0.0035 E_s}$$

where,

x_u = Depth of neutral axis from extreme compression flange

x_u^* = Depth of neutral axis of balanced section

α = Inclination of diagonal reinforcement in the coupling beam

β = Soil foundation factor as per IS 893-2002

ρ = Vertical reinforcement ratio

A_{st} = Area of uniformly distributed vertical steel

E_s = Elastic modulus of steel

P_u = Axial compression load on the wall.

f_y = Yield stress of steel

Case II.

For $\quad \frac{x_u^*}{l_w} < \frac{x_u}{l_w} < 1.0$

$$\frac{M_{uv}}{f_{ck} \cdot t_w \cdot l_w^2} = \alpha_1 \left(\frac{x_u}{l_w} \right) - \alpha_2 \left(\frac{x_u}{l_w} \right)^2 - \alpha_3 - \frac{\lambda}{2} \qquad \text{...(19.5)}$$

where,

$$\alpha_1 = \left[0.36 + \phi \left(1 - \frac{\beta}{2} - \frac{1}{2\beta} \right) \right]$$

$$\alpha_2 = \left[0.15 + \frac{\phi}{2} \left(1 - \beta - \frac{\beta^2}{2} - \frac{1}{3\beta} \right) \right]$$

$$\alpha_3 = \frac{\phi}{6\beta} \left[\frac{1}{x_u/l_w} - 3 \right]$$

The value of $\frac{x_u}{lw}$ to be used in this equation can be determined from the following quadratic equation.

$$\alpha_1 \left(\frac{x_u}{l_w} \right)^2 + \alpha_4 \left(\frac{x_u}{l_w} \right) + \alpha_5 = 0$$

$$\alpha_4 = \left(\frac{\phi}{\beta} - \lambda \right) \text{ and } \alpha_5 = \frac{\phi}{2\beta}$$

Equations (19.2) and (19.5) have been derived assuming the wall section as rectangular of depth L_w and thickness t_w that is subjected to combined uniaxial bending and axial compression. The use of these equations depends on whether the section fails in flexural tension or in flexural compression. The vertical reinforcement is represented by an equivalent steel plate along the length of the section. For concrete the stress-strain curve is assumed as per IS 456-2000 and that for steel as bilinear.

19.9. BEHAVIOUR OF SHEAR WALLS

The behaviour of shear walls particularly with reference to their typical mode of failure is same as those of beams, influenced by their proportions as well as their support conditions. The behaviour of small height to length ratio shear walls is quite different from those of high height to length ratio shear walls. The small height to length ratio shear walls are expected to fail in shear like a deep beam. For such walls shear is critical.

On the other hand shear walls of high rise buildings usually behave as a vertical cantilever beam Fig. 19.6 (*b*). The strength of such shear walls is

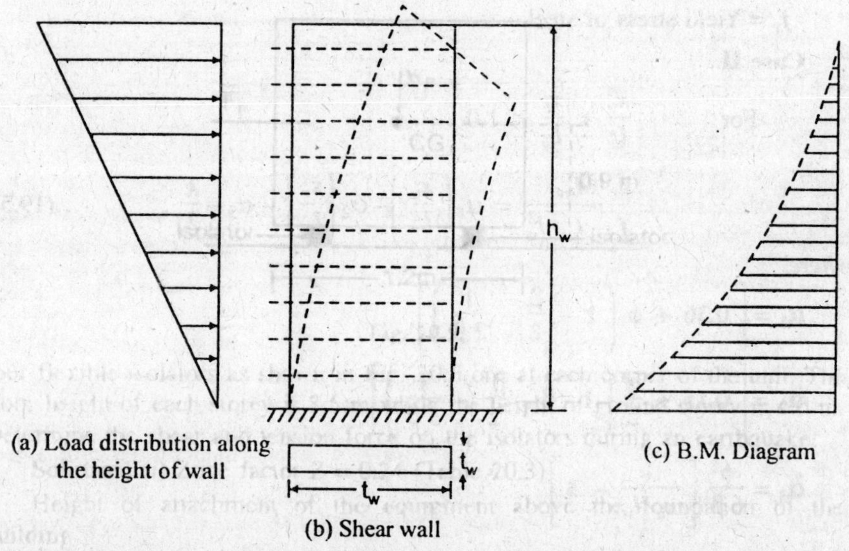

Fig. 19.6. Behaviour of shear wall (Courtesy: Prof. Duggal)

controlled by flexure rather than shear. Such walls are subjected to B.M. and shears produced by lateral loads and to axial compression caused by gravity. Thus such shear walls may be designed as regular flexural elements. When acting as a vertical cantilever beam, the behaviour of a shear wall properly reinforced for shear (diagonal tension) will be governed by the yielding of the tensile reinforcement located near the vertical edges of the wall and to some extent by the vertical reinforcement distributed along the central part of the wall.

Thus it is evident that tall shear walls are mainly controlled by flexural requirements particularly if only uniformly distributed reinforcement is used. Where as for small height to length ratio shear walls shear is critical. A typical shear wall of height *hw*, length L_w and thickness *tw* is shown in Fig. 19.7. It is

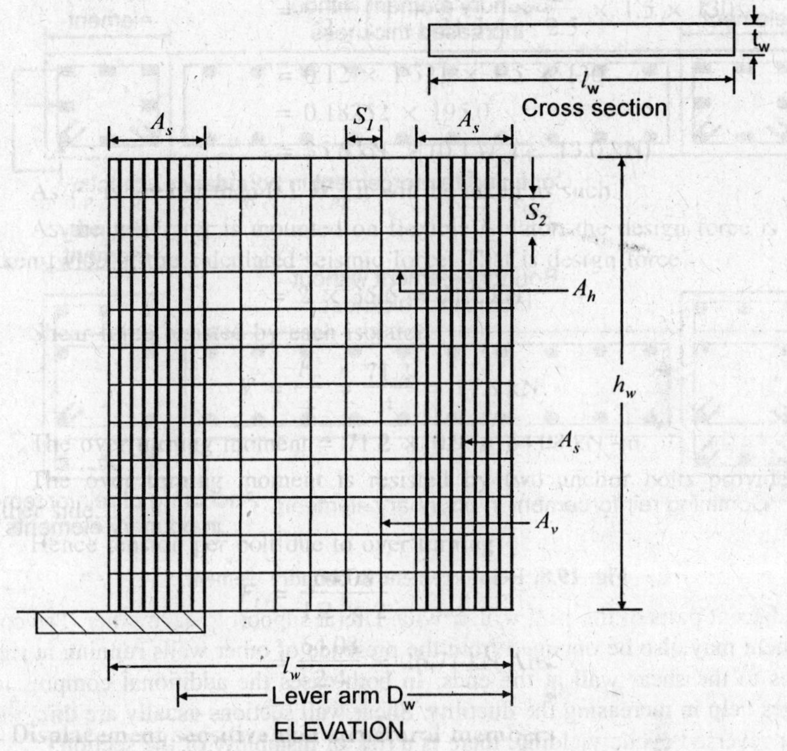

Fig. 19.7. Behaviour of cantilever shear wall

assumed that the shear wall is fixed at its base and loaded horizontally along its left edge. The vertical flexural reinforcement A_s is provided on the left edge, with its centroid at a distance d_w from the extreme compression face. Identical reinforcement is also provided along the right edge to take care of the reversal of the load. Horizontal reinforcement of area A_h at a spacing S_2 and vertical reinforcement A_v at a spacing S_1 is also provided as a shear reinforcement The provision of minimum distributed reinforcement horizontally and vertically helps in controlling the width of the inclined cracks. Such minimum distributed reinforcement normally is placed in two layers parallel to both faces of the wall.

The ductility of a flexural member such as a tall shear wall can be significantly affected by the maximum usable strain in the compression zone of concrete, hence the confirefinement of concrete at the ends of the shear wall section would improve the performance of such shear walls. Such confinement of reinforcement is done in the large section at the boundary as shown in Fig. 19.8. These elements are called boundary elements. In the flanged wall sections,

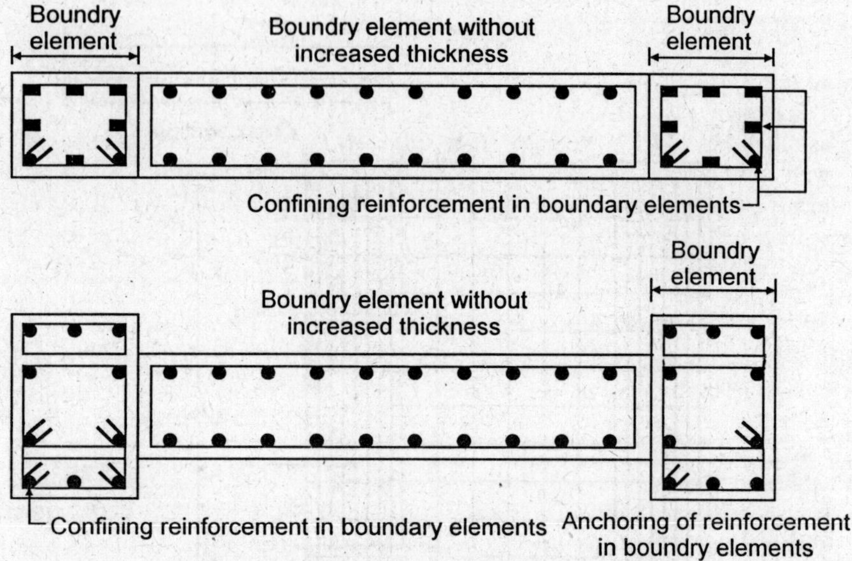

Fig. 19.8. Reinforcement in boundry element

the adjacent parts of the wall will provide lateral support to each other. The confinement may also be obtained from the presence of other walls running at right angles to the shear wall at the ends. In both cases the additional compression flanges help in increasing the ductility. Shear wall sections usually are thin, thus under reversed cyclic yielding, there is a risk of instability of the section.

Thus to increase the stability between the ground and first floors of a

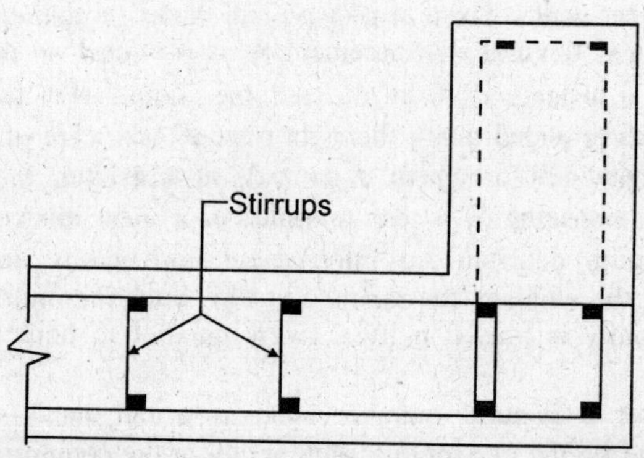

Fig. 19.9. Return wall (Flanged shear wall)

building introduction of return wall as shown in Fig. 19.9 may prove useful. It is also required that vertical (longitudinal) forces produced by seismic loads are entirely resisted by the boundary elements. The design of such boundary elements is similar to the design of steel I section beams, where flanges resist the flexural stresses and the web (wall panel in shear walls) bears the entire shear. In shear walls of high rise structures sufficient shear capacity is provided so that shear failure may not take place before a flexure failure.

However a portion of a shear wall which inter acts with the frames may act as a low height to length ratio shear wall depending upon the proportions of the walls and the location of point of contraflexure along the height of the all. The location of point of contraflexure is dependent primarily on the relative stiffness of the frame and the shear wall elements in a structure. Fig. 19.10 shows layout of main reinforcement in shear walls as per IS 19320-1993.

19.10. CONSTRUCTION JOINTS

In cantilever shear walls there are two likely locations where failure by sliding shear may occur. One of the likely locations is a horizontal construction joint and the other is plastic hinge zone, usually immediately above the foundation level. Due to the inelastic response of the mechanism associated with the sliding shear a drastic loss of stiffness and strength for the reversed cycling loading takes place. Thus in earthquake resistant structures sliding shear should be considered as unsuitable mechanism for energy dissipation.

In shear walls damage due to earthquake is more common at construction joints along which sliding movements may take place. It has been found more common in low shear walls which carry small gravity loads. Thus to check the sliding, it becomes essential to provide sufficient vertical reinforcement. The amount of shear force which can be safely transferred across a well prepared rough horizontal joint can be estimated by the following relation

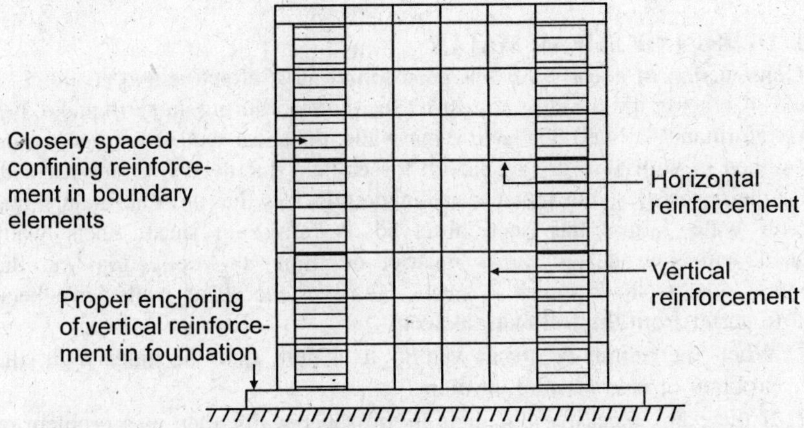

Fig. 19.10. Layout of main reinforcement in shear walls as per IS 19320-1993

$$V_j = \mu [P_u + 0.87 f_y \cdot A_v] \quad ...(19.6)$$

where,

V_j = Shear force at joint

f_y = Yield stress of steel

P_u = Design estimated axial force on the section. it is positive if it produces compression.

A_v = Vertical steel to be provided.

μ = Coefficient of friction at the joint. Usually $\mu = 1.0$.

For shear walls, gravity loads with 20% reduction to account for negative vertical acceleration are given

$$V_j = 0.8\, P_u + 0.87 f_y \cdot A_v \quad ...(19.7)$$

Strength of construction joint is given by the relation

$$\tau_{vf} = \frac{V_j}{A_g} \quad ...(19.8)$$

Where A_g is gross concrete areas of the section. This strength should be equal to, but preferably greater than diagonal tension shear strength of the shear wall.

The steel content across construction joint is given by

$$\rho_{vf} = \frac{A_v}{A_g}$$

The vertical reinforcement ratio ρ_v across a horizontal construction joint should not be less than

$$\left(\tau_v - \frac{P_u}{A_g}\right)\frac{0.92}{f_y} \geq 0.0025$$

Where τ_v is the designed shear stress at the joint and P_u is designed axial force (positive for compression) and A_g is the gross cross sectional area of the joint.

19.11. DESIGN OF SHEAR WALLS

Construction of shear walls has been found most effective and economical method of bracing the building to restrict the damage during an earthquake. For good performance of well designed shear walls, the shear wall structures should be designed to withstand greater lateral forces than ductile R.C.C. frames with similar characteristics. Shear walls are inherently less ductile. The main mode of shear walls failure has been observed as failure in shear. Shear walls designed with low design stress, restrict or limit the deflection, *i.e.* the deflection due to shear forces is small. However the shear walls have been found to suffer from the following defects:

1. When the height of shear wall to its length ratio becomes high, the problem of over turning develops.
2. If there are excessive openings in the shear walls, then also problem of over turning arises.

3. If the soil below the foundation of the shear walls is relatively soft, the entire shear wall may rotate at this juncture causing localized damage around wall.

19.11.1. General Design requirements of shear walls

Here the design aspects are discussed as per provisions of IS 13920-2002.

1. To avoid usually very thin sections, the minimum thickness of the shear wall should not be less than 150 mm. Very thin sections are susceptible to lateral instability areas where inelastic cyclic loading may have to be sustained.
2. For flanged wall sections the width of the flange from the face of the wall called web should be taken lower of the two values:
   (*a*) 10% or one tenth of the total height of the wall.
   (*b*) Half the distance to an adjacent shear wall web.
3. The minimum amount of reinforcement in the longitudinal and as well as in transverse direction in the plan of the wall should be taken as 0.25% of the gross area in each direction. The reinforcement should be uniformly distributed across the cross sectional area of the wall. This reinforcement helps in controlling the width of the inclined cracks developed due to the shear.
4. In case the design estimated shear stress in the wall exceeds $0.25 \sqrt{f_{ck}}$ or if the wall thickness exceeds 200 mm, the reinforcement should be provided in two layers, each layer having bars running in both longitudinal and transverse directions in the plane of the wall. The provision of reinforcement in two layers reduces the fragmentation and premature deterioration of the concrete under cyclic loading.
5. The maximum spacing of reinforcement bars in either direction should be $l_w/5$, $3\ t_w$ or 450 mm, which ever is lowest where lw is horizontal length and t_w is the thickness of the web of the wall.
6. The diameter of the reinforcement bars should not exceed 10% or one tenth of the thickness of that part where reinforcement is provided. This provision limits the use of large diameter bars in thin wall sections.

19.11.2. Shear Strength

The provision for shear strength of shear wall is same as those of R.C.C. beams. The increase in shear strength may also be considered. For the increase in shear strength only 80% of the designed axial force is considered as effective. This reduction of 20% axial force is made to accommodate the possible effect of vertical acceleration.

(*a*) The nominal shear stress τ_v is given by

$$\tau_v = \frac{V_u}{t_w \times d_w} \qquad \ldots(19.9)$$

where, V_u = Design estimated shear force

t_w = Thickness of wall web

d_w = Effective depth of the wall section. It may be taken as 0.8 l_w.

(*b*) The design shear stress of concrete τ_c may be taken as per IS 456-2000.

(*c*) The nominal shear stress τ_v should not be greater than $\tau_{c\,max}$, the minimum shear reinforcement of 0.25% should be provided in the horizontal direction. If $\tau_v > \tau_c$, the area of horizontal shear reinforcement A_h, at a vertical spacing S_v can be determined from the relation

$$V_{u_s} = \frac{0.87 f_y \cdot A_h \cdot d_w}{S_v}$$

where,

V_{us} = Shear force to be resisted by the horizontal reinforcement whose value is given by the relation

$$V_{us} = V_u - \tau_c \cdot t_w \cdot d_w$$

(*d*) Uniformly distributed vertical reinforcement not less than horizontal reinforcement should be provided. This provision is important when the height to width ratio is about 1.0. In this case both vertical as well as horizontal reinforcement are equally effective in resisting the shear force.

19.11.3. Flexure strength

For short shear walls the moment of resistance is calculated as for columns subjected to combined bending and axial loading. The procedure for calculation of moment of resistance M_{uv} of tall rectangular shear walls is same as discussed in section 19.8.

For walls with out boundary elements, the vertical reinforcement is concentrated at the ends of the wall. A minimum of four bars of 12 mm diameter arranged in two layers are provided at each end.

19.11.4. Boundary elements

The portions along the wall edges are known as *boundary elements*. The boundary elements may have the same or greater thickness than wall web as show in Fig. 19.8. The boundary elements are provided through out the height with special confining reinforcement. Wall sections having stiff and well confined boundary elements develop substantial flexural strength. Such shear walls are less susceptible to lateral buckling and have better shear strength and ductility in comparison to plane rectangular wall not having stiff and well confined boundary elements.

1. The ends of a wall during a severe earthquake are subjected to high compressive and tensile stresses. Hence to sustain the load reversal with out a large deterioration in strength, concrete needs to be well confined. Thus when the extreme failure compressive stresses due to the design

gravity load plus design earthquake force exceed 0.2 f_{ck}, the boundary elements are provided along the vertical boundaries of the walls. These boundary elements may be discontinued where the calculated compressive stresses become less than 0.15 f_{ck}.

2. The boundary elements are assumed to be effective to resist the designed moment due to earthquake forces induced along with the web of the wall. The boundary element should be capable to carry the axial compression due to the designed gravity load plus compressive load due to the earthquake load. Thus the boundary elements should be designed as a short column. The compressive force or load to be resisted by the boundary element is given by the relation

$$P_c = \frac{M_u - M_{u_v}}{C_w}$$

where, M_u = Design moment on the entire wall section

M_{uv} = Moment of resistance provided by the distributed reinforcement across the wall section

C_w = Centre to centre distance between the boundary elements along the two vertical edges of the wall.

3. Higher moment capacity of the wall is developed by the moderate axial compression. Thus, due to possible reduction in the magnitude of the axial compression by vertical acceleration of the seismic forces, total effect of axial compression should not be taken in the design. When the gravity loads add to the strength of the wall, a load factor of 0.8 may be adopted.
4. The percentage of vertical reinforcement in the boundary elements may range between 0.6 to 8.0%. However for practical purposes the upper limit may be 4.0%.
5. During a severe earthquake, the boundary elements may be subjected to stress reversals. Hence they have to be confined adequately to sustain the cyclic loading without a large degradation in strength. Thus these elements should be confined through out their height.
6. If the entire wall section is provided with special confining reinforcement, then there is no need of providing boundary elements.

Example. The plan of a ten storey building is shown in Fig. 19.11. In each direction to resist the seismic forces two shear walls are provided. On each shear wall an axial load due to both live and dead load is 6000 kN. The height between floors is 3.2 m. The dead load per unit area of the floor which includes floor slab and finishes etc. as 4.25 kN/m^2 and the weight of partition etc. on the floor is 2.0 kN/m^2. The intensity of live load on each floor is 3 kN/m^2. The live load intensity on roof may be taken as 1.5 kN/m^2. The soil below foundation is hard moorum. The seismic zone of the building may be taken as IV. Determine the following:

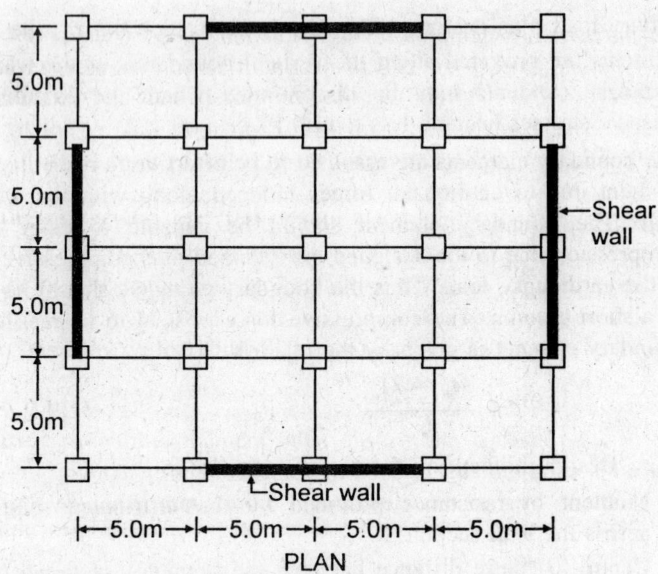

Fig. 19.11.

(*a*) Seismic forces and shear forces at different floors.

(*b*) Design ductile shear wall to resist the seismic forces.

The density of concrete may be taken 25 kN/m^3 and strength of concrete as 250 kg/cm^2 or 425 grade and steel Fe 415. The cross sections of beams and columns as 60 × 30 cm.

Solution. From the study of the plan, it will be seen that there are forty (40) beams of 5 m span and 25 columns of 60 × 30 cm dimensions.

1. Determination of seismic weight of the building

For the calculation of load as per the provisions of the code, no live load is considered on the roof of the building and for the floor 25% load is taken upto the intensity of 3 kN or 3000 N and above that 50% is taken.

Hence effective weight at roof including dead weight and finishing weight

$$= 4.25 \text{ kN/m}^2$$

Effective weight at each floor including partition and live load

$$= 4.25 + 2.0 + 3.0 \times 0.25 = 7.0 \text{ kN/m}^2$$

Weight of 40 beams each of 5 m span and 30 cm × 60 cm section at roof and each floor

$$= 0.3 \times 0.6 \times 5 \times 25 \times 40 = 900 \text{ kN}$$

Weight of 25 columns at each floor

$$= 0.3 \times 0.6 \times (\text{Height of col}) \times 25 \times 25$$

$$= 0.3 \times 0.6 \times (3.2 - 0.6)\, 25 \times 25$$

$= 0.18 \times 25 \times 25\ (3.2 - 0.6)$

(Depth of beam = 0.6)

$= 0.18 \times 25 \times 25 \times 2.6 = 292.5$ kN

Weight of columns at roof $= \frac{1}{2} \times 292 = 146$ kN

Plan area of the building $= 20 \times 20 = 400\ m^2$

∴ Weight of roof $= 4 \times 400 = 1600$ kN

Hence equivalent load at roof level = Weight of roof + wt. of beams + half weight of columns

$= 1600 + 900 + 146 = 2646$ kN

Equivalent weight at each floor $= 7.0 \times 400 + 900 + 292$

$= 3992$ kN

∴ Seismic weight of building $= 2646 + 3992 \times 9 = 38574.0$ kN

The fundamental natural period of vibrations (T) for the walls of the building is given by the relation.

$$T = \frac{0.09\ h}{\sqrt{d}}$$

where h is the total height of building and d is the base or depth of the building. Here $h = 32.0$ m and $d = 20$ m.

$$\therefore \quad T = \frac{0.09 \times 32}{\sqrt{20}} = \frac{28.8}{\sqrt{20}}$$

$$= \frac{2.88}{4.47} = 0.644$$

From table response acceleration coefficient $\frac{S_a}{g} = \frac{1.0}{T} = \frac{1}{0.644}$

$$\therefore \quad \frac{S_a}{g} = 1.553$$

For seismic zone, IV zone factor $z = 0.24$

Importance factor $I = 1.0$

Response reduction factor for ductile shear walls = 4.0

∴ Design horizontal seismic coefficient $A_h = \frac{Z \cdot I \cdot S_a}{2 \times R \times g}$

$$\therefore \quad A_h = \frac{0.24}{2} \times \frac{1}{4} \times 1.553$$

$$= \frac{0.37272}{8} = 0.0466$$

∴ Base shear $= A_h \times$ Seismic weight $= 0.0466 \times 38574$

$= 1800$ kN

Lateral loads and shear forces at different floors levels

Design lateral force or weight is given by the relation

$$Q_i = V_B \times \frac{W_i h_i^2}{\sum_{J=1}^{n} W_j h_j^2}$$

Lateral loads and shear forces at different floor levels are shown in Table 19.1.

Table 19.1.

Mass no.	w_i (kN)	h_i (m)	h_i^2 (m)	$w_i h_i^2$	$\frac{w_i h_i^2}{\Sigma w_i h^2}$	Q_i (kN) ($V_B \times$ col 6)	v_i kN
(1)	(2)	(3)	(4)	(5)	(6)	(7)	(8)
10.	2646	32.0	1024.0	2710.0×10^3	0.1882	338.80	338.8
9.	3992	28.8	829.44	3311×10^3	0.2299	413.82	752.62
8.	3992	25.6	654.4	2613.0×10^3	0.1814	326.62	1079.20
7.	3992	22.4	501.76	2003.0×10^3	0.1391	250.38	1329.58
6.	3992	19.2	368.64	1475.0×10^3	0.1024	184.40	1514.0
5.	3992	16.0	256.0	1022.0×10^3	0.0711	127.80	1641.82
4.	3992	12.8	163.84	654.0×10^3	0.0454	81.72	1725.5
3.	3992	9.6	102.16	408.0×10^3	0.02833	51.00	1774.5
2.	3992	6.4	40.96	163.5×10^3	0.0114	20.52	1795.0
1	3992	3.2	10.24	40.87×10^3	0.002915	5.11	1800.0
				$\Sigma w_i h_i^2 = 14400 \times 10^3$			

Bending moment and shear force

As given in the problem, two shear walls are provided on each side to resist the seismic forces. Thus lateral forces acting on one shear wall will be half of the calculated values shown in Table 19.1. The shear wall will be designed as a cantilever fixed at base and free at the top.

For calculating the B.M., the forces at the wall, distribution of seismic forces is shown in Fig. 19.12.

Maximum shear force at the base of one shear wall

$$= \frac{1800}{2} \text{ kN} = 900 \text{ kN}$$

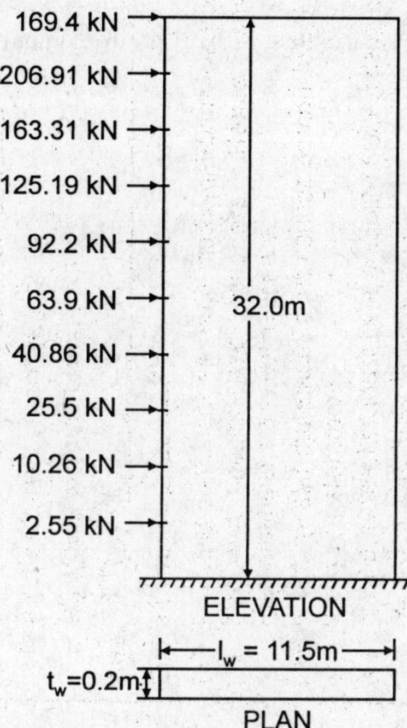

Fig. 19.12.

Maximum B.M. at base

$$= (2.55 \times 3.2) + (10.26 \times 6.4) + (25.5 \times 9.6) + (40.86 \times 12.8) + (63.9 \times 16.0) + (92.2 \times 19.2) + (125.19 \times 22.4) + (163.31 \times 25.6) + (206.91 \times 28.8) + (169.4 \times 32.0)$$

$$= 8.16 + 65.664 + 244.80 + 523.0 + 1022.4 + 1770.24 + 2804.26 + 4180.73 + 5959.0 + 5420.8$$

$$= 21998.8 \text{ kN–m}$$

Taking a partial factor of safety as 1.5, then

Design shear force = 1.5 × 900 = 1350 kN

Design B.M. = 1.5 × 21998.8 = 32998.2 kN.m

Design axial load = 1.5 × 6000 = 9000.0 kN

R.C.C. structures in seismic zones should be designed as per provision of IS 13920-2002. According the code the concrete should be used of grade M25 *i.e.* its 28 days compressive strength f_{ck} = 25 N/m^2 and steel stress f_y = 415 N/mm^2, Modulus of steel $E_s = 2 \times 10^5$ N/mm^2

Flexure strength of the shear wall

Take the length of the shear wall l_w = 11.5 m

Wall thickness $t_w = 0.2$ m

Provide uniformly distributed vertical reinforcement ratio $P = 0.25\%$.

Case I.

For $\dfrac{x_u}{l_w} = \dfrac{x_u^*}{l_w}$

$$\frac{M_{ux}}{f_{ck} \cdot t_w \cdot l_w^2} = \phi\left[\left(1 + \frac{\lambda}{\phi}\right)\left(\frac{1}{2} - 0.416\frac{x_u}{l_w}\right) - \left\{\left(\frac{x_u}{l_w}\right)^2\left(0.168 + \frac{\beta^2}{3}\right)\right\}\right].$$

where,

$$\frac{x_u}{l_w} = \frac{\phi + \lambda}{0.36 + 2\phi}$$

$$\frac{x_u^*}{l_w} = \frac{0.0035}{0.0035 + \dfrac{0.87 f_y}{E_s}}$$

$$\phi = \frac{0.87 f_y \rho}{f_{ck}}$$

$$\lambda = \frac{P_u}{f_{ck} \cdot t_w \cdot l_w}$$

$$\rho = \frac{A_{st}}{t_w \cdot l_w}$$

$$\beta = \frac{0.87 f_y}{0.0035 E_s}$$

where,

x_u = Depth of neutral axis from extreme compression flange.

x_u^* = Depth of neutral axis for balanced section.

α = Inclination of the diagonal reinforcement in the coupling beam

β = Soil foundation factor (IS 1893-2002)

ρ = Vertical reinforcement ratio

A_{st} = Area of uniformly distributed vertical reinforcement

E_s = Elastic modulus of steel

P_u = Axial compression on the wall.

Case II

For $\dfrac{x_u^*}{l_w} < \dfrac{x_u}{l_w} < 1.0$

$$\frac{M_{uv}}{f_{ck} \cdot t_w \cdot l_w^2} = \alpha_1 \left(\frac{x_u}{l_w} \right) - \alpha_2 \left(\frac{x_u}{l_w} \right)^2 - \alpha_3 - \frac{\lambda}{2} \qquad \ldots(2)$$

where,

$$\alpha_1 = \left[0.36 + \phi \left(1 - \frac{\beta}{2} - \frac{1}{2\beta} \right) \right]$$

$$\alpha_2 = \left[0.15 + \frac{\phi}{2} \left(1 - \beta - \frac{\beta^2}{2} - \frac{1}{3\beta} \right) \right]$$

$$\alpha_3 = \frac{\phi}{6\beta} \left[\frac{1}{x_u / l_w} - 3 \right]$$

The value of $\frac{x_u}{l_w}$ to be used in the equation can be computed from the quadratic equation.

$$\alpha_1 \left(\frac{x_u}{l_w} \right)^2 + \alpha_4 \left(\frac{x_u}{l_w} \right) + \alpha_5 = 0$$

$$\alpha_4 = \left(\frac{\phi}{\beta} - \lambda \right) \text{ and } \alpha_5 = \frac{\phi}{2\beta}$$

The flexural strength of the section may be obtained with the help of the equation (1) and (2). The use of the equation depends whether the section fails in flexural tension or flexural compression. The stress-strain curve is assumed for concrete as per IS 456-2000.

$$\text{Now} \quad \phi = \frac{0.87 f_y \cdot P}{f_{ck}} = \frac{0.87 \times 415 \times 0.0025}{25}$$

$$\left[\text{M25 grade has strength } \frac{250\,kg}{cm^2} = \frac{250 \times 10\,N}{10 \times 10} = 25\ \text{N/mm}^2\right]$$

$$\therefore \quad \phi = 0.03611$$

$$\lambda = \frac{P_u}{f_{ck} \cdot l_w \cdot t_w} = \frac{9000 \times 10^3}{25 \times 11.5 \times 10^3 \times 200} \text{ (Al dimension in mm))}$$

$$= 0.157$$

$$\beta = \frac{0.87 f_y}{0.0035 E_s} = \frac{0.87 \times 415}{0.0035 \times 2 \times 10^5}$$

$$= \frac{314 \times 0.87}{700} = \frac{4.15 \times 0.87}{7} = \frac{3.611}{7} = 0.516$$

$$\frac{x_u}{l_w} = \frac{\phi + \lambda}{2\phi + 0.36} = \frac{0.03611 + 0.157}{2 \times 0.03611 + 0.36} = \frac{0.193}{0.432} = 0.447$$

$$\frac{x_u^*}{l_w} = \frac{0.0035}{0.0035 + \dfrac{0.87 f_y}{E_s}} = \frac{0.0035}{0.0055 + \dfrac{0.87 \times 415}{2 \times 105}}$$

$$= \frac{0.0035}{0.053} = 0.66$$

Hence $$\frac{x_u}{l_w} < \frac{x_u^*}{l_w}$$

Hence the moment of resistance M_u will be given by the following equation.

$$M_u = f_{ck} \cdot t_w \cdot l_w^2 \cdot \phi \left[\left(1 + \frac{\lambda}{\phi} \right) \left(\frac{1}{2} - 0.416 \times \frac{x_u}{l_w} \right) - \left(\frac{x_u}{l_w} \right)^2 \left(0.168 + \frac{\beta^2}{3} \right) \right.$$

Putting the proper values in the above relation we get.

$$M_u = 25 \times 200 \times (11500)^2 \times 0.03611 \left(1 + \frac{0.157}{0.03611} \right)$$

$$(0.5 - 0.416 \times 0.447) - (0.447)^2 \left(0.168 + \frac{(0.516)^2}{3} \right)$$

$$= 23808.24 \times 10^6 \, [(1 + 4.347)\,(0.5 - 0.1926)$$
$$- (0.2)\,(0.168 + 0.0888]$$
$$= 23808.24 \times 10^6 \, [(5.347 \times 0.31)\,(0.2 \times 0.257)]$$
$$= 23808.24 \times 10^6 \, [1.66 - 0.0514]$$
$$= 23808.24 \times 10^6 \times [1.611] = 38356.67 \times 10^6$$

Design B.M. $= 38356.67 \times 10^6$ kN–m

$\approx 384 \times 10^8$ kN–m

Assume effective depth of shear wall $= 0.9 \times 11500 = 10350.0$ mm

$= 10350$ mm

Areas of steel to be provided $$A_{st} = \frac{M_u}{0.87 f_y \cdot z}$$

$$= \frac{384 \times 10^8}{0.87 \times 415 \times 10350}$$

[Taking units in mm]

$$= \frac{384 \times 10^8}{87 \times 103.5 \times 415} = \frac{384 \times 10^8}{373.7 \times 10^4}$$

$$= \frac{384 \times 10^4}{373.7} = 1.029 \times 10^4 \text{ mm}^2$$

$$= 10290 \text{ mm}^2$$

Let us provide 20 mm bars in 10350 mm length of the wall at each end. Equal amount of reinforcement should be provided at the vertical edges of the wall which act like flanges of a steel beams.

Cross sectional area of 20 mm dia steel bar

$$= \frac{\pi}{4} \times (20)^2 = 314.2 \text{ mm}^2$$

Total steel required = 10290 mm²

$$\therefore \quad \text{No of steel bars required} = \frac{10290}{314.2} = 32.8$$

Hence provide 33 bars of 20 mm at each and of the wall

Area of 33 bars = 314.2 × 33 = 10368.6 mm²

Thus area of steel provided is 10369 instead of 10290 mm² *i.e.* 79 mm² more. Minimum area of steel required in this portion of wall

$$= 0.0025 \times 11500 \times 200$$

$$= 5750 \text{ mm}^2$$

Minimum steel reinforcement is provided in the vertical direction for a length of $0.8\, l_w = 11.5 \times 0.8 = 9.20$ m or 9200 mm.

Area of minimum reinforcement per metre length of wall

$$= 0.0025 \times 1000 \times 200$$

$$= 500 \text{ mm}^2$$

$$\text{Maximum permissible spacing} = \frac{l_w}{5}$$

or $3\, t_w$ or 450 mm which ever is less,

$$\frac{l_w}{5} = \frac{11500}{5} = 2300 \text{ mm},\ 3\, t_w = 600 \text{ mm and } 450 \text{ mm.}$$

Hence 450 mm is the least value of the above.

Provide 10 mm ϕ bars at 300 mm c/c in the vertical direction in two layers.

Check for shear

$$\text{Design shear force} = \frac{1800 \times 1.5}{2} = 1350 \text{ kN}$$

$$\therefore \quad \text{Nominal shear stress } \tau_v = \frac{V_u}{t_w \times d_w} = \frac{135 \times 10^4}{200 \times 10350}$$

$$= \frac{1350}{2070} = 0.652 \text{ N/mm}^2$$

Permissible shear stress for M-25 grade concrete and steel ratio $P = 0.25\%$.

$$\tau_c = 0.36 \text{ N/mm}^2$$

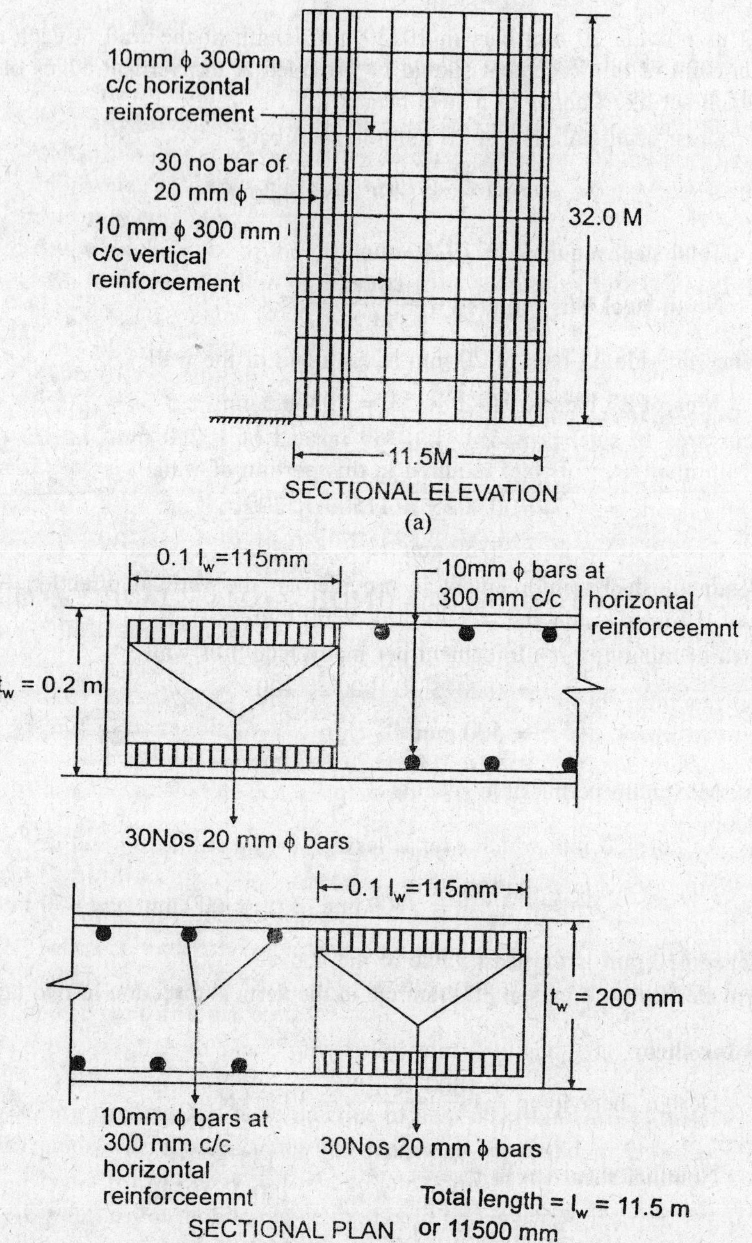

Fig. 19.13. Reinforcement details of shear wall

As $\tau_v > \tau_c$, the area of horizontal shear reinforcement A_h at a vertical spacing S_v is given by the relation

$$S_v = \frac{0.87 f_y \cdot A_h \times d_w}{V_{us}}$$

$$V_{us} = 135 \times 10^4 - \tau_c \times d_w \times t_w$$

$$= 135 \times 10^4 - 0.36 \times 10350 \times 200$$

$$= 135 \times 10^4 - 745200 = 604800$$

$$\therefore \quad S_v = \frac{0.87 \times 415 \times \pi/4\,(10)^2 \times 10350 \times 2}{604800}$$

$$= \frac{0.87 \times 830 \times 78.55 \times 10350}{604800}$$

$$= \frac{5871 \times 10^5}{6048 \times 10^2} = \frac{5871 \times 10^3}{6048} = 971.0 \text{ mm c/c}$$

Thus reinforcement provided in horizontal direction

$$= \frac{78.55 \times 2 \times 1000}{971} = \frac{157100}{971} = 162.0 \text{ mm}^2$$

This reinforcement is much less than the minimum reinforcement required. Hence a minimum specified reinforcement of 0.25% of the gross area of the wall should be provided in horizontal direction. Hence provide 10 mm ϕ bars at 300 mm c/c as horizontal reinforcement on both faces and in full height of the wall.

Reinforcement details are shown in Fig. 19.13.

QUESTIONS

1. Define a shear wall and discuss its architectural aspects.
2. Discuss the importance of shear walls.
3. Discuss squat shear walls.
4. A shear wall should be provided
   (*a*) On one side of the building (*b*) Symmetrical on both axis
   (*c*) In any location
5. Shear walls are subjected to
   (*a*) Vertical compressive loads (*b*) B.M.
   (*c*) Variable shear force (*d*) All the three
6. Usually shear walls fail in....
   (*a*) Shear mode (*b*) Bending mode
   (*c*) Deflection mode (*d*) In any of the above mode
7. Usually over turning problem develops in shear walls due to
   (*a*) Due to high height to length ratio
   (*b*) Due to more openings in the shear wall
   (*c*) Due to relatively soft soil below the foundation of shear walls
   (*d*) Due to all the above factors

8. The minimum thickness of the concrete shear wall should be
   (*a*) 25 cm (*b*) 20 cm
   (*c*) 15 cm (*d*) 10 cm
9. The maximum diameter of reinforcing bars of shear wall should not exceed its thickness
   (*a*) 25% (*b*) 20%
   (*c*) 15% (*d*) 10%
10. The shear force on a shear wall is maximum at
    (*a*) At the top of the wall (*b*) At the middle level of wall
    (*c*) At the bottom of the wall (*d*) At any level
11. The moment of resistance for short shear walls is calculated as for
    (*a*) Slab (*b*) Beam
    (*c*) Columns (*d*) All are true
12. The maximum thickness of shear wall may be kept
    (*a*) 75 cm (*b*) 60 cm
    (*c*) 40 cm (*d*) 35 cm
13. Identify the correct statement/statements
    (*a*) Shear wall should be constructed symmetrical on both axis of the building
    (*b*) Shear wall is made of R.C.C.
    (*c*) Usually shear wall is made rectangular
    (*d*) All are correct
14. the cross-section of shear wall are of the type except
    (*a*) Circular (*b*) Rectangular
    (*c*) L shaped (*d*) C shaped
15. Usually shear wall is constructed of
    (*a*) Thick brick masonry wall (*b*) Ashler stone masonry
    (*c*) R.C.C. wall (*d*) Steel wall
    (*e*) 15 cm timber wall

ANSWERS

4. (*b*)	7. (*d*)	10. (*c*)	13. (*d*)
5. (*d*)	8. (*c*)	11. (*c*)	14. (*a*)
6. (*a*)	9. (*d*)	12. (*c*)	15. (*c*)

20

Effects of Non-structural Elements

20.1. INTRODUCTION

The non load bearing elements of a structure are known as non structural elements. All buildings have numerous non structural elements. Though in some buildings the non structural elements represent a high percentage of total cost of the building, but seismic behaviour of non structural elements or members has not received adequate attention and thus no effective design specifications have been drawn in codes. Hence no effective design specifications for non structural elements are available. The failure of these elements can affect the safety of the occupants of the building and others who are immediately out side the building.

Now it has been well recognised that during an earthquake the good performance of non structural elements in buildings such a Hospitals, emergency disaster management centres, fire stations etc. is extremely important. In modern buildings the use of non structural elements has increased many fold, hence their failure may involve risk of life and the loss of post earthquake services.

Damage studies of earthquakes have revealed that in many cases, though structural damage suffered by a building is minor, but it has been rendered unfit for living and hazardous to life due to the damage of non structural elements. Thus in the design of non structural elements human safety must be combined with the economy. It has also been observed that cost of providing measures to prevent or reduce the damage of non structural elements is less costly than their repair after the damage. In this chapter kind of non structural elements and their effects on the performance of the buildings during an earthquake has been discussed.

20.2. CLASSIFICATION OF NON STRUCTURAL ELEMENTS

The non structural elements can be classified into the following categories which cater directly to the human needs:

1. Architectural components
2. Mechanical components
3. Electrical. components

1. Architectural non structural members

In this category non bearing walls, partition walls, infill walls in frames parapet walls, ceilings, door and window panes, glasses, decorative layers cladding (exterior plastering) etc. are included in this class. Apart from these elements roofing units such as tiles and other such individually attached heavy roof elements, elevator enclosures, stair cases, racks and architectural equipment also are included in the architectural elements.

2. Mechanical elements

In this category furnaces and boilers, chimneys and smoke stacks, tanks, pressure vessels, and piping systems machinery etc. are included.

3. Electrical elements

In this category, Electrical wire ducts, communication systems, electrical motors, transformers, lighting fixtures, smoke and fire detection systems etc. are included.

20.3. EFFECT OF FAILURE OF NON STRUCTURAL ELEMENTS

Following consequences of failure of non structural elements have been observed.

1. Falling debris due to the failure of ceilings, light fixtures, window panes, exterior wall panels or cladding, parapets and ornamental fixtures not only injure or kill human beings in side and out side of the building, but may also cause critical damage to mechanical and electrical non structural elements.
2. During and after the earthquake, the exit signs and emergency lighting may not work properly.
3. The collapse of stair ways, elevators and damage to exit doors may prevent the escape of people from the building.
4. The fire resistance system may fail.
5. Damaged tanks, boilers and piping system may burst or release inflammable toxics or harmful fluids or steam etc.
6. Damaged boilers may release materials at very high temperature which may cause fire and injuries to human beings.
7. Furniture and equipment may over turn and get damaged.

20.4. FAILURE MECHANISM OF NON STRUCTURAL ELEMENTS

The failure of non structural elements in general may be classified into the following two categories:

1. Due to excessive inertial (seismic) forces
2. Due to excessive deflection caused by deformation of structural members of the system.

1. Effect of inertial forces

The inertial force acting on a non structural element can be predicted, if the response of the structure at the floor level of the storey of a building is known. The non structural elements are installed at the floor level. The ground motion at any level on a multi storey building will be modified by the motion of the building itself. Generally the effect of ground motion is to concentrate the frequency of responce around a band close to the natural frequency of the building. It also amplify the peak acceleration roughly in proportion to the height of the building.

At the roof level the value of the amplification reaches two or three. For any element or contents which are either very stiff or have a natural frequency of their own close to that of the building, would be subjected to greater forces than if they would have been mounted at the ground level. The maximum shear force acting on a flexible element has been found much more than acting on a similar rigid element.

The suspended non-structural items such as light fittings and ceiling systems have been found to perform very poorly or badly. Other unimportant or appendages elements such as parapet walls also suffer high level damage, specially in situations when they function as a single degree of freedom inverted pendulums. On multi storey structures damages increase towards the roof of the building and roof water tanks. The luxury flats at the top of a tall building has been found to suffer greater damages.

2. Non-structural elements subjected to excessive deflections

The non structural elements subjected to forced deflections due to storey drift or inter storey displacement must be capable to deform with out failure, in accordance with the structural deformation. As an design alternative there should not be a rigid bond between the structural and non structural members. In other words the non structural element may be detached from the structural member so that the deformation of the structural element does not affect the deformation of the non structural element or induce force in it *i.e.* in the non structural element. Usually windows and cladding elements are connected rigidly with the structure at more than one level and if there is no provision for movement in the connection, they will fail. Some common failure of non structural elements during an earthquake are shown in the following Table 20.1.

Table 20.1. Common failures of non structural elements due to earthquake

S. No.	*Item*	*Type of damage*
1.	Suspended light fittings	Excessive movements causing damage or failure
2.	False ceiling	Panel falling or racking (voilent movement)
3.	Storage racks	Contents falling, rack toppling
4.	Windows	Glass breaking and frame detaching
5.	Stone and concrete cladding	Separation and falling
6.	Parapets	Toppling

S. No.	*Item*	*Type of damage*
7.	Elevators (tractive type)	Guide rails broken, car and counter weights misaligned
8.	Piping system	Rupture due to excessive movment and failure at bends
9.	Control panels	Over turning of tall units
10.	Motor generators	Isolation support failure
11.	Tanks	Support failure
12.	Pumps and boilers	Movement of anchored support.

20.5. EFFECT OF NON STRUCTURAL ELEMENTS ON STRUCTURAL ELEMENTS

Normally buildings contain various non structural elements which influence the behaviour of structural elements during earthquakes and in some situations can not be ignored. However in the normal practice of structural design the non structural elements are not taken into account. In case flexible non structural elements are added to a stiff structural system, then the influence of non structural elements is found very small. For example if the area of a R.C.C. column is extended beyond the confined core by more than 100 mm as shown in Fig. 20.1 due to architectural requirements only, this area is treated as a non structural element and has no effect on the strength of the column as the contribution of this additional area to the strength of the column has not been considered. On the contrary, for example if the exterior or partition walls made of concrete blocks or masonry are installed in a frame, they influence the behaviour of the frame to a great extent. Generally following effects of non structural elements have been observed:

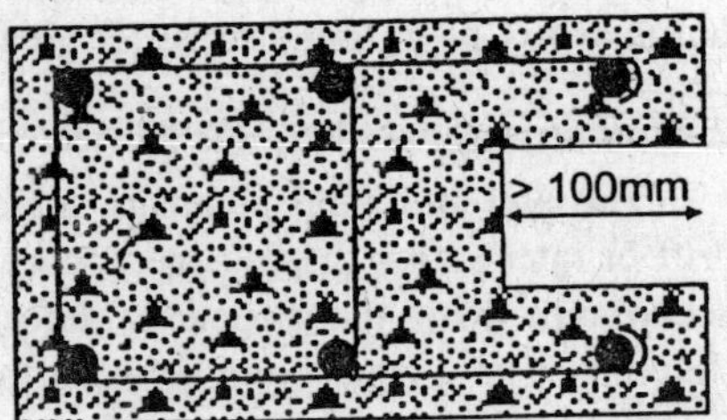

Fig. 20.1.

1. The natural period of the structural system decreases, resulting in a different input level to the system.
2. The distribution of storey shear in columns may change and some columns may sustain more force than assumed in the original design.
3. Significant torsion in the system may develop due to the un symmetrical arrangement of non structural walls.
4. If non structural walls are rearranged non uniformly in height then local force may be concentrated at some particular point.

Usually the effects of non structural elements on structural elements are considered secondary, but the interactive behaviour of non structural and structural elements has been found the cause of structural failure. During an earthquake practically all buildings sway horizontally causing differential movements of each floor relative to the floor just below it. This relative movement is called *storey drift* Fig. 20.2. In addition to horizontal movement,

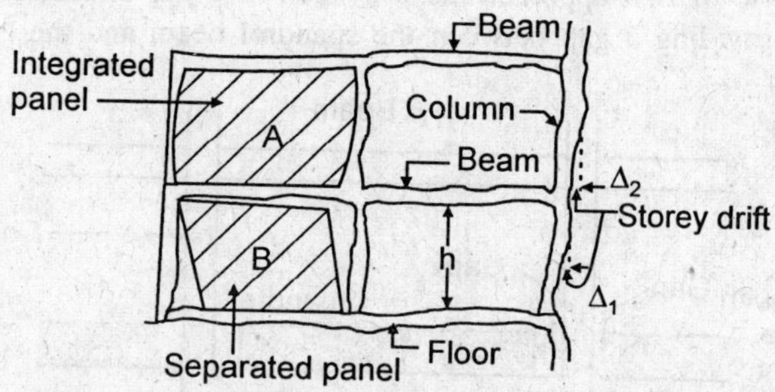

Fig. 20.2. Diagrammatic elevation of structural frame and non structural infill panels

vertical deformations also occur. These vertical deformations cause changes in the clear height '*h*' between the floor and the beam as shown in Fig. 20.2.

To deal the above two movements following two approaches may be adopted:

1. The first approach is to un couple the non structural elements from the structural system. This approach exclusively is adopted in the design of tall buildings. As no reliable movement data of structures is available, these horizontal and vertical movements may be assumed from 20 mm to 40 mm. This type of construction has the following two inherent detailing problems as follows:
   (*a*) To ensure lateral stability against out of plane forces, some awkward details may be required.
   (*b*) In case of providing a gap of 20 to 40 mm, there will be difficulty in accomplishing the sound and fire proofing of the separation gaps. This method of construction is preferred to integral construction when flexible frames are to be used in strong seismic zones.
2. In the second approach, the non structural elements also can be treated as structural members and their characteristics are taken into account in the design. The panels and frames will have effective contact, such that the panels and frames will have equal drift deformations. Such panels must be either strong enough or flexible enough to absorb this deformation and forces. The deformations must be computed properly. This practice makes the noise, heat or water insulation more feasible (possible) than the first approach. In general, stiff and brittle non structural elements such as wing walls have been found more vulnerable than a structural element due to their low deformation capacity. In situations where rigid materials are used appreciably, the panels should be considered as structural elements. In situations where such non

structural elements are included, the hysteric behaviour of the structural system is very complex. This complexity usually results in poor under standing of the true response of the structure.

The example of first approach *i.e.* provision of a gap is illustrated in Fig. 20.3 (*a*). By providing a gap between the spandrel beam and the column, the

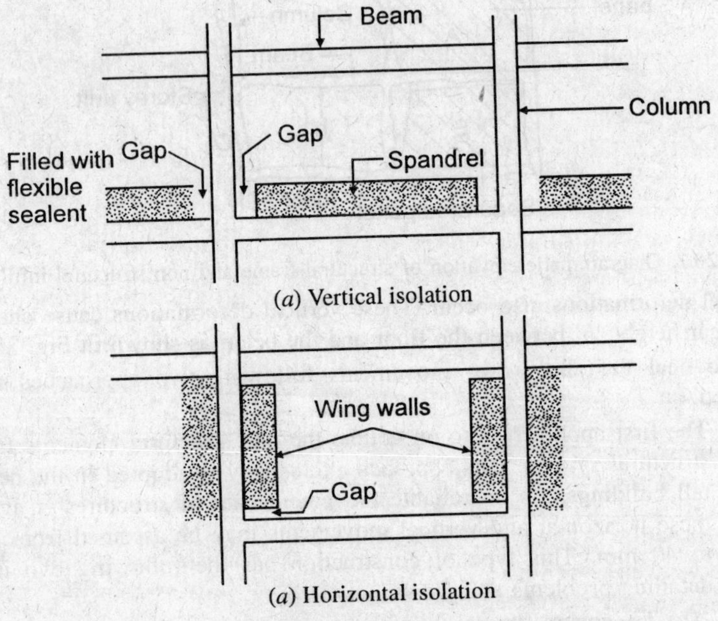

Fig. 20.3: Isolation of non structural walls from structural frame

column is expected to behave in a ductile manner. The same treatment is also possible in wing walls Fig. 20.3 (*b*), so that the adjoined beam does not fail by shear mode.

20.6. ANALYSIS OF NON STRUCTURAL ELEMENTS

When the structural response of the buildings are affected significantly by the non structural elements, then these non structural elements should be treated as structural elements and structural provisions should be applied to them. Depending upon the response sensitivity the non structural elements can be classified as follows:

(*a*) Acceleration sensitive non structural elements

When the non structural elements are mainly affected by the acceleration of their supporting elements, they are known as acceleration sensitive non structural elements. A mechanical unit-anchored to the floor or roof of a building is a good example of acceleration sensitive non structural elements. In such a case the structural and non structural interaction due to deformation of the supporting structure is not significant. The elements are vulnerable to sliding, over turning or tilting. Thus their anchorage or bracing is of prime importance.

(*b*) Deformation sensitive non structural elements

When the non structural elements are affected by the deformation of the supporting structures, specially the inter storey drift, then these non structural elements are called as deformation sensitive non structural elements. Curtain walls, and piping system running floor to floor are good examples of deformation sensitive non structural elements.

(*c*) Deformation and acceleration sensitive elements

There are many elements, which are both deformation and acceleration sensitive elements. Exterior skin of a building as pre fabricated panels is an example of both deformation and acceleration sensitive element.

The classification of non structural elements according to their response sensitiveness is shown in the following Table 20.2.

Table 20.2.

Architectural Components

Architectural Components	*Sensitivity*	
	Acceleration	*Deformation*
Exterior skin		
Anchored veneer	S	P
Adhered veneer	S	P
Glass blocks	S	P
Prefabricated panels	S	P
Glazing systems	S	P
Partitions		
Heavy	S	P
Light	S	P
Interior veneers		
Stone as well as marble	S	P
Cremic tiles	S	—
Ceiling	S	
Directly applied to structure	P	—
Dropped Gypsum, furred	P	—
Board	S	P
Suspended lath and plaster	S	P
Suspended integrated ceiling		
parapets and appendages	P	—

Architectural Components	*Sensitivity*	
	Acceleration	*Deformation*
Canopies	P	–
Chimneys and stacks	P	–
Stair	P	S

Mechanical Components

Mechanical Components	*Sensitivity*	
	Acceleration	*Deformation*
Mechanical Equipment		
Boilers and furnances	P	–
General manufacturing and process machinery	P	–
Vibration isolation	P	–
Non-vibration isolation	P	–
Mounted in line with duck work	P	–
Storage vessels and water heaters		
Structually supported vessels	–	P
Flat bottom vessel	P	–
Pressure vessels	P	S
Fire suppresion piping	P	S
Fluid piping (not fire suppression)		
Hazardous materials	P	S
Non hazardous materials	P	S
Duct work	P	S

P—Primary response
S—Secondary response

For important non structural elements dynamic analysis should be performed using the floor response spectra as input to the sub system. For a less important sub system for public safety, an equivalent static analysis can be used to obtain the necessary information for design or strength requirement verifications. These analysis are described in the following paragraphs.

20.6.1. Dynamic analysis

When a rigid non structural element is tightly clamped on the floor of a structure, the response of the element would be identical to the floor response. The ratio of the element response to the floor response is unity. This ratio is known as *magnification factor*. In case a rigid non structural element is installed on the floor of a structure with a flexible connecting device, the response of the element will be greater than the floor response. Such a behaviour can be represented with the help of one mass system with damping.

A one mass system may have six degrees of freedoms but usually the system may be simplified as one single degree of freedom. The vibrational characteristics of such a system can be found by applying the time history response analysis to the structural system. In case the connecting device is ductile, the magnification factor derived from elastic response analysis may be relaxed or changed according to the ductility.

A long flexible non structural element such as a piping system or a cable can not be simplified to a single degree of freedom system. Therefore for the analysis of a long flexible non structural element a multiple degree of freedom system usually is required with the floor response as input. For the design of such a system usually equivalent static analysis is considered adequate, unless its failure is considered to cause significant damage to the structural system.

20.6.2. Equivalent Static Analysis

In situations where dynamic analysis is not feasible, it is desirable to establish a suitable equivalent static force system. The sub system is modelled as a separate structure with fixed support conditions. Calculations for equivalent static forces for acceleration sensitive as well as deformation or displacement sensitive non structural elements can be done as discussed below:

1. Acceleration sensitive non structural elements

The design seismic force F_P on a non structural element can be determined by the following relation:

$$F_p = \frac{z}{2}\left[1 + \frac{x}{h}\right]\frac{a_p}{R_p} I_p \cdot W_p \qquad \ldots(20.1)$$

where,

z = Zone factor, which indicates the severity of the earthquake. The value of zone factors is shown in Table 20.3.

x = Height of attachment of the non structural element above the foundation.

h = Height of the building or height at which the non structural element is to be attached.

a_p = Component amplification factor as shown in Table 20.4 and 20.5. [The component of amplification factor represents the dynamic amplification of the component relative to the fundamental period of the structure].

R_p = Component response modification factor Table 20.4 and 20.5 [This factor represents ductility, redunancy and energy dissipation capacity of the element and its attachment to the structure].

I_p = Importance factor of the non structural element shown in Table 20.6.

W_p = Weight of non structural element.

Table 20.3. Zone factor-z

Seismic zones	*II*	*III*	*IV*	*V*
Seismic intensity	Low	Moderate	Severe	Very severe
Value of z	0.10	0.16	0.24	0.36

Table 20.4. Amplification factors, and response reduction factors for architectural components

S. No.	*Elements or Architectural Components*	a_p	R_p
1.	Interior non structural walls and partitions plain masonry walls	1.0	1.5
2.	All other walls	1.0	2.5
3.	**Cantilver elements (unbraced or braced to structural frames below its centre of mass)**		
	Parapet and cantilever, interior non structural walls	2.5	2.5
	Chimneys and stacks laterally supported by structures	2.5	2.5
4.	**Cantilever elements (Braced to structural frame above its centre of mass)**		
	Parapets	1.0	2.5
	Chimneys and stacks	1.0	2.5
	Exterior non structural walls	1.0	2.5
5.	**Exterior non strutural wall elements and connections**		
	Wall elements	1.0	2.5
	Body of wall panel connection	1.0	2.5
	Fasteners of the connecting system	1.25	1.0
6.	**Veeners**		
	High deformability elements and attatchments	1.0	2.5
	Low deformability elements and attachments	1.0	1.5
7.	Costly flats of high rise building tops (except when framed by an extension of the building frame)	2.5	3.5
8.	**Ceiling**		
	All types	1.0	2.5
	Cabinets		
	Storage cabinets and labratory equipment	1.0	2.5
9.	**Access floors**		
	Special access floor	1.0	2.5
	All others	1.0	1.5

S. No.	*Elements or Architectural Components*	a_p	R_p
	Appandages and ornamantation	2.5	2.5
	Sign and bill boards	2.5	2.5
10.	**Other rigid components**		
	High deformability elements and attachments	1.0	3.5
	Limited deformability elements and attachments	1.0	2.5
	Low deformability elements and attachments	1.0	1.5
11.	**Other flexible components**		
	High deformability elements and attachments	2.5	3.5
	Limited deformability elements and attachments	2.5	2.5
	Low deformability elements and attachments	2.5	1.5

Note: A lower value for a_p than specified in Table (20.4) above is permitted provided a detailed dynamic analysis is performed which justified the lower value. The value for a_p will not be lower than 1.0. The value of a_p = 1.0 is taken for equipments which are generally rigid and rigidly attached. The value of a_p = 2.5 is taken for flexible components or flexibly attached components.

Table 20.5. Amplification factors and response factors for mechanical and electrical components

S. No.	*Elements of Mech. & Elect. Elements*	a_p	R_p
1.	**General Mechanical**		
	Furnances and boilers	1.0	2.5
	Pressure vessels on skirts and free standing	2.5	2.5
	Stacks	2.5	2.5
	Cantilever chimneys	2.5	2.5
	Others	2.5	2.5
2.	**Manufacturing and Process machinery**		
	General	1.0	2.5
	Conveyors (non personel)	2.5	2.5
3.	**Piping system**		
	High deformability elements and attachments	1.0	2.5
	Limited deformability elements and attachments	1.0	2.5
	Low deformability elements and attachments	1.0	2.5
4.	**High voltage AC system equipment**		
	Vibration isolated	2.5	2.5
	Non vibration isolated	1.0	2.5
	Mounted in line with duct work	1.0	2.5
	Others	1.0	2.5
	Elevator components	1.0	2.5

S. No.	*Elements of Mech. & Elect. Elements*	a_p	R_p
	Escalator components	1.0	2.5
	Trussed towers (Free standing guyed)	2.5	2.5
5.	**General electrical**		
	Distributed systems	2.5	5.0
	Equipment	1.0	1.5
	Lighting fixtures	1.0	1.5

Note: A lower value than specified in Table 20.5 for a_p is permitted, provided a detailed dynamic analysis is carried out, which justify the lower value. However value less than 1.0 for a_p shall not be permissible. Value a_p = 1.0 generally is taken for equipment regarded rigid and rigidly attached. The value of a_p = 2.5 is considered for flexible components or flexibly attached components.

Table 20.6. Importance factor of non structural elements

S. No.	*Description of non structural element*	I_p
1.	Components containing hazardous contents	1.5
2.	Life safety components needed after an earthquake as fire protection sprinkler system)	1.5
3.	Storage racks in structures open to the public	1.5
4.	All other components	1.0

Note: regarding seismic force F_p

1. The value of F_p is the horizontal force for the vertical non structural elements and for horizontal non structural elements it will be vertical force.
2. While choosing the values of a_p and R_p, it is expected that the component will act as a flexible body. (The value of a_p should be taken = 2.5). In general the value of R_p is taken as 1.5, 2.5 and 3.5 for low, limited and high deformable structures respectively.
3. Mechanical components often are fitted with vibration isolation mounts to prevent transmission of vibrations to the structure. By increasing their flexibility, the vibration isolation mounts can alter the dynamic properties of the components, resulting an dramatic increase in seismic inertial forces. Thus for a component mounted on vibration isolation systems the value of design force should be taken as twice that of F_p *i.e.* $2F_p$.
4. Connections and attachments or anchorage of the non structural elements should be designed for twice the design seismic force required for that

non structural element. The method is illustrated by the following examples.

Example 1. A 150 kN equipment as shown in Fig. 20.4 is to be installed on the roof of a four storey building in seismic activity zone IV. It is anchored

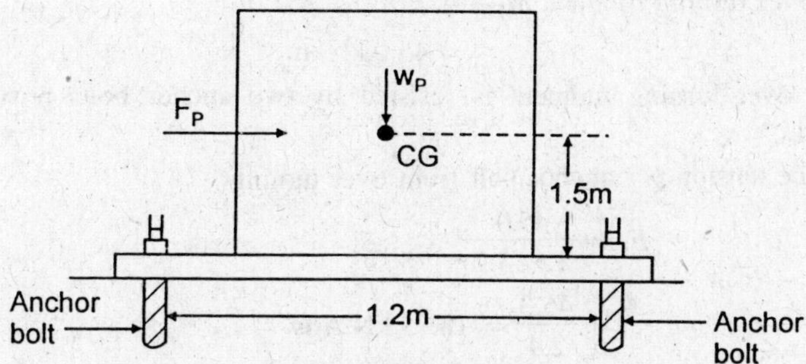

Fig. 20.4. Equipment intalled at roof

with the help of four bolts at each corner of the equipment. The bolts are embedded in the concrete slab. Floor to floor height is 3.5 m for the three storeys and the height of the ground storey is 4.0 m. Find out the shear and tension on the anchored bolts during an earthquake.

Solution. Zone factor z for seismic zone IV from table 20.3 = 0.24

Height of point of attachment of the equipment above the foundation of the building

$$x = (4.0 + 3 \times 3.5) \text{ m} = 14.5 \text{ m}$$

Height of the building = $(4 + 3 \times 3.5) = 14.5$ m

The value of amplification factor of the equipment $a_p = 1.0$

(Being rigid component from table 20.5)

The value of response factor R_p from table 20.5) is 2.5.

Importance factor $I_p = 1.0$ from table 20.6.

Weight of the equipment = 150 kN

$$\therefore \quad \text{Design seismic force } F_p = \frac{z}{2}\left(1 + \frac{x}{h}\right) \times \frac{a_p}{R_p} \times I_p \times W_p$$

$$= \frac{0.24}{2}\left(1 + \frac{14.5}{14.5}\right) \times \frac{1}{2.5} \times 1 \times 150$$

$$= 0.12 \times 2 \times \frac{150}{2.5} = 0.24 \times 60 = 14.4 \text{ kN}$$

0.1 of weight of equipment = $0.1 \times 150 = 15$ kN

$\therefore$ 14.4 < 15.0 *i.e.* F_p is less than 0.1 of the weight of equipment.

Hence the value of F_p will be taken as 15 kN.

The anchorage force of the equipment with the building should be taken double of the calculated seismic force. Thus design force = 2 F_p.

$$\therefore \text{ Shear per anchor bolt } = \frac{2 \times F_p}{4} = \frac{2 \times 15.0}{4} = 7.5 \text{ kN}$$

$$\therefore \text{ Over turning moment } M_{OT} = 2 \times 15 \times 1.5$$

$$= 45.0 \text{ kN–m}$$

The over turning moment is resisted by two anchor bolts provided on either side.

Hence tension per anchor bolt from over turning

$$F_t = \frac{45.0}{2 \times 1.2}$$

$$= \frac{45.0}{2.4} = 18.75 \text{ kN } \textbf{Ans.}$$

Example 2. 130 kN electrical generator is to be installed on the third floor of a six storey hospital in Delhi of seismic zone IV area. It is to be mounted on

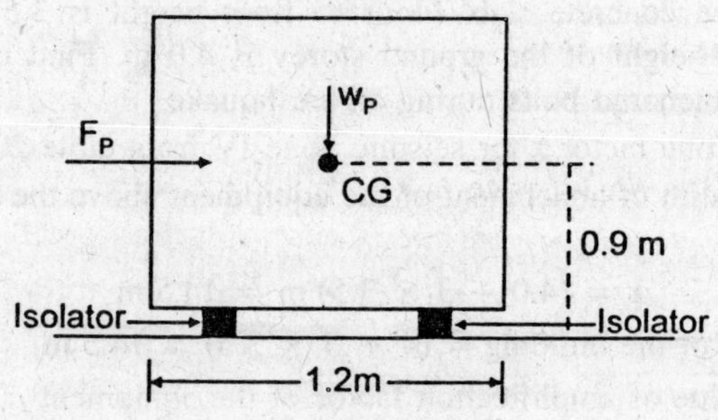

Fig. 20.5.

four flexible isolators as shown in Fig. 20.5 one at each corner of the unit. The floor height of each storey is 3.5 m while the height of ground storey is 4.0 m. Determine the shear and tension force on the isolators during an earthquake.

Solution. (*i*) Zone factor Z = 0.24 (Table 20.3)

Height of attachment of the equipment above the foundation of the building

$$x = 4.0 + 2 \times 3.5 = 11.0 \text{ m}$$

Height of building $h = 4.0 + 5 \times 3.5 = 21.5$ m

Amplification factor for the generator $a_p = 2.5$

(Vibration isolator Table 20.5)

Response modification factor $R_p = 2.5$ (Table 20.5)

Importance factor $I_p = 1.5$ (It is a life safety component table 20.6)

Weight of generator = 130 kN

∴ Design seismic force on the generator

$$F_p = \frac{z}{2}\left(1 + \frac{x}{h}\right)\frac{a_p}{R_P} \times I_p \times W_p$$

$$= \frac{0.24}{2}\left(1 + \frac{11.0}{21.5}\right) \times \frac{2.5}{2.5} \times 1.5 \times 130$$

$$= 0.12 \times 1.521 \times 1.5 \times 130$$

$$= 0.18252 \times 195.0$$

$$= 35.6 \text{ kN} > (0.1\, w_p\ i.e.\ 13.0 \text{ kN})$$

As F_p is greater than 0.1 W_p, it will be taken as such.

As the generator is mounted on flexible isolator, the design force is to be taken twice of the calculated seismic force. That is design force

$$= 2 \times 35.6 = 71.2 \text{ kN}$$

Shear force resisted by each isolator,

$$V = \frac{F_P}{4} = \frac{71.2}{4} = 17.8 \text{ kN}$$

The over turning moment = 71.2 × 0.9 = 64.08 kN–m

The over turning moment is resisted by two anchor bolts provided on either side.

Hence tension per bolt due to over turning

$$F_t = \frac{64.08}{1.2 \times 2}$$

$$= \frac{64.08}{2.4} = 26.71 \text{ kN } \textbf{Ans.}$$

2. Displacement sensitive non structural members

Many elements such as stair cases, cladding, piping system, sign boards and sprinkler system etc. are connected to the buildings at various levels. When the two connection points are on the same building say A. The seismic relative displacement D_P may be calculated by equation (20.2)

$$D_p = \delta_{xA} \cdot \delta_{yA} \qquad \ldots(20.2)$$

where,

δ_{xA} = Deflection at building at level x.

δ_{yA} = Deflection at the building at level y.

These deflections due to design seismic load are determined by elastic analysis and are multiplied by response reduction factor R of the building. Equation (20.2) gives an estimate of the actual structural displacement as determined by elastic analysis.

The seismic relative displacement D_p should not be taken to be greater than DP_1 given by the following relation.

$$D_{P1} = R\,(h_x - h_y)\,\frac{\Delta_{aA}}{h_{sx}} \qquad \text{...(20.3)}$$

where,

h_x = Height of level x to which the upper connection point is attached.

h_y = Height of level y to which the lower connection point is attached.

Δ_{aA} = Allowable storey drift for structure A.

h_{sx} = Storey height below the level x.

Equation 20.3 allows the use of storey drift limitations. The elastic displacements are not always defined.

When the two connection points are on two separate structures or structural system say A and B, one at height h_x and the other on height h_y, then relative displacement D_p can be determined by the following equation.

$$D_p = |\,\delta_{xA}\,| + |\,\delta_{yB}\,| \qquad \text{...(20.4)}$$

D_p should not be greater than D_{P1} given by the relation.

$$D_{P1} = R\left[h_x\,\frac{\Delta_{aA}}{h_{sx}} + h_y\,\frac{\Delta_{aB}}{h_{sy}}\right] \qquad \text{...(20.5)}$$

where δ_{yB} is the deflection at building level y of structure B due to design seismic load determined by elastic analysis and multiplied by response reduction factor R of the building. Similarly δ_{xA} is deflection for building A.

and Δ_{aB} is the allowable storey drift for structure B.

Δ_{aA} = Allowable storey drift for structure A. Other terms same as in equation (3).

Calculation of relative displacement D_p is illustrated with the help, of the following example.

Example 3. An electronic sign board is attached to a six storey building consisted of special-resisting frame system in Delhi of seismic zone IV.

The sign board is attached by two anchors at heights 14.0 m and 10.5 m.

The deflections obtained from elastic analysis under design seismic force for the upper and lower anchor of the sign board are found as 40 mm and 32 mm respectively. From the given data, determine the design relative displacement D_p.

Solution. A sign board is a displacement sensitive non structural element. Hence it should be designed for seismic relative displacement.

The height of level x to which the upper connection point is attached

$$h_x = 14.0 \text{ m.}$$

The height of level y to which lower connection point is attached

$$h_y = 10.5 \text{ m}$$

Deflection at building level x of structure A due to design seismic force

$$= 40 \text{ mm}$$

Deflection at building level y of structure A due to design seismic force

$$= 32 \text{ mm}$$

Response reduction factor for special R.C.C. moment resisting frame Table 20.5.

$$R = 5.$$

Using equation (20.6) the relative displacement

$$D_p = \delta_{xA} - \delta_{yA} \quad \text{...(20.6)}$$

The values of δ_{xA} and δ_{yA} are determined as

$$\delta_{xA} = 40 \times 5 = 200.0 \text{ mm}$$

$$\delta_{yA} = 32 \times 5 = 160.0 \text{ mm}$$

$$\therefore \quad D_p = 200 - 160 = 40.0 \text{ mm}$$

The connections of the sign board shall be designed to accommodate the relative displacement of 40.0 mm.

Alternative method

In case it is not possible to determine the deflections under seismic forces, then storey drift method may be used. This method can be used if the building complies the seismic code.

Under the provisions of seismic code, the maximum permissible storey drift is 0.004 times the height of the storey.

i.e.

$$\frac{\Delta_{aA}}{h_{sA}} = 0.004$$

$\therefore$ then

$$D_p = R\,(h_x - h_y)\,\frac{\Delta_{aA}}{h_{sA}}$$

$$= 5\,[14000 - 10500] \times 0.004$$

$$= 5 \times 3500 \times 0.004$$

$$= 70.0 \text{ mm}$$

In this case the electronic sign board will be designed to accommodate a relative displacement of 70 mm. **Ans.**

Example 4. A glow sign board of 10 m length is to be fixed on the front side of a seven storey building in Chandigarh (Seismic zone IV). It is attached by four anchors at 15 m and 9 m levels respectively. The deflections at the upper and lower fastening of the glow sign board are found as 40 mm and 28 mm by the elastic analysis. Determine the design relative displacement of the hoarding. (The building is a special R.C.C. frame building).

Solution. As a sign board is a displacement sensitive non structural element, it shall be designed for seismic relative displacement.

Height of level x to which the upper connection point is attached

$$h_x = 15 \text{ m}$$

Height of level y to which the lower connection point is attached

$$h_y = 9.0 \text{ m}$$

Deflections at building level x determined by elastic analysis for design seismic force = 40 mm

Deflection at building level y determined by elastic analysis for design seismic force = 28.0 mm

The response reduction factor $R = 5$ for special R.C.C. moment resisting frame

$$\delta_{xA} = 40 \times 5 = 200 \text{ mm}$$

$$\delta_{yA} = 28 \times 5 = 140$$

For two bolt anchored board, the relative design displacement is given as

$$\delta_{xA} = (200 - 140) = 60.0 \text{ mm}$$

In the present case, there are four anchors, two at upper level and two at lower level. Hence the relative displacement would be = 2×60

= 120 mm **Ans.**

Example 5. An air conditioning unit weighting 120 kN is to be installed on the roof of a eleven storey building. The dimension of the unit at base is 1.25 m and height 2 m as shown in Fig. 20.6. The fundamental period of the air conditioning unit is 0.05 second. At each corner of the unit, there are four anchor bolts of 24 mm diameter. These bolts are embedded in the roof concrete slab upto a depth of 180 mm. The building is situated in seismic zone IV. The height of each storey may be assumed as 3.1 m and that of ground storey as 4.0 m.

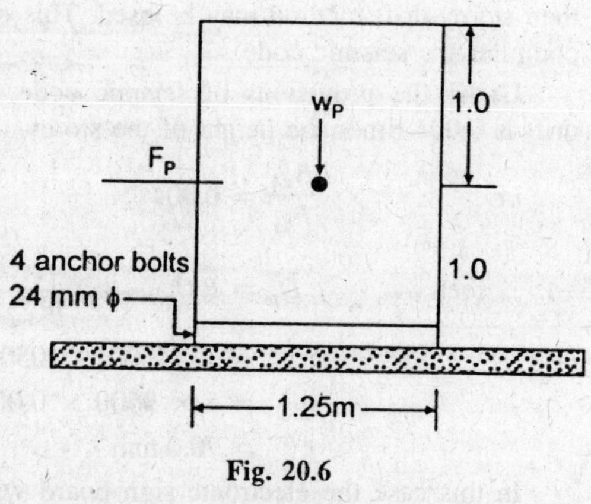

Fig. 20.6

Solution. The structure is of small natural period,

Hence it is rigid structure. The value of a_p will be taken as 1.0 and that of R_p is 2.5 as per Table 20.5.

$\therefore$ $Z = 0.24$ and importance factor $I_p = 1.0$

$$x = (4.0 + 10 \times 3.1 - 0.18 \text{ m})$$

$$= 35 - 0.18 = 34.82 \approx 35 \text{ m}$$

Height of building = $4.0 + 3.1 \times 10 = 35.0$ m

$$\therefore \quad F_p = \frac{z}{2}\left(1 + \frac{x}{h}\right)\frac{a_p}{R_p} \times I_p \times W_p$$

$$= \frac{0.24}{2}\left(1 + \frac{34.82}{35.0}\right) \times \frac{1}{2.5}\, 1 \times 120 \qquad \left(\frac{34.8}{35} \approx 1.0\right)$$

$$= \frac{0.24}{2} \times 2.0 \times \frac{1}{2.5} \times 120$$

$$= \frac{0.24 \times 120}{2.5} = \frac{288}{25}$$

$$= 11.52 < 0.1\, W_p$$

i.e. $F_p < 0.1\, w_p \ (11.52 < 12.0)$

Hence the value of F_p will be taken as 12.0 kN.

For design the value of F_p will be taken as $2 \times F_p = 24.0$ kN.

$\therefore$ Shear per bolt $V = \dfrac{2 \times F_p}{4} = \dfrac{2 \times 12}{4}$

$= 6.0$ kN

(Total bolts being 4, one at each corner)

$\therefore$ Over turning moment $= 2 \times F_p \times$ distance from base

$= 2 \times 12 \times 1.0 = 24.0$ kN–m

The over turning moment is resisted by two anchor bolts provided on either side.

$\therefore$ Hence tension per anchor bolt

$$F_t = \frac{M_{OT}}{\text{No. of bolts} \times \text{distance between them}}$$

$$= \frac{24}{2 \times 1.25} = \frac{24}{2.5}$$

$$= 9.6 \text{ kN}$$

$$\left.\begin{aligned} \text{Shear } V &= 6.0 \text{ kN} \\ F_t &= 9.6 \text{ kN} \end{aligned}\right\} \textbf{Ans.}$$

Example 6. A trussed tower 7 m high and 1.5 × 1.5 m in cross-section at the base and 50 kN in weight is to be installed on the roof of a six storey multiplex building for signal transmission. The building is situated in a seismic zone III. The tower is attached by 16 anchored bolts, four at each corner of the tower base embedded in the concrete block. The height of the ground storey is 4.3 m and the height of other floors is 3.0 m. Determine the shear and tension on the anchored bolts during an earthquake.

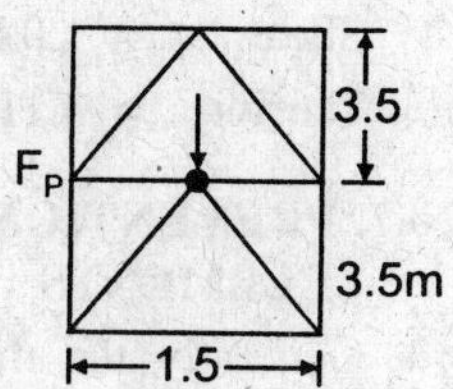

Fig. 20.7

Solution. Given

Weight of the tower = 50 kN

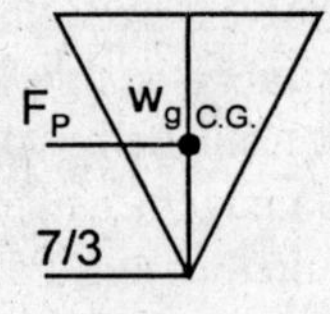

Fig. 20.8

Zone factor $z = 0.16$

For truss towers the value of

$$a_p = 2.5$$

and $R_p = 2.5$

Important factor $I_p = 1.0$

$$\therefore \quad x = 4.3 + 5 \times 3.0 = 19.3 \text{ m}$$

also $h = 4.3 + 5 \times 3.0 = 19.3$

$$\therefore \text{ Design seismic force } F_p = \frac{z}{2}\left(1 + \frac{x}{h}\right)\frac{a_p}{R_p} \times I_p \times W_p$$

$$= \frac{0.16}{2}\left(1 + \frac{19.3}{19.3}\right) \times \frac{2.5}{2.5} \times 1 \times 50$$

$$= \frac{0.16}{2} \times 2 \times 50 = 8.0 \text{ kN}$$

In this case $F_p > 0.1\, w_p$. Hence the value of F_p will be taken as 8.0 kN. For design purposes the value of shear will be

$$2 \times F_p = 16 \text{ kN}$$

$$\therefore \text{ Shear per bolt} = \frac{2 \times 8.0}{16} \quad \text{(As there are total 16 bolts)}$$

$$= 1.0 \text{ kN}$$

$$\text{Over timing moment} = 2 \times 8 \times \frac{7}{3}$$

$$= \frac{112}{3} = 37.33 \text{ kN–m}$$

This over timing moment is resisted by 8 anchored bolts as 4 bolts are provided at each corner.

$$\text{Hence tension per anchor bolt} = \frac{2 \times 8 \times 7}{1.5 \times 8 \times 3} = \frac{112}{36} = 3.11 \text{ kN}$$

Shear = 1.0 kN

Tension = 3.11 kN **Ans.**

20.7. PREVENTION OF DAMAGE TO NON STRUCTURAL ELEMENTS

Generally the damage during earthquakes to non structural elements is caused due to excessive lateral movement of the building. The first and fore most important requirement for all non structural components is that they are well anchored to the building structure. For the safety of life, the objective should be to limit the severity of the damage to the components, so that they do not topple, slide, move gently backward and forward (rock) or detached themselves from the structure and fall. The prevention of loss of this type invariably is simple and inexpensive. Usually floor anchorage and angle ties linking tall items to the structure is needed. For higher performance objectives the damage to components must be controlled, so that functionality of the structures is not disturbed or damaged.

20.7.1. Architectural components

Each storey of a building during an earthquake undergoes a shear distortion. The shear distortion is a horizontal movement of the upper storey with respect to the lower floor, known as storey drift. If a partition in a storey is connected in such a way that it is forced to undergo the same shear distortion as that of the structure it will be safe. In case this distortion is great enough, the partition will be cross cracked *i.e.* will be damaged. This cracking can be prevented if a gap at the top or bottom and at the sides is provided to permit the calculated drift to occur without the involvement of the partition in the movement. An other way of preventing this cracking is to provide sufficient stiffening to the building by providing shear walls to it, so that the magnitude of the shear distortion does not develop enough to crack the plaster of the partition.

An other ill effect of shear distortion of partitions is the racking of door frames. Due to this effect either the doors are jammed shut or will not close. Doorway may become jammed, when the walls surrounding a door way are subjected to large deformations.

As the doors are vital means of egress (entrance and exit) they should be designed properly so that they remain functional even after a strong earthquake. Similar is the case of window frames. Hence proper clearance must be provided to door and windows as shown in Fig. 20.9 (*a*) and (*b*).

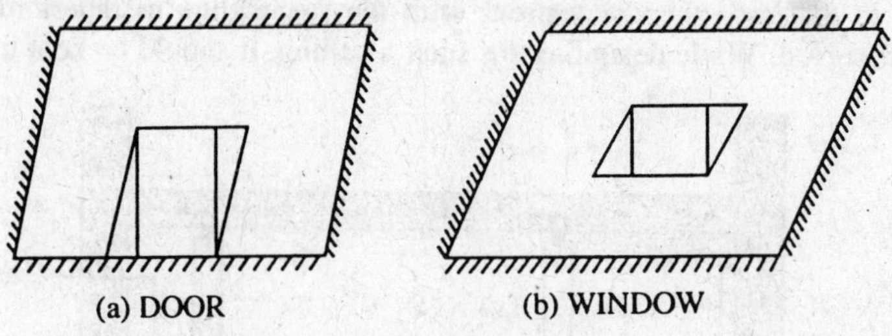

Fig. 20.9.

Many non structural components are attached to the building at different levels. Thus these components must be able to resist the applied accelerations and accommodate the differential displacements without failure. For example, windows frequently need to accommodate inter storey displacements with out failure or fracturing the glass. The cause of breaking glass of windows is due to shear distortion of a storey. The glass of windows break as the windows are connected rigidly to structure of the building. The breaking of window glass is very dangerous as falling pieces of glass can injure people below. If the expected maximum frame deformation is considered small, the glass can be fixed with soft putty. If the frame deformation is large, a provision of the movement of the glass in the frame must be provided. to accommodate racking distortions of 0.5% as shown in Fig. 20.9 (*b*) above. The connection of the frames to the structure should provide for the yield of a similar amount.

Some times the protection of window panes from the lateral distortions of the structure has been achieved by mounting the window frames on springs that hold them against the structural frames. Very often to allow the movement of the glass panes in the window frames, mastic materials have been used. Beside checking the movement of panes in the window frame these materials retain their plasticity. In every case it is essential to design against a force perpendicular to the partition or window irrespective of the origin of this force *i.e.* whether this force is caused by the earthquake or strong wind.

In case of flexible buildings, rigid precast concrete cladding should be mounted on specially designed fixing devices. These fixing devices should fully separate the rigid cladding from horizontal drift movements. Brick or other rigid cladding either should be fully integral and treated as infill walls or should be properly separated with details similar to those for rigid partitions shown in Fig. 20.3 (*a*). Ducts and pipe work crossing movement joints in the building should also be able to accommodate the movement without failure.

Some times ceilings fall down during an earthquake, but now a days these are not so hazardous as in olden days, because now generally ceilings are made of acoustical tiles not of plaster as before.

These tiles are mounted on *T* members or on narrow channels. These tiles must be securely fastened with their supports. If suspended ceiling is to be provided, in that case the connections with the suspending members must be properly designed. While designing for such a ceiling, it should be kept in mind

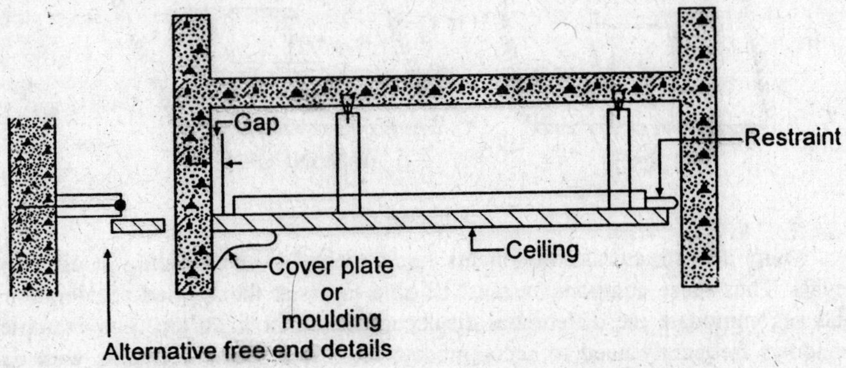

Fig. 20.10. Details at periphery of suspended ceilings to prevent hammering and excessive movement. (Courtesy—BERRY)

that during horizontal movement ceilings do not strike against the surrounding walls. The striking of ceilings may be checked by providing a gap and sliding cover as shown in Fig. 20.10.

20.7.2. Mechanical and Electrical Components

All equipments and furnishings etc. such as light fixtures, ducts, piping and heating units that are hung from ceiling should be braced so that they may not swing. Long pendant (hanging) mounted fluorescent lighting fixtures are free to swing. Hence usually such fixtures break loose. The equipments such as water heaters, boilers, furnaces, storage tanks and air conditioning units etc. that are not securely fastened to the floor fall down or may move horizontally due to the strong motion during earthquake vibrations. Generally utility lines to such units breakdown. Vibration isolation supports particularly are vulnerable to earthquake forces. Storage racks and cabinets should be securely anchored to the walls or partitions. *The basic design requirement is that services should not fail before the failure of the building during an earthquake.*

20.8. ISOLATION OF NON STRUCTURAL ELEMENTS

The failure of non structural elements during an earthquake is of great concern as they affect the loss of human life to a great extent. Non structural elements such as perimeter in fill walls, cladding, and partitions etc. become structurally very responsive during earthquakes. When these non structural elements are made of flexible materials, then these non structural elements do not affect the structure significantly. However if these non structural elements are made of rigid materials such cement concrete blocks, bricks etc. then they affect the structure significantly. There are following two approaches to take care of these non structural elements in the design and analysis of structures.

1. **First approach.** In this approach non structural elements are taken as a part of the structure to be analysed *i.e.* the non structural elements are made in the actual structure.
2. **Second approach.** In this approach the non structural elements are isolated from the actual structure *i.e.* the stiffness of the non structural elements is not included in the stiffness of the structure. A gap is left between the non structural elements and the main structure. Sometimes restraint at top against overturning by out of plane forces may also be applied. Isolation of non structural elements is appropriate when a flexible structure is to be constructed in a low seismic response region.

20.8.1. Architectural Components

When a non structural wall is tightly clamped in a structural frame, the wall is forced to deform in a compatible manner with the frame. If the wall is forced to deform beyond its allowable limit by the frame, then the wall will fail.

To avoid such a failure, the wall may be un coupled from the frame, so that the wall may slide freely in the wall plane, but resist strongly out of plane deformation.

20.9. METHODS OF ISOLATION

For the isolation of architectural non structural elements usually floating partitions are applied as shown in Fig. 20.11. Usually this method is simple and

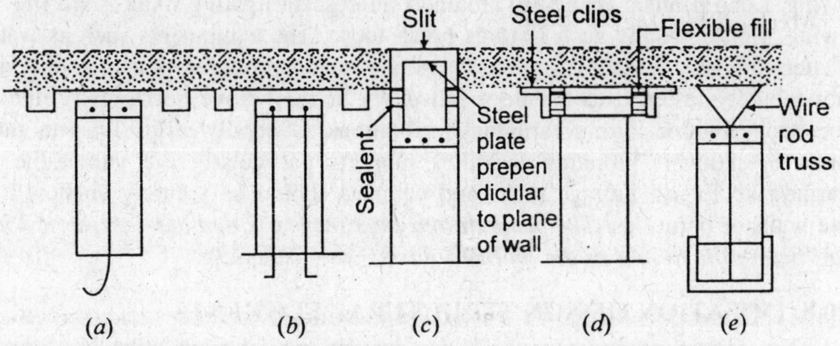

Fig. 20.11. Common isolation partitions (New mark etal-1971)

economical when the partitions are placed in planes that do not contain columns. In this way only the top and the bottom of every partition requires a special treatment to allow movement between partition and the structure. When there is a gap visible between the partition and the structure, it should either be filled or hide to prevent the un sight lines and dust gathering there.

Specially in those buildings which have been repaired and strengthened

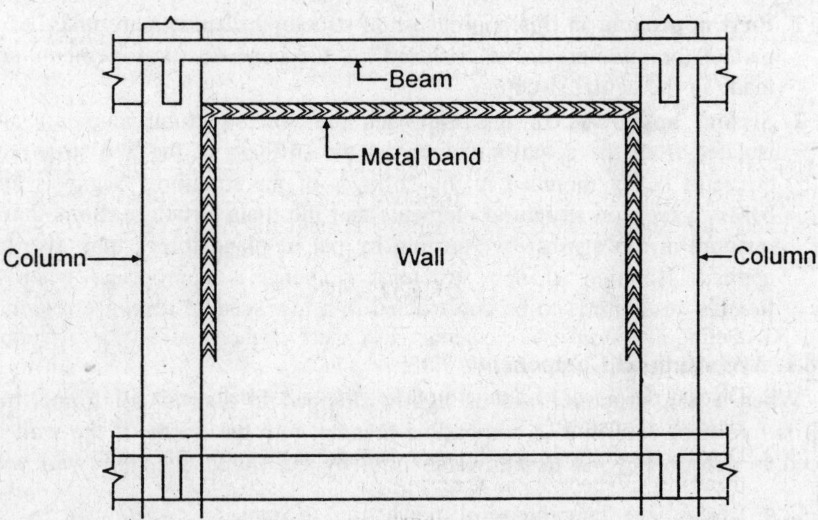

Fig. 20.12. Metal band to protect partition (New mark etal-1971)

after suffering damage during an earthquake use of pheripheral metal band has been found useful as shown in Fig. 20.12. If the normal and shear forces required to yield the band are chosen properly, then it is possible to limit the lateral forces that will be transmitted to the partitions by the structure. At the same time the advantage of the capacity of the partition to resist such forces and the advantage of energy absorption capacity of the band may be taken.

Mechanical Components

The best efficient way of achieving seismic safety of mechanical components is by isolating them from the structure by the use of springs. By isolating the components from the structure the components will not be affected by the deformation of the structural system or force in them. Though a spring supported plane may be vulnerable to large displacement and damage during an major earthquake, but an properly designed isolation system will provide adequate protection. The principle used in the design is that the base motion of the building at the point of support is isolated or removed.

A simple method of sliding isolation, suitable for heavy and stable items is to support them on casters. These devices may be subjected to substantial displacements relative to the floor. This sliding method has been improved and

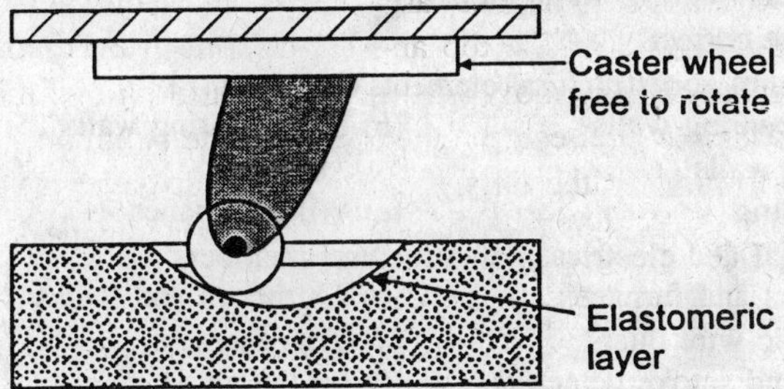

Fig. 20.13. Caster cup isolating support for equipment

a caster cup is used as shown in Fig. 20.13. This method is quite simple and limits the displacement. The eleslomeric layer on the caster contact area provides additional damping between the caster and the support.

QUESTIONS

1. Define non structural elements. How these elements affect the performance of a structural system.
2. Discuss the effect of a structural system on the behaviour of a non structural element or member.
3. Discuss the common earthquake damage in non structural elements. Suggest measures to check these damages.
4. Discuss the importance of prevention of damages to the non structural elements and their repair after the damage.

5. Draw neat sketches to show the isolation of the following non structural element.
   (*a*) Equipment (*b*) Door and windows
   (*c*) Partition walls
6. Identify the incorrect statement/statements
   (*a*) The non structural members are architectural, mechanical and electrical components of buildings.
   (*b*) The non structural components cater directly to the needs of human beings
   (*c*) The failure of non structural component has no effect on the safety of human beings and buildings
   (*d*) Effective design specifications of non structural elements are practically non existent
7. Identify the correct statement/statements
   (*a*) The failure mechanism of non structural elements is due to either excessive inertial forces or excessive deflection
   (*b*) Due to the failure of non structural elements fire resistance system may collapse
   (*c*) In normal structural design practice the non structural elements are not taken into account
   (*d*) The non structural elements influence the behaviour of structural elements during an earthquake
   (*e*) All are correct
8. Architectural non structural elements are except
   (*a*) Non bearing walls (*b*) Load bearing walls
   (*c*) In fill walls
   (*d*) Cladding (*e*) Window panes
9. Mechanical and electrical non structural members are
   (*a*) Boilers and furnaces (*b*) Chimneys and stacks
   (*c*) Electric wire ducts (*d*) Transformers
   (*e*) Fire and smoke detectors (*f*) All the above
10. An air conditioner of weight 140 kN is to be installed on the roof a five storey building in seismic zone III. The air conditioner is anchored by four bolts, one at each corner of the equipment. It is embedded in the concrete slab. Floor to floor height of each storey is 3.1 m and for the ground storey it is 4.0 m. Distance of C.G. from base = 1.0 m.
    Determine (*i*) Shear, (*ii*) Tension on the anchored bolts during an earthquake. **[Ans.** Shear force = 7 kN, Tension = 21 kN]
11. An electrical generator of weight 140 K is to be installed on the third floor of a five storey building in seismic zone III. The generator is to be mounted on four flexible vibration isolators, one at each corner of the unit. The height of the each four floor is 3.1 m and ground floors is 4.0 m. Determine the shear and tension of each isolator during an earthquake. Take C.G. of generator at 0.8 m above base. **[Ans.** Shear = 13.65, Tension = 18.2 kN]

ANSWERS

6. (*c*) 7. (*e*) 8. (*b*) 9. (*f*)

21

Low Cost Seismic Resistant Buildings

21.1. INTRODUCTION

People with limited income or resources not only live in developing countries, but many people with limited income also live in developed countries. There is no specific area or time for occurring a earthquake. Thus there is a need to develop techniques to construct earthquake resistant structures in developed as well as in developing countries. In India about 80% population live in villages. Thus there is a big challenge to construct cheap earthquake resistant structures. As per world available statistics about 20% of all the big earthquake occur in India. In this chapter some techniques and materials shall be discussed to construct cheap earthquake resistant buildings.

21.2. EARTHQUAKE RESISTANT BUILDINGS FOR LOW INCOME GROUP PERSONS

Earthquake resistant buildings for low income group persons can be constructed by using mud blocks and bamboo. Here mud houses constructed in Guinea (West Africa) and Gujrat (India) have been discussed. Mud block with bamboo mat construction has been widely adopted in Guinea.

21.2.1. Advantages of mud blocks

Following advantages of mud blocks have been observed:

1. Mud blocks have been found to have a long life.
2. Mud blocks are stable under normal conditions.
3. Mud block walls can be reinforced with bamboo or with wooden frames to provide earthquake resistance. Fig. 21.1. Shows mud block wall in bamboo frame.
4. They are comparatively cheaper than bricks or stone walls.
5. They (mud blocks) are found abundantly near the site of construction.
6. Mud block construction is appropriate for hot tropical conditions.
7. If smooth surface is desired, the mud block construction can be plastered.
8. The foundation depth of mud block wall is shallow. Hence there is no effect of ground water on the foundation and walls.
9. Mud block walls are constructed in mud mortar. Generally the width of

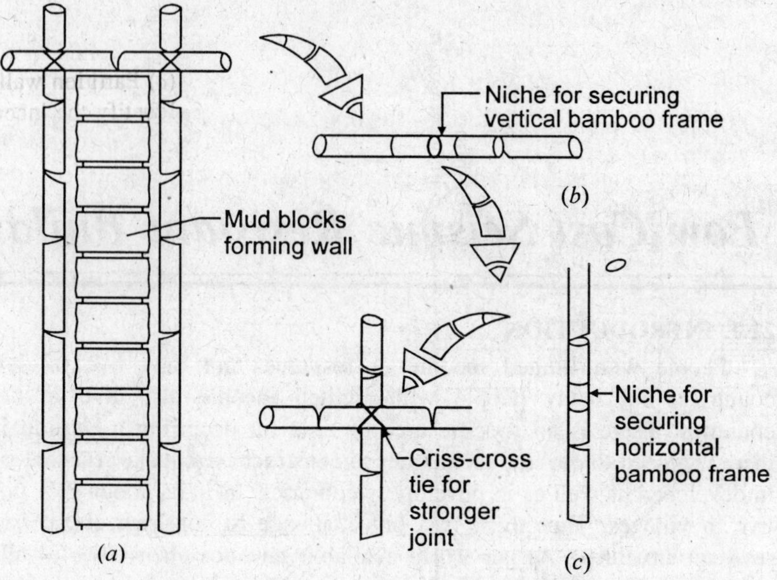

Fig. 21.1. Details of mud wall construction

the wall is kept equal to the width of one block as per local practice.

10. The walls are load bearing. These walls support ring beam and roof frame. Fig. 21.1 shows wall construction with details of preparing bamboo reinforcement, while Fig. 21.2 shows plan and section of the building.

21.2.2. Bamboo reinforcement

1. A horizontal and vertical bamboo lattice (jali) is placed on both sides of the wall.
2. The bamboo lattice on both sides of the wall are tied together by wire passing through the wall.
3. Mud walls are plastered before attaching the bamboo lattice.
4. The bamboo lattice is provided intentionally in such a way so that it can be seen fully from out side.
5. Junctions between the bamboo frame work on adjacent walls are important. Particularly they are important on the external corners.
6. Over the horizontal joint of the bamboo frame an additional vertical bamboo is placed.
7. As far as possible lintels are eliminated in such constructions.
8. The door and windows in such constructions are carried upto the top of the wall.
9. Ring beam provides horizontal continuity.

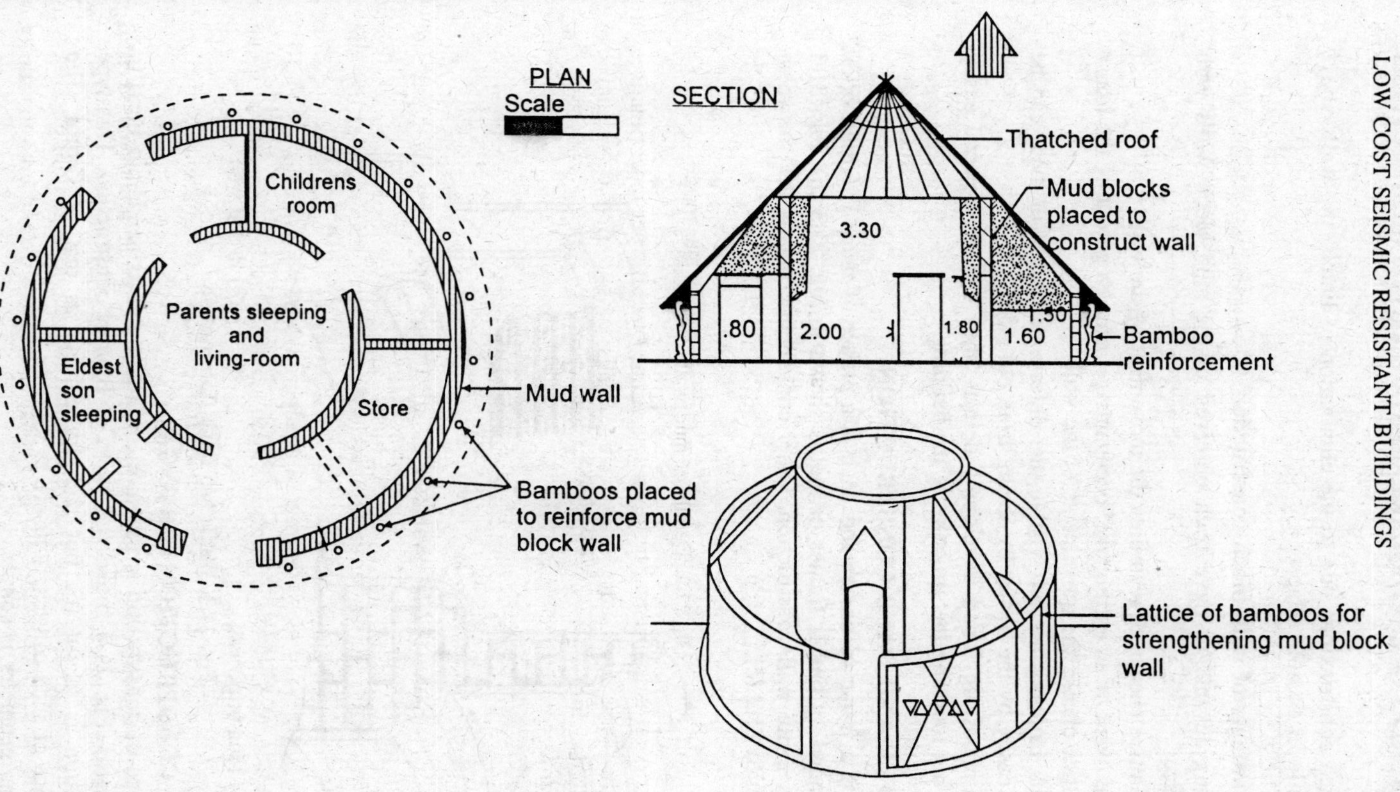

Fig. 21.2. Showing plan, section and bamboo lattice

10. In such constructions due to the elimination of lintels, the walls above lintel level do not collapse.

21.2.3. Advantages of mud block construction

Following advantages have been observed of the mud block walls with bamboo lattice:

1. The lattice checks or restraints the movement of the wall.
2. In the event of an earthquake, occupants get time to go out of the house as lattice checks the movements of the walls.
3. As the bamboos are left visible, the defects developed in them can be seen easily by the owner by seeing from out side.
4. If bamboos are found developing defects, they can be replaced easily with out touching the structure of the building.

21.3. WATTLE AND DAUB CONSTRUCTION

Wattle is a frame of timber and daub is a plaster of mud. The mud brick wall surrounded by timber frames or mat is shown in Fig. 21.3 (*a*). Fig. 21.3 (*b*) shows a insitu wall construction. Other construction details are shown in Fig. 21.3 (*c*) to 21.3 (*k*).

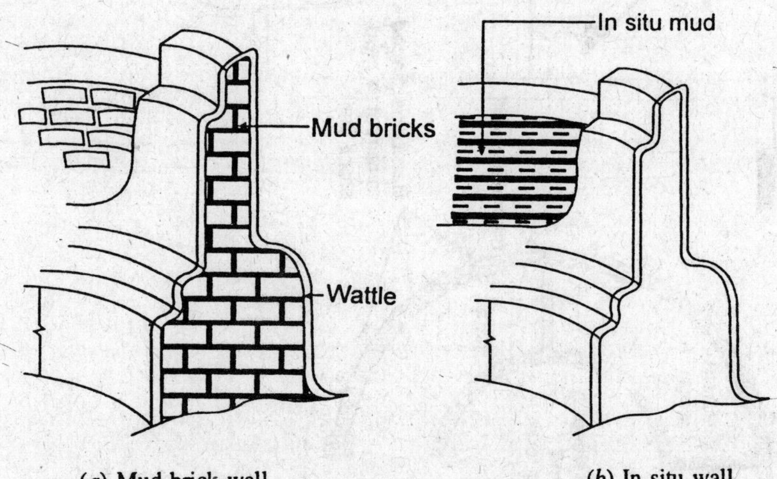

(*a*) Mud brick wall (*b*) In situ wall

Fig. 21.3. Wattle and Daub Construction

21.4. MUD CONSTRUCTION (BHUNGA)

This type of construction is prevalent in Gujrat and its neighbour hood in Rajesthan areas. Fig. 21.4 shows the views of Bhunga construction. This type of construction is useful for hot and dry climate as that of Gujrat. The characteristics of such constructions are as follows:

1. It plan geometry is simple.
2. Its unit edge is defined by the plinth and cluster edge by the fence.

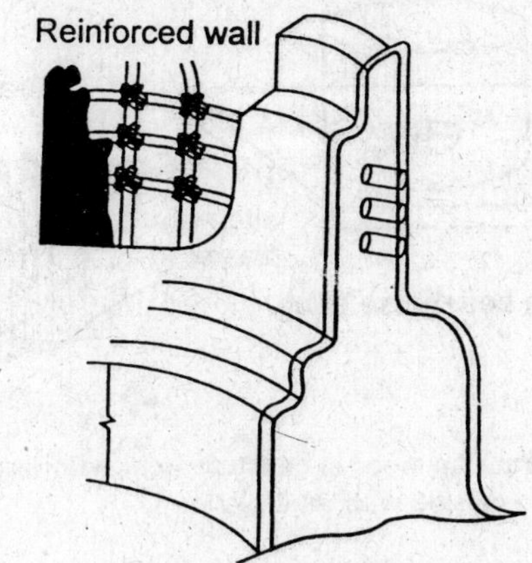

Fig. 21.3 (*c*) Reinforced wall

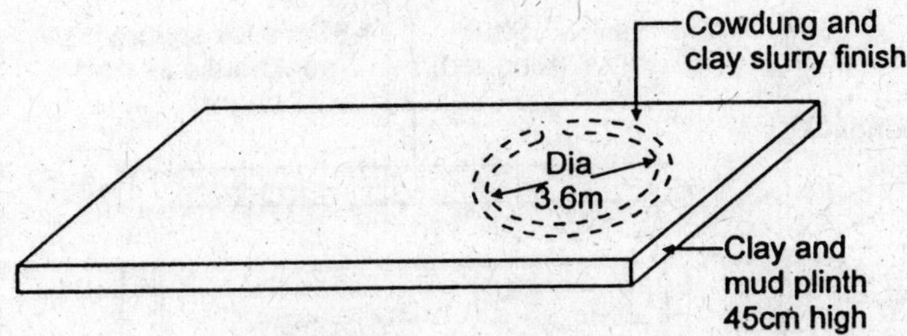

Fig. 21.3. (*d*) Preparation of plinth

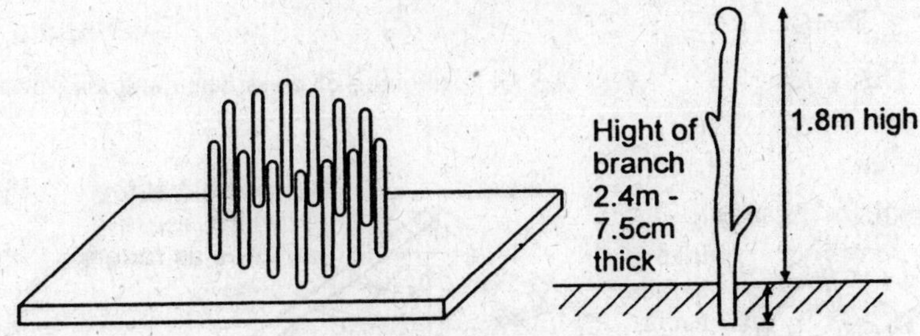

Fig. 21.3. (*e*) Making enclosure with branches embedded in plinth

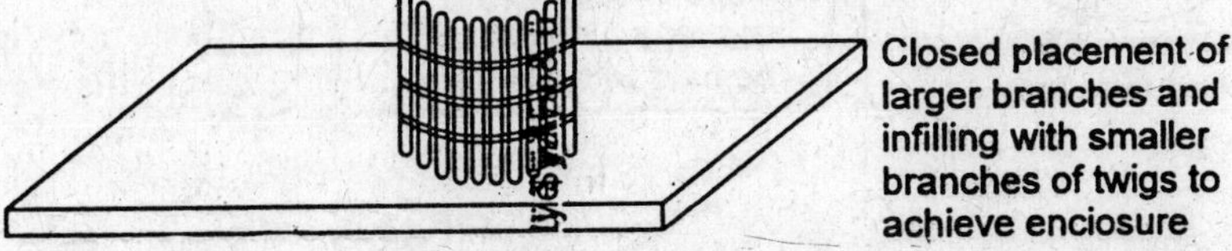

Fig. 21.3. (*f*) Binding wooden closure in straw rope for stability

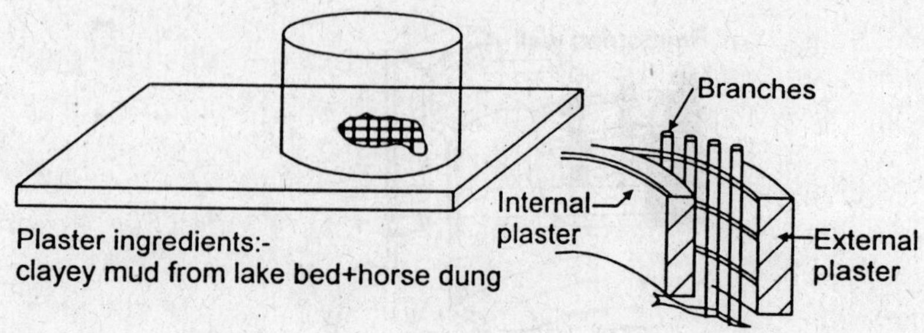

Fig. 21.3. (*g*) Packing wooden structure from with in and outside with mud plaster

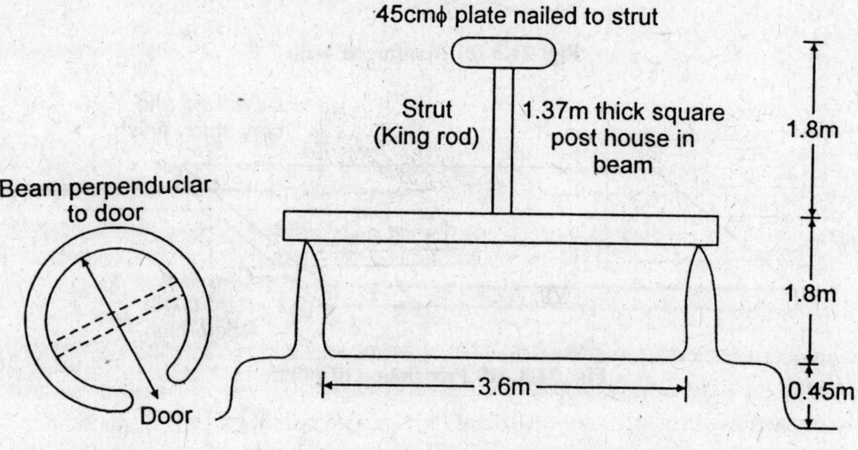

Fig. 21.3. (*h*)

Fig. 21.3 (*i*) Positioning of cross beam and king post

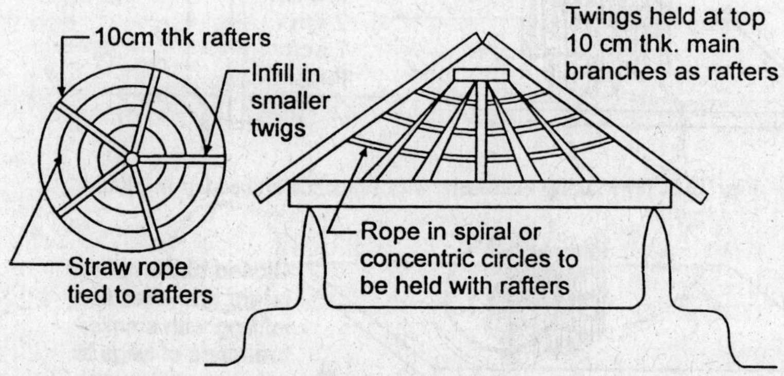

Fig. 21.3. (*j*) Laying of Rafters and Tieing with rope for stability

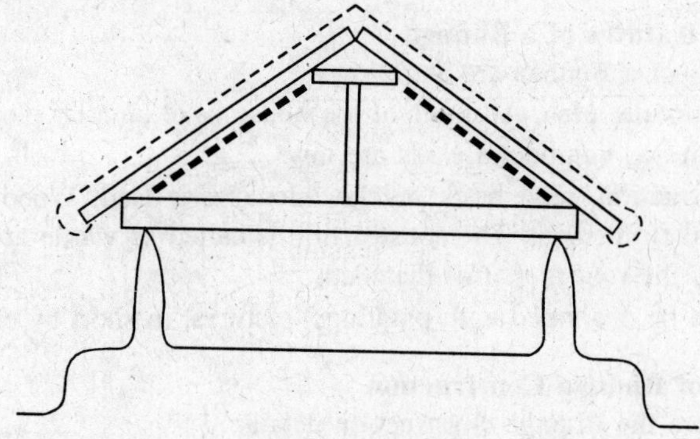

Fig. 21.3. (*k*) Laying of straw in 15 cm to 22.5 cm thick layer and binding it with rope to rafters

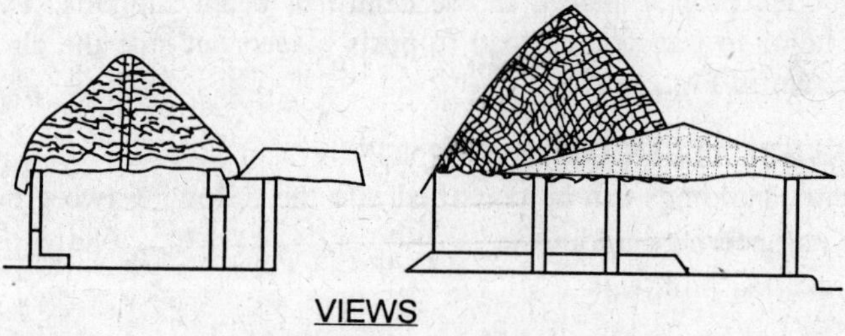

Fig. 21.4. View of Bhunga

3. The growth of the unit and cluster is incremental.
4. A dwelling unit consists of Bhunga and Choki as shown in Fig. 21.5.

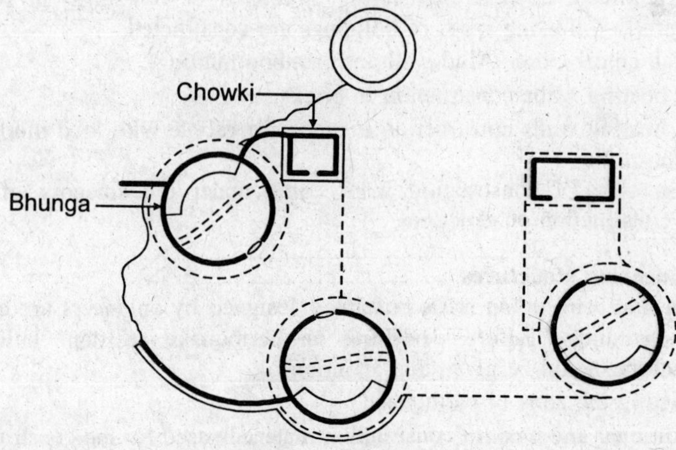

Fig. 21.5. Typical features of bhunga

21.4.1. Typical features of a Bhunga

The features of a Bhunga are as follows:

1. It has a circular plan. All units of the house have circular plan.
2. The plinth and compound walls are low.
3. For construction, mud brick or clay blocks are used. Wood usually is used as reinforcement. The construction is called as wattle and daub.
4. Generally the roof is that of thatched.
5. Walls can be decorated with paintings, pictures, in short by craft.

21.4.2. Details of Bhunga Construction

Following are the Bhunga construction details:

1. The Bhunga enclosure is made of a mud wall.
2. The diameter of a Bhunga varies from 3 to 5 m.
3. The compressive forces are born by the round shape of the Bhunga.
4. A wooden prop is placed in the centre of beam supports. The conical roof helps to transfer the load to posts placed out side the circular wall as shown in Fig. 21.6.

21.5. CLASSIFICATION OF BUILDINGS

In general, buildings can be classified into the following two groups:

1. Non engineering buildings
2. Engineering buildings

21.5.1. Non Engineering buildings

In India about 80% buildings come under this category. The structures constructed by unskilled labourers by traditional construction methods using traditional material of construction with out using any engineering expertized technique are known as non engineering structures or buildings. In Indian villages generally following types of buildings are constructed:

1. Kuccha construction (Mud wall and bamboo matting).
2. Load bearing walls construction in bricks.
3. Load bearing walls construction in stones or rubble with mud mortar or cement mortar.

All these type of construction work come under the category of non engineering construction of structures.

21.5.2. Engineering structures

In urban and semi urban areas buildings designed by engineers are called engineering buildings. Before designing an earthquake resistant building, following factors should be given due attention:

(*a*) Enlisting the zone of earthquake.

(*b*) Traditional and modern construction materials used for the construction as same constructional materials can not be used in different type of climate. For example construction materials useful in Assam for

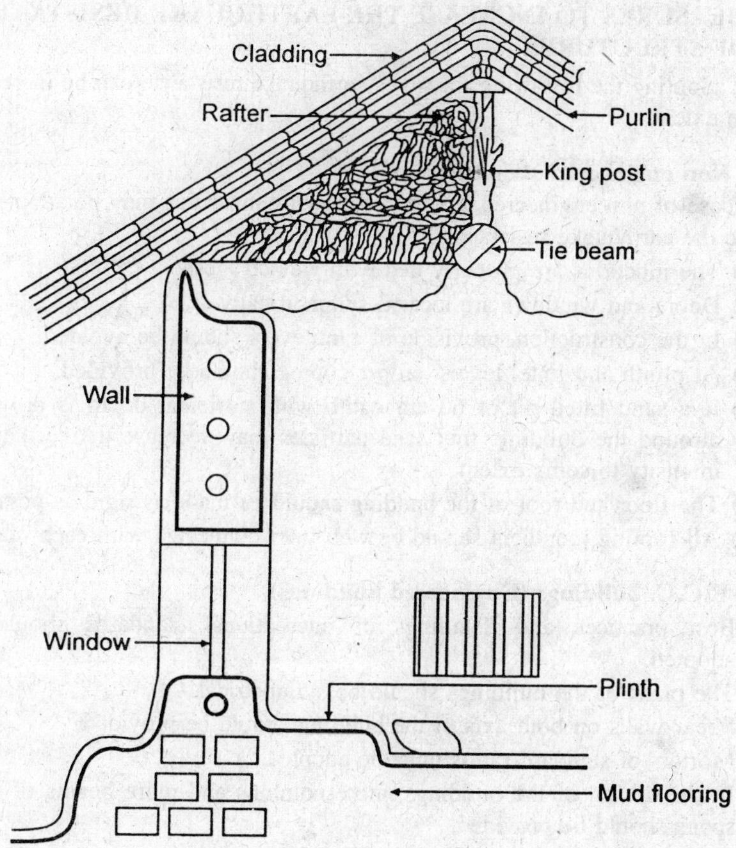

Fig. 21.6. Construction details of a Bhunga

earthquake resistant structures can not be useful in Bombay. Hence following variables should be studied before use.

Following variables will be as per various criterions mentioned below:

1. Region for which the design is to be applied.
2. Nature of soil and its condition.
3. Near hood to large water body as dams, lakes, rivers, and sea etc.
4. Availability of material locally and skill and expertise of local labour.
5. Cultural and socio economical values of the region.
6. Topographic study of the region.
7. Design solutions suitable for local conditions.

Generally the non engineered structures have load bearing brick walls and a foundation. In black cotton soil regions generally pile foundations are adopted, where as in alluvial soils foundations may be as spread or raft foundation.

21.6. MEASURES TO INCREASE THE EARTHQUAKE RESISTANCE OF STRUCTURES

By adopting the following measures earthquake resistance can be increased to some extent.

21.6.1. Non engineered structures

In case of non engineeredstructures following measures may be adopted to increase the earthquake resistance:

(*a*) The junctions are properly tied with welded mesh.

(*b*) Doors and windows are located symmetrically.

(*c*) In the construction, provision of cantilevers should be avoided.

(*d*) At plinth and lintel levels, proper coping should be provided.

(*e*) If a sand filled pit of 60 cm width with sufficient depth is provided alround the building, thin send particles may decrease the earthquake intensity to some extent.

(*f*) The floor and roof of the building should be made as rigid as possible.

(*g*) All roofing members should be well inter connected with each other.

21.6.2. R.C.C. buildings (Engineered buildings)

1. Best practices and detailings of international standards should be adopted.
2. The plans of the buildings should be symmetrical.
3. Shear walls on both axis of the building should be provided.
4. Mortars of standard ratios must be adopted.
5. In the design of the buildings, more columns and more beams of short spans should be provided.
6. Cantilevered balconies should be properly detailed.
7. Loose fittings of the items and decorative items provided as parapet walls and compound walls should be avoided as they are likely to be damaged during an earthquake.
8. Soft storeys should be avoided.
9. At stilt parking level shear walls must be provided to avoid collapse of the building.
10. Continuity of the structure must be maintained properly as lack of continuity results in maximum damage to the building.
11. Developmental works should not be carried on water logged soils as that of dried lake or river as they are most dangerous soils during earthquakes.

21.7. EFFECT OF DIFFERENT ELEMENTS ON SEISMIC PERFORMANCE OF BUILDINGS

1. **Effect of plan.** The effect of geometry of plan or shapes of the plan of a building has a marked effect on the seismic performance of a building.

It has been discussed in detail in chapter 13.

2. **Soft storey effect.** In multi storeyed buildings usually the ground storey is called the soft storey. It has discussed fully in chapter 13.
3. **Corners of the building.** The corners of the building have their own seismic problems. Out side corners experience problem due to the orthogonal effects. Diagonally oriented ground motion may stress the rest of the structure less, but it can stress corners more than principal axes. Corner columns of the frame of the buildings should be given special attention with the consideration of simultaneous motions in both vertical and horizontal direction. The design of corner columns should be conservative.

   The deflection of wall in one plane must-inter act with an incompatible deflection of a wall in a plane at rightagle. This may be more clear or noticeable in case there is no solid wall at the corner.
4. **Circular plan.** In the seismic region the direction of shacking is not certain. Thus circular plan of equal resistant capacity in all directions is the response to the inherent uncertainty in seismic design. It is impossible to predict the direction of shaking in a earthquake. Thus while dealing with seismic forces, the direction of shaking is always uncertain, where as in case of gravitational forces their direction is quite predictable. In gravitational forces, the direction of force being predictable, the beam section is used as I section in stead of circular section. In case of beams circular section will prove quite inefficient in comparison to I section. Thus the circular plan shape in seismic regions is a compromise rather than an ideal one. The circular plan minimises the maximum negative event that may occur.

21.8. EARTHQUAKE RESISTANT MATERIALS (FIBRE REINFORCED POLYMERS)

With the advancement in the development of new construction materials, research in concrete technology is gaining momentum with the development of materials like polymers. Advanced materials are playing greater role in the construction of R.C.C. structures. The research on fibre reinforced polymers is of prime concern to many institutions of the world dealing with Civil Engineering applications. U.S.A., Canada, Germany, Japan and U.K. have developed these advanced materials.

Now a days due to the construction of Nuclear power plants and other such buildings, high performance concrete is in great demand through out the world. There are numerous applications of fibre reinforced polymers in civil and structural engineering. These materials are in great demand for retrofiting the structures due to their performance.

Polymers are used to improve the properties of concrete. Polymers have distinct advantage due to their long life and strength to withstand the operating loads. Polymer concrete has superior qualities than ordinary concrete.

21.8.1. Advantages of polymers

Following are the advantages of polymers:

1. Polymers are light in weight.
2. They have good tensile strength.
3. They have good resistance to moisture.
4. They have good resistance to chemical attacks.
5. The earthquake resistance of polymer concrete is about 3 times more than the ordinary concrete.
6. Polymers can also be used in road construction.

The quality and strength of polymers depend on the type of polymers or monomers used.

21.8.2. Short Comings of Polymers

1. Their longitudinal compression, lateral and torsion strength is less. However their longitudinal tension strength is quite good.
2. Their torsion and lateral load bearing capacity is only 20% of the longitudinal bearing capacity.
3. There are no code and specifications on their use.
4. Temperature has direct effect on the durability of the polymer.
5. On burning, polymers produce toxic smoke.

Thus polymers with low ignitability, low flammability and less flame spread must be developed. Low heat transfer to the surroundings is also most desirable.

21.9. SOME DEFINITIONS

1. **Monomers.** A monomer is an organic molecule, which is capable of combining chemically with similar or different kind of molecules to form a high molecular weight material called polymer.
2. **Polymer.** A polymer is consisted of numerous monomers which are linked together in a chain like structure.
3. **Polymerization.** The chemical process which develops or causes the linkage between monomers to form polymer is called polymerization.
4. **Thermoplastic polymers.** These polymers have long, linear and parallel chains which do not have cross links. These polymers exibit reversibility on heating and cooling *i.e.* they are reversible on heating and cooling.
5. **Thermoset polymers.** These polymers have randomly oriented chains, which are cross linked. These polymers are not reversible on heating and cooling. However thermoplastic polymers can be converted into thermoset polymers by the use of cross linking agents.

In general polymers are chemically inert materials. They have higher tensile and compressive strength than conventional concrete. However the creep of polymers has been found high and modulus of elasticity low than the ordinary concrete.

21.10. CLASSIFICATION OF POLYMER CONCRETE

Polymer concrete can be classified in the following categories:

1. Polymer concrete (PC)
2. Polymer cement concrete (PCC)
3. Partially impregnated and surface coated polymer concrete.
4. Polymer impregnated concrete (PIC)

21.10.1. Polymer Concrete.

It is a composite (material of different particles) in which cement water matrix of cement concrete is replaced by a polymer binder. The main technique in producing polymer concrete is to minimise the volume of voids in the aggregate mass, so that minimum quantity of binder polymer is needed to bind the aggregates. This can be achieved by properly grading and mixing the aggregates to obtain the maximum density and minimum volume of voids.

The graded aggregates are pre packed in a form and vibrated. After this operation, the monomer is diffused through the aggregates and polymerization is initiated by chemical or radiation process. To improve the bond between the monomer and aggregates a adhesive agent is added to the monomer. In case polyester resins are used, then no polymerization is required.

Polyester resin concrete with binder content varying from 20 to 25% have shown tensile strength in the range of 9 to 10 MPa at 7 days. The compressive strength of polymer concrete has been found of the order of 140 MPa with a short curing period.

21.10.1.1. Necessity of developing polymer concrete

The most important reason for the development of polymer concrete is to over come the short comings of the conventional concrete under the following situations:

(*a*) The alkaline portland cement concrete forms internal voids on curing. Water may entrapped in these voids. On freezing this water expands, resulting cracks in concrete.

(*b*) The alkaline portland cement is easily attacked by chemically aggressive (reactive) materials, causing rapid deterioration of the concrete.

(*c*) The polymer concrete can be made compact with minimum voids and hydro-phobic (water repellent) and resistant to chemical attack.

The tensile strength and toughness of polymer concrete can be increased by the dispersion of the fibre reinforcement. The use of fibrous polyester concrete (FPC) in the compressive regions of a reinforced concrete beam provides a high strength and ductile concrete at reasonable cost. The polymer concrete is also visco-elastic in nature and will fail under sustained compressive loading stress at 50% higher than the ultimate stress. Thus the polymer concrete can be used for structures with a high ratio of live load to the dead load and composite structures in which polymer concrete may relax during long term loading.

21.10.1.2. Short coming of polymer concrete

The main short coming of polymer concrete is its brittleness.

21.10.2. Polymer Cement Concrete

Polymer cement concrete can be prepared by mixing cement, aggregates, water and monomers as used in ordinary concrete. The plastic mixture is cast in moulds, cured dried, and polymerized. In polymer cement concrete following polymers may be used:

(*a*) Epoxy styrene (*b*) Polyester-styrene

(*c*) Furans (*d*) Vinylidene chloride

How ever polymer cement concrete produced in this way has shown a very modest improvement in strength and durability. Russian authors have reported recently that a superior polymer cement concrete can be produced by using furfuryl alcohol and aniline hydro-chloride in the wet mix. This product has been found specially dense, non shrinking, and high resistant to corrosion. U.S. researchers have found that the use of epoxy resin has produced polymer cement concrete having some superior characteristics over ordinary concrete. The polymer cement concrete using polymer latex has given tensile strength of 5.8 MPa with w/c ratio of 0.25 compared with control specimen of 4.4 MPa. The increase in tensile strength is very modest.

Uses. Polymer cement concrete can be used for flooring in deck steel over bridges, food processing and chemical industries where wear resistant flooring is required. It is also useful for repair of sea defence structures due to easily development of strength.

21.10.3. Partially impregnated and surface coated (SC) concrete

In situations where in addition to strength increase, the major requirement is surface resistance to chemical and mechanical attack, the partial impregnation may be sufficient. Partial impregnation has been found quite- effective in the increase of the strength of the original concrete.

The partially impregnated concrete can be produced by soaking the initial dried specimens in liquid monomer like methyl methacrylate and then sealing them by keeping under hot water at 70°C to prevent or minimise the loss due to evaporation.

The polymerization can be done by using thermal catalytic method. Benzoyal peroxide is added as a catalyst to the monomer. The depth of penetration of the monomer depends upon the following factors:

1. Pore structure of the hardened and dried concrete.
2. The viscosity of the monomer.
3. The duration of soaking of specimens in the monomer.

21.10.3.1. Use of Partially impregnated and surface coated concrete

The main use of partially impregnated concrete has been found to improve the durability of concrete where the abrasive wear, freezing and thawing, spalling of concrete and corrosion of reinforcement are the main causes of deterioration as in the case of deck bridges. Bridge deck deterioration is a major problem every where. Excellent penetration can be achieved by ponding the monomer on the concrete surface. While ponding monomer on the concrete surface, due care should be taken to prevent the evaporation of monomer. By soaking a 5 cm thick slab for 25 hours with methyl metha crylate (MMA), the polymer was found to penetrate upto 2.5 cm *i.e.* upto 50% depth of the slab. By surfacing treating and partial impregnation of the concrete surface, its tensile and compressive strengths, modulus of elasticity and resistance to acid attack can be increased significantly.

21.10.3.2. Application of the monomers in the field

The application of monomers in the field like bridge decks, impregnation is more difficult than laboratory application and poses more problems. A typical procedure for surface treatment in the field may be adopted as follows:

1. First dry the surface for several days with electric heating blanket.
2. After drying the surface, remove the heating blanket and cover the slab with over dried light weight aggregate at the rate of 0.64 m^3 per 100 square metre of surface.
3. Initially apply monomer system at the rate of 2.0 to 3.0 litre per square metre of the surface.
4. To retard the evaporation of monomer, cover the surface with polythene sheet.
5. To check the temperature-rise, which may initiate the polymerization prematurely, shade the surface. Premature polymerization will reduce the penetration of monomer into the concrete.
6. To keep the aggregates moist for the minimum soak time of 8 hours, additional monomer should be added on the concrete.
7. Now apply heat to polymerise the monomer. For this purpose steam, hot water, or heating blanket may be used.

21.10.3.3. Monomer system to be used for field application

For field application of impregnation following monomers system may be used

(*a*) Methyl Methacrylate (MMA). 1.0% Benzoyal peroxide (B.P.) and 10%. Trimethol-propane -trimethyl crylate (TMPTMA). TMPTMA acts as a cross linking agent which helps in polymerization at low temperature of 52°C and BP acts as catalyst.

(*b*) Iso decylmetha crylate (IDMA). 1.0% BP and 10% TMPTMA.

(*c*) Iso butyl methacrylate (IBMA). 1.0% BP, 10% TMPTMA.

21.10.4. Polymer Impregnated Concrete

It is one of the widely used polymer concrete. It is nothing, but a conventionally precast concrete. It is cured and dried in oven or by dielectric heating. The air in the open cells of the concrete is removed by vacuum process. Then a low viscosity liquid monomer is diffused through the open cells and polymerised by using radiation, or by application of heat or by chemical initiation. The partial or surface impregnation improves the durability and chemical resistance, but the overall improvement in the structural properties is modest where as full impregnation improves structural properties considerably.

A hardened concrete even after considerable period of moist curing contains sufficient amount of free water in voids. The water filled voids form a significant component of the total volume of the concrete ranging from 5% in dense concrete to 15% in gap graded concrete. In polymer impregnated concrete these water filled voids are filled with polymers. The air and moisture in voids affect the monomer loading or filling.

21.10.4.1. Process of impregnation

1. Well designed and adequately moist-cured of optimum strength concrete specimens are taken.
2. The moisture of specimens is removed by drying the concrete by heating at a temperature of 120°C to 150°C. The small specimens can be heated in a air oven. For large cast in situ surfaces a thick blanket of sand usually 10 mm thick can be used to check a steep thermal gradient. Infra red heaters may also be used. To expel the large part of the free water in the concrete about 6 to 8 hours heating is required.
3. To avoid flammability, the concrete surface is cooled to about 35°.
4. The air from the dry concrete specimens is removed by vacuum process. The degree of vacuum and its duration have been found to have a significant influence on the quantity of monomer that can be impregnated. In other words the degree and duration of vacuum influence the depth of impregnation.
5. To achieve the desired depth of penetration of monomer, the specimens can be soaked in monomer. The soaking duration in monomer depends on the viscosity of monomer, characteristics of the concrete and preparation of specimen prier to soaking. The soaking duration for the desired depth may be reduced by exerting external pressure by the use of nitrogen gas. Generally air is used for this purpose.
6. To prevent evaporation of the monomer, the surface should be covered with polythene sheet.
7. Now polymerization of the monomer is initiated. Polymerization can be effected by thermal catalytic technique or by ionizing radiation. For polymerization by thermal catalytic technique the catalyzed monomer is heated to a temperature between 60°C to 150°C depending upon the

type of monometer. The heating should be done under water or by low pressure steam injection or by infra red heater or in an air oven. The duration of heating may vary from 2 to 6 hours depending upon the polymer used.

Heating decomposes the catalyst and initiates the polymerization reaction. This reaction is called *thermal catalytic reaction.* When monomer has penetrated into the concrete, polymerization can also be initiated using ionizing radiation such as gamma rays. Fully polymerized or cross linked polymers become solid and occupy the full volume in which they have been impregnated. At the impregnation stage, the polymer has to be in a pre polymer liquid form, which is generally called monomer. The state of polymerization of monomers or pre polymer resins is brought about also by adding initiators and cross linking agents.

21.11. POLYMERS USED FOR IMPREGNATION

Broadly following polymers are used for impregnation:

1. **Thermaplastics.** Usually these polymers soften between 100°C and 150°C called glass transition temperature. Thus at such temperatures the advantage of using thermoplastic impregnated concrete is lost. Thermoplastic monomers have low viscosity and can penetrate well into the hardened concrete and fill large parts of the pores. Their polymerization is achieved by addition reactions not leading to low molecular weight products.
2. **Thermosetting resins.** These polymers are more viscous and difficult to impregnate into the concrete. They can withstand higher temperatures with out softening, but the condensation reaction occurs. These reactions may lead to the formation of low molecular weight by products, which would occupy some of the space.

Thus it is necessary that a monomer or its polymer to be used for concrete impregnation should be chemically compatible with the compounds of cement and constituents of the hydrated cement paste to prevent their adverse effects. Monomers/resins used for polymer impregnated concrete are as follows:

1. Styrene
2. Methyl metha crylate (MMA)
3. Butyl acrylate
4. Acrylonitrite
5. Epoxies and their copolymer combinations
6. Polyesters

The amount of monomer that can be impregnated into the concrete specimen depends on the amount of water and voids that occupy the total void space.

21.12. USE OF POLYMER IMPREGNATED CONCRETE

The polymer impregnated concrete can be used for following works:

1. For surface impregnation of bridge decks

Impregnation of bridge decks renders them impervious to the ingrass of moisture, deicing chemicals and chloride ions etc.

2. Application in Irrigation structures

The effect of cavitation (vibrations) and erosion in dams and other hydraulic structures is catastrophic (very dangerous). Conventional repair of such damages is very expensive and time consuming, resulting in huge losses due to loss of benefits from irrigation, flood control, and power generation. In such situations the polymer impregnated treatment may prove cost effective. The concrete may be removed from the damaged portion, the damaged area patched up dried and treated by polymer impregnation.

3. Use as structural members

Polymer impregnated concrete has a bright future to be used as a structural material. Polymer impregnated concrete beams have shown remarkable high performance over conventional concrete. The maximum tendon force in case of impregnated concrete could be upto four times that of ordinary concrete. The creep deflection was found of the order of 1/9 to 1/16 that of static deflections. The shear strength also improved by the same factor as that of compressive strength.

The compressive strength of polymer impregnated concrete being of the order of 100 to 140 MPa, it can be used for heavier loads and longer span bridges and prefabricated sections.

4. Marine and under water application

Greatly improved structural properties and low water absorption and permeability makes the polymer impregnated concrete an excellent material for marine and under water application such as sea floor structures, desalination plants etc. It has also been observed that even partial impregnated concrete piles in sea water reduced the reinforcement corrosion by 24 times *i.e.* reinforcement corrosion reduced to 1/24 that of ordinary R.C.C. works. The materials to be used in the construction of flash distillation plants have to with stand the corrosive effects of distilled water, brine and vapours at a temperature upto 143°C. The carbon steel plants used at present for desalination are costly and deteriorate after prolonged use. The use of PIC will prove economical over the conventional carbon steel plants.

5. Nuclear power plants

To meet the power requirement demand for industrial purposes, most of the countries have resorted to nuclear power generation. For the generation of nuclear power, pressure plants are required to withstand the high temperature and at the same time to be able to provide shield against radiation. To avoid radiation hazards, nuclear power generation also needs the containment of spent fuel rods which remain radio active for a long time. The present high density concrete shield is very effective. Polymer impregnated concrete having high strength and durability coupled with high impermeability can be used to solve these problems.

6. Sewage disposal works

Sewer pipes when buried under sulphate infested soils deteriorate due to the attack of effluents. The sewage treatment works made of concrete are also attacked severely from corrosive gases. Polymer impregnated concrete being highly resistant to sulphate and acids may prove to be a most suitable material for this purpose.

7. Impregnation of ferro cement products

Ferro cement products being thin, generally 1 to 4 cm thick are liable to corrode. The impregnation of polymer will improve the functionally efficiency of ferro cement products.

8. Water proofing of structures

Seepage and leakage of water through structural elements such as roof and slabs is a perpetual problem and has not been fully solved by the use of conventional water proofing methods. The use of polymer impregnated mortar may solve this problem.

9. Industrial use

In dairy farm product buildings, tanneries and chemical factories the concrete of the floor has to withstand the chemical attack. The performance of conventional concrete has not been found very satisfactory. It is hoped the polymer impregnated concrete will provide durable flooring in such situations.

21.13. SEARCH FOR NEW EARTHQUAKE RESISTANT MATERIALS

For the development of new materials, work on fibre reinforced polymer concrete is going on for a long time. At the university of Coloumbia (Canada). Dr. Nem Kumar Banthia is working on developing cement based and polymer based repair materials. He has developed a fibre reinforced polymer. It has been reported that by the use of this fibre reinforced polymer on the deck of a bridge, the structural strength of the deck was found double and the energy absorption three times of the original material. The effective age of this polymer was found 25 years. This development is quite significant in road repair and earthquake proofing for maintaining the integrity of the concrete. The material being plastic, and the fibre mix can be applied quickly with a high pressure hose. By the use of this technique the labour cost and disruption to the user are minimized to a great extent.

Dr. Banthia has developed a family of durable steel fibres that is now commercialized and used to reinforce cement based concrete materials.

Another important study is undergoing on the use of fibre reinforced polymers for maintaining masonry walls subjected to seismic loads.

21.13.1. Use of Bamboo in building construction

About 30% population lives below poverty line through out the world.

Hence there is a need to develop cheap houses for these people. After independence, government of India created a National Building Organisation (NBO), under the ministry of housing and development. This organisation held a exhibition of cheap houses in exhibition ground Mathura Road, Delhi. Now it is known as Pragati ground. In this exhibition 65 houses were built by different organisations and states. Author had a chance to study the Thermal behaviour of these houses under Central building Research Institute, Rookee.

In 1950 also, Central Building Research Institute started a project on the use of bamboo as reinforcement in R.C.C. structures. The bamboo reinforced members showed good performation in tension, but their deflection under sustained loads was found excessive, which gave unsightly look of the member. The deflection was measured with the help of strain gauges.

In 1974 an developing country sought technical advice on building bamboo trusses for schools and ware houses from the university of Eindhoven, but it had no experience on the subject. However they found some information from their former Royal Dutch files, which was found useful. Since then university established a laboratory to examine the structural properties of bamboo and find ways to use the material in erecting structures. Especially in construction of trusses for roofs and bridges. This laboratory encouraged researchers in other countries also to develop the use of bamboo as building material.

Villagers were trained in spliting the bamboo and weave the strips into 1.2 m by 2.4 m mats. These mats were sold to the factory. Factory made bamboo ply from these mats by glueing and pressing them. This bamboo ply proved to be very useful for house construction and in preparing other house hold furniture etc. Villagers also learned making bamboo flooring, wall panels and furniture etc.

During 1980-1990 in the country side (villages) of Central America Construction of low cost houses was under taken. Under this project 30 experemental houses of bamboo under the command of Dr. Jorge Gutierrez were constructed near Limon Costarica. This place is near the expicentre of 1991 Costarica earthquake. The intensity of this earthquake was 7.5 on Richter scale. The houses were built under a program of united nations. The project was funded by Netherlands.

During this earthquake hundreds of houses, bridges and other structures made of concrete were found collapsed like buildings of cards. However these 30 experimental bamboo houses were found intact with out even a minor damage or even a single crack. The reason of this miracle happening can be described as bigger the mass, bigger the earthquake force it will attract. Hence concrete structure, having bigger mass collapsed, while light weight bamboo houses remained intact.

21.13.2. Details of experimental houses

Three bed room house on a plot of 47 m^2 area were constructed from thick bamboo pole frames covered with a woven mesh of split bamboo coated with mortar. The bamboo provided support and flexibility, while the mortar provided strength.

21.13.3. Advantages of bamboo houses

Besides flexibility bamboo houses also have the following advantages:

1. Houses made of bamboo are found about 20% cheaper than those built with concrete blocks.
2. Bamboo homes are simple to build.
3. They are eco-friendly as no destruction of forests is required. As a 20 m $\times$ 20 m plot can grow bamboo in 5 years which is enough to construct 2 houses of 8 m $\times$ 8 m of area.

21.13.4. Properties of bamboo

1. It has been observed that a short, straight column of bamboo with a top surface area of 10 cm^2 can support 5000 kg weight.
2. A variety of bamboo called Bambusa vulgaris can withstand 78 neuton/mm^2 of compression force. This means that bamboo can with sand double the compressive force than concrete before it breaks.
3. The maximum height of Bambusa vulgaris variety can be 15 m and maximum diameter as 10.2 cm.

To test the properties of bamboo, compression machines, shear testers bending machines, tension machines and creep gaugers have been used.

QUESTIONS

1. Explain the advantages and disadvantages of mud block masonry.
2. Explain with sketch the bamboo reinforced mud block wall.
3. Explain the construction of Bhunga with neat sketch.
4. What factors should be given attention before design of an earthquake resistant structure.
5. What measures should be taken to increase the earthquake resistance of non engineering buildings.
6. Discuss the effect of different elements on the performance of buildings in seismic regions.
7. Discuss the merits and demerits of polymers as construction material.
8. Explain the necessity of developing polymer concrete.
9. Discuss the process of impregnation of concrete fully.
10. Discuss the situations where the use of polymer impregnated concrete has been found more advantageous.
11. Write a detailed note on the use of bamboo as building material.
12. The best construction material in seismic regions for cheap houses is ....
    (*a*) Teak (*b*) Sal
    (*c*) Shishim (*d*) Bamboo
13. Identify the correct statement/statements

(*a*) During the ground motion the bamboo lattice check the movements of the wall

(*b*) Damaged bamboos can be seen from out side. They can be replaced with out any damage to the wall

(*c*) During earthquake, bamboo houses do not collapse suddenly. Hence residents get time to go out safely

(*d*) All are correct

14. Identify the incorrect statement/statements

(*a*) In houses constructed with bamboo and mud blocks, bamboo provides flexibility and plaster durability to the house

(*b*) During earthquake, bamboo houses attract least seismic forces or loads

(*c*) During earthquake bamboo houses attract largest seismic loads

(*d*) In seismic regions by digging an 60 cm wide pit alround the house and filling it with sand, seismic motion or vibrations can be reduced considerably

15. Identify the incorrect statement/statements

(*a*) The earthquake resistance of the house can be increased by constructing rigid floors and roofs

(*b*) The construction of rigid floors and roofs reduces their earthquake resistivity

(*c*) The earthquake resistivity of the house can be increased by ensuring good connectivity amongst all elements of the roof

(*d*) The earthquake resistivity of the house is reduced considerability by providing good connectivity of the different elements of the roof

16. Identify the incorrect statement/statements

(*a*) Thermoplastic polymers have long, linear and parallel chains. They also not have cross links

(*b*) Thermoplastic polymers do not exhibit reversibility on heating or cooling *i.e.* they can not be converted to thermoset polymers

(*c*) Thermoset polymers have randomly orientated chain which are cross linked

(*d*) Chemically polymers are inert materials

ANSWERS

12. (*d*)
13. (*d*)
14. (*c*)
15. (*b, d*)
16. (*b*)

22

Guidelines for Seismic Rehabilitation of Existing Buildings

22.1. INTRODUCTION

From the study of seismic damaged buildings during the past few decades, it has been realized that the seismic risk to life and property can be reduced to a great extent by improving the seismic performance of existing seismic deficient buildings. The investigations of past failures of structures during an earthquake have provided considerable information to Engineers to design and construct earthquake resistant buildings. The repair techniques of damaged buildings also have been developed which can help to rehabilitate a damaged building. During earthquakes some times fire also breaks out, which causes severe damage to concrete structures and completely destroy masonry and thatched hutments. In this chapter technique to rehabilate damaged buildings from earthquake and fire damage have been discussed.

22.2. SEISMIC VULNERABILITY

The vulnerability of a building subjected to an earthquake depends on the seismic deficiency of that building relative to the required performance objective. The seismic deficiency can be defined as the condition that will prevent the building from developing the ability to acquire the required performance objective. A building evaluated to provide full occupancy after an event, may have more deficiencies than evaluated to prevent collapse. Depending upon the vulnerability assessment, a building may be condemned and demolished or rehabilitated to increase its capacity so that the seismic short comings of the building can be minimized. Thus the structural rehabilitation of a building can be accomplished in a number of ways depending on the specific merits and limitations related to the improving seismic deficiencies.

22.3. COMMON SEISMIC DEFICIENCIES

Regardless to the method of evaluation adopted, failure to meet the stipulated performance objective implies certain seismic deficiencies. These deficiencies have been discussed below:

1. Global strength

It refers to the lateral strength of the vertically oriented lateral force resisting system. For reducing or degrading structural systems characterized by a negative post yield slope on the push over curve (Easy curve) a minimum strength requirements may be applied. In some cases the strength will also affect the total expected inelastic displacement. The added strength may reduce non-linear demands (effects) into acceptable ranges. A deficiency in global strength is common in older buildings due to any of the following reasons.

(*a*) Due to total lack of seismic design.

(*b*) Due to design based on early building code with inadequate strength requirements.

In case prescriptive equivalent lateral force methods or linear static procedures have been adopted for evaluation, inadequate strength will directly relate to unacceptable demand or need to capacity ratios with in elements of the lateral force resisting system.

2. Global stiffness

It refers to the stiffness of the entire lateral force resisting system, though the lack of stiffness may not be critical at all levels. For example, in a building with thin walls critical drift level will develop in upper floors. On the other hand, in frame buildings the critical drifts generally occur in the lowest levels. The stiffness in the building must be added in such a way that drifts are sufficiently reduced in the critical levels. Though strength and stiffness are often controlled by the same existing elements or the same retrofit techniques, the two deficiencies are considered separately. Failure to meet evaluation standards is often the result of a building placing excess drift demands or needs on existing poorly detailed components.

3. Configuration deficiency

In this category of deficiencies all configuration irregularities are covered, which adversely affect the performance of the building. In codes for new buildings, the configuration features are divided in the following two groups:

(*a*) **Plan irregularities:** Plan irregularities are those features, which may highly affect the elements due to torsional effect or shape of the diaphragm effect.

(*b*) **Vertical irregularities.** Vertical irregularities are created by uneven vertical distribution of mass or stiffness between the floors that may result in concentration of force or displacement at certain levels. In older existing buildings such irregularities are seldom taken into consideration in the original design. Hence normally require the rehabilitation measures to rectify the defect.

4. Load path

The inadequate strength in the load path or a discontinuity in the load path may be considered very important as it may negate the many useful qualities of the seismic system. Load path is considered to extend from each mass in the building to the supporting soil. For example for a panel of external plastering called cladding, the load path will include its connection to the supporting floor or floors, the diaphragm and collectors that deliver the load to the components of the primary lateral load resisting system as walls, columns, braces, frames etc. These components extend upto foundation. Finally the loads are transferred from foundation to soil below. To categorise many load deficiencies is difficult as the strength deficiency may be considered to be a part of another element. For example an inadequate construction joint in a shear wall could be considered a load path deficiency or a shear wall deficiency in the category of global strength.

5. Inadequate component detailing

Here detailing refers to design decisions that affect a component or system's behaviour beyond the strength determined by nominal effort (demand) usually in the non linear range. A good example of detailing deficiency is poor confinement of concrete in concrete gravity columns. Often in older concrete buildings, the expected drifts from the design event will exceed the deformation capacity of such columns leading to degradation and collapse. Though primary gravity load design is adequate, but the post elastic behaviour is not adequate due to inadequate confinement and spacing of ties. In the selection of mitigation (removing) strategies of seismic effects, the identification of detailing deficiencies is very important as acceptable performance of the element may be achieved by local adjustment of detailing rather than by adding new lateral force resisting elements. In the case of of gravity concrete columns acceptable performance can be achieved by increasing the deformation capacity of the column by adding confinement rather than reducing global deformation effect (demand) by adding lateral force resisting elements.

6. Diaphragm deficiencies

In a seismic system the main purpose of a diaphragm is to act as a horizontal beam spanning between the lateral force resisting systems. Diaphragm deficiencies include the following factors:

(*a*) Inadequate shear or bending strength.

(*b*) Inadequate stiffness or reinforcing around the openings or re-entrant corners.

Inadequate local shear transfer to lateral force resisting element or missing or inadequate collector are categorize as load path deficiencies.

Foundation deficiencies

Such deficiencies can occur with in the foundation element itself due to inadequate transfer mechanism between foundation and soil. Foundation element deficiencies include:

(*a*) Shear or bending strength of the spread foundations and grade beams.

(*b*) In adequate axial capacity or detailing of piles and piers.

(*c*) Weak and degrading connections between piles, piers, and caps.

II. Transfer deficiencies include:

(*a*) Excessive settlement or bearing failure.

(*b*) Excessive rotation.

(*c*) Inadequate tension capacity of deep foundations or loss of bearing capacity due to liquefaction.

Other deficiencies

The deficiencies not included in the above-mentioned deficiencies are as follows:

(*a*) Adjacent buildings.

(*b*) Geological hazards.

(*c*) Deteriorated structural material.

22.4. PLANS (STRATEGIES) FOR REHABILITATION OF DEMAGED STRUCTURES

1. Technical considerations. In technical considerations, the selected techniques must eliminate deficiencies preferably more than one deficiency. In the first instance the enhancement of existing elements such as shear walls, moment frames, and bracing frames must be considered. The deformation compatibility between the existing elements and new elements must also be considered. In some cases the use of base isolators or damping devices is the most effective way to eliminate deficiencies.

2. Non technical consideration. The solution to be chosen for the rehabilitation always mostly is dictated by the building user based issues rather than mearly based on technical considerations. Following issues are of concern to building owners or users:

(*a*) Cost of construction.

(*b*) Seismic performance.

(*c*) Short-term disruption of occupants.

(*d*) Effects on long-term functionability of building.

(e) Historic preservation and aesthetic considerations.

All these factors are always considered and an importance has to be given to each of these factors and a combination of weightage has to decide the scheme chosen.

1. Cost

Cost of construction is always an important factor and it is balanced against one or more other considerations seems to be significant. However some times other economic considerations such as the cost of disruption to building users or the value of contents to be seismically protected. The cost may be the only criterion applied when choosing among equivalent rehabilitation options.

2. Seismic performance

Before putting emphasis on design-based performance, known qualitative differences between the probable performances of different schemes should be utilized for selecting a scheme. Specific performance objectives are often set before the development of schemes. The objectives that require a limited amount of damage or continued occupancy will severely limit the method of retrofit that can be used and may control the other issues.

3. Short term disruption of occupants

When the seismic rehabilitation is done at the time of major building remodeling, disruption issue is not a major issue or it is minimized. However when the building is partially or completely occupied, this factor or parameter becomes important and controls rehabilitation scheme.

4. Effect on long term functionability of building

Usually the effect of this factor is considered less important than others. The planning flexibility only is changed slightly. How ever this parameter may be significant in building occupancies that need open spaces such as parking garages and shops etc.

5. Aesthetics

In monumental and historic buildings, usually the consideration of historic fabric controls the design of rehabilitation. Performance objectives are controlled by limitations imposed by preservation. In non-historic buildings, though aesthetic is commonly stated as a criterion, but is often sacrificed in favour of minimizing cost and disruption to tenants.

22.5. REHABILITATION TECHNIQUES

Different types of buildings require different techniques of mitigation for a specific seismic deficiency. Depending upon the type of building and associated seismic deficiencies, alternative recommendations are made to satisfy the performance objective of rehabilitation. Rehabilitation techniques are developed for common building types. Followings are the common type of buildings.

1. **Wooden light frame buildings.** These are one or two storeys detached dwellings.
2. **Multi-storey, multi unit residential wooden frames buildings.** These are large residential buildings with commercial space at the ground floor.
3. **Steel moment frame buildings.** These buildings consist of steel beams and columns. Moment frames resist the lateral forces.
4. **Steel braced frames buildings.** These buildings consist of frame assemblies of steel beams and columns. The lateral forces are resisted by diagonal steel members placed in selected bays.
5. **Steel frames with infill masonry shear wall buildings.** Buildings of this category are normally older buildings. These buildings consist of

gravity frames with un reinforced masonry, tightly infilling the space between columns.

6. **Concrete moment frame buildings.** The complete system of such buildings consists of concrete beams and columns. The lateral loads are resisted by cast in place moment frames.
7. **Concrete shear wall buildings (Bearing wall system).** Usually such buildings consist of concrete flat slab or precast plank floors and bearing walls. Gravity loads if any are resisted by beams and columns. Lateral loads are resisted by shear walls.
8. **Concrete shear wall buildings (Gravity frame system).** The buildings have columns and beams or columns and slabs that essentially carry all gravity loads. Lateral loads are resisted by concrete shear walls surrounding shafts, at the building perimeter or isolated walls placed specifically for lateral resistance.
9. **Concrete frames with infill masonry shear walls buildings.** Normally such buildings are older buildings. They consist essentially of complete gravity frame assemblies of concrete column and floor systems. These floors may be of a variety of concrete system such as flat plates, two way slabs, beam and slab etc. Exterior walls are constructed of un reinforced masonry, tightly infilling the space between columns horizontally and between floors structural elements vertically, such that the infill interacts with the frame to form a lateral force resisting system.
10. **Tilt up concrete shear wall buildings.** These buildings are constructed with concrete perimeter walls cast at the site and tilted up to form the exterior of the building. Usually such buildings are of single storey buildings with wood roof framing. However a good number of multistory buildings also exist with composite deck floors and a wood or steel framed roof.
11. **Precast frames with shear walls buildings.** These buildings consist of concrete columns, girders, beams, and slabs. The elements are cast away from the site and erected at the site to form a complete gravity load system. The lateral load or force resisting system of such buildings is of concrete shear walls. These walls may be cast in place or may be of precast. The method of joining floor system vary from place to place. In California, precast floor T beams or hollow core planks are covered by a cast implace-topping slab, reinforced to provide diaphragm action. At some places welded insert plates are used to join the floor system elements.
12. **Reinforcement masonry bearing wall buildings (similar to tilt up concrete shear wall buildings).** Such buildings are constructed with reinforced masonry (Brick cavity wall or concrete units) perimeter walls with a wood or metal deck flexible diaphragm.

13. **Reinforced masonry bearing wall building (Similar to un reinforced masonry bearing wall building).** Such buildings are multistorey buildings. They have interior of concrete masonry unit walls and shorter diaphragm spans.
14. **Reinforced bearing walls buildings (Similar to concrete shear wall buildings with bearing walls.** These buildings consist of reinforced masonry walls and concrete slab floors. The floors may be cast in place or pre cast. These types of buildings often are used as Hotel and Motels. These are similar to concrete wall type buildings.
15. **Un reinforced masonry bearing wall buildings.** Such buildings consist of unreinforced masonry bearing walls. The perimeter of the building usually is made of brick masonry. The floors are typically of wooden joists and wood sheathing supported on the walls and on interior post and beam construction.

22.6. Method of rehabilitation

Any appropriate method suitable for the building may be chosen from the following suggested methods:

1. Add new elements to damaged buildings.
2. Enhance the existing elements of the damaged buildings.
3. Improve connections between the elements of the damaged buildings.
4. Reduce effects (demands) of the damaged building.
5. Remove deficient element of the damaged building.

The seismic rehabilitation techniques are not necessarily related to a specific building type, such as those related to foundations, diaphragms, and non-structural components. The global significant techniques could be applied to any building. These techniques are seismic isolation (base isolation) or addition of damping devices discussed in chapter 18.

22.7. REHABILITATION TECHNIQUES OF MASONRY STRUCTURES

Here some of the methods of strengthening of cracked structures have been discussed in brief:

1. Cracks in masonry structures. The cracks in masonry structures can be strengthened by the following methods:

(*a*) **By grouting the cracks.** The cracks of masonry walls can be filled with cement mortar or concrete by fixing wooden plank or steel plate on one side and pumping of filling concrete or mortar from the other side as shown in Fig. 22.1.

(*b*) **Replacing damaged bricks by concrete blocks.** The damaged bricks are removed and concrete blocks are inserted in their place. Some authors suggest the insertion of concrete blocks in every third course while some other authors suggest the insertion of concrete blocks in every fifth or sixth course *i.e.* at an vertical interval of about 50 cm as

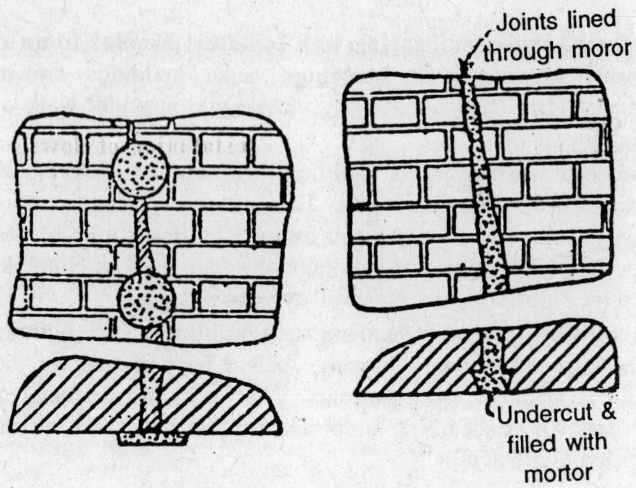

Fig. 22.1. Cut and concrete filling

shown in Fig. 22.2. These blocks may be laid in 1:1:6 cement-lime-sand mortars.

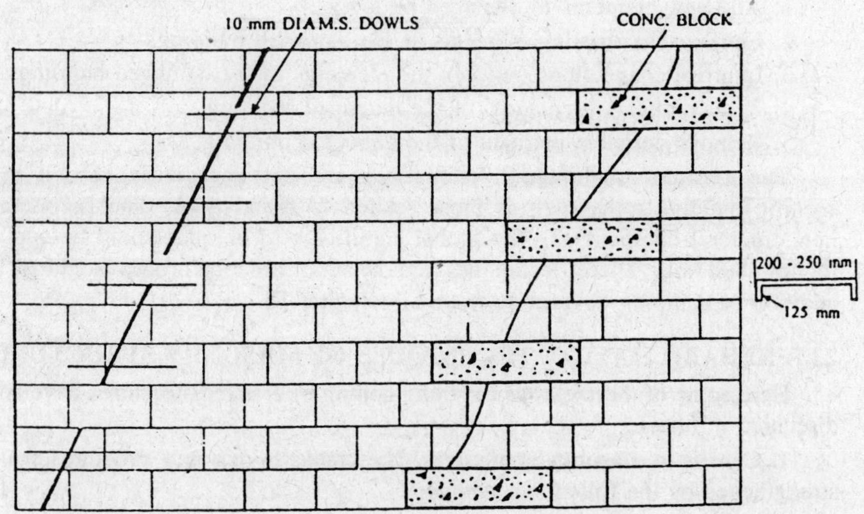

Fig. 22.2. Treatment of cracks (Stitching and use of concrete blocks)

(*c*) **Cement grouting.** By drilling 2 to 4 holes per square meter of area of the wall, a cement water grout of 1:! ratio can be pumped under a pressure of 0.1 to 0.25 Mpa.

(*d*) **By fixing wire net on the crack.** The crack may be strengthened by fixing a 5 × 5 cm dimension wire net piece on both sides of the crack by nails. This wire mesh is plastered with a 2 to 4 cm thick cement sand mortar. This wire net works as a vertical plate. This wire net should be attached with iron rods at an interval of 30 to 40 cm.

(*e*) **Pre stressing of the wall.** Drilling holes on both sides of the crack through out the thickness of the wall, a steel plate may be fixed with the wall on both sides with the help of bolts.

(*f*) **External tightening.** 1st a wire mesh on the wall is fixed and then it is covered with the cement sand mortar or by shotcrete. The continuity of the process should be ensured at the ends.

(*g*) **By stitching crack.** Stitching of cracks can be adopted for brick masonry as well as concrete works. In this technique, holes are drilled on both sides of the crack and a stitching dog is inserted into the holes. The legs of the stitching dogs should be fixed in the hole either in non-shrinkable grout or in epoxy.

A stitching dog is a 20 to 25 cm long, 10 mm thick iron piece. It is bent at right angle at both ends. The length of the bent pieces may vary from 1.25 to 12.5 cm. Stitching does not close the cracks, but it only helps to prevent the further opening of the crack. If water seeps through the crack, it should be sealed before stitching. It will protect the reinforcement from corrosion. Fig. 22.5

22.8. REHABILITATION OF CONCRETE STRUCTURES

Every concrete structure has joints and develops cracks. Thus all joints and cracks have to be sealed to save them from further disintegration. Hence for concrete structures to seal joints and cracks sealers are used. The crack sealers should ensure the structural integrity and serviceability. They should also provide protection from penetration or ingression of harmful liquids and gases.

Method of sealing

For sealing a crack, it should be enlarged along its length on the exposed surface. The process of doing enlargement of the crack is known as chasing or routing. After the enlargement of the crack, it is sealed with a suitable sealer as shown in Fig. 22.3.

The non-routing operation may affect the permanency of the repair. The routing operation consists of cutting a sufficiently large groove to receive the sealer on the surface. The groove may be cut by a concrete saw or hand tool. The maximum surface width of routing of 6mm is sufficient as repair of narrower groove is difficult. The surface of the routed joint should be cleaned with air jet and allowed to dry before placing sealer or sealant.

Functions of the sealant

The functions of a sealant or sealer are as follows:

1. To prevent water from leaking to reinforcement.
2. To prevent the development of hydrostatic pressure with in the joint.
3. To check the development of stains on the surface of the concrete.

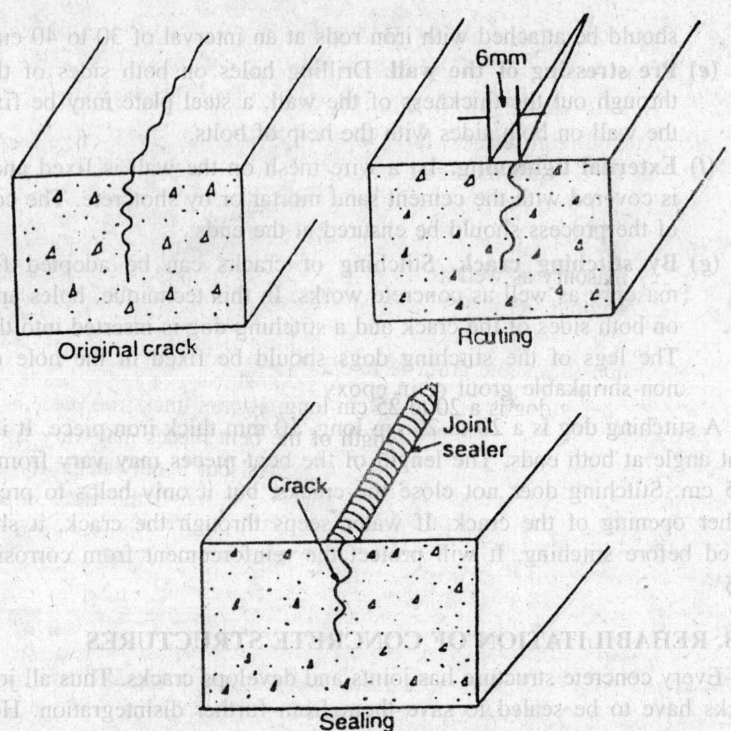

Fig. 22.3. Crack repair by routing and sealing

4. To prevent the development of moisture problems on the far side of the member.

Usually epoxy compounds are used as sealant materials. When appearance is not important and water tightness of the joint is not required, hot poured joint sealants are used. Urethanes which remain flexible over a wide range of temperature have been used successfully for sealing the cracks upto 20 mm in width and of considerable depth.

Flexible sealing

For repairing an active crack, it is necessary to provide for its continuing movement *i.e.* its movement is not checked. This can be achieved by following the crack along its length. The process is known as to rout or chase the crack. The surface of the crack is prepared as follows:

The cracks are cleaned by removing all dirt, oil, grease, fine particles of concrete etc. These elements may prevent the penetration of epoxy and development of the bond between the filling materials and the surface of the crack. The contaminants should preferably be removed by flushing the surface with water or solvent. The solvent is then blown out using compressed air or by air-drying.

After preparation of the surface, the crack is filled with a suitable field moulded flexible sealant. The strain capacity of sealant should be of the same order as that of the crack material. A wide crack spreads movement over a greater width so that the resulting strain is compatible with the sealant to be used. The sealant should adhere to the sides of the rout or chase, but it should not be bonded from the bottom, so that the movement in the crack spreads over the full width of the chase. This can be achieved by providing a bond breaker or debonding strip of a material such as polythene or pressure sensitive tape at the bottom of the chase before applying the sealant. This debonding strip does not bond the sealant during or before the hardening of the sealant and allows the sealant to change its shape with out stress concentration at the bottom. A sectional view of a typical movement joint flexible sealing is shown in Fig. 22.4. With an increase in the width of the chase, the crack movement, which induces tension or shear in

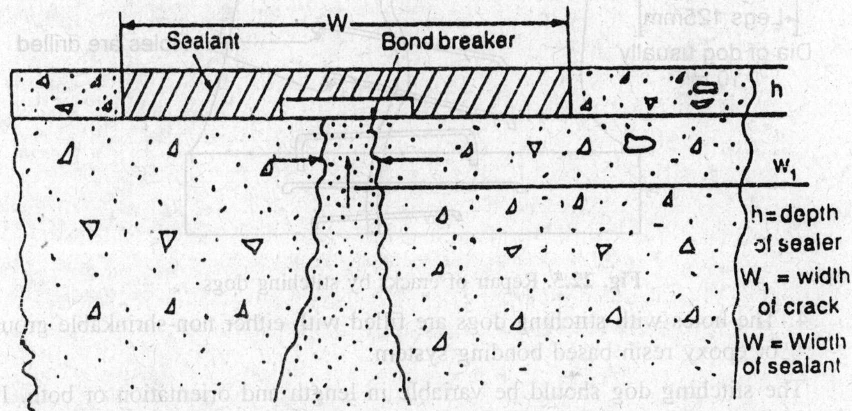

Fig. 22.4. Repair of an active crack by flexible sealing

sealant, will exert considerably reduced stress on the adhesive interface with the concrete, enabling the face seal to cope with the extensive movements.

22.9. STITCHING OF CRACKS IN CONCRETE STRUCTURES

Stitching of cracks process in concrete is adopted when the tensile strength of the member is to be restored across the major cracks. Stitching does not close the crack; it only prevents it from further spreading. Stitching tends to stiffen the structure, which may concentrate the over all structural restraint, developing cracks in concrete somewhere else. Thus it is necessary that the adjacent section to be stitching should be strengthened by using external reinforcement embedded in a suitable overlay.

Procedure of stitching

A stitching unit is a *U* shaped metal unit with short lags. This unit is called stitching dog unit. The length of the dog varies from 20 to 25 cm. Usually it is made of 10 mm thick iron sheet. The legs at both ends are bent at right angles. The length of bent portion varies from 1.25 cm to 12.5 cm.

Working procedure is as follows:

1. 1st holes are drilled on both sides of the crack in a staggered way.
2. The holes are fully cleaned either by air jet or otherwise.
3. After clearing the holes, the stitching dogs are placed in the holes so prepared across the crack as shown in Fig. 22.5.

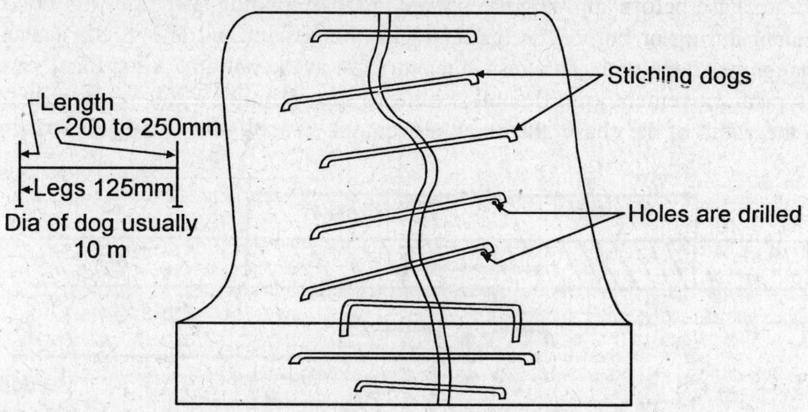

Fig. 22.5. Repair of cracks by stitching dogs

4. The holes with stitching dogs are filled with either non-shrinkable grout or epoxy resin based bonding system.

The stitching dog should be variable in length and orientation or both. It should be so located that the tension transmitted across the crack is not concentrated to a single plane with in the section, but spread over a large area. The spacing of stitching dogs near the ends of the crack should be reduced.

22.10. STRENGTHENING OF SLABS, BEAMS AND COLUMNS BY ADDITIONAL INTERIOR REINFORCEMENT

A common method of strengthening of slabs, beams and columns is by providing additional reinforcement across the cracked surfaces as shown in Fig. 22.6. In this method holes are drilled perpendicular to the crack surface to insert new reinforcement in the member. This reinforcement is called dowel. The entire length of the dowel is fixed to the concrete with the help of a bonding matrix. In order to relieve the member from the dead load stresses and to share the original dead load by the added reinforcement after repair, the structure must be shored and jacked. The added reinforcement has been found to be optimally effective in sharing the full load at yield stress. For bonding the added reinforcement Portland cement grout, available epoxy materials and other chemical adhesives may be used. While selecting the adhesive material, creep

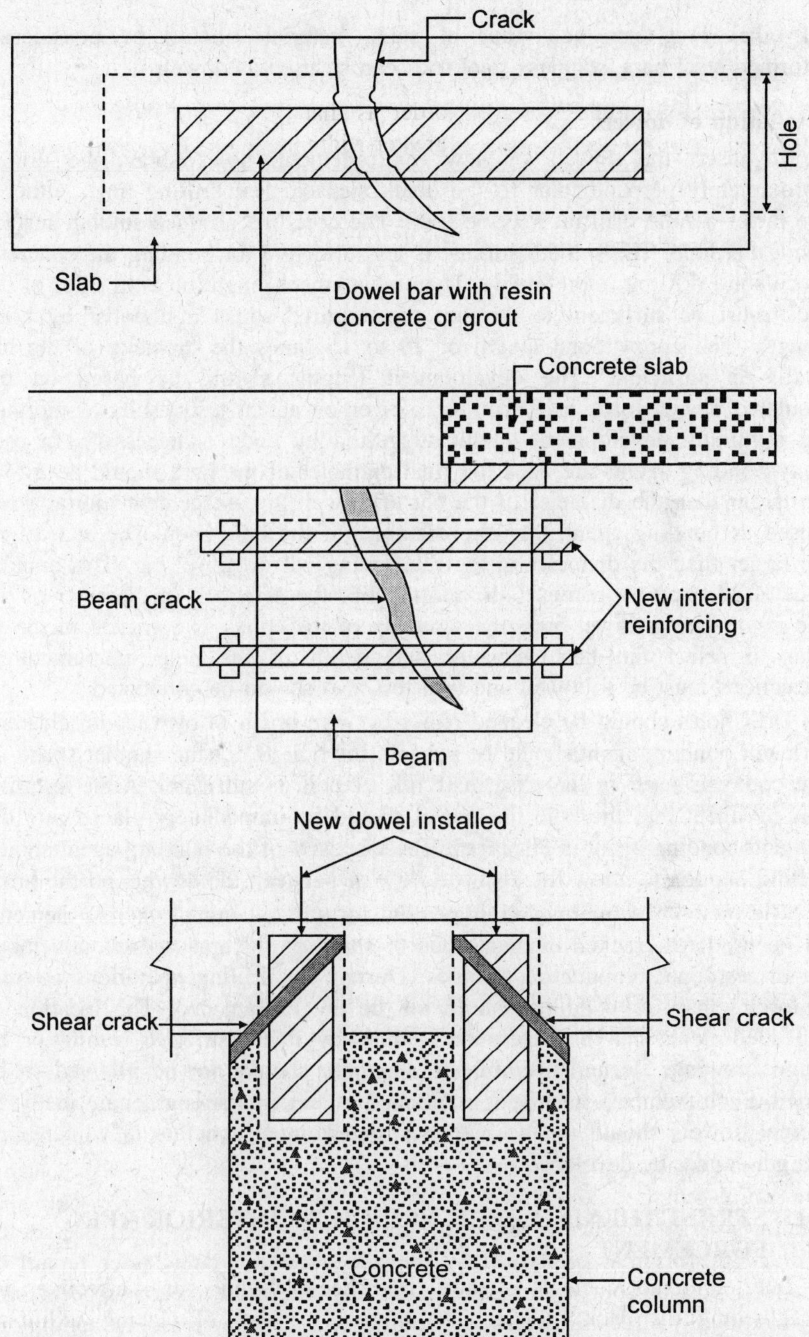

Fig. 22.6. Interior reinforcing in different elements

and other long-term behaviour of such materials should be considered. Deformed steel bars, stainless steel rods can be used as dowels.

Installation of dowels

To insert the dowels or new reinforcement, holes should be drilled approximately perpendicular to the crack surface. For drilling holes either a core bit or a solid drill bit may be used. The core bits produce smooth surface in side the hole. The smooth surface is less effective for bonding the concrete. Hence solid drill bit is preferable. The embankment length on both sides of the crack must be sufficient to develop the required stress in the bar by bond strength. The epoxy bond length of 10 to 15 times the diameter of the bar usually is sufficient. The development lengths should be based on the calculated design loads and bond stresses or on actual test results of mortars. The minimum development length suggested by code is necessary. In case epoxy-bonding agents are used the final diameter of the hole should be 3 to 6 mm larger than the diameter of the bar or dowel. In case cement mortar grout is used as bonding agent, then the diameter of the hole should be at least 50 mm larger than the diameter of the reinforcing bar or dowel bar. This annular space is adequate to compact the mortar. For the selection of diameter of the hole for inserting dowel bars, the viscosity of the epoxy is a critical factor. In order to select the best diameter and depth of the hole, manufacturers instructions must be followed and trial test also should be conducted.

Drill holes should be cleaned either by wire brush or by vacuum clearers, sufficient bonding agent should be put into the hole to fill the annular space. In case epoxy is used in that case half full of hole is sufficient. After inserting bonding agent into the hole the dowel should be immediately placed into the hole and bonding agent is displaced. The viscosity of the bonding agent should be fluid enough to allow the agent to flow in between the dowel and the hole.

The method of internal reinforcement for strengthening concrete elements can be used for cracked elements due to shear or flexural stresses developed due to restrained volumetric changes. During the drilling operations internal reinforcing bars or conduits should not be cut or punched. The location of embedded items can be determined either by non-destrictive testing or by design drawings. Heavily reinforced members should not be allowed to be drilled. Such members may be strengthened by external strengthening methods. Internal dowels should not be placed in deteriorated concrete in which bond strength cannot be developed.

22.11. STRENGTHENING DECK BRIDGE BY INTERIOR REINFORCEMENT

Interior reinforcement method has been found very effective for strengthening the deck bridges. The method consists of placing additional reinforcement and injecting the epoxy resin into the hole to provide bond between the dowel and concrete.

Procedure. The procedure is as follows:

1. First the crack is sealed by epoxy injection.
2. After sealing the crack, holes of 20 mm diameter are drilled at 45° angle to the surface of the element and crossing the crack plane approximately at right angle as shown in the Fig. 22.7.
3. 12 to 16 mm diameter reinforcing bars are placed in the drilled holes. These bars should extend at least 50 cm on each side of the crack. The spacing of these bars may be adopted as per need or as per design.

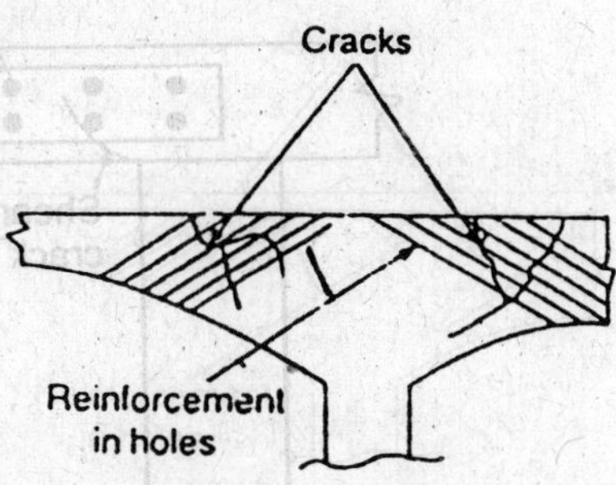

Fig. 22.7. Repair of bridge deck by internal reinforcement

4. The hole and crack plane is filled with an epoxy injection under low pressure varying from 0.35 to 0.55 Mpa. This epoxy bonds the bars to the sides of the hole and fills the crack plane. In this way the cracked concrete surface becomes to a monolithic form.

For an successful repair, an elastic exterior crack sealant is required. For this purpose jel type epoxy crack sealants have been found useful. These sealants should be applied in a uniform layer of 1.5 to 2.5 mm thickness extending upto approximately 20 mm on each side of the crack.

For local strengthening resin bonding of flat steel plates to the external surface of the critical structural member of the bridge or building has been found most practical and economical.

22.12. EXTERIOR REINFORCING

Before applying the external strengthening, the damaged portion due to over load, erosion, abrasion or chemical attack must be removed and new reinforcement is installed around and adjacent to the remaining concrete. Rusting of the existing reinforcement also should be removed before treatment and placing additional reinforcement bars.

Steel elements such as deformed bars, welded wire fabric steel plate, steel rolled sections, steel trappings and specially fabricated brackets may be used as the reinforcing elements.

For strengthening, suitable element may be placed on the exterior of an existing concrete member as shown in Fig. 22.8. The new steel member may be encased with shotcrete, mortar or other material.

The new reinforcement is encased in conventionally laid concrete or shot crete. In case the existing concrete is in good condition, the new reinforcement may be bonded directly to the existing surface after preparing the surface. And enclosing with stirrups specially in case of beams and columns. In case of beams and columns the steel plates may be attached with bolts as shown in Fig. 22.8.

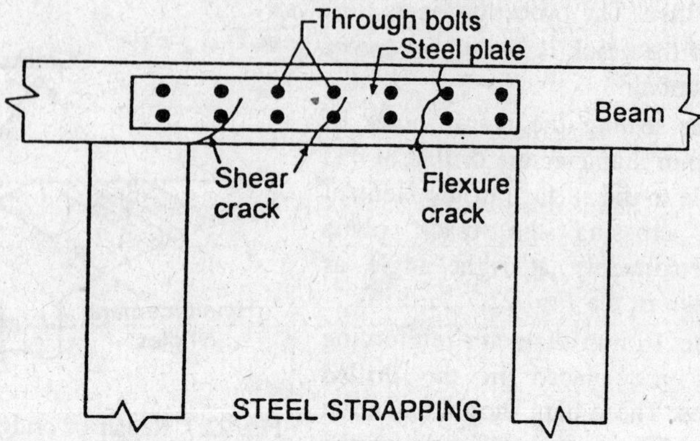

Fig. 22.8. Exterior reinforcing

For bonding the new reinforcement, epoxy, Portland cement mortar or concrete, or other chemical adhesive substances may be used.

The exterior reinforcement placement method is the most convenient method for repair and strengthening concrete elements where carrying equipment needed for placement of interior reinforcement is not possible due to limited space.

External reinforcement for flexural, shear and torsion for beams and girders may be provided by bonding deformed bars or plates to the surface of concrete girder with shot crete, or cast in place concrete or epoxy and polymer concrete. Anchorage may be required in the repair method to ensure composite action.

Steel plates may be attached to the existing girders using bolts. In case adhesive is used to encase the steel member to the concrete, then adequate surface preparation for both steel and concrete is required. For surface preparation for both steel and concrete, sand blasting method is the best method. Surface cleaning with solvents or high pressure water blasting is adequate. Beams, girders, columns, and walls can be strengthened by placing longitudinal reinforcing bars and stirrups or ties around the members and thin encasing the members with shot crete or cast in place concrete. Shot crete bonds the new reinforcement to the existing members. The added shot crete also increases the size of the member and adds strength and stiffness to it.

However increase in dead weight of the member must be kept in view while carrying out such operations. Both R.C.C. and masonry walls can be strengthened by adding external reinforcing bars or welded wire fabric and by the application of shot crete. As stated above also, the shot crete develops bond with the new reinforcement and the wall. Sometimes dowels are embedded in holes drilled in perimeter columns and beams for connection between the frame members and walls. Anchoring dowels are strengthened by filling the dowel holes along with shot creting of wall.

22.12.1. Exterior post tensioning

Slabs and Girders both can be strengthened in flexure and shear by the addition of external tendons, rods or both which are pre-stressed. The strands may be straight or curved. Fig. 22.9. In post tensioning the end plates must be properly designed and securely seated.

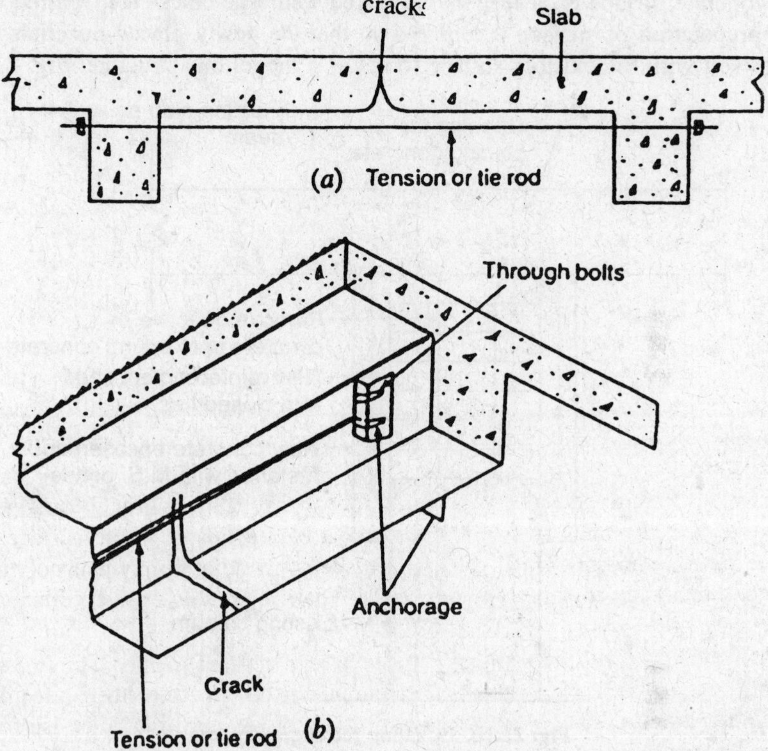

Fig. 22.9. Repair of flexural cracks in slab and beam by post tensioning

22.13. JACKETS, BRACKETS AND COLLARS

Jacketing. Jacketing is the process of restoring an existing structural member to its original dimensions or to be increased in size by encasement with cement or polymer modified cement concrete. Jacketing should be adopted when the existing structure is fairly sound and does not show sign of distress. Before starting jacketing all cracks should be thoroughly sealed.

22.13.1. Materials to be used for Jacketing

Following materials may be used for Jacketing:

1. Conventional cement concrete and mortar.
2. Epoxy mortars grout.
3. Latex modified mortar or concrete.

4. Fero cement.
5. Rubber and plastics.

22.13.2. Process of Jacketing

First of all the deteriorated concrete is removed. The existing reinforcement and concrete surface is cleaned and prepared well. The cracks are repaired well. The preparation of surface is required so that the newly placed materials may bond well with the existing surface to act as a monolithic structure. Fig. 22.10.

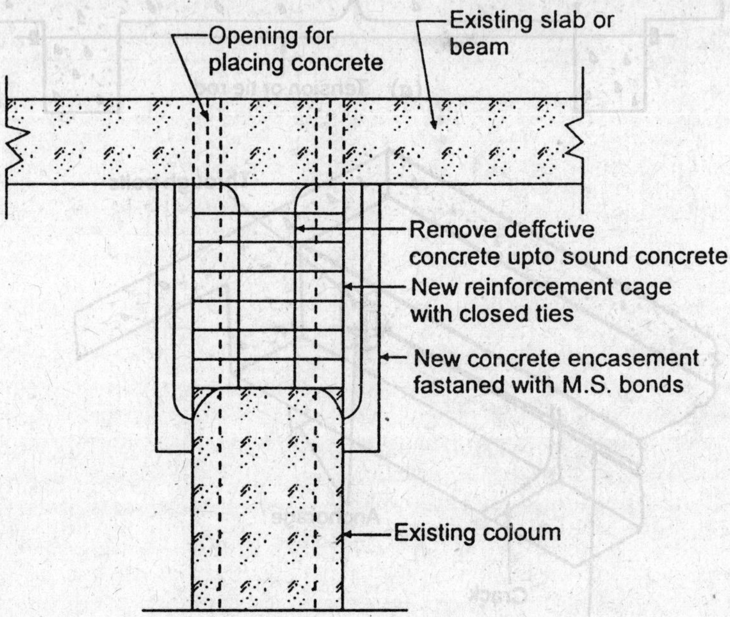

Fig. 22.10. Jacketing technique process

After preparing the surface a steel reinforcement cage is formed around the damaged section in which shot crete or cast in place concrete is laid. Some times brackets are cast externally along with jackets to encase the damaged members.

The jacket form is placed around the damaged section to be repaired. The dimension of the form or diameter of the form is kept larger than the section to keep a uniform annular space between the section and the form. This space should be equal to the desired increase in the dimension of the damaged section. To ensure equal annular clearance around the existing member the form should be provided with spacers.

The form for the jacket may be temporary or permanent. It may be made of timber. Corrugated metal, precast concrete, rubber, fibre glass or special fabric depending upon the purpose and type of exposure. Permanent forms are advantageous in marine environment where added protection from weathering, abrasion and chemical pollution is desired.

Now the selected encasing material is filled in the annular space. Technique for filling the jacket include pumping, tremie or pre placed aggregate concrete.

Jacketing is particularly applicable for repair of deteriorated piers, columns and piles, where full or portion of the section to be repaired is under water. This method is suitable for protecting concrete steel or timber sections against further deterioration as well as for strengthening. When the jacket is provided around the periphery of a column it is called as collar.

Collars are effective in providing new capitals supports on the existing columns for supporting slab floors. The collar provides increased shear capacity for the slab, and it decreases the effective length of the column. Collars may also help to satisfy architectural constraints better than jacketing the column for its full height.

In most of the applications, the main function of the collar is to transfer the vertical load to the column. Circular reinforcement can be used for load transfer. The practice of transferring load through dowel bars embedded into columns or shear keys has a disadvantage. The disadvantage is that they require drilling of holes for dowels or cutting shear keys, which are costly and time consuming. They can also damage the existing column. Reinforcement encircling the column can be used to transfer the load through shear friction. The expansion of collar as it slides along the roughened surface causes the tensioning of circular reinforcement resulting in radial compression, which provides normal force needed for load transfer. The shear transfer strength is provided by both frictional resistance to sliding and dowel action of reinforcement crossing the crack.

Collar can also be used as mid column bearing surface acting as circumferential beam to distribute the concentrated load around the column. The collar is subjected to shear and bending along the collar circumference as well as direct bearing stress under concentrated load. Thus in addition to shear transfer reinforcement, the collar should be provided with reinforcement for shear and moment within the collar. The repair can be used as an alternate load path from the column to the collar and then to the connecting structural component.

Jackets generally are provided under water, as such the preparation of their surface is expensive and difficult. Even then the applicability of jackets and collars is wide spread and generally is cost effective, especially if the alternative is replacement of the deteriorated member.

Jacketing usually is adopted for under water structures as piers of bridges. The jacketing of a pier of a bridge is described as follows.

As stated above before starting jacketing all cracks should be thoroughly grouted. For effective functioning, the jacketing should be taken right upto the foundation and at this level it should be integrated with the existing foundation.

To avoid the endangering of safety of the structure, the foundation should be exposed for only a limited width at a time and for the shortest time necessary for strengthening. While deciding the width of foundation to be exposed at a time, site and soil condition including water table should be kept in mind. The minimum thickness of jacketing should not be less than 150 mm. For railway bridge piers, the speed of trains should be restricted to 8 km/hour during the period of strengthening.

Procedure. The face of existing concrete or masonry should be cleaned thoroughly of all dirt etc. Before laying new concrete, neat cement slurry should

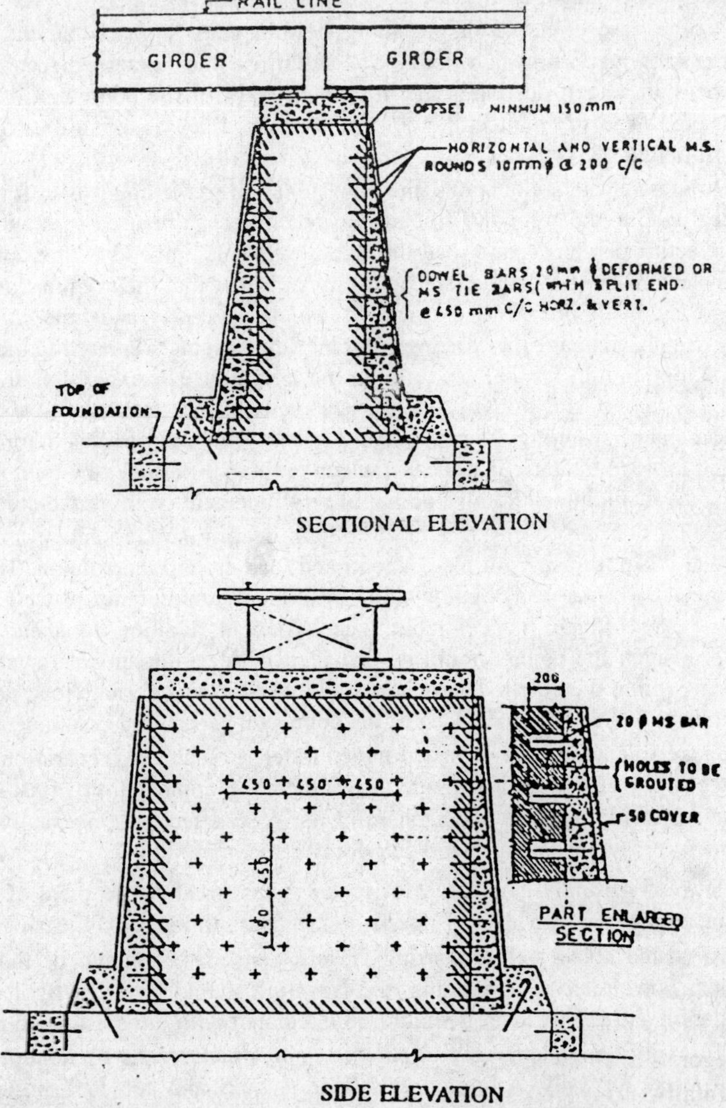

Fig. 22.11. Strengthening of substructure by Jacketing

be applied uniformly over the face of the old masonry. The dowel bars of M.S rods of 20 mm diameter and hooked at exposed end are fixed in the old masonry.

M.S bar flats with split ends can also be similarly fixed into the old masonry. These dewls should be taken upto the depth of not less than 200 mm in side the masonry as shown in Fig. 22.11.

Some times holes are required to be drilled in the masonry. The vertical and horizontal spacing of the dowls should not be more than 450 mm. The dowls should be staggered. The 28 days cube strength of new concrete should not be less than 150 kg/cm^2. A mat of steel reinforcement with maximum diameter of 10 mm, spaced at 200 mm horizontally and vertically may be provided as distribution reinforcement.

22.14. STRENGTHENING OF FOUNDATIONS

The bearing power of foundations may be increased by the following measures:

1. By adding new load bearing element to the foundation.
2. By increasing the dimensions of the existing foundation.
3. By improving the water drainage of the area. In alluvium soils the higher ground water level develops liquefaction of the soil. The liquefaction of soil reduces the load bearing capacity of the soil to a great extent, resulting in collapse of buildings.
4. By providing apron all-round the structure.
5. By increasing the load bearing capacity of the foundation.

Before starting improving foundation load bearing capacity, soil properties of the area must be investigated fully.

22.15. REPAIR OF STEEL STRUCTURES

In case of multi storeyed-framed structures, the damage to the weld in the moment resisting members can be avoided by the following measures:

1. Use of fully welded connections (flange and web both welded).
2. Reduction of stresses in weld itself.
3. The buckled braces should be replaced and their strength is ascertained.
4. The cover of damaged concrete is replaced by new concrete.
5. The damaged riveted joints are rectified by replacing the old gussets plates by new one and riveting.
6. The claddings either replaced or repaired.

22.16. REHABILITATION OF FIRE DAMAGED STRUCTURES

Usually during earthquakes, fire breaks out due to gas lines damage or short circuit of electric fittings. Fire damaged structures may be classified into two categories as follows:

1. **Totally destroyed or burnt.** In this category thatched or wooden structures get totally burnt. In case of concrete structures major portion

has to be rebuilt.

2. **Slightly damaged or deformed.** In this case only repair and finishing of the damaged portion is sufficient.

The extent of damage caused to a R.C.C. structure during a fire depends on the following two factors:

(*a*) Duration of the fire.

(*b*) Temperature experienced by the structure during the fire. High temperature during the fire reduces the strength of the concrete structures due to the following factors:

(*i*) Due to change in strength and deformity of materials.

(*ii*) Reduction in cross-sectional dimensions of the structural members.

(*iii*) Weakening of bond between the reinforcement and the concrete.

This factor determines the structural action under load.

Normally the maximum temperature reached during a fire is estimated indirectly *i.e.* from the melting of metallic or other non-combustible articles. From the available statistics on the damaged R.C.C. structures by the fire, the duration and maximum temperature reached during the fire are shown in the Table 22.1 below:

Table 22.1. Showing duration of fire and max. Temperature reached

S. No.	*Type of structure*	*Duration of fire in hours*	*Range of temp reached in °C*
1.	Residential and administrative buildings	1 to 2 hours	1000°C to 1100°C
2.	Theaters and departmental stores	More than 2 to 3 hours	1100°C to 1200°C
3.	Industrial buildings and ware houses where considerable quantities of solid and liquid combustible materials are stored	More than 2 hours	1300°C

Thus the duration of fire and the maximum temperature reached vary over a wide range. Temperature of 1000°C to 1100° C in fires lasting to 2 hours has been observed more frequently than 1300°C.

An accurate estimation of the performance characteristics of the structure damaged in a fire helps in taking effective measures of restoration. The performance characteristics take into account the physico-chemical and mechanical properties of the materials burnt and that of heated concrete. There is an accumulation of irreversible damages of mechanical and physico-chemical factors. Under mechanical factors creep, cracking, shrinkage and plastic deformations may be classified. While under physico-chemical factors, corrosion, absorption, and degradation etc. may be classified. These informations enhence the reliability of estimation of residual load carrying capacity of the structural members resulting in a considerable saving in the cost of restoration of the structure. However from this information the determination of the physico-chemical characteristics of the materials and geometric dimensions of the structure is difficult.

The strength and stiffness of concrete and steel decreases as the temperature of the material increases and dimensional changes take place.

The changes in strength and stiffness of the concrete are influenced by the constituent elements of the concrete such as type of cement, aggregate and water content. The cracks or spalling develop in beams, columns, and slabs due to the development of stresses caused by the thermal strains. The development of cracks and spalling decreases the area available to resist the applied load or forces. The behaviour of different structural elements damaged in fire is discussed below.

Axially Loaded Columns

Normally the failure of axially loaded columns takes place at mid height due to brittleness. The failure occurs due to the disintegration of concrete in the whole centre of section accompanied by buckling of longitudinal bars. Due to the fire, a large variation in temperature between the concrete of periphery and concrete of the section takes place. The range of variation of this temperature has been found 800°C or even more. This variation in temperature causes variation in the strength of concrete. The strength of concrete varies along the cross section. The central portion of the section keeps its original strength, while it reduces to zero at the peripherical surface.

The temperature at which the crushing strength of concrete reduces to 50% of its original value is known as the *critical temperature.* The value of critical temperature depends upon the nature or type of aggregate used in concrete. The value of critical temperature of concrete made with sand stone or granite aggregate is 550°C and that of made with lime stone is 700°C.

It has been observed that quartz, and gravel expand steadily upto about 573°C. At this temperature they go a sudden expansion of about 0.85%. This expansion develops a disruptive action on the stability of concrete. At this temperature the fire resisting properties of the concrete are least if quartz is the principal or dominant mineral in the aggregate.

Amongst the igneous rock aggregate, the best fire resistant aggregates are dolerites and basalts. The lime stone expands steadily upto a temperature of about 900°C and then begins to contract due to decomposition and libration of carbon dioxide. As the decomposition of limestone takes place at a very high temperature of 900°C, the dense lime stone aggregate has been found a good fire resistant aggregate. The blast furnace slag aggregate is regarded as the best fire resistant aggregate. Broken brick aggregate also has been found as good fire resistant aggregate. On the basis of extensive research work, it has been found that even the best fire resistant concrete will fail, if it is exposed to a temperature more than 900°C for a considerable period. The serious reduction in strength takes place at a temperature of about 600°C. Upto a temperature of about 300°C concrete does not show appreciable loss of strength, but at about 500°C the 50% strength is lost.

Due to non-uniformity of temperature in the cross-section, the hottest layers of concrete and main reinforcement bars near the surface of the columns are separated due to the following factors:

1. Thermal creep
2. Loss of strength
3. Contraction of concrete

Thus the stresses in the center of the section are increased due to the above factors. In the central part of the section moderately hot concrete retains its strength and elasticity. The complete failure of the column takes place when the stresses in the central portion of the cross-section become equal to the initial prism strength of the concrete and deformation approaches its limiting value of 0.0025 to 0.0030.

22.17. Methods of rehabilitation of fire damaged concrete elements

1. Eccentrically loaded columns

The failure of eccentrically loaded columns takes place when the reinforcement bars in tension get heat up. In such cases, the fire resistance of the structural elements can be increased by increasing the thickness of the protective cover to the reinforcement.

2. R.C.C. slabs

The behaviour of R.C.C. slabs exposed to fire is governed by the temperature of the bottom reinforcement and heat transmission in concrete. The reinforcement bars are assumed to retain 50% of their original strength. The carrying capacity of the slab can be increased by increasing their thickness.

3. R.C.C. beams

Due to heating up, the bond between the transverse reinforcement and concrete is weakened considerably. The weakening of bond between the concrete and transverse reinforcement reduces the residual shear load carrying capacity of the beam to a great extent. The depth and width of the beam can be increased. The required increase in the dimensions of the beam, longitudinal and transverse reinforcement should be calculated by taking into account the changes in compressive strength of concrete and modulus of elasticity of concrete and steel.

4. Axially loaded columns

The load carrying capacity of axially loaded columns depends upon the cross-section of the column, coefficient of the change in strength of concrete due to high temperature and corresponding critical temperature. The carrying capacity can be restored by increasing the cross-section with suitable increase in the longitudinal reinforcement.

For restoring the damaged structures, the reinforcing bars can be anchored conveniently into the existing concrete walls and foundations by drilling holes in the concrete somewhat larger than the diameter of the bar and epoxy gel coated bar is set in the hole.

In case of slab also, the epoxy coated reinforcement may be used, but the thickness of epoxy coating should not be more than 0.25 mm.

QUESTIONS

1. Discuss common seismic deficiencies of structures.
2. Discuss the factors, which influence the rehabilitation plans of structures.
3. Discuss the methods of rehabilitation of masonry-cracked buildings in detail with neat sketch wherever possible.
4. Explain the process of strengthening beams and slab by inserting internal reinforcement and post tensioning methods.
5. Explain the process of Jacketing a member in detail.
6. Write a note on the rehabilitation of fire damaged R.C.C. buildings.
7. Strengthening of a member by..... jackating is done.
   (*a*) By inserting the internal reinforcing bars
   (*b*) By fixing plates by bolts or Epoxy etc.
   (*c*) By enlarging the cross-section of the element applying material all-round the element in full height.
   (*d*) By post tensioning the member.
8. Foundations can be strengthened by
   (*a*) By adding new load bearing elements to foundation.
   (*b*) By increasing the dimensions of the existing foundation.
   (*c*) By providing apron alround the structure
   (*d*) By improving the drainage of area
   (*e*) By any of the above methods.
9. Jacketing process usually is adopted for restoring the dimensions of the ......
   (*a*) Beam (*b*) Slab
   (*c*) Columns or pliers (*d*) Walls
10. Temperature upto......have no influence on concrete characteristics
    (*a*) 100°C (*b*) 300
    (*c*) 350°C (*d*) 450°C
11. Even the best quality concrete is affected at...... temperature
    (*a*) 600°C (*b*) 750°C
    (*c*) 825°C (*d*) 900°C
12. At a temperature of...... the strength of concrete reduces to 50%
    (*a*) 175°C (*b*) 420°C
    (*c*) 500°C (*d*) 375°C
13. The best fire resistant aggregate is......
    (*a*) Blast furnace aggregate (*b*) Gravel
    (*c*) Basalt (*d*) Sand stone aggregate
14. Lime stone expands at a constant rate upto a temperature......
    (*a*) 650°C (*b*) 900°C
    (*c*) 1050°C (*d*) 1250°C
15. In igneous rocks the best fire resistant aggregate is
    (*a*) Basalt (*b*) Dolerite

(*c*) Both are correct (*d*) Both are in correct

16. Concrete column collapse when the stress in the central portion of the cross-section develops deformations limiting to prism initial values of prism
(*a*) 0.0025 to 0.0030% (*b*) 0.025 to 0.035%
(*c*) 0.01 to 0.2% (*d*) 1.5 to 2.0%
17. The bond between the reinforcement and concrete near the surface of the concrete elements is destroyed due to
(*a*) Thermal creep (*b*) Loss of strength
(*c*) Contraction of concrete (*d*) Due to all the above factors
18. Fire damaged concrete elements can be rehabilitated by the......
(*a*) By increasing the thickness of the protective cover to the reinforcement
(*b*) In case of slabs they can be rehabilitated by increasing its thickness *i.e.* depth
(*c*) R.C.C. beam can be rehabilitated by increasing the area of cross-section of the beam, *i.e.* by increasing the dimensions of the cross-section of the beam it can be rehabilitated
(*d*) In case of columns, by increasing the area of cross-section of the column
(*e*) All are correct
19. Usually structures have earthquake deficiency
(*a*) Global strength deficiency (*b*) Global rigidity deficiency
(*c*) Load path deficiency (*d*) Shape deficiency
(*e*) Foundation deficiency (*f*) Plan deficiency
(*g*) All are correct
20. Buildings can be rehabilitated by......
(*a*) Adding new elements
(*b*) By increasing load bearing capacity of the existing elements
(*c*) By increasing the bond strength of different elements
(*d*) By removing the damaged elements
(*e*) All the above measures are correct
21. Cracks in buildings can be scaled by
(*a*) By filling concrete or cement sand mortar in wide cracks
(*b*) By stitching the cracks
(*c*) By inserting concrete blocks in every third or fifth course at a vertical interval of about 50 cm
(*d*) All are correct
22. The functions of sealer materials are
(*a*) To check the seepage to reinforcement
(*b*) To check the development of static pressure in joints
(*c*) To check the development of stains on the surface of the concrete
(*d*) To check the seepage problem on the far off surface of the concrete
(*e*) All are correct

ANSWERS

7. (*c*)	11. (*d*)	15. (*c*)	19. (*g*)
8. (*e*)	12. (*c*)	16. (*a*)	20. (*e*)
9. (*c*)	13. (*a*)	17. (*d*)	21. (*d*)
10. (*b*)	14. (*b*)	18. (*e*)	22. (*e*)

23
Tsunami

23.1. INTRODUCTION

Tsunamis are waves of water generated by rapid and large-scale disturbances of the sea. Tsunamis mainly are caused by under sea earthquakes. However Tsunamis may also be generated by land slides above land or under water or even by volcanic eruptions. Thrust earthquakes (opposite of strike slip) are far more likely to generate Tsunamis, but in a few cases small Tsunamis have occurred from large *i.e.* $M > 8.0$ strike slip earthquakes. The earthquake must be a shallow marine (sea) event that displaces the sea floor. In every case a large volume of water is displaced, leading to the generation of a series of long waves. After the generation of a Tsunami, its energy is distributed through out the water column irrespective of water depth. In deep oceans the speed of a Tsunami wave may be 800 km/h, but slows down to 30 to 60 km/h in shallow water zones.

23.2. GENERATION OF TSUNAMIS

Mainly Tsunamis waves are generated by rapid, large-scale disturbances of the sea, caused by under sea earthquakes. However Tsunamis waves can also be generated by above ground landslides or under water landslide, or volcanic eruptions. Thrust earthquakes are found generating more Tsunamis. The earthquake that generates Tsunami must be a shallow marine event that displaces the sea floor. In every case a large volume of water is displaced resulting in the generation of a series of long waves. After the generation of a Tsunami, its energy is distributed through out the water column, irrespective of water depth. The waves travel out wards on the surface of the ocean in all directions away from the source, similar to the ripples caused by throwing a piece of rock in the pond. The wavelength of the Tsunami waves and their period is governed by the generating mechanism and dimensions of the source event. The height of a Tsunami wave from trough to crest can vary from few centimeters to one metre or more in deep Ocean depending on the generating source. In deep ocean Tsunami waves can travel with high speeds for long periods over thousands of kilometers and lose very little energy in the process. The greater is the depth of water; greater is the speed of the Tsunami waves. In deep Ocean the speed of a Tsunami wave is found more than 800km/h, but slows down to 30 to 60 km/h in shallow water near the land.

Though Tsunamis occur at long interval, *i.e.* the frequency of Tsunami is not large, but their devastating effect is very large. At a coastline Tsunamis arrive as a series of successive crests (high water levels) and troughs (low water levels) usually at an interval of 10 to 45 minutes. As the Tsunamis waves enter the shallow waters of coastlines, bays or harbours, their speed decreases. For example in 15 m water depth the Tsunami wave speed may be about 45 km/h. However the speed of a second Tsunami wave traveling in deep water towards the same shore about 100 km behind the first wave may have much higher speed than the first wave. Similarly a third Tsunami wave behind the second wave may be travelling even with higher speed than the second one. As the Tsunami waves get compressed near the coast, their wave length gets shortened and their wave energy is directed upwards resulting in the increase of height and the force of the waves considerably.

Tsunami waves may hit the shore like a wall of water or move ashore as a fast moving tide or flood and carry everything along with them which comes in their way or path. The historic record shows that many Tsunamis have struck the shore with devastating force. Some times the height of Tsunami waves have been observed as high as 30 to 50 metres. It should be remembered that the Tsunami height (run up) of more than 1.0 m is dangerous, as the flooding by individual waves lasts from 10 to 30 seconds, but the danger can last for hours.

Tsunami waves can be distinguished from ordinary waves by their great wavelength often exceeding 100 km. (The distance between the two crests of a wave is called its wave length). The time lag between these crests may vary from 10 to 60 minutes. Usually the crest of a Tsunami wave is not distinuishable from rest of the wave. It is not seen by people abroad ships or noticed by any one sitting in a aeroplane. On the other hand waves generated by wind have wavelength varying from 100 to 200 m with time lag between crests varying from 5 to 20 seconds.

On the basis of available data, the history of Tsunamis is given in crononical order in the following paragraph.

The most ghastly Tsunami occurred in 1755 in the Atlantic Ocean due to Lisbon earthquake. In this mishap, due to actual earthquake and the resulting fire more than one lakh people were killed. In 1782 the fatalistic recorded Tsunami occurred in South China Sea. In this Tsunami 40,000 people were killed. The 1883 Tsunami caused by eruption of Korakatoa resulted in 36000 deaths. In 1908 Tsunami occurred in Messina (Italy) on the Mediterranean Sea, where 70,000 people were killed by Tsunami and earthquake.

Since 1900, the earthquakes recorded with a magnitude greater than 9.0 are as follows:

(*a*) 1960 Great Chilean earthquake (Magnitude 9.5)

(*b*) 1964 Good Friday earthquake in prince william sound (M-9.2)

(*c*) 9th March 1957 earthquake in the Andean Islands (M-9.1)

(*d*) 1952 off the south east coast of Kamchatka (M-9.0)

All these mega thrust earthquakes occurred in Pacific Ocean and caused Tsunamis. Alaskan earthquake in 1964 generated Tsunami with waves between 3 to 6 m high along the parts of the California, Oregon and Washington coasts. This caused more than 84 million dollar damage in Alaska with 123 deaths. Although Tsunamis are rare along the Atlantic coast line, a sever earthquake on November 18, 1929 in the Grand banks of New found land generated a Tsunami that caused considerable damage and loss of life at placenta Bay New found land In 1946, a Tsunami with waves of 6 to 9.5 m crest crashed into Hilo-Hawaii, flooding the down town area and killing 159 people.

23.3. 2004 TSUNAMI

According to records this Tsunami was the most devastating Tsunamis so far.

The 2004 Indian Ocean earthquake was of magnitude 9.3. This earthquake is known as Sumatra-Andaman earthquake. This earthquake occurred at 00:58:53 GMT and 07:58:53 local time under sea on 26.12.2004. The focus or hypocenter of the main earthquake was 3°-19′ N and 95°, 51.24′ E, some 160 km west of Sumatra at a depth of 30 km below sea mean level. This is at the extreme western end of the ring of fire, an earthquake belt that accounts for 81% of the world's largest earthquakes.

The earthquake of 26th December 2004 was felt as far away as Bangladesh, India, Malaysia, Mayannar, Thailand, Singapore and Maldives. This earthquake generated a series of devastating tsunamis, whose waves height

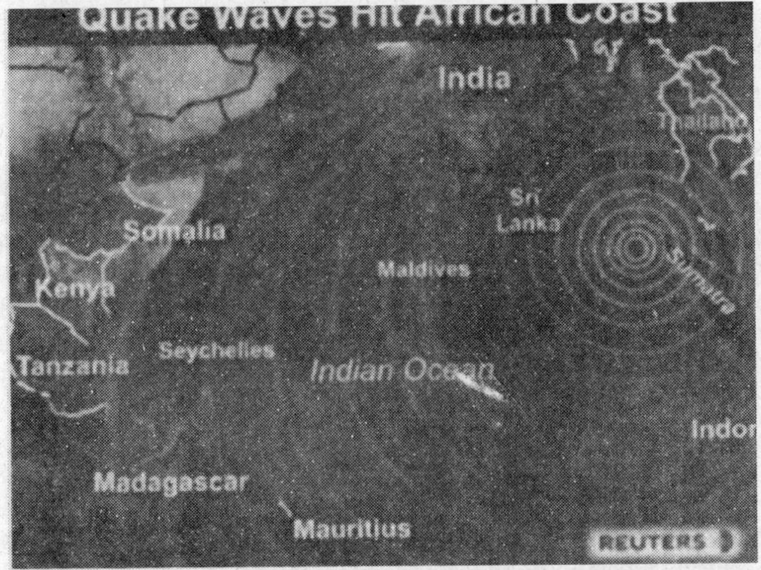

Fig. 23.1. Spread of the earthquake influence far away from the epicenter

was upto 30 m as shown in Fig. 23.1. These tsunami waves spread through out the Indian ocean, killing large number of people and inundating coastal communities across south and south east Asia, including parts of Indonesia, Sri Lanka, India and Thailand. This tsunami caused deaths and serious damage upto the coast of Africa; Deaths were recorded at 8000 km from its epicenter at port Elizabeth in South Africa. In this tsunami about three lakh (3,00,000) peoples have been killed in 11 countries of the region, including nationals of other 55 countries. About 7 billion U.S. dollars were donated by the world wide community to help the affected people by the earthquake.

Most of the major bridges, roadways and civil buildings were survived in the inundation of the waves of the coastal areas of India, Sri Lanka and Thailand. However low lying coastal resorts, businesses and private homes were severely damaged. Despite the low frequency of tsunami events, their severity and extreme consequences make the design of civil engineering structures in tsunami prone regions critical. In Japan efforts are under way at great cost and expense to ensure that ports are tsunami proof and populations living near the sea area are protected through appropriate construction and alerted through warning system.

23.3.1. Causes of 2004 Sumatra-Andaman Tsunami

Tectonic plate movement is believed to be the main cause of 2004 Indian Ocean earthquake and associated tsunami. The 26th December 2004 earthquake occurred along a subduction zone in which the Indian plate an oceanic plate is being subducted underneath the Burma plate. A general diagram of an oceanic subduction zone in the Sumatra-Andaman region is shown in Fig. 23.2. This figure explains, how the mega-thrust earthquake of Sumatra-Andaman occurred along the subduction zone and how the tsunami waves followed.

Fig. 23.3 shows the subduction zone where the Indian plate dives under the Burma plate. Here the water depth ranges from 1000 m to 4000 m.

The India plate is a part of the great Indo-Australian plate, which under lies the Indian ocean and Bay of Bengal. This India plate is drifting northeast at an average speed of 5 cm per year. The India plate meets the Australian plate at the Sunda Trench. (The Australian plate is considered a part of great Eurasian plate). At this point the India plate subducts the Burama plate, which carries the Nicobar Islands, the Andaman Islands and northern Sumatra. During this 26 Dec. 2004 earthquake an estimated 1200 km of fault line slipped about 15 m along the subduction zone where the India plate dives under the Burma plate.

It is believed that the direction of convergence shown by thick arrow in Fig. 23.4 of India plate relative to the over riding plate of subduction zone is oriented oblique to the trench axis. For an oblique subduction zone such as this, the strain can be partitioned in one of the two ways as shown in Fig. 23.4 (*b*).

Fitch in his paper has described the Sumatra subduction zone as a

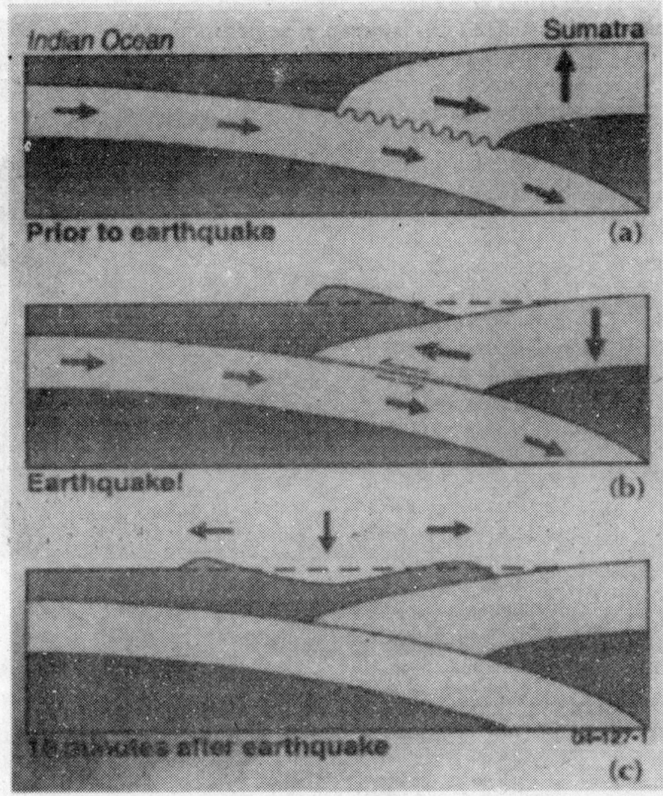

Fig. 23.2. Mechanism of formation of tsunami wave during 2004 Indian ocean earthquake

decoupled fault, in which nearly pure thrust faulting occurs along the inter plate thrust and trans current, strike slip faulting occurs in the over riding plate.

Krishna, Sanu and Milson have described the seismo tectonic environment of Sumatra subduction zone in detail. According to them, the Dec. 26, 2004 slip did not happen instantaneously, but took place in two phases over a period of several minutes. Seismographic and acoustic data shows that in the first phase a rupture of about 400 km long and 100 km wide was formed about 30 km beneath the sea bed. This rupture was the longest ever thought to have been caused by a earthquake *i.e.* this rupture was longest in the history of earthquakes. In the first instance the rupture proceeded with a speed of about 2.8 km/sec (10,000 km/hour) beginning from the coast of Aceh and proceeded in north-westernly direction over a period of about 100 seconds. It stopped or paused for about 100 seconds before starting again. After the pause of about 100 seconds the rupture continued again northwards towards the Andaman and Nicobar Islands. However the northern rupture occurred more slowly than the south. The speed of rupture was about 2.1 km/sec. It continued in north

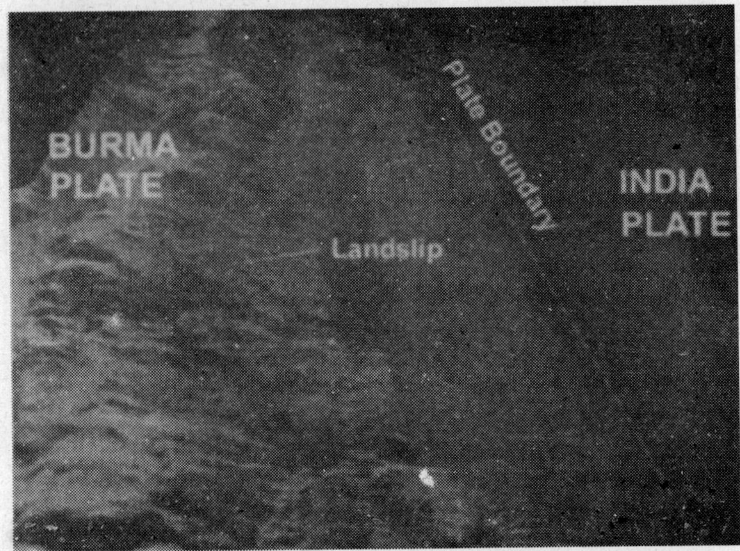

Fig. 23.3. Subduction zone where the Indian plate dives under the Burma plate

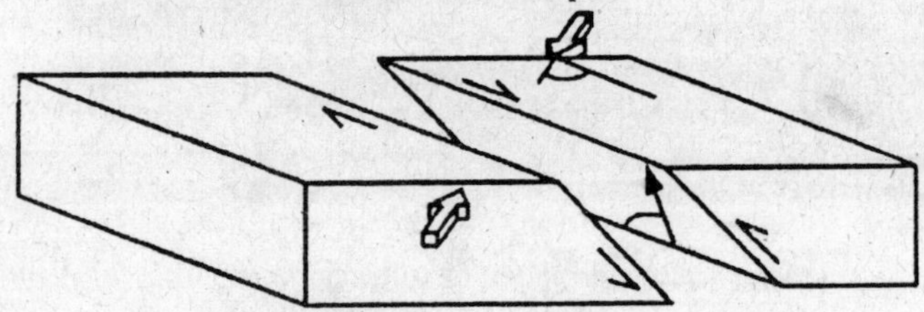

(*a*) Oblique Faulting: thrust/right-lateral faulting

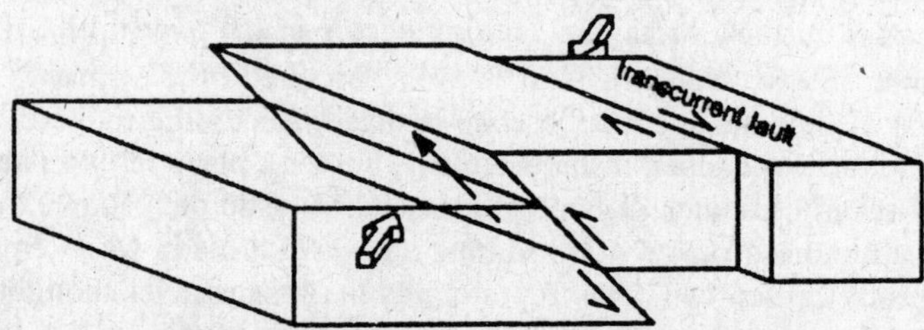

(*b*) Decoupled Faulting: pure thrust faulting

Fig. 23.4. Faulting modes of Tectonic plates of Sumatra Subduction zone

direction for about an other five minutes to a plate boundary, where the fault changes from subduction to strike slip (where the two plates push each other in opposite direction). This resulted in the reduced speed of the water displaced, hence reducing the size of the tsunami that hit the northern part of the Indian Ocean.

Further due to the sideways movements of the two plates, the sea bed is estimated to have risen by several metres, displacing an estimated 30 km^3 of water and generating devastating tsunami waves. The tsunami waves did not originate from a point source, but radiated out wards along the entire 1200 km length of the rupture. This greatly increased the geographical area over which the waves were observed reaching as far as Mexico, Chile and Arctic. The raising of the sea bed significantly reduced the capacity of the Indian Ocean (Big ship could not pass the Indian Ocean). This rise in sea bed has produced permanent rise in the global sea level by about 0.1 mm.

23.4. CHARACTERISTICS OF TSUNAMI WAVES

(*a*) Speed of travel of tsunami waves

Tsunamis displace a large volume of water resulting in the generation of series of long waves. The amplitude of these waves is small (less than 1m) in deep water, but the speed of these waves is very high. The speed of tsunami is found approximately proportional to the square root of the depth of water. The magnitude of velocity is given by the following equation.

(*a*) $$V = (g.D)^{1/2} \text{ in deep sea water for } \left(\frac{D}{L} < \frac{1}{20}\right)$$

(*b*) $$V = \left(\frac{g.L}{2H}\right)^{1/2} \text{ for } \frac{D}{L} > \frac{1}{2}$$

where

D = Water depth in m

L = Wavelength in m from crest to crest of the wave

H = Depth of wave from crest to trough in m

g = Gravitation of earth. Its value is 9.81/sec^2 but for simplicity in calculations, it may be taken as 10.0.

Waves break when approximately D = 1.28 H or L = 7 H.

For the average depth of the Pacific Ocean basin 4300 m, the speed of tsunami would be about 740 km/hour, while for the basin's greatest depth (10912 m at Marianas trench) the speed would be about 1180 km/hour.

When a tsunami approaches a coastline, its speed decreases drastically and its height increases substantially often reaches 15 m or more.

The velocity and wavelength given in the following Table 23.1 are calculated on the basis of shallow water approximation. However with the rapid accelerations and accelerations associated with turbulent flow in fast moving tsunami bore and surges, *Keuleugen* has revised the shallow water relation as follows:

$$V = 2\,(g.D)^{1/2}$$

From the normal shore line bathymetry features, as the tsunami approaches the land, the speed of the wave decreases, but the height of the wave increases

Table 23.1. Velocity and wave length of Tsunami wave for given depth of ocean

Depth in m	*Velocity km/h*	*Wave length in km*
7000	943	282
4000	713	213
2000	504	151
200	159	48
50	79	23
10	36	10.6

and wave length decreases. It has been observed that the off shore and coastal features can change the size and impact of tsunami waves. Deep water close to the shore hampers the build up of a very high wave. A coral reef can act as a breakwater reducing tsunami's energy to some extent. However a V shaped bay can act as a funnel, concentrating the energy of the tsunami into a smaller area. When tsunami waves hit the mouth or delta of a river or harbour inlets, they often form a bore, a steep rapidly advancing wave with almost a vertical face. In this process an enormous wall of water builds up and then inundate the land like a tide flood. The surge momentum may increase the height of the waves at shoreline to give a run up height upto 2 to 5 times, when particle velocity with in the wave exceeds wave velocity for a breaking wave. A non-breaking wave does not amplify the run up height. This build up may be higher than 30 m for tsunami waves generated near the epicenter of the earthquake. For distant origin tsunami the height of waves may be 15 m or so.

It has been observed that 3 to 6 m height of tsunami waves are very distructive. A non-breaking wave un like breaking wave develops a large inundation distance due to limited drag forces. The energy of a wave becomes less concentrated as the wave spreads. Hence a tsunami has more energy when it strikes the shore line that is relatively close to its point of origin, than when it reaches a distant coast.

Usually tsunami inundation is restricted to a narrow strip of land along the coast. Prior 2004 Indian ocean tsunami, coastal planners opined that tsunami would never inundate land more than 3.2 km (2 miles). But satellite imagery of the Indonesia coastline suggests that 2004 Indian ocean tsunami inundated sufficiently more than 3.2 km land in some areas.

Tsunami typically reach the coast in the form of multiple waves. The first wave may seem to be a negative (it seems to be a receding water) but often is not the wave of largest magnitude. There might be three or four waves of considerable magnitude. The smaller wave might occur for a day or longer period. After inundation the draw down of water may create even stronger currents with severe consequences for coastal structures from both direct impact and scouring around piers and piles.

When tsunamis are generated by a local earthquake, the impact of tsunami is compounded by the earthquake impact. Prior to the arrival of the tsunami wave, severe ground shaking may take place. This may cause potential loss of life and damage to buildings and infrastructure including bridges and evacuation routes. In case the local earthquake leads to substantial coastal subsidence, the impact of the tsunami is compounded by long-term changes in vertical elevations, leading to potential submergence of important infrastructure and resources.

23.5. TSUNAMI MAGNITUDE SCALES

Similar to earthquake intensity scales, tsunamis are also quantified by magnitude scales, which are derived from the measurements of run up (maximum wave height on shore). This height is measured above the normal height of seawater. Two measures are widely used for tsunami magnitude as follows:

The comparison of the two scales is shown in Table 23.2.

1. Iida method of tsunami magnitude m.
2. Ambrasey's, tsunami intensity K_0.

1. Tsunami magnitude m = log 2 H.

where H is the maximum observed or measured run up height in metres.

2. Tsunami intensity method K_0 = log 2 $H^{1/2}$

K_0 is known as modified sieberg seismic sea wave intensity scale.

The development of various wave height (run-up) in different global regions is shown in the following Table 23.3.

Table 23.2. A comparison between Iida's and Ambrasey's tsunami magnitude, defining degree of damage

m	*K*0	*Run up (Height in m)*	*Disciption*
– 2	i	0.25	Very light, smallest tsunami perceptible on very sensitive tide gauge.
0	ii	1.00	Light, noticed by those living along the flat shore and familiar with sea.
1	iii	2.00	Rather strong. Generally noticed due to flooding of gently sloping coasts. Light sailing vessels carried away on shore. Slight damage to light structures situated near the coast. In estuaries reversal of river flow for some distance up stream.
2	iv	4.0	Strong, flooding of the shore to some depth. Light scouring of man made ground. Embankments and dykes damaged. Light structures near the coast damaged. Solid structures on the coast damaged, big sailing vessels and small ships drifted inland or carried out to sea. Coasts littered with floating debris.

m	K_0	*Run up (Height in m)*	*Disciption*
4	v	16.00	Very strong. General flooding of the shore to some depth. Quay walls and solid structures near the sea damaged. Light structures damaged. Severe scouring of cultivated land and littering of the coast with the floating items and sea animals. With the exception of big ships all other types of vessels carried inland or out to sea. Big bores in Estuary Rivers. Harbour works damaged. People drowned. Wave accompanied by strong roar.
6	vi	64.00	Disastrous. Partial or total destruction of man made structures for some distance from the shore. Flooding of coast to great depths. Big ships severely damaged. Trees uprooted or broken. Many causalvalties.
8	–	256.00	Catastrophic damage on transoceanic scale. Typical oceanic island collapse, generated tsunami.
10	–	1000.00	Large asteroid effect generated tsunami.

23.6. TSUNAMI HAZARD RISK ASSESSMENT AND WORKING SYSTEM

23.6.1. Introduction

Tsunamis hazards risk assessment and other coastal hazards is a critical component of a global over all warning and mitigation system. Hazard assessment and risks are characterized based on documentation of historic events and impacts, wave propagation and inundation modeling of an expected range of hazards, modeling and traditional knowledge. Hazard maps are developed and used to communicate risk to vulnerable coastal communities. For the proper analysis of risk assessment, data on critical life line infrastructure, marine port facilities, population demographics and land use is required. The results of hazard risk assessment serve as the basis for decision-making support mechanisms and to identify and implement a range of mitigation measures that will reduce the vulnerability of coastal communities to tsunami and other hazards.

Similar to the existing system in the North Pacific Ocean, a warning net work in the Indian ocean would need the following components:

(*a*) Sensors to detect earthquakes and ocean waves. Computers and scientists to analyse the data and issue warnings.

(*b*) Communications equipments to transmit a warning.

(*c*) Local emergency action teams to translate the warning into quick evacuation.

The objective of the pacific Tsunami warning system (PTWS) is to detect, locate and determine the magnitude of potentially tsunamigenic earthquakes occurring in pacific basin or its immediate neighbourhood. Earthquake

Table 23.3. Run up in metres with their return periods in years for various seas

Run up m	*Mediterr-anean sea*	*Black Sea*	*Indian Ocean*	*Notth American Oean*	*Caribean Sea*	*South Amrican Sea*	*Hawii Sea*	*New Zealand Sea*	*SW Pacific Sea*
10	250	1000	1000	1000	1000	200	200	250	200
15	1000	—	—	—	—	750	—	1000	—
20	—	—	—	—	—	1000	1000	—	1000

information is provided by seismic stations operated by PTWC, Asian Tsunami warning centre (ATWC), the U.S. Geological Survey's National Earthquake information centre and international sources. If the location and magnitude of a earthquake meet the known criteria for generation of a tsunami, then a tsunami warning is issued to warn of an imminent tsunami hazard.

The warning includes the predicted tsunami arrival times at the selected coastal sites with in the geographic area defined by the maximum distance the tsunami could travel in a few hours. If a significant tsunami is detected by sea level monitoring instrumentation, the tsunami warning is extended to the entire pacific basin. Sea level or tidal information is provided by National Ocean Atmospheric Administration (USA) service, PTWC, ATWC. University monitoring networks and other participating nations of the PTWC. The international tsunami information centre, part of the intergovernmental oceanographic commission monitors and evaluates the performance and effectiveness of the pacific tsunami warning system. This effort encourages the most effective data collection, data analysis, tsunami impact assessment, and warning dissemination to all tsunami warning systems participants.

In the India ocean region most countries have only limited information to support the hazard risk assessment of tsunami. In many countries historical record of earthquake is available, but not historic records of tsunami due to the rare nature of these events. Few countries have incorporated local and traditional knowledge of evaluation of tsunami risks.

Now there is a general trend to improve the risk assessment capabilities in the region with in the frame work of overall disaster management and to produce a uniform guideline for risk assessment based on the wide experience available among countries of the region. The capabilities of the respective countries vary considerably based on the availability of expertise, tools for analysis, and quality of data. All these elements are essential for risk assessment. The need to develop mathematical models for tsunami wave propagation near the shore and onshore that can accommodate all local feature and for training on the use of such models for risk assessment has been identified. Development of evacuation maps based on hazard risk assessment and traditional community knowledge are essential as one part of an over all ·al to reduce vulnerability and to promote coastal community resilience.

Following activities should be included in the plan on hazard assessment.

1. Prepare guidelines for tsunami risk assessment as part of a multi hazard risk management framework.
2. Provide guidance to emergency response managers on the preparation of risk assessment activities.
3. Facilitate the use and application of the model outputs for the tsunami hazard and risk assessment.
4. Facilitate the data sharing, including access to and development of database, incorporating exposure tsunami hazard and vulnerability.

5. Facilitate capacity building, including knowledge transfer in the form of training programme, workshops, and case studies for risk assessment in all Indian Ocean countries.
6. Promote and facilitate the process of developing cost effective and practical measures and options for mitigation of risk.
7. To have liason with other modeling committees and organizations or professional bodies engaged in developing models and data for their implementation.

23.6.1.1. Results expected from above activities

Following results are expected from the above activities:

(*a*) **Inundation maps.** These maps show the inundated (flooded) areas and the height of waves. These maps are useful to assess the maximum areas to be affected by the tsunami waves.

(*b*) **Hazard maps.** These maps show the areas to be inundated by the tsunami waves.

(*c*) **Risk maps.** These maps show the total potential impact of all tsunami effects on the build environment, population, local and regional economy.

(*d*) **Evacuation maps.** These maps include safe areas and shelters against tsunami, how to reach there and where to go based on hazard risk assessment.

(*e*) **Decision-making.** For appropriate mitigation option decision making support has to be given.

23.6.2. Modeling

Numerical modeling, forecasting and scenario development are integral and important components of an overall tsunami warning and mitigation system. One of the main objects of the numerical simulation is the prediction of arrival time and height of tsunami waves. In other words the aim is to forecast the tsunami event before its actual attack. Though since 1990 much advancement has been made through collection of post tsunami survey data, that is used to improve the model, but accurate predictions still are not possible as many of the crucial parameter values are not available till some times after the event. In spite of all these draw backs the simulation of worst-case scenarios are important components of planning for emergency response as well as for preparedness and mitigation.

Some countries have the capacity to carry out numerical modeling, but accurate bathymetric and topographic data required for inundation models are absent for the most vulnerable coasts. Inundation maps are required as the basis for risk assessment and emergency response.

To develop the expertise to conduct tsunami inundation modeling in the region will be a challenge. In addition to training programs and advanced degrees trough universities, the other promising tool to reach a large community will be through computation portals or other web base technologies that can offer ways to transfer modeling expertise and capabilities to many. In the Indian Ocean region technical assistance and training in numerical modeling is one of the most required activities. The action plan should include planning, on going, and proposed actions for modelling as part of regional implementation plan.

23.6.3. Warning centers

For achieving the overall objective of establishing an exhaustive tsunami warning and mitigation system for the Indian Ocean region, warning centers are required to be established. These warning centers should be capable to collect, analyse the information, formulate, and disseminate the appropriate warnings. Warning centers will include Regional Tsunami watch provider (RTWP) and National Tsunami Warning Centres (NTWC).

23.6.3.1. Capabilities required of a RTWP

For a Regional Tsunami Watch Provider Centre following capabilities are required:

1. It should be capable to be operated as multi hazard or multi purpose center.
2. It should be capable to be operated as a contingency plan centre to secure infrastructure and uninterruptible power supply to ensure continuous operation.
3. It should have capacity to back up another RTWP and continue the other provider's full capabilities.
4. It should have the capacity to collect all available data in seismic and oceano graphic field, analyse and interpret the information, and it should have the ability to under take numerical modeling.
5. It should have communication infrastructure capable of effective disseminating all information to all recipients.

For providing the relevant information to the final recipient, radio and Internet is a community-based system in developing and remote locations.

23.6.4. Mitigation, Preparedness and Response

A tsunami cannot be prevented, but its impact can be reduced through community and emergency preparedness, timely warning, effective response and public education. mitigation, preparedness, and response to tsunamis and other coastal hazards are key components of a warning and mitigation system for the Indian Ocean region.

Structural mitigation measures must be incorporated into the site selection, design and construction of structures and support infrastructures. Non-structural mitigation measure such as establishment of coastal buffer zones and protection of coastal vegetation and habitats, reduce vulnerability of coastal populations to tsunami and other hazards.

Preparedness activities initiated by responsible government agencies along with community organizations and other private establishments are essential for developing advance capacity to respond to the consequences of tsunamis. For receiving and responding tsunami, warnings system and infrastructure must be in place and it should be tested regularly.

Evacuation plans based on hazard risk assessment are required. To check the awareness of the public regular drills of evacuation response must be carried out. To respond to disaster events caused by tsunami and other coastal hazards, National emergency recovery plans and mechanism must be established. These measures include regular assessment of critical infrastructure and lifeline support facilities, rescue operation capacity, and emergency assistance etc.

The regional goals for Indian Ocean emergency response, preparedness, and mitigation are in the process of being developed. The interim regional goals are given below.

1. To develop, promote and share best practice of information of tsunami. development of capacity and resilience, and emergency management to improve the management of tsunami risk through mitigation. preparedness, response and recovery activities.
2. To develop main stream tsunami warning and mitigation system. This should include policy and project identification, sector policies, risk mitigation and recovery processes.
3. To lead, monitor and coordinate the emergency response, inter agency coordination committees and organizations responsible for disaster reduction and management must be established in countries through out the Indian Ocean region.
4. For coastal regions, National and local emergency response plans must be prepared and regular drills and exercises should be undertaken for preparedness in countries through out the Indian Ocean.
5. Coastal communities should undertake the sustained efforts to reduce the risks from tsunami and other coastal hazards.
6. To educate the people about tsunami risks, warning system and response, massive campaigns should be under taken in coastal regions.

Further to reduce the risk from tsunami and other coastal hazards special attention must be given to develop and practice tsunami evacuation plans based on hazard risk assessment. Community and local government preparedness should be assessed on regular basis. Structural and non-structural reduction measures must be main streamed *i.e.* they should be given main attention. But most of the coastal areas in the Indian Ocean region do not have emergency response plans that could effectively reach all vulnerable coastal and rural communities. The key activities of a mitigation, preparedness, and response plan are as follows:

(*a*) Developing capacity of national and local agencies and institutions to prepare for and respond to emergencies.

(*b*) To develop national and local tsunami emergency response plans with evacuation maps.

(*c*) To assess critical and infrastructure for emergency response.

(*d*) To conduct emergency response drills for all stake holders including public.

(*e*) To conduct regular public awareness campaigns. Tsunami and disaster preparedness should be included in education curricula of schools.

(*f*) For the effective communication of risk, warning and response partnership should be developed with communication media.

(*g*) To reduce tsunami impact, structural and non-structural measures must be implemented.

23.6.5. Capacity Building

To achieve an effective and durable tsunami warning and reducing or mitigation system capacity must be developed in the Indian Ocean region. Capacity development activities required to be planned and programmed both at regional and individual country levels. The capacity development must contain a broad spectrum of activities including training, institutional development, technology development, enhancement and transfer for all components of a comprehensive tsunami warning and mitigation system.

Regional goals for capacity building are in the process of being developed. The interim regional goals are as follows. They are tentative and may be revised when needed.

(*a*) The long and intermediate term plans are developed and resources allocated to develop capacity to sustain a comprehensive warning and reducing or mitigation system.

(*b*) The working groups should identify capacity development activities. They should be executed through international, bilateral and national funds.

(*c*) Tsunami related capacity development activities should be developed so that they may be integrated with in the national disaster management frame works.

UNESCO-IOC has incorporated following principles for capacity building:

1. Capacity development help or interventions are required to be incorporated in the ongoing regional projects that contribute directly to the larger Indian Ocean Centres mandate *i.e.*. "To promote international cooperation in protection of the marine environment and preservation of human life and property in the ocean and coastal areas and work to wards sustainable developments."
2. Capacity development programs should be prepared based on proposals drafted by regional scientists who define and determine their own capacity development programs.

These proposals should be as follows:

(*a*) Identify the areas for regional collaboration.

(*b*) Select partners through clear enunciation of their requirements.

(*c*) Seek funds in a business like manner by delivering products of public good.

In short the capacity development or building help or interventions should be structured to have long term impacts. This requires interventions both in know how and know why. Further the help or interventions should target development of both research and operational capabilities. The capacity development must be done in wholehearted manner involving appropriate decision makers, directors of institutes, scientists, technicians and civil society. Interventions should be treated as investment. Active contacts must be maintained with participants, strategic partners, collaborating institutions, key decision makers, funding organizations and thought leaders in relevant scientific disciplines are also important elements in capacity development. Thus active contacts must be maintained with all of them.

The capacity development interventions must optimize the limited resources and eliminate duplication and over lap. For this purpose-maintaining liasion closely is required with other agencies that also provide capacity development services to improve coordination and increase efficiency. The majority of capacity development initiatives should focus on developing regions. The implications of these principles are that with the limited resources Inter Governmental Oceano graphic Commission (IOC) cannot and should not address all capacity development requirements.

The existing capacity development deficiencies have been identified in national assessments conducted with Indian Ocean member countries. Some of the identified regional capacity development requirements are as follows:

1. To develop inundation maps and evaluate tsunami hazards and vulnerability, training and software for numerical modeling is required.
2. To achieve instrumentation standards and requirements for regional seismic and sea level monitoring, core stations and proper training is required.
3. To develop or build capacity up grade and maintain tsunami detection instrumentation warning centers and dissemation system requires long-term capacity development program.
4. To develop coastal community resilience to tsunami and other coastal hazards requires a long-term capacity development program.

23.7. CAPACITY WARNING SYSTEM

When ever our (earth) planet flexes its natural muscles, it often creates hazards for those who live on its surface. The tsunami of December 2004, which struck in south East Asia and parts of Africa is a reminder of earth's power. Though we are unable to control the flexing of earth's muscles, but we should be able to provide necessary resources and warning to people to minimize the losses of life and property from the natural disasters. Though during December 2004 tsunami, its impact was felt after a time lag of several hours after the generation of the earthquake, which generated tsunami. But almost all its victums were taken completely by surprise. The reason for this was the fact that there were no tsunami warning systems in the Indian Ocean to detect tsunamis and equally important warning system to warn the general public living around the ocean. Tsunami detection is not easy because in deep waters the height of tsunami waves is very low and network of sensors is required to detect it. Setting up a communication infrastructure to issue timely warnings is an even bigger problem.

The tsunami warning system is a system to detect tsunamis and issue warning to prevent loss of life and property. It contains two equally important components as follows:

1. A network of sensors to detect tsunamis.
2. A communication infrastructure to issue timely warnings to allow evacuation of coastal areas.

In the Indian Ocean an warning system would require the following three components.

(*a*) Sensors to detect earthquakes and ocean waves, and computers, scientists/technicians to analyse the data and issue warnings.

(*b*) To transmit warnings, a communification equipment.

(*c*) To translate the warning to quick evacuation local emergency response teams.

23.7.1. Types of warning systems

There are two distinct warning system as follows:

1. International tsunami warning systems
2. Regional warning systems.

Both these systems depend on the fact that tsunamis in open water travel at a speed about 0.14 and 0.28 km/s, while earthquake waves travel with a typical speed of 4.0 km/sec, which is much more than tsunami waves. Thus tsunami waves can be detected easily from those of seismic waves on the basis of their speed. This gives time for possible tsunami forecast to be made and a warning to be issued to the threatened areas if needed. Untill a reliable modal capable to correlate earthquakes to tsunami is available; alarm raised by measuring seismic waves only should be treated as warnings. To be sure, tsunami waves must be observed in open water as far as possible from the coast, using real time operating sea floor observatories.

The first elementary tsunami warning system to warn the communities of impending tsumani was tried in Hawaii in 1920. More advanced working systems were developed after 1.4.1946 and 23.5.1960 tsunamis which caused massive destruction in Hilo, Hawaii.

Americans felt the real power of tsunamis on March 28, 1964 when an earthquake of magnitude 8.4 caused tsunami, which caused massive devastation in Alaska. This earthquake was the largest earthquake of twentieth century in the Northern Hemisphere. In this earthquake some areas were raised as much as 15 m and other subsided. The resulting pacific wide tsunami destroyed Alaska's port facilities and affected entire California coast line. In this tsunami 120 people were killed.

After 1964 tsunami, the west coast tsunami-warning center was built at palmer, Alaska in 1967. Subsequently this center was combined with a center built in 1949 in Hawaii to protect people living along the U.S. pacific coast. These two centers have combined observations and monitoring with research into the mechanics of tsunami to offer warning when a tsunami might strike. The center in Hawaii has become a partner of the United Nations intergovernmental Oceanographic Commission (IOC) and international coordination group (ICG) to provide timely tsunami warnings to other pacific nations.

These warning centers are connected to seismic monitors around the globe and sea level monitors in Deep Ocean and harbours around the Pacific Ocean. Whenever a earthquake occurs, scientists are alerted to analyse the earthquake rapidly. In case the earthquake exceeds a magnitude of 7.5, and is near a coastline, a tsunami warning is issued immediately for the area around the earthquake. The warning center then monitors sea level instruments to ascertain the actual generation of the tsunami.

If the instruments detect that the tsunami is small, then the warning is cancelled. If the tsunami detected is a large one, the warning is expanded to all coastlines of the pacific.

The National Oceanic and Atmospheric Administration (NOA) has been conducting research on the causes and consequences of tsunamis and to help detect and warn of their presence for more than thirty years.

The first deep sea assessment and reporting tsunamis (DART) "tsunami meter" or buoy, was developed in engineering laboratory of NOAA's Pacific Marine Environmental Laboratory (PMEL) in Seattle (Washington). DART systems use bottom pressure recorders capable to detecting and measuring a tsunami with amplitude as small as 1 cm in 6000 m depth of water. The data is then relayed by acoustic modem to a surface tsunami meter or buoy, which transmits the information to a ground station via satellite.

PMEL started work on developing DART system in 1987 and a prototype system was deployed for two months off the Washington oregon coast in the summer of 1995. The surface buoy performed well but the data loss of approximately 5% was noted. In 1997 a redesigned system was developed in deep water off Oahu (Hawaii). This new system was designed to reduce the data loss. The deep-water test was found successful and two demonstration systems were subsequently fabricated and tested.

Lack of warning in the ocean coasts caused many unnecessary deaths when the tsunami occurred there. Many analysts claimed that the disaster would have been mitigated, had there been an effective warning system in place. In January 2005, in United Nations Conference in Kobe (Japan) it was agreed to establish an Indian Ocean tsunami warning system to provide a warning to inhabitants bordering the Indian ocean of approaching tsunamis as an initial step towards an international early warning program. Thus an interim tsunami warning system was established in Indian Ocean in April 2005. At present twenty-six countries in the region have established official Tsunami Warning Focal Points (TWFP) to receive interim advisory information based on seismological and sea level information from the operation centers serving the pacific in Hawaii and Tokyo. The Indian Ocean tsunami warning system became active in June 2006 following the lead by UNESCO.

The Intergovernmental coordination group for the Indian ocean tsunami warning and mitigation system at present is serving as the regional body to plan and coordinate the design and implementation of an effective and durable tsunami warning and mitigation system. It consists 25 seismographic stations relaying information to 26 national tsunami information centers as well as three deep ocean sensors. However UNESCO has asked more coordination between governments and methods of relaying information from the centers to the civilians at risk are required to make the system more effective. The over all objective of Indian Ocean Tsunami warning system (IOTWS) is to efficiently identify and effectively mitigate the hazards posed by the local and distant tsunamis. To achieve this objective an end-to-end tsunami warning system is required. The system includes hazard detection and forecast, threat evaluation and alert formulation, alert dissemination of public safety massages and preparedness and response.

In order to achieve the over all objective of establishing a comprehensive tsunami warning and mitigation system for the Indian Ocean region, warning centers are required to collect and analyse the information and formulate and disseminate appropriate warning. Warning centers will include Regional Tsunami Watch Providers (RTWP) and National Tsunami Warning Centres (NTWC). The capabilities of an RTWP are as follows:

1. Where ever feasible RTWP should function as a multi hazard or multi purpose center.
2. It should be capable to secure infrastructure and un interruptible power supply to ensure continuous operation.
3. It should have the capacity to back up another RTWP and continue the other provider's full capabilities.
4. It should have the capacity to collect all data in real time (seismic and oceano graphic situation), analyse and interpret the information. It should also have the ability to undertake numerical modeling.
5. It should be capable of effectively dissemating all informations to all recipients.

Amongst several systems developed for providing the relevant information to the final (last) recipient, a system known as RENET has been found effective for the purpose. This system is a community based communications program designed to reach the last destination in developing nations and remote locations. The program is a collective effort of meteorological services, related national agencies and non-governmental organizations to make weather, climate and related information available and useful to rural or remote communities. To transmit critical information from city centers to rural population, the RENET program has combined unique satellite broadcast capacities with Internet applications and the use of FM radio, HF radio and other terrestrial broadcast capacities.

23.8. PLANNING PROTECTION GUIDELINES FOR TSUNAMIS

23.8.1. Principles

Tsunamis are much more frequent i.e. frequency of tsunamis in the pacific ocean is very high due to the occurrence of earthquakes in the region known as "Ring of fire". In this region about 81% earthquake occurs. In this region an effective tsunami warning system also exists. Though the western edge of the "Ring of fire" extends into the Indian Ocean where 2004 tsunami struek, but no warning system of tsunami exists in this region or ocean. In spite of frequent occurrence of earthquakes in Indonesia, tsunamis are relatively rare. In Indonesia the last major tsunami was caused by the Kraktoa eruption of 1883.

It should be remembered that all earthquake do not produce large tsunami waves. For example on March 28, 2005 a 8.7 magnitude earthquake hit roughly the same areas of the Indian Ocean (where 26th December 2004 tsunami occurred) but did not cause major tsunami.

It is estimated that in U.S.A. almost all the 500 cities with in the pacific states of Alaska, California, Oregon, Hawaii and Washington are susceptible to tsunamis. In these states about 9 lakh people live under the shadow of 15 m high tsunami. These statistics led the states and federal agencies to a joint effort under the umbrella of the National Tsunami Hazard Mitigation program to improve the design and planning of coastal communities for tsunami hazards.

Efforts were made to prepare the guidelines for the use of officials involved at the local and state level in "planning, zoning, drafting regulations, community development and related land use and development in the coastal regions". These guidelines are based on the following principles:

1. Know your community's tsunami risk, hazard, vulnerability and exposure.
2. To minimize future tsunami losses, avoid new development in tsunami run up areas.
3. To minimize future tsunami damage and loss of life, relocate and configure the new plans for existing development in tsunami run up areas.
4. To minimize the tsunami damage, new buildings should be designed and

constructed in such a way so that they may be least affected by tsunami.

5. The existing development must be protected from tsunami losses through modifications, redevelopment, retrofit and land reuse plans and projects.
6. Special precautions must be taken in locating and designing infrastructure and critical facilities to minimize tsunami damage.
7. To plan for evacuation at short notice.

23.8.2. Public Awareness and Protection Planning

23.8.2.1. Community education and awareness

To reduce the loss of life and property, hazard community education and awareness programs are essential both for tsunami and earthquakes. In U.S.A., Oregon is one of the states that is exposed to the threat of a mega tsunami from a large earthquake originating from the Cascadia Subduction Zone (CSZ). But as yet no devastating CSZ tsunami has occurred in modern times. A survey conducted in mid 1980's showed that most of the Oregon coastal population was unaware of tsunami as a threat.

The increased scientific evidence over the time has started suggesting the history of infrequent occurrence of tsunamis. Oregon estate agencies and coastal planners started collaborating with the scientific community and with federal agencies particularly with the National Oceanic and Atmospheric Administration (NOAA) and the Federal Emergency Management Agency (FEMA) to under stand and address the "new" threat. The role of community education and awareness as essential tools for effective mitigation of tsunami became truly clear only with the 1992 Nicaragua and 1993 Okushiri (Japan) tsunamis, and associated post tsunami surveys. Though these both events caused approximately equal number of deaths (200 each), but the deaths occurred in totally different circumstances.

In the case of Okushiri, event population had the knowledge of tsunami occurrence. They reacted in minutes to the ground shaking as sign of tsunami and to tsunami sirens and used preplanned evacuation routes to reach the safe places and prevented death of thousands of people. Where as in the case Nicaragua, an unprepared population suffered the loss of life that could have been easily avoided. Since early 1990's Oregon has become a USA leader in community education and awareness for tsunamis. Learning from the experiences of Hawaiians and Japanese, Oregon sate agencies have collaborated with the local communities and with federal agencies to implement programs that include the followings:

(*a*) Dissemination of literature to residents and tourists.
(*b*) Class room education.
(*c*) Public oriented web sites.
(*d*) Tsunami sirens.
(*e*) Street signs directing the population to tsunami evacuation routes.

(*f*) Coastal offices with mandates to provide technical support to coastal planners on tsunami issues. Now similar initiatives are being taken by the pacific states of USA and Japan.

The December 26, 2004 tsunami gave a grim remainder that such basic and relatively in expensive measures must be taken world wide and must be sustained over a period of time, as tsunamis are rare events in most of the region of the world. The recurrence interval of tsunamis has been found of centuries. When they do not occur for decades, they are easily forgotten.

23.8.2.2. Hazard Risk Assessment

To identify and implement the mitigation measures that will reduce the vulnerability of coastal communities to tsunami and other hazards, hazard risk assessment is essential. The following two rules are the basic rules for the safety from tsunami. These rules are based on past experience.

(*a*) As soon as you learn about tsunami's occurrence, run to a place higher than 15 m above sea level.

(*b*) This higher place or ground must be at leat 3.2 km away from the shore line.

These two rules may provide basic first order guidance to individuals. But the planning and designing for a coastal community needs for more sophisticated information and a high level details are required.

The hazard assessment and risks are characterized and based on documentation of historical events and their impacts, wave propagation and inundation modeling of a region for an expected range of hazards. A proper analysis of risks includes the following factors:

(*i*) Assessment of critical lifelines

(*ii*) Infrastructure.

(*iii*) Marine port facilities.

(*iv*) Inclusion of traditional and community knowledge.

The knowledge of all these factors help to reduce the vulnerability of coastal communities to tsunami and other hazard. The results of hazard risk assessment serve as the basis for decision support mechanisms and to identify and implement a range of mitigation measures as preparation of evacuation maps based on hazard risk assessments results. Hazards maps show areas of high potential for tsunami inundation. These maps are used to prepare evacuation plans, which include safe areas and shelters, how to reach there and where to go.

23.8.2.3. Inundation maps

Tsunami inundation maps are an effective tool or means to provide necessary details to coastal planners. The experience in preparation of inundation maps of Oregon has been used and spread in other USA pacific states. The same could be done in other parts of the world.

In general, the inundation maps of the coastal region are essential. They can be prepared by using contour maps of the region developed by the geo-survey department of the country if the run up wave heights are known or estimated. These inundation maps can be used to plan tsunami escape routes for the coastal people. These maps are portable and easy to integrate in various applications.

23.8.2.4. Zoning

A major application of tsunami inundation maps has been found in the preparation of zoning maps. In fact the first tsunami hazard maps for Oregon were prepared based on the beginning of tsunami simulation. Tsunami simulation was tried to help implement limits of construction of new facilities and special occupancy structures such as schools, hospitals, police and fire stations in tsunami hazard zones. The detailed inundation studies have provided opportunity to refine zoning locally. The simulation with initial (beginning) models usually differ from those with detailed inundation models. The original inundation maps generally proved robust.

This is a proof of the good judgment used by the state official in interpreting modeling results and applying appropriate safety margins.

23.8.2.5. Evacuation plans

In preparing evacuation plans, tsunami inundation maps are used as guiding tools. Though each coastal community can choose a specific format for their evacuation maps but under the National Tsunami Hazard Mitigation program standardization efforts are quite distinct, designating areas of tsunami hazard potential or pointing towards specific escape routes or tsunami shelters. By using inundation maps, the planners can designate escape routes to higher grounds or elevations.

23.8.2.6. Tsunami Mitigation, Preparedness and Response

Though a tsunami cannot be prevented or checked, but its impact can be reduced through community and emergency preparedness, timely warnings, effective response, and public education. Mitigation or reduction, preparedness, and response to tsunamis and other coastal hazards are key elements of an overall tsunami warning and mitigation system for tsunami vulnerable regions. A tsunami early warning system should be put into a risk management framework, which can be applied at global, regional, national and local levels.

Some countries have incorporated local and traditional knowledge in the evaluation of risk. Now there is a general trend to improve the risk assessment capabilities in the region with in the framework of over all disaster management. Though considerable work related to risk management of the country as a whole, region and cities with in the country has been done, but there is not uniform structure to define the risk assessment, implementing risk assessment work and preparation of report from such studies. The capabilities of the different countries vary considerably based on the availability of expertise, tools for analysis and quality of data, which are all essential requirements for risk assessment.

Structural mitigation measures should be incorporated into the site selection, design and construction of the structures and support infrastructures. Non-structural mitigation measures such as establishment of coastal buffer zones and protection of vegetation and habitats reduce vulnerability of coastal populations to tsunamis and other hazards.

Preparedness activities include implementation of rules laid down by responsible government agencies together with community organizations. The non-government organizations are essential in developing advance capacity to respond to the consequences of a tsunami. Systems and infrastructures for receiving and warning must be in place and regularly tested for its effectiveness.

The evacuation plans based on hazard risk assessment are essential to help people to reach safer places. Regular drills must be conducted to ensure that people known how to respond to tsunami warnings.

National emergency response and recovery plans and mechanism are needed in each country to respond to disaster events caused by tsunamis and other coastal hazards. These include the following works:

(*a*) Regular assessment of critical infrastructure and lifeline support facilities.

(*b*) Capacity for rescue operations and emergency assistance.

In he Indian Ocean regional goals, stress has been concentrated on the following goals.

(*i*) To establish a 24 hour warning station.

(*ii*) To develop multiple ways to receive tsunami warnings and to alert public about the occurrence of tsunami.

(*iii*) To develop a formal tsunami hazard plan and conduct emergency drills.

(*iv*) To promote public readiness through community education.

23.9. NEW CHALLENGES

23.9.1. Coastal Construction Valuation for tsunami

Almost all post tsunami surveys have revealed that inundation zones buildings and harbour support structures and piers should have scour resistant foundations. The other small projected elements exposed to the horizontal flow of the wave should be adequately anchored to their foundations.

Flow of water through the structures is critical in reducing the hydrodynamic forces on the structures. The fatalities can also be reduced by designing the buildings for habitation on upper floors and using the ground floor for less important functions. In many regions of the world, tsunami events are infrequent, i.e. they occur in these parts once in centuries and practically no catastrophic damages. Hence to include tsunamis as a mandatory design consideration for all urban buildings in such areas will be unwise and uneconomic. Thus the objective of designing buildings and other critical transportation infrastructure (such as bridges) in such areas should be that they should be able to resist the ground shaking from the earthquake and to resist the local scour from tsunami induced water velocities.

However there are several coastal communities for which it in not feasible or economical to prepare evacuation routes. A common and major hurdle in the preparation of evacuation routes is the local topography of the area. The local topography being very flat, eleminates the opportunity for high ground regions for providing natural tsunami shelters. In such situation, as in the case of essential or large facilities located in inundation zones, tsunami resistant structures should be constructed. Massive protection sea walls (as in Japan in a part of coast massive wall has been constructed) are an example of such structures.

In general, the construction of a specific tsunami resistant buildings such as large high rise hotels to serve as vertical escape route is more challenging. In this case the biggest challenge is to determine the appropriate design loads.

Federal Emergency Management Agency (FEMA) has suggested some guidelines to distinguish tsunami loads due to hydro static water pressure (assuming slow water flow or motion) from hydro dynamic tsunami load (assuming fast flow of water and turbulence). Both loads or forces are computed as for any other flood load. However for computing the hydrodynamic tsunami load, the value of velocity is taken as double that of propagation of tsunami wave. The hydrodynamic load is given by the following equation.

$$F = \frac{1}{2} \rho C_d V^2 A$$

Where,

F = Force developed in the building

ρ = Density of salty water.

C_d = Drag coefficient.

A = Surface areas of obstruction perpendicular to the flow.

V = Design velocity of water. Its value is taken as double of $\sqrt{gh}$ normal velocity.

i.e. $2\sqrt{gh}$

h = Inundation depth.

The value of V can easily attain a value of 10 to 20 m/sec and more. The cost for such high design velocities is significant. Thus it would be advisable to use tsunami inundation models to refine the estimate of local velocities. Before using this approach consistently, more progress in the modeling of inundation and fluid structure interaction for a complex situation of tsunami run up is essential.

23.9.2. Environmental Impacts

The December 26, 2004 Sumatra tsunami has increased the awareness that sediment transported and the subsidence of coastal area due to local tsunami can have a major impact not only on urban communities but on eco system also. These eco system impacts so far have been ignored. But now it has been felt that ecosystem impacts may have very long time lasting effects both on environmental quality and regional economy.

23.9.3. Other considerations

For more than two decades there has been significant progress in the understanding of tsunami generation, propagation and inundation. Preparation on protecting human life first and fore most has been correctly focused.

In the five pacific states of USA, maps of predicted inundation for a range of source scenarios have been produced for may communities. These inundation maps have served the basis for coastal zoning and planning of evacuation routes.

In coastal planning the construction of tsunami resistant buildings might become a more important field, in particular in areas where horizontal (ground) escape routes are unfeasible and selected buildings serve as tsunami shelters. The greatest challenge is to estimate the appropriate loads for the design of buildings. An other area which needs substantially more attention in the future is the environmental impact of tsunami and its generating coastal deformation.

23.10. PROTECTION AGAINST TSUNAMI DAMAGE

Coastal structures have to be planned and designed to withstand or survive the effects of tsunami. In order to achieve this goal, the vulnerability assessment of the built up environment in the tsunami prone areas to be done, followed by mitigation measures of the tsunami structural damage.

23.10.1. Vulnerability to Tsunami

The vulnerability assessment of built up environment in tsunami prone region should include the following factors.

1. Number of storeys in each building

Single storey buildings are more vulnerable as vertical evacuation in case of single storey buildings is not possible. Where as in multi storey building vertical evacuation is possible. It is important for disaster planners to identify the buildings which are likely to contain large number of injured or trapped survivors for peramedical personals to go there directly, if there is no possibility of vertical evacuation in such buildings.

2. Description of ground floor

Open plan storey with movable objects are highly vulnerable to tsunamis, where as completely open plan storeys with columns and without peripherical walls are very low vulnerable to tsunamis. But this type of planning contradicts the earthquake resistant design concept. Thus the cross bracing between columns of the ground floor open plan must be provided perpendicular to the direction of wave front to act as shear walls.

3. Building materials, age, and design etc.

Buildings of adobe (dry lumps of soil) bricks and stone masonry with mud mortar are highly vulnerable to tsunamis, where as ordinary brick masonry structures with cement mortar are medium vulnerable and pre cast or R.C.C. structures have low vulnerability.

4. Access routes

Disaster mitigation planners must ensure that access roads to the coastal areas are not inundated or blocked. Trunk roads telecommunication lines are to be laid above maximum flood levels and emergency shelters should be provided.

5. Land use data

The existence of residential, business (shops, restaurants, hotels) services (Hospitals, schools, power stations, marine works etc.) areas are important for insurance companies, as premiums are set for buildings considering the extent of content loss and loss of business due to interruptions.

6. Sociological data

At the time of planning for tsunami mitigation measures, the sociological data of the coastal resorts should be studied and taken into account for example variation of the population during summer and winter, during day and night is important. Further there will be high variation of tourists during the season. The beaches will be vacant during winter and most of the people would like to stay away from beaches in inland. The number of people per building is also of importance. Changes in population in hospitals and schools are of great importance and must be considered at the time of planning.

7. Land Vegetation Cover

Land areas with out any cover of vegetation are highly vulnerable to scouring, while bushes or grass covered areas are moderately vulnerable where as areas covered with trees are low vulnerable. On the other hand large engineered coastal barriers may have negative impact. Thus the detailed information of buildings, infrastructure works and group of people who are particularly vulnerable to tsunami impact is essential. On the basis of such data, cost effective tsunami mitigation measures may be developed and adopted. This can be used as a tool for local planning and to evaluate post tsunami emergency disaster response.

23.11. MITIGATION MEASURES OF TSUNAMI STRUCTURAL DAMAGE

A survey of recent tsunami damaged coastal areas has revealed some facts about the structural design in a tsunami prone region. Most of the well designed, R.C.C. buildings with good foundations withstood the fury of the waves attack. The survival percentage of elevated buildings was even higher, allowing the water to flow under the structure. In addition to the above, if the structure was constructed in such a way that water could flow through the first floor, the structural damage was found minimum. However the interior contents were damaged.

In Thailand this type of design actually was adopted (accidentally) in the construction of many resort R.C.C. buildings. These buildings contained apartments with sliding glass doors facing the sea and the backs of the buildings. These buildings suffered little structural damage as the force of tsunami broke through all of the doors and windows, reducing the force of water on the building it self. On the other hand concrete buildings with solid masonry in fill walls and no flow capability through the ground storey of the buildings, have been found to suffer more destruction of walls and in many cases severe damage to load bearing frame.

The December 26, 2004 tsunami has shown that R.C.C. buildings performed well with out structural damage by waves to the buildings, where as most of the timber buildings in the inundation zones were completely destroyed. Multi storey R.C.C. buildings played a life saving role by providing a vertical evacuation route that enabled some people to take shelter in upper floors above the flood waters.

The foundations of such buildings were designed well to prevent scour from over passing waves at the corners of the building. Foundations at the corners were kept about one metre deeper than other parts so that no foundation problems could be created.

From the study of tsunami damaged buildings it has been observed that buildings in inundation zones such as piers, and harbour support buildings should have scour resistant foundations. Small sea walls or small projected areas or elements exposed to the horizontal flow of waves should have a good anchorage to their foundations. For reducing hydrodynamic forces on buildings, flow through structures is critical. Designing buildings with habitats on upper floors and using the ground floor for less important functions can also reduce fatalities.

However the structural engineer must be aware with the fact that buildings capable to with stand the wave attacks as suggested above may not be able to survive the onslaght of earthquake which are the generator of the tsunamis unless special precautions such as providing cross bracing between the columns in the direction perpendicular to the direction of waves front at the ground floor, are taken in the design and construction of earthquake resistant elements.

Earthquake resistance and flow through ground floor is not compatible to each other, but opposite. Thus in active earthquake and tsunami prone zones the design of structures is a multi hazard concept and needs good judgment on the part of structural engineers.

QUESTIONS

1. Define tsunami and causes of their generation.
2. Discuss 2004 tsunami in detail.
3. Discuss cause of generation of 2004 tsunami.
4. Discuss the tsunami hazard risk assessment and warning system.
5. What activities should be included in the tsunami hazard assessment plans?
6. Write a note on the mitigation, preparedness and response on tsunami.
7. Identify the incorrect statement/statements.
   (*a*) Tsunamis are generated by thrust earthquakes.
   (*b*) Tsunamis are also generated by strike slip earthquakes of more than 8.0 magnitude.
   (*c*) The earthquake occurs at a very great depth to cause tsunami.
   (*d*) Tsunami is a shallow marine event.
8. Identify the correct statement/statements
   (*a*) Mainly tsunamis are generated by rapid large-scale sea disturbances caused by earthquakes
   (*b*) Over ground land slide
   (*c*) By eruption of volcanoes
   (*d*) Under water land slide
   (*e*) All are correct
9. In deep water the speed of tsunami waves is
   (*a*) 200 km/h (*b*) 500 km/h
   (*c*) 800 km/h (*d*) 1200 km/h
10. In shallow waters the speed of tsunami waves is
    (*a*) 50 to 100 km/h (*b*) 70 to 150 km/h
    (*c*) 65 to 120 km/h (*d*) 30 to 60 km/h
11. Generally the height of tsunami waves is
    (*a*) 10 m (*b*) 15 m
    (*c*) 20 m (*d*) 25 m
12. Generally the time interval between successive waves is ...... minutes
    (*a*) 4 to 25 minutes (*b*) 10 to 45 minutes
    (*c*) 15 to 60 minutes (*d*) 12 to 48 minutes
13. Usually tsunamis are generated due to......
    (*a*) Atmospheric disturbances
    (*b*) High-speed wind disturbances
    (*c*) Large scale disturbances by under sea earthquake
    (*e*) Breaking of mountains
14. Identify the incorrect statement/statements
    (*a*) Tsunamis are usually a shallow marine event
    (*b*) Tsunamis may also be generated by ground level slide

(*c*) Tsunamis may also be generated by volcanic erruption
(*d*) Tsunamis are generated by atmospheric disturbances

15. Identify the incorrect statement/statements
(*a*) Generally tsunami waves come in a series of long waves
(*b*) Generally tsunamis come in a single long wave
(*c*) Tsunami waves travel outwards on the surface of the ocean in all direction away from the source
(*d*) Tsunami waves travel in a opposite way of waves produced when a stone is thrown in the water
(*e*) The wave length and the period of tsunami waves depends on the generating mechanism of the waves
(*f*) When tsunami waves reach the shore their velocity is reduced considerably

16. Tsunami waves can flood land upto a distance from the coast......
(*a*) 2.0 km (*b*) 3.2 km
(*c*) 4.5 km (*d*) 6.0 km

17. Generally the flood period of an individual wave of tsunami is ......
(*a*) 10 to 30 seconds (*b*) 5 to 15 seconds
(*c*) 15 to 40 seconds (*d*) 20 to 40 seconds

18. Tsunami waves can be identified from ordinary waves by
(*a*) By their lengths (*b*) By their shape
(*c*) By their speed (*d*) by all the above

19. Some times the crest to crest length of tsunami wave is
(*a*) 25 km (*b*) 50 km
(*c*) 80 km (*d*) 100 km or more

20. Usually the wave length of waves produced by air is......
(*a*) 50 to 75 m (*b*) 80 to 80 m
(*c*) 100 to 200 m (*d*) 120 to 240 m

21. The travel period from crest to crest of wave produced by air is...... seconds
(*a*) 1 to 10 secs (*b*) 5 to 20 seconds
(*c*) 10 to 30 seconds (*d*) 15 to 40 seconds

22. The tsunami of 2004 was produced at a depth of...... km under water
(*a*) 10 km (*b*) 15 km
(*c*) 20 km (*d*) 30 km

23. In 2004 tsunami...... caused damage upto a distance from its epicentre
(*a*) 2000 km (*b*) 4000 km
(*c*) 6000 km (*d*) 8000 km

24. In 2004 tsunami...... people lost their lives
(*a*) One lakh (*b*) 1.5 lakh
(*c*) 3.0 lakhs (*d*) 5 lakhs

25. Tsunami waves travel in...... direction
(*a*) Only in vertical direction (*b*) Only in horizontal direction
(*c*) In all directions (*d*) All are correct

26. The tsunami of 2004 was generated due to
(*a*) by striking two tectonic plates
(*b*) By passing side by side of two tectonic plates

(*c*) By diving Indian Ocean plate under Burma plate
(*d*) All are correct

27. Indian plate moves towards North east every year by......
(*a*) 5 cm (*b*) 10 cm
(*c*) 15 cm (*d*) 12 cm

28. For tsunami protection works the land level above sea level should be higher by
(*a*) 5 m (*b*) 10 m
(*c*) 12 m (*d*) 15 m

29. The minimum distance of protection site from sea shore should be......
(*a*) 3.0 km (*b*) 5 km
(*c*) 7.5 km (*d*) 10 km

30. The velocity of wave generated by earthquake
(*a*) 1000 km/h (*b*) 1500 km/h
(*c*) 14400 km/h (*d*) 200200 km/h

31. In open waters the velocity of tsunami waves is......
(*a*) 100 to 200 km/h (*b*) 300 to 600 km/h
(*c*) 400 to 800 km/h (*d*) 500 to 1000 km/h

32. For protection from tsunami the ground storey ...... in direction of tsunami should be constructed as
(*a*) Leaving open space between the columns or providing glass walls
(*b*) By providing stone wall
(*c*) By providing concrete wall
(*d*) All are correct

33. The zone where 2004 tsunami occurred is called the ring of fire. In this zone ......% of world earthquake occurred
(*a*) 31% (*b*) 41%
(*c*) 61% (*d*) 81%

34. Identify the correct statement/statements
(*a*) In 2004 tsunami most of the R.C.C. buildings remained undamaged
(*b*) Most of the timber structures totally destroyed
(*c*) The foundations of structures near the shore should be safe against scouring
(*d*) In areas susceptible to flooding during tsunami, the residence should be made on the upper floors and the ground floors should be used for other works
(*e*) All are correct

35. Identify the incorrect statement/statements
(*a*) The areas where there is no vegetation cover, they are more unsafe or susceptible to tsunami damage
(*b*) In tsunami prone areas buildings made of mud adobe, stone or brick masonry are more prone to tsunami damage
(*c*) Buildings having ground storey either totally open or the space between columns covered with glass are more safe during a tsunami
(*d*) Construction of stonewalls between columns has been found totally safe during a tsunami

ANSWERS

7. (*c*)
8. (*e*)
9. (*c*)
10. (*d*)
11. (*b*)
12. (*b*)
13. (*c*)
14. (*d*)
15. (*b, d*)
16. (*b*)
17. (*a*)
18. (*a*)
19. (*d*)
20. (*c*)
21. (*b*)
22. (*d*)
23. (*d*)
24. (*c*)
25. (*c*)
26. (*c*)
27. (*a*)
28. (*d*)
29. (*b*)
30. (*c*)
31. (*d*)
32. (*a*)
33. (*d*)
34. (*e*)
35. (*d*)

24

Guidelines for Earthquake and Tsunami Preparedness and Checklists

24.1. INTRODUCTION

As stated earlier also, earthquakes are natural Phenomenon and they strike suddenly, violently and without warning. For this reason humen are afraid of earthquakes. Earthquakes do not kill any body themselves. The results of deaths, injuries and loss of property during earthquakes are man made. Damage, injury and loss of life can be prevented by adopting appropriate earthquake resistant design and preparedness measures. In this chapter some guide line, for earthquake and Tsunami preparedness and checklists have been discussed.

24.2. PLANNING PREPAREDNESS

Think if earthquake strikes when you are out of your home driving a car or you are in a store doing shopping or at work or public place or say at home, what you can do in such situations. Your mind set and planning may enable you to act camly and constructively in such an emergency.

Planning and earthquake schemes for individual, family and neighborhood can help to improve our chances of surviving an earthquake with out injury or serious damage. Plan to check your family, friends and neighbours after an earthquake. After preparing the guidelines, educate them about the measures to be taken before, during and after the earthquake to reduce or avoid their sufferings caused by injuries, loss of life and damage to property.

24.3. FAMILY EARTQHAUKE PLAN

We all know that we live in a very compact space and many earthquake hazards cannot be eliminated. How ever they can be reduced considerably. Be aware of the dangers during an earthquake. Protect your self and your family or your eightbourhood from their particular dangers. Windowpanes may shatter and scatter. Glass pieces may fly in the neighborhood. Similarly picture frames and mirrors also may be a source of danger. Thus keep your bed and table or desk away from windows.

Before an earthquake plan

Before an earthqauke the family plan consists of knowing the layout of your house and its surroundings fully. Special provisions for children, elderly and disabled persons should be included in your contingency plan. Prepare a plan with your family, friends and neighbours and assign a specific responsibility to each individual to take care after the earthquake. Arrange your house hold articles in such a way that heavy articles are placed at lower levels. Shelves should be fastened securely with the walls. Spaces under tables and desks should be clear, so that you can take shelter under them in case an earthquake occurs. Your family plan should lay emphasis on the following specific items.

24.3.1. Know your environment

Choose safest place in the house

1. Choose the safest place in each room of your house. During a major earthquake it will be difficult to move from one room to another room to choose the safest place. During an earthquake remain away from heavy furniture, appliances, large panes of glass and shelves having heavy objects. These items may fall or break and can injure you. Usually the corridor or way to hall in the house is one of the safest places if it is not croweded with objects. Kitchen and garages are considered to be the most dangerous places and should be avoided.
2. Always locate the possible ways to leave your house or work place in an emergency situation.
3. Know the location of the shut off valves for gas, water and electricity. You should know fully the operation of these valves. Besides this, following special provisions should be made:
   (*a*) Special arrangements should be made for sick, elderly and disabled persons.
   (*b*) These persons may have difficulty in moving around after the earthquake. For them, arrangements to evacuate must be made if necessary. They may also need some medicines and special food. Hence several days' supply of their special needs be stored.
   (*c*) After an earthquake you should try to be safe your self than your pets. Storing extra food and water for your pets is always a good idea. After an earthquake keep your pets in a safe place at home. In case you are evacuated, your pets will not be allowed at emergency shelter.

24.3.2. Know your Community Resources

1. During an earthquake, police, fire brigade and social workers will provide necessary guidance to you.
2. Know the location of nearest fire brigade station and police station.
3. After an earthquake find out the plan of your area, contact your local center of emergency area, as temporary medical services and other emergency services will be operating from these centres.

4. Know your neighbours and their skill, so that they may be helpful after an earthquake. It is important to help each other during an emergency as out side, help may reach late.

24.3.3. Plan to meet

1. Prepare the plan where and how family members should unite, in case they are separated during the disaster. Better choose a person out side your area to contact, as long distance telephone services will be restored sooner than local service. After an earthquake you should not engage the telephone, as some one may need it more than you. Make locai calls only in emergency.
2. Know the policies of the school or day care center your children attend. Plan to take your child or children from the school or day care center in case you are unable to do so after an earthquake.

24.3.4. Plan Responsibilities

There will be many things to take care before and after the earthquake. Make plan with your family friends, and neightbours and assign specific responsibility to each of them. Train them how to avoid injury and panic during earthquake. After an earthquake it would be difficult to go around the area. Hence each person should be given task related to his neighbourhood.

24.4. INDIVIDUAL, FAMILY, HOME AND COMMUNITY PLANNING GUIDELINES

If a major earthquake occurs in your area, try to be calm, and reassure others also. You might be without direct assistance from Government or non-government agencies upto 2 to 3 days. Hence you, your family and neighbourhood should be prepared to be self sufficient. Some guide lines are given below to cope with such a situation.

24.4.1. Individual and family preparedness

1. Identify the safe spots in each room of your house, under sturdy tables desk or against inside walls.
2. The space under the table and desk should be kept clear all the time.
3. Identify the danger spots like windows, mirrors, tall furniture, hanging objects, and fire place etc.
4. Have practice to place physically your self and your children in safe locations.
5. Learn first aid and have practice to help others in case of need.
6. Decide where your family will reunite, if separated.
7. Keep a list of emergency phone numbers.
8. If you have a mobile phone, it should be kept fully charged.
9. Choose a friend or relative out side your state, whom family members

can contact after the eartqhauke to report their where about and conditions.

24.4.2. Home Preparedness

1. Learn to shut off gas, water and electric mains in case lines are damaged.
2. Check roof and wall foundations for stability.
3. Water heater and other appliances that may damage utility lines during the earthquake, should be secured properly.
4. Heavy and breakable objects should be kept on the lower shelves.
5. To avoid injuries from the falling of shelves, they should be secured or fastened well with the walls.
6. Heavy picture frames, Mirrors and hanging plants etc should be secured properly.
7. During shaking, cabinet doors should be kept closed by putting latches on them.
8. Flammable liquids such as paints, pest sprays or cleaning products etc should be put in cabinets or secured on lower shelves.
9. A battery powered transistor radio and flesh light should be kept in the house ready for use at all times.
10. Maintain Emergency food, water, medicines, first-aid kit and clothing.

24.4.3. Community preparedness

1. The local organization of which you are a member should under take a specific preparedness programme, which may be of assistance in the event of a damaging earthquake.
2. A neighbourhood preparedness program must be organized.
3. Training in fire fighting, first aid, damage assessment, search and rescue etc. must be given to the neighbourhood residents.
4. Develop a self-help network between the families and neighbourhood, which may include listing tools, equipments, materials and neighbourhood members, who have special skills and resources to share.
5. Identify the neighbours who have special need or will require special assistance.
6. Have agreement on a sign like a white flag after the disaster to indicate that every one and every thing is O.K.

24.5. COMMUNITY RESPONSE TEAM PLANNING GUIDE

After an earthquake or disaster like fire, police and other disaster response agencies may be over burdened and may not be able to reach your community. Hence you and your neighbours should take initial emergency responsibilities for at least 72 hours. It has been observed that first rescuers are usually from the neighbourhood.

Volunteers from the neighbourhood community have played a vital role immediately after the earthquake in putting out small fires, providing first aid and searching and rescuing the trapped persons. The volunteers must be trained as untrained volunteers may endanger their own as well as the lives of those individuals who are trapped and they are trying to help.

Local municipalities should formulate plans to organize and train volunteer community response teams in basic emergency response techniques. The various activities included in the community response team-planning guide are discussed in the following paragraphs.

24.5.1. Training

The members of the community response team should learn the followings:

(*a*) How to assist themselves and families for injuries.

(*b*) Their homes and work place for hazards or damage.

(*c*) Their neighbours for injuries, hazards and available resources.

For arranging training staff and training workshop contact your local police and fire department, city office of emergency services.

24.5.2. Inventory of neighborhood skills

1. Preparation of inventory of neighbourhood skill is a part of the community response team planning. A list of persons should be prepared who have some special skill as a medical, electrical, firefighting, child care etc.
2. Prepare a list of persons who own vehicles and equipment as chain saw, cutters, and power generator.
3. Prepare a list of persons who own four wheelers, Motorcycles, Water purifiers etc.
4. Prepare a list of persons who are physically fit to become a runner/ cyclist to deliver messages if telephone lines are out of order.
5. Prepare a list of kind of business in the neighbourhood.

This list is essential for an efficient and effective response during an earthquake.

24.5.3. Evaluate special needs

Every home/office or neighbourhood has individuals with special needs. Some one may be blind, hard of hearing; some one may be sick requiring oxygen. There may be some homes where children remain alone during daytime as their parents go to work. The community response team should work with such people in advance to determine their extra supplies assistance they may require after an earthquake or any other emergency.

24.5.4. Store supplies

In addition to food, water and other supplies, the community response team should store tools such as gloves, Goggles, crescent wrenches, hard hates, flashlights, and other items that team thinks will be useful after an earthquake. These items should be stored in a central and easily accessible location.

24.6. RESIDENTIAL CARE FACILITY EARTHQUKE PLAN

The residential care plan should be designed for all residents living there with the objective to educate them that what could happen during an earthquake. The training programmes should be designed for their safety incorporating their suggestions. Their active participation in the programmes should also be ensured. For this purpose periodic drills should be planned. Following steps are involved in such plans.

24.6.1. Plan

Each plan may be unique. When developing the plan, it may be beneficial to work with others, but ensure that the plan you adopt fits your situation. If you are in a facility in which there is only one care taker at a time, in that case convince your staff members to coordinate family plans with that of residential care home. Families of the staff should be allowed to use the facility as meeting place. This step will give peace of mind to the staff members and at the same time will provide extra hands to help at the crucial time. Inform residents that what can happen during an earthquake and what steps have been taken to provide for their safety. Residents should be involved in the process, incorporating their suggestions.

Employee training programme must be developed. In the training following topics should be included.

1. Procedure of providing first aid
2. Securing utilities
3. Suppressing fire
4. Calming residents
5. Conducting search and rescue operations
6. Evacuation of residents
7. Providing emergency power, water and food etc.
8. Providing residents with special needs.

24.6.2. Prepare

Evaluate each action in the facility to determine its performance during an earthquake and elimination of hazards. Secure properly medical equipments, heavy appliances, bookshelves, plants and other items that might fall. Beds should be placed away from windows. Examine the passage or exit routes and clear them of items which may block the safe passage after the earthquake. Identify the gathering place out side the house far enough from the building to be clear of falling debris and safe in case of fire.

Stock supplies, which may include the following items:

(*a*) Canned fruits and vegetables.
(*b*) Glucose or its equivalent.
(*c*) Sturdy but light weight folding chairs.
(*d*) Blankets, carpets or bamboo mats or similar item.
(*e*) A plastic toilet with a seat, waste paper bags and toilet paper
(*f*) Cards, games and books to pass time.

24.6.3. Protect

Identify a safe spot in each room where the inmates or residents can take shelter during an earthquake. They should be trained to get down on the ground or as low as possible if they are unable to reach the safe spot. They should cover their heads with their hands and arms.

Hold at least annual drills to test the earthquake preparedness plan in the facility. After each drill, discussions should be held with the staff about the deficiencies and measures to improve on the deficiencies.

At the time of earthquake, staff should protect itself-first. If they are injured, who will help others? Priority to be given to help those who are less injured.

24.6.4. Special tips

A list of medicines, and equipment needed for each resident should be kept ready. Name, address and phone numbers of each patient's doctor and a list of their relatives along with details of phone number, names and address etc.

24.7. PRACTICE EARTHQUAKE PROCEDURES

Earthquake preparedness procedures should be tested periodically and updated continuously. Ensure that maximum number of your family members and neighbours take part in the earthquake drills. Review the responsibility of each number after the earthquake. If necessary procedures should be improvised and updated.

24.7.1. Earthquake drill

1. Your family members and co-workers should be encouraged to take part in earthquake drills. Emergency procedures should be reviewed and practised periodically.
2. Practice taking over. By this practice people will know the safe places in their neighbour hood to take shelter during an earthquake.
3. Practice existing facilities. In this practice walk through the possible escape routes from your home to your work place. Ensure that they remain clear and there is no likely hood of their being blocked during an earthquake.
4. Practice shut off. Practice switching off water and electricity mains at your home and office. Ensure that this can be done by each member. One should also know how to switch off the gas.

24.7.2. Review post earthquake plans

Check supply of emergency food and water, medicines, first aid materials etc. for all members. Replenish the expired supplies of food, water, medicines, fire extinguishers and batteries. After the earthquake review the responsiblity of each family member.

Review plans to pickup children and check with school and day time centers to ensure that family plan is still satisfactory.

To update the local emergency plan, contact your local emergency services office.

24.8. SELF DEFENCE TECHNIQUES

During an earthquake, it is important to know certain technique to protect your self, whether you are in your home, office, school, and in a high-rise building or any other type of building. It is quite possible that during an earthquake, you may get panicky, nervous. Under such circumstances you should adopt for quick protection techniques as discussed below.

24.8.1. During an earthquake

During an earthquake remain calm and reassure others. Think about the consequences of any action you take at that time.

Duck, Cover and hold

Whether you are in your home, work place, high rise or any other type of building, it is important that you know, how to protect your self during a earthquake. Practice, what is to be done during an earthquake? Teach your family members and your self what is to be done if an earthquake struck. If you are out side at the time of shaking starts then go to open area away from buildings, walls, tress, electric power poles etc. If you are inside, follow the following steps.

(*a*) **Duck.** Duck (move your head down ward) drop down or lay down on the floor and take shelter.

(*b*) **Cover.** Take cover under a sturdy table, desk or under any other furniture or stand in corner of the building away from the window or under an strong door way. If all this is not possible, stand very close to the interior wall and cover your head and neck with your arms. Avoid danger spots such as near windows, hanging objects, mirrors or tall furniture.

(*c*) **Hold.** If you take cover or shelter under a sturdy table or desk etc. hold on to it and be prepared to move with it. Hold the furniture in that position, till the shaking stops and it is safe to move.

24.8.2. Duck, Cover and hold tips

1. In case you are in high-rise building and it is not possible to cover your self under a table or desk, in that case move against the interior wall and

cover your head and neck with your hands and arms. Do not run towards exit gates or stair or elevators. The stair way may be broken. Exit gate and elevator may be jammed with people. Power for elevators or escalators might have failed. Fire alarms or sprinkler system might have fallen.

2. In case you are out door. Remain away from high buildings, walls; power poles and other objects, which might fall. Do not run-through streets. If possible go to an open area away from all the above hazards.
3. In case you are on a side walk near buildings. Duck into a doorway to protect yourself from falling bricks, glass panes, plaster and other debris.
4. In case your driving come to the side of the road and stop. Avoid flyovers, power lines, and other hazards. Stay in side your vehicle until the shaking stops.
5. If you are in a crowed store or public place. Do not rush for exits as many people may have the same idea. Go away from the display shelves containing objects that may fall.
6. If you are in a wheel chair. Stay in the wheel chair. If possible move to cover your self. If it is not possible, lock your wheels and protect your head with your hands and arms.
7. If you are in the kitchen. Move away from the refrigerator, stove and overhead cupboards.
8. If you are in a theatre or stadium, stay in your seat and cover your head with your hands. Do not try to leave your seat till the shaking is over. After the shaking is over leave the place calmly and in a orderly manner.

24.8.3. After the earthquake

1. Check for injuries in your family and neighbourhood. Do not move serious injured persons unless they are in immediate danger of further injury.
2. Check for any fire hazards.
3. Wear shoes in all areas near the windows, broken glass or debris.
4. Do not touch power lines, or objects in contact with the downed wires.
5. If water is off, emergency water may be taken from water heaters, toilet tanks and melted ice cubes.
6. Before flushing toilets, check whether sewage lines are in working condition.
7. Do not drink water from open containers near the shattered glass. Liquid may be strained through clean cloth or handker chief.
8. Do not use your telephone except for emergency calls. Switch on your radio for public broadcasts and information.
9. Open the door of cupboards cautiously for checking their contents, watch carefully for falling objects from the shelves.
10. Keep the streets clear for the passage of emergency vehicles. Do not go

out for sight seeing.

11. Clean up potentially harmful materials and drugs.
12. After an earthquake be prepared for after shocks. Though after shocks usually are smaller than the main shock. However some after shocks may be large enough to cause additional damage to already vulnerable buildings, which are already in an advanced stage of the limit of their resistance to lateral loads and may bring down the weaker structures.
13. Do not go to the damaged areas unless you are asked for help, but respond to the request for help from police, defense and fire fighting organizations. Cooperate fully with public safety officials.

24.9. SPECIAL TOPICS

In order to make the presentation comprehensive some special topics have been added to provide guidelines for earthquake preparedness for schools, businesses, local governments, childcare centers, senior citizens etc.

24.9.1. Earthquake preparedness for schools, Businesses and local governments

Following guidelines are proposed:

1. Prepare and update disaster plans regularly. Address both response and recovery issues.
2. Institute training programmes in emergency procedures, first aid, cardio arrest, search and rescue, use of fire extinguishers and damage assessment. Hold periodic exercises and drills.
3. To ensure the structural safety of your building, consult local building codes.
4. To find out non-structural hazard in offices, class rooms, stores, laboratories, warehouses, and manufacturing areas search for hazards should be conducted.
5. Determine the main and alternative routes for emergency evacuation of the building if necessary after the earthquake.
6. Educate the staff about earthquake effects on high-rise buildings. (Lower floors will shake rapidly, while movement on upper floors will be slower, but the sway of the building is more i.e. building will move side to side farther).
7. Secure and anchor furniture and equipment such as computers, water heaters, laboratory equipment, gas appliances, bookshelves, cabinets etc.
8. Articles on business and home earthquake safety should be included in the brochures for public distribution.
9. For post earthquake operations arrangements with venders should be made.
10. An inventory of critical supplies and equipment should be prepared.
11. Assemble emergency kits with water, first aid supplies, radios, flash

lights, batteries, heavy gloves, food, sanitation supplies etc. These articles should be kept in a safe and accessible location.

24.9.2. Childcare center earthquake plan

Think for a working plan of a children center with staff and parents input. While developing the plan, fix responsibilities based on specific needs, interest and training. At the time of planning following points must be kept in mind.

1. Know your environment

Ensure safest place in each room. Identify the locations of all exits. Utility shut off valves, storage sites for emergency supplies and equipment. If the child care services are run by social center, school, community center or employer, then your emergency plan and procedures should be compatible with those of these agencies.

2. Maintain routine

Normal diets and routines for all age groups must be maintained strictly.

3. Make special provisions for infants

Infants will not under stand or response to emergency instructions. Thus special emphasis should be put on ensuring safe environment as far as possible. For example cribs should be placed away from unanchored windows and tall unsecured book shelves which may slide or topple over. At least 72-hour supplies of extra water, juice, diapers, food and clothing should be stored.

For the transport of the children, blankets, wagons, crips, trallers etc. should be employed.

Toddlers. Toddlers may understand simple emergency instructions. These children can be taught the command to duck, cover and hold position with the command "KISS YOUR KNEES." For these children also at least 72 hour supply of extra water, juice, diapers, food and clothing must be stored. Also have plenty of toys available for children and plan activities to keep them busy.

Children with special needs require some additional assistance along with the above requirements. You may add need for extra staff, parents and older children to help.

4. Conduct Earthquake drills

Drills can save lives. Hence children center should conduct and document drills every six months. Staff and children should be taught duck, cover and hold with the help of sturdy tables or desks for protection. In case no tables desk are available, then children should be taught to bow down and cover their heads with their hands and arms. The back of their head should be fully covered with arms.

Out doors. In case children are out side, they should be taught to bow (duck) cover and hold in an open area away from the power lines, walls of houses and other hazards. They should also be taught, how, where and when to evacuate.

5. Identify resources

Identify the professional assistance such as Engineers, doctors, nurses etc. that might be utilized at the time of need.

6. Conduct hazard assessment

Generally childcare providers store heavy and breakable articles high and out of reach of the children. However during an earthquake these items may become dangerous missiles for the children. Thus these heavy and breakable items should be stored in low cabinets and properly secured. Take special care to secure or remove any item placed above the head level of children, including T.V., hanging plants, and air conditioners.

Windows should be fixed preventing shattering of glass during an earthquake. Professional surveys of buildings for structural integrity should be conducted. Thus internal and external assessment of the facility should be carried out.

24.9.3. Planning guidelines for seniors

1. Plan. Major earthquakes can kill and injure thousands of persons and damage property. Even moderate earthquake can disrupt seriously all those things we have taken for granted and depend on them forour well being. Developing individual, family and neighbourhood earthquake plan can help to improve the chances of surviving an earthquake with out serious injury or damage.

If you have to leave your home after an earthquake, prepare a list of medicines, special equipment, name, address and phone number of your doctor, a friend and take the list with you.

2. Prepare. Falling objects pose one of the greatest hazards in an earthquake. Older people are less mobile and it is difficult or impossible for them to go quickly under a table or heavy furniture for protection. Hence it is very important to eliminate the hazards in home that could fall and cause injury. Either do it your self or take help of a friend or family member.

(*a*) Anchor securely medical equipment, heavy appliances, bookshelves, cabinets, hanging plants, and other such items.

(*b*) Place heavy objects on low shelves.

(*c*) Beds should be kept away from the windows.

(*d*) Corridors, exits, door ways must be kept clear, so that at the time of evacuation there may not be any hindrance.

(*e*) Cabinets and drawers should be provided with latches, so that they may not open at the time of earthquake.

(*f*) Store 72 hours supply of emergency food and water. Have a well stocked first aid kit, flesh lights and batteries, portable radio, and essential medicines.

Protect. At the time of shaking, you should know the place to take shelter. Either under a sturdy furniture like a table or desk or against the inside wall, or under supported archways. If you can not reach a safe place, sit down or continue sitting where you are till the shaking stops. Cover your head and back of the head with your hands and arms.

Outside. If you are outside, move away from buildings, overhead wires and windows etc.

Special needs

Many senior citizens have special needs. Following steps should be taken to increase the chances of surviving during an earthquake:

1. If you need a walking help as walker, wheel chair, cane etc. keep them near to you at all times.
2. Each room should be provided with a security light.
3. In emergency to signal help, have a whistle with you.
4. Store extra battery, if you use battery-operated equipment.
5. A fire and smoke alarm detector system should be installed.
6. If you use glasses, have an extra pair with you for emergency use.

24.9.4. Planning guidelines for people with disabilities

Plan. Develop a close relationship system with friends, neighbours and co-workers. Plan how each of you can be helped in an emergency.

Make a list of your medicines, special equipment, name, address and telephone no. of your doctor, family members, friends and any other important information. Keep one copy with you and give other copy to the person of your confidence.

Prepare

(*a*) Eliminate hazard in your home. Anchor loose equipment heavy appliances, bookshelves, hanging plants, and other items securely.

(*b*) Move away your bed from the windows.

(*c*) Keep exit door ways, corridors and other areas clear of obstacles. Remove hazards and other obstructions which may impede your safe exit after an earthquake.

(*d*) Get installed security night light to provide emergency lighting in case power failure occurs.

(*e*) Store emergency supplies. At least 72 hours emergency supplies should be stored. It includes water, food, any special diet food, sanitary aids. Cooking and eating utensils, flash lights, radio, blankets, clothes, whistle for signaling for assistance, well stocked first aid kit, wheel chair, and batteries for your hearing aids and other battery operated equipment.

24.9.5. Special tips

If you are hard of heaving, then keep a battery operated television set on hand for receiving emergency information when power is off. Store pencil and pad for communicating. Store flashlights also.

If you have impaired vision or are blind, then keep extra canes in strategic areas in your home. Plan alternative routes for evacuation from home or office.

In case you use wheel chair, then tie to it a light weight bag containing your medicines, your emergency sanitary aids, a small flash light and whistle for emergency use. Decide at least two usable exit doors from each room and from your building. In case of emergency move to cover. In case it is not possible to move to cover your self, in that case lock your wheel chair and protect head with your hands and arms or pillow, book or any handy object available at the time.

24.10. PUBIC PREPAREDNESS OF TSUNAMI HAZARDS

Public should be educated to adopt various measures of safety before, during and after the tsunami event to avoid or to reduce their sufferings due to injuries, loss of life and damage to the property.

24.10.1. Measures to be adopted before Tsunami

Adopt following measures before the tsunami:

1. Find out, if your home is in a danger area.
2. Know the height or level of your street above the sea level and distance of your street from sea coast. The evacuations orders are issued on the basis of the distance and level of the area from sea coast height.
3. Be familiar with the warning signs of tsunami, as tsunami can be caused by under water earthquakes or disturbances. People living along the coast should consider an earthquake or ground rumbling as a warning signal. A noticeable rapid rise or fall in coastal water is also a sign of approaching tsunami.
4. Ensusure that all family members know, how to respond to a tsunami.
5. Prepare evacuation plan.
6. Choose an elevated location of area to go in case of emergency.
7. Teach all family members, how and when to switch off gas, water and electricity connections after an natural disasters.
8. Teach children how and when dial the emergency number 911, police or fire department. Children also be taught which radio station should be listen for official information.
9. Following disaster supplies must be kept on hand:
   (*a*) Portable battery operated radio and extra batteries.
   (*b*) Flash lights and extra batteries.
   (*c*) First aid kit and manual.
   (*d*) Emergency food and water.

(*e*) Essential medicines.

(*f*) Sturdy shoes and umbrella.

(*g*) Cash and credit card.

24.10.1. (*b*) Emergency communication plans

Following emergency communication plans should be developed:

(*a*) If during a tsunami, family members are separated from one another, develop a plan to reunite them after the event. (The situation of separation may arise during the day when you are in office or work place and children are in school).

(*b*) In such a situation choose an out of state relative or friend to act as "family contact" after the disaster. Usually long distance phone lines are early put to use than local lines. Hence it is easier to contact long distance contact. Ensure that each member knows the name, address, phone no. of the contact person.

(*c*) Contact your local emergency management office or local Red Cross office for more information about tsunami. During a tsunami roads in and out of the vicinity may be blocked, so choose more than one evacuation route.

24.10.2. During tsunami

Following responses should be adopted:

(*a*) To get the latest emergency information, keep your radio or television set on. Be ready for evacuation if asked to do so.

(*b*) If you detect sign of tsunami or hear tsunami warning, evacuate at once. Go to higher land or ground. A tsunami warning is only issued when the authorities are certain that tsunami threat exists.

(*c*) Keep away from the beach during a tsunami.

(*d*) Never go to watch a tsunami near the beach. If you can see a tsunami wave, think that you are very close to death and you are unable to escape from it. In 2004 tsunami in Chennai some spectators were sucked away from the marina beach when they came to watch the tsunami waves.

(*e*) Return to your home only after authorities advise to do so.

(*f*) Tsunami comes in a series of waves. When one wave is over, never assume that the tsunami danger is over. The next wave may be larger than the first one. Stay out of the area. Tide record of Phuket (Thailand) showed that the tsunami arrived as a negative wave that dropped the sea level to a level corresponding to low tide with in 20 minutes. This was followed by two major wave crests in quick succession (20 minutes apart).

(*g*) In case you are trapped in a building during an tsunami, then stand in the corner of the room away from the window or door of the room. Go to the roof of the house if possible and safe.

(*h*) Help children and old people to vacate the building and guide them to climb to higher land or place.

24.10.3. After tsunami

1. Keep your battery operated radio 'on' to listen the latest emergency information.
2. Help injured or trapped persons.
3. Provide first aid wherever appropriate. Do not move seriously injured persons, unless they are in immediate danger of further injury. Call for help.
4. Remember to provide help to your neighbours, who may require special assistance, elderly people, infants, and people with disabilities.
5. Remain out of damaged buildings. Return home only when authorities declare it safe.
6. Enter your home with caution.
7. While entering a damaged building, use a flash light. Check for electric shorts and live wires. Do not use lights and appliances till electrical system has been checked by an electrician.
8. Doors and windows should be kept open to help the building to dry properly.
9. To help the walls and floor to dry quickly, remove the mud from the building while the mud is moist.
10. Check food supplies and drinking water.
11. Food which has come in contact with flood water may be contaminated, hence it may be thrown away. Get tap water tested by the local health department.
12. Utilities of the damaged house should be fully checked before use.

24.11. EARTHQUAKE PREPAREDNESS CHECKLIST FOR INDIVIDUALS AND FAMILIES

Identifying the potential hazards ahead of time and advance planning may reduce the danger, loss of life and serious injuries from an earthquake.

1. Before earthquake

A. Checking hazards at home. Under this head following steps should be taken to check the hazards:

(*i*) Place large or heavy objects on the lower shelves.

(*ii*) Fasten wooden or steel shelves to wall securely.

(*iii*) Store breakable articles as glass and crockery, bottled food etc. in the low closed cabinets with latches.

(*iv*) Hang pictures, mirrors, and paintings away from the beds. Couches may be placed anywhere people sit.

(*v*) Secure overhead fixtures securely.

(*vi*) Get repaired defective electrical wiring and leaky gas connections. These items are potential fire risks.

(*vii*) Secure water geyser by strapping it to the wall properly.

(*viii*) Store flammable and poisonous products securely in closed cabinets with latches on the bottom shelves.

(*ix*) Get repaired cracks in the building, specially if these cracks are of structural importance.

B. Identify safe places in each room. These places may be under the sturdy furniture such as heavy table or desk or against interior walls. These places may be chosen away from where glass could shatter around windows, mirrors, pictures or heavy bookcases or heavy furniture could fall over.

C. Location of safe places out side the house. These places may be in the open away from buildings, trees, telephone and electric lines and flyovers.

D. Ensure that all the family members know, how to respond after the earthquake.

E. Teach to all family members, how and when to switch off the gas, water and electricity connections. Children and family members should also be taught when to make emergency calls to police and fire stations and to listen to all radio broadcast for emergency instructions and information on your battery operated radio.

F. Contact your emergency management cell or neighbourhood for more information on earthquake.

G. Have following disaster supplies on hand:

(*i*) Flash lights and extra batteries.

(*ii*) Portable battery operated radio and extra batteries.

(*iii*) First aid kit and manual.

(*iv*) Mobile cellular phone if possible.

(*v*) Emergency food and water.

(*vi*) Essential medicines and can opener.

(*vii*) Cash and credit card.

(*viii*) Pair of emergency clothes.

(*ix*) Sturdy shoes.

H. Develop an emergency communication plan. In case family members are separated from one another during an earthquake, develop an plan for reuniting them after the disaster. Choose an out of state relative or friend to act as "family contact". After a disaster usually it is easier to contact or call at long distance. Ensure that each member of the family knows the name, address and phone number of the "family contact person".

During an Earthquake

During an earthquake follow the following instructions:

A. If indoor

(*i*) Take cover under a sturdy piece of furniture as table or desk or against an inside wall away from a window and hold on.

(*ii*) Stay in side.

(*iii*) Do not try to go out the building. It is most dangerous as objects like bricks, stones etc, may fall on you.

B. If you are out side. Go to the open space away from buildings, walls, electric and telephone poles. Stay there till the shaking stops.

C. If you are in a moving vehicle:

(*i*) Stop driving quickly and remain inside of your vehicle.

(*ii*) Stop your vehicle on one side of the road, away from buildings, trees, fly over or downed wires.

(*iii*) After the shaking has stopped, proceed with caution. Avoid bridges, ramps, etc. They might have been damaged during the earthquake.

After an earthquake

(*i*) Be prepared for after shocks. Though after shocks are usually smaller than the main earthquake, but aftershocks can cause severe damage as some buildings are already in advanced stage of limit of their resistance to lateral loads and weaker structures may fall down. Aftershocks can occur after a hour, days, weeks or even months after the quake.

(*ii*) Help trapped and injured persons. Do not try to move seriously injured persons, unless they are in immediate danger of further injury.

(*iii*) Give first aid where appropriate.

(*iv*) For the latest emergency information, listen to battery operated radio.

(*v*) Remember to help your neighborus, who need special assistance like infants, elderly and people with disabilities.

(*vi*) Remain out of damaged buildings. Return home only when authorities declare it safe.

(*vii*) Inspect utilities in damaged home.

Pets after an earthquake

After an earthquake usually behaviour of pets changes dramatically. Normally friendly and quite dogs and cows etc may become aggressive or defensive. Hence watch pets (animals) closely.

Checklist for schools

A. Preparedness and Mitigation.

1. Does your school have a disaster plan. Is the staff of the school aware of their roles and responsibilities under the plan? Do they realize that they

may be responsible for the students for upto 72 hours after a disaster occurs.

2. Is the staff aware of the fact that under the rules of ethics, all staff members are supposed to be disaster service workers. If disaster occurs during school hours, their initial responsibility will be with the school.
3. Does the staff know the location of the water, gas and electricity shutoff valves? Who has been given the responsibility of checking the status of these valves and switch off if need be.
4. Has a map of the school and its grounds been prepared? This map should also include the basic evacuation procedures and potential earthquake hazards avoidance procedures. Such maps should be given to all staff members.
5. Has a list and map of the location and availability of first aid kits, sleeping bags and other emergency supply has been prepared?
6. Whether non-structural hazard mitigation measures have been completed at the school. Under this head following measures should be taken.
   (*i*) Have the book shelves, file cabinets and free standing cup boards been bolted to the wall properly or arranged to support each other?
   (*ii*) Have heavy items been removed from the top of book shelves and cup boards?
   (*iii*) Have the windows of the classrooms and other campus buildings been covered with safety glass or covered with protective fibre?
   (*iv*) Have the ceilings, overhead lights and air ducts been secured to the structure of the building?
7. Have the inventories of hazardous chemicals in science laboratories and maintenance building been prepared? Has any person been appointed to check these items after the earthquake?
8. Has the school made any arrangement with the structural engineer or local contractor to report to the school directly after the disaster to determine the damage and the need to evacuate?
9. Do you know that your school has been designated as a potential mass care shelter? Has the staff been trained to manage such as shelter?
10. Does the school have a paging system? Who has been trained to use it?
11. Is there any earthquake preparedness programme in the curriculum?
12. Where and how you are storing vital data and records? Do you have back up of important data sotred in an off site location?

Emergency Responses

1. Identify an central planning area which contains maps of the campus facilities and hazards, enrolment of the current year, first aid materials and other tools necessary to manage response activities after the disaster.
2. Teachers must follow the operating procedures as follows:

(*i*) Know how to implement the basic "duck and cover" actions when an earthquake starts.

(*ii*) Have an emergency kit near the desk, which contains a roll sheet, special medical information and student release information.

(*iii*) Students should know when to evacuate and when to remain in the class room after an earthquake.

(*iv*) Know how to administer first aid to the seriously injured and how to comfort those in shocks and frightened.

(*v*) If some students are seriously injured and an evacuation is in process, staff should know how to handle the situation.

(*vi*) Staff should known the procedure to be followed before releasing a student to a person.

3. Have the emergency sanitation procedure developed?
4. What are your immediate assessment procedures?
5. Has a liaison person been appointed who can have contacts with the press after the disaster?
6. Who have been deputed for search and rescue? Are they trained in the work?

QUESTIONS

1. Discuss the following plans
   (*a*) Individual and family preparedness plan
   (*b*) Home preparedness plan
   (*c*) Community prepared plan
2. Discuss the residential care facility earthquake plan.
3. Discuss self defence techniques during an earthquake in the following situations
   (*a*) During an earthquake
   (*b*) After the earthquake
4. Write a note an earthquake preparedness for schools and businesses.
5. Discuss the measures to be taken
   (*a*) Before a tsunami
   (*b*) During a tsunami
   (*c*) After the tsunami
6. Identify the incorrect statement/statements
   (*a*) During an earthquake one should remain calm and reassure other.
   (*b*) One should adopt duck, cover and hold principle
   (*c*) One should remain away from windows, hanging mirrors or other items
   (*d*) One should run on roads out side
7. Identify the incorrect statement/statements
   (*a*) During a tsunami one should take shelter on a elevated land or upper storeys of the multi storey building
   (*b*) It is dangerous to visit sea shore during an tsunami
   (*c*) To visit the sea shore during tsunami is not dangerous

(*d*) The requirements of earthquake resistant and tsunami resistant buildings are contradictory to each other

8. The safe shelter land from sea shore should be at a distance
   (*a*) 5 km (*b*) 7.5 km
   (*c*) 10 km (*d*) 15 km
9. The level of safe shelter land should be atleast higher than sea shore level
   (*a*) 50 m (*b*) 25 m
   (*c*) 15 m (*d*) 10 m
10. The recession of tsunami waves are more dangerous due to
    (*a*) Development of higher K-E
    (*b*) Development of higher potential energy
    (*c*) Development of vaccum pressure into wave
    (*d*) All the above
11. Usually a tsunami may in undate land upto a distance from sea shore
    (*a*) 1.5 km (*b*) 2.5 km
    (*c*) 5.3 km (*d*) 3.2 km

ANSWERS

6. (*d*)	8. (*a*)	10. (*c*)
7. (*c*)	9. (*c*)	11. (*d*)

Appendix-1

Second Order effects (*P*-Δ effect)

Due to the inelastic response, most of the structural systems under go large horizontal displacements under the action of seismic forces. This horizontal displacement develops large secondary effects in the members. In general for evaluating the over all stability of the structural frame, it is necessary to consider the second order effects (*P*-Δ effect).

The movement induced by (*P*-Δ effect) is a secondary effect and may be ignored if less than 10% of the primary action of lateral loads. This effect need not be considered if the storey drift ratio does not exceed $0.02/R$ where R is the response reduction factor discussed in chapter 13.

For evaluating (*P*-Δ effect) consider the following Fig. A-1.

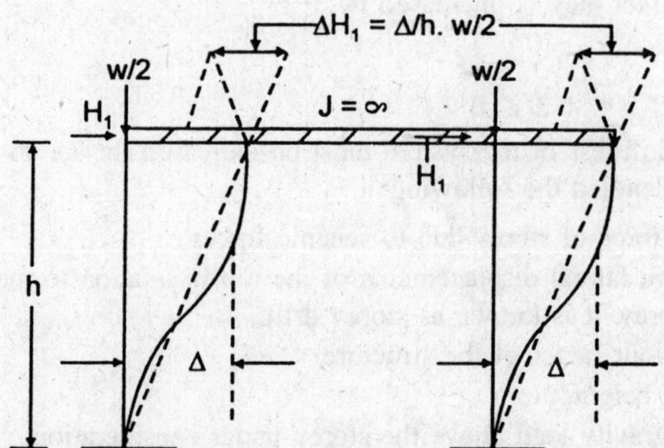

Fig. A-1. Deflected shape of a typical frame showing secondry effects

Let the frame is displaced by Δ due to an earthquake force.

Then each of the two $W/2$ column loads may be taken as axial force on the column for analysis with the value of $W/2$ and a horizontal value one, then from above figure where H_1 is the seismic force or load.

$$\Delta H_1 = \frac{\Delta}{h} \cdot \frac{W}{2}$$

Thus at the floor an additional horizontal force acts, whose value is given by the relation

$$\Delta H = \Delta H_1 + \Delta H_1 = 2\,\Delta H_1$$

$$= \frac{\Delta}{h} \cdot W \qquad \ldots(1)$$

In case of seismic action, the displacement Δ is taken as per code as Δ_{el}, multiplied by a behaviour factor 'q' of the structure, then

$$\Delta = \Delta_{el} \times q$$

Thus the additional shear force induced due to second order effect will be equal to

$$\Delta_v = \frac{\Delta_{el} \times q}{h} \times W \qquad \ldots(2)$$

Case (1)

For $\theta = \frac{\Delta_v}{V} = \left(\frac{\Delta_e\, l \times q}{h}\right) \times \left(\frac{W}{V}\right) \leq 0.10 \qquad \ldots(3)$

Where θ = ratio of Δ_v and V. In this case second order analysis is not required.

Case (2)

When $0.10 \leq \theta \leq 0.20 \qquad \ldots(4)$

In this case second order effect must be taken into account. In this case the seismic action effect may be increased by $\frac{1}{(1-\theta)}$

Case (3)

$0.2 \leq \theta \qquad \ldots(5)$

The lateral stiffness of the system must be increased. In the above relation different letters denoted the following:

V = Shear force of storey due to seismic forces.

Δ_{el} = Relative lateral displacements of the top in relation to the bottom of the storey. It is known as storey drift.

q = Behaviour factor of the structure.

h = Storey height.

W = Total gravity load above the storey under consideration.

To prevent the second order effects, the structural system must be provided a high degree of lateral stiffness.

Appendix-2

Salient features of Indian Standards on Earthquake Engineering

Bureau of Indian standards is a statutory organization under the bureau of Indian standard act 1986. One of the activity of this organisation is to formulate Indian standards on various subjects of Engineering through various division councils. The Civil Engineering Divisions council is responsible of standardization in the field of Civil Engineering including structural Engineering, Building materials, and components, Planning, Design, Construction and maintenance of Civil Engineering structures, construction practices, and safety of buildings. These standards are evolved based on consensus principle through a network of technical committees comprising representatives from Research and development organizations, Industry, Consumers, Testing laboratories, and Government organizations etc.

Earthquake Engineering Sectional committee

The Civil Engineering Division Council is working to achieve the above goals through 41 sectional committees covering vide range of subjects. One of the sectional committee is earthquake Engineering sectional committee. This sectional committee is engaged for the standardization work in the field of design and construction of earthquake resistant structures and in the field of measurements and tests connected with the earthquake.

The need to rationalize the earthquake resistant design and construction of structures based on the studies of past earthquake data has been felt since long. Following standards have been formulated under this committee.

IS 1893-1984 Criteria for earthquake resistant Design of structures

This standard deals with earthquake resistant design of structures and is applicable to the following type of buildings:

1. Elevated structures
2. Dams
3. Bridges

It also gives a map, which divides the country into five seismic zones based on seismic intensity. Shown in Fig. 1.1.

This standard initially was published in 1962 and revised in 1966. As a result of additional seismic data collected in India and enhancement in the knowledge and experience, this standard was further revised in 1970, 1975 and in 1984.

After the publication of this standard, earthquake occurred in different parts of the country including Latur and Utter Kashi. Thus based on the study of data of past earthquake and technological advancement in the field of earthquake, the sectional committees have decided to revise this standard breaking it into five parts, which deal with different types of structures.

Part 1. It deals with the general provisions and buildings.

Part 2. Liquid retaining tanks. Elevated and ground supported water tanks.

Part 3. Bridges and retaining walls.

Part 4. Industrial structures including stacks like structures.

Part 5. Dams and embankments.

Part 1. Contains provisions that are general in nature and applicable to all structures. It also contains provisions that are specific to buildings only. It covers general principles and design criteria, land combinations, design spectrum, main attributes of buildings, dynamic analysis. It also shows seismic zoning map and seismic coefficients of important towns, maps of epicenters and tectonic features and lithological map of India.

Revision of part 1 has been finalized by the committee and is likely to be out shortly. Other parts are under review.

Major and important modifications of part-1 are as follows:

1. The seismic zone map has been revised to have only four zones instead of five zones. Erstwhile zone 1 has been merged to zone II. Hence no zone I appears in the new zoning map. Only zones II, III, IV and V appear in the zone map. The level of zone II has been enhanced to zone III.
2. This revision adopted the procedure of calculating the actual force first, that may be experienced by the structure during the probable maximum earthquakes if it were to remain elastic. Then the concept of response reduction due to ductile deformation or frictional energy dissipation in the cracks is brought into the code explicitly, by introducing the response reduction factor in place of earlier performance factor.
3. The values of seismic zone factors have been changed. Now these factors reflect more realistic values of effective peak ground acceleration considering maximum considered earthquake (MCE) and service life of structure in each seismic zone.
4. A clause has been introduced to restrict the use of foundations vulnerable to differential settlement in severe seismic zones.

In this standard no regulation has been laid that no structure shall suffer any damage during the earthquake of all magnitudes. It has been attempted to ensure that as far as possible structures are able to respond, with out structural damage to shocks of moderate intensities and with out total collapse to shocks of heavy intensities.

IS 1893 (part-1) 2003. Criteria for earthquake resistant design of structures

Part-1. General provisions and buildings. This standard deals with assessment of seismic loads on various structures and earthquake resistant design of buildings. Its basic provisions are applicable to buildings, elevated structures, Industrial and stack like structures, bridges, concrete masonry and earth dams, embankments and retaining walls and other structures.

This standard contains provisions that are general in nature and applicable to all structures. It also contains provisions that are specific to buildings only. It covers general principles and design criteria, load combinations, design spectrum, main attributes of buildings dynamic analysis, apart from seismic zoning map and coefficients of important towns, showing epicenters, map showing tectonic features and lithological map of India.

The important aspects covered by this standard are as follows:

They are same as explained under IS 1893-1984.

IS 4326. Earthquake resistant design and construction of buildings

Code of practice. This standard provides guidance in selection of materials, special features of design and construction for earthquake resistant buildings including masonry construction, timber construction, pre fabricated construction etc.

In this standard, it is intended to cover the specified features of design and construction for earthquake resistance of buildings of conventional type.

The general principles to be observed in the construction of such earthquake resistant buildings as specified in this standard are lightness, continuity of construction, avoiding reinforced projecting and suspended parts. Buildings configuration, strength in various directions, stable foundations, Ductibility of structures, connection to non-structural parts and fire safety of structures.

Special construction features like separation of adjoining structures, foundation design, crumple section, Roofs and floors and stair cases have been elaborated in this standard. It also covers the details pertaining to the type of construction, masonry construction with rectangular masonry units, masonry bearing walls, opening in bearing walls, seismic strengthening arrangements, framing of thin load bearing walls, reinforcing details for hollow block masonry flooring or roofing with precast components and timber construction.

IS 13827-1993. Improving earthquake resistance of earthen Buildings Guidelines

The guidelines covered in this standard deal with the design and construction aspects for improving earthquake resistance of earthen houses with out the use of stabilizers such as lime, cement, asphalt etc.

The provisions of this standard are applicable to seismic zone III, IV and V. No special provisions are considered for zone I and II. However considering inherently weak against water, and earthquake, earthen buildings should be avoided preferably in flood prone, high rain fall areas and seismic zone IV and V.

It has been recommended that such buildings should be light, single storeyed and simple rectangular in plan. Qualitative tests for the suitability of soil have been suggested.

Guidelines for block or adobe construction, Rammed earth construction seismic strengthening of bearing wall buildings. Internal bracing in earthen houses and earthen constructions with wood or cane structure have been elaborated in this standard.

IS 13828-1993. Improving Earthquake resistance of low strength Masonry buildings-Guidelines

This standard covers the special features of design and construction for improving earthquake resistance of buildings of low strength masonry.

The provisions of this standard are applicable in all seismic zones-No special provisions are considered necessary for buildings in seismic zones I and II if cement sand mortar not leaner than 1:6 has been used in the masonry and through stones or bonding elements are used in stone walls.

The various provisions of IS 4326-1993 regarding general principles, special construction features types of construction, categories of buildings and masonry construction with rectangular masonry units, buildings of low strength are dealt with in this standard. However there are certain restrictions, exceptions and additional details, which are specifically included here in.

IS 13920-1993. Ductile detailing of reinforced concrete structures subjected to seismic forces-Code of Practice

This standard covers the requirements for designing and detailing of monolithic R.C.C. buildings so as to give them adequate toughness and ductility to resist severe earthquake shocks with out collapse.

The provisions for reinforced concrete construction given in this standard apply specifically to monolithic reinforced concrete construction; precast and/or prestressed concrete members may be used only if they can provide the same level of ductility as that of a monolithic reinforced concrete construction during or after an earthquake.

Provisions on minimum and maximum reinforcement have been elaborated which include, the requirements of beams for longitudinal reinforcement in beams at joint face, splices and anchorage requirements. Provisions also have been included for calculation of design shear force and for detailing of transverse reinforcements in beams.

Material specifications are indicated for lateral force resisting elements of frames. The provisions are also given for detailing of reinforcement in the wall web, boundary elements, coupling beams, around openings, at construction joints and for the development, splicing and anchorage of reinforcement.

IS 13935-1993 repair and seismic strengthening of buildings-Guidelines.

This standard covers the selection of materials and techniques to be used for repair and seismic strengthening of damaged buildings during earthquake and retrofittings for up grading of seismic resistance of existing buildings.

The provisions of this standard are applicable to seismic zones III, IV and V of IS 1893-1984, which are based on damage intensities VII and more on MSK scales.

The buildings affected by earthquake may suffer both structural as well as non-structural damages. This standard lays down guidelines for non-structural/ architectural as well as structural repairs, seismic strengthening and seismic retrofitting of existing buildings. Guidelines have been given for selection of materials for repair work such as cement, steel, epoxy resins, epoxy mortar, quick setting cement mortar, and special techniques such as shot crete, mechanical anchorage etc.. Seismic strengthening techniques for the modification of roofs or floors, inserting new walls, strengthening existing walls, masonry arches, random rubble masonry walls, strengthening long walls, strengthening reinforced concrete members and strengthening of foundations have been elaborated in detail.

IS 6922-1973 criteria for safety and design of structures subjected to under ground blast

This standard deals with the safety of structures during under ground blasting and is applicable to normal structures like buildings, elevated structures, bridges, retaining walls, concrete and masonry dams constructed with materials like concrete, brick work and stone masonry.

An under ground blasting operations have become almost a must for excavation purposes, this standard lays down criteria for safety for such structures from cracking and also specifies the effective acceleration for their design in certain cases.

IS 4991-1968 criteria for blast resistant design of structures for explosions above ground

This standard covers the criteria for design of structures for blast effects of explosions above ground excluding blast effect of nuclear explosions.

IS 4967-1968. Recommendations for seismic instrumentation for river valley projects

This standard covers recommendations for instrumentation for investigation of seismicity, study of micro tremors, and predominant period of a dam site and permanent installation of instruments in the dam and appurtenant structures and in surrounding areas. Bureau of Indian standards has also formulated a handbook on codes for earthquake engineering. These standards have tried to provide guidelines for designing and repair of buildings for damages under seismic forces.

Bibilography

1. Dr. Jai Kishan, A.R. Chandra Shekharan. 'Elements of Earthquake Engineering', South Asian Publishers, New Delhi.
2. Dr. D.V. Mallik. 'Protection Against Earthquakes and Tsunamis, South Asian Publishers Pvt. Ltd. New Delhi-110014
3. Sunil S. Toye. 'Earthquakes and Building, 'Central Techno Publications, Nagpur
4. S.K. Dugal. 'Earthquake Resistant Design of Structures, Oxford University Press, New Delhi
5. I.I.T.K. Earthquake (Tips) Earthquake Design and Construction.
6. Dr. A.S. Arya, National Seismic Adviser. Earthquake Resistant Structures (Earthquake safe design and construction of multistorey R.C.C. buildings) Journal CE & CR Dec., 2007
7. Dr. Shalesh Kumar Aggarwal, C.B.R.I. (Rookee). Seismic Resisting and Strengthen measures for brick masonry, Journal CE & CR, Dec., 2007
8. Prof. S. Prabavathy, Dr. M.S. Palanichamy, Dr. M. Sekar. Behaviour of R.C.C. frame with masonry infill subjected to lateral cyclic loading (Earthquake resistant structures) Journal CE & CR, Dec., 2007
9. Pankaj Aggarwal, Manish Shrikhande. Earthquake resistant design of structures, Princtice Hall of India, Pvt. Ltd. New Delhi-110001
10. S.R. Damodaraswamy, S. Kavita. Basics of structural dynamics and seismic design, Phi-Learning Pvt. Ltd., New Delhi-110001
11. Civil Engineering and construction journal, New Delhi.
12. Dr. V.L. Shah & Dr. S.R. Karve, Illustrated Design of Reinforced Concrete Buildings, Structures Publications, Pune.

Index

G

H

I

J

T